SWEET PROMISES

A Reader in Indian-White Relations in Canada

Edited by J.R. Miller

In the aftermath of Oka, Canadians are once more pondering the nature of relations between whites and native peoples. In his earlier work, *Skyscrapers Hide the Heavens*, J.R. Miller explored the history of those relations. *Sweet Promises* is a companion volume. It brings together the work of a number of scholars on a wide range of issues in Indian-white relations, and develops many of the themes identified in the earlier work.

The articles, all previously published, are concerned with developments in the various regions of Canada from the days of New France to the present. They deal with the early military alliances, relations at the time of the fur trade, civil Indian policy, treaties and reserves, the Northwest Rebellion, the impact of religion and agricultural and educational policies, the emergence of native political organization, differing attitudes towards the environment, and the struggle for aboriginal rights and contemporary land claims disputes.

In a new introduction Miller provides an overview of the history of Indian-white relations over five centuries, and in the conclusion he draws together the themes discussed in the volume.

J.R. MILLER is Professor of History at the University of Saskatchewan. In addition to *Skyscrapers Hide the Heavens: A History of Indian-White Relations in Canada* he is also the author of *Equal Rights: The Jesuits' Estates Act Controversy*.

SWEET PROMISES

A Reader on Indian-White Relations in Canada

Edited by J.R. Miller

University of Toronto Press
Toronto Buffalo London

Toronto Buffalo London
Printed in Canada

ISBN 0-8020-5945-7 (cloth)
ISBN 0-8020-6818-9 (paper)

Reprinted in paper 1992, 1999

Printed on acid-free paper

Cover illustration by Dennis Smokeyday

Canadian Cataloguing in Publication Data
Main entry under title:

Sweet promises :
a reader on Indian-white relations in Canada
ISBN 0-8020-5945-7 (bound) ISBN 0-8020-6818-9 (pbk.)
1. Indians of North America – Canada – History.
2. Indians of North America – Canada – Government relations.
I. Miller, J.R. (James Rodger), 1943-
E78.C2S94 1991 971'.00497 C90-095805-7

Publication of this book was assisted by a
generous gift to the University of Toronto Press from Hollinger Inc.
Further financial assistance was provided by the
University of Saskatchewan.

Contents

Introduction by J.R. Miller / vii

New France

BRUCE G. TRIGGER, The Jesuits and the Fur Trade / 3
CORNELIUS J. JAENEN, French Sovereignty and Native Nationhood during the French Régime / 19

Colonial Atlantic Canada

OLIVE PATRICIA DICKASON, Amerindians between French and English in Nova Scotia, 1713–1763 / 45
L.F.S. UPTON, The Extermination of the Beothucks of Newfoundland / 68

Military Alliance

BARBARA GRAYMONT, The Six Nations Indians in the Revolutionary War / 93
GEORGE F.G. STANLEY, The Indians in the War of 1812 / 105

Emergence of Civil Indian Policy

JOHN L. TOBIAS, Protection, Civilization, Assimilation: An Outline History of Canada's Indian Policy / 127
JOHN S. MILLOY, The Early Indian Acts: Developmental Strategy and Constitutional Change / 145

Emerging Relationship in Western Canada

E.E. RICH, Trade Habits and Economic Motivation among the Indians of North America / 157
SYLVIA VAN KIRK, The Impact of White Women on Fur Trade Society / 180

Treaties and Reserves

JOHN LEONARD TAYLOR, Canada's North-West Indian Policy in the 1870s: Traditional Premises and Necessary Innovations / 207
JOHN L. TOBIAS, Canada's Subjugation of the Plains Cree, 1879–1885 / 212

Northwest Rebellion

J.R. MILLER, The Northwest Rebellion of 1885 / 243
A. BLAIR STONECHILD, The Indian View of the 1885 Uprising / 259

Relations on the Pacific

ROBIN FISHER, Indian Control of the Maritime Fur Trade and the Northwest Coast / 279
JEAN USHER (FRIESEN), Duncan of Metlakatla: The Victorian Origins of a Model Indian Community / 294

The Policy of the Bible and the Plough

J.R. MILLER, Owen Glendower, Hotspur, and Canadian Indian Policy / 323
SARAH CARTER, Two Acres and a Cow: 'Peasant' Farming for the Indians of the Northwest, 1889–1897 / 353

Emergence of Native Political Organization

STAN CUTHAND, The Native Peoples of the Prairie Provinces in the 1920s and 1930s / 381
HAROLD CARDINAL, Hat in Hand: The Long Fight to Organize / 393

Contemporary Disputes

J.R. MILLER, Aboriginal Rights, Land Claims, and the Struggle to Survive / 405
DONALD PURICH, The Future of Native Rights / 421

Native Peoples and the Environment

DIAMOND JENNESS, The Indian's Interpretation of Man and Nature / 441
WORLD COMMISSION ON ENVIRONMENT AND DEVELOPMENT (THE BRUNDTLAND REPORT), Population and Human Resources / 447
PETER JULL, Lessons from Indigenous Peoples / 452

Conclusion by J.R. Miller / 459

J.R. MILLER

Introduction

In the millennium since Europeans made contact with the northern portion of North America, relations between the indigenous peoples and newcomers have evolved through several distinct phases. In general, relations began promisingly on a cooperative, harmonious note, but later they degenerated into conflict and confrontation. To some extent, clashes between Canada's aboriginal peoples and the strangers from across the water stemmed from profound differences in the attitudes and values of the two peoples. But the shift of the native-newcomer relationship from harmony to discord was also largely attributable to changes in the motives that the two parties had for interacting.

Certainly Europeans and the indigenous peoples were so different that at least misunderstanding, if not friction, was inevitable. The disparate groups of aboriginal inhabitants of Canada shared values and practices that provided an underlying unity to their existence at the same time that those aspirations and activities differentiated them sharply from the mariners, traders, missionaries, and officials who began to visit the continent regularly in the seventeenth century. This is not to say, as was implied by the Europeans' application of the term 'Indian' to all native inhabitants, that the people who met the ships or exploration parties were a single civilization or culture. On the contrary, there were sharp differences in ways of associating and earning a living among fishing folk on the Atlantic and Pacific, agriculturalists in the eastern woodlands, and hunter-gatherers in the northern forests and in the still more northerly arctic regions. But the native peoples did share a few social, political, and ideological traits that were noticeably different from those of the newcomers.

Aboriginal society, though it differed between sedentary agriculturalists and nomadic hunters, shared a common emphasis on autonomy and consent.

Bands and even larger groupings accorded to individuals, even to children, a large amount of freedom to determine for themselves what they would and would not do. Mechanisms of social control relied more on group censure and exclusion than on force and punishment to ensure that anti-social behaviour did not threaten the whole community. The same attitudes were reflected in political arrangements that also tended to emphasize elaborate consultation and consensual decision-making, both of which were designed to secure voluntary compliance. The use of instruments of coercion, such as police or army, to enforce decisions of the political apparatus was rare. Most important of all the indigenous peoples' shared attitudes, however, was their outlook on creation.

Where the Christians who came to North America from western Europe were the products of a lengthy Judeo-Christian tradition that emphasized humankind's dominance of the created world, the indigenous peoples saw everything including themselves as part of an integrated pattern of existence on a single level. Diamond Jenness's discussion of 'The Indian's Interpretation of Man and Nature' is focused on Indians in eastern North America, but what he says about natives' perception of their relationship with the natural world applies to indigenous peoples in other parts of Canada as well. Indians' outlook was shaped by their religious views, usually classified as 'animistic,' which held that everything possesses a force from the Creator that animates and motivates it. Not only did humans have these life-forces – souls, in Christian parlance – but so did animals, marine life, objects in the natural environment, and even items of human manufacture. Humans were only one of a multitude of beings; they held no special place in the created world. On the contrary, they had to observe proper behaviour – taboos, to use the technical term – in their relationship with the other things the Creator had placed on the earth. Did they wish to catch fish for a meal? Then they had to offer a prayer to the spirit of the fish, informing it they meant no harm, explaining they needed to eat to survive, and asking the fish to allow itself to be taken. Afterwards they had to observe proper behaviour – such as refraining from disposing of the bones carelessly, perhaps in the fire – so as not to offend the spirit of the fish. If the fish-spirit were offended, it would warn other fish and prevent their being captured in the future. Animistic belief, as Jenness explains, conditioned North American native peoples to respect those with whom they shared the world; to do otherwise meant not just offending the spirits but want, hardship, and perhaps extinction.

If Europeans and North Americans were so different in their attitudes and social and economic organization, how did it come to pass that the early centuries of native-newcomer contact were generally cooperative and fruitful? Until the nineteenth century in eastern Canada, relations between strangers and natives were on the whole positive. Relations were generally good because the indigenous people, who far outnumbered the intruders, refrained from driving them away. That tolerance, in turn, was conditioned both by aboriginal ethics and economic motives. Indigenous religion, shaped by the need to distribute widely resources that often were scarce, placed a premium on sharing. Indeed, hoarding or miserliness was regarded in eastern woodland societies as evidence that the anti-social person was a witch. And witches did not benefit from the usual prohibition on coercion: witches could be put to death without compunction or delay. The ethical imperative to share made it difficult for Canada's native peoples to refuse the Europeans' demands for part of their fish, a share of the furs they took, assistance in exploring and mapping the land and waterways, and, somewhat later, military aid.

The force of the sharing ethic was augmented by a different motive: economic gain. These strange – some thought ugly – people in their large ships might be pitiable in their inability to do anything right in the North American wilderness, but they did have wonderful products that could be obtained by exchanging relatively worthless animal skins. From the fur commerce that began in the fifteenth century with casual contacts between European fishing boats and Atlantic Indians there evolved by the seventeenth century an exchange from which Indians were able to obtain iron products, firearms (in some cases), and even valuable recreational aids such as distilled alcohol products. In other words, Indian peoples found that substantial economic benefits were obtainable from the trade in beaver and other pelts that the fashion industry of European demanded. The first article in this collection illustrates aspects of the cooperative commercial relationship that developed. Bruce Trigger's 'The Jesuits and the Fur Trade' explains how both French and Indians found Christian missionaries a useful link in this important commerce. Some scholars place more weight on non-economic factors to explain the missionary-Indian association,[1] and one important school of interpretation argues that the fur commerce undermined the Indians' view of their relationship to the animals and other life forms.[2] Whatever the relative importance of ideas and material attractions, the early commercial phase of European-native contact was surprisingly cooperative and mutually beneficial.

A major reason for what might seem to the modern reader to have been surprisingly harmonious relations during the New France period was that the French interlopers posed no serious threat to natives or their lands. As Cornelius Jaenen points out in 'French Sovereignty and Native Nationhood during the French Régime,' the French seldom trespassed on areas that the indigenous peoples used regularly, whether on the St Lawrence or Atlantic. So far as French assertion of sovereignty was concerned, it was only in regard to the pretensions of other European powers in the area. French 'sovereignty' did not impair native nationhood. The constitutional significance of French claims would prove vitally important for twentieth-century disputes about land ownership. More immediately, in the eighteenth century when a new motive for interacting began to figure in the relationship between native and newcomer, it was the fact that French use of lands had not harmed Indian interests that would matter.

After 1700 relations were modified, not radically transformed. It was still true that Europeans and Indians participated in a cooperative commerce in peltries, shared a fishery and whaling industry, cooperated in exploring and mapping the interior of the continent, and faced each other with sometimes friendly and sometimes sullen demeanour across the altar of the missionary priests. However, in the eighteenth century, France's decision to employ a strategy of containing Anglo-American colonies by means of posts and Indian alliances led to a greater emphasis on military alliance as a motive for dealing with the native peoples. Alliance, whether commercial or military or a mixture of both, had certainly been present since early in the seventeenth century. But in the eighteenth century it increasingly dominated the thinking of officialdom both in the French colony north of the St Lawrence and the British settlements and towns in the Thirteen Colonies. Both European powers and their American colonies sought to build and maintain military alliances with the indigenous people to overawe their Euro-American adversary and enhance their own power on the continent.

As it turned out, it was easier for the French and Canadians to fashion these alliances, in part because they had more elaborate commercial and missionary links on which to build the military partnership, and in part because they were less of a danger to the native peoples. Because New France, including both Acadia on the Atlantic and Canada on the St Lawrence, was more a commercial than an agrarian colony, it was sparsely populated and posed little threat to the Indians. Parts of the Thirteen Colonies, however, were agrarian; and farming menaced the Indians' control of and benefit from the land. If Canadian traders and missionaries posed no threat to the Indians, the same could not be said of the Americans. Farmers levelled the forests, stopped the Indians from ranging freely throughout the region, and drove off the game on which the aboriginal economy and peoples depended. Olive Dickason's 'Amerindians between French and English in Nova Scotia, 1713–1763' shows how the Micmac in particular manoeuvred between the competing strategies of the European powers, recognizing that the Acadians were not a serious danger, and that French power and Roman Catholicism represented effective means of protecting both their land and their way of life.

The Atlantic Indians' response to new demands for their military support – coolly appraising their self-interest and acting accordingly – was behaviour that was repeated in other regions of the country over the next century and a half. Both Barbara Graymont's examination of 'The Six Nations Indians in the Revolutionary War' and George Stanley's 'Indians in the War of 1812' show how and why most Indians preferred the British-Canadian alliance, as well as how critical to military success such native military support was. Graymont also illustrates the heterogeneity of even a supposedly single group, the Six Nations; and her essay serves as well to remind us of the importance of women in Iroquois society. Although some of Dr Stanley's language ('primitive peoples,' 'use') might suggest a view of Indians as instruments of European generals, the gist of his argument is that native peoples were shrewd strategists and that they were not used by Europeans. To their sorrow, Indians learned that military partnership was not effective in protecting aboriginal interests. While it lasted, however, the military relationship was one in which Indians were at least as important as European generals and colonial militiamen.

The shift of Indian-European relations to a new, more malevolent phase in the nineteenth century is illustrated well by the essays of Upton, Tobias, and Milloy. The problem now was that Europeans and Euro-Americans no longer found the native peoples directly useful to them. As the fur trade declined in relative importance as immigration and agricultural settlement speeded up, the Indian as commercial partner became a much less attractive figure to the colonist. The Rush-Bagot Convention of 1817, the real end of the War of 1812, demilitarized the Great Lakes and ushered in enduring peace between the United States and British North America (BNA), and Indians were no longer needed as allies and military partners. The consequence was what one historian has referred to as the 'onset of irrelevance' of the Indians to Euro-Canadians.[3] In an age when the native peoples were no longer central to the settlers' needs, it was easy to let them wither away largely as a consequence of disease brought by the European, maladies to which they had no acquired immunity. Leslie Upton's study of 'The Extermination of the Beothucks of Newfoundland' shows clearly how native peoples who no longer mattered for practical purposes to the newcomers and who competed for resources with the intruders could decline and disappear. Upton's perceptive analysis puts to rest old canards, such as the legend that Beothuck died out because they were hunted by Newfoundlanders, or that Europeans somehow 'used' the Micmac to weaken and eliminate the indigenous population of Newfoundland.

Still, what to do about those that remained, especially in the central colonies of British North America where British immigration was surging in during the 1820s and later? As John Tobias explains in 'Protection, Civilization, Assimilation: An Outline History of Canada's Indian Policy,' officialdom's answer was to convert the Indians into imitation white people. Now that the fur trade was declining in importance and war seemed to have been banished from North America, the natives' skills in fur commerce and forest warfare were unimportant to agricultural immigrants. Moreover, the newcomers coveted the lands that the indigenous people used extensively in hunting, fishing, and gathering. A quick response was to try to change indigenous nomads into sedentary agriculturalists by experiments in reserve farming and Christian missions. John Milloy's 'The Early Indian Acts: Developmental Strategy and Constitutional Change' explains how the central British North American colony followed the logic of the new policy departure to a legislative program of defining, controlling, and ultimately hastening the disappearance of Indians as a distinct category of people. By the time the new Dominion of Canada turned to the task of integrating the vast northwest it acquired soon after Confederation, the state was equipped with legislation, policy, and attitudes for dealing with the native peoples by changing them into non-natives.

E.E. Rich and Sylvia Van Kirk introduce us to the most important feature of native-newcomer relations in the west down to the early nineteenth century: the western and northern fur trade.[4] In spite of its occasionally offensive language ('savage people'), Rich's 'Trade Habits and Economic Motivation among the Indians of North America' is useful as a reminder that western and northern Indians, like their eastern counterparts, dictated the pattern of commerce in the first, fur-trade phase of relations in the west. Van Kirk's 'The Impact of White Women on Fur Trade Society' informs the modern reader that the trade in pelts was a social as well as an economic phenomenon. In this article, as in her book on the same subject,[5] Professor Van Kirk illustrates how a study of the social aspects of the western commerce of the eighteenth and nineteenth centuries illuminates the degree to which Indian women influenced events, and also how the Europeans' racial attitudes hardened as the Victorian era began.

The west that joined Confederation in 1869–70 was no longer primarily a fur-trading region, at least not in its southerly portions, where white-skinned agricultural colonists were expected to go. A further complication for the federal government as it contemplated how best to integrate the west into the dominion was the accelerating decline of the bison herds of the plains. These animals had, along with the horse, been the mainstay of the Plains Indian culture that had emerged in a distinctive form in the eighteenth century. However, overhunting by both Euro-American and native groups had begun to reduce the millions of buffalo to numbers that could no longer sustain even the indigenous population. As the 1870s opened, Canada was contemplating what its response should be to these twin western challenges: tens of thousands of migratory Indians in what was intended to become Canada's granary; and the imminent likelihood of those Indians' being reduced to want or even starvation.

For a response to these challenges Canada fell back on a policy of treaty-making that had emerged in the late eighteenth century. The Royal Proclamation of 1763 had established two concepts of critical importance: first, it noted there were interior lands that were being used by the Indian inhabitants, and, second, it said that only the state could negotiate with Indians for ownership and use of the lands under their control. (The proclamation largely codified what was supposed to be state practice in the colony of Nova Scotia.) From this emerged later in the eighteenth century and again early in the nineteenth century a state policy of negotiating with indigenous peoples on behalf of European newcomers for access to lands under native control. This had been done in Upper Canada (Ontario) in preparation for settling Loyalists on lands controlled by the Mississauga following the American Revolution, and the same practice was observed as British immigration began to pour into Upper Canada in the 1820s. By mid-century, when the two Robinson Treaties secured Euro-Canadian access to lands east of Lake Huron and Lake Superior, the state's practice of negotiating in advance of white economic penetration of a native-controlled region was well established.

So it was that Canada negotiated and signed seven so-called 'numbered treaties' with the Indians of the western plains between 1871 and 1877. The role of the Indians in the making of these treaties has until recently been underestimated. However, John L. Taylor's 'Canada's North-West Indian Policy in the 1870s: Traditional Premises and Necessary Innovations' corrects the older picture by emphasizing the important contributions that Indian negotiators made. Whether the two parties had the same understanding of what they were negotiating – whether they were, as the government thought, land surrender treaties; or whether the numbered treaties were, as the Indians understood them, pacts of friendship and mutual assistance – is more doubtful.[6] In any event, misunderstanding of the western treaties has been an irritant to relations between natives and non-natives from the 1870s to the present.

One implication of John Tobias's work is that the meaning of the treaties was irrelevant to government policy towards western Indians from 1879 until the Northwest Rebellion of 1885. His 'Canada's Subjugation of the Plains Cree, 1879–1885' shows clearly, indeed chillingly, how federal officers failed to observe and even deliberately violated the promises made in the treaties. Indian petitioners complained in 1884 that they had been taken in by 'sweet promises' from the government's treaty negotiators, but the situation was even worse than the complainants recognized. Ottawa's objective, as Tobias argues, was to 'subjugate' the Cree in particular. Ultimately, it was the 1885 rebellion and its aftermath that allowed Ottawa temporarily to achieve its goal of overawing and controlling the powerful Cree of the prairies and western woodlands.

Was ill-advised federal Indian policy responsible for the outbreak in 1885 that is usually called the Northwest Rebellion? Traditional interpretations have emphasized federal mistreatment of Plains Indians and neglect of the mixed-blood people called the Métis as the cause of the armed resistance to Canadian authority in the valley of the South Saskatchewan in the spring of 1885.[7] More recent research, however, has insisted on the necessity to distinguish between the situation of the Indians and that of the mixed-blood people, and one scholar stresses the particular role of Riel.[8] Blair Stonechild helps to clarify the role of the Indians in the rebellion in 'The Indian View of the 1885 Uprising,' and J.R. Miller summarizes the debate and seeks to draw a balance on it in his chapter on 'The Northwest Rebellion of 1885.' Although scholarly consensus seems now to favour the view that 1885 was principally a Métis insurrection and that the Indians were mainly quiescent, debate will probably continue. The reason for this is that Riel, the central figure in the drama in the northwest, has become a mythic symbol to which a variety of groups have attached significance that goes far beyond his historical acts.[9]

On the Northwest Coast, relations between indigenous peoples and newcomers went through patterns similar to those found to the east of the mountains, though there was no resort to rebellion as there had been on the prairies. Contact led immediately to a lively fur trade, first as a shipboard commerce and later as a land-based exchange. In the Pacific trade, as Robin Fisher explains in his 'Indian Control of the Maritime Fur Trade and the Northwest Coast,' Indian traders exercised a great deal of control over the relationship. Indian independence was weakened, however, when the fur-trade relationship on the Pacific was supplanted, first by the arrival of the mining frontier, and then by missionaries and agricultural settlers.[10] As had been the case in central British North America in the decades after the War of 1812, the development of settlement on the Pacific led to concerted efforts to convert and assimilate many of the native peoples. British Columbia was noteworthy for at least two types of extreme assimilationist programs, the Catholic 'Durieu System' that was named after its Oblate founder and the ministrations of Church Missionary Society missionary William Duncan.[11] Both the ideological roots and the practical methods of the Anglican missionary's career are depicted in Jean Usher (Friesen)'s 'Duncan of Metlakatla: The Victorian Origins of a Model Indian Community.'[12] What is too easily forgotten is how long British Columbia, in spite of a Durieu or a Duncan, remained 'Indian territory.' It was only about the time that Riel and his compatriots confronted the Canadian government that the non-native population surpassed native numbers in the province.

On both the Pacific and the prairies, part of the aftermath of the 1885 insurrection was an ambitious program of controlling and assimilating native peoples. Perhaps too much should not be made of the role of the rebellion in precipitating government efforts to discourage native religious practices and force the adoption of Euro-Canadian ways through missions and schools. Precedents for coercive policies towards Indians could be found at least as far back as the 1820s, and the increasingly evangelical outlook of Canadian Protestantism in the late nineteenth century would probably have brought increased attention to Indian missions even without Riel's rising. After all, the period from about 1880 until the First World War was an era when Canada's Christian denominations participated energetically in a worldwide campaign to change the indigenous peoples, usually referred to collectively as 'the heathen,' into Christians. So far as Indians in Canada were concerned, these efforts took the form of controlling prairie Indians' mobility, interfering with native self-government, discouraging traditional practices such as the Sun and Thirst dances of the plains and the Potlatch of the Northwest Coast, and pursuing an aggressive program of assimilation through residential schools. This group of measures is usually referred to as Canada's 'policy of the Bible and the plough.'[13]

What needs to be asked about this policy, which Canadians a century later usually find offensive, is, 'Did it work?' Most writing on the subject tends to assume that Ottawa's coercive grasp was as extensive as its interfering reach. Such an interpretation is usually the result of concentrating on the *motives* of the policy-makers rather than the *impact* of the policies on the targets – the native peoples. In 'Owen Glendower, Hotspur, and Canadian Indian Policy,' J.R. Miller suggests that the conventional view needs revision: the pass system and prohibitions on traditional practices were often ineffective; and residential schooling was not some totalitarian edifice erected by the missionaries and occupied by the native peoples. Sarah Carter introduces another revisionist view in her analysis of Ottawa's policy to turn prairie Indians into farmers. 'Two Acres and a Cow: "Peasant" Farming for the Indians of the Northwest, 1889–1897' demonstrates that Indian Affairs agricultural policy was neither the benign program its advocates claimed nor productive of much good for the Indians at whom it was directed.

Native resentment at the high-handed elements of the 'policy of the Bible and the plough' contributed in the twentieth century to the emergence of native political organizations. The most important cause of native organization was resistance to the loss of their lands, and the first stirrings in pursuit of what today would be called land claims were heard in British Columbia. Between the two world wars, as Stan Cuthand explains in 'The Native Peoples of the Prairie Provinces in the 1920s and 1930s,' the Indians of the prairie provinces gradually assumed a prominent role in native politics. Another account of the tangled tale of Indian political organization that brings the story closer to the present is Harold Cardinal's 'Hat in Hand: The Long Fight to Organize.' Cardinal, who is still active in Indian politics in Alberta, gives a first-hand account of the oppressive atmosphere that helped to spawn political movements among Indians, Métis, and Inuit.

During the last two decades these native political bodies have concentrated on two major issues: land claims and the constitutional status of aboriginal peoples within Canada. In 'Aboriginal Rights, Land Claims, and the Struggle to Survive,' J.R. Miller explains the close connection between native demands for recognition of their status as self-governing peoples and their search for recognition and satisfaction of their claims for land and resources. Donald Purich's view of 'The Future of Native Rights' outlines more specifically what aboriginal self-government might mean in practice. The debates over self-government and land claims have been extremely important in Indian-white relations in the 1970s and 1980s, and they promise to remain so through at least the first part of the 1990s. Accommodating the demands of aboriginal peoples that Canada recognize and respect their unsurrendered right to conduct their own affairs places strains on Canada's federal fabric, not to mention the tolerance of a largely uncomprehending non-native citizenry. The contention by Inuit and other natives in the north, by Northwest Coast Indian peoples, and by the mixed-blood communities of the prairies that they have unresolved claims to territory with which Canada and Canadians must come to grips is similarly a difficult item on the agenda of public affairs.

If there are any clues for the future that can be discovered in the last four hundred years of Indian-white relations in Canada, one of them is undoubtedly that misunderstanding and ignorance have usually compounded difficulties. More fundamental is the conclusion that the quality of relations between the indigenous peoples and the newcomers to Canada has usually depended on the motives that the two sides had for interacting. In the New France period the major motives of the intruders – fishing, fur-trading, and exploration – were compatible with the interests of the indigenous population. During this phase of the relationship, as during the commercial era in the western interior and the two-stage fur-trade epoch on the Pacific, relations were reasonably good. The relationship was, on the whole, mutually beneficial, though disease and alcohol were immediate threats to native society. Christian proselytization, which undermined the belief systems of many indigenous peoples, perhaps constituted a longer-term threat. Even during the military phase that dominated the eighteenth century the relationship was positive, because each side needed the other and because of the martial alliance in which they faced each other. It was only in the nineteenth century, after the 'onset of irrelevance' of the Indians to the increasingly numerous Europeans, that relations soured. Then the relationship was characterized by the dispossession of the treaties, the coercion of assimilative policies, and the interference of programs aimed at controlling native peoples. It has really only been since the Second World War, thanks in large part to the emergence of effective Indian political organizations, that Inuit, Indian, and Métis have been able to force the majority population to consider their views.

Some observers believe that the growing environmental crisis will compel non-natives to pay heed and learn from the indigenous peoples. 'The Indian's Interpretation of Man and Nature,' as Diamond Jenness explains in the first selection in the last group of essays, is the basis of natives' distinctive relationship with the natural world. As humankind begins to face up to the consequences of centuries of environmental degradation, some of its leaders have begun to notice that the indigenous peoples around the globe live more in harmony with nature than do the 'advanced,' industrialized countries. The United Nations' World Commission on Environment and Development's *Our Common Future*, more commonly referred to as the Brundtland Report after the chairperson of the commission, brought the need to study and learn from indigenous peoples' views of nature dramatically to the world's attention in 1987. Peter Jull, a Canadian senior research fellow at the North Australia Research Unit, explains the impact of the Brundtland Report on some of Canada's native leaders and urges acceptance of its views by non-native interest groups in advanced countries in his essay 'Lessons from Indigenous Peoples.' Jull and Brundtland tell non-natives what they can learn from Indian religious beliefs: there is a better way to relate to the environment.

The essays that follow illuminate the general pattern of native-newcomer relations in Canada by referring to specific processes, events, people, and policies. They are designed to illustrate the several eras and themes that distinguish the history of Indian-white relations. Because the selections are drawn from the last sixty years of scholarship, they also collectively provide an opportunity to study some of the shifts of attitudes of the people who have studied native peoples. Succeeding generations of scholars build on the work of their predecessors, at times amplifying and at other times nullifying the legacy of those who have preceded them. It is in the debate within and between generations of investigators that understanding of the past evolves. Consequently, not everything that once was written about native peoples or about Indian-white relations is still held to be valid today. Reference has already been made to the fact that interpretations of Indian fighting forces as instruments 'used' by European powers no longer are generally accepted by those who study Indian-white military relations. Similarly, students of New France now would not write, as Bruce Trigger did, that Francis 'Parkman's careful use of historical sources is highly admirable.' Indeed, Professor Trigger himself no longer holds that view.[14] Similarly, today's students of western Indians do not accept Rich's strictures of western Indians' habits of 'consumption and waste.' Readers of the following essays, by considering the development of the scholarly understanding of native peoples and their relations with Euro-Canadians, can learn a great deal both about the evolution of Indian-white relations in Canada and about the ways in which anthropologists, historians, and others have interpreted that pattern.

The essays in this collection have been reproduced largely as they first appeared. Consequently, the reader will find some inconsistencies of style. The spelling of Indian names, such as Beothuck (Beothuk), often varies from author to author. Similarly, some writers render the names of Indian culture groups or nations into the plural by the addition of an 's' (Hurons), while others use the same form of the proper noun (Huron) for singular and plural. (Adding an 's' to names that are already plural, such as Inuit or Micmac, is an error, but a frequent one.) There are few rules covering such matters, and what few rules exist are often ignored.

NOTES

1 For example, Nancy Bonvillain, 'The Iroquois and the Jesuits: Strategies of Influence and Resistance,' *American Indian Culture and Research Journal* 10(1) (1986), 29–42
2 Calvin Martin, *Keepers of the Game: Indian-Animal Relationships and the Fur Trade* (Berkeley and Los Angeles: University of California Press 1978). The responses to Martin's interpretation are usefully collected in Shepard Krech III, ed., *Indians, Animals and the Fur Trade: A Critique of Keepers of the Game* (Athens, Ga: University of Georgia Press 1981).
3 E. Palmer Patterson, *The Canadian Indian: A History since 1500* (Don Mills: Collier-Macmillan 1972), 25
4 An excellent introduction to the early history of the western interior is G. Friesen, *The Canadian Prairies: A History* (Toronto: University of Toronto Press 1984), chaps. 1–5.
5 Sylvia Van Kirk, *'Many Tender Ties': Women in Fur-Trade Society, 1670–1870* (Winnipeg: Watson & Dwyer nd)
6 For a useful examination of the terms and significance of two of these treaties see Richard Price, ed., *The Spirit of the Alberta Indian Treaties*, 2nd ed. (Edmonton: Pica Pica Press 1987; first published by Institute for Research on Public Policy 1979), especially the essays by J.L. Taylor and R. Daniel.
7 See, for example, George F.G. Stanley, *The Birth of Western Canada: A History of the Riel Rebellions*, 2nd ed. (Toronto: University of Toronto Press 1960; first published 1936), Book Two.
8 For a work that distinguishes between the Métis and Indians see B. Beal and R. Macleod, *Prairie Fire: The 1885 North-West Rebellion* (Edmonton: Hurtig 1984).

Thomas Flanagan, *Riel and the Rebellion: 1885 Reconsidered* (Saskatoon: Western Producer Prairie Books 1983), holds Riel almost totally responsible for the outbreak. Readers should also consult Flanagan's more persuasive *Louis 'David' Riel: Prophet of the New World* (Toronto: University of Toronto Press 1979), which seeks to explain Riel's motivations in detail.

9 See D. Owram, 'The Myth of Louis Riel,' *Canadian Historical Review* 63(3) (Sept. 1982): 315–36.

10 The best account of this story is Robin Fisher, *Contact and Conflict: Indian-European Relations in British Columbia, 1774–1890* (Vancouver: University of British Columbia Press 1977).

11 A good introduction to Oblate missions in British Columbia is David Mulhall, *Will to Power: The Missionary Career of Father Morice* (Vancouver: University of British Columbia Press 1986), especially chaps. 1–2. The best account of Duncan's missionary career is Jean Usher [Friesen], *William Duncan of Metlakatla: A Victorian Missionary in British Columbia*, Publications in History, no. 5 (Ottawa: National Museums of Canada 1974).

12 For another view of the conversion of the Tsimshian see Clarence R. Bolt, 'The Conversion of the Port Simpson Tsimshian: Indian Control or Missionary Manipulation?' *BC Studies*, no. 57 (spring 1983): 38–56.

13 See J.R. Miller, *Skyscrapers Hide the Heavens: A History of Indian-White Relations in Canada* (Toronto: University of Toronto Press 1989), chap. 11.

14 See the much more restrained evaluation in Bruce G. Trigger, *Natives and Newcomers: Canada's 'Heroic Age' Reconsidered* (Kingston and Montreal: McGill-Queen's University Press 1985), 10–14, 19.

NEW FRANCE

BRUCE G. TRIGGER

The Jesuits and the Fur Trade

In the past hundred years two major studies of the Jesuit missions in Huronia have attracted widespread attention. The first is Francis Parkman's *The Jesuits in North America in the Seventeenth Century*. Parkman viewed these missions as a keystone in the Jesuits' effort to win North America for the Roman Catholic faith, an effort doomed by Divine Providence to failure as the ancient and bloody wars among the tribes of eastern North America were intensified with the arrival of European traders and European guns. In these wars the Huron were destroyed by their fierce and implacable neighbours, the Iroquois. The second book, George T. Hunt's *The Wars of the Iroquois*, interprets the events of these years in a very different fashion. To him the Indian wars of the seventeenth century were not the climax of an ancient struggle, but instead a competition for furs that arose between the tribes that traded with the Europeans on the St Lawrence and those that traded with them on the Hudson. While admitting the religious motives of the Jesuits, Hunt's book stresses their role as 'clerks of the fur trade' and as agents of French interests. It was they who in Huronia spied out the Huron trading networks and sought to influence Huron policies that were favourable to the Quebec fur trade. 'The priests knew,' he says, 'that the most effective way to serve the missions was to serve the trade.'[1]

Each generation of scholars tends to interpret the past in the light of new experience. The economic determinism of the 1930s is different from the historical teleology of the nineteenth century. Each of these books, while an important contribution to the study of the Jesuit missions, betrays serious weaknesses. Parkman's careful use of historical sources is highly admirable, but his lack of understanding of Indian ways and his contempt for the Catholic sentiments which motivated many of the settlers and missionaries in New France are major shortcomings. Hunt's book is marred by minor errors in his interpretation of his sources[2] and, in his attempt to explain everything in terms of economics, he seems to lose sight of the broader network of factors that were at work. Because of this and because archaeological findings have greatly changed our conception of Iroquoian prehistory, I think that the time has come to begin re-examining the historical data concerning the Jesuit missions to the Huron country. A re-evaluation of these data requires not only adherence to a model of the social forces that were at work but also a more humanistic attempt to understand the manner in which individuals and groups perceived the situation in which they found themselves and responded to it. These two approaches to history are not, and should not be considered, mutually exclusive or opposed to one another, but rather as complementary. Every age is dominated by forces that are not of one man's making and may well be beyond the control or understanding of individuals or even nations. In spite of this, the events which make up history are the results of actions not of men who are the mindless instruments of these forces, but of individuals with different backgrounds, abilities, and convictions. The pressure for conformity is great and men often may prefer to yield to it rather than to defend what they believe is right. In spite of this, the freedom which reason gives us to assess the results of our actions, however limited the choice of action may be, requires that a balanced historical explanation deal not merely with the actions of particular groups or individuals, as Parkman tended to do, or with abstract social and economic trends, as Hunt has done. Instead it must attempt to make meaningful a web of relationships that includes individuals, social processes, and the beliefs and ideas that animate men's lives.

My purpose in writing this paper is not to discourse on the charges of venality that were made against the Jesuits. These charges were made in France during the period of the Huron missions and in 1972 Louis de Buade, comte de Frontenac, governor of New France, asserted that the Jesuits were more interested in converting beaver than souls.[3] It is true that the Jesuits used furs as a means of exchange, as did all the colonists, and that they bought supplies from the Company of New France, some of them with furs they obtained from the Indians. They were also required, however, to give away much trade goods to the Indians as presents and in return for favours. It is unlikely that even in years when their relations with the Indians were good they broke even on this trade. Moreover, many of the lay workers who were attached to the mission and who were licensed to trade appear to have used their profits to support the priests. The Jesuits were neither partners nor rivals of the fur company. Parkman, who was never one to gloss over the Jesuits' shortcomings, is certainly correct when he concludes that 'to impute mercenary motives [to these men] is manifestly idle.'[4]

Nevertheless, close relations did exist between the Jesuits and the Company of New France. My aim here is to examine the history of the tripartite relationship among priests, fur traders, and Indians which constituted the foundation for the Huron missions. To begin with, we must say something about the fur trade between the Europeans and the Indians in general.[5] This trade began considerably earlier than is generally realized. Early in the sixteenth century, Western European fishermen began to penetrate the coasts of the Maritime provinces and the north shore of the lower St Lawrence. Those who landed to dry their fish soon began to trade for furs with the Indians, and gradually this trade grew. The original trade was in skins of all varieties. During the sixteenth century, however, an old process for felting beaver hair began to revive and beaver pelts rapidly outstripped all other kinds of fur in popularity. There is relatively little definite information about the beginnings of trade on the eastern seaboard, but when the French navigator and explorer Jacques Cartier first visited the Gulf of St Lawrence in 1534, his arrival caused no stir among the Indians there who were already accustomed to trading with the Europeans. Neither did his visit to the Laurentian Iroquois settlements near Quebec City, since many people from these villages spent their summers fishing and hunting seals farther east where Europeans were already trading.

The beads, cloth, and metal implements of the Europeans were very popular among the Indians. In particular the Indians soon came to recognize the superiority of European tools and weapons over their native ones. While such goods were scarce, they were in great demand as novelties, but soon many tribes grew used to having these tools and became dependent on them.

The tribes that first had access to trade goods were the ones living along the lower St Lawrence. As tribes living farther away came to want trade goods, these tribes along the lower St Lawrence strove to acquire a monopoly over the passage of goods back and forth through their territory. Such a practice may even have been a characteristic of native trade prior to this time. Each tribe that enjoyed a position as a middleman in such an arrangement could profit from trading furs it did not have to trap for European goods it did not have to manufacture. The concern of such a tribe was to prevent direct contact between the French and the tribes living in its hinterland. Already in 1535 the Indians at Quebec City tried very hard to discourage Cartier from going further upriver to Hochelaga, located at the site of the present city of Montreal. The hostility of the Indians in this area kept Europeans from travelling upriver again until 1581 and it seems to have been motivated only in part by the cruel treatment they received at the hands of Cartier and the Sieur de Roberval, who was in command of the third expedition made by

Cartier. As the tribes living farther inland were attracted by the profits of this trade and became increasingly dependent on trade goods, they would attempt, if they were strong enough, to seize control of the monopoly held by the tribes downriver. This resulted, as Hunt has indicated, in a new form of tribal warfare, economically motivated and more deadly than it had been prior to the fur trade when it was a small-scale business concerned with blood revenge, individual prestige, and obtaining prisoners for human sacrifice.

Although the details remain unknown, it is more than likely that quarrels over access to trading spots along the St Lawrence played an important part in the disappearance of the Laurentian Iroquois and perhaps may have strengthened or even brought into being the Five Nations Confederacy of the Iroquois. Trade goods began arriving among the Iroquois in the second half of the sixteenth century, but the Iroquois were prevented from having direct contact with the traders at Tadoussac, located at the mouth of the Saguenay River, first by the Laurentian Indians and later by the Algonkians who took control of the St Lawrence.

By the time the Europeans had arrived on the upper St Lawrence in 1603, the tribes living along the Saguenay, St Maurice, Ottawa, and Richelieu rivers were already drawn into fur trading and embroiled in conflicts over direct access to the European traders. Until this time, most of the trade took place at Tadoussac; with the arrival of the French explorer Samuel de Champlain it was soon to spread upriver to Quebec, Three Rivers, and Montreal.

Although trade goods probably reached Huronia earlier, by way of the Algonkians, there is no reason to doubt the Huron claim that they first made contact with the French when some of them visited the Ottawa River early in the seventeenth century.[6] Trading, however, was already playing an important role in the economy of Huronia. From 1615 onward French references indicate that the Huron were trading corn, tobacco, Indian hemp, and squirrel skins with the Algonkians in return for dried fish, meat, skins, native copper, clothing, and charms. Algonkians and Nipissings wintered in the Huron country, living outside their villages and trading fish for corn. The Hurons had elaborate rules governing trade with other tribes, and actions which imperiled good relations with these tribes were punished more severely than they would have been if the incident involved only Huron. It seems unlikely that these patterns could have evolved in a few short years, and I have argued elsewhere that the Huron were engaged in trade with the northern hunting peoples prior to the start of the fur trade.[7] Huronia has rich, easily worked soil and it borders on the Canadian Shield where corn agriculture could not support the indigenous population. Moreover, Huronia stood at the southern end of an along-shore canoe trail that penetrated far to the north. It was thus an ideal spot for trade between an agricultural population and a hunting and gathering one. Through time, as the Huron confederacy grew, more and more of the Iroquoian population of central and eastern Ontario appears to have settled in this region.

As the fur trade penetrated west, the sheer size of the Huron confederacy made it apparent that it, and not the Algonkian tribes of the Ottawa Valley, would dominate this trade. The Huron had only to expand and intensify existing patterns and to add French trade goods to their line. The corn which they grew in abundance was already in high demand among the northern peoples, who often went hungry in winter. In this manner, the Huron were able to capture a major portion of the fur market in northern Ontario and become the major trading partners with the French. The French, Algonkian, and Huron cooperated in the early years of the seventeenth century in clearing the Mohawk raiders from the St Lawrence Valley,[8] but the Huron 'wars' with the other Iroquois tribes were still of the traditional type, as Champlain discovered to his dismay. The Mohawks were probably happy to have extra furs to trade with the Dutch, who had arrived on the Hudson, and hence profited from looting Huron and Algonkian boats on the Ottawa. The Iroquois were still able to hunt beaver inside their tribal territory, however, and it was not until 1640 that the depletion of beaver made outside sources a vital necessity.[9]

It appears that when Indians of different tribes in this area traded with each other, often they exchanged children as guarantees of friendship.[10] Champlain conformed to this practice and in 1609 several French boys were sent inland to live with the Algonkian and the Huron. Champlain's visit to Huronia in 1615 served to strengthen alliances with a number of Huron chiefs who had already indicated their willingness for such alliances by sending gifts downriver. From Champlain's time onward there were young Frenchmen living in Huronia, travelling with the Huron and much in demand as 'relatives' and go-betweens in the fur trade. The most famous of these first *coureurs de bois* was Etienne Brûlé, who travelled with Huron parties all the way between Lake Superior and the Susquehannah country. The religious historians of this period largely ignore the activities of these men, but many appear to have led a rough and ready life among the Huron, often living with Indian women and in many ways resembling the traders of the North-West Company in later times. Their role in organizing the fur trade remains a subject to be investigated. Although they gathered furs on their own, their main importance to the company must have been in encouraging trade in general and in building up confidence and good will among the Indians. The Huron determination to maintain a monopoly of trade with surrounding regions is shown by their behaviour when a French mission was sent to the Neutral country in 1623. When Father de la Roche Daillon, who led the mission, was adopted by the

Neutral and the French suggested leading them to trade, the Huron cleverly frightened off these potential rivals by spreading malicious rumours concerning the diabolical nature of the French.

While the early *coureurs de bois* were respected as hunters and fighters and became participating members of Huron society, the missionaries who came to Huronia were quite different. Although sometimes respected as powerful and important men, they neither took to the Huron way of life nor were they accepted as part of it. French prayers were sought to supplement Huron ones much as shadow pictures gained a reputation for bringing good luck in fishing. But while both Recollets and Jesuits continued to work in Huronia and Father Jean de Brébeuf became personally popular, Father Nicolas Viel was murdered by the Huron and there is little evidence of success in proselytizing.

Although the Huron admired French trade goods, their respect for the French themselves was far from universal. The inability of many of them to master the Huron language and their awkwardness in their new surroundings were subjects of ridicule, and their readiness to overlook serious Indian offenses, for fear of injuring trade gave rise to the quip that Frenchmen could be killed cheaply. While wanting French goods, the Huron saw no reason for altering their way of life. Their contacts with the traders provided desirable new implements and luxury goods but were no challenge to their way of life. The missionaries, on the other hand, provided nothing the Huron wanted, yet they criticized their behaviour and challenged their most cherished beliefs. They were tolerated only because the Huron wished to preserve good relations with the traders.

During this period the trading company gave little support to the missionaries, since the Recollets' policy of persuading migratory Indians to settle down and adopt French ways conflicted with its own interest in furs. Neither the Indian nor the trader needed or welcomed missionary activity. Champlain's interest in missionary work was exceptional and in part related to the ambitious plans he had for developing the infant colony of New France. The suggestion that later the French traders needed the missionaries as their agents is clearly disproved by the situation that existed during these years. The *coureurs de bois* were adequate to this task and, unlike the priests, they were welcomed by the Huron.

When Quebec was returned to the French in 1632 after a brief period of British occupation, considerable changes were made in the nature of missionary work. The Recollets were not allowed to return and this left the Jesuits free to develop a coordinated plan. Cooperation on the part of the fur company was essential if any progress was to be made. Huguenot interests had been strong in the Quebec fur trade prior to that time, but the new trading company, formed just before the British occupation, was owned by zealous Catholics who were more than sympathetic to missionary work.

In 1633 three Jesuits attempted unsuccessfully to reach the Huron country. The Huron refused to take them, giving as their reason threats made against the priests' lives by the Algonkians along the St Lawrence. Since they objected again the next year, it seems more likely that the French defeat at the hands of the English made the Huron bold enough to object to taking *persona non grata* with them. They were eventually won over, however, by gifts and by Champlain's insistence that to accept the missionaries and treat them well was an integral part of their friendship with the French.[11] Once the decision was made to accept the missionaries, the Rock and Bear tribes vied to get the missionaries to return with them.

The policy that the Jesuits worked out in their dealings with the Huron seems in retrospect to have been a wise one.[12] In general they did not seek to alter the Huron way of life more than was necessary to allow them to live as Christians. Frontenac was later to denounce the Jesuits for not trying to make the Indians adopt the dress and manners of the French, for keeping them isolated, and for teaching them in their own language. The desire to convert an Indian nation, rather than to turn Indians into Frenchmen, was foremost in their minds. One of the first steps taken by the Jesuits was to prevent *coureurs de bois* from living in Huronia, since their moral behaviour was felt to be prejudicial to the success of the mission.[13] In their place the Jesuits accepted lay helpers who were maintained by the mission and were allowed to trade with the Indians. The lay assistants who were accepted appear to have been men who shared the zeal and high principles of their employers.

During their first year in the Huron country the Jesuits remained popular and their presence was sought after by different families and villages. They were invited to the war councils as representatives of the French and their favour was sought in connection with the fur trade. French food and trinkets were given to the Indians in return for their services, and religious instruction was welcome since it was accompanied by liberal dispensations of tobacco.

The period between 1634 and 1640 was a bad one for the Huron. In 1634 an unidentified disease, either measles or smallpox, which was then raging in Quebec, followed them upriver. This was the start of a series of epidemics of unusual proportions which persisted over the next six years and culminated in the smallpox epidemic of 1638 to 1640. During these years over half the population of Huronia died out; about 10,000 survived.[14]

The Huron accurately noted that the disease had come from Quebec and, following their own beliefs, they began to accuse the priests of practising witchcraft or seeking to avenge the death of Brûlé, and some villages refused to let them come near. Sinister stories about the black robes, which were said to have been told the Indians by Protestants trading on the Hudson, were passed on to the Huron by the Wenro Indians when they fled to Huronia from New York State about 1638. These and similar stories served to fan Huron resentment. Trade was growing, however, and the Huron desire to murder the Jesuits was held in check by their desire to continue trading with the French. The Jesuits noted that their persecution diminished before the Huron made their annual trading expedition to Quebec and when the trade had been successful. It is an important comment on the importance of French trade goods among the Huron that only one village went so far as to reject the use of French goods during this period of crisis.[15] One Huron said that if they should remain two years without going to Quebec they would be very badly off.

When the Jesuit fathers Brébeuf and Joseph-Marie Chaumonot visited the Neutral country in 1640–1, the Huron attempted to bribe these Indians to kill the missionaries. By doing so, they hoped to have the Jesuits killed without hurting the fur trade and probably at the same time to put the Neutral in a bad light. The older chiefs seem to have seen through the offer, however, and prevented the deed from being carried out. In any case, the men of the Neutral confederacy, who did not have trading relations to worry about, treated the missionaries with much less respect than did the Huron.

At home, the Huron did not hesitate to harass the Jesuits in the hope that they would leave. Children were set on them, their food supply was threatened, and their religious objects were befouled. One of their few converts, a man of outstanding ability, was killed, possibly by the Huron themselves, after he had led the Jesuits on a trip to the Petun country.[16]

By 1637 the Jesuits had given up making special efforts to convert children and to provide intensive training for some of them in Quebec. From now on they sought to baptize older men and the heads of families. Many of their converts were traders who had been to Quebec and who wanted preferred treatment in their trade there. The French in Quebec appear to have gone so far as to intimate that the Huron had only four years to become Christians or the trade might be cut off.[17] The Jesuits did not capitalize on such pressures to make mass conversions, but would baptize only those candidates who demonstrated their ability to lead a Christian life. There were only about sixty professing Christians among the Huron at the end of this period.

By 1640 many changes had taken place in Huronia. Half of the population had died in the preceding six years. Many of these were children and this probably means that during the final years of the Iroquois attacks the number of young men was small, relative to the size of the population. Many of the old people died too, and with them many of the best leaders and craftsmen were lost. The Jesuits note that a good deal of the mythology and religious lore of the Huron had been the property of the aged and that it had perished at this time.[18] The political organization also appears to have suffered from the loss of many of the traditional leaders. Non-hereditary chiefs who survived the epidemic appear to have played a more active role in the councils than they had previously.[19] It also appears that the fur trade may have been producing increased status differentiation and the development of a *nouveau riche*.[20] With the loss of old skills, and a possible weakening of traditional leadership, the Huron dependence on the French increased.

By 1640 the Iroquois had exhausted the supplies of furs in their own country and began to look around for sources elsewhere. By this time they were also obtaining guns from the various European colonies to the south. The Huron, on the other hand, could trade only with the French, who preferred to send French soldiers to protect their Indian allies rather than to sell them guns. It is also possible that the epidemics among the Iroquois were not as severe as they had been among the Huron. In 1642 an Iroquois war party burned the Huron village of Contarea and the Mohawk ambushed the Huron fleet on its way to Quebec.[21] The growing weakness of the Huron and the increasing desire of the Iroquois to capture the Huron fur trade, or at least to force the Huron to share it with them, increased Huronia's dependence on the French. It is little wonder then that when in 1640, which was also a year of health and good harvests, Charles-Jacques Hualt de Montmagny, the governor of New France at this time, took action against the Huron to punish them for the bad treatment the missionaries had received, the persecution of the Jesuits ceased. At the same time he offered to reaffirm the French alliance with the Huron, and stressed the importance that he placed on the Jesuits' remaining in their country.[22]

In 1639 the Jesuits founded a permanent centre for missionary activity near the mouth of the Wye River. The new headquarters, named Ste Marie, was designed to offer shelter to the Jesuits and their assistants and to permit the construction of buildings that were more permanent than was feasible in the shifting Huron towns. The centre was to have a hospital, a retreat for Indians, and a place where Christians could assemble on feast days. By 1649 it was the headquarters for over sixty Europeans, including twenty-three priests. Pigs, cows, and fowl had been brought up from Quebec, and European crops were grown in the fields nearby.

In the years that followed 1640, the Jesuits were no longer persecuted and Christianity was more popular than it had been before. Three important chiefs were baptized in 1642 and 1643 and this won more converts. The number of Christians in Ossassane, where the Jesuits had done much of their early work, was growing and the Jesuits had as an immediate goal the conversion of an entire village. Christian Indians now wore their rosaries in public and some of them went on a lay mission to convert the Neutral. It may be that the Indians undertook this mission themselves because the Huron as a whole were not encouraging French contact with the Neutral Indians at this time.

The Huron gave a variety of reasons for becoming Christians. An admiration for the missionaries was not the least of these. Others were converted because relatives were Christian and they did not want to be separated from them after death. At least some of the conversions were prompted by economic considerations. It is significant, for example, that in 1648, when about 10 per cent of the population was Christian, half of the Indians in the Huron fleet were either converts or in the process of being converted. Some Indians hoped for preferential treatment in Quebec, while others hoped to avoid having to give away their property at pagan feasts.[23] This latter reason also suggests an acquisitiveness that was new to Huron culture.

Despite Jesuit desires to missionize the Huron country without destroying those Huron institutions that were compatible with Christianity, many difficulties presented themselves. The Jesuit missionary Jérôme Lalémant observed that 'to be a chief and a Christian is to combine water and fire,' for the business of chiefs if to preside over pagan ceremonies.[24] Christians were no longer expelled from the village councils, but Christian warriors refused to take part in the pagan divinations associated with war and fought in separate units. It was said that the bonds of Christianity should be stronger than the bonds of kinship, and some Christians refused to be buried beside the pagan members of their tribe.

Because of the increasing rate at which Hurons were being converted, the pagans were becoming fearful for their old ways of life and probably for their power. While the Jesuits were left alone, converts were taunted, expelled from their houses by their families, and threatened with torture or death. Pagan women attempted to seduce Christian men and, in one village, the Jesuits had to reprimand their followers for offering the pagan leaders a bribe to stop trying to seduce Christians. New pagan cults arose in 1645 and 1646 which attempted to marshal opposition to Christianity. One was the cult of a forest spirit; another was based on the alleged revelation of a Christian woman whose ghost had returned from the dead to report that Huron Christians who went to heaven were tortured there by the French. Often, however, the Christians were reproved more gently, being told that they should not attack the ways of their forefathers so openly. As time went on, important men ceased to give up their offices when they became Christian, but transferred their pagan religious functions to a subordinate deputy.[25] Occasionally pagan chiefs would tell Christians not to attend a feast that involved pagan rites.

These events were taking place against a background of deepening concern. In 1642 and 1643 the Mohawk raided Huron boats along the Ottawa River and in 1644 they blockaded the waterway. That year a band of twenty French soldiers was sent to Huronia to protect the region. In 1645 a peace was patched up between the French, their Indian allies, and the Iroquois which the Iroquois expected would cause the Huron and Algonkian to come to them to trade.[26] The Huron were not inclined to become satellites of the Iroquois, however, or to endanger their alliance with the French. In 1645 over sixty, and in 1646 over eighty boat loads of furs arrived in Montreal. The latter shipment amounted to over 32,000 pounds of beaver pelts.

Mohawk anger increased and, in the fall of that year, Father Isaac Jogues was accused of spreading disease and corn worm among the Iroquois and killed by a faction of this easternmost tribe. At this point the Iroquois began to develop their master plan to eliminate the Huron as rivals in the fur trade. The leaders in this were the Mohawk, the chief fur dealers with the Dutch, and the Seneca, who lived closest to the borders of Ontario. The Onondaga, who resented Mohawk attempts to dominate the League of the Five Nations, were the least anxious to participate. The Iroquois raids and the growing power of the confederacy began to frighten the Huron. After 1640 over 200 of them left Huronia to settle under French protection near Quebec. In 1645 more began to retreat into remote areas along the southern edge of the Canadian Shield. In 1647, when the Iroquois were blockading the St Lawrence, the Rock tribe, which lived in the eastern part of Huronia, abandoned its villages and moved nearer to Ste Marie. Nevertheless, the Huron were still not despondent. In 1647 they solicited help from the Susquehannah in an attempt to divide the Iroquois league. As a result of their first efforts, 300 Onondaga, who were planning to join a Seneca expedition, were persuaded to turn back. In January 1648 the Mohawk slew a party of Huron on their way to negotiate with the Onondaga, and this brought the negotiations to an end.

Events now began to move more swiftly. St Ignace suffered heavy losses in March 1648 and the survivors withdrew to a location just east of Ste Marie, where the Jesuits helped them to establish a new village. On 4 July the Iroquois attacked St Joseph, where Father Antoine Daniel was celebrating the mass, killing or capturing over 700 people. The village of St Michael, which the Hurons had deserted, was also burned. With the growing insecurity, many of the Huron began to turn to the Jesuits for help and leadership. Thirteen hundred conversions are recorded between 1646 and the spring of 1648, and 2700 between July 1648 and March 1649. In the year 1647–8 over 3000 Indians visited Ste Marie and 9000 meals were dispensed. A dispute over policy between the Bear tribe, which was relatively sheltered and preferred war, and the Rock tribe, which had suffered heavy losses and preferred to negotiate with the Iroquois, must have helped to increase this uncertainty.

The growing number of converts and the prestige of the Jesuits had by now thoroughly alarmed some of the more extreme members of the pagan faction. We may never know what, if any, connection there was between this pagan group and the elements that favoured peace with the Iroquois, but it may be significant that the Bear tribe, which was the one most opposed to peace with the Iroquois, was also the most Christian of the tribes. The pagan party was not only anti-Christian but also anti-French. Perhaps their real aim, which has been left unrecorded, was to break the Huron alliance with the French and to make peace with the Iroquois by agreeing to trade their furs with them. In April 1648 six chiefs from three villages got together and decided to provoke an incident involving the French. They did this by murdering a lay helper of the Jesuits, Jacques Douart. When the Christians of the area rallied outside Ste Marie, the conspirators made no secret of their involvement, but demanded that all Christians be banished from the country. After several days of debate, the French faction among the Indians prevailed and the Jesuits were persuaded to settle for the payment of a heavy indemnity, the traditional Huron penalty for murder.[27] The Christian faction had won a major victory.

By this time the town of Ossossane was largely Christian. That winter the Christian majority refused to allow the performance of pagan rituals in the village and the advice of the priests was sought on issues involving moral considerations. The Jesuit dream of a Christian Huronia was being realized, but so far only in one village.

In spite of the increasing danger, the fur trade recovered after the summer of 1647. In 1648, 250 Huron set out for Quebec in fifty to sixty canoes. A few French soldiers were sent to Huronia to garrison Ste Marie and to assure trade the next spring. The trading was more than successful and Ste Marie was stocked with enough provisions to last three years.

The last year of the Jesuit mission is well known. In March 1649 about 1000 Seneca and Mohawk warriors fell on the villages of St Ignace and St Louis, capturing Father Brébeuf and Father Lalémant who had refused to flee. The death of these priests, at once horrible and triumphant, needs no retelling. An Iroquois advance on Ste Marie was halted by 300 Christian warriors from Ossossane, many of whom fought to the death. The Iroquois, impressed by their own heavy losses, left Huronia, taking their prisoners and plunder with them. The Huron, while suffering rather small loss of life, had lost five villages to the Iroquois in a short space of time. The Iroquois were well armed, and the prospect of a secure life in Huronia, or even of being able to grow crops there, seemed remote indeed. As a result of this last raid, the Huron were obliged to concede defeat. Soon after this they burned fifteen of their villages and scattered among their neighbours, the Petun and Neutral, or fled to the forests and islands of Georgian Bay. By May 1649 over 300 families were living on Christian Island not far from the mainland. Some of the leaders of the Christians still living in the area asked the Jesuits to settle there. The Jesuits had wished to direct the refugees to Manitoulin Island in Lake Huron, where they hoped to be able to reorganize the Huron communities and to preserve the fur trade.[27] They agreed, however, to destroy Ste Marie and follow the Huron to Christian Island.

They built a fort there and, together with the Huron, tried to clear new fields and plant corn. The tiny population of New France, itself threatened by the Iroquois and having bad harvests, sent back no aid. By winter, 6000 Indians are said to have crowded onto the island, and their numbers were increased by refugees from the Petun, whom the Iroquois attacked that winter. The Jesuits made heroic efforts to deal with the situation, even buying up stores of acorn from the Algonkian. The bulk of the population on the island was now Christian, nominally or in fact, and masses and religious instruction were well attended. Soon, however, the food supplies began to run out and disease and starvation took a gruesome toll. In late winter the Huron were reduced to cannibalism to survive. Hunger drove many of them from the island, where they died crossing on the thin ice or were killed by roving bands of Iroquois. By spring, 300 Indians were left on the island. They asked to be taken to Quebec, and the Jesuits consented. There they continued to be harassed by the Iroquois, but some have remained at Lorette to the present day.

Not all the Huron went to Christian Island. Many remained scattered for a time in the vicinity of Georgian Bay and among these were Indians who blamed the ruin of their country on the French and were bitterly anti-Christian.[28] Others fled to the Petun and together they survived to form the Wyandot tribe. Sill others went farther afield to the Neutral and Erie, only to suffer a second dispersal at the hands of the Iroquois within a few years. The villagers of St Jean Baptiste and St Michael surrendered to the Iroquois and settled in a body among the Seneca. Disease and hunger had of course killed many more Huron than had Iroquois bullets.

I have been able to present only a brief outline of the Jesuit missions to the Huron country. While I have not been able to discuss personalities, I have been able to sketch certain general trends. In conclusion I would like to draw together a few observations concerning the nature of the Huron missions. As I noted at the outset, there has been a tendency in the literature to hint at certain dark purposes as playing a leading role in the work of the Jesuits. According to some, they were busy among these tribes as political agents; according to others, they kept their mission going by acting, first and foremost, as agents of the fur trade. Such interpretations are the product of a secular society. Indeed, it is curious that scholars who are trained to take great pains to understand the thoughts and motives of non-Western peoples are often the least willing to understand people of their own culture who happen to hold views different from their own. There is, and can be, no doubt that the primary aim of the Jesuits was to convert the Huron to Roman Catholicism. In the spirit of their order, they saw a chance to make good in the New World the losses which their church had suffered in Europe as a result of the Reformation. The Jesuits sought to promote close relations between the Huron and the French, not simply because they themselves were French but because France was the only Catholic power that had established a colony in eastern North America. There is no evidence that the Jesuits sought to undermine the political institutions of the Huron or to manipulate their leaders as instruments of French policy. Indeed, they appear to have feared that unguarded contact with the French might be prejudicial to the development of the Christian state at which they were aiming. As Frontenac said, they kept that Indians apart and taught them in their own language; in short, they did not try to turn them into Frenchmen. Their aims in this respect seem to resemble closely those of their colleagues in Paraguay. If the Jesuits failed the Huron in any particular, it was in not persuading the officials in Quebec that they needed guns in greater quantities than they were able to obtain them.

Nor were the Jesuits agents of the trading company. Unwanted by the Huron, their only way to live and preach among them was for the trading company to persuade the Huron to accept them as part of the terms of trade. In Huronia they replaced the *coureurs de bois,* whom they felt set a bad moral example for the Indians, with their own lay assistants. Any commitment to the fur trade that was involved in this action can be seen as taken for religious, not monetary ends. In short, whatever activities the Jesuits may have performed on behalf of the government or fur trade of New France was action taken because it made the Jesuits' work in Huronia possible and did not conflict with their principles. There can be no question that religious motives, combined with a rare sense of responsibility for the welfare of a primitive people, were the considerations that were uppermost in their minds.

NOTES

This article is from *Ethnohistory* 12 (1965). Reprinted with permission.

This paper was read on 30 January 1965 at the Huron Symposium held in Orillia, Ontario, as part of the Huronia Exhibition organized by the local Chamber of

Commerce to mark the 350th anniversary of Champlain's visit to the region. It is an attempt to draw together certain lines of my research on the Huron and to focus on issues I have not emphasized before. It is part of a projected study of French-Huron relations in the first half of the seventeenth century which it is hoped will culminate in a book-length report.

1 George T. Hunt, *The Wars of the Iroquois: A Study in Intertribal Trade Relations* (Madison 1940), 70
2 Bruce G. Trigger, 'The Destruction of Huronia: A Study in Economic and Cultural Change, 1609–1650; *Transactions of the Royal Canadian Institute* 33(1)(1960): 15; Elisabeth Tooker, 'The Iroquois Defeat of the Huron: A Review of Causes; *Pennsylvania Archaeologist* 33 (1963): 122
3 Gustave Lanctôt, *A History of Canada,* vol. 2: *From the Royal Regime to the Treaty of Utrecht,* 1663-1713 (Toronto 1964), 63
4 Francis Parkman, *The Jesuits in North America in the Seventeenth Century* (Boston 1927), 466
5 References for statements made in this section and further details may be found in Bruce G. Trigger, 'Trade and Tribal Warfare on the St. Lawrence in the Sixteenth Century,' *Ethnohistory* 9 (1962): 240-56. There are additional notes on the Laurentian Iroquois in Elisabeth Tooker, 'An Ethnography of the Huron Indians, 1615–1649, 'Bureau of American Ethnology, *Bulletin 190* (Washington 1964), 3 and 4.
6 Reuben G. Thwaites, ed., *The Jesuit Relations and Allied Documents,* 73 vols. (Cleveland 1896–1901), 16: 229. For additional documentation and discussion of prehistoric Huron trade and settlement, see Bruce G. Trigger, 'The Historic Location of the Hurons,' *Ontario History* 54 (1962): 137–48.
7 Trigger, 'Historic Location'
8 Harold A. Innis, *The Fur Trade in Canada* (New Haven 1930), 20
9 Hunt, *Wars,* 33–4
10 See Thwaites, ed., *Jesuit Relations,* 20:59; 27:25. Further citations concerning the role of friendship and alliances in trade are given in Trigger, 'Destruction,' 23. This same paper gives citations for many of the statements made below.
11 Thwaites, *Jesuit Relations,* 10:27
12 It may also be noted that it conformed to Jesuit policy elsewhere. This general policy is discussed in Peter Duignan, 'Early Jesuit Missionaries: A Suggestion for Further Study,' *American Anthropologist* 60 (1958): 725–32. For the Frontenac reference see Christian Le Clercq, *The First Establishment of the Faith in New France,* trans. John G. Shea (New York 1881), 256.
13 Parkman, *Jesuits,* 465, 466
14 The population of Huronia prior to the epidemics was estimated by various people to be between 30,000 and 40,000, but little basis is given for these calculations and they may be wide of the mark. The population survey of 1639 no doubt gives fairly accurate figures for that year.
15 Thwaites, ed., *Jesuit Relations,* 15:21
16 Bruce G. Trigger, 'Chihwatenwa,' *Dictionary of Canadian Biography* (Toronto 1966), 1:211
17 Thwaites, ed., *Jesuit Relations,* 17:171
18 Ibid., 19: 123, 127; 8: 145–7
19 Parkman, *Jesuits,* 209

20 Brébeuf's comments on the behaviour of chiefs at the Feast of the Dead might support the assumption of increased status differentiation. Thwaites, ed., *Jesuit Relations,* 10:303–5. New attitudes towards property are noted in ibid., 17:111; 23:129.
21 For a discussion of the Iroquois defeat of the Huron see Tooker, 'Iroquois Defeat.'
22 Thwaites, ed., *Jesuit Relations,* 21:143
23 See ibid., 17:111; 23:129.
24 Parkman, *Jesuits,* 452
25 Thwaites, ed., *Jesuit Relations,* 28:89
26 Hunt, *Wars,* 76-82
27 Thwaites, ed., *Jesuit Relations,* 34:205
28 Ibid., 25: 175–7

CORNELIUS J. JAENEN

French Sovereignty and Native Nationhood during the French Régime

Our generation has become aware of the fact that the Vikings and the early European fishermen, who preceded such adventurers as John Cabot and Jacques Cartier, were not the 'discoverers' of North America. This paper will concern itself with the French intrusion and colonization in the context of Amerindian occupation and exploitation of the Americas. In other words, we shall examine how in this early colonial period concepts of French sovereignty and native nationhood were reconciled. Europeans, of course, had a long-established experience with colonization and the occupation of new lands. Ancient and medieval history are replete with instances of conquest and annexation.

The first historical fact that must be kept in mind in dealing with the matter of sovereignty and nationhood is that the early whalers, walrus hunters, and cod fishers from the French Atlantic ports did not find an uninhabited New World. Virtually from the moment of first contacts, those in authority, both civil and ecclesiastical, were aware of the native peoples, or 'new men,' of the Western hemisphere. The first record of Amerindians being taken to France for official presentation and public display dates from a fishing expedition undertaken by Thomas Aubert of Dieppe in 1508.

Presumably, the Amerindians had migrated into *terra nullius* and, as first occupants, had established undisputed possession of North America – at least so it now appears in terms of international law as subsequently canonized by European jurists. There is no archaeological evidence, or corroborating scientific evidence, to suggest that the remains of earliest humans on this continent are not of Mongoloid origin and predecessors of the native peoples 'discovered' by Europeans in the tenth and following centuries. Whether the *Skraelings* contacted by the Norsemen or the *sauvages* encountered by the crews of fishing vessels were lineal descendants of the first peoples to inhabit northeastern America is problematical. Oral tradition and archaeological research point to major displacements of Amerindian cultural and ethnic groups before European contact. Major migrations and traumatic demographic shifts occurred both at the time of and subsequent to first French contact. The disappearance of the Laurentian Iroquois, between Cartier's departure in 1542 and the reappearance of his nephews at the sites of Quebec and Montreal in the 1580s, is probably the best-known example of such important demographic change. Important territorial redistributions render unreliable even so basic a cultural boundary as the demarcation between the territories of the nomadic Algonkian hunting bands and the sedentary Iroquoian tribes.

The second historical fact which will need to be kept in mind in dealing with the matter of sovereignty and nationhood is that the French established beachheads for settlement in largely unoccupied lands. The valleys of the St Lawrence and the Annapolis, where they started settlements in the early seventeenth century, were not at that time inhabited. The presumed annihilation, or adoption and assimilation following conquest, of the Iroquoian peoples who had met with Cartier and Roberval's expeditions in the 1530s and 1540s, and shunning by Algonkian Micmac bands of the salty marshlands along the Bay of Fundy which attracted de Monts and Champlain, gave initial French colonization a unique and important characteristic. In these restricted areas, the French, not unlike the Amerindians who had migrated from Asia to North America, were able to move into *terra nullius* from another continent. The immediate consequence of this rather unique situation was that from the outset there was no question of displacement of aboriginal residents or of concern about legitimate title to lands appropriated. The colonization of New France, therefore, began without evident concern about territorial occupancy as a factor in French-Amerindian relations. Hospitality, sharing of possessions, and exchange of gifts – all Amerindian cultural qualities – marked the initial French intrusion into Amerindian America. Even when pursuit of trade and missionary work resulted in deep penetration into the heartland of North America, neither was associated with land acquisition.

The objectives of French intrusion into North America are well documented. By contrast, we know virtually nothing of the Amerindian motives for migration to this continent, the pressures that may have been exerted upon them to leave Asia, or the circumstances of their arrival. The French came in the first instance in search of walrus, whale, and cod, then of fabulous riches similar to those found by the Spaniards in Central and South America, and of the route to the exotic Orient. None of these necessitated extensive settlement. Religious motivation developed only later in the French contact. Cartier's third commission, that of 1541, ordered him to penetrate inland and 'converse with the said peoples thereof and live among them, if need be' in order to facilitate the spread of the Christian religion.[1] Yet none of the French expeditions to the New World was accompanied by missionaries before 1610.

By the late 1690s, however, it was becoming clear that France's chief interest in North America was no longer commercial but rather strategic. The priority given military matters in Europe during the closing decades of Louis XIV's reign was mirrored in New France. This significant shift in colonial policy placed new emphasis on holding the *pays d'en haut*, conciliating native inhabitants, associating the fur trade with military operations, and opening career opportunities to the Canadian nobility in the Marine contingents. In this context the need to reconcile native self-government with French claims remained imperative.[2]

This historiography of this question of sovereignty and ancestral rights during the French regime is neither extensive nor particularly illuminating. The Department of Indian Affairs assumed that the French had never concerned themselves with aboriginal rights, the concept of guardianship, or ancestral territorial rights. Consequently, writers such as T. MacInnis could assert that the French government 'never recognized them as having special legal rights.' Robert Surtees perpetuated the traditional view by asserting that 'since the French had never recognized Indian title to land,' no agreements had been entered into. He also confused seigneurial grants to missionaries for reserves, as described by George F.G. Stanley, with ancestral hinterland territories inhabited by Amerindian bands and tribes. Not surprisingly, these erroneous views were repeated by Francis Jennings in works which reached American readers principally. Bruce Trigger also cited Olive Dickason to conclude from a supposed lack of acknowledgment of aboriginal rights, 'French lack of sensitivity,' that they 'claimed ownership as well sovereignty over it be right of discovery.' Such a view could apply to the sixteenth- and early seventeenth-century ('heroic age') ventures but scarcely to the period following Louis XIV's assumption of direct rule in the metropole (1661) and in New France (1663).[3]

Of little help in clarifying the issue was Peter Cumming and Neil Mickenburg's magisterial study, *Native Rights in Canada*, which reasserted the 'non-recognition by the French of any aboriginal proprietary interest in the soil,' yet concluded that the French had vigorously defended Iroquois independence from Great Britain and their right to negotiate their own prisoner-of-war exchanges. An otherwise competent study of aboriginal, treaty, and human rights by Russel Barsh and James Henderson followed the same line of reasoning and began its exposition with 1763, presuming that the French regime was irrelevant. Native groups such as the Ontario Métis and Non-Status Indian Association have repeated the same views. Bradford W. Morse's

Aboriginal Peoples and the Law is largely silent on the French role.[4] Perhaps there is some consolation in the fact that these are not historians' interpretations.

W.J. Eccles muddied the waters somewhat by affirming that 'the French kings most certainly did recognize Indian land title and sovereignty,' that the French claimed sovereignty for their crown, although they were never able to exercise it, and that therefore the sovereignty and title to native lands later accruing to Canada 'were not acquired by virtue of France having ceded a non-existent title to the British Crown in 1763.' Eccles made the important observation that sovereignty comprised the right to levy taxes, to enact laws and enforce them, to demand military service and the right of eminent domain. Beyond demonstrating that the French did not exercise these rights over the Amerindians of New France, he argued that the native peoples 'could, and did, maintain that they satisfied all those requirements.' Amerindian societies, including the Iroquois confederacy, were not equipped either institutionally or ideologically to assume sovereign rights as defined in the European context. Indeed, even the assumption that any claim to sovereignty required 'occupation and military force to impose the will of the occupying power' distorts the relationship that the French developed with the native peoples.[5]

More pertinent is Lloyd Barber's cautious observation that 'France, as a colonizing nation, did not form an explicit theory of aboriginal title and did not treat with indigenous people for the surrender of their rights in the land.' A.G. Harper had observed in 1947 that 'it was assumed when a tribe or band of Indians assented to French rule, the title to their land passed to the French sovereign, including their right of occupancy.' The few treaties that were negotiated were not land cessions but were designed 'to formalize the Indian's consent to the authority of the King of France and to acknowledge that sovereign as the rightful ruler over themselves and the territory they occupied.' Brian Slattery has argued that not only did the French assert sovereignty over the vast expanse of New France but also they exercised their rights through the allied 'nations' as vassals of the crown in a quasi-feudal relationship. Slattery has also drawn attention to 'the coexistence and interaction' of two levels or 'diplomatic spheres' – a French-native context and an international context – while affirming that the doctrine of aboriginal rights in Canada draws from French as well as British sources.[6]

All of which brings us to a consideration of the concept of sovereignty. By the thirteenth century, French and British monarchs were using the right of eminent domain (ie, power of state expropriation of private property in the public interest) and levying taxes and armies whenever enemies threatened the realm. There is much truth in Francis Jenning's observation that sovereignty 'had been invented to justify kings' conquests of their own peoples,

[and] lent itself readily to export.'[7] Jean Bodin (1530–96) defined sovereignty as unitary and indivisible, a monopoly of power in the sense of control and creation of law. But he made an important distinction between the location and exercise of power. Thus France, without renouncing the doctrine that sovereignty was its exclusive possession in the colony, could exercise its power in various ways and could bring it to bear, or not to bear, upon its inhabitants. Sovereignty was conceived as residing in the crown; nevertheless, Bodin pointed out that the monarchy, while above human positive law, was subject to divine and natural law. By the time France began to colonize North America, sovereignty was thought of in terms almost exclusively of diplomatic and political overlordship. Economic control was perceived as being somewhat different. Also, sovereignty was seen as being subject to limitations since an authority might have full power in one sphere and none in another. On this basis we are prepared to submit that, although indispensable to any concept of the sovereign state is the attribute of its own constitutional or public law, in relations with the Amerindians of New France the French had arrived at a more complex arrangement. Indeed, metropolitan France itself was neither centralized nor unified during the seventeenth and eighteenth centuries in the sense of contemporary sovereign states. The French had come to the conclusion, faced with their inability and the undesirability of imposing universally their metropolitan concepts and laws, that the colonists in New France would be governed only by selective and modified French laws and customs and usages. This dualism, it will be argued, did not mean that the French did not assert sovereignty or that the British did not regard New France as being under French sovereignty. Amerindians did not share European concepts of either sovereignty or property; their perceptions did not and do not fall within the realm of Western European legal definitions. However, the French and Amerindians had reached a mutually satisfactory working relationship which is worthy of consideration and record.

In order to review the French relationship with the Amerindian peoples in juridical, political, and military terms, four aspects of the question of sovereignty and native nationhood need to be considered. First, we shall consider European traditions respecting colonization and the acquisition of new territories. Secondly, we shall examine formal French claims and acts of possession in the light of European legal formulations. Thirdly, we shall review French definitions of Amerindian nationhood and their reconciliation of such a view with their own claims of sovereignty. Finally, we shall consider briefly the question of native possessory and territorial rights. These are all relevant to contemporary issues of aboriginal rights and native self-government.

By what right did France come into possession of New France? Her invasion of America, to employ a term popularized by Francis Jennings, seemed justified by a European tradition that evolved out of classical Roman, medieval Christian, and feudal concepts. Roman civil law clearly set forth the rules to be observed in settling disputes between individuals over ownership of lands previously unclaimed. Hugo Grotius in 1625 applied this Roman legal concept of lands previously unclaimed to nations: 'as to things without a master, if we follow nature alone, they belong to him who discovers and occupies them.' On the basis of this argument in *Droit de la Guerre et de la Paix*, the 'vacant lands' of America could legally be claimed by the nation which first discovered and took possession of them. Colonization was seen as a normal expansion of European law and government into a legal vacuum and of European peoples into vacant lands.[8]

Roman civil law seemed to uphold the occupation and appropriation of newly discovered territory that was virtually uninhabited and not extensively cultivated. Europeans did not believe that nomadic, loosely organized native societies with communal land-sharing constituted sovereign states which could be recognized as such in international diplomacy. Northwestern America was 'vacant land' either in the Roman sense of *vacuum domicilium*, or the sixteenth-century term *terra nullius* for lands unoccupied by any other sovereign state, concepts which in our day Robert Berkhofer has described as lands devoid of extensive human occupation and cultivation and which Olive Dickason calls 'lands not already under Christian control.'[9] In other words, the European powers adopted the concept that the 'laws of nature' permit a nation to settle an unoccupied territory and to develop its own society. This would have been the Amerindian claim to North America had it been made in European juridical terms.

That the argument to justify European occupation of the Americas could also be used to affirm the prior rights of the Amerindians had not passed unnoticed. Francisco de Vitoria, a theologian at the University of Salamanaca in the mid-sixteenth century, argued in two famous treaties entitled *De Indis* and *De Jure Belli* that the Amerindians were the true possessors of the Americas by virtue of their occupation of these lands from time immemorial. This was the initial statement of aboriginal rights. However, he qualified it with the judgment that all nations had the right of visiting, sojourning, and trading in newly discovered lands and that the high seas were open to all nations. There was emerging a concept of international law, which Vitoria described as 'having been established by the authority of the whole world.'[10] It was a view that a number of Catholic theologians at the time, and later, employed to decry the exploitation and despoiling of native peoples.

Christian theology and medieval musings about the rights of infidel and non-Christian populations, nevertheless, contributed a second element to European justifications for taking possession of America. While Pope Innocent IV had opined in the early thirteenth century that non-Christian states enjoyed the same rights and authority as Christian states, and Thomas Aquinas taught that legitimacy of dominion did not depend on the religious beliefs of those exercising authority, the church undertook Crusades and used the Ostiensian thesis to justify its actions. Henry of Susa, cardinal of Ostia (d. 1271), held that infidel nations were not legitimate, their rulers lacked recognized jurisdiction, and the lands of such states could be appropriated without compensation. He argued in favour of universal papal dominion over pagans, whom he alleged had lost their sovereignty to Christ.[11]

Gallican theologians were willing to go along with the dispossession of pagan rulers but they regarded the Christian prince, not the Pope, as the instrument for bringing the entire world under Christian dominion in expectation of Christ's second advent. The Spanish monarchs had consulted churchmen on the manner of taking possession of 'new found lands,' but the French ignored papal claims and used the religious justification to bolster royal claims. Marc Lescarbot, New France's first historian, explained France's claim to Acadia in the following terms in 1618:

> The earth pertaining then, by divine right to the children of God, there is here no question of applying the law and policy of nations,by which it would not be permissible to claim the territory of another. This being so, we must possess it and preserve its natural inhabitants, and plant therein with determination the name of Jesus Christ and of France, since today many of your children have the unshakable resolution to dwell there with their families.[12]

Lescarbot was aware that the Micmacs had some legitimate claims to Acadia also, but he restricted himself to observing that they should not be exterminated 'as the Spaniard has those of the West Indies.' Even the Protestant Jacques de Charron supported the French claim to 'inherit' the New World in the name of Jesus Christ, adding the argument that the Gauls were the descendants of Gomar, of Japheth, and of Noah.[13] The extension of the kingdom of God and of the kingdom of France were seen as concurrent.

Feudalism held that the acquisition of a territory presupposed the possibility of holding it effectively, so that if 'positive rule and legal authority' were not exercised, all legitimate claim was lost. On such grounds Francis I had challenged the papal division of the New World between Portugal and Spain with the celebrated phrase, 'Show me Adam's will!' The royal commission to Roberval in 1541 commanded him to take possession of regions 'uninhabited and not possessed or ruled by any other Christian princes.'[14] Effective occupation was the only recognized claim to possession. International law eventually pronounced in favour of such an interpretation. In 1672 Pufendorf expanded on Grotius's concept of the rights of discovery to include physical appropriation because ''twould be in vain for you to claim as your own, [that] which you can by no means hinder others from sharing with you.' The Swiss legal scholar, Emmerich de Vattel, in *Le Droit des gens* (*The Law of Nations*) held that it was not ancient occupation of the land, as consecrated in the phrase 'from time immemorial,' that was the basis of title and right, but the use made of the land which was the ultimate justification for its possession.[15]

Emmerich de Vattel thought that the majority of the native peoples of 'those vast tracts of land rather roamed over them than inhabited them' and by pursuing 'this idle mode of life, usurp more extensive territories than, with a reasonable share of labour, they would have occasion for'; therefore, it was just 'if other nations more industrious and too closely confined, come to take possession of a part of those lands.' He concluded of the native inhabitants of New France that 'their unsettled habitation in those immense regions cannot be counted a true and legal possession,' whereas Europeans 'were lawfully entitled to take possession of it, and settle it with colonies.'[16] This view represented the culmination of conceptualization, based on Roman, Christian, and feudal principles, regarding the European right to colonize. The philosopher-encyclopedist Diderot could not help but wonder if his compatriots would defend the thesis had some Amerindians by chance landed on French soil and 'had written on the sand of your beaches or on the bark of your trees: This land belongs to us.'[17]

By what means did France establish and proclaim her sovereignty over New France? The official view of the French administration in the eighteenth century was that Jean da Verrassano had taken possession for Francis I in 1523 and Jacques Cartier had reaffirmed this *prise de possession* in 1535.[18] The formal taking possession of a territory was usually expressed through some symbolic act such as erecting a cross, posting the king's arms, burying inscribed lead plates, and reading a proclamation in the name of God and the king. The French did not read a *requerimiento* as did the Spaniards on approaching new lands, but it has been stated that they erected crosses in Brazil with the intention of imposing French laws and customs and the Catholic religion, as well as laying formal claim to the land. Cartier planted many crosses on his journeys to North America but most of these, as Brian Slattery has demonstrated, were markers or navigational aids, religious symbols, or commemorative pillars without any symbolic taking of possession of the country.[19]

Nevertheless, as Slattery has also noted, there were formal French claims in the sixteenth century which tended to support the view that New France was acquired through right of conquest. The royal commission to Roberval, dated 15 January 1541, said explicitly that he was to 'descend and enter these lands and put them in our possession, by means of friendship and amicable agreements, if that can be done, or by force of arms, strong handed and all other hostile means,' to destroy its strongholds and establish French control. Roberval was instructed to acquire the region either through voluntary cession or 'consent and tuition of the said countries.'[20] These instructions must be understood in the light of Cartier's rather troubled relations with the Laurentian peoples during the six previous years and the fact that settlement was going to be undertaken in an inhabited region.

This aggressive approach continued throughout the remaining years of the sixteenth century. The Marquis de la Roche received authority in 1577 to 'invest and make his all lands which he can make himself master of' and not previously claimed by other Europeans. The following year he was named governor of 'new found lands and countries which he shall take and conquer from the said barbarians.' In the letters-patent of 1588 to those who had inherited Jacques Cartier's privileges in New France, 'conquests under our name and authority by all due and licit means' were authorized. The commission to La Roche for Sable Island in 1598 authorized him to acquire possession 'by means of friendship and amicable means' and, failing that 'by force of arms, strong handed and all other hostile means' as had been the directive to Roberval.[21] Fortunately for French-Amerindian relations, these early colonization attempts failed.

The seventeenth century witnessed a very different approach. The planting of a trading post of Tadoussac in 1600, the founding of 'habitations' at Port Royal (1605) and Quebec (1608), and the inauguration of missionary work in Acadia (1611) and Canada (1615) were accompanied by a policy of pacification and reconciliation. De Mont's commission of 8 November 1603 did stipulate that he was 'to establish, extend and make known our (royal) name, power and authority,' but there was no longer any mention of coercive measures. The commissions of 1612 and 1625 for Champlain employed the same conciliatory tone, and the articles establishing the Company of New France in April 1627, with full title to the 'property, justice and seigneury' of the colony, made no mention of acquisition of title or imposition of French sovereignty, but contented itself with granting converted Amerindians the same rights as natural-born French subjects when in metropolitan France.[22] Thus, under royal charter company rule (1627–63) as drawn up by Cardinal Richelieu for Louis XIII, it would appear that those natives who accepted the king's religion (and by extension his sovereignty?) were granted the same status as other colonial subjects.

What knowledge the native inhabitants had of these European legalities is uncertain. Although missionaries interpreted actions such as presenting gifts to the king as 'paying homage' when Amerindians were presented at court, their own reception in Iroquois country suggested a different perspective. The successful diplomatic mission, so-called, of Jean Bourdon and Father Isaac Jogues to the Mohawk in May 1646, for example, extracted only the promise that the French would always have 'an assured dwelling place' among them and that the missionary personally 'will always find his mat ready to receive him.' The continued hostility of the Iroquois in the 1660s, however, resulted in several military raids on their villages, described by the colonial bishop at one point as a kind of crusade. The several Iroquoian tribes found themselves obliged to adhere to a series of peace treaties in 1665–6 by which Louis XIV was acknowledged 'from this time as their Sovereign,' the Huron and Algonkian allies of the king as being 'not only under his protection but also as his proper subjects' and with whom they pledged 'to live fraternally for their mutual defense under the common protection of the said Lord the King.' This treaty, which ended a war regarded somewhat as a baronial struggle and which involved no territorial appropriation, also provided for exchanges of families between the French colonists and the Five Nations and explicitly provided that the Iroquois should provide French exchange families with agricultural land and hunting and fishing rights in their territory.[23] The language of the treaties would appear to substantiate the interpretation that the Iroquois, under the protection of His Most Christian Majesty, were bound by fealty and allegiance, while enjoying seigneurial rights under the crown.

The charter of the Compagnie des Indes Occidentales, issued in May 1664, reflected the troubled relations with the Iroquois. The company was instructed to establish its commercial activities 'by chasing or submitting the natives or natural inhabitants of the said countries' who were not allies of the crown, to develop 'all lands it shall be able to conquer and inhabit,' and to enter into negotiations with 'the kings and prices of the country' for 'peace and alliances in our name.' As it turned out, the crown assumed direct control of the colony and limited the opportunities for its corporate subjects to exploit the native peoples.[24]

In the interior of the country, as exploration, missions, and trade progressed, more formal claims of possession through symbolic acts occurred. Saint-Lusson's *prise de possession* at Sault Ste Marie on 14 June 1671 is probably the best-known ceremony. As the representative of Louis XIV and special envoy of the Intendant Jean Talon, Saint-Lusson with Nicholas Perrot as chief interpreter and in the presence of four Jesuit missionaries, fourteen native chieftains, and about two thousand spectators took formal possession of the upper country 'bounded on the one side by the oceans of the north and west, and on the other side by the South Sea.' He did so 'declaring to all nations therein that from this time henceforth they are subjects of His Majesty, bound to obey his laws and follow his customs.' In return for what the French called a submission to the king of France, the assembled 'nations' were promised 'all succour and protection against their enemies.' A great wooden cross had been planted, and Saint-Lusson made the declaration with sword drawn in one hand and a symbolic handful of soil in the other. A religious celebration followed and in the evening the fourteen 'nations' were treated to a large bonfire, the distribution of the 'King's presents,' and a *Te Deum* sung in their name to thank God for having made them 'the subjects of so great and powerful a Monarch.' No dissenting voices were recorded as the native people joined in a celebration which cemented commercial and military relations.[25]

Formal claims appear to have been directed more at European competitors than at Amerindians who were theoretically becoming French subjects. When Sieur de Villieu was sent in 1693 'to post the King's coat of arms along a line separating New France from New England,' he underscored the fact that the Iroquois insisted they had never been subjects of Britain and he opined that such a categorical statement should be kept in the French archives for use at an appropriate time. Sieur de Louvigny, in concluding a treaty with the Fox in 1716, gave them 'a copy on a sheet of paper as an authentic testimonial of our convention and the taking possession of a conquered land by the King's arms' for the benefit of English, whom he described as 'ever jealous of the success of French arms' and liable to challenge the French claim to the western interior. In 1732 Joseph Normandin undertook to mark the boundary along the height of land north of Lac St Jean separating the French territory from that of the Hudson's Bay Company. He made a formal claim of possession for Louis XV, placing four *fleurs de lys* on four trees and in the middle of a portage three crosses on the largest red pine. In 1743 Louis Fornel erected two large crosses on a promontory at Baie St Louis in Labrador, kneeled before them singing hymns of thanksgiving, and then raised a royal standard as a sign of 'the Taking of possession which we make in the name of the King and the French nation of land which has never yet been inhabited by any nation and among whom we are the first to take possession thereof.'[26]

Sometimes the French were challenged when they sought to take formal possession of a region. La Vérendrye the elder, among the Mandan, gave a chief a flag and an inscribed lead tablet decorated with ribbons. He recorded that 'this tablet was placed in a box, so that it might be kept forever, in memory of my having taken possession of their lands in the name of the King.' But in the explanation he offered the Mandans concerning its significance he merely said, 'I made them understand as best I could that I was leaving this token in memory of the visit of the French to their country.' His son penetrated even farther westwards to the Arikaras where he erected a pyramid of stones, as he told them 'in memory of the fact that we had been in their country' but under which he had managed to deposit secretly a lead table 'bearing the arms and inscription of the King.' In 1749, in order to forestall British claims to the Ohio Valley, Celoron de Blainville buried a series of six lead plates asserting French claims to the region, as well as posting the king's arms on prominent trees along the river bank. The native people, even those allied with the French, wondered about the significance of these objects, removed them, and asked the English about their meaning.[27]

It seems evident that the French never doubted their right to acquire lands not already under Christian control. In asserting their sovereignty, they directed their claims against European rivals in particular, while with native nations they formed alliances and observed many traditional ceremonies in cementing good relations. The role of the king's presents was an important component of this special relationship.[28] Only with the Iroquois and Fox in the *pays d'en haut,* both of whom were regarded as being under British influence and against whom they waged war, did they sign treaties. Relations in the lower Mississippi region, emanating from the government of Louisiana, were of a different order, marked notably by military action directed at the Chicakasaw and the Natchez. This region of French America, characterized by plantation agriculture, slavery, and the intermingling of French colonists with slaves and indigenous peoples, in terms of relations with the Amerindians should be studied in the context of the French Antilles and Guiana, not Acadia, Canada, and the *pays d'en haut.*

How did the French view the status of Amerindian 'nations' and how did they reconcile native nationhood and self-government with their own claims of sovereignty in North America? There seems to have been no conceptual problem for the French because they distinguished between nationhood as understood in the international family of nations, where *states* were organized under sovereign governments possessing coercive powers to maintain order in their communities, and nationhood as understood locally, where collectivities organized as bands and tribes could conclude agreements, enter into alliances, and wage wars.

Thus, while the French claimed sovereignty in terms of international law, they conceded self-determination to native 'nations.' Native 'nations' were seen as independent in the sense of retaining their own forms of social and political organization, customs, and practices. The intention was to restrict French settlement in Canada to the St Lawrence Valley, where some domiciled natives might come voluntarily to live on reserves under missionary guidance, and to permit only small French communities at trading posts, military forts, and mission stations in the vast Amerindian territory. There was, in other words, a French area with limited native settlement, and there was a native area with limited French settlement. Royal instructions in 1716 not only required leaving the native peoples to govern themselves but also forbade the

French from settling and clearing land above the Montreal seigneuries.[29] This dualism had far-reaching consequences and moved a Lower Canadian judge to make the following observation in his judgment in the famous *Connolly* v. *Woolrich and Johnson et al.* case:

> Neither the French Government, nor any of its colonists or their trading associations, ever attempted, during an intercourse of over two hundred years, to subvert or modify the laws and usages of the aboriginal tribes, except where they had established colonies and permanent settlements, and, then only by persuasion.

In answer to the rhetorical question whether 'the territorial rights, political organization such as it was, or the laws and usages of the Indian tribes, were abrogated,' he opined: 'In my opinion, it is beyond controversy that they did not – that so far from being abolished, they were left in full force, and were not even modified in the slightest degree in regard to the civil rights of the natives.'[30]

Royal policy was outlined for Governor Courcelles soon after the crown abrogated government by charter companies in 1663. He was reminded that although the primary objective remained the Indians' rapid conversion to Catholicism, it was imperative that 'the officers, soldiers, and all his adult subjects treat the Indians with kindness, justice and equity, without ever causing them any hurt or violence.' The second objective was the Indians' eventual assimilation into French civil and commercial life, provided 'all this be carried out in goodwill and that these Indians take it up out of their own interest.'[31]

This innovative dualism of native self-determination under French sovereignty was remarked upon by an observant Spanish visitor to eighteenth-century Louisbourg. He wrote:

> These natives, whom the French term savages, were not absolutely subjects of the King of France, nor entirely independent of him. They acknowledged him lord of the country, but without any alteration in their way of living; or submitting themselves to his laws; and so far were they from paying any tribute, that they received annually from the King of France a quantity of apparel, gunpowder and muskets, brandy and several kinds of tools, in order to keep them quiet and attached to the French interest, and this has also been the political practice of the crown with regard to the savages of Canada.[32]

It was not merely a European interpretation of the unique French relationship with the Amerindians but the native peoples themselves were explicit in their declarations. When British officers tried to get Micmac headmen to swear allegiance to King George I in 1715, they consulted their councils and concluded that 'they did not want any king to say that he had taken possession of their land.' They affirmed that the French could not have ceded their rights to Britain by the Treaty of Utrecht since they had always been allies and 'brothers' of the French and independent.[33] The Abenakis made the same affirmations ten years later, and as late as 1752 responded to the official delegate of the governor at Boston in these terms: 'We are entirely free; we are allies of the King of France, from whom we have received the Faith and all sorts of assistance in our necessities; we love that Monarch, and we are strongly attached to his interests.'[34]

In the autumn of 1748 Governor La Galissonière and Intendant François Bigot met with eighty Iroquois delegates in the audience hall of the Chateau St Louis in Quebec. As a result of this conference, officials at Versailles could reaffirm their belief that 'these Indians claim to be and in effect are independent of all nations, and their lands incontestably belong to them.' La Galissonière was congratulated for having 'induced them to maintain their rights' against British claims. 'These nations govern themselves alone,' said a report, noting that they were becoming 'more friends and allies of the French.' In fact a number of Iroquois did choose to leave their territory to take up residence in the French colony at that time.[35]

The other side of this coin, so to speak, was well illustrated by an incident which occurred at the reserve at La Présentation (Ogdensburg). The abbé Picquet had had to obtain 'the consent necessary from the Iroquois nations' to proceed with his project to found this reserve in 1748. The grant was made without any thought of alienation of lands but with the idea simply of extending the rights and privileges to others which they themselves enjoyed on ancestral lands given them by the Great Spirit. No payment was made for such lands. When Governor Vaudreuil made the mistake of recognizing as 'chief of the cabin' at La Présentation a certain Onondaga who had not been chosen in the traditional way, the abbé Picquet went with a delegation of sixty Iroquois to wait on the governor and protest an action 'which seemed to them to be contrary to the rights of a free and warlike people, which recognizes as chiefs only those they give themselves and for the term they wish.' Vaudreuil backed down hurriedly, said there had been a 'misunderstanding,' reaffirmed the native council's authority, and made suitable presents of pikes and stiff collars to the seven war chiefs to wash away the stain of his momentary lapse of good judgment.[36]

While it seems clear that the French had succeeded in having their sovereignty in New France recognized in international circles, and never having it seriously contested by the Amerindians, the right to native self-determination was never denied by Versailles. Recognition of French sovereignty was usually expressed in terms of receiving the French as 'brothers,' the governor-general as Onontio, and His Most Christian Majesty as Onontio-Goa, their 'Father.' The acceptance of missionaries, the concluding of military pacts, and the conduct of trade were intertwined aspects of mutually beneficial and mutually binding relations from which it became almost impossible for either the French or the Amerindians to extricate themselves. Although the French never doubted that sovereignty resided in their crown, they sensed that Amerindian independence and self-esteem would never permit a political relationship that went beyond voluntary association. In exchange for the recognition of their nationhood, native collectivities submitted to what European nations considered to be French sovereignty.

This dualistic approach was not unique in European dealings with an expanding known world. Two different treaty systems evolved: a European continental system in which the Great Powers dealt among themselves, and an extended treaty system in which they dealt with the rest of the world using 'a different timetable than the strictly European system.'[37]

Finally, one might ask what was the status of native possessory and territorial rights under the sovereignty-association arrangement just described. Even if the French recognized and legitimized existing native customs and practices in this domain, there remains much obscurity. Little is known about the diverse and flexible patterns and concepts of Amerindian property rights, hunting territories, and territorial delimitation. Although various clans, bands, tribes, and confederacies differentiated themselves from one another in their occupancy of land, all seem to have recognized some territorial limits. Hunting territories and traditional homelands each had their boundaries. From the days of Jacques Cartier's crossing the 'boundary' between the Stadaconans and Hochelagans, and the exacting of tribute by Algonkin bands from Huron and French canoe brigades passing on the Ottawa River, through to the end of the French regime, care was taken about crossing various frontiers.

All native peoples allocated resources within their territory among themselves, whether in terms of horticultural plots or hunting ranges. Since there are no modern survivals of the aboriginal systems of tenure, or of the social and ecological conditions which formed their historical context, we are obliged to rely on native oral tradition and scholarly reconstructions. For the Algonkian hunters it may even be that the game animals were reckoned to be the true 'owners' of the hunting grounds. Land was no more 'owned' by human beings than was the air or the sea. Whether exclusive hunting territories were aboriginal in origin or traced their beginnings to European intrusion and the advent of the fur trade with its demands, a matter of continuing debate among anthropologists, the fact remains that a spiritual relationship to an area as well as practical concerns (sometimes even economic) regulated behaviour. Scholars seem agreed that ownership was not conceived in terms of modern land tenure; therefore, modern courts have sometimes refused to recognize any native proprietary rights.[38]

The French administration has been depicted by W.J. Eccles and L.F.S. Upton, among others, as avoiding all definition of native property and territorial rights, as well as avoiding the Dutch and British ambiguity of purchase. Slattery argued, on the contrary, that recognition of native possessory and territorial rights was the keystone of French sovereignty. He stressed the fact that France's primary concern was to extend its dominions in North America and it did this by incorporating native nations under its rule rather than by acquiring lands for European settlement or attempting to extinguish aboriginal title. Through alliances and trading arrangements the French hoped 'to attach the Indian nations to the French Crown as subjects and vassals, and thereby obtain dominion over their territories.' Consequently, he concluded, 'the Crown's rights to the soil were to be held, not to the exclusion of the indigenous peoples, but through them. This approach was consonant with the economic gains initially sought for the establishment of French colonies in America, which centred upon the fur trade, and depended upon the Indians' retention of their hunting territories.'[39]

Property has two aspects. There are first of all the privileges and benefits which derive from the exclusive use of property. Secondly, there is the power which control of property puts into the hands of a seigneur or feudal owner. In the area of French settlement the seigneur enjoyed both revenues from their *censitaires* and privileges and honours under the crown. In the native regions, however, the aspects of property were separated with the Amerindians retaining their territories and enjoying the fruits of their property, yet remaining theoretically subject to the rights of the king of France as superior lord. This relationship flowed naturally from Samuel Pufendorf's definition of usufruct, 'a right in a thing which belongs to another,' in *Du Jure Naturae et Gentium* (1688). He wrote: 'For although whoever is the owner of a thing is regularly the owner of its fruits, yet nothing prevents the separation of these two, so that dominion lies with one, and the right to enjoy the fruits with another.'[40] Pufendorf, on the other hand, had also observed that although 'usufruct cannot be alienated,' it terminated with the death of the usufructuary, or if it had been 'left in legacy to a state' Roman law had ruled that 'it should terminate after one hundred years.'

Among the many affirmations made by French officials, two important declarations, one made during the early years of royal government in Canada and the other in the closing years of the French régime, stand out. The royal instructions to Governor Courcelles in 1665 said that no one was to 'take the lands on which they are living under pretext that it would be better and more suitable if they were French.' In 1755 the Ministry of War issued a directive governing relations with the 'allied nations' of America. It said: 'The natives are jealous of their liberty, and one could not without committing an injustice take away from them the primitive right of property to the Lands on which Providence has given them birth and located them.'[41]

Access to food resources for Algonkian bands often required the mobility offered only by nomadism. Royal instructions in 1755 repeated views which had been expressed when the French first established forts in the hinterland. The pertinent passage said: 'The allied Natives must be deemed well everywhere ... and Sieur de Vaudreuil must leave to certain nations the liberty to wander and go about the lands of the colony, provided that they do not receive foreigners, for that last point is the most essential.'[42]

When the Amerindians, like the French inhabitants of Canada, came under British rule in 1760 the French did not forget their 'brothers.' Article 40 of the Articles of Capitulation of Montreal stated: 'The Savages or Indian allies of his most Christian Majesty, shall be maintained in the Lands they inhabit; if they chose to remain there; they shall not be molested on any pretence whatsoever, for having carried arms, and served his most Christian Majesty; they shall have, as well as the French, liberty of religion, and shall keep their missionaries.'[43] Article 4 of the definitive Treaty of Paris (1763) permitted the inhabitants of Canada, 'French and others,' to emigrate and protected their property rights. The laws and customs by which the Amerindians had been governed in New France would remain in force until specifically abrogated or changed by the new sovereign.

It was a well-established principle of international law by 1763 that the laws and civil rights of subjects acquired by conquest or cession continued in force unless repugnant to the crown's sovereignty. In other words, the ancestral rights of Canada's native peoples were protected as much as the laws and private rights of the French-Canadian 'new subjects.' Just as the Canadian seigneurs and censitaires continued to possess and use their land under their customary law, so the native peoples as agriculturalists, hunters, and fishermen continued to possess and use their ancestral territory according to their group customs under the French régime. The Royal Proclamation of 1763 was the British crown's formal declaration of adoption of a policy similar to French imperial policy regarding the native peoples of the upper Canadian region. Just as the French had restricted seigneurial tenure to the St Lawrence lowlands, with the crown through its marine officers regulating all French acquisition of property in the hinterland which had no western boundary, so the British declared a virtually identical area 'reserved' to 'the several Nations or Tribes of Indians, with whom We are connected, and who live under Our

Protection,' and closed to European settlement except when voluntarily ceded to the crown and opened to colonization.[44]

Royal instructions sent to Governor James Murray in December 1763 directed him to gather information concerning the several bodies of native peoples, 'of the manner of their lives, and the Rules and Constitutions by which they are governed and regulated.' There was some recognition that under the French régime they had enjoyed a generous measure of independence and non-interference with their indigenous system of internal order. Murray was instructed as follows: 'And You are on no Account to molest or disturb them in the Possession of such Parts of the said Province, as they at present occupy or possess; but to use the best means You can for conciliating their Affections, and uniting them to our Government.'[45]

In 1765 the Montagnais asked their missionary, Father Coquart, who had served them since 1746, to intervene with the British authorities to assure that the Royal Domain would not be broken up and lands parcelled out to private owners and that native hunting and trapping rights not be permitted to lapse. They said, 'we have always been a free nation, and we would become slaves, which would be very difficult after having rejoiced for so long in our liberty.' General Amherst ordered that matters should 'continue on the same footing as previously' under the French régime.[46]

Similarly, the chiefs of the Wabash peoples agreed to the British 'taking possession of the Posts in our Country' in 1765 but warned that 'we have been informed that the English where ever they settle make the Country their own.' They disputed the claim that 'when you Conquered the French they gave you this Country.' Instead, they said: 'that no difference may happen hereafter, we tell you now the French never Conquered [us] neither did they purchase a foot of our Country, nor have [they a right] to give it to you. We gave them liberty to settle for which they always rewarded us & treated us with great Civility while they had it in their power, but as they are become your People, if you expect to keep those Posts, we will expect to have proper returns from you.'[47] A few years later the Huron of Detroit made similar statements asserting they had previously informed Sir William Johnson at Niagara that the lands on which the French were settled there belonged to the native people and 'they never had sold it to the French.'

The British interpretation seems to have been, as it had been earlier in Nova Scotia following the cession of 1713, that all lands had belonged to the French crown and that the native 'nations' had enjoyed a usufructuary and personal interest in the land.[48] The French had done all they could to guarantee a continuation under British rule of their special relationship with the Amerindians. The transfer of sovereignty, nevertheless, seemed to imply that legally the native peoples could only make good such rights as the new sovereign through his officers recognized.

In summary, the French claim to New France was based on concepts of Christian appropriation, settlement of vacant lands, and effective cultivation and 'policing.' The establishment of French sovereignty through symbolic acts met with little overt opposition; nevertheless, in the early decades the French did indicate a willingness to resort to the use of force if necessary to establish their claims. French claims were asserted against European rivals. They were not directed against the native peoples because French settlement was geographically restricted to areas largely uninhabited by them. There were no spectacular confrontations which might have indicated the degree to which the Amerindians understood and accepted French concepts of sovereignty.

Instead, a type of dualism evolved as some native people accepted the hospitality of the reserves in the French seigneurial tract of the riverine colony and as some French accepted the hospitality offered in the Amerindian hinterlands. The recognition of the independence and rights of native 'nations' under an umbrella of French sovereignty posed no major problems for either Quebec or Versailles. In seventeenth-century France, sovereignty was generally deemed to be undivided and indivisible. The realm was governed by an unalterable set of fundamental rules and the monarch was sovereign by divine right. Yet in New France there emerged the concept of sovereignty being divided. In other words, an authority might have full power in one sphere and none in another. This followed closely the geographic division of the Canadian sector of New France into a Laurentian colony of European settlement and a vast *pays d'en haut* or Amerindian region claimed and exploited for commercial, strategic, and missionary purposes. Three components of aboriginal rights had been recognized in this upper country: self-rule, as evidenced in the negotiation of alliances and inapplicability of French laws to native peoples; possessory and territorial rights as evidenced in the need to acquire property for emplacements for forts, missions, and a few French agriculturalists; usufructuary rights, specifically unhampered hunting and fishing rights.

The term 'nation' was employed for what later would be called a 'tribe,' to designate an ethnic group and a geographical location. European powers were nation-states whose peoples were politically organized under sovereign governments which possessed coercive powers to maintain order, impose laws, and exact dues. The French did not see the Illinois or Micmacs as possessing coercive governments, but they did envisage them as 'nations' in the sense that they were ethnic identities, that they were bound by ties of consanguinity, that they thought and acted as a group in terms of defence, trade, religious observances, and that each 'nation' had its own distinctive unwritten laws, customs, and traditions.

The French operated on different levels of diplomacy in dealing with members of the 'family of nations' and the native 'allied nations.' On the international level, France like other European powers involved in colonization of America asserted her sovereign rights over a vast continental expanse. At the regional level, dealing with 'independent' peoples, she refrained from interference with original territorial rights, customs, and mode of life. French laws since 1664 applied only to colonists and were not imposed on native inhabitants. The relationship with the latter was couched in terms of military alliances, trading arrangements, and the annual payments of the king's presents rather than in terms of the exercise of coercive social and legal powers, taxation, and military service.

The Janus-like French position can be understood only when account is taken of the two diplomatic levels or spheres in which French statements must be situated. Sovereignty was stressed in interactions with other nation-states, whereas independence was stressed in the context of continental coexistence. The genius of French native policy was therefore that no inherent contradiction was perceived between these two positions. Nevertheless, pursuit of this line of conduct did require the French to do two things: first, to restrict Canadian settlement almost exclusively to the Lower St Lawrence Valley below the junction of the Ottawa River; secondly, to instruct its marine commandants at upper country posts to be circumspect in their statements and actions when dealing with the 'allied Nations.' So long as this relationship was maintained it would appear that France could assume responsibility under international law for colonists and aboriginal peoples. Native nationhood was protected by French sovereignty and French sovereignty was exercised through native nationhood and self-government.

NOTES

This article is from *Native Studies Review* 2 (1) (1986). Reprinted with permission.

Revised version of a public lecture given at the Native Studies Department, University of Saskatchewan, 4 October 1984.

1 H.P. Biggar, ed., *A Collection of Documents Relating to Jacques Cartier and the Sieur de Roberval* (Ottawa 1930), 128
2 Cornelius J. Jaenen, *The French Relationship with the Native Peoples of New France* (Ottawa 1984), 158–212
3 T.R.L. MacInnis, 'The History of Indian Administration in Canada,' *Canadian Journal of Economics and Political Science* 12 (3) (1948): 387; Robert J. Surtees,

The Original People (Toronto 1971), 60; Francis Jennings et al., *The History and Culture of Iroquois Diplomacy* (Syracuse 1985), 71; Bruce G. Trigger, *Natives and Newcomers: Canada's 'Heroic Age' Reconsidered* (Kingston/Montreal 1985), 330–1

4 Peter A. Cumming and Neil H. Mickenberg, *Native Rights in Canada* (Toronto 1972), 14–16, 80; Russel L. Barsh and James Youngblood Henderson, 'Aboriginal Rights, Treaty Rights, and Human Rights: Indian Tribes and "Constitutional Renewal," ' *Journal of Canadian Studies/Revue d'Etudes canadiennes* 17 (2) (1982): 55–81; Ontario Métis and Non-Status Indian Association, *Final Report of the Department of Research for Aboriginal Title* (Toronto 1980), 5; Bradford W. Morse, ed., *Aboriginal Peoples and the Law: Indian, Metis and Inuit Rights in Canada* (Ottawa 1985), passim

5 W.J. Eccles, 'Sovereignty-Association, 1500–1783,' *Canadian Historical Review* 65 (4) (1984): 475, 478, 505, 510

6 Lloyd I. Barber, 'Indian Land Claims and Rights,' in Marc-Adelard Tremblay, ed., *Les Facettes de l'identité amérindienne/The Patterns of Amerindian Identity* (Quebec 1976), 67; A.G. Harper, 'Canada's Indian Administration: The Treaty System,' *America Indigena* 7 (1947): 131; Brian Slattery, 'The Hidden Constitution: Aboriginal Rights in Canada,' *American Journal of Comparative Law* 32 (1984): 363, 367

7 Francis Jennings, *The Ambiguous Iroquois Empire* (New York 1984), 4

8 Cited in Walter B. Scaife, 'The Development of International Law as to Newly Discovered Territory,' *Papers of the American Historical Association* 4 (3) (July 1890); Hugo Grotius, *Droit de guerre et de la paix* (Paris 1867), II, ch. 2, art, ii, 5; Christopher C. Joyne, 'The Historical Status of American Indians under International Law,' *The Indian Historian* 2 (4) (1978): 30–6; James Simsarian, 'The Acquisition of Legal Title to *Terra Nullium*,' *Political Science Quarterly* 53 (1) (1938): 111–28

9 Robert F. Berkhofer, Jr, *The White Man's Indian* (New York 1978), 120; Olive P. Dickason, 'Europeans and Amerindians: Some Comparative Aspects of Early Contact,' Canadian Historical Association, *Historical Papers/Communications historiques, 1979* (Ottawa 1980), 192

10 Francisco de Vitoria, *Leçons sur les Indiens et sur les droits de guerre* (Geneve 1966), 82–4; James B. Scott, *The Catholic Conception of International Law* (Washington 1934), 89

11 Olive P. Dickason, 'Renaissance Europe's View of Amerindian Sovereignty and Territoriality,' *Plural Societies* 8 (3–4) (1977): 97–107; Olive P. Dickason, *The Myth of the Savage and the Beginnings of French Colonialism in the Americas* (Edmonton 1984), 127–32; Neville Figgis, *The Divine Right of Kings* (Cambridge 1914), 45–65; Lewis Hanke, *The Spanish Struggle for Justice in Conquest of America* (Philadelphia 1944), passim.; Fred. H. Kimney, 'Christianity and Indian Lands,' *Ethnohistory* 7 (1960): 44; James Muldoon, *Popes, Lawyers and Infidels: The Church and the Non-Christian World, 1250–1550* (London 1979), passim.; Kenneth J. Pennington, Jr, 'Bartolome de Las Casas and the Tradition of Medieval Law,' *Church History* 39 (June 1970): 149–61; Walter Ullmann, *Medieval Papalism: The Political Theories of the Medieval Canonists* (London 1949), 129–37

12 W.L. Grant, ed., *The History of New France by Marc Lescarbot* (Toronto 1907), I, 17

13 Jacques de Charron, *Histoire universelle de toutes nations et specialement des Gaulois ou François* (Paris 1621), Ch. XII, 13. Catholics often interpreted their

discovery of the New World as a special grace of God, who revealed the existence of 'Adam's other children' to them in order to compensate for the losses suffered through the rise of Islam and the Protestant Reformation. It was unusual, therefore, for a Huguenot to use an essentially Catholic argument of universal Christian dominion.

14 Biggar, *Collection of Documents*, 178

15 Samuel Pufendorf, *De Jure Naturae et Gentium* (Oxford 1934), 600–1; Emmerich de Vattel, *Le Droit des gens; ou, principes de la loi naturelle* (Washington 1916), III, 38

16 Emmerich de Vattel, *The Law of Nations or the Principles of Natural Law* (London 1758), I, 35–6, 98–100

17 Yves Benot, *Diderot: De l'athéisme à l'anticolonialisme* (Paris 1970), 197

18 National Archives of Canada (NA), MG 4, C1, article 14, vol. I, no. 6, 'Droits de France sur le Canada' (1755), 41–2

19 Arthur S. Keller et al., *Creation of the Rights of Sovereignty through Symbolic Acts, 1400–1800* (New York 1938), 148; Joyne, 'Historical Status,' 30–6; Scaife, 'Development,' passim; Simsarian, 'Acquisition,' 111–28; Friedrich A.F. Von der Heydte, 'Discovery, Symbolic Annexation and Virtual Effectiveness in International Law,' *American Journal of International Law* 29 (1935): 448–71; and for the initial discovery period especially Brian Slattery, *French Claims in North America, 1500–59* (Saskatoon 1980), 8–13

20 Biggar, *Collection of Documents*, 180

21 M. Michelant and M. Rame, eds., *Relation originale du voyage de Jacques Cartier* (Paris 1867), II, 6, 8, 41–2; *Edits, ordonnances royaux, déclarations et arrêts concernant le Canada* (Quebec 1854–6), III, 8–9

22 Marc Lescarbot, *Histoire de la Nouvelle-France* (Paris 1618), II, 490; E.H. Gosselin, ed., *Documents authentiques et inédits pour servir à l'histoire de la Marine normande et du Commerce rouennais pendant les XVIe et XVIIe siècles* (Rouen 1876), 18–19; *Edits et ordonnances*, III, II, 13; I, 5

23 E.B. O'Callaghan, ed., *Documents Relating to the Colonial History of the State of New York* (Albany 1855–77), I, 51–2; IX, 46; III, 121, does not give the text of the treaty.

24 NA, MG 1, series C11A, vol. I, 'Extrait de diverses relations qui peut servir à établir le droit de la France sur le pays des Iroquois, 1646 à 1681,' 427; *Edits et ordonnances*, III, 41, 46

25 R.G. Thwaites ed., *The Jesuit Relations and Allied Documents* (New York 1959), LV, 104–14; J. Tailham, ed., *Mémoire sur les moeurs, coutumes et religion des sauvages de l'Amérique septentrionale de Nicolas Perrot* (Paris 1864), 126–8; *Collection de manuscrits contenant lettres, mémoires et autres documents historiques relatifs à la Nouvelle-France* (Quebec 1883–5), I, 213, 217–18; NA, MG 4, C, article 14, vol. I, no. 5, 'Droits de France sur le Canada,' 32–3

26 NA, MG 5, vol. 6, Extracts from a letter of Sieur de Villieu, 16 Oct. 1700, 205–6; MG 1, series C11A, vol. 37, Lovigny to Comte de Toulouse, 1 Oct. 1717, 387; MG7, 1, A3, Nouv. acq. fr., vol. 9275, Journal de Joseph Normandin, 1732, 149–50; Journal of Louis Forhel, 1743, 368

27 C. Hubert Smith, *The Explorations of the La Vérendryes in the Northern Plains, 1738–43* (Lincoln 1980), 49, 63, 113; NA, MG 1, series F3, vol. 13, pt 2, Campaign journal of Celoron, Nov. 1749, 472; MG 21, Egerton MSS, vol. 2694, 11

28 Cornelius J. Jaenen, 'The Role of Presents in French-Amerindian Trade,' in Duncan Cameron, ed., *Explorations in Canadian Economic History* (Ottawa 1985), 231–50
29 NA, MG 1, series C11A, vol. 36, 'Mémoire instructif,' 1716, 33–9; see also J. Clinebell J. Thompson, 'Sovereignty and Self-Determination: The Rights of Native Americans under International Law,' *Buffalo Law Review* 27 (1978): 713.
30 Cited in Brian Slattery, *Canadian Native Law Cases* (Saskatoon 1980), I, 77
31 *Collection de manuscrits*, I, 125
32 Jorge Juan y Antonio d'Ulloa, *A Voyage to South America* (London 1806), 376–7, as cited in Dickason, 'Europeans and Amerindians,' 193
33 NA, MG 1, series C11A, vol. 35, Ramezay to Governor, 16 Sept. 1715, 120
34 E.B. O'Callaghan, ed., *Documents Relative to the Colonial History of the State of New York* (Albany 1855), X, 5 July 1752, 253
35 *Rapport de l'Archiviste de la Province de Québec pour 1921–22* (Quebec 1922), 'Acte authentique des Six nations Iroquoises sur leur Indépendence,' 2 nov. 1748, 108; Archives des colonies (AC) (Paris), series B, vol. 89, Rouille to La Jonquère, 4 mai 1749, f. 67; NA, MG 5, B1, vol. 24, 'Discussions sur les limites du Canada,' 9 mai 1755, 354
36 NA, MG 18, G1, La Jonquière Papers, King to La Jonquée, 30 avril 1749, 12; AC, series B, vol. 87, Maurépas to La Galissonière, 23 juin 1748, f. 7; André Chagny, *François Picquet Le Canadien (1708–1781)* (Paris 1913), 304–7
37 Dorothy V. Jones, *License for Empire: Colonialism by Treaty in Early America* (Chicago 1982), 5–18
38 Ralph Linton, 'Land Tenure in Aboriginal America,' in O. Lafarge, ed., *The Changing Indian* (Norman 1943), 53–4; John C. McManus, 'An Economic Analysis of Indian Behaviour in the North American Fur Trade,' *Journal of Economic History* 32 (1) (March 1972): 39, 43, 49; Adrian Tanner, *Bringing Home Animals* (St John's 1979), 182, 187, 190; Daniel Francis and Toby Morantz, *Partners in Furs* (Montreal 1983), 95–7, 120, 126–7, 170; A.H. Snow, *The Question of Aborigines in the Law and Practice of Nations* (Northbrook 1972), 72–5
39 Brian Slattery, 'The Land Rights of Indigenous Canadian Peoples, as Affected by the Crown's Acquisition of Their Territories' (Diss. Oxford University 1979), 91–2
40 Pufendorf, *De Jure Naturae et Gentium*, 600
41 Biggar, *Collection de Manuscrits*, I, 175; NA, MG 4, C1, article 14, vol. I, no. 8, 'Moyens pratiques pour concilier la France et l'Amérique' (1755), 72
42 H.R. Casgrain, ed., *Extrait des archives* (Quebec 1890), Instructions to Vaudreuil, 1755, 33
43 Adam Shortt and Arthur G. Doughty, eds., *Documents Relative to the Constitutional History of Canada, 1759–1791* (Ottawa 1918), I, 2, 25–30; NA, MG 17, A4, vol. 4, Articles of Capitulation, 1760, 288
44 *The Royal Proclamation of 7 October 1763* (London 1763), passim.
45 NA, MG 17, A4, vol. 4, 'Mémoire du Canada, 1745–60,' 288; Shortt and Doughty, *Documents*, I, 2, 25, 27, 199
46 Lorenzo Angers, *Chicoutimi, Poste de Traite (1676–1856)* (Montreal 1971), 60
47 Clarence V. Alvord, ed., *Collections of the Illinois State Historical Library*, XI: *The New Regime 1765–1767* (Springfield 1916), Crogan's Journal, 30 Aug. 1765, 47–8
48 Sir Francis Bond Head in 1836 made an assessment which indicated that the British following the Conquest had adopted a policy similar to the French

relationship. He said: 'Over these lands His Majesty has never exercised his paramount right except at their request, and for their manifest advantage – within their own communities they have hitherto governed themselves by their own unwritten laws and customs. The lands and property have never been subject to tax or assessment or themselves liable to personal service. As they are not subject to such liabilities, neither do they yet possess the political privileges of His Majesty's subjects generally.' NA, RG 10, vol. 60, Head's reply to House of Assembly, nd

COLONIAL ATLANTIC CANADA

OLIVE PATRICIA DICKASON

Amerindians between French and English in Nova Scotia, 1713-1763

The Treaty of Utrecht (1713) has been called 'la plaque tournant' (the turntable) of the French empire in North America. Until that point, France had been aggressive and expanding; afterward, she was on the defensive, determined to prevent further dismemberment of her North American empire. Nowhere was this change more evident than along the Atlantic coast, where French peninsular Acadia was transformed into English Nova Scotia, while Ile Royale (Cape Breton) and Ile St-Jean (Prince Edward Island), as well as adjacent mainland areas such as the Gaspé and the St John River, remained in the hands of the French. These regions were mostly inhabited by the Micmac, an Algonkian-speaking hunting and gathering people, with their close relatives the Malecite (including the Passamaquoddy, who spoke a variety of the same language), and later some Abenaki, living along the St John River. To the south were Abenaki.[1] In contact with Europeans for more than two centuries, and allies of the French for half that time, these peoples were usually the ones indicated by the expression 'French and Indians' of colonial war fame.

The Treaty of Utrecht profoundly modified their position, particularly that of the Micmac in Nova Scotia (with whom this paper is principally concerned). As the rival colonial powers squared off against each other in preparation for what would become the final round of imperial hostilities in the northeast, Micmac and Malecite found that their position to play off one against the other had been greatly strengthened. This was a vital matter for them, because as allies of the French they had been fighting the English ever since the first decades of the seventeenth century. At the beginning, they had fought for traditional reasons of prestige and booty, even when helping their allies, but the defeat of the French in Acadia in 1710 and the advent of English settlement had put another cast entirely upon the conflict, which at that point was already nearly one hundred years old. Micmac and Malecite were now fighting for their lands and for their very survival as a people. Not only was their struggle the longest in Canadian history (a fact which is not generally recognized); in its last phase it came the closest to fitting into the pattern of American frontier wars. It can be seen as the northern extension of the Abenaki confrontation with the British to the south, sharing with it the characteristic of being largely fought on the sea.[2]

The prolonged hostilities, combined with such factors as the slow rate of settlement in the northern regions, meant that the Micmac (as well as the Malecite, and to a lesser extent in Canada, the Abenaki), were able to maintain their traditional way of life within their aboriginal territories much longer than the coastal peoples to the south. In fact, although they were among the earliest in Canada to be colonized by Europeans, Micmac and Malecite are still to be found in their ancestral lands (although admittedly on only a tiny fraction of what had once been theirs), and retain a lively sense of their cultural identity. The pressures of colonization soon made them aware of the importance of asserting their sovereignty, which the Micmac declared very early (in 1715, and probably earlier). Viewed by the British at the time as 'extravagant,' such claims nevertheless influenced perceptions of Amerindian rights to their lands, and explicit acknowledgement of those rights began to appear in treaties involving the Micmac and Malecite. This in turn helped pave the way for the proclamations of 1761–3. The definition of those rights is if anything an even thornier issue in Canada today than in 1763, a consequence of having been recognized, but not defined, in the Constitution in 1982. What was once a regional issue is now freighted with constitutional considerations. In this new context, the war assumes a historical significance that was not evident in the past; it has been transmuted from an episode in local history into a confrontation of national, and possibly even supranational, importance (insofar as it may have an influence on aboriginals of other states). It is therefore pertinent to re-examine the conflict in the light of its role in winning recognition for aboriginal rights.[3] Winning those rights was not a result that could have been foreseen, or even contemplated, by the architects of the Treaty of Utrecht.

Consistent with the European view that conquest was primarily concerned with territorial right, Britain saw the Treaty of Utrecht as giving her clear sovereign title to Acadia, on the grounds that since it had been recognized as a French possession, France must have extinguished aboriginal title. This was not a belief shared by the original inhabitants who, far from having been conquered by the French, had welcomed them as allies. Long ago, the Micmac and their neighbours had accepted the French king as their father, because he had sent missionaries to teach them their new religion; but the idea that he had any claim on their lands, or that they owed him any more allegiance than they owed their own chiefs, was foreign to them. In Acadia, France remained too dependent upon her allies, for reasons of trade and war, to ever make an issue of these points; rather, colonial officials were carefully instructed to make sure that Amerindians were not disturbed on lands they occupied or otherwise used.[4] Nor did the Micmac consider that this alliance automatically implied their subjugation when France was defeated in Acadia in 1710. Even if they had been conquered, in the Amerindian view that would have involved a complex web of rights and obligations that related principally to persons and only secondarily, if at all, to territories.[5] The British were equally firm in their belief that whatever title the Micmac (or any other Acadian Amerindians) might have had had been lost in the two-fold process of French colonization followed by French defeat.[6] In any event, in the British view the whole issue was irrelevant as the Micmac and their neighbours had never possessed sovereignty anyway, being migratory or semi-sedentary peoples who had not organized into a nation-state. Their difficulty, as they would quickly learn, would be in convincing the Amerindians of all this.

The irony of such a position lay in the fact that when the British took over Acadia, they had a long history of recognition of aboriginal land rights, in contrast to the French, who had never formally acknowledged such rights, except where it was useful for annoying the British. Originally, there had been little to choose between the positions of the two colonial powers: as Christian nations, they both considered their claim to sovereignty over lands pre-eminent to that of non-Christian peoples. In principle, the French had not found it necessary to modify this position, even though in practice they took care to respect the territories of their allies, as we have already seen. The fur trade, upon which their colony was economically based, meant capitalizing on the hunting skills of the indigenous population rather than competing over territorial rights; coupled with the smallness of the French population, that had meant that land had never become an issue in New France. The English, however, first colonized in territories where the Amerindians were farmers, very much as the English were themselves; the latter soon became entangled in the legal absurdity of claiming one set of land ownership principles for themselves and a different set for Amerindians. This had become painfully evident in Virginia, where thoughtless and insensitive actions of colonists had goaded Amerindians into bloody retaliation in 1622. The Dutch had pointed to a solution in 1623 by purchasing Manhattan Island and lands along the Hudson River from the Amerindians, a move which dealt with proprietary right while sidestepping that of sovereignty. The English, after first ridiculing the idea, quickly adopted it; after all, it accorded with a traditional principle of their Common Law that there be no expropriation without compensation. In 1629 John Endecott, governor of Massachusetts Bay Colony (1628–30), was instructed to purchase title to desired lands.[7] The first deed which has survived dates from 1633; there are claims in the documents to earlier purchases.[8] Although the principle of compensation at that time was more honoured in the breach than in the observance, it managed to survive through a morass of fraudulent dealings, some of which were difficult to distinguish from outright theft. The resultant tensions had contributed not a little to the wars between colonists and Amerindians which were to become characteristic of the American frontier; by the time the British took permanent possession of Acadia, they had already experienced several, of which King Philip's War (1675) is the best known. Despite their failure to colonize in peace, the English continued to recognize the principle of compensation; for example, Colonel Thomas Dongan, governor of New York (1682–8), was instructed in 1683 'to take all opportunities to gain and procure from the Indians upon reasonable rates and terms such tracts and quantities of ground as are contiguous to any other lands or convenient for any territories in trade ... thereby to enlarge and secure any territories.'[9]

Clear as this principle might have appeared in the Thirteen Colonies, where most of the aboriginal peoples had lived in agriculturally based communities long before the arrival of the Europeans, the British did not at first consider it applicable to Acadia. They appear to have taken for granted that their defeat of France, besides winning them sovereignty, also had absolved them from the necessity of compensating Amerindians for lands. Never clearly enunciated as a policy, this reflected the popular colonial view that the Acadian natives, as hunters and gatherers, did not have as strong a claim to the land as did farmers. Consequently, they did not have the same proprietary rights. Proclaiming George I as king of Acadia, the British asked the Amerindians for an oath of fidelity, and to share their lands peacefully with the settlers they hoped would soon be coming. In return, they promised more generous annual gifts than the Amerindians had received from the French, but relied mainly on the prospect of better trade values at government-backed 'truck-houses.' They also promised not to interfere with the Amerindians' religion (the French had declared the Micmac of Acadia all Catholicized by the end of the seventeenth century). The Amerindians replied that they were pleased to have religious liberty, but also wanted to have the same in trade – they did not want truck-houses or, for that matter, any more European forts on their lands. Trade could continue as it had for the most part in the past, from shipboard. As for the oath of allegiance, they had never taken one to the French king, and did not see why they should do so for the British. As far as the Micmac were concerned, Acadia was their land, which they called Megumaage and which they had divided into seven districts. All they wanted was to live in their traditional territories without fear of English encroachment.[10]

Both English and French had a lively awareness of the need to maintain good relations with Amerindians. It was not their importance as allies that mattered so much as the difficulties they could cause if they were not.[11] The attempt to get the natives of Acadia to swear allegiance to the British monarch galvanized the French. Pontchartrain (minister of the marine, 1699–1715) had visions of the unthinkable: that the Amerindians might transfer their loyalties to the British and wage war against the French.[12] With their intimate knowledge of Acadia, Amerindians could easily isolate remaining French territories. In Pontchartrain's view, the best way to avoid such an eventuality would be to persuade the Micmac of Nova Scotia and the Abenaki of the borderlands to go and live on territory that was indisputably French (at least in the European, if not the Micmac, view), preferably Ile Royale.[13] When the British heard what the French were planning, they foresaw dire consequences for themselves, since such an Amerindian move would not only greatly increase Ile Royale's military strength, it would put Acadia's trade under French instead of English control.[14] Pontchartrain called upon two men with proven records for effective Amerindian relations to implement this program: the Canadian-born missionary Antoine Gaulin (1674–1740) and the half-Abenaki Bernard-Anselme d'Abbadie, Baron de Saint-Castin (1680–1720). Loyal as they both were to the French cause, and despite a lavish use of gifts,[15] neither of these men was successful. Saint-Castin could not dislodge the Abenaki from their farms on the Penobscot; as for Gaulin, the closest to French territory he could persuade his migratory Micmac flock to include regularly in their rounds was at Antigonish, on the British side of Baye d'Artigoniche (George Bay). Their claim that there was not enough game on Ile Royale to support them for any length of time appears to have been confirmed by a stay there in 1715–16. It would be a decade before the harassment of war made it possible for Gaulin to persuade the Micmac to establish a gardening community on Ile Royale's Bras d'Or Lake. Faced with this kind of intransigence, the French did the next best thing and concentrated on the proven method of maintaining alliances by annual ceremonies featuring feasting, dancing, endless oratory accompanied by gift-giving, and awards of medals and honours. They also met English prices in trade.[16]

The French held a trump card in this contest to win Amerindian loyalties: their missionaries. Of the approximately one hundred who worked in Acadia during the French regime, three who had been sent by the Missions Etrangères to the Micmac stand out during New France's later period. Gaulin served from 1698 until 1731, when he retired because of ill-health; Spiritan Pierre-Antoine-Simon Maillard (c. 1710–62) was in Acadia from 1735 until his death in 1762; and Spiritan Jean-Louis Le Loutre (1709–72), whose missions included Acadians as well as Micmacs, 1737–55. The effectiveness of these missionaries stemmed at least in part from the fact that traditionally, among Amerindians, the most highly respected leaders were also shamans. This was recognized by the French: in the words of Governor Saint-Ovide, 'It is only these men [the missionaries] who can control the Savages in their duty to God and the King.'[17] Maillard put it another way: only through religion, he wrote, could Amerindians be rendered docile.[18] The record supports this; for one thing, the Micmac complained incessantly about the lack of missionaries, particularly after Gaulin's retirement, when the French had difficulties in finding suitable candidates.[19] In spite of such deficiencies, Micmac, Malecite, and Abenaki remained faithful to the French cause for the 150 years that France was a colonial presence in North America. To this day, most of them are Catholic.[20] All of this adds up to a record that stands in striking contrast to the popular stereotype of the 'fickle' Amerindian. French success was based as much on the nature of Amerindian societies as it was on the Christian message and the character of the missionaries themselves. The seventeenth century, when the French became active in Acadia, was also the period when Catholic evangelical zeal reached its peak in the Counter Reformation, and its message and practices struck a responsive chord among the peoples in Acadia. In the words of an eighteenth-century observer, the Micmac 'use ritual to fill the times that are not occupied with satisfying their needs. They had already developed much before we knew them; in modifying their orientation, we cannot claim to have entirely changed their taste in these matters.'[21]

Neither can it be doubted that the French used missionary influence for political ends: this was evident with Gaulin, and above all with Le Loutre. Gaulin, born on Ile d'Orléans near Quebec City, appears to have been something of a maverick; he espoused the interests of the Micmac so thoroughly that he managed to run afoul not only of the English, which perhaps was to be expected, but also of the French. 'Sieur Gaulin is not a settled spirit in whom one can have confidence,' was the verdict.[22] Still, French officials admitted, although belatedly (after his retirement), that Gaulin had been one of their most effective missionaries in the field.[23] As for Le Loutre, he concentrated so thoroughly on the political side of his functions that in 1749 the English put a price on his head[24] Capturing him in 1755, they took care to keep him in England until after the Peace of Paris, 1763.

The Micmac were far from being passive in this struggle for their control. Quickly realizing the strength of their position *vis-à-vis* English-French rivalry, they pressured both French and English in the matter of gifts. Presents were essential in Amerindian diplomacy, in which they had designated roles; metaphorically, they could, for example, dry tears, open doors of foreign countries, appease anger, ask for fair value in trade, or bring the dead back to life. The Micmac complained if presents were deficient in quantity or quality, in accordance with their own custom of exchanging gifts of value. In 1716 Governor Costebelle found himself in difficulties at the annual rendezvous at Port Dauphin (Englishtown, NS) when he had one-third less than the usual quantity to distribute: the Amerindians accused him of withholding goods, particularly powder and shot, and refused to accept anything at all. Thanking the French for having sent them missionaries, they said they would go to the English to obtain what they needed.[25] The threat was not an idle one; the year previous, Pierre-August de Soubras (commissaire-ordonnateur for Ile Royale, 1714–19) had warned that 'the policy of the Savages appears to be to maintain neutrality, conserving the liberty to go to both the French and the English to obtain merchandise at the lowest price.' He hoped the missionaries would be able to use 'motifs de la religion' to prevent that from happening.[26] He was to be disappointed: in 1718 Nova Scotia's Lieutenant-Governor John Doucett (1717–26) wrote to Richard Philipps (governor of Nova Scotia, 1717–49) that a chief had visited him at Annapolis Royal to say that if the English expected to be friends with the Micmac, they must give presents as was done every year by the French king. Doucett expected visits from other chiefs with the same message.[27]

As incidents accumulated, such as the raid and counter-raid on Canso, 1718–20, the French were eventually led in 1720–1 to reorganize their system of distribution. Governor Saint-Ovide was informed that everything he had requested for the Amerindians was being sent in order to end their complaints.[28] The English adapted reluctantly to this form of diplomacy, placing more importance on good value in trade than on gifts as such, as they tended to regard presents as a form of bribery rather than as an acknowledgment of an active alliance. In other words, the English considered gift distribution as paying Amerindians to keep the peace; the French looked on it as reimbursement for support against the enemy. In neither case did gifts automatically ensure success for a particular purpose, as the unsuccessful French attempt to persuade the Micmac and Abenaki to move to Ile Royale so clearly illustrates. But without presents, negotiations or alliances were hardly possible, as Philipps realized when he deferred convening chiefs to a peace conference until the arrival of gifts for the occasion.[29]

Looming hostilities eventually loosened British purse strings, and Philipps was able to hold a feast and distribute presents in 1722, a month before the outbreak of the English-Indian War (Râle's War or Dummer's War; the Abenaki were the principal Amerindians involved). But the occasion turned out to be a concession rather than a change of heart; it took the prospect of peace in 1725 to bring about British gift distributions on a scale calculated to influence the course of events. This occurred not only during the treaty negotiations in Boston, but continued later at the ratifications at Annapolis

Royal in 1726 and 1728, at Halifax and the St John River in 1749, and again at Halifax in 1752 and 1760.[30] In trade also, the British found themselves accommodating Amerindian preferences and customs.[31]

Adaptation was less evident in the question of sovereignty, as here the British saw no reason to equivocate with the Amerindians as the French had done. The Micmac responded by reaffirming their sovereignty over Megumaage, and by announcing that they could make war or peace as they willed.[32] As the final round of the North American colonial wars got under way, the Micmac pitched into the fray on both land and sea. Between 1713 and 1760 Louisbourg correspondence refers to well over one hundred captures of vessels by Amerindians. This activity peaked in 1722, the year the English-Indian War broke out.[33] Revivals of lesser proportions in the 1750s followed the establishment of Halifax in 1749 and the expulsion of the Acadians in 1755.[34]

The turning point came in 1725, when the British took advantage of the Abenaki suit for peace following the destruction of Norridgewock to obtain Amerindian acknowledgement of their claim that the Treaty of Utrecht had made the British crown 'the rightful possessor of the Province of Nova Scotia or Acadia according to ancient boundaries,' even though the natives had not been consulted or even informed beforehand. Such a move was made possible because the negotiations involved Micmac from Cape Sable and Malecite from the St John River, as well as the Abenaki. The British in return promised to respect native hunting and fishing rights. Both agreements were signed on the same day, 15 December, the one for peace known as the Treaty of Boston (or Dummer's Treaty), including hunting and fishing rights; the other known as Treaty No. 239, although sometimes called Mascarene's Treaty, detailing how the Amerindians were expected to behave as British subjects.[35] Treaty 239 is not, as has been alleged, a different version of the peace of 1725, since it is not directly concerned with the cessation of hostilities. Ratification of these agreements with the Micmac proceeded slowly, perhaps because the British were more concerned with recognition of their sovereignty claims than they were about acknowledging Amerindian rights. The process was not helped by the fact that each side had a different understanding of what a treaty meant. The European concept of a few acting for a whole people was strange to the Micmac, in whose non-state society every man was expected to speak for himself. To the Amerindians, treaties were covenants between groups of individuals that did not have to be written, and, far from being permanent, were ritually renewed from time to time with appropriate ceremonies in which gift exchanges played an essential part. The English insisted on written treaties which theoretically were to be honoured in perpetuity, but conceded to Amerindian practice to the extent of arranging for ratifications and confirmations, as they had soon learned that unless all the chiefs considered themselves included, treaties of any kind were ineffective. There were also problems of language; apparently the British were not always scrupulous about how proposed terms were translated and explained during negotiations.[36] At first they sought to avoid subsequent challenges by including general statements, as they did in a treaty signed with Abenaki in 1693, to the effect that the terms had been carefully read and interpreted to the Amerindians, who had agreed they understood what was involved, By the Treaty of 1725, it was noted that the terms had been 'read distinctly' by 'sworn interpreters'; in 1749 a renewal with the Amerindians of the St John River included the acknowledgement that its terms had been 'faithfully interpreted to us by Madame de Bellisle, inhabitant of this river, nominated by us [the native signers] for that purpose.[37] The problems, however, continued. Even when interpreters were conscientious, there were grave difficulties in translating concepts, such as that of exclusive land ownership, which had no counterpart in native languages.[38] Neither were the two 1725 treaties always clearly distinguished. Such confusions, or deceptions, did little to allay the suspicions of Amerindians. They considered each ratification a separate agreement, which concerned the signees and their bands alone. In this they were encouraged by the French, who signed no written treaties with their allies.

The 1725 peace treaty was a blow to the French, and their immediate reaction was to disclaim that the English-Indian war had been of any concern to them, even as they arranged for 150 of the refugees to be established at Bécancour on the south shore of the St Lawrence opposite Trois-Rivières and at St François on the Chaudière River. They hoped the Abenaki would use these bases to continue contributing to the French war effort.[39] An apparently unfounded report from Quebec, to the effect that Gaulin was encouraging his Micmac to sign also, so annoyed the minister of the marine, Maurepas,[40] that Saint-Ovide had to come to Gaulin's defence.[41] Maurepas was inclined to think the Boston peace treaty had been inspired more by war-weariness than by a weakening of Abenaki attachment to the French.[42]

But measures had to be taken to counteract the threat the treaty so obviously presented, particularly in the face of repeated Amerindian complaints that the all-important gift distributions often did not have enough goods to go around. The amount budgeted by the French for 'présents ordinaires' in the early days of the British period had been 200 *livres* a year for Acadia; not included were expenditures for 'présents extraordinaires,' which varied according to circumstances. The intensifying colonial conflict tended to transform the latter category of gift into the former, contributing to a steady rise in costs that was further aggravated by inflationary pressures.[43] By 1756, 37,000 *livres* was listed for 'présents ordinaires'; the extra-budgetary expenditures were only hinted at by Drucour, Louisbourg's last French governor: 'it is not possible to refuse certain extraordinary expenses which are entailed when we are obliged to employ Savages.'[44] He added that promises of gifts to come were no longer sufficient; the allies would be led only when they had goods in hand. What had started as a matter of protocol to cement alliances and trade agreements had ended as a means of subsistence for the Amerindians and a form of protection for the French. An increasing number of Amerindians were journeying to Port Toulouse (St Peters, NS) on Ile Royale for its distributions; in the words of Edward Cornwallis (governor of Halifax, 1749–52), 'the Micmacs go every year to Canada, to be clothed at the expense of the French King.'[45] When numbers were unexpectedly large, officials sometimes took matters into their own hands. In one reported case, Commandant Des Herbiers and Commissaire-Ordonnateur Prevost personally supplemented an insufficient supply of goods form the king's stores; in other cases as well, presiding officials, English as well as French, found themselves paying for goods out of their own pockets.[46] There were also transportation costs and the need to feed Amerindians at these rendezvous, a need which became more pressing as game diminished and the size of the assemblies grew.[47] The irony of this for both French and English lay in the fact that such expenses could only increase, as the effectiveness of the gifts was relative not only to quantity and quality, but also to the numbers who received them.

When the British besieged and took Louisbourg in 1745, they felt they had won the day in Acadia. But the French had taken Madras from the British in India, so an exchange was effected at the bargaining tables in Europe and Louisbourg was returned to the French in the Treaty of Aix-la-Chapelle in 1748. The British reacted by founding Halifax in Chebouctou (Chebucto) Harbour in 1749, partly to appease the New Englanders who had played a major role in Louisbourg's fall. But in doing so, they again neglected to consult with the Micmac, whose territory (a district they called Segepenegatig) was involved. Asking, 'Where can we go, if we are to be deprived of our lands?' the Micmac claimed that the area was particularly good for hunting and declared war.[48] The English reciprocated by calling the Micmac 'rebels,' on the grounds that they were British subjects, whether they agreed or not.[49] The ensuing harassment of settlers hampered the plans of Governor Cornwallis, who asked that arms be provided the colonists as 'at present above ten thousand people are awed by two hundred savages.'[50] Lawrencetown, a palisaded settlement to the east of Halifax, had to be abandoned for a time.[51] Cornwallis issued a proclamation commanding all 'to Annoy, distress, take or destroy the Savages commonly called Mic-macks, wherever they are found,' and encouraged soldiers to stay in Nova Scotia and homestead after they had finished their service. For a short while. marriage with Amerindian women was officially encouraged.[52]

That fall the Micmac again attacked Canso, taking twenty prisoners whom the French eventually released; when the English attempted to build a fortification at Minas, Micmac killed nine of the workers.[53] Suspecting French complicity, the English responded by stepping up their efforts to counter French gift diplomacy and to boost trade. This was effective, and a group of Micmac under a ranking chief defected and signed a peace treaty at Halifax in 1752.[54] Major Jean-Baptiste (Joseph) Cope (Coppe, d. 1758/60), chief of a Shubenacadie band, told the Halifax Council during negotiations that peace could be renewed if 'the Indians should be paid for the land the English had settled upon in this country.'[55] The final treaty made no mention of such a payment, but did explicitly acknowledge the right of Amerindians to the 'free liberty of Hunting and Fishing as usual' (presumably on their lands, although it does not explicitly say so), acknowledged the natives' right 'to trade to the best Advantage,' and provided for regular gift distributions, the first of the treaties to do so.[56] In these measures, it was a precursor of things to come: in the first case, of the Proclamation of 1763, and in the second, of the numbered treaties of the west. Only recently, in 1985, the Supreme Court of Canada ruled that its guarantee of hunting and fishing rights is still valid.[57] At the time of its signing, its concessions were discounted by Rouillé, minister of the marine, who believed that the peace treaty did not reflect general Micmac sentiment but was the fruit of gifts lavished on certain individuals, and that in any event it would not be observed for long.[58] And in truth, the Halifax Council had presented Cope with a gold belt and two lace hats for himself and his son, along with a promise of 'handsome presents of such Things whereof you have the most need.'[59] Rouillé's judgment proved sound for the short run, as within a few months an incident in an English fort set off another series of reprisals and counter-reprisals with the Micmac.[60]

In the midst of these mounting rounds of vengeance, or perhaps pursuit of scalp bounties (both English and French by this time were paying such bounties, no questions asked),[61] the fall in 1755 of Forts Beauséjour and Gaspareaux on Chignecto Peninsula marked the opening of the last phase of the French-English colonial wars in North America. The English expulsion of the Acadians also played a part; their blood ties with Micmac, Malecite, and Abenaki triggered a series of vengeance raids. As Louisbourg prepared itself for its second and final siege, which came in 1758, a full-scale war dance was staged, the last of its kind in Nova Scotia. The arrival of the French navy in the harbour provided the occasion. Continuing for several days, it featured both Catholic and Amerindian ritual, including the endless speeches characteristic of such events. Abbé Maillard sang a High Mass, accompanied by a choir of Amerindians. The appearance of Charles Deschamp de Boishébert et de Raffetot (1727–92) with a detachment of Malecites and Canibas (Abenaki), 'strong men, very tall, who had already fought with distinction in Canada,' added a striking note. The chiefs prostrated themselves at the feet of the naval squadron commander, Comte Dubois de la Motte, who raised them up. A Malecite chief advanced and placed at the comte's feet four scalps woven into a wampum collar, which the commander received, expressing the hope that there would be more to come. He added that the moment was near when the French would be counting on their allies' bravery and valour. The assembled warriors responded with their cry 'heur.' Several days later Drucour held a feast, consisting of salt pork, raisins, wine, and biscuits, which the warriors received with a restraint that impressed the naval officers; the warriors kept most of their food to take to their wives and children. More speeches were followed by war games and finally a dance, which to the audience was characterized by the 'singularity of [the dancers'] postures and cries, the strangeness of their accoutrements.' Their war paint added to the colourfulness of the occasion.[62]

A major role as scouts and coastal lookouts was seen for these Amerindians.[63] But in the hurly-burly of events, plans miscarried or were not carried out at all; for example, when Boishébert had arrived with 500 Acadians and Amerindians, he had found that expected food and ammunition depots had not been set up, which had caused his men considerable hardship.[64] The influx of Le Loutre's Amerindians to Ile Royale after the loss of Beauséjour and Gaspareaux put unforeseen demands on supplies,[65] a situation that was not eased when Maillard's Amerindians helped themselves without permission from a depot outside the fortress.[66]

Growing sentiment that the presence of Amerindians within the fortress was a liability as far as treating with the British was concerned reached its climax at this time. In 1757 Louisbourg learned of the recent massacre of English prisoners by French allies at the fall of Fort William Henry (at Lake George, New York). When Louisbourg in its turn fell the following year, capitulation terms offered by the English made no mention of Amerindians, which was interpreted as not boding well for them.[67] When the British took over the fortress, none was present.

If the Amerindian factor had simply faded away at Louisbourg during its capitulation, the same could not be said for Acadia generally. As with the 1725 treaties, the British had to make sure that all the chiefs felt themselves to be included in this new arrangement. Accordingly, the British set about obtaining submissions through the intercession of French missionaries such as Maillard, Jesuit Joseph-Charles Germain (1707–79), and Jean Manach (c. 1717–66) of Les Missions Etrangères, all of whom were allowed to stay with their Amerindian flocks after 1760. The British officer in charge of this mission eventually reported that he had received the submissions of Paul Lawrence

(Laurent in the French documents) of La Hève (La Have, NS) and of Augustine Michael (Michel) of Richibouctou and had sent them to Halifax to complete formalities. Along with two other submissions he had received previously, he hoped these would clear up the Amerindian question. Alas, it was not to be so. He was taken aback to be informed by Abbé Manach that there were others to be seen 'upon the same business, as soon as their spring hunting is over; and enquiring upon how many, he gave me a list of fourteen chiefs, including those already mentioned, most of which he said would come.' Surprised to hear of such a number of chiefs in this part of America, the colonel added that "Mr. Manach further told me they were all of one nation, and known by the name of Mickmackis.'[68] Despite this collaboration with British authorities, Manach was eventually accused of causing unrest among the Amerindians, arrested, and sent to England in 1761. The British also doubted Germain, and in 1762 detained him in Quebec. Maillard was allowed to remain, but died in August 1762.

Ratifications finally completed, the ceremonial conclusion of peace between the British and the Micmac took place on 25 June 1761, with Lieutenant-Governor Jonathan Belcher presiding. Micmac confirmed their acknowledgment of British sovereignty and promised good behaviour; they were assured that British laws would 'be a great Hedge about your Rights and properties.'[69] The peace was to be effective 'as long as the Sun and the Moon shall endure.'

Thus concluded the military phase of the long fight of the Micmac, Malecite, and Abenaki of Acadia to remain masters of their own territories. In this struggle, they had shown themselves to be astute in turning imperial rivalries to their own advantage. When it came to self-interest, there was not much to choose between the Amerindians and the colonial powers.[70] The difference lay in the fact that both France and Britain were building empires, whereas the Amerindians, after a brief initial period when some attempted to use European alliances to expand their own hegemonies, had soon found themselves struggling simply to survive. French and English encouraged Amerindian alliances because of the commercial and imperial benefits they would bring; Amerindians sought trade alliances because of the usefulness of European goods, and also because of the prestige these brought in fulfilling social obligations within their communities as well as in their diplomatic relations with other tribal groups. At first, such goods enhanced traditional lifestyles. But as the growth of European settlement exacerbated colonial rivalries, particularly in Acadia, Amerindians became aware that the trading aspect of the alliance had become eclipsed by its military aspect, and that they could best assure their survival as a people by acting as guerrillas for the colonial powers. Their capacity to keep those powers off balance was their most formidable weapon.[71] In this context, Louisbourg's role was vital: for the French, whatever their original intentions for building the fortress, its greatest military usefulness turned out to be as headquarters for the maintenance of Amerindian alliances and in encouraging and abetting guerrilla warfare; for the Micmac and Malecite, it represented a reprieve from European economic and cultural domination, because as guerrillas they were able to dictate to a surprising extent their own terms as allies, particularly with the French.

The Peace of Paris of 1763 did not exorcise the spectre of French return to Canada, which remained to haunt the British and to give hope to the Micmac until the defeat of Napoleon in 1815. Upon hearing of the French investment of St John's, Newfoundland, in 1762, the Micmac became restive and gave the settlers of Lunenburg a severe fright (Lunenburg was near La Hève, a major settlement for Amerindians and Métis). Such fears were fuelled by reports that the Micmac were being supplied secretly from St Pierre and Miquelon, islands off the southern coast of Newfoundland that were France's only remaining foothold in Canada. These reports have not been substantiated; officially, at least, France instructed her representatives on the two islands not to receive Micmac from Cape Breton, since that 'would only be disagreeable to the English, and expensive and useless to the French.'[72] The Micmac appear to have gone to the islands in search of the services of priests, as much as anything. They were also looking for new hunting grounds; thrown back on their own resources when their traditional territories on the mainland had long since been overhunted, they further alarmed British authorities by going to southern Newfoundland.[73] The movement, which had been desultory as long as colonial rivalries provided Micmac with the means of subsistence, took on a new dimension with the loss of French support. Despite attempts of British officials in Newfoundland to dislodge these unwanted immigrants, they had come to stay.

The American War of Independence led the Micmac to investigate its potentialities for their interests, and in 1776 a group of them even signed a treaty of Watertown, Massachusetts, to send men to the American army. But the majority of their people opposed the idea, and the treaty was quickly disavowed on the grounds of misunderstanding. Hope again flickered when the French joined the American cause, but by this time it was all too clear that whatever happened in the south, the British were going to be in Nova Scotia for a long while. During the War of 1812–14, the Micmac promised the British to be neutral in return for not being required to take up arms.

The major effect of this protracted period of uncertainty was to persuade the British to continue with gift distributions, albeit in fits and starts. A scare or a crisis turned on the flow, its resolution reduced it, or even turned it off. No longer in a position to bargain, the Micmac had to take what they could get. This once-assertive, far-ranging people now asked only to be left alone, to live their lives in their own way. But the pressures of incoming settlers would not allow for even that, and the long neglected need to regulate land transfers and titles became urgent. The principle that Amerindians had a right to the use of their lands (expressed as hunting and fishing) had been explicitly recognized in the Treaty of Portsmouth, New Hampshire (1713), the Treaty of Boston (1725), and the Halifax Treaty (1752), as well as implicitly in others.[74] The move to realize this in practice came in the Proclamation of 1761. This was in the form of instructions to 'the Governors of Nova Scotia, New Hampshire, New York, Virginia, North Carolina, South Carolina and Georgia, forbidding them to Grant Lands or make Settlements which may interfere with the Indians bordering on those Colonies.'[75] The governors were told they were no longer to grant licences to individuals for the purchase of Amerindian lands without the express approval in each case of the commissioners for trade and plantations in London.[76] Whitehall hoped that this reaffirmation of a long-standing policy would encourage its enforcement.

The proclamation had little effect in Nova Scotia; among other things, Amerindians complained that their relatives and erstwhile allies, the Acadians, were invading their lands and disrupting their hunting. Lieutenant-Governor Belcher saw this as a move on the part of the Acadians to keep the Amerindians stirred up against the English;[77] it is also possible that since their dispossession and expulsion by the English, the few Acadians who remained were simply moving onto Micmac lands, to which they considered they had a claim because of their blood ties with the natives. There is evidence that Acadians were not always considerate of their Amerindian relatives.[78]

Belcher issued a second proclamation, specifically for Nova Scotia, in 1762.[79] It ordered the removal of all persons illegally settled on Amerindian lands, and reserved the colony's northeastern coast from the Musquodoboit River to the Baie des Chaleurs for the Micmac to hunt, fowl, and fish. The good intentions of this measure did not last past the scare caused by the French occupation of St John's that summer. Memories of Micmac depredations were much too recent to allow for such a gesture; if the Micmac were to be given land anywhere, so the argument went, it should be in the interior, away from the strategic coast. The reference in the proclamation to lands of Amerindians, 'the Property of which they have by Treaties reserved to themselves,' may refer to clauses in earlier agreements assuring Amerindians of their rights to hunt and fish as usual on their lands. In Nova Scotia and the Maritimes generally, treaties were not used as vehicles for the acquisition of Amerindian lands. It is possible that the much more sweeping Proclamation of 1763, which designated lands west of the Appalachians as Amerindian territory and reserved to the crown the sole right to extinguish Amerindian title, was foreseen by Belcher as applying to the Atlantic colonies. There are some grounds for believing that this had been Whitehall's intention; but on the scene in the Maritimes, as in the St Lawrence Valley, colonial officialdom stood firm in its position that the French had extinguished aboriginal title and there was no need to repeat the process.

When Loyalist refugees from the English colonies flooded into Nova Scotia and the St John River following the Peace of Paris of 1783, lands were opened for homesteads without further ado. Aboriginal proprietors had to protest very loudly for their voices to be heard. There were those who listened, however, and lands were set aside for the Micmac as well as for the Malecite, but by government grants or legislative acts, not by negotiated treaties. Any compensation Micmac or Malecite received for land used for settlers' homesteads was by sale of portions of these reserves.

Thus ended the last, and perhaps most intense, phase of the 150-year-old fight of the Micmac, which had started in the traditional pattern of raiding the enemy and had ended as a struggle for the right to continue to live in their own way on their own lands. The war remains a unique episode in Canada's history, since it was the only one in which Amerindians fought on their lands for their lands. Other confrontations that might be considered comparable, such as the clashes during the gold rush in British Columbia (1857–64), were isolated incidents that did not develop into warfare, despite some hysterical reporting. The conflict of the French with the Iroquois (1609–1701), which certainly was a war, was fought for reasons of trade and power; and not only did the Iroquois not lose territory because of it, they even managed to keep most of the fighting off their lands, at least until towards the end. The 1885 confrontation with the Métis in the Canadian northwest must also be placed in another category: in that case the struggle was for a recognized place within the dominant society. The Amerindian participation in that showdown, which was minimal, was a desperate protest against Ottawa's parsimony at a time when starvation stalked the plains as a consequence of the near-extermination of the buffalo.

If the Micmac's success was not unqualified as far as they themselves were concerned, their long struggle did much to set the scene for the Proclamation of 1763, which was issued two years after they had signed the peace.[80] Although the disturbances in the Ohio Valley known as 'Pontiac's Uprising' may have precipitated matters, they did not initiate its policy. Rather, it had slowly developed as Amerindian land rights came to be acknowledged in earlier treaties arising out of the eastern war and out of earlier proclamations, particularly the one of 1762. The implementation of the Proclamation of 1763 began in southern Ontario, when incoming settlers obtained lands by means of negotiated treaties. In this case, at least, the native peoples of central and later of western Canada benefited from the protracted confrontation that had been fought out in the east. European settlement also benefited, as a way had been found to avoid a repetition of a costly exercise. And in the long view, the proclamation would be a factor in incorporating Amerindians into the Canadian mosaic, since the process of negotiated settlement that it inaugurated has meant that almost all Amerindians in Canada have a continuing presence in their aboriginal homelands. But aboriginal right still remains to be defined; in this, Canada has the unique distinction of having raised the issue to the constitutional level.

NOTES

This article is from *American Indian Culture and Research Journal* 10 (4) (1986). Reprinted with permission.

This paper is an expansion and reinterpretation of research originally done for 'Louisbourg and the Indians: A Study in Imperial Race Relations 1713–1760,' *History and Archaeology* 6 (1976): 3-206; the French edition appeared in 1979. This version was prepared with the aid of a grant from the Social Sciences and Humanities Research Council of Canada.

1 Concerning the fluidity of tribal boundaries, see Harald E.L. Prins, 'Micmacs and Maliseets in the St. Lawrence Valley,' *Actes du dix-septème Congrès des Algonquinistes*, ed. William Cowan (Ottawa: Cartleton University Press, 1986), 263–78.

2 On the Abenaki war, see Kenneth M. Morrison, *The Embattled Northeast* (Berkeley: University of California Press, 1984).

3 The best general account of the war to date is that of L.F.S. Upton, in *Micmacs and Colonists* (Vancouver: University of British Columbia Press, 1979), 31–60. The war's marine aspect is dealt with by Olive Patricia Dickason, 'La "querre navale" contre les Britanniques, 1713–1763,' in *Les Micmacs et la Mer*, ed. Charles A. Martijn (Quebec: Recherches amérindiennes au Québec, 1986), 233–48. See also Horace Palmer Beck, *The American Indian as a Colonial Sea Fighter*(Mystic, Conn.: Maine Historical Association Publication #35, 1959), and John S. McLennan, *Louisbourg from its Foundation to its Fall 1713–1758* (Toronto: Macmillan, 1918), ch. 4.

4 For example, the king's instructions in 1665 to Daniel Rémy de Courcelle (governor of New France, 1665–72). *Collection de manuscrits contenant lettres, mémoires et autres documents historiques relatif à la Nouvelle-France*, 4 vols. (Québec: Coté, 1883–5), 1:75

5 National Archives of Canada (NA), Archives des colonies (AC), C11B 1: 340–1, lettre de Michel Bégon de la Picardière (intendant of New France, 1712–14), 25 sept. 1715, dans déliberations de Conseil, 28 mars 1716; ibid., lettre de Philippe Pastour de Costebelle (first governor of Ile Royale, 1713–17), 7 sept. 1715, 335–6; *Collection de manuscrits*, 1: 46–7, lettre des sauvages à Monsieur le Général Philipps, aux Mines, 2 oct. 1730

6 NA, Colonial Office (CO) 217/31: 115–115, Lt. Col. Lawrence Armstrong (lieutenant-governor of Nova Scotia, 1724/25–39), to Board of Trade, 19 June

1736. See also Upton, *Micmacs and Colonists*, 37–9; and R.O. MacFarlane, 'British Indian Policy in Nova Scotia to 1760,' *Canadian Historical Review* 19 (2) (1938): 154–67.

7 Francis Jennings, *The Invasion of America* (Chapel Hill, NC: University of North Carolina Press, 1975), 135

8 Ibid., 138

9 Peter A. Cumming and Neil H. Mickenberg, eds., *Native Rights in Canada* (Toronto: General Publishing, 1972), 67

10 NA, CO 217/1: 364–6, 'Answer of Indians of Penobscot to the Commissioners,' April 1714; NA, AC, C11B 1: 340v–2, lettre de Bégon, 25 sept. 1715, dans les déliberations de Conseil, 28 mars 1716; ibid., lettre de Costebelle, 7 sept. 1715, 335–6. Amerindian hostility worried the British, who warned Philippe de Rigaud de Vaudreuil (governor general of New France, 1703–25) that unless guerrilla harassment ceased, they would respond in kind. NA, Nova Scotia A 3: 22. See also Upton, *Micmacs and Colonists*, 37–8.

11 Les sauvages sont peu de chose, étant nos alliées, mais pourraient devenir quelque chose de considérable, étant nos ennemis.' NA, AC, C11B 4: 251–6, 17 nov. 1719

12 NA, AC, B 35/3: 239, Louis de Phélypeaux, Comte de Pontchartrain et de Maurepas (known as Pontchartrain), à Saint-Ovide, 20 mars 1713. See *Collection de manuscrits* 3: 399–400, de la Galisonnière, 6 nov. 1747.

13 Dickason, 'Louisbourg and the Indians,' 82–5; NA, AC, F3 50: 4v, 10 avril 1713; NA, AC, B 35/3: 262v–3, à Baron de Saint-Castin, 8 avril 1713

14 Thomas B. Akins, ed., *Selections from the Public Documents of the Province of Nova Scotia* (Halifax: Annand, 1869), 6; letter from Colonel Samuel Vetch (commander at Annapolis Royal, 1710–13) to Lords of Trade, 24 Nov. 1714. A facsimile edition of this work was published by Polyanthos in 1972 under the title *Acadia and Nova Scotia: Documents Relating to the Acadian French and the First British Colonization of the Province, 1714–1758.*

15 NA, AC, B 35/3: 239, Pontchartrain à Saint-Ovide, 20 mars 1713; ibid: 260 v, à Gaulin, 29 mars 1713; AC, B 36/7: 430, à Jacques l'Hermitte (king's second lieutenant and engineer at Ile Royale, 1714–15), 21 mars 1714; ibid: 443-443, à Costebelle, 22 mars 1714; NA, AC, B 36/1: 84, Conseil à Besnard, 26 fév. 1716

16 NA, AC, C 11 B 1: 343-4, Conseil, 3 mars 1716

17 NA, AC, C11B 12: 37 v, Joseph de Monbeton de Brouillan *dit* Saint-Ovide (governor of Ile Royale, 1718–39), à Jean-Frédéric Phélypeaux, Comte de Maurepas (minister of the marine, 1723–49), 25 nov. 1731

18 NA, Nova Scotia A 32: 222, Maillard to Peregrine Hopson (governor of Nova Scotia, 1752–5), 11 Sept. 1748. French civil officials concurred: 'Religion is a rein which truly holds them in our interest.' NA, AC, B 64/3: 425, Maurepas à Charles de La Boische, Marquis de Beauharnois (governor general of New France, 1726–46), et Gilles Hocquart (commissaire-ordonnateur for New France, 1729–31; intendant, 1731-48), 17 avril 1736. Maillard was not always so positive, however. See his 'Lettre sur les missions de l'Acadie et particulièrement sur les missions Micmaques,' *Les Soirées canadiennes* 3 (1863): 294. Similar doubts were expressed by others: 'Were it not for other concurring circumstances that indispose the savages against the English, religion alone would not operate, at least not so violently, to that effect.' 'Letter from Mons. de la Varenne,' in *An Account of the Customs and Manners of the Micmakis and Maricheets, Savage*

Nations Now Dependent on the Government of Cape Breton (London: Hooper and Morley, 1758), 86

19 NA, AC, C11B 12: 36–9, Saint-Ovide au ministre, 25 nov. 1731; ibid., 14: 55–55v, 15 oct. 1733; ibid., 18: 38–38v, 23 oct. 1736; ibid., 20:85–90v, François Le Coutre de Bourville (king's lieutenant for Ile Royale, 1730–44) à Maurepas, 3 oct. 1738

20 According to Abbé Noël Alexandre de Gléfien, Micmac regarded non-Catholics as enemies. Letter from Mons. de la Varenne, *Customs and Manners*, 85

21 Thomas Pichon, *Lettres et mémoires pour servir à l'histoire naturelle, civile et politique du Cap Breton* (London 1760), 101–2. The Amerindians 'ont besoin d'un culte qui remplisse la durée des momens qu'ils ne donnent pas à leurs besoins. Ils en avoient déjà trouvé l'emploi de ces momens avant que nous les connussions, et en changeant le genre de leurs occupations à cet égard, nous ne devons pas prétendre changer entièrement les goûts qui leurs avoient fait choisir.'

22 NA, AC, C11B 2: 44–44v, Conseil, 10 avril 1717; ibid., 1: 337v, 345-66, Conseil, 28 mars 1716; ibid., 2: 39, lettre de Soubras, 8 jan. 1717, dans les déliberations du Conseil, 10 avril 1717. One observer thought that missionaries generally appeared to be under the control of the Amerindians. NA, AC, C11B 29: 367, de Jean-Pierre Roma (fisheries entrepreneur, fl. 1715–57), 11 mars 1750

23 NA, AC, C11B 1: 249v, 'Mémoire sur la mission des sauvages Mikmak et de l'acadie,' sans signature, c. 1739

24 Gérard Finn, 'La carrière de l'Abbé Jean-Louis Le Loutre et les derniers années de l'affrontement anglo-français en Acadie' (thèse de doctorat, troisième cycle, Université de Paris I, 1974, 86–91); Akins, ed., *Public Documents of Nova Scotia*, 178–9, Cornwallis to Captain Sylvanus Cobb, 13 Jan. 1749

25 Louis Chancels de Lagrange, 'Voyage fait a Lisle Royalle ou du Cap Breton en Canada,' *Revue d'histoire de l'Amérique française* 13(3) (1959): 431; NA, AC, C11B 2: 188–9v, de Costebelle au Conseil, 1717

26 'La politique des Sauvages semble estre de s'entrenir neutres et de se conserver la liberté d'aller chés les françois et les anglois prendre les marchandises ou ils le trouvent à plus bas prix.' NA, C11B 1: 343–343v, lettre de Soubras, le 19 déc. 1715, en déliberations du conseil, le 28 mars 1716

27 NA, CO 217/31:63, Doucett to Philipps, 1 Nov. 1718

28 Dickason, 'Louisbourg and the Indians,' 83; NA, AC, B 45/2: 267; B 45/2: 267, 13 mai 1722

29 Akins, ed., *Public Documents of Nova Scotia*, 33, Philipps to British Secretary of State for the Southern Department, James Cragg, Annapolis Royal, 26 May 1720. The Jesuits had learned this very early. In 1636 they had come empty-handed to a parley in Huronia, and had been rebuked by an Old Man. Reuben Gold Thwaites, ed., *The Jesuit Relations and Allied Documents* (Cleveland: Burrows Bros., 1896–1901), 9: 231. In the realms of trade and politics, French governors quickly learned to give back speech for speech and present for present. Thwaites, ed., *Jesuit Relations*, 40 165–9. For the English view, see E.B. O'Callaghan and J.R. Brodhead, eds., *Documents Relative to the Colonial History of the State of New York*, 15 vols (Albany, NY: Weed, Parsons, 1853–87), 7: 650, Sir William Johnson (superintendent of Indian Affairs for the Northern Department, 1755–74) to Lords of Trade, 30 Aug. 1764. For a general, although somewhat dated, treatment of the subject, see Wilbur S. Jacobs, *Diplomacy and Indian Gifts* (Stanford, Calif.: Stanford University Press, 1950).

30 NA, CO 217/30: 14, abstract of letter from Doucett, 16 Aug. 1729; *Canadian Indian Treaties and Surrenders*, 3 vols. (Ottawa 1891–1912; facsimile, Coles Canadiana Collection, 1971), 2: 199–204; William Daugherty, *Maritime Indian Treaties in Perspective* (Ottawa: Indian and Northern Affairs Canada, 1983), 81–93. The negotiations for the 1749 ratification are reported in Akins, ed., *Public Documents of Nova Scotia*, 573–4, Council aboard the *Beaufort*, 14 Aug. 1749. The French were especially annoyed with the St John River people, as they had been courting them with particular care. A recent influx of Abenaki from New England may have been a factor, as well as substantial gifts from the English. Ibid., 581, Council aboard the *Beaufort*, 1 Oct. 1749. Governor Raymond sent René, Micmac chief from Naltigonish, to break the ratification. NA, AC, C11B 31: 62–3, Raymond à Rouillé, 19 nov. 1751

31 NA, CO 217/30: 14–14v, abstract of letter from Colonel Armstrong, 24 Nov. 1726. thomas Caulfield, lietuenant-governor at Annapolis Royal, 1711–17, complained; 'The Indians of Pennobscot, St. Johns, and Cape Sables, trade chiefly on ye several coasts with furrs and feathers, who never come here but when necessity obliges them and ye reasons they assign are that there is noe Kings Magazine here for them, as was in ye time of ye french, or as there is now at Cape Breton, wch: if there was they would bring in their peltery to us and I believe would prove a great advantage.' Akins, ed., *Public Documents of Nova Scotia*, 9, Caulfield to Board of Trade and Plantations, Annapolis Royal, 1 Nov. 1715

32 NA, CO 217/2: 5 extract of letter from David Jefferies to Captain Robert Mears, 6 July 1715

33 NA, AC, C11B 6: 46, Saint-Ovide to minister, 4 nov. 1722

34 At one point the British were urged to be cautious about 'extirpating the French Neutrals that inhabit the Coast from Mirimachi to Canso for fear of giving umbrage to the Indians.' Akins, ed., *Public Documents of Nova Scotia*, 486, General Edward Whitmore to Lawrence, Louisbourg, 20 June 1760

35 The texts of these treaties are in Daugherty, *Maritime Indian Treaties*, 75–8; Cumming and Mickenberg, eds., *Native Rights in Canada*, 300–4; *Canadian Indian Treaties and Surrenders*, 2: 198. the chief British negotiator was army officer Paul Mascarene, administrator for Nova Scotia (1720–51, off and on). The Cape Sable Micmac, supplied with arms and equipment from Louisbourg, had been particularly effective as sea-raiders against English shipping. NA, AC, CO 217/31: 46, extract of letter from Joseph Dudley (governor of Massachusetts, 1702–15), 31 July 1719. A Malecite view of these agreements, particularly in regard to hunting and fishing rights, is by Andrea Bear Nicholas, 'Maliseet Aboriginal Rights and Mascarene's Treaty, not Dummer's Treaty,' *Actes du dix-septième Congrès Algonquinistes*, 215–29. The first treaty affecting Canadian Amerindians that specifically acknowledged hunting and fishing rights had been signed in 1713, of which more later.

36 Concerning the Abenaki's difficulties in this regard, see David L. Ghere, 'Mistranslations and Misinformation: Diplomacy on the Maine Frontier, 1725 to 1755,' *American Indian Culture and Research Journal* 8(4) (1984): 3–26.

37 Daugherty, *Maritime Indian Treaties*, 69, 77, 83

38 Nicholas, 'Maliseet Aboriginal Rights,' 225–6. Eventual acceptance of British sovereignty is witnessed by the treaty of the Miramichi Micmac of 1794, in which the Micmac 'King' John Julian and his brother 'begged His Majesty to

grant them a portion of land for their own use.' The request was granted. Cumming and Mickenberg, ed., *Native Rights in Canada*, 308–9

39 *Collection de manuscrits* 3: 125, Charles Le Moyne de Longueuil (acting governor of New France, 1715–26), et Bégon au ministre, 31 oct. 1725; ibid., 111–14, lettre de Vaudreuil au ministre, de Québec, 16 nov. 1725

40 NA, AC, B 49/2: 705–7, de Maurepas, 28 mai 1726. The charge was in a letter from Longueuil and Bégon, 31 oct. 1725. *Collection de manuscrits*, 3: 126

41 NA, AC, C11B 8: 34–8v, 18 sept. 1726

42 NA, AC, B 52/2: 487-487v, Maurepas à Saint-Ovide, 20 juin 1728

43 When the Micmac asked that the extra gifts they had been receiving be included in the regular distribution, the request was granted. NA, AC, C11B 31: 63, Jean Louis, Comte de Raymond et Seigneur d'Oye (governor of Ile Royale, 1751–3), au ministre, 19 nov. 1751

44 NA, AC, C11B 35: 125, Chevalier Augustin de Boschenry de Drucour (governor of Ile Royale, 1754–8), au ministre, 18 nov. 1755

45 Akins, ed., *Public Documents of Nova Scotia*, 183, Cornwallis to the Duke of Bedford, 19 March 1749/50

46 NA, AC, C11B 28: 40v, Charles Des Herbiers, Sieur de La Ralière (commandant at Ile Royale, 1749–51), et Jacques Prevost de La Croix (commissaire-ordonnateur for Ile Royale, 1749–58), au ministre, 19 oct. 1749; NA, CO 217/30: 14, abstract of letter from Doucett, 16 Aug. 1721

47 NA, AC, C11B 15: 12–14, Conseil, 25 jan. 1735

48 There are two versions of this declaration. The earlier one is reproduced in *Report Concerning Canadian Archives, 1905*, 3 vols. (1902), 2: appendix A, pt III, in 'Acadian Genealogy and Notes' by Placide Gaudet, 293. The later one is in *Collection de documents inédits sur le Canada et l' Amérique publiés par le Canada Français*, 3 vols. (Québec: Demers, 1888–90), 1: 17–19. Similar complaints had been heard when the English had planned Lunenburg. NA, AC, C11B 10: 187–92, Saint-Ovide à Maurepas, 1 nov. 1729.

49 Akins, ed., *Public Documents of Nova Scotia*, 581, Council aboard the *Beaufort*, 1 Oct. 1749; ibid., 581–2, Proclamation of Governor Cornwallis, Oct. 1749

50 NA, Nova Scotia A 35: 4, Cornwallis to Secretary of State, 20 Aug. 1749

51 Adam Shortt and Arthur G. Doughty, eds., *Canada and its Provinces*, 23 vols. (Toronto: Glasgow Brook, 1914–17), 13: 99

52 NA, Nova Scotia A 17: 129–32; Nova Scotia B 1: 53–5; J.B. Brebner, 'Subsidized Intermarriage with the Indians,' *Canadian Historical Review* 6(1) (1925): 33–6

53 NA, AC, C11B 28: 84, de Des Herbiers, 5 nov. 1749; Beamish Murdoch, *History of Nova Scotia or Acadie*, 3 vols. (Halifax: James Barnes, 1865–7), 2: 161

54 NA, AC, C11B 32: 163–6, Prevost à Antoine Louis Rouillé, Comte de Joüy (minister of the marine, 1749–54), 10 sept. 1752; ibid., 33: 159v, Prevost à Rouillé, 12 mai 1753; Akins, ed., *Public Documents of Nova Scotia*, 672–4, Council minutes, Halifax, 16 Sept. 1752; Murdoch, *History of Nova Scotia*, 2: 219–22

55 Akins, ed., *Public Documents of Nova Scotia*, 671. Council minutes, Halifax, 14 Sept. 1752. Amerindian resistance to land surveys had long been troubling the British. Ibid., 99, Council minutes, Halifax, 4 Sept. 1732

56 Akins, ed., *Public Documents of Nova Scotia*, 682–5; Daugherty, *Maritime Treaties*, 50–1, 84–5; Cumming and Mickenberg, eds., *Native Rights in Canada*, 307–9

57 'Court Rules 1752 Treaty Still Valid,' *Micmac News* (Dec. 1985), 1, 5; 'Ruling Says Indian Treaty Has Priority Over N.S. Law,' *Edmonton Journal*, 22 Nov. 1985
58 NA, AC, B 97: 313, Rouillé à Raymond, 17 juil. 1753
59 Akins, ed., *Public Documents of Nova Scotia*, 673
60 NA, AC, C11B 33: 160–1, Prevost à Rouillé, 12 mai 1753. See also *Collection de documents* 2: 111–26, Anthony Casteel's Journal.
61 Akins, ed., *Public Documents of Nova Scotia*, 682. Hopson to the Lords of Trade, 16 April 1753
62 NA, Archives de la Marine, B4, Article 76:41–2, Mémoire concernant les Sauvages Mickmacs, malechites et Cannibas rassembler sur la côte de L'ile Royale en 1757, de Emmanuel-Auguste de Cahideuc, Comte du Bois de la Motte, lieutenant général des armées navales
63 NA, AC, C11B 37: 289–91, Louis Franquet (military engineer in New France, 1750–8), au ministre, 18 juin 1757; Pre-Conquest Papers, L8, letter from Captain Henry Pringle, 31 July 1757, 54
64 NA, AC, C11A 103: 140-1, Vaudreuil au ministre, 3 août 1758
65 NA, AC, C11B 35: 59–61v. Drucour et Prévost à Machault, 11 nov. 1755
66 NA, AC, C11C 10: 52–3, Journal du siège du Louisbourg, 1758
67 Le Courtois de Surlaville, *Les derniers jours de l'Acadie*, ed. Gaston du Boscq de Beaumont (Paris: Emile Lechevalier, 1899), 223–4, 238
68 Colonel Frye to the Governor of Nova Scotia, dated Fort Cumberland, Chignecto, 7 March 1760. *Massachusetts Historical Society Collections*, first series, 10: 115
69 NA, CO, 217/18: 277–84, 'Ceremonials at Concluding a Peace,' 25 June 1761
70 That the French were well aware of this is evident in official correspondence. Typical was the observation that 'au fonds, tous ces gens là ne sont amis de personne' [fundamentally, these people are not friends of anyone]. NA, AC, C11B 29: 367, mémoire de Roma, 11 mars 1750
71 Dickason, 'Louisbourg and the Indians,' 31–2. See also Upton, *Micmacs and Colonists*, 39.
72 NA, AC, C 12, 1: 30, Mémoire du Roy pour servir d'instruction au Sr Dangeac nommé au gouvernment des Iles St Pierre et de Miquelon, 23 fév. 1763
73 While there is no doubt that Amerindians had crossed Cabot Strait in prehistoric times, it is also evident that the eighteenth-century migration to Newfoundland was facilitated by sea-going shallops acquired from Europeans. The Micmac had been using such craft since the beginning of the seventeenth century. Samuel Purchas, *Hakluytus Posthumus or Purchas His Pilgrimmes*, 20 vols. (Glasgow: McLehose, 1906), 18: 304; R.T. Pastore, 'Micmac Colonization of Newfoundland,' paper presented at Canadian Historical Association conference, Fredericton, NB, 1977
74 Although the Portsmouth Treaty principally concerned New England Abenaki, it included some St John River Amerindians. Its partial nature prevented it from being effective. There is some irony in the fact that it was signed in the same year as the Treaty of Utrecht, which ignored Amerindian rights. The text is in Daugherty, *Maritime Indian Treaties*, 70–2; and Cumming and Mickenberg, eds., *Native Rights in Canada*, 296–8.
75 Cumming and Mickenberg, eds., *Native Rights in Canada*, 285
76 Ibid., 286

77 Ibid., 286–7, letter of Jonathan Belcher (lieutenant-governor of Nova Scotia, 1761–3) to the Lords of Trade, 2 July 1762

78 For instance, in 1717 Doucett reported that as far as Acadian claims that fear of Amerindian reprisals prevented them from taking the oath were concerned, 'I am far from believing what they [the Acadians] say, for to my knowledge if an Indian is att any time insolent in their House's, they not only turn them out, but beat them very severely. 'However, Amerindians did not 'revenge themselves on 'em for such usage.' The most likely explanation for such behaviour on the part of the Micmac would be that they considered the Acadians kin. NA, CO 217/2: 175v–6

79 The text of this proclamation, along with Belcher's explantory letter, is in Cumming and Mickenberg, eds., *Native Rights in Canada*, 286–8.

80 See, for example, the letter of the Earl of Egremont (Sir Charles Wyndham, 1710–63), to the Lords of Trade, 5 May 1763, and the latter's response, 8 June 1763. These letters make clear the official desire to avoid placing colonists in the unpleasant position of facing 'frequent Incursions of Amerindians' such as had occurred in Acadia and on the fishing grounds following the Treaty of Utrecht. Adam Shortt and Arthur G. Doughty, *Documents Relating to the Constitutional History of Canada 1759–1791*, 2 vols (Ottawa: King's Printer, 1918), 1: 127–47. Egremont's concern that Amerindian land rights be respected had no parallel in the negotiations for the Treaty of Utrecht.

L.F.S. UPTON

The Extermination of the Beothucks of Newfoundland

The extermination of native people as the result of white contact was a recurrent feature of European expansion. Certain well-defined causes are offered to explain the process: the first informal contacts spread disease; missionaries arrive to challenge tribal customs and disrupt traditional lines of authority; settlers come to farm on the lands of people already decimated by epidemics, and kill those who resist; the surviving natives move on to be absorbed by other indigenous groups on the fringes of white settlement. Where there is no hinterland to serve as a refuge, as in the Caribbean Islands or Tasmania, the aborigines are destroyed completely.

The natives of Newfoundland were exterminated, but events there do not follow this pattern. The whites who made the first contact were fishermen, as was usual for the area, but no missionaries followed to challenge and disrupt tribal society. No farmers settled in Newfoundland, so the usual reason for dispossessing the natives did not operate; nor, consequently, did the customary rationale for wars of extermination. The insular situation of Newfoundland meant that there was no retreat for the natives, yet, while they were being annihilated, another Amerindian people, the Micmacs, successfully established themselves there in the face of the white presence.

The natives of Newfoundland were the first North Americans to come into contact with Europeans, who called them Red Indians because of their liberal use of ochre on bodies, clothing, food, and weapons. The Beothucks were equipped for life in a taiga economy, in common with the other peoples of the northeastern boreal forest. They used the full range of equipment to be found in the region: bark canoes, snowshoes, moccasins; they wore skin clothing, lived in bark or skin-covered shelters, ate out of bark dishes and containers. Their diet was almost entirely animal, caribou from late fall to early spring, fish, shellfish, waterfowl, and berries in the relaxed months of summer. Their ability to preserve food was superior to that of the mainland Indians, for they had storehouses fifty feet long, covered with deerskins and birch bark, with a ridge pole and gable ends. These stores may have been a late development, inspired by the sheds of the white fishermen; and the elaborate deer fences that stretched for miles to control the caribou during the hunt may also be of post-contact origin.[1]

It is impossible to know what the population of any part of northeastern America may have been at the time of first contact; before the first written estimates were made, in the seventeenth century, there had already been a hundred years of exposure to new European diseases. Estimates of the Beothuck population in 1500 range anywhere from 500 to 20,000. The ability of the northeastern forest to support hunters and gatherers has been calculated by Eggan as being one person per hundred square kilometres. Koerber suggests that the resources of one mile of coastline, in association with interior land, could support the same number of persons as one hundred square kilometres.[2] These criteria would give Newfoundland a pre-contact population somewhere between 1123 and 3050 persons. Given that the ability of the northeastern forest to support life decreased as man moved north, the lower figure would seem more reasonable; but as Newfoundland had a climate mild by comparison with the mainland in the same latitude, I would place the pre-contact population at 2000.

The relationship between whites and Beothucks passed through three well-defined stages. The first lasted from 1500 to 1612 and was marked by occasional kidnapping, casual trade, sporadic pillage, and mutual retaliation. This period saw the introduction of European goods and, presumably, European disease. The second stage began when the Beothucks withdrew into the interior to live beyond the restricted range of the European fishermen who visited the coast. This strategy of withdrawal has no parallel elsewhere in the region and its cause cannot be known: epidemic disease may have been the catalyst that prompted the decision. The third and final stage began in the middle of the eighteenth century when whites moved in from the north coast to use the resources of the interior along the line of the Exploits River, the very area to which the Beothucks had withdrawn. The resulting competition saw the extermination of the Beothucks despite attempts by British officials and a few belated humanitarians to stop the process.

The first description of the Beothucks was written in 1500 by Alberto Cantino; fifty-seven of them had been brought to Lisbon for display:

> I have seen, touched, and examined these people ... they are somewhat taller than our average, with members corresponding and well-formed. The hair of the men is long, just as we wear ours, and they wear it in

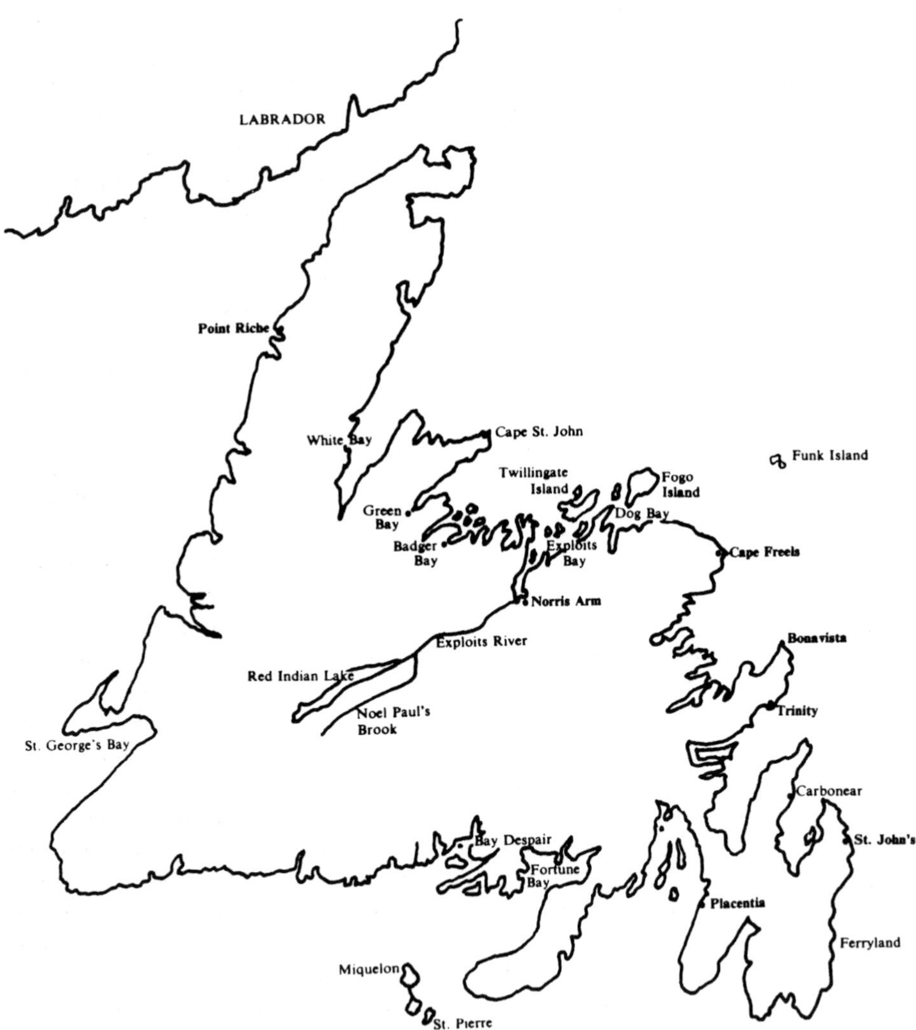
LABRADOR
Point Riche
White Bay
Cape St. John
Funk Island
Twillingate Island
Fogo Island
Green Bay
Dog Bay
Badger Bay
Exploits Bay
Cape Freels
Norris Arm
Exploits River
Bonavista
Red Indian Lake
Noel Paul's Brook
Trinity
St. George's Bay
Carbonear
Bay Despair
St. John's
Fortune Bay
Placentia
Ferryland
Miquelon
St. Pierre

> curls, and have their faces marked with great signs ... Their eyes are greenish and when they look at one, this gives an air of great boldness to their whole countenance. Their speech is unintelligible, but nevertheless is not harsh but rather human. Their manners and gestures are most gentle; they laugh considerably and manifest the greatest pleasure. So much for the men. The women have small breasts and most beautiful bodies and rather pleasant faces. The colour of these women may be said to be more white than otherwise, but the men are considerably darker.[3]

Other Beothucks were reported to have been brought to England as early as 1502, but it is not always possible to tell at this distance who the marauding Europeans actually brought home with them. In 1509 a French ship landed six or seven natives at Rouen, together with their clothes, weapons, and canoes. These men were described as being 'of the colour of soot ... tattooed on the face with a small blue vein from the ear to the middle of the chin, across the jaws.'[4] By the middle of the century an uncomplimentary note had crept into the scattered references accorded the Beothucks. 'The people are large & somewhat dark. They have no more God than beasts, & are evil folk,' noted Jean Alphonse de Saintonge in 1559. André Thevet heard that they were 'extremely inhuman and intractable: according to the experiences of those who have gone there [Newfoundland] to fish for cod.'[5]

The difference between the laughing captives in Lisbon in 1500 and the intractable natives of mid-century was precisely the result of their exposure to those who came to fish for cod. The explorer with his quest for human souvenirs was an occasional invader, but from 1500 on European fishermen were a permanent feature of the summer landscape. Their contacts with the Beothucks have gone unrecorded, but they must have included the occasional trade and pillage that took place elsewhere on the northeast coast of America. But there was an aggravating circumstance peculiar to Newfoundland: the cod fishery required that the catch be dried and cured before carrying it back across the Atlantic, and this meant that some rudimentary works had to be erected on the shoreline in the form of fish-flakes (drying racks), cabins (tilts), sheds, and landing stages. These buildings were used for only a few weeks in the year, and it saved considerable time, labour, and expense if they were all to be found standing when the next fishing season came around. These abandoned structures were a natural attraction to natives eager to acquire European goods by salvaging what had been left behind; and such salvage would be regarded as theft by the Europeans on their return. From salvaging during the off-season it was a short step to theft during the fishing season itself.[6] This situation did not prevent the growth of a casual fur trade, but it did not make for mutual trust. Cartier stopped at Quirpon in 1534 and exchanged goods with some Red Indians, but two years later came the first report of the natives fleeing at the sight of white men. Fighting must have taken place, as implied in Thevet's comment of 1557 that the Beothucks 'are little prone to warfare if their enemies do not search them out. Then they defend themselves completely in the fashion and manner of the Canadians.'[7] It would seem that the cycle of Indian provocation and white revenge began early.

Whether by trade or salvage or theft, the Beothucks acquired European goods in the sixteenth century. When John Guy established contact with a band in 1612 he noted that they had a brass kettle, sailcloth, and a fishing reel; the sail was being used as covering for a tepee. In the last friendly contact ever recorded, Guy sent one of his men ahead to meet two Indians who were waving a white skin as a sign that they wished to parley. Small gifts were exchanged, 'a chaine of leather full of small periwinkles shels [sic], a splitting knife, and a feather,' a linen cap and a knife; then, 'hand in hand they all three did sing and dance.' The whites made further small gifts, for they did not carry a trading stock with them: a shirt, two table napkins, a hand towel, bread, butter, raisins, beer, and brandy. Two days later, the Red Indians left 'twelve furres of beauers most, a fox skin, a sable skin, a bird skin, and an old mitten, set euery one upon a seueral pole' in exchange. Obviously they were familiar with trade and the items most favoured by the whites.

Guy's success was not to be repeated. In the following year another ship arrived at the same place, and the captain, knowing nothing of the earlier peaceful trade, opened fire on the Beothucks as they assembled.[8] Never again did the Beothucks attempt to trade with the white man. The withdrew from all voluntary contact and remained hidden to the end. Presumably the first phase of contact had had the same results in Newfoundland as elsewhere in the northeastern coastal region. European disease had been introduced there by casual trade, and there is no reason why the Beothucks should have been exempt. Estimates of the impact of these diseases have been made for seventeenth-century New England, where some population figures are available, Cook states that the effect of new endemic diseases, quite apart from epidemic or warfare, was to reduce a northeastern population by 80 per cent in one hundred years.[9] If the Beothucks suffered loss on this scale, their numbers would have been about 400 when Guy made contact with them, even less if epidemic or warfare had ravaged them to any significant extent.

The Beothucks do not re-emerge into the written record until Sir Joseph Banks made a few notes on them in his journal for 1766.[10] The obscurity that surrounds them is part of the greater obscurity that surrounds Newfoundland itself. Development was stifled by a deliberate British policy to keep the island an unpopulated fishing station; settlement was officially forbidden and the bulk of the white population were summer transients. From ten to twelve thousand men made the return crossing of the Atlantic every year. Not until 1785 did the resident population overtake the transient, growing quickly to 20,000 by 1804 and 60,000 by 1832. The exercise of authority was proportioned to the needs of the fishery. Ordinary fishermen, styled fishing admirals, maintained a seasonal control harbour by harbour. In 1729 the British government appointed the naval officer commanding the North Atlantic squadron as governor, with the power to appoint justices of the peace throughout the island. His jurisdiction was seasonal, ebbing when the year's fishing and the need for a naval presence ended. Between 1764 and 1830 there were twenty-one such governors, few of whom stayed more than one season. They chose to live for a few weeks at St John's, but their choice did not make the town into a capital city. There was no person or place of authority in Newfoundland.[11]

As long as the resident population remained small and totally oriented towards the needs of the Atlantic fishery, the whites made no demands on the native peoples except to be left alone. However, as the number of residents increased, some began to seek profit within Newfoundland itself, and at that point it became obvious that the lack of government created an anarchic vacuum. English settlers first appeared in the north at Fogo Island in 1729 and Twillingate in 1732; by the 1740s they were well established in the Exploits Bay area. By mid-century there were some four hundred settlers in tiny communities scattered along the north coast. These whites were salmon fishers, and from this base they began to enter into direct competition with the Red Indians for the resources of the land. On their annual migrations down the Exploits River the Beothucks took salmon; so did the whites, and in the same season. The whites sold the feathers of sea birds slaughtered on Funk Island, the very place to which the Indians went for their seasonal diet of wild fowl and eggs. Even more valuable to the whites was the fur trade, which led them inland along the same routes that the Indians used along the Exploits River and its tributaries.

Thus the period of withdrawal ended and the final phase of the Beothucks' existence began. Their refuge had become a source of profit. The diversity of interests available in the north meant that this was the only part of Newfoundland where year-round employment in extractive industry was available as a basis for permanent settlement. Salmon-catchers in the summer became furriers (fur-trappers) in the winter. They laid their traplines across the Beothucks' deer runs, thus disrupting the caribou hunt. They destroyed campsites and stores of food, and stole the Red Indians' stocks of fur. They made no attempt to open a trade, and the Beothucks, true to their strategy of withdrawal, made no known overtures to open one. Travelling through and living off the land, the furriers became wise in its ways: they learned how to identify Indian trails and campsites, to calculate the age of a track or the length of time a fire had been abandoned. This knowledge made them dangerous enemies, as much at home in the interior as the Beothucks themselves. The salmon-feathers-fur industry threatened the natives where they lived at all seasons – in their hunting grounds, on their migrations to the bays and river mouths, even to their voyage over open water to Funk Island. The Beothucks resisted as best they could by taking the traps and converting the iron to their own uses, by stealing from the tilts and cottages and boats, and by the occasional ambush. But their main defence was to remain invisible, and it became increasingly difficult to hide from the furriers. This was a hard country in which to make a living. The profit of one group left little room for the survival of the other. It made sound business sense to shoot an Indian.

The most graphic description of the relationship between whites and Beothucks was recorded in a series of interviews conducted by Lt Pulling, RN, in 1792. He heard tales of Indian ambush: eight men in a punt struck by thirty arrows; Thomas Rousell shot from a blind and beheaded; Thomas Frith, a clerk, similarly dispatched while picking berries; a boy about to have his throat cut and saved at the last moment by his father. These attacks and the pilfering of sails, nets, traps, and other durables led to punitive raids. Eight whites revenged the death of Rousell, travelling eighty miles before finding an encampment. According to their account, they let the Indians run away, all except two women. They found a tin tea kettle, an iron pot, traps, and nets. They ate the Indians' food, burned three canoes and three of the four wigwams covered with stolen sails. That was in February, with months of winter yet to come. Several veterans of that expedition went looking for stolen nets in the following year, 1791; they found an empty punt and assumed its crew had been killed. Discovering a wigwam, they let two women run away but shot down a man who emerged carrying a child. Both were left to die. This deed, so the murderer explained, was in revenge for the death of his father. That same summer one of the principal employers of the area, John Peyton, led a group whose members were most reluctant to talk about what happened. Three days' travel up Main Brook brought them to their quarry; they fired into the midst of the Beothucks – Peyton had thirty-six pistol balls in his gun – but did not report their kill. They found a wounded Indian lying in a wigwam; the man tried to defend himself and Peyton beat his brains out with a stolen trap.[12] These stories covered a period of only two years.

Governor Hugh Palliser was the first British official to comment on these practices. In 1766 he informed the secretary of state that the 'barbarous system of killing prevails amongst our People towards the native Indians ... whom our People always kill, when they can meet them.'[13] He hoped to find a way of making contact with these hidden people and offered a reward for any taken alive. He proposed to welcome the captive with liberal presents and return him to his band overwhelmed at the benevolence of the whites and ready to open trade with them. But the furriers had no wish to see government officials interfering with their trading practices or sharing their knowledge of the interior. One small boy was brought to the governor, and he was obtained by the simple expedient of shooting his mother; the child was of no use, Palliser wrote, 'not even to get a word of their language out of it.' As a result of this failure, Palliser commissioned two brothers, George and John Cartwright, army and navy officers, respectively, to lead an expedition with the object of capturing some natives 'in hopes of effecting thereby a friendly intercourse with them, in order to promote their civilization, to afford them the means of conversion to christianity, and to render them in the end useful subjects to his majesty.' The Cartwrights travelled sixty miles along the Exploits River, finding numerous wigwams, abandoned canoes, and deer fences; what they saw suggested that the Beothucks numbered between 400 and 500.[14] Following their return, a proclamation was issued enjoining friendship with the natives and directing magistrates to seize those guilty of murder and send them for trial in England.[15]

Official policy towards the Beothucks was now set. Their right to live had been recognized by proclamation but, since they would not show themselves voluntarily, they would have to be kidnapped into civilization either by individuals acting for a reward or through officially sponsored search parties. Neither plan was followed with any energy or consistency, and it was not until 1803 that a Beothuck woman was actually captured and brought to St John's. Governor James Gambier introduced her to a large gathering at a party, where she showed some interest in the music but none in dancing. 'She squatted on the floor, holding fast a bundle, in which were her fur clothes, which she would not suffer to be taken away from her.' Still clutching the bundle, she went shopping, and was allowed to take whatever she liked. And then, as had been proposed long ago, she was returned to her people together with the tokens of white generosity. William Cull of Fogo, who had brought her in, received £50 for his trouble.[16]

The Beothucks were not to be drawn out of hiding. A painting that depicted Indians and whites exchanging furs for blankets and hatchets was left off by a naval expedition, together with some trade goods. Surely the Beothucks would understand?[17] The British government agreed to a full-scale search. William Cull was hired to reconnoiter and reported finding large storage sheds on each bank about sixty miles up the Exploits River.[18] Lt David Buchan, RN, was ordered to winter at the mouth of the river, find the Beothucks, and 'induce them to hold a communication.'[19] He set out on 12 January 1811 with twenty-four marines, two guides – one of them the ubiquitous William Cull – and twelve sledges of provisions and presents. After ten days he divided his party: half were to stay with the sledges and half were to accompany him with supplies for four days. At 6:30 on the morning of 24 January Buchan's party sighted three wigwams and achieved complete surprise; they opened the flaps and found dozens of frightened Beothucks, thirty-five adults and as many children. Speech was useless; Buchan made friendly gestures, shook hands; the Indians offered food and the whites exchanged a few personal items for furs. After three-and-a-half hours Buchan decided to go and fetch the trade goods on the sledges twelve miles back; four Indians agreed to accompany him and two of his own men volunteered to stay behind unarmed. Only one of the four Beothucks stayed with Buchan until he reached the sledges, and when the expedition returned to the camp on the following day they found it deserted. All spent a restless night there and in the morning placed blankets, tin pots, and shirts in each wigwam before leaving. After two-thirds of a mile on the return journey the lone Beothuck ran off, and Buchan discovered the naked headless corpses of his two men stretched out on the ice. The expedition beat a fearful retreat, conscious of their small size and the unknown hundreds of Indians that might be all around them. They reached the *Adonis* on 30 January, rested for a month, and went off on a second search. They retraced their route but this time found no Beothucks.[20]

The Red Indians resumed their hidden ways and the evidence for their continued existence lay in the continuing loss of traps, fishing nets, sails, and tackle from the settlements. There were, presumably, more reprisals. Following a particularly daring raid on John Peyton's establishment in 1818, a punitive party overtook some fifteen Indians, captured one woman, and killed her husband when he tried to resue her.[21] The captive's name was Demasuit but she was dubbed Mary March to commemorate the month of her capture. She was placed in the care of the Rev. John Leigh, minister of the Society for the Propagation of the Gospel, at Twillingate. Leigh, hoping for help from the society, took her to St John's to be trained as an interpreter.[22] The governor, however, decided that 'every feeling of humanity' required her immediate return to her family.[23] There were delays, and it was not until late in 1819 that Buchan, fortuitously back in Newfoundland waters, was able to make the return journey. Demasduit's health had been failing fast, and she died aboard the sloop *Grasshopper* on 8 January 1820, 'seized with a sort of suffocation.' Buchan set out with fifty men, supplies for forty days, presents, and Mary March in a coffin 'handsomely covered with red cloth ornamented with copper trimmings and breastplate.' Their approach was obviously watched, for they found signs of hasty retreat in their path. When Buchan reached a spot close to his earlier discovery of the Beothuck camp he left the coffin suspended six feet high in a special tent containing presents and displaying the Union Jack.[24]

Public reaction to the capture of Mary March showed that for the first time 'feelings of humanity' were no longer confined to visiting British officers. This new concern reflected the fact that by 1819 Newfoundland was becoming a community in its own right and no longer a mere appendage of the cod fishery: what happened on the island was beginning to be perceived as the responsibility of those who lived there. For the first time in an Indian killing, judicial process was followed. Leigh, who was a justice of the peace, had the murder of Demasduit's husband, Nonosabuit, presented to the Grand Jury. They found that the act had been committed in self-defence, but at the same time asked for more information; Chief Justice Forbes suggested that new evidence be laid before the next assizes. It was not, but an important gesture had been made.[25] Another innovation was the holding of a town meeting at St John's that resolved to undertake 'the opening of a friendly communication with the Native Indians.' There was also a real effort to learn something of the Red Indians and their language; it was from Demasduit that whites first heard the name 'Beothuck.' Leigh compiled a vocabulary and taught Mary March some English, so that she was able to consult with those who tried to return her home.[26] The mere fact that she was referred to by her own name showed that some at least realized she was a person and not just a curiosity. All this is in marked contrast with the attitude towards the woman brought in by William Cull: then there had been no judicial enquiry into the circumstances of her capture, nobody had tried to learn her tongue, no one had bothered to give her a name let alone think of establishing a society to reach her people.

Feelings of humanity had come too late to save the Beothucks, for the last scenes of their life were about to be played out. In June 1823 the Grand Jury of St John's returned a true bill against the furriers James Carey and Stephen Adams for the murder of two Red Indians at Badger Bay. Only Carey stood trial; he was the sole witness to the events and pleaded self-defence. Forbes, in his charge to the jury, 'pointed out particularly that it is Murder to Kill an Indian' unless there were mitigating circumstances. Was the act necessary for the accused's safety? He claimed to have fired out of fear, and his guilt 'could not *exceed Manslaughter*.' The jury returned a verdict of not guilty.[27]

Within a week of this trial John Peyton, Jr, brought three Beothuck women to St John's. They had been seized by Carey and Adams, William Cull, and other furriers.[28] One of the women, the youngest, the only one accorded a name, was in perfectly good health: Shanawdithit was to be the last of the Beothucks. The Rev. William Wilson saw all three of them in the street: 'The ladies had dressed them in English garb, but over their dresses they all had on their indispensable deer-skin shawls; and Shanawdithit thinking the long front of her bonnet an unnecessary appendage had torn it off and in its place had decorated her forehead and her arms with tinsel and coloured paper.' She enjoyed herself chasing the onlookers, laughing as they fled. Wilson showed her his watch, and, in approved savage fashion, she was amused at its tick; 'but when a black lead pencil was put into her hand and a piece of white paper laid upon the table, she was in raptures ... in one flourish she drew a deer perfectly.'[29] After two weeks' lodging at the court house, the women were sent back with presents under the care of Peyton. He left them off at Charles Brook on 12 July.[30] They wandered back to the settlement at Exploits Bay and Petyon built them a tilt on his property. Shortly thereafter the two older women died, and Shanawdithit, renamed Nancy, was taken into the Peyton household. If the Rev. John Leigh had still been alive she might have gone to live under his roof, as had Demasduit, and Leigh's enquiring intelligence would have elicited a great deal of useful information. Peyton was not interested. What little information did leak out was startling enough: Shanawdithit claimed that there were no more than fifteen of her people alive in the early winter of 1823; three had since perished, three had been captured, leaving nine Beothucks all told.[31]

After the natives of Newfoundland had passed over the edge into extinction, a determined effort was made to rescue them. John Inglis, bishop of Nova Scotia, made a tour of the furthest corners of his diocese in 1827 and met Shanawdithit at Peyton's home. She told him some very interesting stories: that she had been in the camp surprised by Buchan in 1811, as were all her people; that the marines had been killed when one of them refused to give up his jacket and both ran away. Inglis realized that Shanawdithit was too important to be left a mere servant. He thought a new attempt should be made to reach the surviving Red Indians, with Shanawdithit as an interpreter. Money for this venture could be sought by subscription both in England and Newfoundland.[32]

Bishop Inglis sent his ideas to William Epps Cormack, a man who had already established himself as an authority on Newfoundland. Born in St John's, Cormack had received a thoroughly modern education at Edinburgh University in botany, geology, and mineralogy; and, further, he had access to the outside world through the *Edinburgh Philosophical Journal* edited by his old tutor, Professor Jameson. The journal had published Cormack's account of his crossing Newfoundland by land in 1822, the first such exploration by a white; he had recorded the topography, climate, minerals, flora, and fauna, but had found none of the elusive native Indians. His educated mind could not accept that a whole race might have been exterminated, and he was convinced that Shanawdithit came from but one band of a still numerous tribe.[33]

Spurred by Inglis's suggestions, Cormack decided to do something to prove his theory. He established the Beothuck Institution at Twillingate in October 1827 for the purpose of 'opening a communication with, and promoting the civilization of the Red Indians of Newfoundland.'[34] The first task was to discover some Beothucks with whom to communicate, and by the end of the month Cormack was off on the search. He travelled as far as Red Indian Lake, finding many traces of the Beothucks, including the grave of Mary March. He passed through a dead land and spent 'several melancholy days ... surveying the remains of what we now contemplated to have been an unoffending and cruelly extirpated race.' Even so, he continued to hope, surmising that a few survivors might have moved south of White Bay or down to the southwest of the island. But it was not to be, and two further search parties failed to find any survivors.[35]

The institution's other main purpose was to train Shanawdithit to act as an interpreter. Resolution 15 of the inaugural meeting stated that she should be placed under the institution's 'paternal care' and be educated at its expense. The institution having moved to St John's, its January 1828 meeting resolved to bring her there too. She arrived on 20 September, stayed a few days with Cormack, and was then lodged with Charles Simms, member of the institution and acting attorney general. Cormack found her command of the English language to be very poor, but as she improved and gained confidence in her new surroundings he was able to compile a vocabulary of Beothuck words. However, Cormack realized that there was no longer any point in training her as an interpreter and concentrated on her artistic talents. The result was a series of drawings, five of them basically sketch maps and the rest depictions of wigwams, storehouses, tools, and various kinds of preserved food. The maps told the story of Buchan's expedition of 1811, of the capture of Mary March, Buchan's return with the body, Shanawdithit's own capture, and one hitherto unknown double murder about the year 1816. Cormack was able to follow the demise of the Beothucks, from seventy-two in two camps in 1811 to thirty-one in one camp in 1819; in that year their numbers were reduced to twenty-seven and by the spring of 1823 only thirteen were left. At that point Shanawdithit's knowledge of her people, all knowledge of the Beothucks, ceased. She herself died of consumption on 6 June 1829 at the age of twenty-three.[36]

Cormack's inaugural address to the Beothuck Institution identified two villains responsible for the extermination of the Red Indians: not the English, but the French and the Micmacs. 'About a century and a half ago,' he said, without offering any proof, the French put a bounty on Beothuck heads; some Beothucks found two severed heads in a Micmac canoe and, pretending to know nothing of the crime, invited the Micmacs to a feast and there killed them all. From then on there was open war, and since the French supplied the Micmacs with guns, the Beothucks with their bows and arrows were doomed. It was only after this warfare had shattered the Beothucks that the English started shooting them. This was a very comforting explanation, since it relegated the English to the minor role of finishing off what others had begun. Moreover, the French were still present in Newfoundland, much to the disgust of the English residents. France had acknowledged British sovereignty in 1714, but she kept the exclusive use of long stretches of coast for her fisheries until 1904. Any story that involved her in evil doings would be very acceptable to Cormack's audience. The tale was sedulously repeated to such diverse people as the bishop of Nova Scotia and a visiting Cambridge don.[37] The story received wide currency when *Ottawah: Last Chief of the Red Indians of Newfoundland* appeared in twenty double-columned penny issues in Roscoe's Series in London in 1848. The work was reprinted in Philadelphia and even translated into German. In spite of the title's reference to 'last,' the story dealt with the early seventeenth century and the destruction of the Beothucks by the Micmacs. Tales of Micmac hostility have been repeated ever since.[38]

The English of Newfoundland had suffered much more from the French and the Micmacs than they ever had from the Beothucks, and Cormack's accusation has that measure of poetic justice about it. The Micmacs had survived the first phase of white contact and learned to accommodate themselves to the newcomers' trade goods, firearms, and brandy. They had made their peace with the French missionaries and amalgamated Christian rituals with their own. They had learned to live with white settlers, the Acadian French scattered in small numbers across Nova Scotia. There had been much intermarriage in the seventeenth century and there was an awareness of close blood ties; an 'almost symbiotic relationship of mutual tolerance and support grew up between the two cultures.'[39] This strength was to serve the Micmacs well as they established themselves in Newfoundland; it was a strength the Beothucks never knew.

The Micmacs had been occasional visitors to Newfoundland, along with Mountaineer Indians and Eskimos from Labrador, for hundreds of years. The French first employed them against white settlers in 1705: 'Je les ay Envoyé deux fois sur les Costes Angloises,' Governor Subercase informed his minister; 'ils ont donnés aux Ennemis une terreur qu'il n'est pas jamais de croire.' The Micmacs were so indiscriminate in their slaughter that Subercase's successor, Costebelle, tried to rein them in, threatening to deny them brandy unless they fought 'alafrançaise.' They promised they would do so, but the attempt to introduce humane warfare was unsuccessful, and so were Costebelle's subsequent efforts to ship the Micmacs back to Cape Breton. Only the collapse of the French position at Placentia and Port Royal put an end to the scourge.[40]

In 1720 a few Micmacs settled at St George's Bay on the southwest coast of Newfoundland. They kept in touch with the Catholic priests and French traders of Cape Breton. The situation changed in 1763 with the final explusion of France from Acadia, the return to her of the islands of St Pierre and Miquelon, and a shift in the limits of the French fishing shore so that St George's Bay lay within its bounds. In 1765 some Micmacs landed on the Newfoundland coast near St Pierre, and Governor Palliser was outraged to learn that they carried passports from the British commander at Louisburg who had been, apparently, only too glad to get rid of them. The next year it was the turn of Lieutenant-Governor Francklin of Nova Scotia to write Palliser; alarmed at the pagan-Christian mix of the St Anne's Day festivities, he reported that Micmacs were assembling in large numbers with 'Holy Water Relicts, Books & other Articles' of the Roman faith and requested Palliser to prevent their communicating with the missionaries at St Pierre.[41] But there was no stopping the Micmacs; there were 175 of them on the coast in the Bay of Despair area, and there they remained, trading with French merchants.[42] From then on there was a circuit from Cape Breton to St George's Bay to Bay of Despair and thence to St Pierre. When the British reoccupied that island in 1793 they found that the Indians from St George's Bay were coming there regularly to have their children baptised; further, wrote the British commander, the 'Political humanity' of the French had paid handsome dividends in ensuring that the Micmacs brought the produce of their winter hunt to them for sale.[43]

English officials regarded the Micmacs with grave suspicion because of these contacts with the French. The Micmacs, having lost their accustomed market with the French for the duration of the war, were forced to trade with the English; they thus became more visible, They were apparently accepted by the furriers on an equal footing, for there is not one story of a white firing on a Micmac encampment, possibly because it was well known that the Micmacs would shoot back. Officials took a sterner line: in 1808 Governor Hamilton tried to stop the Micmacs from crossing Newfoundland, not only because they took fur 'at improper Seasons' but also because of their presumed hostility to the Beothucks. The same alarm was sounded by Governor Keats in 1815 when he wrote that the 'thriving and populous' Micmac settlements at St George's Bay 'should prove fatal to the Native Indians of the Island.'[44] These charges probably derived from George Cartwright's unsupported assertion, published in 1792, that the Micmacs were the implacable enemies of the Red Indians.[45] Officials included that accusation as one in a long list of complaints against the Micmacs, and on that basis the notion that the Micmacs destroyed the Beothucks became the conventional wisdom of the day.

Micmac folklore does speak of hostility towards the Beothucks: once upon a time both peoples lived in harmony, and then two boys quarrelled over the killing of a squirrel; the Red Indian boy was killed, his tribe tried to revenge his death and was defeated. This story is so similar to the one explaining Micmac hostility with the Iroquois that it may simply be one variant of a general hostility legend told to satisfy a persistent white.[46] But there can be no doubt that the Micmacs regarded the Beothucks as an inferior people. One communicative Micmac, who stopped a river boat by firing his musket into the air, was asked if the Red Indians, like himself, looked up to God? 'No; *no lookee up* GOD: Killee all men dat dem see. Red Indians no good.' 'Do you understand the talk of the *Red Indians?' 'Oh, no; me not talkee likee dem: dem talkee all same dog, "Bow, wow, wow!"'* The Micmac 'appeared so much offended at our last question, that we did not think it prudent to renew the dialogue.'[47] Some of this contempt came out in identifying with the whites' bravado: 'I see Red Indian I shoot him all the same as one dog.'[48] The Micmac, Noel Boss, was reputed to have killed ninety-nine Red Indians, and Shanawdithit had the scars to show that he narrowly missed making her his hundredth victim; but a Micmac long after recalled that Boss had always been ready to give a helping hand to the Beothucks. There were several stories of the kindness shown by Micmacs to those who were, indisputably, their inferiors. The Rev. Silas Rand of the Micmac Mission in Nova Scotia recorded a legend showing how the Micmacs had long tried to prove their friendship to the timorous Beothucks but had only been able to convince one woman and save her from starvation.[49]

It is highly unlikely that the Micmacs played any significant part in the destruction of the Beothucks, either at the bidding of the French or on their own account. The French did not use that part of their fishing shore contiguous with Red Indian territory and would not have suffered from the pilfering and other annoyances that might have led them to offer a bounty for dead Beothucks. Nor did the Beothucks challenge the Micmacs' self-interest. Their point of arrival in Newfoundland was distant from Beothuck territory, their hunting grounds were in the south, their whole orientation was towards the French of Cape Breton or, later, St Pierre and Miquelon. Moreover, the natural flow of the rivers in the Micmacs' area is southerly, and it would require considerable portaging to journey north to the centre of the island. Some Micmacs were to be found in the north: William Cull took two with him on his expedition from Exploits Bay in 1810. But there are no reports of families or hunting parties of Micmacs in that area. Cormack met numerous Micmacs on his traverse of the island in 1822, but he was following a southerly route. He found the remains of a Micmac canoe on the shore of Serpentine Lake, surmised that it had been brought up from the Bay of Despair along the Cod

Roy River, and that this was a route to the centre of the island. John Peyton, Jr, knew of an access: he claimed that the Red Indians used to point out a tributary of the Exploits River by which the Micmacs came north. Since the Beothucks, he said, called the Micmacs 'Shannock' – bad Indians – he named it Shannock Brook (now Noel Paul's Brook).[50] There is no doubt that the Micmacs could have gone north had they wished to do so, but the fact remains that there was no reason why they should. And if by chance they had gone, they would not have found Beothucks enough to kill in any quantity.

In reviewing the reasons for the destruction of the Beothucks, Cormack did admit that 'the terror of the ignorant European has [sometimes] goaded him on to murder the innocent.'[51] The misdeeds of the whites were linked with the greater culpability of the Micmacs from the first, but at the present day the responsibility for exterminating the Beothucks has been laid squarely on the settlers. This interpretation is exemplified by an article titled, 'The people who were murdered for fun,' which cites as evidence reports that 400 Beothucks were massacred at Bloody Lake, another 100 at Red Indian Lake, and so on.[52] These assertions were offered without support, and it goes against all probability that there were ever enough Beothucks in one place at one time to be slaughtered on this scale, or, indeed, enough whites to perpetrate the deed.

Indian killing occurred as part of the whites' drive to use the resources of the Exploits River area and as a defence against intrusions on their isolated and scattered settlements. The Rev. Leigh testified to the universal fear of the natives and the fact that the whites habitually went armed: in the twenty years before 1823, he said, only three Red Indians had been killed by whites, yet eight settlers had been murdered and three badly wounded in the same period. Leigh was as sober and impartial a witness as could be desired.[53] Yet killing an Indian was definitely a source of pride. The man who 'has shot an indian values himself upon the feat, and fails not to speak of it in the mad hours of drunkenness,' noted John Cartwright.[54] As the rum flowed, so the stories must have grown by competitive exaggeration from isolated encounters to wholesale massacres. The stories collected by J.P. Howley in the 1880s show that a common fate for the first settler in any given locality was to be killed by the Red Indians, sometimes under the guise of friendship. Indian killing was usually presented in the context of revenge, with the avenger seeking out the guilty party.[55]

Folklore concerning the Beothucks is still being gathered in the outports. It is still bloody in content. Sandy Cove has the story of Michael Turpin, who was out swimming with William Murray when attacked by Red Indians in a canoe. Turpin was killed and beheaded on a rock that bears his name to this day; Murray escaped thanks to a woman working in a garden who pointed a spade at his pursuers as though it were a musket.[56] An old man living near St

Philips recalled that the brother of one of Buchan's murdered marines told his grandfather that in the year following the expedition he and his five brothers loaded a boat with artillery and grape shot, sailed up the Exploits River, and massacred the Red Indians they found. Comfort Cove remembers its first resident, John (William?) Cull, who shot many Indians: his grandfather and uncle had been killed at Comfort Island, and Cull himself had been one of the few men in the party to escape with his life. One day Cull and some friends left a loaded musket on the ground, primed to fire. After a while some Beothucks came along; they picked up the gun and it went off. Terrified, they ran away, only to be shot down by Cull and his men from ambush. A resident of Brown's Arm heard about the Indians from his aunt, who lived to 112: she used to keep a chain which she rattled to scare them off, for they thought the noise was gunfire. He told of an ambush by whites at Charles Brook: 'dey opened fire, and dey levelled, nothing alive, nothing got ashore, men, women and children, twas barbarous you know. And dey sunk everything right where twas too. Dey cleared away all, dats all was dere see in Charleses Brook at dat time ... So dere was no Injuns heared talk of dereafter.'[57]

Despite these tales of slaughter, common to all North American frontiers, the decrease in the Beothuck population over a period of three hundred years was unspectacular. From 2000 in 1500 to seventy-two in 1811 is an annual rate of decline of 1.01 per cent, far less than the 1.5 per cent that Cook found to be the norm for the New England Indians wasted by endemic diseases alone.[58] We may assume a rapid loss of population as a result of first contact diseases followed by a period of recovery and stabilisation, with the Beothuck people adapting to new, smaller, hunting grounds. Renewed contacts with the whites in the mid-eighteenth century brought not only death by gunfire but also fresh exposure to disease. Epidemics were spread amongst the populations of neighbouring Greenland and Labrador in this period as a result of white contact.[59] Endemic disease was taking its toll amongst the Beothucks, for all the captive women had tuberculosis at the time they were taken, except Shanawdithit, and she died of it at an early age. Buchan's visit in 1811 may have been the final calamity for her weakened people. She told Cormack that in the second winter following, twenty-two out of seventy-two died, 'and the third year also numbers died of hardship and want.' The fact that she thought it worthy of note that Demasduit was married four years before bearing any children may point to an unprecedented decline in fertility.[60]

The strategy of withdrawal may have prolonged the life of the Beothuck people, but the success of the Micmacs raises some question about its validity as a response to the white presence. Could it be that the Beothucks died because they did not have enough contact with the whites? There was no missionary to plead for their souls, no trader anxious to barter for their furs, no soldier to arm and use them as auxiliaries in his wars, no government to restrain the settlers. The presence of all these white intruders served to strengthen the Micmacs. Perhaps those same intruders could have saved the Beothucks from extinction.

NOTES

This article is from *Canadian Historical Review* 58 (2) (1977). Reprinted with permission.

1 For the general conditions of life in the area see John M. Hooper, 'The Culture of the Northeastern Indian Hunters: A Reconstructive Interpretation,' in Frederick Johnson, ed., *Man in Northeastern North America* (Andover, Mass. 1946), 272–305. The standard work on the Beothucks is James P. Howley, ed., *The Beothucks or Red Indians* (Cambridge, Mass. 1915), reprinted Coles Canadiana Collection (Toronto 1974). This book is a compilation of forty years' search for material concerning the Beothucks and has been the source for everything written about them since 1915. The best review of the subject is to be found in W.H. Oswalt, *This Land Was Theirs,* 1st ed. (New York 1966), 65–80. A 'Bibliography of the Beothuck Culture of Newfoundland' has been prepared by Francoy Raynauld and published in typescript by the Ethnology Division, National Museum of Man, Ottawa, 1974.

2 Diamond Jenness, *The Indians of Canada,* 3rd ed. (Ottawa 1955), 266, asserts without explanation that they 'could hardly have numbered much more than five hundred' when Cabot arrived. Much higher estimates, equally without foundation, are more common – for example, Leo F. English, 'Some Aspects of Beothuk Culture,' *Newfoundland Quarterly,* St John's (Dec. 1959, summer 1960), who places them in the 15–20,000 range. See also Barbara Whitby, 'The Beothucks,' ibid. (summer 1963); James Mooney, *The Aboriginal Population of America North of Mexico* (Washington 1928), places the Beothuck population in 1600 as '500(?).' This figure is repeated without question and transposed to the year 1500 in A.L. Kroeber, *Cultural and Natural Areas of Native North America* (Berkeley and Los Angeles 1939), 171. Fred Eggan puts the land support capacity of the area at one person per 100 square kilometres in 'Indians, North America,' *International Encyclopedia of the Social Sciences,* VII, 180–200. Kroeber suggests the relationship between capacity and coastline (169). Archaeology is no help in determining numbers, since no 'pure Beothuck occupation site has been excavated' and the burials found are post-contact, containing European items; see Elmer Harp, Jr. *The Cultural Affinities of the Newfoundland Dorset Eskimo* (Ottawa 1964), 153.

3 Quoted in Bernard G. Hoffman, *Cabot to Cartier* (Toronto 1961), 29

4 Howley, ed., *Beothucks,* 7–8; Hoffman, *Cabot to Cartier,* 31–2

5 Hoffman, *Cabot to Cartier,* 168–9, 177–8. Alphonse noted that the people were named Tabios, the only known reference to this term.

6 Recalling the situation in 1582, Captain Richard Whitbourne, *A Discourse and Discovery of the New-found-lannde* (London 1622), quoted in Howley, ed.,

Beothucks, 20, wrote: 'Many of them come secretly every yeare, into Trinity Bay and Harbour, in the night time, purposely to steale sailes, lines, hatchets, knives and such like.'

7 Howley, ed., *Beothucks*, 10, 11; Hoffman, *Cabot to Cartier*, 177–8

8 John Guy's narrative is in Howley, ed., *Beothucks*, 15–18. Gillian T. Cell, *English Enterprise in Newfoundland* (Toronto 1969), 68, considers that the offer of furs shows that 'the Beothucks were more accustomed to the fur trade, presumably with the French, than were the English.'

9 Sherburn F. Cook, 'The Significance of Disease in the Extinction of the New England Indians,' *Human Biology*, 1973, 485–508

10 A.M. Lysaght, ed., *Joseph Banks in Newfoundland and Labrador, 1766* (Berkeley and Los Angeles 1971), 132–3

11 See Keith Matthews, *Lectures on the History of Newfoundland* (St John's 1973), for a review of the situation in the eighteenth century.

12 John Bland to J.P. Rance, 1 Sept. 1797, with enclosure, CO 194/39, ff. 219–29, Public Records Office, London (microfilm, National Archives of Canada, Ottawa [NA]). A slightly different version, entitled 'The Liverpool Manuscript,' is in the Centre for Newfoundland Studies, Memorial University, St John's, in photostat. Another copy of Pulling's report was submitted in G.C. Jenner to Gov. William Waldegrave, 28 Sept. 1797, but the document was too lengthy for the clerk to transcribe into the Colonial Secretary's Letter Books, GN2/1/13, 298–9, Public Archives of Newfoundland and Labrador [PANL], St John's.

13 Palliser to Grafton, 31 March 1766, CO 194/27, ff. 178–180

14 Palliser to Hillsborough, 20 Oct. 1768, CO 194/28, ff. 25–6. Lt John Cartwright to Dartmouth, 13 Jan. 1773, with 'Remarks on the Situation of the Red Indians,' William Legge Dartmouth Papers, MG 23, AI, series 1, vol. 16, NA; printed with variations in F.D. Cartwright, ed., *Life and Correspondence of Major Cartwright*, 2 vols. (London 1826), II, 307-25, and in Howley, ed., *Beothucks*, 29–45. A second expedition met with no greater success; see George Cartwright, *A Journal of Transactions and Events*, 3 vols. (Newark 1792), 1, 3–5; Howley, ed., *Beothucks*, 46–9.

15 Review of Instructions for Gov. John Byron, CO 195/10, at ff. 4, 76–8

16 Gambier to Hobart, 23 Nov. 1803, CO 194/43, ff. 169–70; Rev. Lewis A. Anspach, *A History of the Island of Newfoundland* (London 1819), 245–6; Howley, ed., *Beothucks*, 63–4

17 Gov. John Holloway to Castlereagh, 20 May 1808, CO 194/47, ff. 33–5; Howley, ed., *Beothucks*, 66–7. A 'Reproduction from description of the picture painted for Governor Holloway' is the frontispiece of Howley's book.

18 'Substance of the Narrative of Wm. Cull of Fogo,' CO 194/49, ff. 116–17; Howley, ed., *Beothucks*, 69–70

19 Eleventh Instruction to Sir J.T. Duckworth, CO 194/49 at ff. 87–90; Duckworth to Castlereagh, 24 July 1810, ibid., ff. 24–5; proclamations, 24 July, 1 Aug. 1810, ibid., ff. 26–7, 113–14; Howley, ed., *Beothucks*, 71; Duckworth to Buchan, 26 July 1810, GN2/1/21, 29–30, PANL; Duckworth to Buchan, 1 Oct. 1810, CO 194/49, ff. 115–16

20 Buchan's narrative, 12–30 Jan., 4–19 March 1811, paper endorsed 'Mr. Buchan's Notes,' CO 194/50, ff. 153–88; *The Times*, London, 27 Nov. 1811; Howley, ed., *Beothucks*, 72–91, 104. Buchan's sketch map of River Exploits, CO 194/50, map G859

21 Howley, ed., *Beothucks*, 91–129, has a very extensive account of this event.
22 Letter of Rev. John Leigh, 12 July 1819, before Committee of the SPG, SPGFP, vol. 32, 140–4 (microfilm, NA). The society was appalled at Leigh's tangential involvement in an act of violence: Leigh to Rev. Anthony Hamilton, nd [1820], before Committee of SPG, ibid., 342f–342g.
23 Orders to Captain Glascock, RN, 3 June 1819, GN2/1/30, 156–9, PANL; Howley, ed., *Beothucks*, 110–11, 112 List 1
24 Instructions to Buchan, 8 Aug., 22 Sept. 1819, GN2/1/30, 260–2, 229–302; Howley, ed., *Beothucks*, 116–18, 121–6; Buchan to Hamilton, 10 March 1820, CO 194/63, ff. 64–78; 4 June 1820, ff. 79–80
25 'Result of the Enquiry into Peyton's affair with the native Indians,' 25 May 1819, GN2/1/30, 125–6; Hamilton to Glascock, 3 June 1819, ibid., 156–9; Howley, ed., *Beothucks*, 105, 111. Hamilton to Forbes, 26 June 1819, Forbes to Hamilton, 29 June 1819, GN2/1/30, 180–1, PANL
26 Howley, ed., *Beothucks*, 108; Hercules Robinson, 'Private Journal kept on board H.M.S. Favourite, 1820,' Royal Geographical Society, *Journal*, 1834, 207–20, portions in Howley, ed., *Beothucks*, 127–9
27 The King *v* James Carey, in the Supreme Court, St John's, 20–23 June 1823, CO 194/66, ff. 73–7
28 Ibid.; other accounts in Howley, ed., *Beothucks*, 169–70, 179–81; Buchan to Hamilton, 10 June 1823, CO 194/66, ff. 63–4; Peyton to Buchan, 18 June 1823, ibid., ff. 68–9; Buchan to Peyton, *i.d.*, ibid., ff. 69–70
29 Rev. William Wilson, *Newfoundland and its Missionaries* (Cambridge, Mass. 1866), 312–14; Howley, ed., *Beothucks*, 171–2. Buchan was also impressed, sending two of her drawings to Wilmot Horton at the Colonial Office, 24 Nov. 1824, CO 194/68, ff. 249–50.
30 Buchan to Peyton, 28 June 1823, CO 194/66, ff. 70–2; Peyton to Buchan, 23 July 1823, GN2/1/33, 200–1, PANL; Howley, ed., *Beothucks*, 173. Peyton received £51.15.4 for his troubles, CO 194/66, f. 143.
31 R.A. Tucker to R.W. Horton, 29 June 1825, CO 194/71, ff. 395–8; Howley, ed., *Beothucks*, 174–5
32 Journal, 2, 4 July 1827, John Inglis Papers, Public Archives of Nova Scotia, Halifax; Inglis to Cormack, 10 Aug. 1827; Howley, ed., *Beothucks*, 205–6
33 W.E. Cormack, *Narrative of a Journey across the Island of Newfoundland in 1822* (St John's 1856); Howley, ed., *Beothucks*, 130–68, 232–7; Cormack to John Barrow, 22 July 1823, CO 194/66, f. 313; Cormack to Bathurst, *i.d.*, ibid., f. 315
34 *Royal Gazette*, St John's, 13 Nov. 1827; Howley, ed., *Beothucks*, 182–7
35 'Mr. Cormack's Journey in search of the Red Indians,' *Edinburgh New Philosophical Journal*, Jan. 1828, 408–10; 'Report of Mr. W.E. Cormack's Journey,' ibid., March 1829, 318–29; Howley, ed., *Beothucks*, 188–97, 216–19; Cormack to Peyton, 28 Oct. 1828, Provincial Reference Section, Public Library, St John's
36 W.E. Cormack, 'History of the Red Indians of Newfoundland,' Howley, ed., *Beothucks*, 222–9, 231–2, 238–49; Cormack to Inglis, 10 Jan. 1829, ibid., 210; see also 186, 197. Her obituary appeared in the *Public Ledger*, St John's, 12 June 1829; *Newfoundlander*, St John's, 11 June 1829; *The Times*, London, 14 Sept. 1829.
37 Howley, ed., *Beothucks*, 182–4; Journal, 2 July 1827, John Inglis Papers; J.B. Juke, *Excursions in and about Newfoundland in the Years 1839 and 1840*, 2 vols. (London 1842), II, 128. The fact that Bishop Inglis heard the story from Peyton a

year before Cormack's address indicates that the idea may have originated with Peyton.

38 E.J. Devereux, 'The Beothuck Indians of Newfoundland in Fact and Fiction,' *Dalhousie Review*, 1970, 350–62. Stories of Micmac hostility received a form of official sanction when they were repeated in the Geographic Board, Canada, *Handbook of Indians of Canada* (Ottawa 1912), 61–2.

39 Andrew H. Clark, *Acadia* (Madison 1968), 361. For a survey of the effect of initial contact on the Micmacs see Calvin Martin, 'The European Impact on the Culture of a Northeastern Algonquian Tribe,' *William & Mary Quarterly*, Jan. 1974, 3–26.

40 Subercase to minister of marine, 22 Oct. 1705; Costebelle to minister, 8 Nov. 1706, 10 Nov. 1707. Archives des colonies, Paris, Amérique du Nord, C11C, IV, ff. 195–226, V, ff. 30–70, 118–55 (microfilm, MG1, NA)

41 Palliser to Lt-Col. Pringle, 22 Oct. 1765, GN2/1/3, 345; Francklin to Palliser, 11 Sept., 1766, GN2/1/4, 40, PANL

42 Palliser to Lords of Trade, 21 Oct. 1766, CO 194/27, ff. 287–92; Palliser to Shelburne, 5 Dec. 1767, ibid., ff. 320–1

43 Enclosure in Major P.F. Thorne to John Sullivan, 25 June 1793, CO 194/43, ff. 261–4; Thorne to Dundas, 26 May 1794, CO 194/41, ff. 80–2; 'Facts respecting the Fishery at the Islands of St. Pierre and Miquelon,' in W.H. Miles to Addington, 10 Oct., 1802, CO 194/43, ff. 239–42. There were about 100 Micmacs living at St George's Bay in 1797, Abrose Crofton to Waldegrave, 10 Jan. 1798, CO 194/40, ff. 17–34.

44 Hamilton to Castlereagh, 8 Nov. 1808, CO 194/47, ff. 61–9; Keats to Bathurst, 10 Nova. 1815, CO 194/56, ff. 105–14

45 Cartwright, *Journal*, I, 12–13

46 Compare the stories in Frank G. Speck, *Beothuck and Micmac* (New York 1922), 27–9, and in W.D. and R.S. Wallis, *The Micmac Indians of Eastern Canada* (Minneapolis 1955), 449

47 Lt Edward Chappell, *Voyage of His Majesty's Ship Rosamond to Newfoundland and the Southern Coast of Labrador* (London 1818), 71; Howley, ed., *Beothucks*, 288. Chappell may not be the most reliable of reporters, but it is unlikely that this exchange is simply a figment of his imagination; the next quotation corroborates his account.

48 Quoted in James Dobie to Sir G. Cockburn, 10 Sept. 1823, CO 194/66, ff. 324–9

49 Howley, ed., *Beothucks*, 181, 279, 284–6

50 Ibid., 69–70, 146, 270. The names Cormack used and the natural features he depicted in no way tally with those on present-day maps, so that it is impossible to evaluate his surmise. Cormack's map is among the end papers of *The Edinburgh Philosophical Journal*, 1824.

51 Howley, ed., *Beothucks, 183*

52 Harold Horwood in *Maclean's Magazine*, 10 Oct. 1959: see also his *Newfoundland* (New York 1969), 72–8. The Bloody Bay story is based on three lines in Howley, ed., *Beothucks*, 269.

53 Testimony in King v James Carey, St John's, 20–23 June 1823, CO 194/66, ff. 73–7

54 Cartwright, 'Remarks,' *Journal*, I

55 Howley, ed., *Beothucks*, 265–81, *passim*

56 MS C-77/64–13, 15–16; also 70–24, 23, Memorial University of Newfoundland Folklore Archives [MUNFLA]; MS 69–19, 80 has it that a little girl was beheaded on the rock, which is still stained with her blood. Evidently the stories were invented to explain an unusually reddish rock. The Turpin legend is the only one at MUNFLA to be recorded in Howley, ed., *Beothucks* (268).

57 MS 72–69, 5–6; MS 75–207, 20–2; MS C-320/66–25, 3, MUNFLA. The only legend that has been checked out referred to three brothers named Pardy, killed by the Red Indians: a visit to the local graveyard revealed a headstone recording that the three died in a blizzard on 27 February 1791. 'A Burin Legend about Beothucks,' *Evening Telegram*, St John's, 16 April 1969

58 Cook, 'Significance of Disease,' 502, prints a formula for establishing the rate of decline. My figure was reached by correcting that equation to read $\log p_i = \log p_0 - tk$, where p_0 is the population in the base year, p_i population in the ith year, t is time elapsed, and k the rate of population decline. I am indebted by my colleague Richard Unger for advice on this point.

59 Robert Fortuine, 'The Health of the Eskimos at the Time of First Contact,' *Bulletin of the History of Medicine*, 1971, 97–114

60 Howley, ed., *Beothucks*, 227

THE NEW OCTOPUSBOOK ST
116 THIRD AVE K1S2K1
OTTAWA ON
21073718

'''' ACHAT ''''

09-14-2010 09:34:27
No compte '''''''''''2022 C
Date exp. ''/'' Type carte VI
Nom: VERONIQUE LABONTE
A0000000031010 VISA Desjardins

No repère 560004
FS2107371801
No facture 6081
No aut. 044465 RRN 001653004

Total $35.65

(00) Approuvé-Merci

Conservez cette copie pour vos dossiers
Copie client

THE NEW OCTOPUS BOOK ST
116 THIRD AVE K1S2K1
OTTAWA ON
21073718

|||| ACHAT ||||

09-14-2010 09:34:27
No compte ************2022 C
Date exp **/** Type carte VI
Nom VERONIQUE LABONTE
A0000000031010 VISA Desjardins

No repère 560004
F52107371501

No facture 6081
No aut 044465 RRN 001653004

Total $35.65

(00) Approuvé-Merci

Conservez cette copie pour vos
dossiers
Copie client

MILITARY ALLIANCE

BARBARA GRAYMONT

The Six Nations Indians in the Revolutionary War

In 1863, when the United States was undergoing its most trying period in history, President Abraham Lincoln memorialized the achievement of a previous generation that in 1776 had 'brought forth on this continent a new nation, conceived in liberty, and dedicated to the proposition that all men are created equal.' And in dedicating the battlefield at Gettysburg, Lincoln reminded his hearers: 'Now we are engaged in a great civil war testing whether that nation or any nation so conceived and so dedicated can long endure.' Two hundred years after the revolution we are now engaged in a reassessment of our history; from the vantage point of two centuries' distance, we can deal more objectively with aspects of the revolutionary war that our ancestors overlooked in their fervent patriotism glorifying the victorious achievements of white participants in that war.

Historians in recent years have given far more attention to the role of black Americans and Indian Americans in the revolution. We know now, as Indians have always known, that Indians fought, bled, and died to make the white man free. We know also that other Indians fought, suffered, and eventually lost their homes and their lands as loyal allies of King George III. And, we know that, tragically, Indian nations were frequently divided among themselves during that war – brother against brother. Indians were then 'engaged in a great civil war' that had powerful repercussions in their society, testing whether their nations could long endure. Worthy of particular consideration is the role of the Six Nations, or Iroquois Confederacy, in the conflict.

The American Revolution sundered the British Empire; it also sundered the Six Nations Confederacy. At the same time that it brought forth 'a new birth of freedom' for the people of the thirteen colonies, it led eventually to the decline of freedom for the Iroquois people. For these reasons, the American Revolution is one of the most profound events in both American and Iroquois history.

Why did the Iroquois become involved in the war? A careful examination of the documentary sources indicates that most of them actually wanted to remain neutral. In fact, the Americans had concluded a neutrality treaty with the Six Nations in 1775. Furthermore, General George Washington was not eager to have Indians in the war on the side of the Americans because the expense of maintaining an Indian department would be enormous, and both supplies and money were scarce. The British were more eager for Indian support in the early stages of the war and they placed much pressure on the Indians of Canada to declare themselves for the British and to provide warriors to repulse the American invasion of Canada.[1] By and large, however, the British could not nudge most of the Six Nations Indians into the hostility in the early stages of the war. Some few among them, though, took sides immediately. Mary Brant, Mohawk widow of Sir William Johnson, was active as a conveyor of intelligence to the British. She also sheltered and fed British Loyalists.[2] Her younger brother, Joseph Brant, did his utmost to persuade the Six Nations to break their treaty of neutrality with the Americans. Various Oneidas also carried intelligence to Americans during the early stages of the conflict. In the end, it was a combination of several factors which determined Indian allegiances in the revolution. These included long-standing connections and friendships of the various Iroquois nations with their white neighbours, religious preferences of the Indians and influence of missionaries, military needs of the British and of the Americans, and the availability of trade goods and other services from whites.

The strong Iroquois warrior tradition also played a significant part in drawing respective nations into the war. Being a warrior was a large part of being a man in Iroquois society. Hunting, fishing, waging war, diplomacy, and oratory were prized male virtues. Iroquois warriors actually had been involved in all intercolonial wars between the English and French fought on the American continent. Once before the Iroquois Confederacy had been partially split when, in the French and Indian War, some Senecas supported the French and the Mohawks supported the British.

Their success on the warpath had made the Iroquois fearsome to white and Indian alike, and it established their confederacy as a power to be reckoned with. But constant warfare had also reduced drastically their numbers. The Mohawks, who had been most active for the British in wars against the French, suffered a population decline as a result of continuing casualties among their warriors. The Senecas, however, seemed to have gained population as a result of warfare, for their losses were replenished by large-scale adoption of neighbouring tribes whom they had defeated.

Although individual Iroquois were fighting in Canada for the British or actively spying for one side or another, the actual break in their neutrality did not come until 1777 with Burgoyne's invasion of New York. A number of Oneida and Tuscarora warriors, under the leadership of the Caughnawaga, Louis Atayataghronghta, offered their services to the Americans and assisted General Horatio Gates at the Battle of Saratoga.[3] In the western part of the confederacy, Colonel John Butler, with the assistance of a number of militant Indian leaders, persuaded the Iroquois, particularly the Senecas and Cayugas, to break their treaty of neutrality with the Americans. He accomplished this feat by means of persuasive oratory, the display of an old covenant belt linking the Iroquois and British in an alliance of perpetual friendship, and a large bribe of rum and trade goods.[4] This successful manipulation of the Iroquois netted the British a large number of Indian allies for St Leger's campaign against Fort Stanwix and for the Battle of Oriskany. The presence of Oneida warriors on the side of Americans at Oriskany assured a continuing enmity throughout the war between pro-American and pro-British factions among the Iroquois.

Confederacies are structurally the weakest form of government. A large measure of autonomy is retained locally and the central government frequently has difficulty enforcing its authority. In the Iroquois Confederacy, decisions affecting the entire organization had to be unanimous. When unanimity broke down, the confederate form of government broke down and the league separated into its various national, and even village, components. For instance, Big Tree, a Seneca chief, supposedly maintained a friendly neutrality towards the Americans, even though other Seneca villages ultimately enlisted in the British cause. The invading army of Generals Sullivan and Clinton, however, evidently did not put much stock in Big Tree's alleged neutrality, for the American soldiers destroyed his village, along with the others, in 1779. Also, early in the war, the Onondagas had split into pro-American, pro-British, and neutral factions. The Van Schaick expedition of 1779 destroyed the neutral Onondaga village and thus thrust all Onondagas into the British column.

Oneidas and Tuscaroras favoured the Americans largely because of the availability of American trade goods and the long-standing influence of their missionary, Samuel Kirkland; and of James Dean, who had been raised among the Oneidas and spoke their language perfectly. Both men were American patriots. Support for the Oneida mission had come also from the New England churches and the missionary society at Boston. The Oneidas and Tuscaroras throughout most of the war maintained a loyal support for those who had shown them this friendship. A serious break in their loyalty did not come until 1780.

Mohawks were influenced not only by the Brants and Guy Johnson and Sir John Johnson, successors to Sir William Johnson, but also by the Loyalist Anglican missionary John Stuart. These personal and family ties and religious preference were decisive in drawing their allegiance to the British government. Even so, a handful of Mohawks at Fort Hunter refused to follow their pro-British brethren to Canada but instead remained behind in a friendly neutrality to the Americans.

Families also were divided at times. An Oneida named Hanyost Thaosagwat received a lieutenant's commission in the Continental army and accompanied the Sullivan-Clinton expedition as one of several Indian guides and scouts. He was captured in Seneca territory by Indian allies of the British, along with Lieutenant Thomas Boyd's advance scouting party. His brother, enlisted with the British, confronted and upbraided him for making war against the Six Nations, telling him he deserved death but that, as a brother, he could not perform the deed. The Seneca Little Beard thereupon dispatched Lieutenant Thaosagwat. The Americans subsequently found his body hacked to pieces and gave him and his luckless companions a burial with full military honours.[5]

As allies, the Iroquois were of inestimable value to both the Americans and the British. General Horatio Gates praised his 150 Oneida, Tuscarora, and Caughnawaga warriors at the Battle of Saratoga. He reported after the battle: 'The Six Nations Indians having taken up the hatchet in our favour has been of great service and I hope the Enemy will not be able to retreat from them.' A New Yorker who knew many of these Indians and who fought beside them at that battle said that they were all 'brave men and fought Like Bull dogs' until Burgoyne surrendered.[6] In 1780, sixty Oneida warriors, under the command of Colonel Louis Ataytaghronghta, joined Colonel Marinus Willett and the militia in pursuit of the invading force of Major John Ross, Captain Walter Butler, and their Indian allies; it was an Indian who subsequently shot and killed Butler. Willett considered Indians to be 'the best cavalry for the wilderness.'[7]

About 500 Indians served with St Leger in his 1777 campaign against Fort Stanwix. According to the adopted Mohawk, John Norton, 'there was not provided a sufficient Quantity of Arms for these Warriors, so that nearly one half of them fought with no other arms than a Short Spear or Tomohawk.' When word came of the advance of General Herkimer with 800-900 Tryon County militia to relieve Fort Stanwix, 400 Indians, John Butler and twenty Rangers, and John Johnson and fifty Royal Yorkers detached themselves to ambush the Americans. The force was about half the size of the American militia contingent. Because of the shortage of firearms, the Indians would have to fight the Americans in close combat. During the engagement, the vastly outnumbered Indians and Tories inflicted a devastating slaughter upon the Americans and thwarted their plan to relieve the fort. John Norton, evidently repeating what he had heard from his friend Joseph Brant or one of the other participants, said 'that in the commencement, the Warriors of the Five Nations immediately advancing in the front, were much annoyed by the Loyalists in the rear keeping up an inconsiderate Fire, – which they were mixed in combat with the Enemy, did equal injury to both: A celebrated War Chief of the Ondowaga [Seneca], – (of the Ottigaumi race,) appeared to have fallen by their Fire, – as he was found after the Battle shot through the Back, with his face towards the Enemy.'[8]

In all seasons of the year, pro-British Iroquois warriors continued to carry on a deadly guerrilla warfare against American frontier settlements and American forces in New York, Pennsylvania, Virginia, and Ohio. Their effectiveness can be gauged from a report by Governor George Clinton to Congress concerning New York's tribulations since the beginning of the war. Speaking of the year 1778, he said: 'In the course of the Campaign the native Barbarians conflagrated the antient and valuable Settlements of Burnetsfield, German Flatts, and German Town, and reduced a People who had lived in Comfort and Ease, in a Country on which nature had bestowed inexhaustible Fertility, to Indigence and Want. This Disaster was followed by the entire Destruction of Kobell's Kill, the thriving district of Cherry Valley, Anderson's Town and Wagoners Town, and reduced almost the whole of Tryon County on the South Side of the Mohawk to the Settlements on the Banks of that River.'[9]

The year 1779 saw some respite because of the invasion of Indian country by the Continental army, but the Indians still managed to destroy settlements in Ulster and Orange Counties and areas 'Westward and Northward of Albany.' In 1780, the year after the Sullivan-Clinton expedition that was supposed to have smashed the power of the confederacy, the Indians again devastated much of Tryon County. The districts of Caughnawaga and Canajoharie in Tryon County were destroyed in that year, as was the settlement of Schoharie. The enemy then, continued Clinton's report, 'moved to the Mohawk River and laid waste many valuable Habitations on its Banks, and penetrating to Stone Arabia destroyed great Part of that antient Settlement, and would have completed the entire Destruction of Tryon country, had not the Militia and Oneida Indians overtaken and obliged them to retire with precipitation.'[10] In summarizing the situation in the year 1781, when he was writing his report, Clinton concluded: 'We are now ... deprived of a great Portion of our most valuable and well inhabited Territory, numbers of our Citizens have been barbarously butchered by ruthless Hand of the Savages, many are carried away into Captivity, vast numbers entirely ruined, and these with their Families become a heavy Burthen to the distressed Remainder ... Without help from other states, we shall soon approach the Verge of Ruin.'[11]

The war was often brutal on both sides. Indians fought total war and the British were frequently embarrassed by their attacks on women and children. But Indians always complained that Indian captives in American hands could expect no quarter and the Onondaga women captured on the Van Schaick expedition were shamefully treated. White captives, on the other hand, if they could stand the ordeal of the march back to Indian territory, generally were treated humanely, although torture and burning of captives occasionally did happen right after a battle. Forcing captives to run the gauntlet in Indian villages was common also. Although the British had tried to impress upon the Indians that this war was different and that the king's rebellious subjects were not to be adopted but turned in to British authorities for imprisonment, Indians occasionally disobeyed this injunction and adopted white captives. Those fortunate enough to be adopted had a far more pleasant life in the Indian villages than in British prison camps.

As previously mentioned, the Oneidas and Tuscaroras, with few exceptions, remained for several years staunch allies of the Americans. On 13 September 1779, after the American army's devastation of Iroquoia, General Frederick Haldimand wrote to Lord George Germain expressing fears that their Indian allies in the Ohio region – but not the Iroquois – were being disaffected by the rebels: 'It is not so with the Six Nations, the Oneidas & a great part of the Tuscaroras excepted, who from the beginning have strongly espousd the Interest of the Rebels, their attachment is as affixed as ever, but the regular advances made by the Rebels into their country in force, & the impossibility of their resisting them unassisted has alarmed their fears, but not shaken their fidelity.'[12]

The situation with the Oneidas and Tuscaroras would soon change.

Early in 1780 General Philip Schuyler sent a delegation of two leading men from the Oneidas and two from the Fort Hunter Mohawks to Niagara to persuade the Six Nations in the British cause to make peace with the Americans. The delegates were treated with contempt by the Indians and thrown into prison by the British, where eventually one of them died.

Evidently there was a certain amount of factionalism at Old Oneida, a village several miles distant from the main Oneida settlement of Kanowalohale, for some of the Loyalist Indians had been receiving messages of friendship from some of these Oneidas, promising to join the British. Accordingly, on 24 June 1780, a party under David the Mohawk and John McDonell of the Rangers reached Old Oneida and held council with the chiefs in an attempt to persuade them 'to come off and join the rest of the six nations.'

Instead of the acquiescence expected, the Oneidas expressed resentment at the treatment their chiefs had received at Niagara and asked for their release. The next day, however, the visitors had better luck. Spruce Carrier of the Senecas came in with his party of warriors and held another council with the Oneidas. McDonell reported the favourable outcome to Colonel Mason Bolton at Fort Niagara: 'whether the Spruce-Carrier's arguments were more forcible, or that they had deliberated on what had been told them the day before, I cannot pretend to say – They have, however, unanimously agreed to come off. They beg of me to inform you, that they are very sorry for their past Behaviour; but that they will, for the future, behave like dutiful Children – They request that their Chiefs may be allowed to return, as they have vary large families, and no men in them to take care of them, the instant they arrive the Whole of them are to be set off.'

Eleven warriors of Old Oneida departed immediately to serve with the British. But the chiefs held captive at Fort Niagara were never released to return home. The three of them who survived were forced instead to join Indian war parties going against the Oneidas and the American settlements.[13]

On 2 July 1780 294 men, women, and children who had formerly been pro-American joined the pro-British Iroquois who were living in the vicinity of Fort Niagara. This total included 123 Onondagas from Onondaga, sixty-one Onondagas from the mixed Onondaga-Tuscarora settlement of Ganaghsaraga, seventy-eight Tuscarora from the same village, and thirty-two Oneidas from Kanowalohale. Eighty-eight of this group were men, most of whom presumably were capable of bearing arms. On 11 July 1780 a war party of 314 left Niagara under the command of Joseph Brant. In this party were fifty-nine of the formerly pro-American Iroquois who had just come over to the British side.[14]

Except for the Onondagas, who had recently had their villages destroyed by the Americans, the motives of the other Iroquois in joining the British are more difficult to discover. The break may have been a result of sympathy aroused for the neutralist Onondagas who had their village destroyed and the subsequent American treatment of the Onondaga women. It may also have been a result of some long-standing or recent factionalism within the villages coupled with British offers of supplies and protection, which the Americans obviously could not provide.

Brant's main objective on the July 1780 campaign was the destruction of the Oneida and Tuscarora villages, which he and his party accomplished towards the end of the month. About one hundred more Oneidas were persuaded to desert to the British, but 406 Oneidas, Tuscaroras, and Caughnawagas chose continued loyalty to the Americans and fled to the American settlements for protection.

We have said much of Iroquois warriors. It would not be just to neglect the role of Iroquois women in the war. The Oneida Good Peter aptly described the high esteem in which women were held in Iroquois society when he said: 'Our Ancestors considered it a great Transgression to reject the Council of their Women, particularly the female Governesses. Our Ancestors considered them Mistresses of the Soil. Our Ancestors said who brings us forth, who cultivate our Lands, who kindles our Fires and boil our Pots, but the Women ... they are the Life of the Nation.'[15]

The warrior Silver Heels, in presenting a wampum belt on behalf of the women to Major DePeyster at Detroit during the course of the American Revolution, succinctly summarized the part of the women in the war effort. 'This Belt,' he said, 'is in behalf of the Women who are the Support of us Warriors as they mend their Shoes, plant Corn and without their assistance we would not continue the War.'[16]

Women could block the decision of a party to depart on the war path by refusing to perform these functions. It was therefore entirely necessary for the women to agree to and cooperate in a decision for war. Mary Jemison, the adopted white captive of the Seneca and a resident of Little Beard's village on the Genesee River, has recounted her experience in helping both white and Indian warriors: 'During the revolution, my house was the home of Col's Butler and Brandt, whenever they chanced to come into our neighborhood as they passed to and from Fort Niagara, which was the seat of their military operations. Many and many a night I have pounded samp for them from sun-set till sun-rise, and furnished them with necessary provision and clean clothing for their journey.'[17]

In the matrilineal Iroquois society, it was the elder of the mothers who became the female governesses to whom Good Peter referred. These women were empowered to choose the sachems, or peace chiefs, for their respective clans. It was the clan mother also who could de-horn, or remove from office, a sachem who misbehaved. The women could not only veto a declaration of war, but also free or adopt captives and give their advice on matters of diplomacy. Thus Iroquois women in their own society enjoyed more power and higher status than did white women of the day in their society.

The Iroquois woman who performed the most outstanding service and who wielded the greatest influence during the war was Mary Brant, a Mohawk, who was head of a society of Six Nations matrons. This society, and Mary Brant as its head, had much influence with the warriors.[18]

Although she and Sir William Johnson were undoubtedly married according to Indian rites, Johnson never recognized the legality of the marriage, referring to her in his will as his 'housekeeper' and to his children by her as his natural children. There was, however, no doubt of their affection for each other and of his high regard for her and his children by her, for whom he provided handsomely in his will. Mary Brant was always highly respected by all who knew her, both before and after Sir William's death.

Mary Brant obviously had dual loyalties – to her people and to her husband's king. Although she came from a prominent Mohawk family, she doubly enhanced her status by the connection with such a powerful British official as Sir William. Both as his widow and as a capable leader in her own right, she enjoyed much prestige in the Six Nations. She did not use this power in an opportunistic way. Her support of the British cause was sincere, for she put her life in jeopardy and lost her home, her lands, and her possessions as a result of her decision.

After the battles of Fort Stanwix and Oriskany, when the Iroquois began counting the cost of their service to the British and began wondering aloud if peace would not be the better policy, Mary Brant held them steady to the king's service. She publicly rebuked the noted Seneca war chief Sayenqueraghta in council for wavering in his loyalty to the king and Sir William, and gave an impassioned oration that carried the day. That a woman spoke in council at all was remarkable; usually a warrior was appointed spokesman for the women. But Mary Brant was no ordinary woman, either in status or in ability. Throughout the war, she continued to use her influence to steady the warriors, encourage them after setbacks, and bolster their morale and strengthen their loyalty to the king's interest, which she felt to be the Indians' best interest.[19]

Even an elder white woman who had the respect of the Indians could upon occasion take the initiative in matters of diplomacy. Such an incident happened at Cayuga after the campaign of 1777. General Philip Schuyler had sent a wampum belt westward to the tribes telling of the American victory at Saratoga. A Tory woman named Sarah Magines,[20] widow of Tedy Magines, had fled to St Leger's lines and, after the battle, was settled by the British among the Cayugas where, because of her loyalty and her knowledge of the Indian language, she was expected to render what service she could in keeping the Indians firmly attached to the British. When Schuyler's belt bearing the news of the American victory reached Cayuga, Mrs Magines, availing herself of the prerogative of an Iroquois clan mother, seized the belt and canceled it and had the Indians send on a message more favourable to the British cause.

Upon occasion, Iroquois women accompanied their men on their campaigns, and even, when necessity demanded, fought beside them. There were some women with the pro-British Indians at Fort Stanwix in 1777, and undoubtedly their tasks were to perform the usual camp chores. The Cherry Valley campaign of 1778 entailed a particularly arduous march in inclement weather; we know that there were women along on that fatiguing journey. Cherry

Valley was a sorry affair, which shocked and embarrassed the British greatly, for their Indian allies – except for those under Captain Joseph Brant, who acted humanely – did not confine their attacks to men in arms but spread through the settlement, massacring helpless settlers indiscriminately, making no distinction between Loyalist friends and Whig foes. In the memoirs of Governor Blacksnake, the Seneca chief, there is an interesting but all too brief mention of the Indian women, who, he wrote, had armed themselves with tomahawks for protection and waited in the rear lines until it was safe for them to loot the settlement.[21]

During the battle of Oriskany, approximately sixty Oneida warriors fought on the side of the Americans. In the course of the conflict, the Oneida commander, Thawengarakwen (Honyery Doxtater), was wounded in the right wrist. His wife, who had accompanied the army, came to his rescue, loading his gun for him, and also using her own gun against the enemy, fighting as bravely as any warrior in this furious engagement.[22]

Thus the Iroquois women also shared with their men the rigours, the dangers, and the horrors of war.

Finally, we should not let ourselves be led astray by the contemporary British and American description of Indians as savages. The word 'savage' actually did not not have all of the unfavourable connotations in the seventeenth and eighteenth centuries that it does today. It meant a person who lived in the woods, or who lived in a state of nature. But by the middle of the eighteenth century there was very little difference between the material way of life of the Indians and the white frontier families. Sometimes the homes and farms of the Indians were even superior to those of the whites. A tremendous amount of important ethnological information on Iroquois material culture can be gained from the diaries kept by soldiers on the Sullivan-Clinton expedition and from the very accurate sketch maps made by army surveyors.[23]

Traditional Indian bark houses were still in use, but there were also, throughout Iroquoia, many log houses and even some built of hewn planks. The various house styles indicated a gradual adoption of the building techniques of whites, whenever these suited Indian preferences.[24] The soldiers also remarked favourably upon the very fine and extensive fields of corn, beans, squash, pumpkins, melons, cucumbers, potatoes, and other vegetables that they found everywhere surrounding the Indian villages.[25] At a number of places they also discovered apple and peach orchards, some of them quite old, indicating a long-standing Iroquois development of fruit culture.[26] There is abundant evidence also that the Iroquois were raising not only horses, but cattle and pigs. At least in one village, a large amount of hay had been cut and stacked, indicating adoption of European methods of feeding cattle.[27]

Colonel Peter Gansevoort was ordered by Sullivan to destroy the Mohawk village of Fort Hunter, despite the fact that the few remaining families were friendly to the Americans. Gansevoort arrested the remaining Mohawks but refrained from destruction of the settlement because the whites who had lost their homes wished to move in. In reporting on his actions, Gansevoort noted that the Mohawk village 'is in the Heart of our Settlements, and abounding with every Necessary so that it is remarked that the Indians live much better than most of the Mohawk River farmers their Houses very well furnished with all necessary Household utensils, great plenty of Grain, several Horses, cows and waggons.'[28]

It was this way of life that was entirely destroyed during the war. With the coming of peace, the Iroquois painstakingly tried to recapture and rebuild what they had once known. They succeeded only partially, for peace brought also land speculators and white settlers in droves, gobbling up Iroquoia by the millions of acres. The white man's gain was, inevitably, the Indian's loss.

NOTES

This article is from *The Iroquois in the American Revolution: 1976 Conference Proceedings*. Rochester: Research Division of the Rochester Museum and Science Center 1981. Reprinted with permission.

1 'Journal of Treaties at German Flats and Albany, 15 August-1 September, 1775,' MS 13431, New York State Library; Edmund B. O'Callaghan, ed., *Documents Relative to the Colonial History of the State of New York* (Albany: Weed, Parsons & Co, 1857), 7: 605–31; John C. Fitzpatrick, ed., *The Writings of George Washington from the Original Manuscript Sources, 1745–1799* (Washington: U.S. Government Printing Office), 4: 280; Memorial of Guy Johnson to Lord's Commissioners of His Majesty's Treasury, 28 March 1776, no. 147, British Headquarters Papers, New York Public Library (NYPL); Claim of Guy Johnson, American Loyalists, 44: 58–59, NYPL; Claim of Daniel Claus, American Loyalists, 43: 397–98

2 Claim of Mary Brant's Children, American Loyalists, 44:118, NYPL

3 Draper MSS 11U264, State Historical Society of Wisconsin (SHSW)

4 Ibid., 4F190, 16F121–34, 4S17–23

5 James E. Seaver, Narrative of the *Life of Mrs Mary Jemison* (New York: Corinth Books, 1961), 79–81; 'Journal of Lieut. Erkuries Beatty,' in Frederick Cook, ed., *Journals of the Military Expedition of Major General John Sullivan against the Six Nations* (Auburn, NY: Knapp, Pack and Thomson, 1887), 32

6 Draper MSS 11U264, SHSW; Gates to Hancock, 12 Oct. 1777, Emmet, no. 4347, NYPL

7 William M. Willett, *A Narrative of the Military Actions of Colonel Marinus Willett, Taken Chiefly from His Own Manuscript* (New York: G. & C. Carvill, 1831), 85–7; Jeptha R. Simms, *History of Schoharie County and the Border Wars of*

New York (Albany: Munsell & Tanner, 1845), 479; Jeptha R. Simms, *The Frontiersmen of New York* (Albany: Geo. C. Riggs, 1882, 1883), 2:259

8 Carl F. Klinck and James J. Talman, eds., *The Journal of Major Norton 1816* (Toronto: Champlain Society, 1970), 272–3

9 George Clinton to President of Congress, 5 Feb. 1781, Papers of the Continental Congress (microfilm Columbia University), item 67, 346

10 Ibid., 347, 349–50

11 Ibid., 351

12 Haldimand to Germain, 13 Sept. 1779, Halidmand Transcripts, B 54, 144, National Archives of Canada (NA)

13 McDonell to Bolton, 1 July 1780, B 100, 418–19, NA; Draper MSS 11U204–9, 237–44, SHSW

14 Return of Indians, 2 July 1780, B 100, 422, NA; Return of a Party of Indians who are gone to War, under the command of Capt. Joseph Brant, 11 July 1780, B 100, 438

15 Franklin B. Hough, *Proceedings of the Commissioners of Indian Affairs Appointed by Law for the Extinguishment of Indian Titles in the State of New York* (Albany: Munsell, 1861), 279–80

16 Council at Detroit, 1 May 1782, Indian Records, RG 10, series 2, vol. XII, 103, NA

17 Seaver, *Mary Jemison*, 77

18 Claus Papers, 6 Sept. 1779, vol. 25, 119, NA; Haldimand to Germain, 13 Sept. 1779, B 54, 155–6, NA

19 Claus to Haldimand, 30 Aug. 1779, Claus Papers, vol. 2, 131–3, NA; Anecdotes of Brant, ibid., 51

20 Her name is variously spelled. In 1760, when she bound herself out to Harme Gansevoort in Albany, she signed her name 'Sarah Magines.' In the American Loyalist Transcripts it is 'McGinn.' Daniel Claus spelled it 'McGinnis' and 'Maginnes.' Harme Gansevoort, Letters and Documents, vol. I, 17 Nov. 1760, Gansevoort-Lansing Collection, NYPL; Claus to Haldimand, 30 Sept. 1779, B 114, 76–7, NA

21 Blacksnake Conversations, Draper MSS 4S28–31, SHSW

22 Draper MSS 11U196–7, 200, 215–17, SHSW

23 Cook, ed., *Journals*. Some of these maps have been published as endpapers in ibid. Others are in the Erskine-Dewitt Collection, New York Historical Society.

24 John W. Jordan, 'Adam Hubley, Jr., Lt. Colo. Commandant 11th Penna. Regt., His Journal, Commencing at Wyoming, July 30th, 1779,' *Pennsylvania Magazine of History and Biography* 33 (1909):298–9

25 The observation is made in numerous journals in Cook, ed., *Journals*.

26 'Journal of Major James Norris,' ibid., 233–4; Jordan, ed., 'Adam Hubley,' 294–7

27 'Journal of Sgt. Moses Fellows,' in Cook, ed., *Journals*, 90; 'Journal of Major James Norris,' ibid., 234

28 Gansevoort to Sullivan, 8 Oct. 1779, Gansevoort Military Papers, vol. 5, NYPL

GEORGE F.G. STANLEY

The Indians in the War of 1812

The use of primitive peoples to fight the battles of civilized nations has, from time to time, been condemned by moralists. And yet, despite such condemnation, the practice has been frequent in our history. Certainly today few nations would cavil at the employment of Senegalese by France or Ghurkas by Great Britain – except, perhaps, such nations as do not possess colonies providing coloured man power. In the past, in North America, all nations have been prepared to employ the native Indian peoples as military auxiliaries. Each country, be it France, England, or the United States, while admitting the difficulties of keeping their aboriginal allies within the recognized bounds of civilized warfare, has been prepared not only to use, but to employ every device to solicit the assistance of the Indians. In the seventeenth and eighteenth centuries the French relied to a great extent upon the Indians for the defence of Canada. The British sedulously cultivated the friendship of the League of the Iroquois, and in particular that of the Mohawk nation. During the American Revolution the United States succeeded in detaching many Oneida from the league through the efforts of the Reverend Samuel Kirkland. Thus in 1812 when President Madison declared war upon Great Britain and Henry Clay boasted that the Kentucky militia alone could take Canada, it is not surprising to find both contestants seeking the aid of such Indian warriors as were prepared to take up the tomahawk on their behalf.

As far as the Indians were concerned, Great Britain enjoyed certain marked advantages. The British Indian Department had behind it a long tradition of successful dealing with the Indians ever since the day when William Johnson had been appointed superintendent of the Six Nations in 1755. The department had extended its activities to Canada after the Seven Years' War, and after the American Revolution removed its main office to Montreal. In 1774 Colonel Guy Johnson was appointed to succeed Sir William, and in 1782 Sir John

Johnson, Sir William's son, was appointed superintendent-general of Indian affairs. The expanding needs of the service necessitated a division of responsibility and, at the end of the eighteenth century, the department was divided, with the superintendent-general remaining at Montreal and a new office, that of the deputy superintendent-general, being opened at Fort George.

At the outset there had been a close association between the officers of the Indian Department and those of the military establishment. Indeed, the *raison d'être* of the department was to facilitate the employment of the Indians as military auxiliaries rather than their education or civilization. Control of Indian affairs thus rested ultimately in the hands of the commander-in-chief and disbursements were made out of the military chest. However, in 1796 in Upper Canada, and in 1800 in Lower Canada, the control of Indian affairs was transferred from the military to the civil authorities. It was not until 13 May 1816 that the management of Indian affairs was once more placed under the direction of the commander of the forces in British North America.

One of the most significant features of the Indian Department in its early days was the strong personal hold which the officers of the department acquired over the Indians. For many years, the men who ran the department were men who had been schooled in the tradition of Sir William Johnson; when they passed on, their sons succeeded to their appointments and to their influence. Many of the officers of the department were related to one another and, in some instances, to the very Indians whose affairs they administered. Names like Johnson, McKee, Claus, Elliott, Caldwell, Chew, and others were names familiar to more than one generation of Indians; and they were still names to conjure with in 1812. This fact gave the Indian Department a strong sense of independence, one which brought it into conflict with the military authorities after the war broke out.

To swing the Indians to the British side was not a difficult task. The western tribes, in particular, had never ceased to hate the Americans. They had refused to lay down their arms when the white men had stopped fighting in 1783, preferring to carry on an unequal struggle to preserve the Ohio as the boundary of the Indian territory until they were finally defeated at the hands of 'Mad Anthony' Wayne and compelled to accept the peace of Greenville in 1795. Although the United States claimed territorial sovereignty over their lands, the western Indians continued to look to Great Britain for assistance and advice. And these Great Britain was prepared to give. To have refused would have been to impose unnecessary hardship and undue distress upon the Indians who were completely dependent for their very subsistence upon periodical handouts of ammunition. There is no evidence to show that the British ever used their influence with the western Indians deliberately to stir them up against the United States – and much to the contrary – but there is truth in the charge that the Indians were encouraged by Great Britain never to let the ancient covenant chain of friendship grow brown with rust. Political and military factors made it essential for the British to retain the confidence of the Indians. Against the western Indians the colony of Upper Canada had no defence whatever; against the Americans, unfriendly and threatening, Canada's greatest assurance of protection seemed to lie in the support of the red men. The fur trade, too, still one of the principal economic activities of Canada, required the friendship of the western Indians. That is why the Indians continued to receive presents in large numbers from the British government through the agency of the British Indian Department. Undoubtedly these presents, the official expressions of sympathy, the retention of the western posts until 1796, and the presence of British agents at Indian councils must have worked strongly upon the minds of the Indians to convince them that Great Britain was still their ally and that in a final test of strength with the United States, Great Britain would defend them – even when no official encouragement was actually given them so to believe.

The British might hope for much from the western tribes; from the Six Nations they could expect less. The League of the Iroquois for the greater part, and the Mohawk in particular, had thrown in their lot with the British between 1776 and 1783. They had been assured that their interests would never be forgotten by their 'Great Father' the king when peace should be made and they felt confident that the boundaries fixed at Stanwix in 1768 would be confirmed by victory in arms. When the treaty was finally signed in 1783 it included no mention of the claims of the Indians. There was bitter disillusion among the tribes. They had never accepted the view that they were subjects of the crown: they were allies. The king had no right to cede to the United States lands which were not his to cede.[1] Sir John Johnson, unwilling though he was for obvious reasons to undertake the task, was finally compelled to go to Niagara to face the Indians assembled in council. Even liberal portions of rum and Johnson's evasions of the truth could not calm the fears of the Six Nations that they had been cheated by the British;[2] nor did Haldimand's grant of lands to John Deserontyon's Mohawk at the Bay of Quinte, the traditional home of Dekanawida, the founder of the League, and to Joseph Brant's followers at the Grand River allay the distrust which had been aroused in Indian minds by British neglect of their interests at Versailles.

We do not find among the Six Nations, between 1783 and 1812, the same display of enthusiastic loyalty which had marked their former devotion to the cause of Great Britain and the person of Sir William Johnson. And their attitude was not improved by the disputes which subsequently arose over the extent and nature of the Grand River grant.[3] Even Joseph Brant, whose fidelity and attachment to the crown had elicited the commendation of Haldimand in

1781, was looked upon a few years later with distinct disfavour by the secretary of state in charge of the colonies.[4] Nevertheless, the Six Nations were prepared to fight when war came to their doors and when they became convinced that the British were determined to prosecute the war with real vigour. They had little enough for which to thank the British; from the Americans they could expect even less.

From the Caughnawaga Indians, the 'praying Indians' of the Ancien Régime, the British might hope for, but had little reason to expect, much assistance in the event of war. There had been a strong infiltration of New England blood into the Indians at the Sault St-Louis, as Peter Kalm observed in 1749,[5] and their attitude during the American Revolutionary War had not been one to inspire great confidence in their loyalty to Great Britain. In 1778 the Indian superintendent accused them of having 'listened to the singing of evil birds' and declared that the hatchet which he had given them had 'been rusted by some Dirt which the Rebels wanted to throw in your Eyes.'[6] Iroquois from Caughnawaga formed part of a delegation to the French headquarters at Newport in 1780.[7] 'Colonel' Louis Cook, the half-breed Abenaki from Caughnawaga who had acted as go-between for the Oneida and Caughnawaga[8] during the American Revolutionary War, was alive in 1812. He was too old to fight, but his name still carried weight among the Indians of Lower Canada; when linked with that of the Reverend Eleazar Williams of Caughnawaga, the pseudo-Bourbon heir[9] who endeavoured to seduce the Caughnawaga and St-Regis Indians from their allegience to the Catholic church and to the king of England, he caused considerable alarm in official British circles. Certainly the indifference of the Seven Nations of Lower Canada to the fate of British rule in North America was such that it brought down upon the heads of the Indians the wrath of Sir George Prevost, who told them they 'were like old women, and that if they would not fight willingly where and when they were ordered to, they should be considered unworthy of receiving provisions and presents from their Great Father's Government.'[10]

THE WESTERN THEATRE OF OPERATIONS, 1812–13

The war which broke out in 1812 was preceded by years of uncertainty. In 1807 the threat of hostilities was sufficiently real to cause considerable alarm in Canada, and Sir James Craig, the governor general, entered into a lengthy correspondence with Lieutenant-Governor Gore of Upper Canada with respect to the disposition and possible employment of the western Indians. Craig considered it essential that the Indians be included in any defence plans for Canada and hoped to be able to take advantage of their antagonism towards the Americans. At Gore's instructions, William Claus was sent to Amherstburg to ascertain the intentions of the Indians. He found the Shawnees prepared to take the field against the Americans but reported that the other nations were reserved and noncommittal. He estimated that 'the number of fighting men' in the Miami and Michigan country 'do not exceed fifteen hundred' who, in view of the defenceless state of Amherstburg, might prove 'very backward' in coming forward.[11] Craig was distressed at this apparent lack of enthusiasm and in a letter to Gore requested the lieutenant-governor to impress upon the Indian Department the 'peculiar importance' which he attached 'to the success of our endeavours to conciliate and secure the Indians to our interests.'[12] Reporting to Viscount Castlereagh on 15 July, 1808, Craig deplored that so little interest had been taken in the Indians – a neglect which he attributed to the mistaken idea that 'it has been thought little probable that we should ever have occasion for their assistance': a 'commendable principle of economy' in the matter of Indian presents had, he felt, 'in this instance been attended with ... ill consequence.'[13]

That the Indians must constitute an important component of the defence forces of Canada was always appreciated by Major General Brock. He was aware of the temper of the Shawnee and knew of Tecumseh's efforts to form a western Indian confederacy. Although he took care to direct the officers of the Indian Department at Amherstburg to exert their whole influence to dissuade the Indians from attacking the Americans in 1811,[14] he took equal care to secure that should war break out between Great Britain and the United States, the Indians would be found on the British side. He realized that the best way to engage their active support would be a quick, decisive action against Detroit and Michilimackinac; only in this way would it be possible to convince those Indians who felt they had been deserted by the British when Major Campbell refused to help them against Wayne in 1794 and when the red coats marched out of the western posts in 1796 'that we are earnestly engaged in the War.'[15]

It was in accordance with this policy that Brock wrote in February 1812, four months before the actual declaration of war, to Robert Dickson, a British fur trader then in Wisconsin, asking him 'to ascertain the degree of cooperation that you and *your friends* might be able to furnish, in case of ... an Emergency taking place.'[16] Dickson received this communication in June and hastened to assure Brock of the services of 250 to 300 Indians, seventy-nine of whom he sent at once to Amherstburg while hurrying himself with the remainder directly to St Joseph's.[17]

Meanwhile General Hull at Detroit was engaged in similar efforts to gain Indian support, or at least to ensure Indian neutrality. He had been instructed to 'adopt such measures with the chiefs of the several tribes of Indians as may ... appear to be the best calculated to secure the peace of the country.'[18] He therefore dispatched Huron agents to the Grand River with a promise that the Six Nations would be undisturbed in the occupation of their lands[19] and invited all the Indians in the vicinity of Detroit, including those under Tecumseh and Roundhead who had already joined the British at Amherstburg, to attend an Indian council at the Wyandot village at Brownstown.[20] Both chiefs, however, remained firm in their refusal to have anything to do with the Americans and Colonel Matthew Elliott wrote to Claus that Tecumseh 'has shewn himself to be a determined character and a great friend to our Government.'[21] This was good news to Brock's ears, for he had always been apprehensive lest the scale of American preparations at Detroit should so impress the Indians with the strength and determination of the United States that they would be reluctant to support a side which might appear to have little chance of victory.

The first success of the war went to the British, not to the Americans. The small British force at St Joseph's, taking advantage of a prior knowledge of the official declaration of war, immediately seized Michilimackinac, a fort long known to the Indian trade.[22] The effect of this victory was all that Brock had hoped for: to quote General Hull: 'after the surrender of Michilimackinac, almost every tribe and nation of Indians, excepting a part of the Miamis and Delawares, north from beyond Lake Superior, west from beyond the Mississippi, south from the Ohio and Wabash, and east from every part of Upper Canada and from all the intermediate country, joined in open hostility, under the British standard against the Army I commanded ... The surrender of Michilimackinac opened the northern hive of Indians, and they were swarming down in every direction.'[23] One must make allowances for the fact that Hull, when he penned this report, was seeking to find excuses for his own supine conduct at Detroit in August; but there is no doubt that the initial British success at Michilimackinac made an impact upon the Indians far out of proportion to its broader military significance.

On the Detroit front, Hull made the first move by crossing the river and penetrating into Upper Canada. He issued a belligerent manifesto threatening reprisals against those taken in arms with the Indians but made no hostile move against the British position at Amherstburg. Then came the news of the British success at Michilimackinac, quickly followed by rumours that the British forces on his flank included 5000 Indians![24] The report was false, but Hull was gullible enough to believe it and, finding his line of communications cut by Tecumseh, he succumbed to the war of nerves and surrendered his entire command to General Brock on 16 August without striking a blow. The American frontier was thus thrust a long way back towards the Ohio, the line the Indians sought to establish as their boundary. Brock reaped great credit for his spectacular victory, but without the aid of Tecumseh and the Indians it could never have been so easily achieved, a fact which Brock willingly admitted. From the day the two men met face to face at Amherstburg each respected the other, and Brock wrote of his ally, 'a more sagacious or a more gallant Warrior does not I believe exist.'[25]

During the autumn and winter, Robert Dickson continued to hand out presents and to send Indians to Amherstburg. Behind him was the full support of the fur barons of Montreal. James McGill wrote to Sir George Prevost on Dickson's behalf, pointing out that 'the Indians are the only Allies who can aught avail in the defence of the Canadas. They have the same interest as us, and alike are objects of American subjugation, if not extermination.'[26] He urged that Dickson's requests for further supplies be given favourable consideration. Sir George was more than favourably disposed towards Dickson. Not only was he prepared to compensate him for the sums which had been spent upon Indian presents[27] but commissioned him as a special agent for the Indians west of Lake Huron with a staff of five officers and fifteen interpreters and authority to 'make such requisitions as may be necessary upon H.M. Indian storekeepers and other proper officers for such goods and provisions as from time to time shall be considered needful'; all this 'in the expectation that upwards of 1,000 picked warriors will be collected.'[28]

The Indians, however useful their services may have been at Michilimackinac, Brownstown, and Detroit, were at best unsatisfactory soldiers. They were devoid of discipline. They lacked tenacity and were easily discouraged by failure. They were restless, dissatisfied during periods of enforced inactivity, and yet inclined to fight for only brief periods at a time. Tactically they offered great advantages in ambuscades and forest warfare, but when it came to besieging a fort protected by walls and cannon, they were invariably useless.[29]

This weakness on the part of the Indians as a fighting force became painfully apparent during the campaign of 1813. In January Colonel Procter administered a check to General Winchester at Au Raisin River where the issue was decided by the Indians outflanking the Americans on either side and gaining their rear; at Fort Meigs, however, the Indians drifted away after several days' siege leaving Procter, according to his own report, with 'less than twenty Chiefs and Warriors.' Well might Procter add that 'under present Circumstances, at least, our Indian Force is not a disposable one, or permanent, tho' occasionally a most powerful Aid.'[30] Throughout the spring and summer, western Indians flocked to Amherstburg, adding both to Procter's strength and to his embarrassment. They consumed vast quantities of food and Procter's supplies were never abundant. It was, therefore, as much with the object of finding employment for his Indians as in the hope of administering a defeat to the Americans that he led his force against Fort Stephenson in late July. But a cannon, a stockade, and a determined Irishman stopped the Indian assault and the British force returned to Amherstburg with both Procter and the Indians indulging in mutual recriminations.

During the autumn it became clear that the reverses suffered at Fort Meigs and Fort Stephenson had not been without their effect upon Indian morale. Procter was aware of what was happening and begged that reinforcements of regulars be sent him in order 'that our Dependance on the Indian Force may not appear to so great a Degree as it has hitherto done,' also 'to prevent Defection among the Indian Tribes, which ought strenuously to be guarded against, from the Propensity of Indians to follow each other, on the most unaccountable Impulse at Times.'[31]

If the Indians needed a stimulant for their morale, so too did Procter. He was not a man of great courage nor did he ever enjoy the respect of his redskin allies. He seems to have been very much alarmed at the extent of the American preparations for a counter attack and was inclined to pull out of his exposed position. He feared, however, that such a course might lead to trouble with the Indians and endeavoured to cloak his intentions from his allies. Finally, after Barclay's defeat at Put-in-Bay and the loss of Lake Erie to the Americans, he felt that he had no choice but withdrawal, even though Tecumseh, anxious to fight it out where he stood, likened the British commander to a whipped dog crawling away with its tail between its legs. And there was some aptness to the metaphor. For when Procter was finally shamed into making a stand at Moraviantown on 5 October 1813, it was Tecumseh and the Indians who did the fighting, not Procter's red coats. Tecumseh gave his life; Procter saved his by flight.

The effect upon the Indians of the defeat at Moraviantown was as decisive as that of the victories at Detroit and Michilimackinac. With military defeat and the death of the soul and inspiration of the Indian resistance, organized Indian opposition in the Michigan and Lake Erie region came to an end. Small bands of Indians might harass the American army on its withdrawal from Moraviantown, but no large forces of Indians were again mustered on the Detroit front. Only in the upper reaches of Lake Huron and in Wisconsin, where Robert Dickson continued to hand out large numbers of presents and larger numbers of promises while arranging with Sir George Prevost for still larger supplies of both, did the British influence over the Indians remain unimpaired.

THE NIAGARA FRONTIER, 1812–13

The response of the western Indians to the British appeals for assistance was by no means equalled in alacrity or ardour by that of the Six Nations. The Iroquois tribes had, after the American Revolutionary War, accepted land reserves not only in Canada but in the United States as well and they had little stomach, at this time, to engage in fratricidal war. Hoping to take advantage of this disinclination on the part of the Six Nations to join in the hostilities, the United States prevailed upon the old Seneca chief, Cornplanter, to send a deputation of American Iroquois to Canada to talk in terms of Indian neutrality with their kindred at Grand River. There is no doubt that the Canadian Six Nations were disposed to toy with the idea of neutrality, but to the American deputation they returned the answer: 'It is the President of the United States makes war upon us. We know not your disputes ... The British say the Americans want to take our lands. We do not want to fight, nor do we intend to disturb you; but if you come to take our land, we are determined to defend ourselves.'[32]

Brock was just as anxious to bring the Six Nations into the war as the Americans were to keep them out. On 3 July, 1812 he wrote: 'About 100 Indians from the Grand River have attended to my summons, the remainder promise to come also, but I have too much reason to conclude that the Americans have been too successful in their endeavours to sow dissension and disaffection among them.'[33] Three weeks later he learned to his disgust that only fifty Grand River Indians were willing to go to Detroit; the remainder had determined to follow a cautious policy of wait and see.[34] This was a great source of apprehension to the commanding general, for as long as the Indians remained undecided as to their course of action, the civilian population living in the Niagara peninsula would be reluctant to leave their homes and join the militia at Amherstburg or Fort George.[35] Brock therefore hastened to answer Hull's letter to the Indians by drawing attention to Hull's inconsistency in making threats in his Proclamation while making promises in his letter, and by sending Joseph Willcocks to Grand River to counter the American propaganda.[36]

However cool the Six Nations Indians may have been at the beginning of hostilities, they warmed to enthusiasm after the British victories at Michilimackinac and Detroit. On 7 September Brock reported to Prevost that he had now three hundred Indians assembled at Fort George, with 'two hundred more ... expected tomorrow.' 'They appear ashamed of themselves,' he wrote, 'and promise to whipe away the disgrace into which they have fallen by their late conduct.'[37] Even so he was not inclined to place too much reliance on their loyalty. He felt that so long as he was able to maintain his position at Niagara and keep open the line of communications with Montreal, the Indians would remain firm in their attachment to the crown, but 'the moment they are convinced that we either want the means to prosecute the War with spirit, or are negociating a separate peace, they will begin to study in what manner they can most effectually deceive us.'[38]

When put to the test, the Six Nations Indians fought well. At Queenston Heights they played an important role under the command of John Brant – a son of the immortal Joseph – Captain Jacobs, and Captain Norton, and suffered the loss of two Cayuga chiefs, one Onondaga and two Oneida warriors, and several wounded.[39] Following the traditional Council of Condolence at Fort George on 6 November, the bulk of the Indians, under the command of Major Givins of the Indian Department and Captains Norton and Kerr, proceeded up the Niagara River towards Fort Erie where they assisted in repelling the second attempt made by the Americans to cross the river. Subsequently they returned to Fort George, whence Lieutenant Thomas Ridout wrote to his cousin on 5 January, they 'are encamped on the skirts of the woods back of the town' keeping the troops 'alive with their war dances' and making 'the dark cedar woods echo with savage yells.'[40]

Indian morale suffered something of a slump after the British reverses at Fort York and Fort George, nevertheless a number of Indians remained with the British troops and accompanied them on the retreat towards Burlington. They were therefore on hand to participate in the pursuit of the Americans after the night attack at Stoney Creek. On this occasion they appear to have acquired considerable booty: on 11 June Harvey wrote from Forty Mile Creek that 'the greatest part' of the enemy baggage and equipment 'are in the hands of the *Indians* or scattered throughout the Country.'[41]

Following the setback at Stoney Creek, the Americans withdrew to Fort George closely followed by the troops and the Indians. The latter had, incidentally, received a strong reinforcement from Lower Canada. On 26 May Sir John Johnson had informed Claus that he had succeeded in raising a substantial force in Lower Canada and would send about 300 Indians to Sir George Prevost 'either to attack or defend.'[42] These Indians were led by Captain Dominique Ducharme. At Forty Mile they were joined by John Brant and William Kerr with about 100 Mohawk. On 20 June the combined force of Indians encamped at Twenty Mile Creek, near a spot known as Beaver Dam. Learning from scouts that the Americans were preparing a reconnaissance in force, Ducharme notified Major de Haren and then, placing himself in the centre, Kerr on the left, and J.B. de Lorimier and Isaac Leclair on the right, he set the stage for an ambush. After two hours' fighting the Americans under Colonel Boerstler surrendered. The actual capitulation was received by Lieutenant Fitzgibbon and completed by de Haren, both of whom, however, arrived on the scene with regular reinforcements after the day had been won; it is clear from all contemporary accounts that Beaver Dam was an Indian victory. Indeed, there seems to be more than one grain of truth to Norton's jibe that 'The Cognauaga Indians fought the battle, the Mohawks got the plunder, and Fitzgibbon got the credit.'[43] In the fighting, the Indians suffered five principal chiefs and warriors killed and twenty wounded.[44]

Beaver Dam was an important victory for the British. The old fear of the Indians took possession of the American troops at Fort George and, following Colonel Boerstler's disaster, they did not venture to send a patrol more than a mile from the fort.[45] Perhaps there was justification for such caution, for, despite the return home of the Lower Canada contingent,[46] the Indian forces in the Niagara peninsula had received a new reinforcement with the arrival, on 5 July, of a number of Ottawa Indians under Captain Matthew Elliott and their chief, Blackbird. It was the new arrivals from the west, along with some of Norton's Mohawk, who fought a sharp engagement with the Americans on 8 July at Ball's Farm in an effort to recover a quantity of medicines and surgical instruments which had been buried when the British had abandoned Fort George earlier in the year.[47] Unlike the engagement at Beaver Dam, the proceedings at Ball's were marred by scalping, notwithstanding all that could be done by the officers of the Indian Department to prevent it.[48]

The net around Fort George tightened as the weeks passed. Each day the Indians were employed harassing and teasing the enemy outposts. On 27 July the American General Peter B. Porter wrote disgustedly: 'The truth is ... that we have had an army at Fort George for two months past, which at any moment of this period might by a vigorous and well-directed exertion of three or four days have prostrated the whole of the enemy's force in this division of the country, and yet this army lies panic-struck, shut up and whipped in by a few hundred miserable savages, leaving the whole of this frontier, except the mile in extent which they occupy, exposed to the inroads and depredations of the enemy.'[49] No more eloquent tribute could have been paid to the services of the Indians to the British cause in the Niagara peninsula in 1813 than this.

Meanwhile, the Americans were using every effort to scrape up a few native warriors for themselves. The failure of Cornplanter's mission to the Grand River in 1812 had not, perhaps, been wholly unexpected; but the chilly reply of the Seneca to the American request that they take up the hatchet[50] and the letter sent by a number of Oneida, Onondaga, Stockbridge, and Tuscarora Indians to the president of the United States on 28 September expressing their desire to remain neutral and their regret that they should ever have been asked to take up arms in a white man's war[51] must have been a great disappointment.

Early in 1813 a determined drive was made to enlist Indian support. The United States Indian Department might point out that the president had never authorized the employment of the Indians, but the army needed them and General Dearborn, the commander-in-chief at Niagara, made it clear that he wanted 150 'young warriors of the Six Nations' to meet him at Fort George.[52] The Indians replied by holding council at Buffalo and on 25 July Red Jacket told the American Indian agent, Erastus Granger, that 'the part we take in this war is not voluntary on our part; you have persuaded us into it ... Your voice was for us to sit still, when the war began, but you have beat us – you have got us into the war.'[53] The reluctance on the part of Red Jacket and some of the other Indians to take up the tomahawk was probably promoted less by their distaste for war than the fact that by this time, they had been fully informed of the American reverses at Stoney Creek and Beaver Dam. Under the circumstances neutrality was perhaps the safest course. This, at least, was Granger's explanation of the Indian attitude.[54] Farmer's Brother and Henry O'Bail of the Seneca were, however, less inclined to argue than was Red Jacket, and the American military authorities succeeded in enlisting a number of Indian warriors who took part in the defence of Black Rock and Buffalo in July 1813. A few Seneca and other Six Nations Indians joined the American forces at Fort George but, with the exception of one slight skirmish, their services did not merit much comment.

THE ST LAWRENCE RIVER

The principal theatres of operations were those already discussed. Nevertheless, several engagements took place along the St Lawrence River which might be noted briefly. At St Regis the Indians occupied a unique position living, as they did, upon both sides of the frontier. Neutrality under such circumstances was difficult enough, but it became impossible when the troops of both sides engaged in operations in the immediate vicinity. Thus the Indians became divided in their loyalty, and while some, owing to the influence of 'Colonel' Louis, favoured the Americans, others joined the British and participated in the fighting at Sackett's Harbour, Ogdensburg, and Beaver Dam.

Of more significance was the operation which ended in the defeat of the Americans at Chateauguay. During 1813, plans were laid for a combined movement of two American forces upon Montreal. In September 1813 the right wing of this combined movement got under way with Hampton's advance towards Odelltown. According to Hampton, his force encountered no real resistance but he was constantly annoyed by a 'few despicable Indians' who continued 'to lurk about the distant bushes and frequently crawled up and fired upon our sentries during the day and the succeeding night' despite the fact that 'they were frequently drove off.'[55] Finding it difficult to secure water and fodder for his horses, Hampton shifted his line of advance from Odelltown westward towards the Chateauguay River with 'Cognawaga opposite Lachine, about forty miles from Chateauguay and ten from Montreal' as his objective. The change of route did not rid him of the nuisance of the Indians. They still continued to hover about his flanks and pot away at his sentries, harassing the enemy in the manner best suited to their style of warfare. When Hampton and de Salaberry finally met on 26 October, Captain Lamothe's twenty-two Indians 'behaved well'; the 150 with de Léry only shouted, but their war whoops apparently counted for something when the Americans began to lose their nerve.

THE CAMPAIGN OF 1814

The decisive year was 1814. With the entrance of the allies into Paris and the fall of the French Empire, it was obvious that if the Americans were to achieve victory in Canada they would have to do so before the arrival of the reinforcements from Wellington's armies, which events in Europe would now set free.

The American advance began with the crossing of the Niagara and the surrender of Fort Erie. Moving northwards along the Niagara River, the American troops encountered General Riall near the Chippewa River. With Riall were 300 Indians, including 100 western Indians and 200 Six Nations under Norton. These Indians very nearly succeeded in capturing Winfield Scott, one of the American brigadiers, while he was taking his morning coffee in a Canadian farm house, but Scott and his aides proved to be fleet of foot and succeeded in effecting an escape.[56] In the battle which ensued the Indians penetrated too far into the woods on the British right to afford Riall the assistance he required of them and when the retreat began they melted into the surrounding country in a fashion which drew forth his indignation: 'The Indians ... have behaved most shamefully; literally speaking, not one remaining, of the hundreds that were with him, prior to the retreat.'[57]

This marks the virtual end of the Indian participation in the war in the Niagara area. Only a small number of them took part in the battle of Lundy's Lane and these, together with the light troops, were sent to follow the Americans and harass them during their withdrawal. There were also a few Indians at the siege of Fort Erie but they played no significant role.[58]

Nor did the American Indians play much part in 1814. General Porter had enlisted the aid of Red Jacket and Erastus Granger to raise a force of Indians for his command and 600 Indians appear on the United States payroll.[59] It is hardly likely, however, that anything like this number actually crossed the Niagara River or participated in the battle at Chippewa. When, after the battle, the Indians appeared before Porter and demanded payment for their scalps, Porter indignantly refused and his Indians promptly returned home. There were no American Indians present at Lundy's Lane.

The problem of handling the Indians during the war was not simply a matter of preventing them from indulging in the barbaric practices usually associated with Indian warfare, it was also a matter of preserving good relations between the army and the Indian Department. And these, unfortunately, were never very satisfactory during 1812–14. Even prior to the outbreak of hostilities Captain Norton, an Indianized Scotsman[60] who sought to step into the shoes of Joseph Brant as the principal leader of the Six Nations, had come into conflict with the officers of the Indian Department, and in particular with William Claus, the deputy superintendent-general. Brock was not unaware of this personal antagonism and the effect which it had upon the tribes on the Grand River. As early as May 1812 he had noted that while the Six Nations seemed 'well disposed' they were, unfortunately, divided 'on points which some white people find an interest in keeping alive.'[61]

The issue raised by the quarrel between Norton and Claus was a fundamental one. Norton had proved himself to be a good fighting man, and for that reason he received the support of officers like Prevost, de Rottenburg, Harvey, and others, who felt that the first consideration should be that of winning the war. The political implications of Norton's activities were of no concern to them. On the other hand, the Indian Department and the civil authorities had to look to the future. They were obliged to consider what problems might arise were Norton to achieve his object of becoming the leader of the Six Nations; better by far that the Indians should remain peaceful and submissive than stirred up to make embarrassing demands. For that reason Claus not only attempted to play down Norton's ability as a leader of the fighting Indians, but also endeavoured to undermine Norton's authority with the tribes at Grand River and obstinately opposed all proposals that he be given a free hand in the distribution of presents to the Indians.

It was thus a matter of concern to Claus that Prevost, who was always suspicious of the Indian Department as a jealous clique, agreed in 1813 to give Norton a discretionary power to distribute presents and rewards to Six Nations warriors who fought in the British interest. And events soon proved that Claus had some justification for his alarm. It was not long before Norton, not content with controlling the Six Nations Indians, endeavoured to extend his influence over the western Indians as well by bribing them with liquor and supplies. When Colonel Caldwell, the superintendent of the western nations, addressed his Indians on 14 June, one of their chiefs replied: 'As to the Snipe [Captain Norton] having got some of our young men to join him, I only say, He speaks loud, and has Strong Milk and Big Breasts, which yield plentifully. You know Father, your Children are fond of Milk, and he gives when they go to him, and promises them Provisions as they want and Goods at discretion.

If you will do so Father they will not go to him, but we cannot keep our young men in our hands.'[62]

THE MISSISSIPPI VALLEY

Despite the events on the Thames River in 1813 which had led to the virtual extinction of Indian resistance on the Detroit front, the British still hoped to revive the fighting spirit of the western Indians. Tecumseh's sister was heaped with presents of condolence, his son was given a commission in the British army, and his brother, the Prophet, was given a pension and installed as principal chief of the western Indians. But these investments yielded no dividends, for the Indians were not prepared to take up arms in any large numbers until the British themselves were in a position to send regular troops to reoccupy the abandoned territory. General Drummond was confident that the Indians around Detroit were still loyal to Great Britain and that, could he but spare the men, he could, without difficulty, recover everything that had been lost. But there were no troops available for this task, and the Indians would not fight alone.

Beyond Lake Michigan the British position was still reasonably secure. Michilimackinac was well defended; an Indian store depot had been established at Green Bay and Dickson's agents, Rolette and Brisbois, with the assistance of the loyal Winnebago, maintained British influence throughout the upper reaches of the Mississippi River between Michilimackinac and Prairie du Chien. Against these two positions the Americans directed their western operations during 1814 without success. The little post at Prairie du Chien was taken but quickly recovered and the attempt against Michilimackinac ended in failure. A later effort by Zachary Taylor to dislodge the British from the Mississippi met with failure at the hands of the Winnebago, Sioux, and Sauk Indians. The British thus retained their hold on Prairie du Chien and even began to plan offensive operations for the Wisconsin Indians against St Louis for the spring of 1815.[63]

THE TREATY OF GHENT

One of the great blunders committed by the British delegates to Versailles in 1783 had been failure to secure some guarantees for the Indian allies of the crown in the final treaty of peace. The problem of obtaining Indian assistance during the War of 1812 had kept this lesson before the minds of the British authorities and when their representatives left London for Ghent in 1814 they were bound by instructions to make some effort to arrive at an understanding with the United States over the Indian boundary line. It was to the credit of the British that they would not consent to any arrangement which excluded the Indians, and righteously asserted of Great Britain that 'it is utterly inconsistent with her practice and her principles ever to abandon in her negotiations for peace those who have co-operated with her in war'[64] – an assertion which would have stuck in any Indian throat at that date.

The original British proposal called for the establishment of a clearly defined Indian territory in which the Indians might live their own independent existence, the boundaries to follow those fixed at Greenville in 1795. This was, at least in principle, what the Indians had been fighting for. But the defeat at Moraviantown, and the loss of that territory beyond Lake Erie which the capture of Detroit by Brock and Tecumseh had given them, made it difficult for the British to press their point in the face of the adamant refusal of the American delegates to agree to the setting up of an Indian buffer state. The final compromise was one by which the United States agreed to restore to the Indian nations who had been at war 'all the Possessions, Rights, and Privileges'[65] which they had enjoyed or been entitled to enjoy before the commencement of hostilities. It was not what the Indians wanted nor what the British would like to have gained for them; but, while conceding the United States claim to territorial sovereignty over the area which the western Indians had striven to maintain for themselves ever since the days of Pontiac, the Treaty of Ghent did place the United States under a moral obligation to restore the Indians to the *status quo ante bellum*. If the Indians did not gain anything from supporting the British in 1812–14, at least they did not lose anything.

NOTES

This article is from *Canadian Historical Review* 31 (2) (1950). Reprinted with permission.

1 National Archives of Canada (NA), B 103, 177, Maclean to Haldimand, 18 May 1783

2 Ibid., 280, Maclean to Haldimand, 19 July 1783. See also B 119, 195 ff, and NA, Claus Papers, 3, 246 ff, for the proceedings of the Indian council. Johnson told the Indians that the peace treaty had not included the lands set aside for the Indians at Stanwix and gave them assurances of support should the United States attempt to deprive them of their lands, which he must have known he had no authority to give. It was not surprising that Haldimand should later urge the retention of the western posts; to risk further disillusion would be to risk an Indian war.

3 The two questions at issue were the boundaries of the Grand River reserve and the right of the Indians to a transmissible title. This last was withheld by

Simcoe for the protection of the Indians, much to their annoyance. The Six Nations finally gave Joseph Brant power of attorney to surrender, sell, or transfer their lands for the purpose of forming a fund which would provide them with an annuity when the wild game had vanished. Brant conveyed large tracts of lands by sale and by 999-year lease, in many instances for nominal consideration.

4 B 222, 68, Haldimand to Claus, 19 April 1781; NA, G 53-2, 579, Portland to Hunter, 4 Oct. 1799. See also NA, C 252, 270.

5 Prisoners taken during the Ancien Régime had frequently been adopted by and later married into the Indian tribes. Silas Rice captured at Marlboro, Mass., in 1703; Eunice Williams, one of the captives of Deerfield in 1704; Jacob Hill and John Stacey, two boys taken near Albany in 1755, are outstanding instances of this. See E.J. Devine, *Historic Caughnawaga* (Montreal 1922), 421.

6 B 119, 8-10, Proceedings of a Council held at Montreal, 14 Aug. 1778.

7 Devine, *Historic Caughnawaga*, 321

8 F.B. Hough, *A History of St-Lawrence and Franklin Counties New York, from Their Earliest Period to the Present Time* (Albany 1853), 182. Colonel Louis was commissioned into the American army and went to Plattsburg where he was regarded as 'a firm and undeviating friend of the United States' (ibid., 195). His father was a negro and his mother an Abenaki from St Francis, according to Hough, although other sources suggest he was of mixed French, negro, and Oneida blood.

9 Eleazar Williams, a descendant of one of the Deerfield captives, claimed to be the son of Louis XVI and that he had been smuggled out of the hands of the revolutionists in Paris and brought to North America where he was secretly raised by the Caughnawaga Indians. Although he was an arrant imposter, he was adept at exploiting the credulity of newspaper men and others. For a full account see J.H. Hanson, *The Lost Prince: Facts Tending to Prove the Identity of Louis the Seventeenth and the Rev. Eleazar Williams, Missionary among the Indians in North America* (New York 1854).

10 Quoted in Devine, *Historic Caughnawaga*, 321

11 NA, Q 107, 233, Extract of a letter from Claus to Gore, 20 April 1808. The Craig-Gore correspondence is to be found in Q 107.

12 Ibid., 232, Extract of a letter from Craig to Gore, 11 May 1808

13 Ibid., 202, Craig to Castlereagh, 15 July 1808

14 E. Cruikshank, 'The Employment of Indians in the War of 1812,' *Annual Report*, American Historical Association, 1895, 323

15 C 673, 171, Brock to Prevost, 2 Dec. 1811. See also *Select British Documents of the Canadian War of 1812*, ed. W. Wood, 3 vols. (Champlain Society, Toronto 1920), 1: 271 ff, and *Documentary History of the Campaign on the Niagara Frontier*, ed. E. Cruikshank, 9 vols. (Welland 1896), III, 21.

16 *Select British Documents*, I, 423, Brock to Dickson, 27 Feb. 1812. See also C 256, 209.

17 *Select British Documents*, 424, Dickson to Brock, 18 June 1812; C 256, 211

18 Cruikshank, 'Employment of Indians in the War of 1812,' 328

19 Hull's letter to the Six Nations is printed in *Select British Documents*, I, 359, and in *Documentary History*, III, 132.

20 Cruikshank, 'Employment of Indians in the War of 1812,' 329

21 *Select British Documents*, I, 358, Elliott to Claus, 15 July 1812
22 For the events of the war see C.P. Lucas, *The Canadian War of 1812* (Oxford 1906). A recent American account of the war is F.F. Beirne, *The War of 1812* (New York 1949). Oddly enough, Beirne seems unaware of the existence of Sir Charles Lucas's book.
23 *The Historical Register of the United States from the Declaration of War in 1812 to January 1st 1814*, 2 vols. (Washington 1814), II, 41–2, Hull to Eustis, 26 Aug. 1812
24 Owing to the capture of Hull's orders and dispatches at Brownstown as a result of an Indian ambush, the British were fully informed of Hull's weakness and his fear of the Indians. It was thus possible to play upon his fears by planting a letter purporting to be from Procter to the commanding officer at Michilimackinac asking that no more Indians be sent to Amherstburg since there were already more than 5000 there! Beirne, *War of 1812*, 103
25 *Select British Documents*, I, 508, Brock to Liverpool, 29 Aug. 1812
26 C 257, 31, McGill to Prevost, 19 Dec. 1812
27 A board of commissioners including General de Rottenburg, McGill and his associates, John Richardson and Wm. McGillivray, and officers of the Indian Department awarded Dickson the sum of £1875 to cover the cost of the goods which he distributed among the Indians during the summer and autumn of 1812. NA, C 257, 11. A detailed statement of Dickson's claims may be found in *Select British Documents*, I, 426–7.
28 C 257, 4, Instructions for Robert Dickson, 14 Jan. 1813
29 G.F.G. Stanley, 'British Operations in the American North-West 1812–1815,' *Journal of the Society for Army Historical Research*, 22 (87) (autumn 1943): 95–6
30 *Select British Documents*, II, 35–6, Procter to Prevost, 14 May 1813; C 678, 261
31 *Select British Documents*, II, 262, Procter to Baynes, 19 Aug. 1813; C 679, 456
32 B.J. Lossing, *The Pictorial Field Book of the War of 1812* (New York 1869), 400n
33 *Select British Docouments*, I, 348, Brock to Prevost, 3 July 1812; C 676, 115
34 *Select British Doclùments*, 378, Brock to Prevost, 26 July 1812. Brock attributed this change of sentiment to the agents whom Hull had sent to Grand River with his letter to the Six Nations. See above, note 19.
35 Ibid. Brock wrote: 'I meditated, the moment I could collect a sufficient number of Militia, a diversion to the westward, in the hope of compelling General Hull to retreat across the river, but this unexpected intelligence has ruined the whole of my plans. The Militia, which I destined for this service, will now be alarmed, and unwilling to leave their families to the mercy of 400 Indians, whose conduct afford such wide room for suspicion – and really to expect that this fickle race would remain in the midst of war in a state of neutrality is truly absurd.'
36 Ibid., 517, Willcocks to Macdonell, 1 Sept. 1812; C 688 B, 30. This appears to be the same Willcocks who later went over to the Americans and led a force of renegades calling themselves the 'Canadian Volunteers' who ravaged the Canadian frontier during 1813 and 1814. Willcocks was later killed in a skirmish at Fort Erie, 4 September 1814. An odd selection, to say the least, for the purpose of inducing the Indians to fight on behalf of Great Britain.
37 *Select British Documents*, 587, Brock to Prevost, 7 Sept. 1812; C 677, 64
38 *Select British Documents*, 597, Brock to Prevost, 28 Sept. 1812; C 677, 94
39 Claus Papers, X, 87, Report of William Claus, 4 Dec. 1813. This report is also printed in the publications of the *Niagara Historical Society* 9 (1902): 23–40.

40 M. Edgar, *Ten Years of Upper Canada in Peace and War 1805–1815, Being the Ridout Letters with Annotations* (London 1891), 167
41 *Select British Documents*, II, 153, Harvey to Baynes, 11 June 1813; C 679, 76
42 *Documentary History*, V 245, Johnson to Claus, 26 May 1813. According to a letter written by Ducharme on 5 June 1826, he commanded 340 Indians comprising 160 from Caughnawaga, 120 from Lake of Two Mountains, and 60 from St Regis. See *Documentary History*, VI, 126.
43 *Select British Documents*, III-2, 585, Journal of Events by Captain W.H. Merritt. For various reports on the battle of Beaver Dam see ibid., II, 169, General Order sent to Sir John Johnson, 6 July 1813; *Documentary History*, VI, 110, Claus to Bisshopp, 24 June 1813; ibid., 112, Bisshopp to Vincent, 24 June 1813; ibid., 116, *Montreal Gazette*, 6 July 1813; ibid., 126, Ducharme letter, 5 June 1826. In 1818 Fitzgibbon wrote to Captain Kerr of the Indian Department: 'With respect to the affair with Captain Boerstler, not a shot was fired on our side by any but the Indians. They beat the American detachment into a state of terror, and the only share I claim is taking advantage of a favorable moment to offer them protection from the tomahawk and scalping knife. The Indian Department did all the rest.' *Documentary History*, VI, 120–1. According to Ducharme the only reason that he did not demand the surrender and receive the capitulation was because he did not speak English.
44 *Documentary History*, VI, 110, Claus to Bisshopp, 24 June 1813
45 Ibid., 163, Fulton to Prevost, 30 June 1813
46 Following the victory at Beaver Dam the Lower Canada Indians became restless. They were dissatisfied with the rewards which they had received and the long-standing jealousy between the Iroquois of Caughnawaga and the Iroquois of Grand River flared up. Many of them returned home and the others followed a few weeks later owing to the necessity of looking after their crops.
47 *Documentary History*, VI, 207, de Rottenburg to Prevost, 9 July 1813
48 Ibid., 216, Claus to Johnson, 11 July 1813
49 Ibid., 283, Porter to Tompkins, 27 July 1813
50 W. Ketchum, *An Authentic and Comprehensive History of Buffalo with Some Account of Its Early Inhabitants, Both Savage and Civilized*, 2 vols. (Buffalo 1865), II, 423, appendix 8, Minutes of a Meeting at Buffalo, 8 Sept. 1812
51 Ibid., 424, Address to the President of the United States, 28 Sept. 1812
52 Ibid., 428, Granger to the Chiefs at Alleghany, 22 June 1813
53 Ibid., 430–1, Minutes of Council at Buffalo, by Erastus Granger, 25 July 1813
54 Ibid., 431, Granger to the secretary for war, 9 Aug. 1813
55 *Documentary History*, VII, 159, Hampton to secretary for war, 22 Sept. 1813
56 C.W. Elliott, *Winfield Scott, the Soldier and the Man* (New York 1937), 158
57 *Select British Documents*, III-1, 128, Drummond to Prevost, 13 July 1814; C 684, 90
58 Following the battle of Chippewa, two American Indians bringing with them a Cayuga chief taken prisoner at Chippewa attended a council of the Six Nations at Burlington where they endeavoured to persuade the Canadian Indians to withdraw from the war promising the American Indians would do likewise. 'Whatever those fellow have said,' wrote Riall, 'has caused much dissatisfaction among the Indians, and the western people have reason to suspect the Six Nations of treachery.' *Documentary History*, I, 70, Riall to Drummond, 17 July

1814. In any event, very few Cayuga or Onondaga came forward with the other Indians.

59 L.L. Babcock, *The War of 1812 on the Niagara Frontier* (Buffalo 1927) 147

60 Norton was a Scotsman by birth who came to Canada as a private in the 65th Regiment. He was discharged in 1788 and after a brief stay in Kingston went to the villages of the Six Nations, where he learned the Mohawk tongue. After a period as a trader he made the acquaintance of Joseph Brant and, at Brant's instigation, was appointed interpreter to the Mohawk. He resigned this appointment in 1800 and assumed the habits and manners of an Indian. Q 312-1, 126-8, Gore to Castlereagh, 4 Sept. 1809; see also Claus Papers, VIII, Chew to Selby, 1 Sept. 1800.

61 *Select British Documents*, I, 306, Brock to Liverpool, 25 May 1812

62 Ibid., III-2, 726-7, Extract of a speech delivered to the Western Warriors, 14 June 1814, and the answer of Neywash; C 257, 303

63 See Public Archives of Canada, *Report, 1887*, cv-vii, for correspondence relating to the recovery of Prairie du Chien. For later military events at Prairie du Chien see Bulger-McDouall correspondence in the Bulger Papers in the National Archives of Canada.

64 Quoted in Lucas, *Canadian War of 1812*, 251

65 The terms of the Treaty of Ghent will be found in *Treaties and Agreements Affecting Canada in Force between His Majesty and the United States of America 1814-1925* (Ottawa 1927), 1–6.

EMERGENCE OF CIVIL INDIAN POLICY

JOHN L. TOBIAS

Protection, Civilization, Assimilation: An Outline History of Canada's Indian Policy

Protection, civilization, and assimilation have always been the goals of Canada's Indian policy. These goals were established by governments which believed that Indians were incapable of dealing with persons of European ancestry without being exploited. Therefore, the government of Canada had to protect the person and property of the Indian from exploitation by the European, which meant that the Indian was to have a special status in the political and social structure of Canada. This distinction was made part of the constitutional structure of Canada through Section 91, Subsection 24, of the British North America Act of 1867, which gave the government exclusive jurisdiction over 'Indians and Indian land.' However, the legislation by which the governments of Canada sought to fulfil their responsibility always had as its ultimate purpose the elimination of the Indian's special status. The means to achieve this goal was by training, that is, 'civilizing,' the Indian in European values, to make him capable of looking after his own interests. Eventually, through this training, the Indian identity and culture would be eradicated, and the Indian would be assimilable and no longer in need of special status. However, rather than furthering the ultimate goal of assimilation, such legislation has only served to thwart it. How and why this paradoxical situation arose is the subject of this paper.

COLONIAL ORIGINS OF CANADA'S INDIAN POLICY

The basic principles of Canada's Indian policy pre-date Confederation. They were a carry-over of policies developed by the imperial government during the century preceding Confederation. Protection of the Indian was the first principle of imperial Indian policy, having its roots in the eighteenth-century European struggle for empire in North America. It evolved from the exigencies of the French-British rivalry for dominion in mid-century and from the difficulties experienced by the British with the Indians when British colonials encroached on Indian lands. Realizing that the lack of a uniform system of dealing with the issue of Indian lands and Indian trade often led to the Indians allying with France, the imperial government decided to make relations with the Indians an imperial responsibility.

The British government adopted the policy of protecting the Indians from European encroachment in the use of their lands and of preventing fraudulent trading practices that had been characteristic of much of the Indian-white economic dealings. Therefore, Indian superintendents were appointed and made responsible for these matters, as well as for making the Indians allies of the British through annual distribution of presents.[1] Later, a boundary line was established between Indian lands and European settlement, which could be altered only by the crown making treaties to take the surrender of Indian title to the land. Regulations for trade with the Indians were also made. These policies, adopted in the period 1745–61, were made law when they were incorporated into the Royal Proclamation of 7 October 1763.[2]

Adherence to the principles of the Royal Proclamation of 1763 remained the basis of Britain's Indian policy for more than half a century and explains the success of the British in maintaining the Indians as allies in Britain's wars in North America during that period. Even when Britain lost much of its North American territory after 1781, and its Indian allies lost their traditional lands as a result of their British alliance, the crown purchased land from Indians living within British territory and gave it to their allies who moved north to remain under British protection. The British continued also to purchase Indian title to any lands needed for European settlement and economic exploitation as the population of their North American colony expanded.[3] Such practices became the basis for later Canadian treaties with Indians living in the territories purchased from the Hudson's Bay Company.

It was after 1815 that the British adopted the policy of civilizing the Indian as an integral part of their relationship with the Indians. The policy evolved slowly, as a result of much propaganda in Britain and North America about the need to develop the Indian. Much of the propaganda in North America was made by Protestant sects which were in the throes of Evangelical and Revivalist movements stressing the need to Christianize all men. Many of these sects established missions among the Indians, similar to those the Jesuits and other Catholic orders had been carrying on for generations. Such missions were intended not only to teach the Indian a new religion, but also to encourage him to adopt European or American values. In Britain the Humanitarians, who were responsible for the abolition of slavery in the empire and who supported such causes as the Aborigines' Protection Society, advocated the need to protect and civilize the Indian. Romantic writers on both sides of the Atlantic also joined the chorus which protested the British and American policy of pushing the Indian further into the wilderness, and they tried to induce both governments to instruct the Indian in European civilization.[4]

These protests were effective, for in the 1830's the British initiated several experiments in civilization. Essentially, they entailed the establishment of Indian reserves in isolated areas. Indians were encouraged to gather and settle in large villages on these reserves, where they would be taught to farm and would receive religious instruction and an education. These endeavours became the basis of the reserve system in Canada.[5] The reserve system, which was to be the keystone of Canada's Indian policy, was conceived as a social laboratory, where the Indian could be prepared for coping with the European.

Legislation was passed in the colonial assemblies to facilitate this purpose. In Upper Canada, Indian lands, including the new reserves, were among the crown lands upon which settlers were forbidden by law in 1839 to encroach. By 1850, Indian lands were given special status by being protected from trespass by non-Indians and by being freed from seizure for non-payment of debt or taxes. In fact, Indian lands were designated as being held in trust by the crown and free from taxation. Finally, to protect the Indian from being debauched by certain accoutrements of civilization, a ban on the sale of liquor to Indians was legislated.[6] All these protective measures were incorporated into Indian legislation of the Canadian Parliament and were later expanded.

Legislation for Lower Canada differed somewhat from that for Upper Canada. This difference was primarily a result of the fact that there was much less political involvement in new efforts to civilize the Indian, since the Catholic church had for more than a century been engaged in such work. Some protection was granted to these reserves and Indian lands when a commissioner was appointed to supervise them. What was most remarkable about legislation in Lower Canada was that it defined who was an Indian for the first time. It did so in very sweeping terms, for it included all persons of Indian ancestry and all persons married to such persons, belonging to or recognized as belonging to an Indian band, and living with that band.[7] Subsequent legislation would modify this definition by requiring that ancestry and membership would have to be traced through the male line, and marriage would only grant such status if a non-Indian woman married an Indian. However, this act of 1850 established the precedent that non-Indians determined who was an Indian and that Indians would have no say in the matter.

Disenchantment with the efforts to settle Indians on isolated reserves in Upper Canada became manifest by 1850. An evaluation of the program led to the conclusion that the reserve system as then constituted was impractical and a failure. However, rather than repudiate the ideal of the reserve as a school or laboratory for civilizing the Indian, blame for the failure was placed on the fact that such programs were carried out in isolation from centres of European civilization. American experience in Michigan was believed to have shown that where reserves were surrounded by settlement, Indians not only became civilized, but also were being assimilated into the communities bordering on the reserves. Therefore, the decision was made to try working with smaller reserves for individual bands located next to or near European-Canadian communities. With the change in location it was thought that the civilization policy would work,[8] for the Euro-Canadian would serve as an example of what the Indian should become, and the existence of the town, it was thought, would attract the Indian from the reserve and into the non-Indian community where the Indian's newly learned values would supplant his old values and allow him to be fully assimilated.

This alteration in dealing with Indians and their reserves brought about a change in the ultimate goal of British Indian policy. No longer was the end result simply to teach the Indian to cope with persons of European ancestry; he was to become European and to be fully assimilated into the colonial society. In order to achieve such a goal, it was thought necessary to give the Indian special legislative status in order that he could be indoctrinated with European values and thereby made capable of being assimilated. This was the avowed purpose of the law, 'an Act to encourage the gradual civilization of the Indians in this Province, and to amend the laws respecting Indians,' passed in the legislature of the United Canadas in 1857.[9]

The paradox that was to become and remain a characteristic of Canada's Indian policy was given a firm foundation in this act. After stipulating in the preamble that the measure was designed to encourage civilization of the Indian, remove all legal distinctions between Indians and other Canadians, and integrate them fully into Canadian society, the legislation proceeded to define who was an Indian and then to state that such a person could not be accorded the rights and privileges accorded to European Canadians until the Indian could prove that he could read and write either the French or English language, was free of debt, and of good moral character. If he could meet such criteria, the Indian was then eligible to receive an allotment of twenty hectares of reserve land, to be placed on one-year probation to give further proof of his being civilized, and then to be given the franchise.[10] Thus, the legislation to remove all legal distinctions between Indians and Euro-Canadians actually established them. In fact, it set standards for acceptance that many, if not most, white colonials could not meet, for few of them were literate, free of debt, and of high moral character. The 'civilized' Indian would have to be more 'civilized' than the Euro-Canadian.

CANADA'S INDIAN POLICY

The principles of Canada's Indian policy were thus all established by the time of Confederation. What changed after Confederation was the emphasis placed on these principles. Until Confederation, protection of the Indian and his land was the paramount goal. Civilization of the Indian was gaining in importance but was regarded as a gradual and long-term process. Assimilation was the long-range goal. These priorities were retained for a short period after 1867, for although the British North America Act gave the government of the Dominion of Canada exclusive jurisdiction over Indians and lands reserved for Indians, the first legislation on this subject in 1868 merely incorporated the earlier colonial legislation concerning Indian lands. The only changes were the definition of who was an Indian and the penalties imposed for trespass on Indian lands.[11] In 1869 the goals of civilization and assimilation were formally added by the passage of 'an Act for the gradual enfranchisement of Indians.'[12]

The title of this piece of legislation demonstrates a change in emhasis. Whereas the colonial legislation was 'for the gradual civilization,' this new act was 'for the gradual enfranchisement' of the Indian. This shift is demonstrated by the power the governor-in-council was given to impose the Euro-Canadian political ideal of elected local government on an Indian band and to remove from band office those considered unqualified or unfit to hold it. The elected band council was empowered to make by-laws on minor police and public health matters, but before such regulations could be enforced they had to be approved by the superintendent general (the minister) of Indian affairs.[13] This act, designed for the Six Nations and other Indian people with long contact with Europeans who were supposed to have received a rudimentary training under earlier legislation and missionaries, was to provide further instruction in Euro-Canadian values. This extensive education in what was regarded as the more sophisticated aspects of European civilization was to be provided by a paternalistic government which would lead the Indian away from his 'inferior' political system. It thereby established another criterion of civilization.

The new Dominion of Canada developed its Indian policy during the decade of the 1870s. It extended its authority over the Plains Indian through the treaty system. In doing so, the Canadian government demonstrated its acceptance of the principles established by the old imperial government, for not only did the dominion government purchase Indian title to the land, but it also imposed the reserve system as a laboratory for cultural change on the Plains Indians by means of these treaties.[14] In addition, through the 'Act to amend and consolidate the laws respecting Indians' or, as it was short-titled,

'The Indian Act' of 1876,[15] the foundation for all Canada's future Indian legislation was laid.

The new legislation incorporated all the protective features of the earlier legislation and established more stringent requirements for non-Indian use of Indian lands and for their alienation. It contained slight revisions of the mechanism for enfranchisement which it was thought would facilitate assimilation. However, most of these changes were related directly to furthering the process of civilization and permitting the government to encourage and direct it. Thus, the elective system was no longer to be imposed but was only to be applied if the band asked for it. To encourage this system of government, band councils under the elective system were given increased authority. However, the legislation set out the formula for the number of councillors and chiefs a band could have and who could vote in such elections.[16]

The most important innovation of the new Indian Act, in the eyes of the government, was the introduction of the location ticket. This was regarded as an essential feature of the civilization process and a necessity for enfranchisement. It was a means by which the Indian could demonstrate that he had adopted the European concept of private property. The new policy stipulated that the superintendent general have the reserve surveyed into individual lots. The band council could then assign these lots to individual band members. As a form of title the superintendent general would then give the band member a location ticket. Before an individual received a ticket he had to prove his suitability in the same manner as under the earlier legislation. On passing this first test and receiving his location ticket, the Indian entered a three-year probationary period during which he had to demonstrate that he would use the land as a Euro-Canadian might and that he was fully qualified for membership in Canadian society. If he passed these tests, he was enfranchised and given title to the land. If all band members wished, they could enfranchise in this way.[17]

An alternative means of assimilation was also offered, which required less time and supervision than the one discussed above. An Indian who went to university and earned a professional degree as minister, lawyer, teacher, or doctor could be given a location ticket and enfranchised immediately without going through the probationary period.[18] By earning such degrees, the Indian had demonstrated his acceptance of Euro-Canadian values and his ability to function in Canadian society.

What becomes even clearer is the government's determination to make the Indians into imitation Europeans and to eradicate the old Indian values through education, religion, new economic and political systems, and a new concept of property. Not only was the Indian as a distinct cultural group to disappear, but also the laboratory where these changes were brought about would disappear, for as the Indian was enfranchised, that is, became assimilated, he would take with him his share of the reserve. Therefore, when all Indians were enfranchised, there would no longer be any Indian reserves. The first piece of comprehensive legislation by which the government exercised its exclusive jurisdiction over Indians and Indian lands had as its purpose the eventual extirpation of this jurisdiction by doing away with those persons and lands that fell within the category of Indians and Indian lands.

The new Indian Act, like all previous legislation, was designed for the Indians living east of Lake Superior. The western Indians were excluded from the operation of most sections of the Indian Act until such time as the superintendent general of Indian affairs considered them advanced enough in civilization to take advantage of the act. However, to speed up their advance, and under the guise of protecting them from exploitation, the 1876 Indian Act and subsequent amendments contained provisions which attacked traditional Indian sexual, marriage, and divorce mores and furthered the Christian-European values. Into this category fall the sections relating to illegitimate children, non-band members on the reserve after sundown, non-Indians on reserves and cohabiting with Indians, and Indian women in public houses.[19] In addition, Indian agents were given the powers of a justice of the peace to enforce sections of the criminal code relating to vagrancy, in order that the western Indian could be kept on the reserve where he might be taught to farm and learn the value of work.[20]

The eastern Indians who were to be the beneficiaries of the act rejected it, for they knew that if they adopted the elective system, the superintendent general would not only have supervisory and veto power over band decisions, but also, according to other provisions of the act, he could force the band council to concern itself with issues with which it did not wish to deal. Many eastern bands clearly stated that they would never request an elected band council because they did not wish to be governed and managed by the government of Canada.[21] Such protests were interpreted as demonstration of the fact that the Indian needed more direction and guidance, for subsequent amendments and later Indian acts increased the authority of the superintendent general to interfere in the band and personal affairs of the Indians.

The Indian Act of 1880 provided the means to manage Indian affairs. It created a new branch of the civil service that was to be called the Department of Indian Affairs. It once again empowered the superintendent general to impose the elective system of band government whenever he thought a band ready for it. In addition, this new legislation allowed the superintendent general to deprive the traditional leaders of recognition by stating that the only spokesmen of the band were those men elected according to the provisions of the Indian Act when the elective system was imposed. Otherwise, the Indian Act of 1880 differed little from that of 1876.[22]

The elected band council was regarded as the means to destroy the last vestige of the old tribal system, the traditional political system. The reserve system, other sections of the Indian Act, and missionaries were thought to have dealt effectively with all other aspects of traditional Indian values. The only impediment to civilization and assimilation was lack of training in the Canadian political system. This evaluation was the reason for the stress on the elective system despite Indian opposition to it. It was also the reason for passage in 1884 of 'An Act for conferring certain privileges on the more advanced bands of Indians of Canada with the view of training them for exercise of Municipal Affairs.'[23] This bill came to be known as the Indian Advancement Act.

The Indian Advancement Act was an ideal tool for directed civilization. It extended slightly the powers of the band council beyond those of the Indian Act by giving the band council the power to levy taxes on the real property of band members. It also expanded the council's powers over police and public health matters. At the same time it greatly increased the powers of the superintendent general to direct the band's political affairs. Election regulation, size of the band council, and deposition of elected officials were all spelled out in the act. Moreover, the superintendent general or an agent delegated by him was empowered to call for the elections, supervise them, call band meetings, preside over them, record them, advise the band council, and participate in the meetings in every manner except to vote and adjourn the meetings. In effect, the agent directed the political affairs of the band.[24]

To further encourage the Indians to ask for this form of government, Indians east of Lake Superior were granted the franchise in dominion elections by the Electoral Franchise Act of 1885. Thus, they would be able to participate in the political process off the reserve as well as on it. However, few bands accepted either measure, and in 1896 the franchise was withdrawn from the Indians. Nevertheless, the Advancement Act was retained.

Despite most bands' refusing to come under the Advancement Act, the elective system as provided for in the Indian Act was imposed on them. Many bands merely elected their traditional leaders, who were often unsatisfactory to the government and were deposed as being incompetent, immoral, or intemperate, all grounds for dismissal under the Act. However, these men were usually re-elected, which thwarted the government's intentions in deposing them. Therefore, in 1884 the Indian Act was amended to prohibit persons deposed from office from standing for immediate re-election.[25] A decade later, an amendment was added to the Indian Act which allowed the minister to depose chiefs and councillors where the elective system was not applicable. This amendment was included because the band leaders in the West were found to be resisting the innovations of the reserve system and the government's efforts to discourage the practice of traditional Indian beliefs and values.[26]

Interference in and direction of a band's political affairs led to an increase in the government's control of the band's resources. Because most bands opposed enfranchisement of their members and the alienation of reserve lands that this procedure entailed, they were able to thwart the goal by refusing to allot reserve lands to individual band members. Without a land allotment, no location ticket could be given, and without a location ticket, enfranchisement was impossible. Therefore, in 1879 power to allot reserve lands was taken from the band and given to the superintendent general.[27] Because most bands refused to alienate their land, even for a limited period, persons who held location tickets and wanted to lease their land to non-Indians as a source of revenue could not do so, since the band refused to vote for the required surrender. Consequently, the Indian Act was amended in 1884 and 1894 to allow the superintendent general to lease such lands for revenue purposes without taking a surrender. The first was for the purpose of revenue for those holding a location ticket and desiring to lease their land, while the 1894 amendment allowed the superintendent general to lease the land of orphans or aged who held location tickets, but who did not specifically ask to have their land leased. The 1894 amendment was really a device for cutting the cost of government aid to various bands where the location ticket system was well established. By these means, the government thought it was preventing an 'unenlightened' band council from holding a 'civilized' band member in check.[28] In 1898, as a result of bands' refusing to exercise their police and public health powers and not expending their band funds for this purpose, the superintendent general was empowered to make the necessary regulations and expend band funds for whatever expense was entailed in carrying out the regulations.[29]

While the effort to direct civilization and civilization and assimilation of the eastern Indian led to direct involvement in band affairs, legislation for the western Indian was to further the initial process of the civilization program and was therefore geared much more to the individual. Because the Plains Indians and the Indians of British Columbia attempted to preserve their traditional religious and cultural values, despite pressure from missionaries and the government to repudiate them for being contrary to Christian and European values, the government decided to prohibit many of the traditional practices. The 'Sun Dance,' 'Potlatches,' and all 'Give Away' ceremonials were banned because they promoted pagan beliefs and were anathema to the development of a concept of private property.[30] A similar purpose, to teach the Indian to husband his resources, was behind the legislated prohibition on the sale of produce and livestock from Indian reserves on the Prairies.[31]

The ability of many Indians living in Manitoba and the old Northwest Territories to pursue their old form of livelihood, hunting and fishing, was particularly irksome to the government, for it was regarded as a drawback to the Indian's adopting a more settled economic base, farming. Besides, the hunting Indian was retarding the education of his children, because he took them with him into the bush, which meant they did not attend school. These children were regarded as being the first generation which would become civilized and to whom the full benefits of the Indian Act could be extended. However, if they were kept illiterate by their parent's economic pursuits, the government's plans for them would be thwarted. Therefore, in 1980 an amendment to the Indian Act was made empowering the governor-in-council to declare the game laws of Manitoba and the Northwest Territories to be applicable to Indians.[32]

School attendance was of vital concern to the government, for education of the Indian child was a keystone of the civilizing process the reserve system was to perform. Since schools on the reserve were not well attended by Indian children, they were regarded as ineffectual instruments of this process. Residential and industrial schools, which removed the child from the detrimental influence of uncivilized parents and Indian traditions, were regarded as better instruments of government policy. Indian parents refused to send their children to such schools because they were long distances from the reserve and alienated the child from his culture. Therefore, in 1894 amendments to the Indian Act were made authorizing the governor-in-council to make whatever regulations on the school question he thought necessary and empowering him to commit children to the boarding and industrial schools founded by the government.[33]

The program of directed and aggressive civilization that was a characteristic of Indian policy and legislation in the period after 1870 had spent its force by the turn of the century. By 1900 the reserve system was being questioned as a means of achieving assimilation. In fact, many had come to regard the reserve as preventing assimilation, and to believe that the existence of reserves was a check on the economic development and growth of areas where they were located. This attitude began to find expression in the new or, rather, consolidated Indian Act of revised statutes of 1906.[34] Amendments to this act in subsequent years reinforced this view, for most of them were designed to remove the protection the reserve seemed to provide the Indian and to force the Indian people off the reserve. Assimilation was no longer regarded as a long-term goal; it was one that could be attained immediately if the Indian were removed from the protective environment of the reserve.

The initial attack on the reserve began in the 1890s when the superintendent general was given power to lease land for revenue purposes. Shortly thereafter, amendments were made to ease the permanent alienation of reserve land by allowing the government to distribute in cash up to 50 per cent of the value of the land as an inducement for a surrender for sale.[35] As was expected, much reserve land was made available for sale to non-Indians, particularly on the Prairies. These measures were justified as promoting the economic growth of the country and removing a retarding influence on development of an area. Such arguments were also used when the superintendent general was given the power to lease Indian land without taking a surrender for purpose of mineral exploration, to expropriate for right-of-ways for highways and provincially chartered railways, and to lease for revenue farm lands said not to be used by Indians. These powers were given because Indians had refused to make surrenders for these purposes in the past. Finally, a mechanism was established to deal with situations similar to those of Sarnia, Ontario, and Victoria, BC, where reserves within the boundaries of a city could be abolished when it was found to be in the Indian and public interest.[36]

Dissatisfaction with the reserve system principally resulted from the fact that it only partially fulfilled its functions. It did civilize the Indian, but it did not complete the process as envisioned by encouraging them to enfranchise. In the period between 1857 when the enfranchisement process was first enacted and 1920, only slightly more than 250 persons were enfranchised.[37] To remedy this situation, the government amended the Indian Act to permit Indians living off the reserve to be enfranchised without the required land. This change resulted in the enfranchisement of 500 people within two years after passage of the amendment.[38] Subsequent amendments reduced the number of Indians by making it easier for half-breeds who had taken treaty in the West to be enfranchised and for Indian women married to non-Indians to give up entirely their Indian status.[39]

The civilized Indian who preferred to live on the reserve was untouched by any of these amendments, but this was the individual the government wanted off the reserve, for otherwise the reserve and the Indian would become permanent features of Canadian society. The government found such a thought abhorrent, for it wanted to do away with the reserve and 'make a final disposition of the individuals who have been civilized into the ordinary life of the country.'[40] Therefore, assimilation was not to be a voluntary act on the part of the Indian. The superintendent general, at his discretion, was given the power to establish boards of inquiry to examine the fitness of Indians for enfranchisement, without the people making application, report on their fitness for enfranchisement, and the superintendent general would then recommend to the governor-in-council that they be enfranchised. Such people could then be given title to the reserve lands they occupied, receive their share of the band's monies, and be enfranchised.[41]

The outcry and protests that resulted from the operation of these procedures was so great that two years later the government modified these sections of the act to appoint such boards only after applications for enfranchisement were received. However, when this change failed to achieve the purpose established for the original amendments, power to create such boards was returned to the discretion of the superintendent general, and compulsory enfranchisement was re-enacted.[42]

Forced or compulsory enfranchisement was designed for the Indians east of Lake Superior. In the west, where the Indians were thought to be less advanced, the policy of directed civilization was applied to hasten their development. Because the existing provisions of the act were thought not strong enough to achieve this purpose, amendments were made to ensure compulsory school attendance and to treat chronic non-attenders as juvenile delinquents.[43] Also, stronger efforts were made to put an end to Plains Indians' practice of old ceremonials, so that prohibitions against these Indians appearing in aboriginal garb and performing their traditional dances at fairs and stampedes under the guise of entertaining the non-Indian community were interpreted as being part of the act. Later this section was amended to prohibit such dances in any type of dress, unless prior approval in writing was given by the Department of Indian Affairs.[44] To promote farming on western reserves so that the Indians could become self-supporting landholders, the superintendent general was authorized to use band funds to purchase farm machinery for individual Indians and to establish a fund from which loans might be made to allow Indians to purchase machinery or get started in small businesses.[45]

In an effort to reduce the distinctions between Indian and non-Indian communities, the government also incorporated into the Indian Act authority for the superintendent general to regulate the use and operation of amusement and recreational facilities on Indian reserves in accordance with provincial and local laws which forbade opening such facilities on Sundays. Moreover, provincial laws on general matters, such as on motor vehicles, could be declared to be applicable on reserves, and such laws would have the same effect as though they had been incorporated into the Indian Act.[46]

Enactment of compulsory enfranchisement and the breaking down of the barriers of the reserve boundaries both literally by lease and sale and figuratively by making provincial laws apply there were all to promote more rapid assimilation. However, these acts had only limited success. With the economic crisis followed by a major war in the period 1933–45, little attention was paid to Indian matters. In fact, in that period the government and the civil servants in what became the Indian Affairs Branch appear not to have had any policy.

They left this whole area of government-Indian relations in a state of flux and made only ad hoc decisions. Perhaps this situation was a result of the realization that all previous policies had failed to attain the goal established for Canada's Indian administration. At any rate, there is an obvious lack of policy or policy goal in this period.

This apparent aimlessness changed after 1945, when public interest in Indian affairs was awakened to an unprecedented degree. This interest was largely a result of the strong Indian contribution to the war effort in the years 1940–5. The public was generally concerned with what was regarded as the treatment of the Indian as a second-class person and with the fact that the Indian did not have the same status as other Canadians. In fact, the Indian was not even a citizen. Veterans' organizations, churches, and citizen groups across the country called for a royal commission to investigate the administration of Indian affairs and conditions prevailing on Indian reserves. All wanted a complete revision of the Indian Act and an end to discrimination against the Indian.[47]

No royal commission was appointed, but a joint committee of both the Senate and House of Commons was created in 1946 to study and make proposals on Canada's Indian administration and the revision of the Indian Act. After two years, the joint committee recommended:

1. The complete revision of every section of the Indian Act and the repeal of those sections which were outdated.
2. That the new Indian Act be designed to facilitate the gradual transition of the Indian from a position of wards up to full citizenship. Therefore the Act should provide:
   A. A political voice for Indian women in band affairs.
   B. Bands with more self-government and financial assistance.
   C. Equal treatment of Indians and non-Indians in the matter of intoxicants.
   D. That a band might incorporate as a municipality.
   E. That Indian Affairs officials were to have their duties and responsibilities designed to assist the Indian in the responsibilities of self-government and to attain the rights of full citizenship.
3. Guidelines for future Indian policy were to be:
   A. Easing of enfranchisement.
   B. Extension of the franchise to the Indian.
   C. Co-operation with the provinces in extending service to the Indian.
   D. Education of Indian children with non-Indians in order to prepare Indian children for assimilation.[48]

In essence, the joint committee approved the goal of Canada's previous Indian policy – assimilation – but disapproved some of the earlier methods to achieve it. They assumed that most of the work of civilization was virtually complete, and that therefore many of the protective features of earlier acts could be withdrawn and bands allowed more self-government and less governmental interference. Moreover, since assimilation was soon attainable, the guidelines for the new Indian policy and the new Indian Act stipulated that the dominion government should begin turning over responsibilities for providing services to the provinces. In this way the barriers provided by the reserves and the Indians' special status under the constitution would be further broken down and assimilation made all the easier. Thus, the Indian and the Indian reserve were still regarded as a transitory feature of Canadian society.

In 1951 a new Indian Act was passed which met most of the criteria established by the joint committee. At first glance it appeared to differ greatly from all previous Indian acts back to 1876. Not since the 1876 act had the minister's powers been so limited, for under the new act the minister's 'powers were reduced to a supervisory role' but with veto power. His authority to direct band and personal matters required band approval. The individual bands, if they desired, could now run their own reserves. As many as fifty sections and subsections were deleted from earlier acts because they were antiquated or too restrictive on individuals or the band. Most of the provisions for aggressive civilization and compulsory enfranchisement were deleted.[49]

A closer look at the 1951 Indian Act and a comparison with the Indian Act of 1876 shows that there are only minor differences. In format, content, and intent they are quite similar. Both provide for a cooperative approach between government and Indian towards the goal of assimilation, although enfranchisement is made easier in the 1951 act by eliminating the testing period and the requirement for location tickets or certificates of possession. However, other provisions are virtually the same. The new act definitely differs from the Indian acts between 1880 and 1951, but only because it returned to the philosophy of the original Indian Act: civilization was to be encouraged but not directed or forced on the Indian people. Assimilation for all Indians was a goal that should be striven for without an abundance of tests or the compulsory aspects of the preceding Indian acts. Through the 1951 Indian Act the government managed to extricate itself from the quicksand that a desire to hurry assimilation had mired it in after passage of the 1876 Indian Act.

Speedy assimilation was not repudiated as the goal of Canada's Indian policy – what was repudiated was the earlier means to achieve it. Therefore, when it became obvious that the 1951 Indian Act would not promote the purpose it was designed for any more than earlier acts did, an alternative means to those tried between 1880 and 1950 was sought. This was provided in part by the recommendation by the joint committee to turn over responsibility for services to Indians to the provinces. Therefore, this process was begun in the 1950s and continued in the decade of the 1960s. Then, in 1969, when this transfer was nearing completion, the government announced its intention to absolve itself from responsibility for Indian affairs and the special status of Indians and to repeal special legislation relating to Indians – that is, the Indian Act.[50] By adoption of this policy and by repealing the Indian Act, the Indian would be assimilated by government fiat, and what the Indian Act of 1876 had sought as a long-term goal – the extirpation of the Indian and Indian lands – would be realized.

The announcement of this policy in the 1969 White Paper on Indian Affairs brought such a protest from the Indian people, who had always rejected this goal, that the government was forced to reconsider its policy, delay transfer of services, and in 1973 announced the withdrawal of the policy statement. However, this official withdrawal does not mean that the goal has been repudiated; at least there is no indication of such renunciation to date. It is simply that alternative means to achieve it are being considered. At the moment Canada's Indian policy is in a state of flux, but unlike any earlier period, a more honest effort is being made to involve the Indian and Indian views in the determination of a new Indian policy.[51]

NOTES

This article is from *The Western Canadian Journal of Anthropology* 6 (2) (1976). Reprinted with permission.

1 Robert S. Allen, *The British Indian Department and the Frontier in North America, 1755–1830*, Occasional Papers in Archaeology and History 14 (Ottawa 1975), 1–8; Clarence W. Alvord, *The Genesis of the Proclamation of 1763* (Michigan Pioneer and Historical Society, vol. 36, 1908), 24–6; Duncan Campbell Scott, 'Indian Affairs, 1763–1841,' in A. Shortt and A.G. Doughty, eds., *Canada and Its Provinces*, vol. IV (Toronto 1914), 698–9

2 Alvord, *Genesis*, 31–5, 51–2; Allen, 'British Indian Department,' 17–20

3 Scott, 'Indian Affairs, 1763–1841,' 700–19. The best study of Britain's Indian policy is Allen, 'British Indian Department.' See also Robert J. Surtees, *The Original People* (Toronto 1971), 45–9; Duncan Campbell Scott, 'Indian Affairs, 1840–1867,' in A. Shortt and A.G. Doughty, eds., *Canada and Its Provinces*, vol. V (Toronto 1914), 345–6, and Anna Margaret Wright, 'The Canadian Frontier, 1840–1867' (Ph D thesis, University of Toronto, 1943), 40.

4 Robert J. Surtees, 'The Development of an Indian Reserve Policy in Canada,' *Ontario History* 61 (2) (June 1969): 87–90; Allen, 'British Indian Department,' 207–11; and L.F.S. Upton, 'The Origins of Canadian Indian Policy,' *Journal of Canadian Studies* 8 (4) (Nov. 1973): 51–61

5 Surtees, 'Development.' For a more detailed study of this policy see Surtees, 'Indian Reserve Policy in Upper Canada, 1830–1845' (MA thesis, Carleton University, 1967), on which his article is based. See also John E. Hodgetts, 'Indian Affairs, the White Man's Albatross,' in his *Pioneer Public Service: An Administrative History 1841–1867* (Toronto 1955), 209–10, and Upton, 'Origins,' 51–61.

6 Statutes of the Province of Canada (SPC), 1839, 2 Vict., c. 15; 1840, 3 Vict., c. 13; 1850, 13–14 Vict., c. 74

7 Ibid., 1850, 13–14 Vict., c. 42. The Indian reserves which existed in Lower Canada at this time were those that had been established by the various religious orders on lands granted to them during the French régime. These reserves were therefore within or next to non-Indian communities. Thus, there was often intermarriage or non-Indians living on the reserves, which were run by the religious orders and not by colonial officials, as in Upper Canada. For this reason, it was necessary to define who was being protected by this legislation governing Indian lands. The special circumstances of Lower Canada made this definition necessary, for as was stated above, non-Indians were forbidden by law from living on crown lands used for or regarded as being Indian lands in Upper Canada.

8 Hodgetts, 'Indian Affairs,' 210

9 SPC, 1857, 20 Vict., c. 26

10 Ibid.

11 Statutes of Canada (SC), 1868, 31 Vict., c. 42. Incorporated in this act was a law not mentioned above which dealt with surrender of Indian lands. SPC, 1860, 23 Vict., c. 151.

12 SC, 1869, 32–3 Vict., c. 42

13 Ibid.

14 Alexander Morris, *The Treaties of Canada with the Indians of Manitoba and the North-West Territories* (Toronto 1971). The last chapter of this book provides an excellent summary of the views of the man responsible for making many of the western treaties and his reasons for including the various provisions of the treaties.

15 SC, 1876, 39 Vict., c. 18; National Archives of Canada (NA), RG 10, vol. 1923, file 3007. The latter reference gives some background to this act. From the RG 10 series, vol. 1935, file 3589; vol. 1928, file 3281; vol. 3084, file 3608. All provide information as to reasons various provisions of the act were made.

16 SC, 1876, 39 Vict., c. 18; House of Commons, *Debates*, 2 March 1876, 342–3; 21 March 1876, 749–53

17 SC, 1876, 39 Vict., c. 18; House of Commons, *Debates*, 2 March 1876, 342–3; 21 March 1876, 749–53

18 SC, 1876, 39 Vict., c. 18

19 SC, 1879, 42 Vict., c. 34; 1884, 47 Vict., c. 27; 1887, 50–1 Vict., c. 33; 1898, 61 Vict., c. 34; 1894, 57–8 Vict., c. 32; NA, RG 10, vol. 2378, file 77, 190; vol. 2004, file 7728; vol. 3947, file 123, 264–1; vol. 1596; vol. 6809, file 470-2-3, vol. 11, part 3

20 SC, 1890, 53 Vict., c. 24; 1895, 58-9 Vict., c. 35; NA, RG 10, vol. 3832, file 64,009; vol. 2446, file 93,503; vol. 2497, file 102,950; vol. 3378, file 77,020; vol. 6809, file 470-2-3, vol. 22, part 4

21 SC, 1876, 39 Vict., c. 18; NA, RG 10, vol. 2077, file 11,432
22 SC, 1880, 43 Vict., c. 28. Further amendments regarding the minister's power in elections and band government were included in SC, 1884, 47 Vict., c. 27. See also NA, RG 10, vol. 2378, file 77,190.
23 SC 1884, 47 Vict., c. 28
24 Ibid. This amendment included provisions which gave band councils most of the powers, except taxation, provided in the Indian Advancement Act.
25 NA, RG 10, vol. 3947, file 123, 764-2; SC, 1884, 47 Vict., c. 27
26 Ibid., vol. 6809, file 470-2-3, vol. 11, part 4; SC, 1895, 58–9 Vict., c. 35
27 SC, 1879, 42 Vict., c. 34; 1884, 47 Vict., c. 27; NA, RG 10, vol. 2378, file 77,190
28 SC 1894, 57-8 Vict., c. 32; 1895, 58–9 Vict., c. 35; NA, RG 10, vol. 6809, file 470-2-3, vol. 11, part 4; vol. 2378, file 77,190
29 SC, 1898, 61 Vict., c. 34; NA, RG 10, vol. 6809, file 470-2-3, vol. 11, part 4. Earlier acts, such as SC, 1887, 50–1 Vict., c. 33, allowed leases for cutting hay and timber without a surrender.
30 SC, 1884, 47 Vict., c. 27; 1895, 58–9 Vict., c. 35; NA, RG 10, vol. 6809, file 470-2-3, vol. 11, part 4
31 SC, 1884, 47 Vict., c. 27; 1890, 53 Vict., c. 24; NA, RG 10, vol. 2446, file 93,503; vol. 2497, file 102,950. The government had found that the Plains Indians disposed of all their agricultural and livestock produce each fall in order to get cash which was, in turn, expended for foodstuffs. However, since other purchases were also made, by mid-winter many of the Indians were destitute, having no food on hand and no means by which to procure it, for their money was completely expended. This situation meant that the government had to provide rations to keep these people alive. Rather than do this, the government thought that the Indian should be prevented from disposing of his crop all at once. It was assumed that the Indian, having seen that husbanding his crop would mean that he would be able to feed himself and have cash at intervals throughout the year, would then voluntarily limit himself to selling only a portion of his produce in the fall and that he would have learned the efficacy of husbanding his resources.
32 SC, 1890, c. 29; NA, RG 10, vol. 2378, file 70,020; vol. 3832, file 69,009; vol. 2446, file 93,503; vol. 2497, file 102,950
33 SC, 1894, 57–8 Vict., c. 32; NA, RG 10, vol. 3947, file 123,764–3; vol. 6908, file 470-2-3, vol. 11
34 SC, 1906, revised statutes c. 81. See NA, RG 10, vol. 6810, file 470-2-3, vol. 12, part 7, for the correspondence concerning the new attitude towards the reserve.
35 SC, 1898, 61 Vict., c. 34; 1906, 6 Ed. VII, c. 20; NA, RG 10, vol. 6809, file 470-2-3, vol. 11, parts 4, 5
36 SC, 1910, 9–10 Ed. VII, c. 20; 1910, 1–2 Geo. V, c. 14; 1918, 9–10 Geo. V, c. 50; NA, RG 10, vol. 6809, file 470-2-3, vol. 2, part 6; vol. 6810, file 470-2-3, vol. 12, part 10
37 NA, RG 10, vol. 6810, vol. 470-2-3, vol. 12, part 7; memo on enfranchisement
38 SC, 1918, 8–9 Geo. V, c. 26; NA, RG 10, vol. 6809, file 470-2-3, vol. 11, part 6
39 SC, 1914, 4–5 Geo. V, c. 35; 1919–20, 10–11 Geo. V, c. 50; NA, RG 10, vol. 6810, file 470-2-3, vol. 12, part 7
40 NA, RG 10, vol. 6810, file 470-2-3, vol. 12, part 7; memo on enfranchisement
41 Ibid.; SC, 1919–20, 10–11 Geo. V, c. 50

42 SC, 1922, 12–13 Geo. V, c. 26; 1932–3, 23–4 Geo. V, c. 42; NA, RG 10, vol. 6810, file 470-2-3, vol. 12, parts 7–9
43 SC, 1914, 4–5 Geo. V, c. 35; 1919–20, 10–11 Geo. V, c. 50; 1930, 20–1 Geo. V, c. 25; NA, RG 10, vol. 6809, file 470-2-3, vol. 11, parts 5 and 6; vol. 6810, file 470-2-3, vol. 12, parts 7–8
44 SC, 1914, 4–5 Geo. V, c. 26; NA, RG 10, vol. 3825, file 60,511, vols. 1 and 2
45 SC, 1918, 8–9 Geo. V, c. 26; 1922, 12–13 Geo. V, c. 26; 1938, 2 Geo. VI, c. 31; NA, RG 10, vol. 6809, file 470-2-3, vol. 11, part 6; vol. 6810, file 470-2-3, vol. 12, parts 8 and 10
46 SC, 1922, 12–13 Geo. V, c. 26; 1930, 20–1 Geo. V, c. 25; 1936, 1 Ed. VIII, c. 20; NA, RG 10, vol. 6810, file 470-2-3, vol. 12, parts 8 and 10
47 NA, RG 10, vol. 6810, file 470-2-3, vol. 12, part 11
48 *Proceedings of the Joint Senate-House Committee on Indian Affairs*, 1948
49 SC, 1951, 15 Geo. VI, c. 29
50 See the *Statement of the Government of Canada on Indian Policy* (Ottawa 1969), presented to the First Session of the 28th Parliament by the Honourable Jean Chrétien, minister of Indian affairs and northern development.
51 Discussions concerning the development of a new Indian policy between government and Indian leaders have been going on since 1974. The chances of success for these discussions hinge to a large degree on whether the traditional dichotomy between Indian and government understanding of some basic concepts, such as reserves and treaties, can be resolved. This difference in views on the question of reserves and treaties is the subject of a paper I have written entitled 'Indian Reserves in Western Canada: Indian Homelands or Devices for Assimilation,' in D.A. Muise, ed., *Approaches to Native History in Canada* (Ottawa 1977), 89–103.

JOHN S. MILLOY

The Early Indian Acts: Developmental Strategy and Constitutional Change

With the fall of New France, the British government seized the opportunity to consolidate its imperial position by structuring formal, constitutional relations with Canadian natives. In the Proclamation of 1763, it announced its intention of conciliating those disgruntled tribes by recognizing their land rights, by securing to them control of unceded land, and by entering into a nation-to-nation relationship with them. Under this policy of conciliation, the agency charged with conducting relations with the tribes, the British imperial Indian Department, was a foreign office in every sense. Departmental agents could not command; they could employ only the ordinary tools of the diplomat: cajolery, coercion, bribery, or, put more politely, persuasion. The well-known success of the Indian Department-cum-foreign office in maintaining friendly and useful military relations with the tribes and in expediting a peaceful and inexpensive transfer of needed tribal territory should not be misread. It was a sign of talented diplomats and of the coincidence of imperial and Indian interest, not of any sure or constitutional control.

This nation-to-nation status quo was maintained even after 1830 when the imperial government added a policy of Indian civilization to that of conciliation, when it began to offer foreign aid in the form of developmental assistance through training in European skills. Despite the influence of Indian Department agents, now dedicated to social engineering, or of God himself represented by Methodist, Baptist, and Anglican missionaries, it was tribal councils who decided the degree and direction of culture change: whether schools would be allowed on the reserves, the rate and type of agricultural or resource development, and the extent to which Indian finances, composed of the annual payments received by the tribes for lands surrendered to the crown, would be devoted to projects of development.

In short, in the period in which the British imperial government was responsible for Indian affairs, from 1763 until 1860 when that responsibility was transferred to the government of the United Canadas, Indian tribes were, de facto, self-governing. They had exclusive control over their population, land, and finances.[1]

This constitutional status was not destined to survive the subsequent phase of imperial reorganization in Canada – Confederation. Under the authority of section 91, subsection 24 of the British North America Act, the Canadian federal government in the first comprehensive Indian Act, that of 1876, took extensive control of reserves and tribal nations. Traditional Indian government was dismissed and replaced by Indian-agent-controlled models of white government. The ultimate control of finance and land use passed into federal hands. Governmental powers left with the tribes placed them, in the multilayered Confederation, well below the position of a respectable municipality. That the mid-century change in the constitutional status of native people was dramatic is apparent; the cause of that change is less obvious.

It might be postulated that the full dismantling of tribal independence which occurred in 1876 was related directly to the process and challenge of nation-building: the Indian nations, like former colonies, were to find new low watermarks in the drive for national consolidation. This is an appealing explanation. With respect to the west, for example, the act of 1876 and treaties of 1871–7 served the need to secure a firm grip over the area in the worrisome light of American pretensions and the post-buffalo days of economic and social crisis that faced the powerful Plains tribes. There is evidence, as well, that some western treaty makers saw their task in just such a political light. Alexander Morris was one. During the negotiations for Treaty Six he explained to Say-sway-kus the government's provision of red coats for chiefs, saying, 'all the other Chiefs of the Queen wear the coats we have bought, and the good of this is that when the Chief is seen with his uniform and medal, everyone knows he is an officer of hers.'[2] Morris's implication that the treaty was more than a land cession but also subsumed tribal authority to that of the crown was made even more explicit in his subsequent writing on the administration of the treaties. He advised the government that 'they [the chiefs] should be strongly impressed with the belief that they are officers of the Crown, and that it is their duty to see that the Indians of their tribes obey the provisions of the treaties,'[3] for it is advantageous 'to the Crown to possess so large a number of Indian officials, duly recognized as such, and who can be inspired with a proper sense of their responsibility to the Government.'[4]

Despite the case that might be made for the foregoing explanation, it can be demonstrated that it was factors other than the varied geopolitical considerations of the 1860s and 1870s which motivated the process of constitutional change. In fact, the events of nation-building are largely irrelevant, for the first step in that process of change was taken by the British with the Gradual Civilization Act of 1857 and was related solely to developmental strategy designed to secure more readily the Christianization and civilization of native people in Ontario, and the destruction of native self-government was completed in the Enfranchisement Act of 1869. Indeed, the path from 1857 to 1869 was marked by a continuing quest for a more perfect developmental strategy in an atmosphere of escalating political conflict involving native leaders and local civilizers, such as Indian agents and missionaries. It was the formulation of what might be termed a developmental logic mainly in the pre-Confederation era which both motivated constitutional change and determined the nature of it. Any understanding of the acts of 1857, 1869, 1876, and no doubt that of 1951, and of the particular constitutional status they forced upon native people is rooted in the historical evolution of that logic – in the deterministic nature of developmental strategy. It is to that evolution one must turn.

The foundations of this constitutionally disturbing developmental logic were put in place by the British with the passage by the Assembly of the United Canadas of the Gradual Civilization Act of 1857.[5] The act was based upon the assumption that the full civilization of the tribes could be achieved only when Indians were brought into contact with individualized property. It had been argued by the Sir Charles Bagot Commission on Indian Affairs in the 1840s[6] and by the Methodist missionaries in the 1850s[7] that this would create industriousness in the breast of the properly educated and thereafter the increasingly self-reliant native farmer. However, there were tactical problems. The fact that in 1846 tribal councils across the colony had firmly rejected the concept of reserve subdivision meant that qualified Indians would have to be brought into the colonial environment where freehold tenure was available; that is, they would have to be enfranchised.[8] Thus, individual tenure and enfranchisement became the heart of developmental strategy, which included the more traditional elements of skill training, education, resource development, and general behavioural modification through conversion to the Christian faith.

The act of 1857 was designed to facilitate this newly reformed strategy. Any Indian, the act stipulated, adjudged by a special board of examiners to be educated, free from debt, and of good moral character could on application be awarded twenty hectares of land within the colony and 'the rights accompanying it.'[9] He was thereby enfranchised, enabled to participate equally with his white neighbours in the political life of the colony, and made amenable to the same laws. As a consequence, he would cut his tribal ties, and, according to this new developmental strategy, he would be rescued from the retrograde influence of reserve life, while his possession of twenty freehold hectares would animate his existence with industry.

The impact of this act was profound in at least three ways. First, it created a constitutional inconsistency in that it allowed that the twenty hectares to be awarded to the enfranchised individual was to be reserve land removed from tribal control on the questionable authority of a colonial act. Since the Proclamation of 1763, colonial legislatures had been excluded from involvement in Indian affairs. They had provided legislation supportive of the policy of civilization, but this had been done by restraining the behaviour of their white colonial constituents towards the native population. Such legislation, since it did not apply to native people or their land, was constitutionally correct.[10] The act of 1857 was not. It represented a direct colonial intervention in Indian affairs. Furthermore, the act gave development a higher priority than traditional constitutional relations anchored to the Proclamation of 1763, for it removed exclusive tribal control over reserves for the sake of enfranchisement.

Second, it changed radically the intent of the British policy of civilization and in so doing further threatened the promises of 1763. From 1830 the goal of the Indian Department's effort, though not often articulated, had been the creation of civilized, Christianized, and self-governing native communities seated securely on reserves protected by the British imperial government.[11] The idea that these civilized communities would be amalgamated with the colony was never discussed, and the idea that individual Indians should become colonial citizens was rejected on the only occasion it was suggested[12] before the policy reformation in the late 1840s and the early 1850s. With the act of 1857 a wholly new course was charted. Thereafter, the goal, full civilization, would be marked by the disappearance of those communities as individuals were enfranchised and the reserves were eroded, twenty hectares by twenty hectares.

Third, the developmental strategy at the heart of the act and its constitutional implications created a political conflict – a crisis in the relationship between tribal leaders and local civilizers – which set the stage in the 1860s for more overt encroachment on native independence and for the consequent statutory destruction of tribal self-government. Immediately upon publication of the act, tribal councils recognized its intent and rejected it. Surely, one tribal leader noted accurately, it was an attempt 'to break them to pieces.'[13] It did not, he continued, 'meet their views'[14] since it was inconsistent with their desire to maintain tribal integrity within customary forms most recently expressed by their insistence on group rather than individual tenure of reserve land. On their part, civilizers were coldly unsympathetic to these views. The head of the Indian Department, Civil Secretary R.J. Pennefather, replied to tribal objections with the curt phrase, 'the Civilization Act is no grievance to you.'[15]

This frank exchange of views symbolizes the breakdown of the generally progressive partnership in development which had existed since the 1830s involving the agents of the department, missionaries, and tribal councils. It had been through the efforts of these men that the on-reserve infrastructure for development – housing, schools, mills, roads, barns, and so forth – had been realized, and through their efforts also that the body of Indians had participated in activities designed to achieve the goals of self-sufficiency on the basis of an agricultural economy. As recently as 1849–50 they had cooperated in the formation of two off-reserve boarding schools, manual labour schools teaching the arts and crafts of European life, which all concerned viewed as a marked improvement over ordinary on-reserve common schools.[16]

The 1860s were not marked by continued cooperation in improving developmental systems which were critical in producing candidates for enfranchisement. Accord was replaced by opposition; allies were now enemies. In the eyes of many chiefs, missionaries and officials of the Indian Department were no longer sympathetic purveyors of the benefits of civilization and staunch defenders of native rights but aggressive and disruptive agents of assimilation. Thus, they threw themselves into a campaign to maintain the pre-1857 status quo. Together they petitioned for the repeal of the act and protested the transfer in 1860 of the responsibility for conducting Indian affairs to the government of the United Canadas, which they dismissed as a government of land jobbers. They also announced in a general council that they would sell no more of their land and organized a lobby to lay their grievances before the Prince of Wales, who was then visiting the province.[17] Individual councils took varied action: some removed their children or financial support from schools; others refused to allow the annual band census or reserve surveys.[18]

A general Indian position emerged in the 1860s. Councils across the colony remained pro-development. They wanted education and agricultural and resource development but would not participate in a system designed, as an Oneida petition said, to 'separate our people.'[19] Civilization, which they might define as the revitalization of their traditional culture within an agricultural context, they would have; assimilation, the total abandonment of their culture, they would not. The policy of civilization, particularly as it was now centred on enfranchisement, was destined to founder upon the rocks of tribal nationalism.

In terms of changing the traditional constitutional relationship between natives and whites, it was the new attitude and policy recommendations of departmental agents and missionaries, not the position of the tribes, that were the most critical, for it was the advice of these men which formed the basis of the second substantial act of the period, that of 1869. Facing the failure of cooperation and yet loyal to the developmental logic of 1857, the need for individual landholding and enfranchisement, they placed their trust in a new strategy to remove all the difficulties. Officials and missionaries placed their trust in the coercive power of the law. For example, a missionary, the Rev. J. Musgrove, wanted a law to 'make it obligatory upon parents to keep the child at the school until 20 years of age,'[20] and agent J. Gilkison prayed that the government would enact legislation giving the department extensive control over on-reserve activities, from the power to imprison Indians for drunkenness to that of compelling them to cultivate the land.[21] In this fashion, it was imagined, the whole range of developmental systems could be made to operate effectively again.

To the department, the difficulty of central importance involved both the core of the old constitutional relationship, native self-government, and the heart of the new developmental logic, enfranchisement. Officials had had high hopes for enfranchisement. To them it was much more than a status change necessitated by off-reserve freehold tenure. It was itself an important inducement to individual development. Pennefather's predecessor, L. Oliphant, held that 'the prospect of one day sharing upon equal terms in those rights and liberties which the whole community now enjoy would operate as the highest stimulant to exertion, which could be held out to young Indians.'[22] All were confident that many Indians would qualify easily and that many were 'desirous even now of sharing the privileges and responsibilities which would attend their incorporation with the great mass of the community.'[23] These assumptions proved unfounded. Between 1857 and 1876 only a handful of Indians came forward and only one application, that of Elias Hill, was accepted.[24] In fact, as early as 1863 one agent admitted that 'the object for which the act was passed is not likely to be attained – for all practical purposes, it is a dead letter.'[25]

The department's analysis of the failure of enfranchisement came quickly. The fault was directly attributable to Indian leaders, who had, after all, stated openly, as had the Six Nations' Council, that they were 'wholly averse to their people taking the advantages offered'[26] by the act. The chiefs were pictured, perhaps quite accurately, as using the traditional authority of their office to dissuade their members from volunteering for enfranchisement.

This specific critique inspired a general missionary and agent campaign against traditional native government. It was, they claimed, the major block on the road to civilization, since it had prevented the prerequisites for progress: reserve subdivision and enfranchisement. It had frustrated the developmental logic of 1857. In addition, it was inefficient, its form cumbersome, and its members rarely qualified to make wise decisions on the proper use of tribal funds and valuable reserve resources.[27] The department's proposed solution to all these problems was again the coercive force of the law. 'Petty chieftainships,'[28] it was recommended, should be abolished and a 'Governor, and a sufficient number of magistrates and officers'[29] should be set over the tribes.

The department's argument can be stated succinctly. If the various systems of development were ever to produce the civilized Indian amenable to enfranchisement, then native self-government had to be abolished. It had to be shouldered aside and replaced by new institutions allowing unchallengeable departmental control.

That this argument was accepted by the newly created federal government is evidenced by the 1869 act for the gradual enfranchisement of the Indians.[30] The Hon. H. Langevin, who piloted the bill through the House of Commons for Sir John A. Macdonald's government, noted in his introductory remarks that though the act also updated the enfranchisement provisions of 1857, its key provision was 'in giving them [the Indians] the benefits of municipal government.'[31] What was given was not only a municipal institution but that degree of departmental control over this new governmental system for which officials had lobbied throughout the 1860s.

The act of 1869 allowed the election of chiefs and councillors by all male band members over the age of twenty-one. However, here all meaningful Indian participation ended, for the time, place, and manner of the election was to be determined by the superintendent general of Indian affairs, and, most critically, public officials served at Her Majesty's pleasure: they could be removed from office before the end of their term 'by the governor for dishonesty, intemperance or immorality.'[32] Apparently, the exact meaning of these terms and the applicability in specific cases would be left to the governor's advisers, departmental agents. Clearly, the problematic independent authority of the chiefs was to be circumscribed.

The intrusion of federal authority did not stop at the electoral system. The newly created 'municipal' council was allotted by the act a specific and very restricted list of jurisdictional concerns. It could make by-laws for the care of public health, the observance of order and decorum at assemblies, the repression of intemperance and profligacy, the prevention of trespass by cattle, the maintenance of roads, bridges, ditches, and fences, the construction and maintenance of school and council houses, and, finally, for the establishment of pounds and the appointment of pound keepers. But having given with one hand, the act took back with the other. The council faced an all-encompassing federal power of disallowance, in that all the rules and regulations it made were 'subject to confirmation by the Governor in Council.'[33]

With the act of 1869, federal control of on-reserve governmental systems became the essence of Canadian-Indian constitutional relations. In the Consolidated Indian Act of 1876 the political formula of 1869 was repeated, and its accompanying implication, that Indians would lose control of every aspect of their corporate existence, was spelled out in extensive and complex terms. Through its control of native government, the department could now institute all the systems of development it cherished. Under the act of 1876 it could create, for example, individualized land holding, determine the use of resources, and create particular educational systems.[34] It now had the political and financial control to make enfranchisement a reality, or so at least the minister in 1869, Hector Langevin, predicted.[35]

Standing back from the complexity of the acts of 1869 and 1876, it can be seen clearly that Indian self-government had been abolished for the sake of the department's developmental strategy, and thus tribal nations entered a wholly new relationship with white authority in Canada. For Indians a unique and unenviable position in Confederation was reserved. For the original people there was to be no partnership, no degree of home rule to protect and encourage the development of a valued and variant culture, as was the case with French Canada. Not only were the Indians not a necessary element in the creation of Confederation as French Canadians were, but their cultural aspirations, their desire to create a new Indian culture on the reserves, was rejected. Responsible white authorities, politicians, departmental officials, and missionaries were convinced that their duty towards the Indian was, as Superintendent General David Laird declared in 1876, 'to prepare him for a higher civilization by encouraging him to assume the privileges and responsibilities of full citizenship,'[36] and that this could only be achieved through a system of wardship, colonization, and tutelage.

NOTES

This article is from *As Long as the Sun Shines and the Water Flows: A Reader in Canadian Native Studies*, ed. I.A.L. Getty and A.S. Lussier. Vancouver: University of British Columbia Press 1983. Reprinted with permission.

1 See chapters 1 and 5 in J.S. Milloy, 'The Era of Civilization – British Policy for the Indians of Canada, 1830–1860' (D.Phil thesis, Oxford, 1978).
2 A. Morris, *The Treaties of Canada with the Indians of Manitoba and the North-West Territories* (Toronto 1880), 226
3 Ibid., 286
4 Ibid., 287
5 *Statutes of Canada,* 20 Vict., c. 26, 10 June 1857
6 National Archives of Canada (NA), RG 10, vol. 36, *Report on the Affairs of the Indians in Canada*, 20 March 1845.
7 Ibid., vol. 209, Enoch Wood to Col. Bruce, 22 April 1854. Enoch Wood was the supervisor of Methodist Missions.
8 For tribal reaction to the subdivision request see ibid., vol. 195, T.G. Anderson to Col. Bruce, 29 March 1852.
9 *Statutes of Canada,* 20 Vict., c. 26, 10 June 1857
10 See, for example, *Statutes of Canada* 1850–1, 13 & 15 Vict., 'An Act to provide more summary and effectual means for the protection of such Indians in the

unmolested possession and enjoyment of the lands and other property in their use or occupation.'

11 Public Record Office (PRO), CO 43/27, no. 95, Sir George Murray to Sir James Kempt, 25 Jan. 1830
12 Ibid., CO 42 349/88, Sir Francis Gore to Lord Castlereagh, 4 Sept. 1809.
13 NA, RG 10, vol. 245, part 1, D. Thorburn to R. Pennefather, 13 Oct. 1858
14 Ibid.
15 Ibid., vol. 519, R.J. Pennefather to Rev. A. Sickles, 11 Nov. 1858
16 These were the Mount Elgin Ojibway Industrial School at Muncey Town on the River Thames and the Alderville Industrial School. Tribal enthusiasm for this initiative is indicated by the fact that every council agreed to devote 25 per cent of its annuity to support the schools. See, for example, ibid., vol. 158, Chiefs, Warriors, etc. of the Tribes of Almwick, Rice, Mud and Scugog Indians to Cathcart.
17 Petitions for the repeal of the Act of 1857 can be found in ibid., vol. 245, part 1, D. Thorburn to R.J. Pennefather, 13 Oct. 1858. In the same source one finds tribal objections to the Transfer Act drafted in 1858. Protests continued during the debate in the colonial legislature and when the transfer took effect. Information relative to the general council's position on future land sales is found in ibid., vol. 247, R.J. Pennefather to Sir E. Head, Draft Annual Report, 11 Jan. 1859, and vol. 256, Bartlett to Pennefather, 25 Sept. 1860, which contains information on the visit of the Prince of Wales.
18 Information on education is plentiful. See, for example, ibid., vol. 258, J. Musgrove Missionary to F. Talfourd, 2 April 1861. For protests against the census see, for example, ibid., Geo. Ironside Manitouaning to R.J. Pennefather, 8 March 1861, and in vol. 256, see Bartlett to R.J. Pennefather, 19 Nov. 1860. An example of the opposition to surveys appears in ibid., vol. 262, part 2, Proceedings of a Council assembly at Manitouaning on the Great Manitoulin Island on Saturday the 5th of October 1861.
19 Ibid., vol. 258, part 2, Memorial to His Excellency Sir Edmund Walker Head from the Oneida Indians of Muncey Town and other Bands on the River Thames, 1858
20 Ibid., M. Musgrove to F. Talfourd, 2 April 1861
21 Ibid., vol. 288, J. Gilkison, Brantford, to W. Spragge, 30 Sept. 1861
22 PRO, CO 42/95, L. Oliphant to Lord Elgin, 3 Nov. 1854
23 Ibid.
24 NA, RG 10, vol. 519, R.J. Pennefather to the provincial secretary, 31 March 1859
25 Ibid., vol. 287, J. Gilkison to the chief superintendent of Indian affairs, 4 March 1863
26 Ibid., vol. 242, D. Thorburn to R.J. Pennefather, 27 May 1858
27 One of the earliest and most complete criticisms of native government is provided by the influential Methodist missionary and departmental adviser, the Rev. T. Hurlburt, in ibid., vol. 239, part 1, Rev. T. Hurlburt to R.J. Pennefather, 22 Dec. 1857.
28 Ibid. Hurlburt's letter also brings forward the department's solution.
29 Ibid.
30 *Statutes of Canada*, 32–3 Vict., c. 6, 22 June 1869
31 House of Commons, *Debates*, 2d session, 1st Parl., 32–3 Vict., vol. 2, 83

32 *Statutes of Canada*, 32–3 Vict., c. 6, 22 June 1869
33 Ibid.
34 *Statutes of Canada*, Revised, the Act of 1876, vol. 1, 1886. See, for example, sections 69–74 on Indian finances, sections 75–6 on Indian government, and section 96 on liquor.
35 House of Commons, *Debates*, 2d session, 1st Parl., 1869, 83–5
36 Annual Report, Department of Indian Affairs, 1876

EMERGING RELATIONSHIP IN WESTERN CANADA

E.E. RICH

Trade Habits and Economic Motivation among the Indians of North America

It was a strange caricature of the Red Indians which emerged as the 'noble savage' from the scrutiny of the statesmen and the *philosophes* of the second half of the eighteenth century. 'Mild and hospitable when at peace, though merciless in war beyond any known degree of human ferocity,' the 'Indian was indebted to no one but himself; his virtues, his vices and his prejudices were his own work; he had grown up in the wild independence of his nature.' So wrote Alexis de Tocqueville,[1] emphasizing a great truth but suggesting an important untruth. For the Indian was indeed independent in spirit, and his vices and many of his virtues were alien to Europeans. But however independent his nature might be, he was not economically independent. The Chipewa chief who met Alexander Henry at Michilimackinac in 1761 expressed much of the splendid independence of the Indians: 'Englishman, though you have conquered the French, you have not yet conquered us. We are not your slaves. These lakes, these woods and mountains, were left to us by our ancestors. They are our inheritance: and we will part with them to none.'[2] Alexander Henry, however, was present at Michilimackinac precisely because he knew that the Indians were not independent economically; he had gone up, and he stayed up through the dangers and vicissitudes of Pontiac's rebellion, because there was no doubt at all that, despite his savagery and despite his independence, the Indian would trade for European goods as soon as they were brought within his grasp.

In modern terms we would say that the dichotomy between the independence of the Indian and his economic subservience, between the defiance of Alexander Henry and his acceptance as a trader, lay in the way in which the frontier of trade had outrun the frontier of administration. The point was expressed even in the Royal Proclamation of 7 October 1763, which decreed that all lands west of the Appalachian Mountains except for the territories of the Hudson's Bay Company and lands which were specifically allotted to the four colonies of Quebec, East Florida, West Florida, and Grenada were to be set aside as a vast reserve for the use of the Indians. The reserve was indeed to be under British sovereignty, but no detailed arrangements for administration were ordered; it was evident that some vague paternal supervision was all that was intended and that the Indians might expect to live their own lives within these lands and that white settlers were to be forbidden. Yet the proclamation itself laid it down that the reserve should be 'open to Trade but not to Grants and Settlements,' and there could be no denying that without trade with Europeans the Indians would have been denied something which was essential to their way of life.

Dependence on trade was not a new thing for the Indian in the eighteenth century. So far was he from preserving an existence which depended on hunting alone that from his first contacts with Europeans he had easily and naturally taken to habits in which the hunt continued to provide him with primary materials but in which trade, and dependence on European goods, played a dominant part; more than this, behind the direct contacts with European traders there spread a network of Indian middlemen who rapidly reached across North America, taking European goods inland and bringing furs out. To a large extent these Indian traders dictated the pattern of European expansion into the continent, and they influenced the character of the European trade even when they could not confine it.

Naturally, the French were the first to meet this phenomenon, as their dependence on the fur trade brought them into alliance with the Hurons, the Montagnais, and the Ottawas, who controlled the fur routes through the Saguenay and the Ottawa rivers. Such alliance brought them hostility from the Iroquois who controlled the fur routes to the south of the St Lawrence and who aimed to direct the furs of the north, by those routes, to their own patrons and allies, the Dutch and the English. Trade rivalry lay at the heart of the Iroquois wars which beset the French colony; and as the Iroquois dominated the region between the Alleghanies and the Great Lakes they cut off the Ottawas and the Hurons from Quebec and Montreal, they spread to the west and the north the tribes who had formerly hunted for the French market, and they made it necessary for the French themselves to voyage out into the west.

The French *coureur* had to break through the Iroquois cordon and to bring the Indians and their furs down to Quebec and Montreal under some sort of European leadership and protection – certainly under strong encouragement. The *coureurs*, moreover, were not only trying to break through the hostile cordon of the Iroquois; they were also trying to break through the possessive cordon of the middlemen, seeking an unspoiled tribe with its savage code of values, to whom furs would be cheap. The constant urge to reach out past the middlemen was a potent factor in French penetration; and it was that same urge which led to the foundation of the English Hudson's Bay Company and to national rivalry in the fur trade. But although it was the need to pass by the intermediary middlemen Indian traders which caused the foundation of the English company, it seems to have taken the English more than a century to realize that the Indians – even the Crees with whom they made contact by the shores of the bay – lapsed easily and naturally into a trading role.

How soon the Crees of the bay adopted this way of life is not clear since the company paid but little attention to the phenomena which would indicate such habits. But from the first foundation of their posts the English had been aware that Indians coming to trade had to run the gauntlet, and they sought a remedy by multiplying their posts on the coast and by sending enterprising young men up-country to bring fresh Indians down to trade. In so doing they were fumbling round the edges of their problem while evidence of the inner reality lay all the time in their hands.

It was some years before the company had a competent traveller ready to send inland, but in 1690–1 Henry Kelsey was sent up to the prairies and proved more than adequate for his task – at least as far as the English company understood that task. The duty laid upon him was to journey up into the country of the Assinipoets (the Assiniboins) with the captain of that nation and to encourage the remote Indians to come down to trade, and his report was throughout pointedly directed to this instruction. He found that the Indians who came down to trade at the bay, and then returned inland armed with guns, used those weapons to terrify their neighbours and to prevent them from breaking into their profitable monopoly. So much was obvious to Kelsey during the first part of his journey, before he reached the Saskatchewan, and as he went further afield he found the pattern repeated. Westwards up the Saskatchewan he made contact with 'Indian strangers' (the 'Eagles brich Indians'), and found they were afraid that the Crees would murder them; and when he met with some 'stone Indians' or 'Mountain Poets' (probably a branch of the Assiniboins) he found that their chief ambition was to get him, and English arms, to help them in their wars. The 'Navywatame Poets' (perhaps the Gros Ventres from the area west of Cumberland House on the Saskatchewan) also were deeply embroiled with the Crees and were so afraid of Cree vengeance that Kelsey was told it was unlikely he would meet with them, and they were also at grips with the Assiniboins with whom he was travelling.

Altogether this built up into a picture of a continent split by endless wars, with the Crees hostile to all the inland peoples. The lesson seemed to be that trade would be vastly increased if the Indians could only be persuaded to give up warfare and to hunt beaver instead, and that the Indians must be convinced that the company did not bring them guns to kill each other but to hunt furs with. This was indeed a part, and a great part, of Kelsey's message, 'that they must not go to wars for it will not be liked by the governor neither would he trade with them if they did not cease from warring.' But there was more in Kelsey's report than this. His realization of the major problem was revealed when he told the Assiniboins that beaver hunting 'will be better liked on then killing their Enemies *when they come to the factory*.' I have italicized a phrase which showed that he accepted the need to bring the distant Indians safe through a hostile cordon. The Assiniboins knew perfectly well what was at issue, for their reply was, 'What signified a peace with those Indians considering they knew not the use of Cannoes?' Kelsey, they implied, was wasting his time trying to make them allow the far Indians access to the bay if the far Indians could not in any case make the journey. This was something of a smooth answer, which left unsolved the question whether the Assiniboins or the Crees would, or would not, allow such access if it should prove possible; and when Kelsey had eventually met the Naywatame Poets, had reassured them, and had got from them a promise to come down to trade at the bay, it was only to find that the Crees 'struck a new fear into them that they would not venture down.'[3]

In that his purpose was to bring the Indians down to trade, not to pioneer a route by which Englishmen could go inland, it did not matter that Kelsey's journal was difficult and inexact, and that to this day it is not possible to tell precisely where he went. The formative thing which he had revealed was that the possessive Crees (and to a lesser extent the Assiniboins), with the prestige and the fire-power got from direct contact with the English, were forbidding access to the bay. The use which the English company made of Kelsey's journal has never been clear, but they do not seem to have understood this reaction of their Indians to trade until it was brought home to them in different form some sixty years later. By that time the preventive cordon had changed its nature and its nationality. No longer was it a cordon of Indians anxious to monopolize the trade of bringing the furs down; it was a cordon of Frenchmen intent to intercept the furs themselves – and for the company the problem did not change when Canada came into English hands and the interceptors became 'new subjects' of the crown.

That the French should so figure was due to the very nature of their fur trade. They had always known what the English company took so long to learn, that the trading Indians were jealous of their monopoly and would exploit it (in their own way) if they could. As early as 1603 Champlain had written of the way in which the Montagnais traded furs with remote Indians and then brought them in to trade.[4] It was well known, too, that the Hurons had an annual rendezvous with the many tribes to the north of Trois-Rivières and that they scared these Indians out of making direct contact with the French.[5] Alongside of the hostility between French and Iroquois there developed a lasting (but not always active) rivalry between the *coureur de bois* and the Indian middleman. The French were always conscious that the Ottawas and the Hurons tried to control the trade as it came down to their posts, and that these great trading tribes got their peltries 'in the North, from the people of the interior.' It was as the French reached out past their middlemen that they came to the Sioux to the south of Lake Superior and to the west of Lake Michigan. They came, too, to the Crees north of Lake Superior and so, with the epic journey of Groseilliers and Radisson in 1659, to a realization of the wealth of Hudson Bay. There was in this movement a recognizable need to outpace the Iroquois, and to keep on the heels of the Indians whom the Iroquois had dispersed westwards; but there was an equally recognizable desire to make direct contact with the primary producers of furs. It was this which took the French up into the focal area of Lake Winnipeg, where they controlled the furs which came down the Saskatchewan and through Cedar Lake to the rivers which would bring them to the English posts by the bay.

The English records, in the meantime, carry no evidence that the conflict between European traders and Indian middlemen was either recognized or accepted. Following after Kelsey, emphasis was on turning the Indians away from warfare and to enthusiastic hunting. But this did not amount to a recognition that much of the warfare was of a peculiar kind, designed to keep rivals away from participation in direct trade. This was not from lack of evidence, however. For instance, when in the period after 1713 the English tried to expand their trade inland they found that the Crees had driven the 'Northern Indians' (the Chipewyans) away from Churchill River, and they had to send William Stewart off from York Fort in the direction of Great Slave Lake to make a peace with the Chipewyans and to bring them down to trade. The Crees were difficult allies in this venture, for they killed the first Chipewyans whom they met.[6] But then they reported prospects of trade from the direction of Lake Athabaska and, acting on their own without white companions, in 1715 they made a journey which opened up a trade in which they acted as middlemen for the Chipewyans.[7]

The Crees, clearly, were still jealously guarding their position as middlemen. But the English company did not seem to realize the position until the French interception of furs led them almost by accident to discover the pattern of Indian trade on which they depended. Then, in 1754, Anthony Henday was sent inland from York Fort in company with a band of Crees who were returning from trade. He was in search of the Earchithinues, members of the Blackfoot, and the company was still harping on its old refrain – these strange

Indians must be persuaded to live at peace with their neighbours, to hunt beaver, and to bring it down to the bay.

Henday's journey has received well-merited praise as an epic of northern travel. He journeyed up the Saskatchewan to the 'Muscuty Plains,' he hunted the buffalo on foot with the Crees and on horseback with the Blackfoot, and he almost certainly got within sight of the Rockies. There is much here which deserves the closest attention, much which presaged a new chapter in the history of the English company. But in many ways the least spectacular parts of the journal which was sent home (it was probably written up by others for the illiterate Henday) were the most interesting. There were no great events as he wandered through the winter on the plains – endless feasts, some desultory hunting of buffalo or of beaver for food, and then canoe-building for the journey down river. It was at this time, however, that Henday recorded the astonishing way in which his Indians refused to hunt beaver to bring down to the bay. He tried his best to urge them to do so. But they merely went their way, enjoying themselves and telling him that when spring came they would have all the beaver they wanted, without the trouble of hunting it. He slowly, almost reluctantly, became convinced that the Assiniboins and Crees who yearly brought furs to the bay caught very little of those furs themselves. When spring came they were able to trade their European goods, many of them soiled and worn out, for all the furs they wanted, and Henday himself carried on a very profitable trade.

The band with which Henday was travelling was only one of many which had returned inland with the company's goods, to trade them with the hunting Blackfoot and the Assiniboins for yet more furs. The system was continent-wide and depended partly on the reluctance of the hunters to travel, partly on obstruction by the middlemen. The Crees with whom Henday was travelling had promised that they also would try to persuade the Blackfoot to come down to the bay. Henday's own persuasions were quite useless, for the Blackfoot told him that they got all they needed without that trouble, that they could not manage canoes, and that they liked their buffalo meat and would not live on fish, as they would have to do on the long journey. But if Henday persuaded in vain, the Crees never opened their mouths on the subject; and Henday quite accepted the reason, which was that 'if they could be brought down to trade, the others would be obliged to trap their own Furs: which at present two thirds of them do not.'[8]

Even then the company read the lesson rather in the light of the French threat than as an indication of the Indians' habits, for Henday had observed the inland French at their trade and he had reported the way in which they took all the best and lightest furs, leaving only the heavy and poor-quality skins to come down to the bay. But his journal was the point from which a policy of penetration to the Saskatchewan stemmed, and as the inland trade gathered momentum, more and more evidence of the trade carried on by the Indians came to the notice of the committee. Moses Norton reported from Churchill in 1765 on the difficulties of getting the 'Far Indians in to trade, that the Northern Indians got nine or ten beaver from them for a hatchet (for which they paid only one beaver at Churchill) which caused him 'to be of Opinion that the Northern Indians will rather be a Hinderance to their coming to the Fort than otherwise in order to keep that Monopoly in their Power as much as they can.'[9] To the south the same story was unfolded as Tomison and his fellows reported from Cumberland and Hudson House that their Indians came to them starving and unable even to kill buffalo because they had traded their guns to the Assinipoets; it was small wonder that they had done so, for they were able to get thirty-six beaver for a good gun and twenty-five to thirty for a half-worn gun when the company's standard was at most fourteen to a new gun. They concluded that few even of those who came to the inland posts trapped their own furs,[10] and they reported much the same sort of life as Henday had done. Their Indians laughed at exhortations that they should 'pitch away a Beaver hunting'; they would see the Assinipoets in the spring and would trade furs with them. In the meantime they were very indolent and spent their time in gaming and smoking. But in spring, sure enough, they got all the furs they wanted from trade, not from hunting.

The Indian way of life was old and deeply ingrained. It did not change as the white men drove their own trade over the Rockies and into the Pacific slope. David Thompson's efforts to find a way across the Rockies brought him up against the opposition of the Piegans. They had been on good terms with the traders as long as posts remained on the east side of the mountains, for so the Piegans could get arms and other European goods, and could bar access to their rivals and enemies further west, especially to the Kootenais tribe. It was a detailed repetition of the classical pattern of Indian trade relations, and it had serious results for Thompson, whose arms and fortified posts made it possible for the Kootenais and Kullyspell Indians to defy Piegan dominance.[11]

The other aspects of this trade system were revealed when Samuel Black in 1824 penetrated to the headwaters of the Finlay and Stikine rivers. He found European goods in the possession of Indians who had never seen white men, and he saw that the Sekani and Thloadinni of the interior were supplied by the 'trading Nahani' who in turn got their goods from the Tlinkit of the coast. It was a jealously guarded trade, and the Thloadinni and Sekani were rigorously excluded from the annual rendezvous with the Tlinkits. When Aemilius Simpson, Ogden, and McLoughlin came to report on the coastal trade which came down from the hinterland of New Caledonia, they filled in this picture, for it was one of the great grievances of the Hudson's Bay men that the furs which the Russians traded at the coast were brought down by Indian traders from lands which were supposed to be under English control.[12]

As knowledge accumulated it became clear that the Russian fur trade on the coast depended far less on the fur seals and sea otters than on the land furs which came, probably down Nass River, to about the vicinity of the Russian post at Sitka.[13] Attention therefore concentrated on 'the Post of Nass which is the grand mart of the coast both for Sea Otters and Land Skins,'[14] and in due course the company set up its post at Nass (or rather Simpson) River. The post set up at Fort Simpson in 1831, however, failed to give direct communication with the interior, the coastal Indians proved shrewd traders, and uncooperative, and by 1834 it was agreed that the post must be moved to Stikine River, where perhaps the route to the Indians of the interior might be found.[15] Ogden's attempt to carry out this plan in 1834 met with opposition from the Russians and formed the subject of almost endless diplomatic correspondence. At least equally significant was the way in which Ogden was opposed by the Indians, who assumed a tone which that doughty trader 'was not in the habit of hearing' and told him they would not permit him to navigate up Stikine River since that would injure their trade with the uplands Indians. This aspect of Ogden's failure was not recounted when the company sent in their narrative of the affair to the British government, for they were anxious above all to make out a case against the Russians. But it was a real element in the correspondence within the company,[16] and further evidence to bear out the Indians' desire to control the posts and their routes to the interior came when Ogden went to shift the unhandy little post of Fort Simpson to a more propitious site. Indian opposition to the move caused scenes which plainly showed the reluctance of the Indians to allow the trade post to pass from their control.[17]

These are a few of the innumerable instances which could be adduced to show that from the middle of the eighteenth century onwards even the English company was at last fully aware of what, in any case, was a basic fact in the North American fur trade. The trading Indians had dictated the pattern of trade, and reaction against the monopoly of the trading Indians had dictated the expansion of the trade from the earliest days. The Indian and his role were all-important, and in straightforward terms they are apt to be taken for granted by the historians of the fur trade. But they were not the accepted commonplaces of the English company for many important years; and when they were at last acknowledged as the normal facts of the trade they were accepted in a somewhat peculiar way because, the French having intervened (and later the Northwesters), English attention was concentrated on European rivals. So, little attention was paid to the need to reach past the trading Indians and to secure better prices by direct access to the hunting tribes. Where the Indians figured in English policy was in a series of attempts to prevent them from diverting furs to European rivals rather than in efforts to penetrate through the trading Indians to the hunters. The result was, of course, much the same, for within a generation of Henday's voyage the 'Inland Trade' had become the main source of furs, the posts by the bay had become chiefly supply depots for the inland posts, and the organization of supply routes had become the main duty of the company's governors.

But in all this development the motive was to counteract European rivalry, as it was later when the company decided to establish the Babine country and the interior of New Caledonia. The trading Indian was easily accepted; it was his task to bring furs down to the coast. This, said the company, 'it is apprehended is better performed by them than could be done by Europeans,'[18] and as long as the trading Indians brought the furs they were worth the cost. That cost was a resultant of the price which the company had to pay for furs, and that in turn resulted from the Indians' habits of trade, many of which were quite alien to a European trade system. But the English accepted the Indians' habits along with their function. With a strange mixture of simplicity and sophistication, English and Indians fell into a system which fitted in with the Indian background. Much that was formal and social rather than primarily economic found a proper place in such interchanges, and trade at the bay-side posts soon developed the formal and public character of a great social occasion. Through the artless description of James Isham there emerges a clear picture of the mixture of formality and cunning, and the characters of the Indians with whom he had to deal. 'They may be Reckon'd a crafty sort of people, cheating, Stealing and Lying they glory in,' he wrote. 'If they grow obstobilious, a Little correction, then sweatning makes them pliant ... they are Cunning and sly to the Last Degree, the more you give, the more they Crave – the generality of them are Loth to part with any thing they have, if at any time they give they Expect Double Satisfaction.'[19] This was a picture of professional traders, obstinate and hard bargainers and without much respect for even the outward observance of European virtues in the way of honesty or truthfulness.

Yet Isham was careful to make it clear that these Indians had their own rules of conduct, and they had reacted to a European idea of price to the extent that they soon got to know the fixed range of the English company's Standard of Trade. They were shrewd enough to get the best both of the company's fixed standard system and of the Canadian flexibility; for whereas the French gave presents, and a dram of brandy before trade began, and then made the best bargains they could (sometimes even leaving small articles such as needles about so that the Indian might steal them and so come easily and sweetly to the actual trade), the English system if rigidly applied would have left no place for such *douceurs* but would have given 'better pennyworths' on the day.

The Indians held the whip hand, with an alternative market open, and the English company not only had to sent out captains' outfits and other presents to attract the Indians but also had to connive at the complicated system of the 'double standard' of trade and the resultant 'overplus trade.' Here the inflexibility of the English system, which was based on the need to maintain central control and the need to eliminate competition between neighbouring posts, was modified so that the traders gave short measure and, while ostensibly maintaining the official standard, built up a reserve of 'overplus' goods from which they could make presents, and put themselves on something of the same footing as the Canadians. There was nothing underhand about the double standard of trade; accounts were kept of it, the committee in London knew all (or almost all) about it, and there never was any feeling that in making an overplus the trader was swindling the company or taking a perquisite for himself. The overplus was applied to the trade on behalf of the company and in practice became a means of mitigating the inflexibility of the fixed standard.[20]

The Indians also knew all about the overplus and the double standard, and within their own conventions they were sophisticated enough to accept it and to work to it. When the company tried to adjust the standard, the Indians reacted strongly and would take their furs elsewhere, and when the traders tried to work the double standard too hard they protested and tried to discount the extortion by exacting more presents and perquisites. Here again Isham sets out the picture with his description of the Indian captain and his gang. The first encounters would be purely formal and social, with an exchange of presents and of a dram and a pipe, and even the trade sessions would begin with a pipe and a ceremonial exchange of compliments. Then the captain would begin his trade talk with exhortations to the Englishman to give sound goods and fair measure. No more should the traders put their fingers into the bowl as they measure out the powder, and the yardstick by which cloth was measured was to be brought out for inspection. The French were enticing the Indians to trade, but they would come to the English if only they could get sound value and fair treatment. 'This is the Cheifest Subjects of their harange tho they talk a great Deal more, of Little signification;'[21] and in itself it embodied the cautious approach of hard bargainers working within a formalized pattern of trade.

But although the trading Indians were so long habituated to their business, and so shrewd in their conduct of it, they were not logical in their reactions. They knew the formal standards of trade, and they gave information (not always reliable) about the standards according to which the French traded. But they accepted the double standard as long as it was applied within known conventions. It was impossible, apparently, to make a clean departure from the standard and to demand excess furs for an article such as a gun or a hatchet for which the price was known. The overplus could only be got from commodities which were measured out as they were traded. The overplus therefore had to be got from the trade in brandy, cloth, powder, and tobacco of the major commodities, and from laces, gartering, beads, and paint from among the minor luxuries. Even here the Indian accepted some variation but would not stand for arbitrary changes or exploitation, and there was no attempt on either side to raise prices in accordance with the laws of supply and demand. The standard, perhaps with some accepted adjustment according to the locality or the personalities involved, was applied whether furs were scarce or plentiful, and whether goods were in supply or not. When the Indians had got used to a convention there was no breaking it with safety; if once they had got used to receiving a yard of tobacco for a beaver – and the company's Brazil tobacco was traded by length, not by weight – they would go elsewhere to traders who would give only a foot rather than abate an inch of the yard to which they thought they were entitled.[22]

This was a strange, but not unlikely, combination of practices; more strange was the way in which the Indians, over the years, preserved the primitive notion of gift exchange in their trade. Whatever was available was to be had for the asking. This led the company to set up its rules that its traders would only trade 'through a hole in the wall.' The Indians were not to be allowed in the trade room at trade time, and Isham's 'Observations on the Trader and a Gang of Indians' fully support the accusation of trade through a hole in the wall. Here, in a lively phrase-book dialogue, the Indian says, 'When shall we trade?' and is answered, 'Come and trade'; to which he replies, 'Open the window.' Trade itself begins with the trader saying, 'The window is open' and then 'Open your bundles of beaver.' Then when trade (and the dialogue) is over, he asks the Indian, 'Have you done?' and gets his answer, 'Yes you may shutt the window.'[23]

Compared with the French habits of trading in the woods, or the description which one of the early 'pedlars' from Montreal gave of himself as trading on the Saskatchewan in the midst of utter confusion 'with two hundred Drunken Vilions about me,'[24] the Hudson's Bay Company's practice was suspicious and unattractive. But it was realistic in that it took into account the Indians' tendency to pilfer, and in that it took into account the lasting notions of property and trade which the Indians accepted. The price element in exchanging goods was not fully accepted. The Chipewyans, for example, were reckoned to be dull, but sober and industrious and not addicted to brandy. But when

Malchom Ross penetrated up to establish Fairford House in 1796 he found that 'they think that where ever they see goods it ought to be given them, whether they have anything to give in return or not. They also make Sacrifices of their property on the death of their relations and then demaunds from the traders such goods as they have sacrificed for the Good of their deceased Relations and doe not looke well on it if denied them.' 'They even had the Impudance to ask what the Goods is brought into their Country for if they are not to get them as they need them,' and they topped off this unanswerable question by stating that 'they had no right to go without the Necessaries for want of furs when goods was at their doors.' Ross, as he recorded, was obliged to drop the subject![25]

Here, it may perhaps seem, is nothing more than a savage people trying to exploit the advantage of finding a well-gooded and defenceless trader in their midst. But something more is evident. When this outspoken attitude to property in exchange is set alongside the other anomalies of the Indian trade it becomes clear that, with all the sophistication which went with knowledge of the set prices according to the Standard of Trade, there went a persistent reluctance to accept European notions or the basic values of the European approach. A glance at the commodities which were traded reveals something of this inherent difference in approach. It was always said[26] that the Indian would only trade for necessaries; but that word did not carry its normal European meaning in this context. Rather, if it had any accurate meaning, it meant goods for immediate consumption. But it did not mean precisely that, for the Indian would always supply himself first with powder and shot. After that would come what the trader would call 'necessaries' and what we would call luxuries – tobacco, spirits, gay cloth of different kinds, beads, and caps, with articles such as ice-chisels, snow-glasses, and hatchets varying in priority.

There was much variation in the demand, from year to year, trader to trader, and Indian to individual Indian. But a significant fact is that, as far as can be ascertained, the Indian never traded oatmeal. From the early days, in 1684, the company had shipped oatmeal out to the bay in the hope that the Indians would take some as they needed 'by way of trade.'[27] But trade time was not a time at which the Indians were thinking of the possibility of semi-starvation during the winter and the need to take a little oatmeal away as a necessity to see them through. Oatmeal did not figure in the Standard of Trade and it never became an item of trade. But it was essential for survival; and since the survival of the Indians was a necessity for the company's trade it was habitually shipped out and given away to starving bands of Indians as they came in to the forts during hard winters. On occasions a postmaster would trade a little oatmeal in exchange for fresh game during a winter, but this again was more nearly akin to gift exchange than to proper trade, a pleasant and friendly interchange of surpluses which made variety of fare possible, and no more. Year after year the Indian had good reason to fear that before winter was out he would need to fall back on oatmeal. If reduced to that extremity he would come in to the post and beg for help. But he would not lay aside that 'necessity' at trade time, and from the start the company was realistic enough to order that although trade was to be hoped for, especially in provisions, yet 'when they are in want we must leave it to your Discretion to give what is fitting.'[28]

The steady refusal to regard oatmeal as a necessity despite the endless instances of the need to fall back on it may, of course, be taken as just another example of the improvidence of the Indian. It certainly was that. Given the power of indiscriminate killing, the Indians almost exterminated the great buffalo herds on which they depended for their meat, they almost exterminated the beaver from many of the most wealthy areas under their control, and they even brought the coverted area inland from Nelson River to such a state that in his 1824 journey to the Columbia George Simpson recorded that in the whole of the Nelson River district he did not see a solitary vestige of beaver.[29] Not only furs were dissipated; much of the buffalo meat went for pemmican and was traded, but much was for the Indians' own consumption and waste. Henday recorded the promiscuous slaughter, and all later accounts confirmed the fact, while Isham had written that 'I have found frequently Indians to Kill some scores of Deer, and take only the tongues or heads, and Let the body or carcass go a Drift with the tide, therefore I think it's no wonder godalmighty shou'd fix his Judgemen't upon these Vile Reaches, and occation their being starvd. and in want of food, when they make such havock of what the Lord sent them plenty of.'

But this improvidence had a deeper significance than would similar improvidence in a European, for it meant that the Indian did not react to the ordinary European notions of property nor to the normal European economic motives. This lay at the root of the whole matter, and this was a problem which was brought to an issue in the Parliamentary Enquiry of 1749. Many interwoven problems were before that committee – whether there was in fact a North West Passage, whether the Hudson's Bay Company was bound by its charter to search for such a passage, and whether it had engaged in such a search or not; whether there were possibilities of founding an agricultural colony by penetrating up the rivers from Hudson Bay, and whether it was the company's interest or policy to attempt such a venture; whether the company treated the fur trade as a monopoly in which equal profits could be got from a limited trade as from expansion and enterprise, and whether an expanded trade would provide a greater market for goods of English manufacture. By their European processes of thought the critics of the company were convinced that the trade could be expanded and many more furs traded. So more English-made goods would be used, and the business would become more of a 'national interest.' Arguments were ranged for and against the many contentions; and after the policy of reaching out to the Indians in the hinterland had been reviewed against the assumption that the Indians brought down to the bay all the furs which they had for trade came the theoretical argument that more furs would be produced if better prices were given.

This would be the normal European reaction, although Adam Smith had not yet enunciated the dogma that when the market price of any commodity rises the quantity brought to market will increase until it is adequate for the effectual demand.[30] But an interesting feature of the report of the 1749 enquiry (as of so much which was written and spoken at that period) was the way in which practising merchants enunciated the classical economic doctrines as part of their rule-of-thumb trading precepts. 'Tis a Maxim in Trade,' said William Wansey, merchant of Bristol, 'that a large Quantity of Goods brought to Market reduces the Price'[31] – and of course he was only uttering the commonplace of every farmer's wife who ever took eggs to market. 'Tis plain a greater Price would encourage the Indians to kill more,' said another merchant.[32] But these English economic rules did not apply to the Indian trade. On the contrary, all who had any knowledge of that trade were convinced that a rise in prices would lead to the Indians bringing down less furs, not more – 'The giving Indians larger Price would occasion the Decrease of Trade.'[33]

The traders who denied the merchants' assumptions were, of course, company men and it may be suspected that their evidence was tainted. But not all of them were still in the company's employ, or friendly to the company. On the whole, when the report is read in relation to the numerous documents in the company's possession there emerges a coherent picture, and the reader is driven to respect the ability of the Parliamentary Committee to get at the truth despite the bias and the ignorance of witnesses.

The company's evidence, in the first place, was clear and definite. It was accepted as a primary consideration that the Indians with whom the company traded at the bay were traders rather than hunters. This did not mean that they had lost the habit of hunting, but it did mean that their chief task was to take European goods inland and to trade them. 'The Natives on the Continent Surrounding the Bay go up into the Inland Countries from the Northernmost Coast the Western Side as also the Eastern Side and in the Months of June and July bring down to the Co's Settlements all the Furs of those Wild Creatures they kill in the Winter, in exchange and Barter for which the Co supplys them with such sorts of European goods as they stand in need of which they carry up to the several Nations that Inhabit these Inland Countries.'[34] The company had at last accepted the facts, and it was established that trade was with Indians well accustomed to exchanges and, indeed, living as professional middlemen. Next came the iniquities of the trade. The double standard and the overplus were revealed, with details of the way in which brandy was watered and short measure was given in cloth, shot, and powder. The assumption at this stage was that the company was exploiting its monopoly to defraud the Indians and that better treatment would bring more furs to the English market. Christopher Bannister, for example, with twenty-two years' service in the bay behind him, told the committee that 'if the Indians were better used, the Company might have more Trade; for the Factors don't give them a sufficient Price, and then they growl and grumble.'[35] He had himself been ordered 'to shorten the Measure for Powder,' and he knew what he was talking about. But even Bannister admitted that it would not be sensible for the company to pay twice the price for its furs unless it was forced to do so, and that despite their treatment the Indians continued to come to the bay.

Joseph Robson, the disgruntled mason and surveyor, William White, for seventeen years clerk at Albany and Churchill, and Edward Thompson, a surgeon with only three years' experience, were the most hostile witnesses with first-hand knowledge. Of them Robson, in answer to the question whether he had ever heard the Indians complain that they did not get a sufficient price for their goods, could merely reply that he was not admitted to talk with them except in the fort. He did, however, give it as his opinion (but not as a fact) that if the Standard of Trade was more advantageous to the Indians, a greater quantity of furs and pelts would be brought.[36] Considering Robson's animosity it is remarkable that he could say no more on this point. William White early in his evidence gave his opinion that it would be for the advantage of the public if the traders would give a better price 'as it would encourage the Natives to bring more Skins down.' But as the problem began to take point he first reiterated his opinion that if the governor would advance the price even for the large furs it would encourage the Indians to bring down the smaller and finer furs which the French were reputed to intercept; then he thought that if the choice lay between sending men up-country or raising the Standard of Trade, sending men up-country would be the more likely to bring in more furs. In the end, he concluded 'that he believes the Indians would kill no more Beasts than what is sufficient to purchase Commodities for the Year, as he has seen them act in the same manner, with regard to Venison; and he does not know, whether, if they could have an advanced Price for their Goods, they would not bring down fewer Skins than they do at present.' Thompson's experience was of much shorter duration, and he had been less concerned with trade than had White. His evidence was largely concerned with the need to explore, both in a search for a Passage and in penetrating up the rivers, and while he spoke of the Double Standard and of ill treatment of Indians he ventured no opinion on the results of a raising of the standard, although he seemed convinced that posts established inland would increase the volume of trade.[37]

The only apposite statement from these three hostile witnesses was, therefore, that of White – that he thought it quite probable the Indians would bring down less skins, instead of more, if they were given a better price. The anomaly required explanation. It was difficult to accept that there were trading Indians, not mere hunters but people who for two or three generations had been in the habit of trading with Europeans and who exercised that function within their non-European society, who reacted in this way. It was nothing to the point for some of the witnesses, such as Robert Pilgrim, to say that the company got as much trade as it needed and wanted no more.[38] That was another question, whether the extension of the trade was desirable or not. On the parallel issue, whether an increase in prices would bring more furs to market, if such an increase should be desired, the not unfriendly Alexander Browne, six years a surgeon at Churchill, was convinced that the company gave better prices than the French but yet thought that 'if they allowed them a better Price, they would certainly bring down more.'[39] But against this stood a solid weight of opinion which emphasized White's doubts. James Isham, the most experienced trader available, an acute observer with a speculative turn of mind, and by no means uncritical of the company, was forthright: 'The giving Indians a larger Price would occasion the Decrease of Trade.'[40] Captain Spurrell was equally emphatic: 'Would not the Natives kill more Game, if more Goods were sent to them for their Fur?' 'They might, but they're too lazy to take any Extraordinary pains, suppose they have their Bellyful.' 'Suppose there were two Markets would not the Indians raise the Price of their Furs?' 'Yes.' 'Would they kill more?' 'No, less.'[41]

As the evidence accumulated (not all of it printed in the official report) there was no escaping the conclusion that in trade with Indians the price mechanism did not work. They were hardened enough traders to exploit competition and an alternative market, but un-European in their reaction to better prices. Struggling to show that even this was a condition which an open trade would remedy, John Hardman, merchant of Liverpool, put forward a thesis which went to the root of the matter – and expressed it in eighteenth-century English terms. The root problem was to inculcate a notion of *Property*. Being asked,

> Whether the Indians would be prevailed upon to kill more Beasts than to purchase Necessaries for themselves for a Year? he said, He did not doubt but that they would, in order to dispose of them to their Neigh-

> bours; that at present perhaps, if they were to kill Furs enough to supply them with Necessaries for Two Years, they would not come down to trade; but if they were once made sensible of the Conveniency of having some Property, they would then desire to carry on a Trade, and supply their Neighbours; for that the Witness did not apprehend that all the Indian Nation came down to trade; that this Notion of Property would increase; though it would not increase their real Necessities, yet it would furnish them with imaginary Wants. [The Indian's] Necessities and Desires would increase in proportion to his Property.[42]

This is the thesis of the English manufacturer seeking a market for his goods; the 'cheap tin trays' approach to underdeveloped peoples, in which imaginary wants eventually provide a market. The trouble with the Indian in trade (from the point of view of a Liverpool merchant in search of a market) was that he knew what he wanted. His 'Necessities and Desires' were well defined and could not be rephrased; they certainly had not yet been rephrased in the course of three generations of continuous trade. The Hudson's Bay Company were perhaps not the most vigorous and imaginative experimentalists in their Indian trade. They relied on their traders to tell them what commodities the Indians wanted, and confined most of their shipments outwards to items which were known to be acceptable. Occasionally they made experiments, with jointed dolls, Nuremburgh toys, raisins and prunes (which proved very popular but which the Indians only accepted as presents, not in trade). Such experiments were almost all complete failures. The one great success was to introduce the English-made blanket. That soon became a traditional article in the trade, and it was tradition which marked the Indian trade and limited the number of articles which were acceptable. To such an extent was the fear of innovation carried that when the Dutch colonies were captured, and the English controlled the Hudson River and its access to furs, even the Navigation Acts were laid on one side and the colonists were granted the right to continue trading to Holland because the Indians had grown so accustomed to Dutch goods that it was to be feared they would cease to trade altogether rather than accept English-made goods.

The Indian would not be tempted into indulging 'imaginary wants.' English merchants were convinced that this was possible, and almost inevitable. Fur traders knew better. The Indians were under no compulsion; they were a free people who were not to be coerced and, said Henry Spurling, fur merchant and shareholder of the company with a lifetime's experience behind him, 'they won't make a Toil of a Pleasure for any Consideration.'[43] There was only one commodity of which they wanted unlimited quantities, spirits. And even of spirits they wanted no more than for their immediate gratification. There may be instances, but in all the fur-trade documents which I have so far studied I have never yet come across a single instance in which an Indian made any attempt to acquire a stock of spirits, either for trade or for future use. The whole literature of the fur trade would emphasize that the Indian was most unlikely ever to have brought himself to deal in spirits in such a way; but to emphasize the point that to the Indian a 'property' in the European sense of the word was an alien notion, it is perhaps worth while to make it clear that he did not attempt to establish a 'property' even in that one commodity for which he had an apparently insatiable demand.

Here the trade in spirits needs to be brought into perspective, for when the documents are read in order to establish whether the Indian would react to the price mechanism as a stimulus to production it becomes clear that even where spirits were involved nothing like the European equation could be established. There was no question of setting a *quantity* of spirits against a *quantity* of furs. Always there persisted something of the idea of gift exchange, and always there persisted something of a ceremonial and social intercourse in the trade between whites and Indians; and spirits had their place in both contexts. It was the presence of spirits, and the giving of spirits rather than the trading of spirits, which brought the Indian down to trade. The quantity given varied according to the circumstances, not in any strict relation to the number of furs. In its nineteenth-century arguments with the British government the Hudson's Bay Company always drew a distinction between giving spirits to Indians and trading spirits for furs. Though the distinction was lost on the British government, and was largely meaningless from their point of view, it was still at that date a real distinction from the point of view of the fur trader; for it meant that in the one commodity for which there was limitless demand the incentive which that demand might be presumed to harness to production was not in fact so applied. The distinction was early appreciated. From Albany in the period of French rivalry in the early eighteenth century came the report that the French did not actually trade brandy. They gave it away in a *régal* and then proceeded to trade.[44] It was the knowledge that brandy was available and would be distributed which took the Indian to one trader or the other. He did not take many skins in order to get more brandy, and he certainly would not have brought more in future years because he knew that the quantity for each skin would be increased. Brandy was indeed a strong incentive to trade, but it was not in any way quantitative in its operation – except perhaps in the disastrous short-term results on the Indians.

As the Hudson's Bay Company's men insisted that they could get more done for a quart of brandy than for ten pounds' worth of trade goods, and as the Northwesters in the climax of their rivalry shipped ever increasing quantities into the Indian country, it still emerges that the spirits were not 'traded' according to European notions and that the quantity given was not in relation to the goods received.[45] The problem was to leave satisfied customers on both sides rather than to set a price in terms of commodities. So although the Indian would not come to the hand-out without bringing furs or provisions, the incentive to hunt was an indirect one. As for the question whether spirits acted as a stimulus to *more vigorous* hunting in proportion as they were more or less generously supplied, the only possible conclusion is that this was not so. Spirits would draw such trade as there was in one direction or the other and would ensure that the Indian had (so to speak) the price of admission, but no more.

As the Hudson's Bay Company pushed its posts up the Saskatchewan in the last quarter of the eighteenth century in rivalry with the Northwesters, it met the full impact of the spirits 'trade.' The Indians, again and again, 'will not Trade out without Liquor.'[46] They kept their young men in touch with the posts so as to have information on this subject; when they heard that all the liquor was gone they could not be brought in to trade, and when they found supplies in both companies' posts they went from one post to the other in a shameless manner, and could hardly be brought to trade at all.[47] These were extreme conditions, in which competition between the Canadian traders, as well as between them and the Hudson's Bay Company, was driving the Indians 'into a state of Debauch and Indolence,' and in which the Europeans' dependence on the Indians for provisions was fully exploited. William Tomison was 'positive that Indians will never trouble themselves with any Laborious duty when they can live without it,'[48] and if ever there was a time at which bidding up prices in terms of spirits should have been evident this was it. But spirits were used in quite a different way. While Robert Longmoor sent off presents of tobacco to Indians 'to keep them from the Canadian traders,' Booty Holmes set up a ten-gallon cask of rum upon the ice on the river, with the head of the cask open so that all might drink. The cask was surrounded by armed men, and Holmes's intention was that every Indian who drank their rum or smoked their tobacco must (if necessary by force) come and trade with them.[49]

This was but one of many examples of the way in which the 'trade' in spirits worked. The basic principle, of enticement rather than of stimulus to effort by high prices, was explained at the 1749 enquiry by Matthew Sergeant. He spoke 'the Indian Language' (presumably Cree), and he had seen the number of Indians who came to trade greatly increased by the gift of a suit of clothes to each chief who brought down a band. His view was that 'if they would give to every Indian Leader a Gallon of Brandy, and for every Indian of the Nation of the *Poets* a Gallon and a Half,' it would bring them down to trade and consequently enlarge the trade.[50] The gift-function of spirits, thus recognized, remained its predominant function notwithstanding the fact that on occasions spirits were undoubtedly traded.

In the nineteenth century, settlement and more rapid transportation increased the number of Indians who had become quasi-employees of white men. They revealed a completely European reaction to prices, but since during that period the fur trade was a monopoly of the Hudson's Bay Company in a way which had never previously been achieved, and for a vast part of the territory of Rupert's Land the aim was to conserve furs by a rigid quota system rather than to encourage trapping by high prices, it is difficult to say when, or why, or even if, the reaction of the hunting Indians to the stimulus of prices changed. The Iroquois who had become professional fur hunters and who composed a large section of the hunting parties in the Snake Country seem to show little change and to be content to work to a set tariff; and where real competition with Americans or Russians was met during this period it was still by the old incentives of spirits and guns that the Indians were attracted.

It is of course true that in their reaction to the price mechanism the Indians were not unique. Other examples from non-European peoples could easily be found, and even in Europe the theory did not always fit the facts; there were elements in European society, from priests to artisans, who were content with their status and with the satisfaction of their necessities. The difference of the Indians from such elements in European society was that the Indians under discussion were by profession traders. They were 'a free people and will go where they find best usage,'[51] they knew how to exploit competition, they took goods to the interior 'for their own Consumption and use, and to dispose of amongst the other Natives there'[52] – and from medieval times onwards it had been accepted that the function of the trader was to buy cheap and to sell dear. But the trading Indian never did this because he had not developed that notion of 'property' which the Liverpool merchant John Hardman had thought it so easy to develop in him.

Some twenty-five years after the 1749 report had brought the question to the attention of Parliament (and had left the Parliamentary Committee convinced that the fur traders were right in their views), Andrew Graham gave his views. Graham was unequalled among the bay-governors of the eighteenth century as a writer of closely reasoned memoranda in which accurate observation was mingled with shrewd reasoning. Whether his conclusions, either in his official volume of 'Observations' or scattered through his voluminous correspondence and journals, were entirely original does not matter; in fact his views should receive even greater weight if they represent a consensus of opinions. His view, as late as 1775, was that the Indian would always only trade what he needed.[53] This was an epitome of a more reasoned and analytical statement. Graham reckoned that the Indian annually could get hold of between seventy and a hundred made-beaver in furs without effort. For seventy made-beaver he could fully satisfy all the wants which he would anticipate before he next came down to trade, and the other thirty for waste and dissipation were all that he had time to spend before he had to leave the plantation and begin his journey inland again.[54] So any consistent increase in the quantity of furs, which would entail a change in the Indians' habits or ideas, was bound to come up against the fact that he could satisfy his wants without effort, and that any extra rewards would be valueless to him.

In itself, as a passing phenomenon, there would have been nothing very peculiar in this attitude of the Red Indian. The peculiarity lay in the way in which the attitude persisted, and in the way in which it persisted despite continuous and active trade, and despite the emergence of professional traders. In those conditions the attitude was peculiar and interesting in itself, and it also set the mould within which the fur trade had to be conducted until the Indian found the Eskimo, with a much more active sense of property, alongside him as a primary hunter. It was the Indian's lack of a sense of property (as the word was used by Europeans) which made the fur trade the only branch of commerce which needed some other control and some other incentive than the European controls and incentives which arose from a sense of property. This was the reality which explained the perpetuation of monopoly in an age to which the very word was anathema. The deviation from established principles tried statesmen hard, but the reality was accepted and the need to deviate was even enshrined in the gospel of freedom of trade itself, the *Wealth of Nations*. For this was the reality which compelled Adam Smith to admit the merits of the Hudson's Bay Company despite the way in which it ran counter to all his generalizations. The company, with its limited capital and restricted interests, could 'engross the whole, or almost the whole trade and surplus produce of the miserable though extensive country comprehended within their charter.'[55] The trade of Rupert's Land, in fact, was not capable of expansion by the normal incentives, which Smith accepted for all other trades. Smith ascribed this largely to the barren territory; but within the limits of the fur trade, which soil and climate made appropriate to that territory, the habits of the Indians, and their lack of a sense of property, forbade expansion on normal lines even in the production of furs.

NOTES

This article is from *Canadian Journal of Economics and Political Science* 26 (1) (1960). Reprinted with permission.

1 *Democracy in America*, chap. I
2 Francis Parkman, *Conspiracy of Pontiac*, 6th ed., 1893, 1:329
3 For Kelsey see A.G. Doughty and Chester Martin, eds., *The Kelsey Papers* (Ottawa 1929), esp. 2–4, 8–10, 15, 16–18.
4 *Works of Samuel de Champlain*, 1:123–4
5 *Jesuit Relations*, 31:209–11. Cf H.A. Innis, *The Fur Trade in Canada* (Toronto 1956), ch. 2
6 Hudson's Bay Company Archives (HBC), B/239/a/3, quoted by kind permission of the governor and committee.
7 A.S. Morton, *A History of the Canadian West to 1870–71* (London, Toronto 1939), 134–5
8 L.J. Burpee, ed., 'York Factory to the Blackfeet Country: The Journal of Anthony Hendry [later Henday], 1754–55,' in *Proceedings and Transactions of the Royal Society of Canada*, third series, 1:1907, sec. II, 350–1; HBC, B/239/a/40, E/2/6, E/23/11
9 HBC, B/239/a/59/6
10 HBC, B/239/a/64/13, 15
11 Morton, *Canadian West*, 481–5
12 Hudson's Bay Record Society (HBRS), vol. 18: *Black's Rocky Mountain Journal*, lxxiv-lxxvi, 111–12, 161–2
13 HBRS, vol. 10: *Simpson's 1828 Journey to the Columbia*, 78
14 Frederick Merk, ed., *Fur Trade and Empire* (Cambridge, Mass. 1931), 288, 300
15 HBC, B/223/b/9/12
16 HBRS, vol. 4: *McLoughlin's Fort Vancouver Letters*, first series, 316–22
17 See Morton, *Canadian West*, 725.
18 HBC, A/9/4/79
19 HBRS, vol. 12: *James Isham's Observations on Hudson's Bay*, 80–1
20 For this system see HBRS, vol. 20: *Letters Outward, 1688–96*, xliv-xlv; and vol. 21: *The Hudson's Bay Company, 1670–1870*, 1: 594–7.
21 HBRS, vol. 12: *Isham's Observations*, 82–8
22 HBC, A/11/43/120d
23 HBRS, vol. 12: *Isham's Observations*, 49, 54
24 HBC, A/11/115/148
25 HBC,.B/66/a/1/22-22d
26 Eg, by Isham; see HBRS, vol. 12: *Isham's Observations*, 177.
27 HBRS, vol. 11: *Letters Outward, 1679–94*, 124; and vol. 9: *Minutes, 1679–84*, first series, 175
28 HBRS, vol. 11: *Letters Outward, 1679–94*, 124
29 HBC, A/12/1/109; Merk, ed., *Fur Trade and Empire*, 14–15
30 Adam Smith, *Wealth of Nations*, book 1, chap. 7
31 Parliamentary Report, 1749, 234
32 Ibid., 233
33 HBC, A/18/1/195d
34 HBC, A/18/1/27
35 Parliamentary Report, 1749 Report, 225
36 Ibid., 216
37 Ibid., 217–19, 222–4
38 HBC, A/18/1/142d

39 Parliamentary Report, 1749 Report, 226, 227
40 HBC, A/18/1/195d
41 HBC, A/18/1/202–202d
42 Parliamentary Report, 1749 Report, 233
43 Ibid., 230
44 HBC, A/11/2/145
45 This is not to deny that on many occasions the spirits were given in direct exchange for goods, especially in exchange for provisions or for canoes, but merely to deny that the *price* of liquor was an incentive to extra endeavour. Cf HBRS, vol. 14: *Cumberland and Hudson House Journals, 1775–82*, first series, 299: 'the Indians that came Yesterday traded a few Furrs for Liquor and got drunk.'
46 Ibid., 288, 323
47 Ibid., 314, 330 n. 1
48 Ibid., 290
49 Ibid., 317.
50 Parliamentary Report, 1749 Report, 220
51 HBC, A/11/114/9
52 HBC, A/9/4/79, Memo to the Lords of Trade, 3 Oct. 1750
53 HBC, E/2/9/89d
54 HBC, E/2/5/13
55 Smith, *Wealth of Nations*, book 5, ch. 1, part 3

SYLVIA VAN KIRK

The Impact of White Women on Fur Trade Society

During the early period of the fur trade, the white man in penetrating the wilds of Western Canada faced a situation in which, for practical purposes, the social norms of European civilization were no longer operable. Since colonization was not envisaged, no white women accompanied the fur traders. Family units which would have reflected, in however rough a state, their former domestic life were impossible. Instead, the traders were forced to come to terms with an alien, nomadic culture; their livelihood depended upon the very existence of the Indian whose way of life gave him distinct advantages in coping with the wilderness environment. In this light, the Indian woman played an important role as a liaison between the two cultures. Trained as she was in the skills necessary for survival, a native woman, while filling the role of wife and mother left void by the absence of white women, was uniquely qualified to help the white trader adapt to the exigencies of life in Rupert's Land.

The men of the Montreal-based North West Company, who had inherited the framework and traditions of the French colonial fur trade, had always appreciated the economic advantages to be gained by forming alliances with Indian women. Besides helping to secure the trade of her tribe or band, the Indian woman did much to familiarize the Nor'wester with Indian life and, in teaching him the native tongue, greatly contributed to his effectiveness as a trader. In contrast, the London Committee, the remote ruling body of the Hudson's Bay Company, had early forbidden any dealings between its servants and Indian women on the grounds that the expense which would accrue from their support plus the possible danger of affronting Indian sensibilities outweighed any advantages to be derived. In practice, this regulation proved difficult to enforce. Although it prevented the practice of taking Indian wives from becoming widespread within the lower ranks of the English company, keeping an Indian woman became the prerogative of an officer in charge of a post.[1]

When forced into open competition with the Nor'Westers in the late decades of the eighteenth century, the Hudson's Bay Company was compelled to modify its policy towards Indian women. In attempting to recruit the highly prized French-Canadian voyageur into its service, the company was made aware that the right to have an Indian helpmate was not one which the Canadian would relinquish lightly,[2] and this attitude influenced its own men. In 1802 the council at York Factory appealed to the London Committee, stressing that their Indian women were in fact 'your Honors Servants' and played an important economic role in the struggle against the rival concern:

> they clean and put into a state of preservation all Beavr. and Otter skins brought by the Indians undried and in bad Condition. They prepare Line for Snow shoes and knit them also without which your Honors servants could not give efficient opposition to the Canadian traders they make Leather shoes for the men who are obliged to travel about in search of Indians and furs and are useful in a variety of other instances.[3]

By the time of the union of the two companies in 1821, taking a native woman for a wife was a widespread social practice, known as marriage *à la façon du pays*. Although it might involve the payment of a bride price, a country marriage was an informal arrangement whereby a couple agreed to cohabit for an unspecified length of time. It derived from the Indian concept of marriage and was but one example of the extent to which the social mores and customs of the Indians influenced the norms of fur-trade society. As the explorer Sir John Franklin remarked, the white man seemed 'to find it easier to descend to the Indian customs, and modes of thinking, particularly with respect to women, than to attempt to raise the Indians to theirs.'[4] The first missionaries, who arrived relatively late in Rupert's Land, were horrified by what they considered to be the Europeans' uncivilized treatment of their Indian wives.[5] Such usage, however, reflected the position of women in Indian society. Partly through economic necessity, they were subjected to an endless round of domestic drudgery, even to the extent of being reduced to beasts of burden. The excuse was advanced that if the white man displayed tender feelings towards his wife, the Indian, to whom such notions were foreign, would despise him.[6] It is likely, however, that within the fur-trade post, European conventions did tend to ameliorate the Indian woman's lot, particularly in the higher ranks of the service where she would have shared in her husband's privileges.

Although there were occasions (especially during the drunken days of the trade war) when Indian women were abused by the traders, in general an unwritten code of honour developed; marriage *à la façon du pays* was considered to be as binding as any church ceremony in the Indian Country. There were many examples of a lasting and honourable relationship developing between the white trader and his Indian helpmate. The domestic pleasures of family life undoubtedly did much to reconcile the European to the isolated and monotonous life of a fur-trade post.[7]

The greatest social problem occurred when the trader retired from Rupert's Land. It became customary to forsake one's Indian family for it proved extremely difficult for the wife in particular to make the transition to 'civilized' living whether in Great Britain or the Canadas.[8] In the early days of the fur trade, when widowed or abandoned, an Indian wife with her children had been welcomed back into her tribe. This became increasingly rare as the structure of Indian society crumbled through the effects of European contact. It was also not feasible for the half-breed woman, who knew little of life outside the fur-trade post, and from whose growing ranks many wives were chosen in the early decades of the nineteenth century. A practice which was dubbed 'turning off' arose, by which the retiring husband endeavoured to assure that his spouse was placed under the protection of or became the country wife of another fur trader. Such had been the fate of the kind-hearted washerwoman Betsey, who when Letitia Hargrave encountered her at York Factory in 1840 was not sure whether her last protector had been her fourth or fifth husband.[9] Although it was fairly common for fathers to bequeath some money for the maintenance of their country-born children, they were not legally compelled to do so. As a result, during the decades immediately preceding the union of the two companies, the number of deserted women and children being maintained at the expense of the posts, especially those of the North West Company, reached alarming proportions. In an attempt to reduce this heavy economic burden, the North West proprietors ruled as early as 1806 that in future its servants were to choose only half-breed women as wives. They also contemplated the creation of a settlement in the Rainy Lake area where their superannuated servants, particularly the French-Canadian voyageurs, could retire with their Indian families.[10]

The whole question was pushed into the background by the struggle for the control of the fur trade, but when the Hudson's Bay Company absorbed its rival in 1821, the London Committee recognized that steps must be taken to solve this pressing social problem if only for reasons of economy and security:

> We understand that there are an immense number of Women and Children supported at the different Trading Posts, some belonging to men still in the Service and others who have been left by the Fathers

> unprotected and a burden on the Trade. It becomes ... a serious consideration how these People are to be disposed of.[11]

Philanthropic considerations also influenced company policy at this time, mainly through the efforts of Benjamin Harrison, a prominent member of the committee and an associate of the Clapham Sect. He played an important part in developing a plan for the settlement of these families in the fledgling colony of Red River which had been founded in the previous decade by the idealistic Lord Selkirk. A Catholic mission already existed to minister to the large French-Canadian sector, and several Anglican clergymen were sent out under company auspices who, with the help of the Church Missionary Society, were to establish a school for orphan children.[12] In a marked change of policy, the London Committee also encouraged those servants who did not wish to retire in Rupert's Land to take their families with them provided they possessed sufficient means for their support.[13]

At the same time, as part of its program of economy and consolidation, the committee endeavoured to divest the company of any further responsibility for the support of the families of the traders who remained at the various posts. Although they acknowledged that those few women who performed really essential services might be paid in goods or provisions, in future each man was to clothe his family on his own private account, and a proportional tax was to be imposed to cover the cost of provisions.[14] They also proposed the creation of a pro-rated benefit fund to provide for the maintenance of a wife and family in the event of the decease of the husband or his retirement from the country.[15] The men, however, objected to being forced to make an annual payment towards the present or future support of their families, the lower ranks, in particular, claiming that their salaries were not high enough to bear this additional expense. The committee eventually acquiesced on this point, but only after it was established as a general rule:

> That no Officer or Servant in the company's service be hereafter allowed to take a woman without binding himself down to such reasonable provision for the maintenance of the woman and children as on a fair and equitable principle may be considered necessary not only during their residence in the country but after their departure hence.[16]

The Hudson's Bay Company gave official status to marriage *à la façon du pays* by the introduction of a marriage contract which emphasized the husband's economic responsibilities. Although there is some variation in the actual format of the certificates which survive in the company's records, usually both parties signed or made their mark on a document which declared that the woman was recognized as one's legal wife.[17] In retrospect, since the

Hudson's Bay Company was vested with governmental power over Rupert's Land, these contracts can be seen as an early form of civil marriage. The prerogative of the church in this sphere, however, was acknowledged by the proviso that the couple would undertake to be married by a clergyman at the first possible opportunity.[18]

The company's first chaplain, the Rev. John West, considered this to be one of his most pressing duties upon his arrival in the Indian Country in the fall of 1820; 'the institution of marriage,' he proclaimed, along with 'the security of property' were 'the fundamental laws' of any civilized society.[19] When he left Rupert's Land three years later, the worthy parson had performed a total of sixty-five marriages, among them those of several prominent settlers in Red River, former company officers who had continued to live with their Indian wives *à la façon du pays*. His success was greeted with approbation by Nicholas Garry, a visiting member of the London Committee, who considered the practices of the Indian Country most demoralizing:

> Mr. West has done much good in persuading these Gentlemen to marry ... thus introducing more proper Feelings and preventing that Debasement of Mind which must, at last, have rooted out every honorable and right Feeling. Perhaps nothing shows Debasement of Mind so much as their having lived themselves in an unmarried state, giving up their Daughters to live the same Life as their Mothers, and this Feeling, or rather its Justification, had become general all over the Country.[20]

Clearly the moral code of fur-trade society was in a state of confusion. It was the missionaries themselves who emphasized the concept of 'living in sin' for many fur traders, and certainly the Indians considered a country marriage to be a legal and honourable union. While officially the company was attempting to introduce accepted Christian standards into fur-trade life, as can be seen in a list of regulations designed to effect 'the civilization and moral improvement' of the families attached to the various posts,[21] it is difficult to estimate the actual success of these measures. Although the social and religious conventions of European society were undoubtedly taking hold in the basically agrarian settlement of Red River, the old norms of fur-trade society persisted, especially in isolated areas. In 1825 George Simpson, the governor of the Northern Department, advised that any missionary appointed to the Columbia District across the Rockies would be wise to let the custom of the country alone: 'he ought to understand in the outset that nearly all the Gentlemen & Servants have Families altho' Marriage ceremonies are unknown in the Country and that it would be all in vain to attempt breaking through this uncivilized custom.'[22]

When Simpson was appointed governor of the vast territories of the Northern Department in 1821, he had had only one year of experience in the Indian Country as a trader in opposition to the Nor'Westers on Lake Athabasca. He soon proved himself a capable administrator, and his hard-headed, often pragmatic approach to business is reflected in his official views on the position of Indian women in fur trade society.

Simpson's journal of his winter in Athabasca reveals his appreciation of the valuable economic role played by Indian women in the functioning of the fur trade. Besides performing such routine tasks as making moccasins and collecting *wattappe* for sewing the birch-bark canoes, they were essential as interpreters. In enumerating the reasons for the strong position of the Nor'Westers at Fort Chipewyan, Simpson declared: 'their Women are faithful to their cause and good Interpreters whereas we have but one in the Fort that can talk Chipewyan.'[23] This one was the crafty Madam Lamallice, the wife of the brigade guide, who was not only adept at hoarding provisions but even managed to carry on a private trade. Simpson, concerned that this couple, who possessed much influence over the Indians, might desert to the rival concern, was forced to wink at these misdemeanours and urged the disgruntled post commander to humour them with flattery and a few extra rations.[24]

In making plans to extend the company's trade into the remote areas of New Caledonia and McKenzie's River, formerly the preserve of the North West Company, the governor emphasized the value of marriage alliances. Early in the spring of 1821 he engaged the French-Canadian Pering [Perrin] to help establish a depot on Great Slave Lake primarily because his wife was 'extensively connected amongst the Yellow Knife and Chipewyan tribes in that quarter ... and will be enabled to remove any prejudice that our Opponents may have instilled on their minds against us.'[25] Viewing the committee's policy of discouraging liaisons with Indian women as detrimental to the company's expansion, he recommended that in New Caledonia the gentlemen should form connections with the principal families immediately upon their arrival as 'the best security we can have of the goodwill of the Natives.'[26]

During his rapid tours of the posts in the early 1820s, however, Simpson became increasingly aware of the problems caused by the large numbers of women and children being supported in established areas, and he favoured the committee's proposed economic reforms.[27] A major source of inefficiency and expense was the practice of allowing families, particularly those of the officers, to accompany the brigades on the long summer journey to and from the main depot at York Factory. Simpson's low opinion of one chief factor, John Clarke, was confirmed when Clarke abandoned some of the goods destined for Athabasca *en route* to make a light canoe for the better accommodation of his half-breed wife and her servant – an extravagance which Simpson estimated had cost the company £500.[28] After his visit to the Columbia in 1824–5, the governor further decried the extent to which family considerations hindered the expedition of business:

> We must really put a stop to the practise of Gentlemen bringing their Women & Children from the East to the West side of the Mountains, it is attended with much expense and inconvenience on the Voyage, business itself must give way to domestick considerations, the Gentlemen become drones and are not disposable in short the evil is more serious than I am well able to describe.[29]

The following year, the annual session of the council passed a resolution stating that gentlemen appointed to the two districts across the Rockies were not to encumber themselves with families.

Although Indian women were relegated by custom to an inferior status, the ladies of the country appear to have exerted a surprising influence over their fur-trader husbands. Simpson was appalled by the widespread power of these 'pettycoat politicians,' whose interests he suspected even affected the decisions of top-ranking officers.[30] In expressing his dissatisfaction with Chief Factor James Bird's management of the company's business at Red River, he lamented, 'I find that every matter however triffling or important is discussed wh. his Copper Colld. Mate before decided on and from her it finds its way all over the Colony.'[31] Likewise, he described Mrs McDonald, the country wife of the officer in charge at Fort Qu'Appelle, as 'a stout good looking Dame not master p. Force but through persuasion & cunning.'[32] In the Columbia District, the governor claimed, two out of the three chief traders were completely under the control of their women. They frequently neglected business in their jealous attempts to 'guard against certain innocent indiscretions which these frail brown ones are so apt to indulge in.'[33]

If the irregularities in the workings of the trade caused by native families disturbed Simpson, he was even more adamant that the Indian Country was no place for a white woman. In a private letter to committee member Andrew Colvile, he expressed concern that the example of three of the company's officers in taking wives from among the Red River settlers in the early 1820s might establish a trend which he considered most undesirable: 'it not only frustrates the intentions of the Company and executors, in respect to the Colony, but is a clog on the gentlemen who take them ... native women are a serious incumbrance but with women from the civilized world, it is quite impossible the gentlemen can do their duty.'[34]

In light of his own subsequent experience, Simpson could perhaps have shown a little compassion for the marital difficulties of some of his contemporaries. His extraordinary private correspondence with his close friend Chief Factor John George McTavish reveals a Simpson curiously different from the person his official pronouncements would lead one to expect. For a novice, he adapted with ease to the social conventions of Rupert's Land, succumbing as readily as any Nor'Wester to the charms of the ladies of the country.

Sometime during his first winter, possibly at Oxford House, Simpson was attracted to a damsel called Betsey Sinclair, a daughter of the later Chief Factor William Sinclair and his native wife Nahovway.[35] Although she accompanied him to York Factory in the fall of 1821, the newly appointed governor soon found her presence bothersome. He left Betsey at York when he embarked on a tour of inland posts in December and shortly afterward instructed McTavish, then in charge of the factory, to see that she was 'forwarded' in the spring to the Rock Depot where her brother-in-law Thomas Bunn was stationed.[36] Simpson's rather cavalier references to this woman as 'my japan helpmate' or 'my article' suggest that he himself may never have thought of her as a country wife in the true sense. That many of his contemporaries considered her as such is revealed by an entry in the York Fort Journal dated 10 February 1822 which reads: 'Mrs. Simpson was delivered of a Daughter.'[37] Although the governor was at York when this infant was christened Maria by the Rev. John West on 27 August,[38] he was still determined to avoid the encumbrance of a family. The proposal to place Betsey under the care of Thomas Bunn had been abandoned, but Simpson departed in early September for an extensive tour of the Athabasca and Peace River districts, leaving it to McTavish to settle the matter expeditiously: 'My Family concerns I leave entirely to your kind management, if you can dispose of the Lady it will be satisfactory as she is an unnecessary and expensive appendage, I see no fun in keeping a woman without enjoying her charms which my present rambling Life does not enable me to do.'[39] He needlessly expressed concern for her virtue. Not long after his departure, Betsey Sinclair became the country wife of the clerk Robert Miles, a high-minded Englishman who had spent the winter of 1820–1 with Simpson in the Athabasca country. The match was celebrated in the customary fashion by a dance and supper where liquid cheer flowed freely, and the couple were reported to be very happy.[40]

Despite protestations that he was too busy to be bothered by domestic considerations, the governor seems to have found time to indulge his inclination during his tours of the company's domains. In fact, he confided to McTavish that he suspected his amours were gaining him a notorious reputation.[41] Although the identities of the recipients of his favours remain obscure, it is known that in 1823 a son named James Keith Simpson was born.[42]

Simpson, however, appears to have made a distinction between the behaviour he considered appropriate in that motley outpost of civilization, the Red

River Colony, and the behaviour acceptable in the rest of the Indian Country. While wintering at Fort Garry in 1823–4 he apparently held aloof from romantic entanglements, describing himself as one of the most 'exemplary Batchelors' in the settlement.[43] Furthermore, in spite of his country romances, the intention of returning to England to marry seems to have been in the back of the governor's mind during this period.[44] Who the object of his affection was is not known, although it is established that Simpson had another daughter in Scotland called Maria, born before he left for Rupert's Land.[45] He was cautioned by his mentor Andrew Colvile against taking any hasty action, however: 'A wife I fear would be an embarrassment to you until the business gets into more complete order & until the necessity of those distant journies is over & if it be delayed one or two years you will be able to accumulate something before the expense of a family comes upon you.'

Simpson acquiesced and set off in the fall of 1824 on his tour across the Rockies to the Columbia. While at Fort George, he was at pains to prevent himself from being drawn into the system or marriage alliances which had helped to secure the loyalty of the powerful Chinook nation, especially the great Chief Concomely. It was considered most prestigious among the 'aristocracy' of this highly complex tribe to claim a fur trader for a son-in-law. A most assiduous social-climber was an influential personage known as 'Lady Calpo,' who on more than one occasion had warned the fort of impending treachery. She proved a valuable source of information for Simpson, but he found himself in a delicate situation when this old dame, in order to reaffirm her rank, endeavoured to secure him as a husband for her carefully raised daughter: 'I have therefore a difficult card to play being equally desirous to keep clear of the Daughter and continue on good terms with the Mother and by management I hope to succeed in both altho' her ladyship is most pressing & persevering.'[46] Simpson seems to have succumbed somewhat, however, for if the Chinooks expressed sorrow at his departure in the spring, 'the fair princess "Chowie,"' he suspected, was not the least grieved.[47]

When Simpson returned to Red River to wind up business prior to sailing for England, he found a situation which likely made him reconsider the feasibility of bringing a European wife to Rupert's Land. The new governor of the settlement, Capt. R.P. Pelly, now felt compelled to return to England owing to the ill health of his wife, who only two short years before had accompanied her husband out to Red River. This was a great disappointment to Simpson, since he had hoped Pelly would be able to effect some order and stability in the chaotic affairs of the colony. While every effort had been made to ensure the material comfort of the family, Simpson himself had noted that 'Mrs. Pelly appears to be a delicate woman and does not yet seem quite at home among us.'[48] When he sailed from York Factory in September 1825, the governor was accompanied by Capt. Pelly and his ailing wife. While it is unknown how he settled any romantic attachments he may have had in Great Britain, Pelly's unhappy example undoubtedly contributed to the fact that Simpson returned to Rupert's Land still a bachelor, apparently prepared to resume former arrangements *à la façon du pays*.

Contrary to the assertions of several authors, it is only now that Margaret Taylor, the half-breed daughter of George Taylor, a former sloop master at York, appears in the governor's life. She was definitely not the mother of either Maria or James Keith Simpson. When Simpson first became attached to her is uncertain, but she was probably introduced to him by her brother Thomas Taylor, the governor's personal servant during these years. As was his practice when embarking on an extensive tour, Simpson left this woman at York in the fall of 1826 under the surveillance of his friend McTavish, to whom he wrote in a jocular, if rather crude fashion: 'Pray keep an Eye on the commodity and if she bring forth anything in the proper time & of the right color let them be taken care of but if any thing be amiss let the whole be bundled about their business.'[49] The lady does ont seem to have warranted his suspicion, and in the spring of 1827 a son was born, named George after his father.[50] Simpson honoured his responsibility for the support of his family at York, allowing Margaret the enjoyment of special rations such as tea and sugar and even providing financial assistance for her widowed mother.[51]

In his brief biography of Simpson, A.S. Morton stated that domestic concerns played no part in the governor's life at this time, but such is not the case.[52] Although she is never mentioned in the official journals, Simpson's private correspondence reveals that Margaret Taylor accompanied him when he left York in July 1828 on another cross-country voyage, this time to New Caledonia. At first she was so unwell that he was afraid he might have to leave her in Athabasca, but she recovered and proved herself a valued companion, for Simpson rapidly found his two associates, Dr Hamlyn and Chief Trader 'Archy' McDonald, rather tiresome. 'The commodity,' he confided to McTavish, 'has been a great consolation to me.'[53] By this time, Simpson himself seems to have regarded Margaret Taylor as his wife according to the custom of the country. While returning in the spring, he speaks of her affectionately as 'my fair one' and although disgruntled at the conduct of her brother Thomas, acknowledges him as a brother-in-law.[54] Simpson, however, was now preparing for another trip to England via the Canadas. On his way east, he left Margaret, now far advanced in her second pregnancy, at Bas de la Rivière under the care of Chief Factor John Stuart, whose country wife was her sister Mary Taylor. There, at the end of August 1829, Margaret gave birth to another boy, later christened John McKenzie Simpson.[55]

John Stuart's letters to the governor during his absence provide a touching picture of Simpson's county wife and her little ones. Young Geordy and his baby brother were thriving; 'I never saw finer or for their age more promising

Children,' claimed Stuart. His praise of their quiet and good-natured mother was also unstinted: 'in her comportment she is both decent and modest far beyond anything I could expect – or ever witnessed in any of her country-women.'[56] Old Widow Taylor was living with the family at Bas de la Rivière, and Stuart credited her with instilling such commendable habits of cleanliness and industry in her daughters. He emphasized that Margaret was counting the days until Simpson's return: 'A little ago when at supper I was telling Geordy that in two months and ten days he would see his father. [His mother] smiled and remarked to her sister that seventy days was a long time and [she] wished it was over.'[57]

It must have been a grievous shock, therefore, when the governor did return to Rupert's Land in May 1830 – a lovely young English bride at his side! There can be little doubt that John Stuart had not the slightest intimation that Simpson intended taking a wife in England. His obsequious attempts to curry favour are much in evidence,[58] and he unquestionably described Simpson's country family in such glowing terms because he thought that was what the governor wanted to hear.

It is extremely difficult to pinpoint the time or cause of Simpsons' change of heart. In a letter dated March 1828, his cousin Aemileus Simpson advised the governor, then contemplating retirement in Rupert's Land, that this was not likely to be a happy course of action: 'rather look for some amiable companion in the civilized world with which to conclude your days in the true comforts of a domestic life.'[59] Whatever his private feelings for Margaret Taylor, Simpson may have decided that her background and lack of education made her unsuitable for the role of 'first lady' of Rupert's Land. Furthermore, his reasoning appears to have been influenced by the experience and counsel of his close friend John George McTavish, who in the winter of 1829–30 was also on furlough in Great Britain searching for a wife.[60]

Before becoming a chief factor in the Hudson's Bay Company in 1821, J.G. McTavish, the son of a Scottish chieftain, had had a long and distinguished career as a Nor'Wester. During his early days at Moose Factory, though in opposition, he formed a union with one of the daughters of Thomas Thomas, the governor of the English company's establishment. It appears to have been a particularly unhappy relationship: the woman was driven to infanticide and McTavish subsequently renounced his connection with her.[61] It should be noted that infanticide was not unknown in Indian society in times of famine or great hardship. In the case of the women of the fur traders it was perhaps symptomatic of their fear of being abandoned, for it usually occurred when the husband was on furlough.

Around 1813, sometime after this unfortunate episode, McTavish took another country wife, young Nancy McKenzie, otherwise known as Matooskie, the daughter of a prominent Nor'Wester, Roderic McKenzie, and an Indian woman. She was to live with him for seventeen years and bear him a lively family of at least six daughters, of whom McTavish seems to have been very fond. In the late 1820s, however, there are signs of a growing estrangement between himself and their mother; McTavish confided to Simpson that he contemplated packing Nancy off to Red River where her uncle, Donald McKenzie, was now governor.[62] Although his wife may have feared the outcome of such a long separation, the fact that McTavish took their young daughter Anne with him when he sailed for England in September 1829 must have been reassuring.[63]

The glimpses of the two friends' quest for a 'tender exotic' in Britain reveal that the rough and ready society of the fur trade left its gentlemen ill at ease in the intricacies of genteel courtship. Simpson wrote encouragingly to McTavish who was in Scotland: 'I see you are something like myself shy with the fair, we should not be so much so with the Browns ... muster courage "a faint heart never won a fair Lady."' Simpson was, in fact, very ill during his sojourn in England, the years of strenuous travelling having caught up with him, but he queried jauntily, 'Let me know if you have any fair cousin or acquaintance likely to suit an invalid like me.'[64] McTavish had little time to offer assistance. A few weeks later Simpson wrote ecstatically, 'Would you believe it? I am in Love.'[65] The middle-aged, hard-hearted governor had fallen completely under the spell of his eighteen-year-old cousin Frances Simpson, who had been but a child when he had first started his career as a clerk in her father's firm. At first it was decided that the wedding should await Simpson's return from America in the fall of 1830, but the prospect of such a separation prompted him to persuade her parents to give their immediate consent.[66] The couple were united on 24 February and embarked on a short honeymoon to Tunbridge Wells.

McTavish, in the meantime, had not met with such immediate success. An attempt to secure the affection of a 'Miss B' failed, but, by February, the old Nor'Wester was able to report, much to Simpson's delight, that he too was to be wed – to a Miss Catherine Turner, daughter of the late Keith Turner of Turnerhall, Aberdeenshire.[67] They were married on 22 February in Edinburgh, their honeymoon being no more than a hasty journey to London to join the Simpsons prior to sailing for North America. Simpson, who appreciated how much the ladies would value each other's company, took pains to ensure their comfort on the voyage, reserving the sole use of the Ladies' Cabin for their party.

Although Frances Simpson was undoubtedly a very pretty and cultivated young lady, her sheltered upbringing and delicate constitution made her an unlikely candidate for the role of governor's lady in the inhospitable wilds of

Rupert's Land. Her diary of the voyage to the Indian Country reveals that parting from the close family circle of Grove House was almost more than she could bear: 'I can scarcely trust myself to think of the pang which shot thro' my heart, on taking the last "Farewell" of my beloved Father, who was equally overcome at the first parting from any of his children – suffice it to say, that this was to me a moment of bitter sorrow.'[68] Shortly after the ship sailed from Liverpool on 10 March the young woman succumbed to a violent attack of sea-sickness; she was so ill that Simpson was prepared to bribe the captain to put her ashore in Ireland, but stormy weather foiled the attempted landing. Fortunately, over the course of the voyage her health improved. The party spent several pleasant days in New York and then proceeded overland to Montreal, where the ladies divided their time between sight-seeing and being entertained by fashionable society.

Before embarking at Lachine for the canoe trip to the interior, however, an incident occurred which threw the contrasting mores of fur-trade society and middle-class gentility into sharp focus. McTavish's open affection and continuing responsibility for his eldest daughters made it inevitable that his new wife would learn of their existence. In fact, his thirteen-year-old daughter Mary was at school near Montreal. One evening after dinner, the governor's servant threw open the door and announced 'Miss Mactavish' to the assembled company:

> [McTavish] rose & took her up to his wife, who got stupid, but shook hands with the Miss who was very pretty & mighty impudent ... [Mrs McTavish] got white & red & at last rose & left the room, all the party looking very uncomfortable except [her husband] & the girl. [Mrs Simpson] followed & found her in a violent fit of crying, she said she knew the child was to have been home that night, but thought she would have been spared such a public introduction.[69]

Simpson seems to have endeavoured to spare his wife similar indignities. Letitia Hargrave, in recounting this episode in 1840, commented wryly that 'Mrs. Simpson evidently has no idea that she has more encumbrances than Mrs. Mactavish, altho' she did say that she was always terrified to look about her in case of seeing something disagreeable.'[70] (This may help to explain Simpson's relative neglect of his mixed-blood children in later years. There is no evidence that they, unlike many of the children of company officers, were ever sent overseas or to Canada to be educated, and all were excluded from Simpson's final will of 1860.)[71]

On the long voyage into the Indian Country, the first ever for British ladies, every precaution was taken to minimize the hazards and inconveniences of canoe travel. Although Frances owned that it was not a trip 'altogether pleasing or congenial to the taste of a Stranger,' her diary displays much youthful enthusiasm and good humour. She was awed by the magnificence of the scenery, professed admiration for the strength and skill of their picked crew of voyageurs, two of whom were entrusted to carry the ladies over the portages, and shook hands with several of the leading Indians, to whom she was an object of great curiosity.[72] At Fort William, however, she was grieved at losing the companionship of the amiable Mrs. McTavish, who was here branching off to her new home at Moose Factory, the headquarters of the Southern Department.

The news that the governor had returned to Rupert's Land with a genteel English wife made a great stir, especially in the upper echelons of fur-trade society. As the party progressed from post to post, the company's officers were assiduous in their attempts to appear hospitable and refined. At Lac La Pluie (which some weeks later was named Fort Frances in honour of Mrs Simpson), Chief Trader Thomas McMurray undertook to play the gallant and escorted the governor's wife on a tour of fort and garden: 'old & weatherbeaten as he was, he surpassed all the Gentlemen I had met with in these wilds, as a Lady's Man; but altho' our walk did not occupy an hour, it quite exhausted all his fine speeches, and the poor man seemed as much relieved when we returned to the house ... as if he had just been freed from an attack of the Night-Mare.'[73] Few were more concerned to create a favourable impression than the obsequious John Stuart who welcomed Simpson's bride to Bas de la Rivière in early June with 'no ordinary degree of kindness.' His efforts to appear the well-read gentlemen are conspicuous in the rapturous way he described the Governor's lady to a prominent member of the London Committee:

> The very first sight of her on landing at Bas de la Rivière strongly reminded me of the Picture Milton has drawn of our first Mother = Grace was in all her steps = heaven in her Eye = In all her gestures Dignity and love, while everything I have seen of her since – seems to denote her such as first Lord Lyttleton represented his first Lady to have been = Polite as all her life in courts had been – Yet good as she the world had never seen.[74]

Governor Simpson, he declared, had performed an immeasurable service in bringing this charming creature to the Indian Country because her coming heralded an improved standard of morality and gentility.

The extent to which Stuart enthused over the virtues of Simpson's new wife is extremely suspect when one considers that this old Nor'Wester had often taken it upon himself to champion the honour of the ladies of the country,[75] and that his own country wife was the sister of the deposed Margaret Taylor. A truer gauge of his feelings is revealed in his hostile reaction to the news that his long-time associate J.G. McTavish had also not considered his country union binding and had returned to Rupert's Land with a Scottish wife.[76]

Indeed, the news of McTavish's marriage was greeted with astonishment throughout the Indian Country. Whatever their opinion of the governor's action, several influential fur traders were loud in denouncing McTavish's shabby treatment of Nancy McKenzie, none more so than her uncle Donald, the governor of Red River, though he himself had quietly 'turned off' his own country wife shortly before marrying a Swiss settler's daughter. Even the young clerk, James Hargrave, who disapproved of country marriages, felt great sympathy for Matooskie when she was quietly told that McTavish was not returning to York: 'The first blow was dreadful to witness ... but the poor girl here bears up wonderfully & is fast acquiring resignation.'[77] McTavish's action added to his unpopularity at York; his opponents circulated rumours, which may have originated with the grief-stricken Matooskie herself, charging him with gross cruelty and drunkeness.[78] Simpson, however, would brook no attack on his friend's character when he arrived at York in the summer of 1830. He packed Nancy McKenzie off to Bas de la Rivière where she spent the winter under the same roof as his 'old concern' Margaret Taylor. Both women, who each had two children with them, were given an allowance of thirty pounds.[79]

Thus John Stuart had become the temporary guardian of both cast-off wives. Much to Simpson's annoyance, the old man now deemed it a question of honour to defend the rights of the pitiable Matooskie. He bitterly attacked McTavish for having so unfeelingly violated the custom of the country:

> what could be your aim in discarding her whom you ... had for 17 Years with you. She was the Wife of your choice and has born you seven Children, now Stigmatized with ignominy ... if with a view to domestick happiness you have thus acted, I fear the Aim has been Missed and that remorse will be your portion for life ... I will never become your enemy, but ... I think it is as well ... our correspondence may cease.[80]

McTavish, now safely isolated at Moose Factory, had delegated Simpson to settle his affairs, and the governor found himself at 'hot war' with McKenzie and Stuart who demanded that Matooskie should at least receive a large financial settlement to compensate for the years she had devoted to McTavish.

Although Simpson acknowledged the necessity of some provision for both women, he considered it both economic and honourable to solve the problem by finding them new husbands. Thus while McKenzie and Stuart raged, Simpson was busy negotiating. Early in January he silenced his opponents by securing a written promise of marriage for Matooskie: one Pierre Leblanc, a respectable French Canadian in the company's service at Red River, had finally succumbed to the offered dowry of £200 sterling.[81] Leblanc was given a week off to go courting at Bas de la Rivière, and Matooskie, although she had declared she would never take another husband, had little alternative but to accept his offer. The couple were formally married by a priest, after Matooskie's baptism, at the Catholic Church of St Boniface early in the morning on 7 February 1831, an event which was duly celebrated by their friends at Red River. Although McTavish's country wife was now safely disposed of, he still continued to provide some financial aid for his youngest daughters who were left under her care.[82]

The details of Simpson's own negotiations are unfortunately lacking. It is recorded, however, that on 24 March 1831 'Margarette' Taylor was married to French-Canadian Amable Hogue by the Rev. David Jones at the Red River church.[83] The opinion was popularly expressed that these arrangements represented quite a come-down for both ladies, particularly the latter.[84] John Stuart, on the other hand, attempting to reinstate himself with the governor, declared his relief at being rid of his charges: 'I am very glad that the recent marriages are over – every one of the two Couples appear perfectly happy.'[85] Simpson, however, was not about to forgive either McKenzie or Stuart for their vexatious meddling. He now considered McKenzie, whom he had come to detest, as a most unsuitable governor for Red River.[86] Old John Stuart, for all his pains, found himself banished to the wilds of the McKenzie River district in the fall of 1832.[87] The whole affair, which illustrates the influence of private matters in the closeknit society of the fur trade, did little to help the governor and his new wife settle comfortably into life at Red River.

In the colony, Simpson endeavoured to adopt a life-style which he considered appropriate to his position as the overseas governor of the Hudson's Bay Company. Such refinements as a pianoforte and a shiny, new carriole appeared, and construction was begun on an impressive stone house which was to be the official residence.[88] The governor's lady was extolled as 'the brightest star' in Red River society, but her very presence tended to reinforce class distinctions in the settlement. As one mixed-blood officer in the company observed, 'things are not on the same footing as formerly.'[89]

By the spring of 1831, however, Simpson had become thoroughly disgusted with the 'high society' of the colony, largely as a result of the gossip and intrigue occasioned by the McTavish affair. He felt there were few women even among the European ladies in Red River with whom his wife Frances could form an intimate acquaintance. The governor lamented to McTavish:

> I am most heartily tired of Red River ... and should be delighted to join you at Moose next Fall, indeed my better half is constantly entreating me to take her there so that she may enjoy the society of her Friend ... Here she has formed no intimacies, [Governor] McKenzie's Wife is a silly ignorant thing, whose common place wise saws with which we are constantly persecuted are worse than a blister; Mrs. Jones [the chaplain's wife] is a good unmeaning Woman whom we merely see for half an hour occasionally & Mrs. Cockrane [the assistant-chaplain's wife] whose assumed puritanism but ill conceals the vixen, shines only when talking of elbow Grease & the scouring of pots & pans.[90]

But if the European women left much to be desired, the ladies of the country were now definitely *personae non gratae*. This self-enforced exclusiveness of the governor had unfortunate repercussions. Those company officers who had mixed-blood wives were much insulted when Simpson indicated that their society was no longer acceptable. No one felt this slight more acutely than Chief Factor Colin Robertson, a proud Scotsman who had had a long if somewhat erratic career in the service of both companies. Robertson had earned Simpson's dislike partly because his genuine concern for the betterment of his half-breed wife Theresa Chalifoux and their family had often resulted in extravagance and a neglect of business. The old chief factor intended to take his country family with him when he retired from Rupert's Land, but his attempt to introduce his wife to the society of Mrs Simpson when passing through Red River met with a scathing rebuff from the Governor: 'Robertson brought his bit of Brown wt. him to the Settlement this Spring in hopes that She would pick up a few English manners before visiting the civilized World ... I told him distinctly that the thing was impossible which mortified him exceedingly.'[91]

At Moose Factory, McTavish had similarly ruffled feelings by refusing to countenance certain of the officers' wives. Even Simpson expressed concern lest McTavish go too far in alienating Chief Factor Joseph Beioley whose capacities he rated highly, although the governor fully sympathized with his friend that it was the height of impertinence for Beioley to expect that 'his bit of circulating copper' should have the society of Mrs McTavish.[92] The mixed-blood, though Anglicized families of former company officers, such as that of George Gladman at Moose, were highly incensed at such treatment as they considered themselves among the upper crust of fur-trade society. Simpson, however, encouraged McTavish to keep these people in their place: 'I ...

understand that the other Ladies at Moose are violent and indignant at being kept at such a distance, likewise their husbands, the Young Gladmans particularly ... The greater distance at which they are kept the better.'[93] Only two half-breed women had been allowed to come within a dozen yards of Mrs Simpson, he informed McTavish, and these in a purely menial capacity.[94] The extent to which the governor found himself avoided caused him to muse: 'They do not even venture within gun Shot of me now – I have seen the time when they were not so shy.'[95]

By this time, the responsibilities of married life weighed heavily on the governor for Frances Simpson, like Mrs Pelly before her, proved unequal to the rigours of frontier life. Despite constant medical care, her health deteriorated rapidly as her first pregnancy advanced. Simpson, who now appears the most attentive of husbands, was distraught at the necessity of leaving her during the summer of 1831 to attend the annual council at York Factory.[96] His speedy dispatch of company business was not his time motivated simply by a desire for efficiency, and he hurried back to Red River in time for the birth of a son, which his wife barely survived. During the winter, Simpson was much heartened by the steady, if slow progress of both mother and child. The christening of George Geddes Simpson in January 1832 was a considerable social event in the colony. But this happiness was short-lived; the sudden death of the little boy a few months later plunged his parents into the depths of despair.[97]

Domestic tribulations had, in fact, brought the governor to the low point of his career: his own health was breaking down, he confessed himself little interested in business, detested most of his associates, and was only prevented from retiring from the fur trade by the loss of a large sum of money.[98] His vision of a comfortable family life in Red River now shattered, Simpson had to accept that his wife, who was desperately in need of skilled medical attention, could no longer remain in Rupert's Land: 'She has no Society, no Friend, no Relative here but myself, she cannot move wt. me on my different Journeys and I cannot leave her in the hands of Strangers ... some of them very unfeeling.'[99] He, therefore, took Frances home via Canada in the summer of 1833, and she never returned to the Indian Country. Simpson's subsequent efforts to divide his time between his family in England and the superintendence of the fur trade in western Canada tended to hamper his effectiveness as governor.[100]

Perhaps it was Catherine McTavish's Scottish constitution which enabled her to withstand the harsh climate of Hudson Bay because she appears to have adapted with less difficulty to life at Moose Factory. A kind, sensible woman, 'tho' not handsome,'[101] she reconciled herself to McTavish's former arrangements. She presented the old fur trader with two more little girls and for a time had the care of four of her stepdaughters.[102] McTavish himself was suffering badly from gout, and Simpson, ever solicitous of his friend's welfare, sought a more amenable situation for the family. Thus, in 1835, McTavish moved to the Lake of Two Mountains, a post about one hundred miles from the Chats on the Ottawa River where he had invested in a farm. The governor declared it the ideal solution: 'Here your Family could be reared and Educated cheaply while Mrs. McTavish & yourself could enjoy the comforts of civilized society in a moderate degree as the country is becoming closely settled all about you, a Steam Vessel plies regularly to your Door & there is a Church within 3 or 4 Miles of it.'[103]

Although neither Mrs Simpson nor Mrs McTavish remained for long in the Indian Country, their coming contributed to the decline in the position of native women in fur-trade society. The implication was apparent that in more established areas, particularly at Red River, a country wife was no longer acceptable. In considering possible successors to McKenzie for the governorship of the colony, Simpson initially discounted the highly competent Alexander Christie because he had an Indian family *à la façon du pays*.[104]

It now became fashionable for a company officer to have a European wife. As Hargrave unfeelingly observed, 'this influx of white faces has cast a still deeper shade over the faces of our Brunettes in the eyes of many.'[105] When Chief Factor James McMillan brought his Scottish wife out to Red River in the fall of 1831, one old fur trader, commenting on this 'novelty of getting H Bay stocked with European Ladys,' conjectured that several others would avail themselves of their furlough 'with no other view than that of getting Spliced to some fair Belinda & return with her' to the Indian Country.[106] Even some of those who had strongly professed a sense of duty to their country wives succumbed. Simpson commented wryly on Chief Factor William Connolly's marriage to his wealthy cousin in Montreal in 1832: 'You would have heard of Connolly's Marriage – he was one of those who considered it a most unnatural proceeding 'to desert the Mother of his children' and marry another; this is all very fine, very sentimental and very kindhearted 3000 Miles from the Civilized World but is lost sight of even by Friend Connolly where a proper opportunity offers.'[107]

The coming of white women to the Indian Country brought into disrepute the indigenous social customs of the fur trade. Marriage *à la façon du pays* was now no longer acceptable, especially with the presence of missionaries intolerant of any deviation. The presence of white women underlined the perceived cultural shortcomings of mixed-blood wives, particularly in more settled areas where their native skills were no longer required. European ladies themselves, by zealously guarding what they considered to be their intrinsically superior status, actively fostered an increasing stratification of fur-trade society. The arrival of the white woman can be seen as symbolic of a new era: the old fur-trade order was gradually giving way to agrarian settlement which was unquestioningly equated with civilization.

NOTES

This article is from *The Neglected Majority: Essays in Canadian Women's History*, ed. Alison Prentice and Susan Mann Trofimenkoff. Toronto: McClelland and Stewart 1977. Reprinted with permission of the Canadian Publishers, McClelland and Stewart, Toronto.

1 Glyndwr Williams, ed., *Andrew Graham's Observations on Hudson's Bay 1767–91* (London: Hudsons' Bay Record Society (HBRS) 1969), 248

2 Hudson's Bay Company Archives (HBC), B22/a/6, Brandon House, f. 8d, 13 Nov. 1798: 'Jollycoeur the Canadian wanted an old Woman to keep ... he says every Frenchman has a woman & why should we stop him.'

3 HBC, B239/b/79, York Factory, fos. 40d-41, as quoted in Alice M. Johnson, ed., *Saskatchewan Journals and Correspondence, 1795–1802* (London: HBRS 1967)

4 John Franklin, *Narrative of a Journey to the Shores of the Polar Sea in the Years 1819–20–21–22* (London 1824), 101

5 John West, *The Substance of a Journal during a Residence at the Red River Colony* ... (London 1827), 16: 'They do not admit them as their companions, nor do they allow them to eat at their tables, but degrade them *merely* as slaves to their arbitrary inclination.' See also 53–4.

6 Franklin, *Narrative*, 106

7 G.P. deT. Glazebrook, ed., *The Hargrave Correspondence*, 1821–43 (Toronto: Champlain Society 1938), 381, Jas. Douglas to Jas. Hargrave, Fort Vancouver, 24 March 1842: 'There is indeed no living with comfort in this country until a person has forgot the great world and has his tastes and character formed on the current standard of the stage ... To any other being ... the vapid monotony of an inland trading Post, would be perfectly unsufferable, while habit makes it familiar to us, softened as it is by the many tender ties, which find a way to the heart.'

8 John Siveright in his letters to James Hargrave as published in the Hargrave Corres. frequently observed that Indian traders who retired with their families to farms in the Canadas were rarely successful. He cited the case of Alexander Stewart's wife, who died soon after her arrival in Montreal.

9 Margaret A. Macleod, ed., *The Letters of Letitia Hargrave* (Toronto: Champlain Society 1947), 72, To Mary Mactavish, York, 1 Sept. 1840

10 W. Kaye Lamb, ed., *Sixteen Years in the Indian Country: The Journal of Daniel Williams Harmon* (Toronto 1957), 5–6. See also W.S. Wallace, ed., *Documents Relating to the North West Company* (Toronto: Champlain Society 1934), 211.

11 E.E. Rich, ed., *Minutes of Council of the Northern Department of Rupert's Land, 1821–31* (London: HBRS 1940), 33–4

12 Ibid., 33–4. See also HBC, B235/z/3, f. 545, for a circular outlining the proposals for the establishment of a boarding school for female children, natives of the Indian Country. A similar institution for boys was not actually established until the 1830s.

13 Rich, ed., *Minutes of Council*, 94–5. See also 382, Simpson to Gov. & Committee, York, 1 Sept. 1822: 'Messrs. Donald Sutherland and James Kirkness have this season requested permission to take their Families to Europe, which I was induced to comply with being aware that they had the means of providing for them so as to prevent their becoming a burden on the Company, and some labourers are in like manner permitted to take their children home.'
14 Ibid., 358–9. See also HBC, A6/20, f. 74, 136d.
15 HBC, A6/62, f. 3–3d
16 Rich, *Minutes of Council*, 94–5. This rule eventually became incorporated into the Standing Rules and Regulations. See also HBC, A6/21, f. 32, 151d.
17 Quite a number of these contracts are to the found in the miscellaneous file (z) under the heading of the various posts, ie, B239/z/1, f. 32d.
18 HBC, B49/z/1, B156/z/1, f. 96
19 West, *Journal*, 26
20 Nicholas Garry, *Diary of ...* (Ottawa: Transactions of the Royal Society of Canada, ser. 2, vol. 6, 1900), 137
21 Rich, *Minutes of Council*, 60–1. There is evidence that Chief Factor James Keith drew up these rules during the winter of 1822–3 at Severn. See HBC, B198/e/6, fos. 5d–6.
22 Frederick Merk, ed., *Fur Trade and Empire: George Simpson's Journal ...* (Cambridge, Mass. 1931), 108
23 E.E. Rich, ed., *Simpson's Athabaska Journal and Report* (London: HBRS 1938), 231
24 HBC, B39/a/16, Ft Chipewyan, Simpson to Wm Brown, 17 Oct. 1820, et al.
25 Rich, ed., *Athabaska Journal*, 264, Simpson to Jn Clarke, Isle à la Crosse, 9 Feb. 1821
26 Ibid., 392, 395–96.
27 HBC, D3/3, f. 35, 7 March 1822, Brandon House: 'no less than 87 people including women & children which is a very serious drawback.' B239/c/1, f. 91, Simpson to McTavish, Isle à la Crosse, 12 Nov. 1822: 'the Deptmt. is dreadfully overloaded with Families no less than 102 women & children & no less than three births since my arrival here.'
28 Rich, ed., *Athabaska Journal*, 23–4
29 Merk, ed., *Fur Trade*, 131
30 Ibid., 11–12: 'they are nearly all *Family Men*.' See also 99.
31 HBC, D3/3, 1821–2, f. 52
32 HBC, D3/3, f. 34
33 Merk, ed., *Fur Trade*, 58, 131–2. These two chief traders were John McLeod, whose wife was a daughter of J.P. Pruden, and John Warren Dease. There is other evidence that jealousy often caused the men to shirk their duty. See HBC, B39/a/22, Ft Chipewyan, f. 42.
34 HBC, Copy no. 160a, Selkirk Correspondence, f. 1157c, Simpson to Colvile, York, 11 Aug. 1824. These three men were Donald Ross, clerk, who took Mary MacBeath, daughter of a Selkirk settler, in 1820; John Clarke, chief factor, who took a Swiss girl Mary Ann Traitley in 1822; and Robert McVicar, chief trader, who took Christy MacBeath at Norway House in 1824. Since there is no record of any of these marriages in the Red River Register of Marriages, it is likely that, initially at least, they were after the fashion of the country.
35 This is a good example of a lasting marriage '*la façon du pays*.' William Sinclair, an Orkneyman who served in the Hudson's Bay Company from 1792

to 1818, spent most of his career at Oxford House which he built in 1798. Little is known about the origin of his wife Nahovway, by whom he had eleven children, but she may have been a daughter of Moses Norton. See Denis Bayley, *A Londoner in Rupert's Land: Thomas Bunn of the Hudson's Bay Company* (Chichester, Eng. 1969), and D. Geneva Lent, *West of the Mountains: James Sinclair and the Hudson's Bay Company* (Seattle 1963), for details of the Sinclair family.

36 HBC, B239/c/1, York Inward Corres., f. 60, Geo. Simpson to J.G. McTavish, Rock Depot, 14 Dec. 1821; same to same, f. 71, 25 Jan. 1822, and f. 83, 4 June 1822

37 HBC, B239/a/130, York Factory, f. 38d. This is a curious entry for it has been crossed out by someone at a later date. However, A.S. Morton in his biography of Simpson is wrong in stating that this child was born in October 1821 for he confused this Maria with another natural daughter also called Maria who was born in Britain before Simpson ever came to Rupert's Land. Simpson received the news that this daughter was to be married to one Donald McTavish of Inverness in 1833 (B135/c/2, f. 110, Simpson to McTavish, 1 July 1833) and if she was then sixteen, as Morton states, she must have been born in 1817. Furthermore, there is no evidence that Simpson ever sent Betsey Sinclair's child to Scotland to be educated; she appears to have been at Mrs Cockran's school for girls in Red River in 1830 (B4/b/1, f. 5v, J, Stuart to Simpson, 1 Feb. 1830) and in the fall of 1837 she married the botanist Robert Wallace at Fort Edmonton (*Hargrave Corres.*, 274, J. Rowand to Hargrave, Edmonton, 31 Dec. 1838). That this daughter was not a child of Margaret Taylor's, as Morton states, is conclusively proved in a letter from Robert Miles to Edward Ermatinger dated 8 Aug. 1839 (HBC Copy no. 23, fos. 304–5) which tells of Betsey Sinclair's grief on learning that her first daughter Maria had been drowned at the Dalles on the Columbia River in the fall of 1838.

38 HBC, E4/la, Red River Register of Baptisms, f. 39

39 HBC, B239/c/1, f. 92, Simpson to McTavish, Isle à la Crosse, 12 Nov. 1822

40 HBC, B235/c/1, Winnipeg. fos. 3d–4, Geo. Barnston to Jas. Hargrave, York, 1 Feb. 1823. This country marriage was a long and happy one. Betsey bore Miles at least eight children and retired with him to Upper Canada. I have found no evidence to support the suggestion of two writers (Lent, *Sinclair*, 30–1, and Bayley, *Bunn*, 46) that Betsey Sinclair was left out of her father's will because of her loose behaviour. Whatever the reason, her actions seem no worse than that of other young ladies growing up in the Indian Country.

41 HBC, B239/c/1, Simpson to McTavish, Red River, 4 June 1822, f. 83

42 Macleod, ed., *Letitia's Letters*, 205, n1. The tombstone of James Keith Simpson records that he died on 28 Dec. 1901 at the age of seventy eight. He is ruputed to have had a very sickly childhood but eventually entered the company's service in the mid-1840s. He was definitely not a son by Margaret Taylor as Morton claims. Macleod suggests his mother may have been the 'country wife' of Chief Factor James Keith; Keith does indeed seem to have had some interest in this child for he bequeathed him the sum of five pounds for the purchase of books in his will of 1836 (HBC, A36/8, f. 58). During this period Simpson may also have had a liaison with Jane Klyne, who later became the wife of Chief Factor Archibald MacDonald. She was the half-breed daughter of a former Nor'Wester, Michael Klyne, who was stationed at Great Slave Lake in 1822–3.

See *Letitia's Letters*, 213: 'poor Mrs. MacDonald was an Indian wife of the Govr's.'

43 HBC, B239/c/1, Simpson to McTavish, Red River, 7 Jan, 1824, f. 136. See also f. 127: Simpson refused to allow Capt. Matthey, one of the leaders of the de Meuron segment of the population, to introduce his wife to the English wife of the colony's governor, R.P. Pelly, because Mrs Matthey was not his legal wife and she had been guilty of some indiscreet amours.

44 HBC Copy no. 112, vol. 2, fos. 638–9, Simpson to A. Colvile, York, 16 Aug. 1822: 'I should certainly wish to get Home for a Season if my inclination continues to lead the same way.'

45 In his biography *Sir George Simpson*, A.S. Morton places much emphasis on a Miss Eleanor Pooler who is kindly remembered in Simpson's letters to her father Richard Pooler (see 124, 161). One can only speculate, however; perhaps he intended to make an honest woman out of the mother of Maria, his Scottish-born daughter.

46 Merk, ed., *Fur Trade*, 104–5

47 Ibid., 122

48 HBC Copy no. 160a, f. 1112, Simpson to Colvile, York, 8 Sept. 1823

49 HBC, B239/c/1, f. 283, S. to McT., Norway House, 28 Aug. 1826

50 HBC, B239/a/136, York Factory, f. 111d. For the date 11 Feb. 1827 there has been added the tiny postscript /G.S. Born/ with a curious comment by Robert Miles 'Say 11th March.' This may well establish the date of the birth of Margaret's son, christened George Stewart; Simpson's letter to McTavish of 15 Sept. 1827 confirms that a son had been born.

51 HBC, B239/c/1, f. 346, Memo for J.G. McTavish

52 Arthur S. Morton, *Sir George Simpson: Overseas Governor of the Hudson's Bay Company* (Toronto 1944), 162. There may also have been another woman in Simpson's life at this time, maintained at his headquarters at Lachine established in 1826. See HBC, D5/3, Aemileus Simpson to Geo. Simpson, Ft Vancouver, 20 March 1828: 'I do not think it improves the arrangements of your domestic economy to have a mistress attached to your Establishment – rather have her Elsewhere.'

53 HBC, B239/c/1, f. 366, Simpson to McTavish, Stuart's Lake, 22 Sept. 1828

54 HBC, B239/c/2, f. 10, S. to McT., Saskatchewan River, 10 May 1829

55 HBC, B4/b/1, fos. 2d–3, Jn Stuart to Simpson, Bas de la Rivière, 1 Feb. 1830. This son was baptized by the Rev. Wm. Cockran at Red River on 26 Dec. 1830 (E4/la, f. 80).

56 HBC, B4/b/1, same to same, 1 Feb. 1830, fos. 2d–3

57 HBC, B1/b/1, same to same, 20 March, f. 7

58 HBC, B4/b/1, same to same, Norway House, 8 Aug. 1825, f. 18: 'permit me my heartfelt acknowledgements for the many Kindness [es] and marks of friendship manifested towards me on various occasions ... before I can cease to be grateful I must cease to be myself.' See also same to same, 1 Feb. 1830, fos. 2d, 6d.

59 HBC, D5/3. AEmileus Simpson to Geo. Simpson, Fort Vancouver, 20 March 1828

60 HBC, B135/c/2, f. 76, Simpson to McTavish, Red River, 3 Jan. 1832: Simpson indulging in mutual congratulation on their choice of wives: 'Now my good friend, we are in great measure indebted to each other for all this happiness, our mutual Friendship having been one of the "primitive" causes thereof.'

61 Macleod, ed., *Letitia's Letters*, 83. This country wife of McTavish was reputed to have smothered two children, one while he was on his way to England. See also HBC, John Stuart Papers, Stuart to McTavish, Bas de la Rivière, 16 Aug. 1830. Stuart reminds McTavish that it was at Moose 'you abandoned the first of your Wives.'

62 HBC, B135/c/2, f. 50, Simpson to McTavish, 10 July 1830. Donald Mckenzie was the brother of Nancy's father Roderic McKenzie, who had retired in the early 1800s to Terrebonne in Lower Canada.

63 Macleod, ed., *Letitia's Letters*, 84, To Mrs Dugald McTavish, York, 1 Dec. 1840

64 HBC, B135/c/2, fos. 33d–34, Simpson to McTavish, London, 5 Dec. 1829

65 HBC, B135/c/2, f. 35d, same to same, 26 Dec. 1829

66 HBC, B135/c/2, f. 42, same to same, 26 Jan. 1830

67 Morton, *Simpson*, 164

68 HBC, D6/4, 2

69 Macleod, ed., *Letitia's Letters*, To Mrs Dugald McTavish, Gravesend, 21 May 1840, 34–6

70 Ibid., 36

71 What little education his sons did receive was at various schools in the Indian Country (HBC, D5/9, f. 236) and this undoubtedly contributed to their lack of advancement in the company's service. Simpson also demanded a standard of conduct, particularly from his son George, which made little allowance for the boy's background or the insecurity of his childhood (D5/10, f. 50). Although a small bequest was made to his sons George, John, and James in a draft will of 1841 (D6/1, fos. 1–11), the Scottish-born Maria, now widowed and living in Upper Canada, was the only natural child to be remembered in his final will. Even she seems to have suffered his neglect. See D5/9, fos. 260–1, Maria McTavish to Geo. Simpson, 22 Nov. 1843: 'Certain you must not be ashamed at countenancing me a little everyone knows I am your acknowledged daughter.'

72 See G.L. Nute, 'Journey for Frances,' *The Beaver*, Dec. 1953, 50–4; March 1954, 12–17; summer 1954, 12–18.

73 Ibid., March 1954, 17

74 HBC, B4/b/1, fos. 8d–9, Stuart to Nicholas Carry, Berens River, 8 Aug. 1830

75 HBC, John Stuart Papers, John Stuart to Capt. Franklin, Lesser Slave Lake, 12 Dec. 1826. Stuart claimed that Dr Richardson's contemptuous remarks about the morality of fur-trade society were unjust, arising merely from ignorance and hearsay. See also B/b/1, f. 14, Stuart to Jas. McKenzie, Lake Winnipeg, 7 Aug. 1831, f. 14: 'much of my present happiness is derived from the belief, that among the human race, are to be found ... women, that are equally chaste and virtuous, as they are acknowledged to be beautiful, not only among the children of nature, the savage race, but in civilized life also.'

76 That the Governor seems to have been above reproach is corroborated by a comment of Richard Grant: 'I will use the saying of our Worthy friend J.G. McTavish many will bark at me, who dare not bark at those who have the power of doing them injury.' *Hargrave Corres.*, 277, R. Grant to Hargrave, Oxford House, 3 Jan. 1839

77 National Archives of Canada (NA), MG 19, A 21(1), vol. 21, J. Hargrave to Donald McKenzie, York, 1 July 1830

78 HBC, B135/c/2, fos. 50–1, Simpson to McTavish, York, 10 July 1830
79 HBC, B135/c/2, f. 54d, same to same, 3 Jan. 1831
80 Stuart Papers, Stuart to McTavish, Bas de la Rivière, 16 Aug. 1830
81 HBC, B135/c/2, fos. 56–7, Simpson to McTavish, Red River, 10–11 Jan. 1831
82 HBC, B135/c/2, f. 63d, same to same, 10 April 1831. For the actual marriage contract see B235/z/3, f. 547a.
83 HBC, E4/1b, f. 230d
84 HBC, Copy no. 23, Ermatinger Papers, Wm Sinclair to Ed. Ermatinger, Ft Alexander, 15 Aug. 1831, f. 271: 'what a down fall is here.'
85 HBC, B4/b/1, f. 13, Stuart to Simpson, Bas de la Rivière, 24 Aug. 1831
86 HBC, A34/2, Simpson's Character Book, f. 4d–5, no. 14
87 HBC, B135/c/2, Simpson to McTavish, Red River, 2 Dec. 1832, f. 95
88 Glazebrook, ed., *Hargrave Corres.*, Alexander Ross to Hargrave, Red River, 18 Dec. 1830, 59
89 HBC, Copy no. 23, Sinclair to Ermatinger, 15 Aug. 1831, f. 271. See also Glazebrook, ed., *Hargrave Corres.*, Jas. McMillan to Hargrave, Red River, 15 Dec. 1830, 58: 'Mrs. Simpson's presence here makes a change in us.'
90 HBC, B135/c/2, Simpson to McTavish, Red River, 10 April 1831, f. 64d
91 HBC, B135/c/2, f. 73, same to same, York, 15 Aug. 1831
92 HBC, B135/c/2, f. 78, same to same, Red River, 3 Jan. 1832
93 HBC, B135/c/2, f. 74, same to same, York, 15 Aug. 1831
94 One of these women was Nancy Leblanc, who nursed Mrs Simpson's infant during her illness. Mrs Simpson unflatteringly described her as 'a complete savage, with a coarse blue sort of wollen gown without shape & a blanket fastened round her neck.' *Letitia's Letters*, To Mrs. Dugald McTavish, Gravesend, 20 May 1840, 36
95 HBC, B135/c/2, f. 74d, Simpson to McTavish, York, 15 Aug. 1831
96 HBC, B135/c/2, f. 70, same to same, York, 7 July 1831
97 HBC, B135/c/2, f. 83, same to same, Red River, 1 May 1832
98 HBC, B135/c/2, f. 85, same to same, York, 19 July 1832
99 HBC, B135/c/2, f. 83, same to same, Red River, 1 May 1832
100 Angus Cameron, for example, was happy to learn that the governor intended to bring his family out to Lachine: 'he will be more conveniently situated to superintend his various important duties than by going backwards and forwards to England every year.' *Hargrave Corres.*, Angus Cameron to Hargrave, Temiscamingue, 25 April 1843, 434
101 NA, MG 19, A 21(1), vol. 3, 813, Ed. Smith to Hargrave, Norway House, 8 July 1834
102 Macleod, ed., *Letitia's Letters*, 84, To Mrs Dugald McTavish, 1 Dec. 1840
103 HBC, B135/c/2, f. 115, Simpson to McTavish, London, 10 Jan. 1834
104 NA, MG 19 A 21(1), vol. 21, Hargrave to Charles Ross, York, 1 Dec. 1830
105 HBC, B135/c/2, f. 106, Simpson to McTavish, Michipicoten, 29 June 1833. Alexander Christie did eventually became the governor of Red River. He appears to have been devoted to his country family, his wife being Anne, the daughter of Thomas Thomas.
106 Glazebrook, ed., *Hargrave Corres.*, 66, Cuthbert Cumming to Hargrave, St Maurice, 1 March 1831
107 HBC, B135/c/2, f. 96, Simpson to McTavish, Red River, 2 Dec. 1832

TREATIES AND RESERVES

JOHN LEONARD TAYLOR

Canada's North-West Indian Policy in the 1870s: Traditional Premises and Necessary Innovations

In 1870 the Government of Canada assumed sovereignty over the 'North-West' of the fur trade. That portion of the territory lying between the mountains on the west, the Great Lakes on the east, the United States boundary, and the Saskatchewan River system was considered ripe for settlement and development. If this was to be undertaken without the danger of the Indian wars experienced in the United States, then the Indians of the region would have to be placated.

The traditional means of doing so in British North America had been through treaties providing compensation in return for land surrender. In whatever way they understood them, the western Indians themselves were anxious to have treaties. Consequently, between 1871 and 1877 treaties numbered from one to seven were concluded between the government and the Indians of the proposed settlement areas. In return for land surrender and the maintenance of peace, these treaties provided the Indian people with a small cash annuity, reserves of land, schools, agricultural assistance, and hunting and fishing supplies. The precise terms varied from treaty to treaty.[1]

These seven numbered treaties laid the foundation of the dominion's Indian policy in the North-West. In fact, during that decade the treaties were almost the only instrument and expression of that policy. Based on the premises and methods of the traditional British North American Indian policy, they were nevertheless innovative in some respects. This only becomes apparent when the treaty-making decade is examined in some detail.

This has been difficult to do because no detailed or well-researched account of the subject has been produced. Some printed primary sources have been readily available. The official record appeared in successive annual issues of the *Sessional Papers*. In 1880 Alexander Morris, who had been chief negotiator for four of the seven treaties, brought out his book entitled *The Treaties of*

Canada with the Indians of Manitoba and the North-West Territories. Much of his material duplicates that in the *Sessional Papers*, but it does include some additional accounts of treaty negotiations and some of his own views. The sketchy secondary accounts in existence have been based on these two sources.[2]

Stanley's chapter on the treaties in his now forty-year-old book, *The Birth of Western Canada*, remains the most thoroughly researched and most detailed account of the subject in print. His purpose in this book, however, was not to expound on the treaties but to explain the causes of the North-West Rebellion. His chapter entitled 'The Indian Problem: The Treaties' is merely prologue to his major thesis. His theory is that, within the context of a culture clash, some Indians joined the Métis in rebellion because of maladministration by the Indian Department. He does not find the causes of Indian discontent in the treaties themselves but in the period which followed. Stanley challenged only half of the conventional wisdom–the quality of the Indian administration. He left the treaties and the treaty-making process largely intact.

The conclusions which emerge from the official records and the secondary literature are:

1 that Canada's Indian policy in the North-West was a further application of the traditional British North American policy which had evolved from British eighteenth-century practice and had come to fruition in Upper Canada;
2 that this policy was deliberate, wise, and benevolent.

Any attempt to question the validity of these conclusions must take into account the manuscript sources which were not used by the authors of the existing literature. These sources include the papers of major participants:

the Sir John A. Macdonald Papers (National Archives of Canada)
the A.G. Archibald Papers (Public Archives of Manitoba)
the Alexander Morris Papers (Public Archives of Manitoba)

and the records of

the Indian Affairs Branch (RG 10, National Archives of Canada)
the RCMP (RG 18, National Archives of Canada)

As far as it goes, there is no reason to doubt the soundness of the first conclusion derived from the existing accounts. Ministers and government officials gave every indication that they intended to adhere to traditional practices as closely as possible. They believed that treaties faithfully observed had been responsible for a successful and peaceful relationship with the Indian people of Canada in contrast to the Indian wars in the United States. Since the Indians themselves seemed anxious to have treaties, the government wished to continue the traditional policy of treaty-making.

Not only was treaty-making the first premise of traditional policy, but there was precedent in old Canada for every significant item which came to be included in the western treaties. Some earlier eastern treaties had provided for reserves and annuities. The Robinson Treaties of 1850 had also included hunting and fishing rights. Agriculture and education had received official encouragement from the Indian Branch, while hunting and fishing supplies were amongst the earliest items supplied to Indians. All of this could be described as traditional Indian policy and practice. What was new in the North-West was the inclusion of all these items in the treaty terms as obligations upon the crown.

These features of the treaties gave a plausible ring to the impression of considered purpose, wisdom, and benevolence behind the government's actions as conveyed in the secondary literature. There the treaties are presented as creations of the government. The Indian contribution was confined to 'intransigence' and the making of 'extravagant demands.' This view is not, however, supported by a closer examination of the evidence. A good case can be made that the Indians, and not the government, were responsible for introducing most of the important treaty terms.

Treaties One and Two were both concluded during August 1871 and contained identical terms. The government's initial offer to the Indians consisted only of reserves and a small cash gratuity and annuity. A draft treaty was sent from Ottawa to the commissioners before they negotiated Treaty One. Ken Tyler found it amongst the Archibald Papers and discovered that it included only those provisions along with a prohibition of alcoholic beverages. Yet what emerged from the negotiations at Lower Fort Garry was a treaty providing not only for these items but also for schools and farm animals, implements and supplies. These additions appear to have been proposed by the Indians, since the commissioners had no instructions to offer them. This view is further supported by the fact that the agricultural aid was not included in the treaty text but in the form of 'outside promises' which were reduced to writing by the commissioners in a memorandum.[3] This memorandum only became a formal part of the treaties in 1875.

The government displayed no intention of offering so much in subsequent treaties. Prior to the negotiation of Treaty Three with the Saulteaux, only annuities and the initial gratuity were discussed in correspondence which passed between Alexander Morris, the treaty commissioner, and the minister, Alexander Campbell. The Saulteaux, however, had demands of their own to make. They had drawn up a list as early as January 1869.[4] It included agricultural aid as well as hunting and fishing supplies. They managed to have these items included in the text of their treaty.

Like Treaties One and Two, Treaty Three carried the marks of its dual origins. In both instances, the Indian parties had added to the government's traditional terms some necessary innovations. To the Indians, these additional treaty terms were necessary because of their fear and anxiety about their own survival. They were necessary innovations to the government because, without them, they would have had even more difficulty getting treaties, if they had been able to get them at all.

None of the secondary literature contains any recognition of this Indian contribution. Some of it notes that there were difficulties getting treaties in some places, but where reasons were given for these difficulties, the official sources are quoted to the effect that the Indians made 'extravagant demands.' This is the major reason given for the failure to make the first treaty with the lakeland Saulteaux between Lake Superior and Red River. Treaty One was made at the Red River Settlement instead. The government concluded Treaty Three with the Saulteaux only after four unsuccessful attempts had been made. Nor was Treaty One concluded easily. Treaties Four and Six also involved difficult negotiations because of extravagant Indian demands, according to the commissioners. Some of those extravagant demands were in fact the provisions for schools, agricultural assistance, and help in making the transition to a new life which give the treaties the appearance of a forward-looking plan for the economic and social well-being of the Indian people.

Once it is realized that those treaty provisions which best support a claim for deliberation, wisdom, and benevolence came from the Indian side, it is evident that no plan meriting the description 'wise and benevolent' was ever produced by the government. In fact, no plan at all was ever produced. The picture is one of a government seeking to forestall potential trouble from the Indian inhabitants occupying the site of its prospective development project, and attempting to do so at the least cost.

In spite of government intentions, the Indians were able to obtain more than they were originally offered. Credit must be given to the treaty commissioners who showed some understanding of the problems and exercised enough flexibility to meet Indian suggestions part way. Nevertheless, it is evident that the Indians themselves displayed an awareness of their situation and had taken the initiative in suggesting the means of coping with it. Their partial success in having their demands included in the treaties was no doubt due largely to their numbers relative to the non-Indian population then in the North-West.

NOTES

This article is from *Approaches to Native History in Canada: Papers of a Conference held at the National of Man, October 1976*, ed. D.A. Muise, National Museum of Man Mercury Series, History Division Paper No. 25 (Ottawa: National Museums of Canada 1977). The foundation for this article is a doctoral thesis written by the author for Queen's University under the direction of Dr Roger Graham. Reprinted with permission.

1 The complete texts of the treaties are most readily available in Alexander Morris, *The Treaties of Canada with the Indians of Manitoba and the North-West Territories* (Toronto 1880), reprinted by Coles Publishing Company (Toronto 1971). They are also to be found for the individual years in Canada, *Sessional Papers*, and, together with the texts of earlier treaties and surrenders, in Canada, *Indian Treaties and Surrenders from 1680 to 1902* (Ottawa 1891), 3 vols., reprinted by Coles Publishing Company (Toronto 1971). The texts of individual treaties are supplied on request by the Department of Indian and Northern Affairs, Ottawa.

2 Alexander Begg, *The Great Canadian North-West* (Montreal 1881), and *History of the North-West*, vol. 2 (Toronto 1894) A.G. Harper, 'Canada's Indian Administration: The Treaty System,' *América Indígena 7(2)* (April 1947); David Laird, *Our Indian Treaties* (Winnipeg 1905); E.H. Oliver, 'Saskatchewan and Alberta: General History,' in A. Shortt and A.G. Doughty, eds., *Canada and Its Provinces* (Toronto 1914); D.C. Scott, 'Indian Affairs, 1867–1912,' in Shortt and Doughty, eds., *Canada and Its Provinces* (Toronto 1913)

3 The Indian parties to the treaty disputed that the memorandum contained all that had been promised them.

4 Morris made reference to this document, of which he had a copy. Morris, *Treaties*, 48

JOHN L. TOBIAS

Canada's Subjugation of the Plains Cree, 1879-1885

One of the most persistent myths that Canadian historians perpetuate is that of the honourable and just policy Canada followed in dealing with the Plains Indians. First enunciated in the Canadian expansionist literature of the 1870s as a means to emphasize the distinctive Canadian approach to and the unique character of the Canadian west,[1] it has been given credence by G.F.G. Stanley in the classic *The Birth of Western Canada*,[2] and by all those who use Stanley's work as the standard interpretation of Canada's relationship with the Plains Indians in the period 1870–85. Thus students are taught that the Canadian government was paternalistic and far-sighted in offering the Indians a means to become civilized and assimilated into white society by the reserve system, and honest and fair-minded in honouring legal commitments made in the treaties.[3] The Plains Indians, and particularly the Plains Cree, are said to be a primitive people adhering to an inflexible system of tradition and custom, seeking to protect themselves against the advance of civilization, and taking up arms in rejection of the reserve system and an agricultural way of life.[4] This traditional interpretation distorts the roles of both the Cree and the Canadian government, for the Cree were both flexible and active in promoting their own interests, and willing to accommodate themselves to a new way of life, while the Canadian government was neither as far-sighted nor as just as tradition maintains. Canada's principal concern in its relationship with the Plains Cree was to establish control over them, and Canadian authorities were willing to and did wage war upon the Cree in order to achieve this control.

Those who propagate the myth would have us believe that Canada began to negotiate treaties with the Indians of the west in 1871 as part of an overall plan to develop the agricultural potential of the west, open the land for railway construction, and bind the prairies to Canada in a network of commercial and economic ties. Although there is an element of truth to these statements, the fact remains that in 1871 Canada had no plan on how to deal with the Indians, and the negotiation of treaties was not at the initiative of the Canadian government but at the insistence of the Ojibwa Indians of the North-West Angle and the Saulteaux of the tiny province of Manitoba. What is ignored by the traditional interpretation is that the treaty process only started after Yellow Quill's band of Saulteaux turned back settlers who tried to go west of Portage la Prairie, and after other Saulteaux leaders insisted upon enforcement of the Selkirk Treaty or, more often, insisted upon making a new treaty. Also ignored is the fact that the Ojibwa of the North-West Angle demanded rents and created the fear of violence against prospective settlers who crossed their land or made use of their territory if Ojibwa rights to their lands were not recognized. This pressure and fear of resulting violence is what motivated the government to begin the treaty-making process.[5]

Canada's initial offer to the Saulteaux and Ojibwa Indians consisted only of reserves and a small cash annuity. This proposal was rejected by the Ojibwa in 1871 and again in 1872, while the Saulteaux demanded, much to Treaty Commissioner Wemyss Simpson's chagrin, farm animals, horses, wagons, and farm tools and equipment. Simpson did not include these demands in the written treaty, for he had no authority to do so, but he wrote them down in the form of a memorandum that he entitled 'outside promises' and which he failed to send to Ottawa. Thus, the original Treaties 1 and 2 did not include those items the Saulteaux said had to be part of a treaty before they would agree to surrender their lands. Only in 1874, after the Indian leaders of Manitoba became irate over non-receipt of the goods that Simpson had promised them, was an inquiry launched, and Simpson's list of 'outside promises' discovered and incorporated in renegotiated treaties in 1875.[6] It was only in 1873, after the Ojibwa of the North-West Angle had twice refused treaties that only included reserves and annuities, that the government agreed to include the domestic animals, farm tools, and equipment that the Ojibwa demanded. After this experience Canada made such goods a standard part of later treaties.[7]

Just as it was pressure from the Indians of Manitoba that forced the government of Canada to initiate the treaty process, it was pressure from the Plains Cree in the period 1872–5 that compelled the government of Canada to continue the process with the Indians of the Qu'Appelle and Saskatchewan districts. The Plains Cree had interfered with the geological survey and prevented the construction of telegraph lines through their territory to emphasize that Canada had to deal with the Cree for Cree lands.[8] The Cree had learned in 1870 about Canada's claim to their lands, and not wanting to experience what had happened to the Indians in the United States when those people were faced with an expansionist government, the Cree made clear that they would not allow settlement or use of their lands until Cree rights had been clearly recognized. They also made clear that part of any arrangement for Cree lands had to involve assistance to the Cree in developing a new agricultural way of life.[9]

In adopting this position, the Cree were simply demonstrating a skill that they had shown since their initial contact with Europeans in 1670. On numerous occasions during the fur trade era, they had adapted to changed environmental and economic circumstances, beginning first as hunters, then as provisioners and middlemen in the Hudson's Bay Company trading system, and finally adapting from a woodland to parkland-prairie buffalo hunting culture to retain their independence and their desired ties with the fur trade.[10] Having accommodated themselves to the Plains Indian culture after 1800, they expanded into territory formerly controlled by the Atsina, and as the buffalo herds began to decline after 1850, the Cree expanded into Blackfoot territory.[11] Expansion was one response to the threat posed by declining buffalo herds; another was that some Plains Cree bands began to turn to agriculture.[12] Thus, when the Cree learned that Canada claimed their lands, part of the arrangement they were determined to make and succeeded in making was to receive assistance in adapting to an agricultural way of life. So successful were they in negotiating such assistance that when the Mackenzie government received a copy of Treaty 6 in 1876 it accepted the treaty only after expressing a protest concerning the too-generous terms granted to the Cree.[13]

While willing to explore the alternative of agriculture, three Cree leaders in the 1870s sought means to guarantee preservation of the buffalo-hunting culture as long as possible. Piapot (leader of the Cree-Assiniboine of the region south of the Qu'Appelle River), and Big Bear and Little Pine (leaders of two of the largest Cree bands from the Saskatchewan River district) led what has been called an armed migration of the Cree into the Cypress Hills in the latter 1860s. All three men were noted warriors, and Big Bear and Piapot were noted religious leaders, but their prowess was not enough to prevent a Cree defeat at the Battle of the Belly River in 1870.[14] As a result, they explored the alternative of dealing with the government of Canada, but in a manner to extract guarantees for the preservation of Cree autonomy. They were determined to get the government to promise to limit the buffalo hunt to the Indians–a goal that Cree leaders had been advocating since the 1850s.[15] When Big Bear met with Treaty Commissioner Alexander Morris at Fort Pitt in September 1876, he extracted a promise from Morris that non-Indian hunting of the buffalo would be regulated.[16]

Big Bear refused to take treaty in 1876, despite receiving Morris's assurances about the regulation of the hunt. Little Pine and Piapot also did not take treaty when the treaty commissioners first came to deal with the Cree. Oral tradition among the Cree maintains that all three leaders wished to see how faithful the government would be in honouring the treaties,[17] but equally important for all three leaders was their belief that the treaties were inadequate and that revisions were necessary. Piapot thought Treaty 4 (the Qu'Appelle Treaty) needed to be expanded to include increased farm equipment and tools, and to stipulate that the government had to provide mills, blacksmith and carpentry shops and tools, and instructors in farming and the trades. Only after receiving assurances that Ottawa would consider these requests did Piapot take treaty in 1875.[18] Big Bear and Little Pine objected to Treaty 6 (Fort Pitt and Carlton) because Commissioner Morris had made clear that in taking treaty the Cree would be bound by Canadian law. To accept the treaties would mean being subject to an external authority of which the Crees had little knowledge and upon which they had little influence. Neither Big Bear nor Little Pine would countenance such a loss of autonomy.

Big Bear had raised the matter of Cree autonomy at Fort Pitt in 1876 when he met Commissioner Morris. At that time Big Bear said: 'I will make a request that he [Morris] save me from what I most dread, that is the rope about my neck ... It was not given to us to have the rope about our neck.'[19] Morris and most subsequent historians have interpreted Big Bear's statements to be a specific reference to hanging, but such an interpretation ignores the fact that Big Bear, like most Indian leaders, often used a metaphor to emphasize a point. In 1875 he had made the same point by using a different metaphor when he spoke to messengers informing him that a treaty commission was to meet with the Cree in 1876. At that time Big Bear said: 'We want none of the Queen's presents: when we set a foxtrap we scatter pieces of meat all around, but when the fox gets into the trap we knock him on the head; we want no bait.'[20] A more accurate interpretation of Big Bear's words to Morris in 1876 is that he feared being controlled or 'enslaved,' just as an animal is controlled when it has a rope around its neck.[21] In 1877, when meeting with Lieutenant-Governor David Laird, Little Pine also stated that he would not take treaty because he saw the treaties as a means by which the government could 'enslave' his people.[22]

The importance of these three leaders cannot be overestimated, for they had with them in the Cypress Hills more than 50 per cent of the total Indian population of the Treaty 4 and 6 areas. By concentrating in such numbers in the last buffalo ranges in Canadian territory, the Cree were free from all external interference, whether by other Indian nations or by the agents of the Canadian government – the North-West Mounted Police.[23] Recognizing that these men were bargaining from a position of strength, Laird recommended in 1878 that the government act quickly to establish reserves and honour the treaties. He was aware that the Cypress Hills leaders had the support of many of the Cree in treaty, and that many of the Cree leaders were complaining that the government was not providing the farming assistance promised. As the number of these complaints increased, so did Cree support for Big Bear and Little Pine.[24]

The Cree were concerned not only about the lack of assistance to farm, but when Canadian officials were slow to take action to regulate the buffalo hunt, Big Bear, Piapot, and Little Pine met with Blackfoot leaders and with Sitting Bull of the Teton Sioux in an attempt to reach agreement among the Indian nations on the need to regulate buffalo hunting.[25] These councils were also the forum where Indian leaders discussed the need to revise the treaties. On learning about the Indian council, the non-Indian populace of the west grew anxious, fearing establishment of an Indian confederacy which would wage war if Indian demands were rejected.[26] However, an Indian confederacy did not result from these meetings, nor was agreement reached on how the buffalo were to be preserved, because the Cree, Sioux, and Blackfoot could not overcome their old animosities towards one another.[27]

When in 1879 the buffalo disappeared from the Canadian prairies and Big Bear and Little Pine took their bands south to the buffalo ranges on the Milk and Missouri rivers, most of the other Cree and Assiniboine bands also went with them. The Cree who remained in Canada faced starvation while awaiting the survey of their reserves and the farming equipment that had been promised. Realizing that many of the Cree were dying, the government decided that those who had taken treaty should be given rations. As well, the government appointed Edgar Dewdney to the newly created position of commissioner of Indian affairs for the North-West Territory; a farming policy for the western reserves was introduced; a survey of Cree reserves was begun; and twelve farming instructors were appointed to teach the Indians of the North-West.[28]

The new Indian commissioner quickly sought to use rations as a means of getting control over the Cree. In the fall of 1879 he announced that rations were to be provided only to Indians who had taken treaty. To get the Cree into treaty more easily and to reduce the influence of recalcitrant leaders, Dewdney announced that he would adopt an old Hudson's Bay Company practice of recognizing any adult male Cree as chief of a new band if he could induce 100 or more persons to recognize him as leader. He expected that the starving Cypress Hills Cree would desert their old leaders to get rations. As a means of demonstrating Canada's control over the Cree, Dewdney ordered that only the sick, aged, and orphans should receive rations without providing some service to one of the government agencies in the west.[29]

Dewdney's policies seemed to work, for when the Cree and Assiniboine who had gone to hunt in Montana returned starving, their resolve weakened.

Little Pine's people convinced their chief to take treaty in 1879, but when Big Bear refused to do the same, almost half of his following joined Lucky Man or Thunderchild to form new bands in order to receive rations.[30]

Taking treaty to avoid starvation did not mean that the Cree had come to accept the treaties as written; rather they altered their tactics in seeking revisions. Believing that small reserves were more susceptible to the control of the Canadian government and its officials, Big Bear, Piapot, and Little Pine sought to effect a concentration of the Cree people in an Indian territory similar to the reservation system in the United States. In such a territory the Cree would be able to preserve their autonomy, or at least limit the ability of others to control them; they would be better able to take concerted action on matters of importance to them.[31]

Soon after taking treaty Little Pine applied for a reserve in the Cypress Hills, twenty-seven miles northeast of the North-West Mounted Police post of Fort Walsh. Piapot requested a reserve next to Little Pine's, while ten other bands, including most of the Assiniboine nation, selected reserve sites contiguous to either Little Pine's or Piapot's and to one another.[32] If all these reserve sites were granted, and if Big Bear were to take treaty and settle in the Cypress Hills, the result would be concentration of much of the Cree nation and the creation of an Indian territory that would comprise most of what is now southwestern Saskatchewan.

Unaware of the intention of the Cree and Assiniboine leaders, Canadian officials in the spring of 1880 agreed to the establishment of a reserve for all the Canadian Assiniboine and reserves in the Cypress Hills for each of the Cree bands that wished them. In 1880 the Assiniboine reserve was surveyed, but the other Indian leaders were told that their reserves would not be surveyed until the following year.[33] In the interim, most of the Cree went to the buffalo ranges in Montana.

The Cree effort to exploit the remaining American buffalo ranges caused them much trouble. The Crow, the Peigan, and other Indian nations with reservations in Montana were upset by competition for the scare food resource, and these people threatened to break the treaties they had made with the American government and to wage war on the Cree if the American authorities did not protect the Indian hunting ranges. These threats were renewed when the Cree began to steal horses from the Crow and Peigan. To add to their difficulties, American ranchers accused the Cree of killing range cattle. American officials, not wishing trouble with their Indians and wishing to placate the ranchers, informed the Cree that they would have to return to Canada. Most Cree bands, aware that if they did not leave voluntarily the American government would use troops to force them to move north, returned to the Cypress Hill.[34]

They returned to find that Canadian officials were now aware of the dangers to their authority posed by a concentration of the Cree. A riot at Fort Walsh in 1880, which the police were powerless to prevent or control, assaults on farming instructors who refused to provide rations to starving Indians, and rumours that the Cree were planning a grand Indian council to discuss treaty revisions in 1881 all caused the Indian commissioner much concern.[35] To avoid further difficulties over rations, in late 1880 Dewdney ordered that all Indians requesting rations be given them, regardless of whether the supplicant was in treaty.[36] There was little that the government could do at this time about the proposed Indian council or the concentration of Cree in the Cypress Hills.

In the spring of 1881, Cree bands from all regions of the Canadian prairies left their reserves to go south to meet with Little Pine and Big Bear. Even the new bands Dewdney had created were going to the council in American territory. What was also disconcerting to Canadian officials were the reports that Big Bear and Little Pine, who had gone to Montana to prepare for the council, had reached an accommodation with the Blackfoot and had participated in a joint raid on the Crow. To all appearances the Blackfoot, the Indian confederacy the Canadian government most feared, would be part of the Indian council.[37]

The Indian council was not held because the raid on the Crow led American officials to intervene militarily to force the Cree to return to Canada. With Montana stockmen acting as militia units, the American army prevented most Cree and Assiniboine bands from entering the United States. As well, the American forces seized horses, guns, and carts, and escorted the Cree to Canada.[38] The Cree-Blackfoot alliance did not materialize, for soon after the raid on the Crow, young Cree warriors stole horses from the Blackfoot and thereby destroyed the accord that Little Pine and Big Bear were attempting to create.[39]

The actions of the American military in 1881 were extremely beneficial to Canada. Not only did the Americans prevent the holding of the Indian council, but by confiscating the guns and horses of the Cree, the Americans had dispossessed the Cree of the ability to resist whatever measures the Canadian authorities wished to take against them. The Canadian authorities also benefited from Governor General Lorne's tour of the west in 1881, for many of the Cree bands that had gone to the Cypress Hills in the spring went north in late summer to meet Lorne to impress upon him the inadequacy of the treaties and the need to revise them.[40] Thus, Lorne's tour prevented the concentration of most of the Cree nation in the Cypress Hills.

The threat posed to Canadian authority in the North-West by concentration of the Cree was clearly recognized by Dewdney and other Canadian officials in late 1881. They saw how the Cree had forced officials to placate them and to ignore their orders in 1880 and 1881. This convinced both Dewdney and Ottawa that the Cree request for contiguous reserves in the Cypress Hills could not be granted. Dewdney recognized that to grant the Cree requests would be to create an Indian territory, for most of the Cree who had reserves further north would come to the Cypress Hills and request reserves contiguous to those of the Cypress Hills Cree. This would result in so large a concentration of Cree that the only way Canada could enforce its laws on them would be via a military campaign. To prevent this, Dewdney recommended a sizeable expansion of the Mounted Police Force and the closure of Fort Walsh and all government facilities in the Cypress Hills. This action would remove all sources of sustenance from the Cree in the Cypress Hills. Dewdney hoped that starvation would drive them from the Fort Walsh area and thus end the concentration of their force.[41]

Dewdney decided to take these steps fully aware that what he was doing was a violation not only of the promises made to the Cypress Hills Indians in 1880 and 1881, but also that by refusing to grant reserves on the sites the Indians had selected, he was violating the promises made to the Cree by the Treaty Commissions in 1874 and 1876, and in the written treaties. Nevertheless, Dewdney believed that to accede to the Cree requests would be to grant the Cree de facto autonomy from Canadian control, which would result in the perpetuation and heightening of the 1880–1 crisis. Rather than see that situation continue, Dewdney wanted to exploit the opportunity presented to him by the hunger crisis and disarmament of the Cree to bring them under the government's control, even if it meant violating the treaties.[42]

In the spring of 1882 the Cree and Assiniboine were told that no further rations would be issued to them while they remained in the Cypress Hills. Only if the Indians moved north to Qu'Appelle, Battleford, and Fort Pitt were they to be given assistance, and at those locations only treaty Indians were to be aided. The Mounted Police were ordered to stop issuing rations at Fort Walsh and the Indian Department farm that had been located near Fort Walsh was closed. Faced with the prospect of starvation, without weapons or transport to get to the Montana buffalo ranges, and knowing that if they were to try to go south the Mounted Police would inform the American military authorities, many Cree and all the Assiniboine decided to go north.[43] Even Big Bear discovered that his people wanted him to take treaty and move north. In 1882, after taking treaty, he, along with Piapot and Little Pine, promised to leave the Cypress Hills.[44]

Only Piapot kept his promise and even he did not remain long at Fort Qu'Appelle. By late summer of 1882, Piapot was back in the Cypress Hills complaining about how he had been mistreated at Qu'Appelle, and making the Cree aware of how they could lose their autonomy if the government could deal with them as individual bands.[45] On hearing this report, the other Cree leaders refused to leave the Fort Walsh region and insisted upon receiving the reserves promised them in 1880 and 1881. North-West Mounted Police Commissioner Irvine feared a repetition of the incidents of 1880 if he refused to feed the Cree and believed that the hungry Cree would harass the construction crews of the Canadian Pacific Railway for food, which would lead to a confrontation between whites and Indians which the police would be unable to handle and which in turn might lead to an Indian war. Therefore Irvine decided to feed the Cree.[46]

Dewdney and Ottawa were upset by Irvine's actions. Ottawa gave specific instructions to close Fort Walsh in the spring of 1883. When Irvine closed the fort, the Cree faced starvation. As it was quite evident that they could not go to the United States, and as they would not receive reserves in the Cypress Hills, the Cree moved north. Piapot moved to Indian Head and selected a reserve site next to the huge reserve set aside for the Assiniboine. Little Pine and Lucky Man moved to Battleford and selected reserve sites next to Poundmaker's reserve. Big Bear went to Fort Pitt.

The move to the north was not a sign of the Cree acceptance of the treaties as written, nor of their acceptance of the authority of the Canadian government. Big Bear, Little Pine, and Piapot were aware that the other Cree chiefs were dissatisfied with the treaties, and were also aware that if they could effect concentration of the Cree in the north they would be able to preserve their autonomy, just as they had done in the Cypress Hills in the 1879–81 period. Therefore, the move to the north was simply a tactical move, for no sooner were these chiefs in the north than they once again sought to effect a concentration of their people.

By moving to Indian Head, Piapot had effected a concentration of more than 2000 Indians. This number threatened to grow larger if the council he planned to hold with all the Treaty 4 bands to discuss treaty revisions were successful. Commissioner Dewdney, fearing the results of such a meeting in 1883, was able to thwart Piapot by threatening to cut off rations to any Indians attending Piapot's council and by threatening to arrest Piapot and depose any chiefs who did meet with him. Although Dewdney, in 1883, prevented Piapot from holding a large council by such actions, Piapot was able to get the Treaty 4 chiefs to agree to meet in the late spring of 1884 for a thirst dance and council on Pasquah's Reserve, near Fort Qu'Appelle.[47]

While Piapot was organizing an Indian council in the Treaty 4 area, Big Bear and Little Pine were doing the same for the Treaty 6 region. Little Pine and Lucky Man attempted to effect a concentration of more than 2000 Cree on contiguous reserves in the Battleford district, by requesting reserves next to Poundmaker, whose reserve was next to three other Cree reserves, which in turn were only a short distance from three Assiniboine reserves. Another 500 Cree would have been located in the Battleford area if Big Bear's request for a reserve next to Little Pine's site had been granted. Only with difficulty was Dewdney able to get Big Bear to move to Fort Pitt.[48] However, he was unable to prevent Big Bear and Little Pine from sending messengers to the Cree leaders of the Edmonton, Carlton, and Duck Lake districts to enlist their support for the movement to concentrate the Cree.[49]

Dewdney was convinced that the activities of Big Bear, Piapot, and Little Pine were a prelude to a major project the Cree planned for the following year, 1884. He was also aware that his ability to deal with the impending problem was severely limited by decisions taken in Ottawa. The deputy superintendent-general of Indian affairs, Lawrence Vankoughnet, was concerned about the cost of administering Dewdney's policies, and he ordered reductions in the level of assistance provided to the Cree and in the number of employees working with the Cree.[50] In making these decisions, Ottawa effectively deprived Dewdney of his major sources of intelligence about the Cree and their plans. It also deprived Dewdney of a major instrument in placating the Cree–the distribution of rations to those bands which co-operated.

Vankoughnet's economy measures led to further alienation of the Cree. In some areas, notably in the Fort Pitt, Edmonton, and Crooked Lakes regions, farming instructors were assaulted and government storehouses broken into when Indians were denied rations. The incident on the Sakemay Reserve in the Crooked Lakes area was quite serious, for when the policy were called upon to arrest those guilty of the assault, they were surrounded and threatened with death if they carried out their orders. Only after Assistant Indian Commissioner Hayter Reed had agreed to restore assistance to the Sakemay band to the 1883 level and had promised not to imprison the accused were the police allowed to leave with their prisoners.[51]

The violence that followed the reductions in rations convinced Dewdney that starving the Cree into submission was not the means to control them. He wanted to use coercion, but this required an expansion of the number of police in the west. Therefore, he recommended that more men be recruited for the Mounted Police. In addition, Dewdney wanted to ensure that jail sentences were given to arrested Indians so that they would cause no further problems. Having seen the effects of incarceration on Indians, Dewdney was convinced that this was the means to bring the Cree leaders under control. However, what was needed in his opinion were trial judges who 'understood' Indian nature at first hand and who would take effective action to keep the Indians under control. Therefore, Dewdney wanted all Indian Department officials in the west to be appointed stipendiary magistrates in order that all

Indian troublemakers could be brought to 'justice' quickly. As Dewdney stated in his letter to Prime Minister John A. Macdonald: 'The only effective course with the great proportion [of Indian bands] to adopt is one of sheer compulsion.'[52]

Dewdney used the policy of 'sheer compulsion' for only a few months in 1884. He found that his efforts to use the Mounted Police to break up the Indian councils and to arrest Indian leaders only led to confrontations between the Cree and the police. In these confrontations the police were shown to be ineffectual because they were placed in situations in which, if the Cree had been desirous of initiating hostilities, large numbers of Mounted Police would have been massacred.

The first incident which called the policy of compulsion into question was the attempt to prevent Piapot from holding his thirst dance and council in May 1884. Assistant Commissioner Hayter Reed, fearing that the council would result in a concentration of all the Treaty 4 bands, ordered Police Commissioner Irvine to prevent Piapot from attending the council. Irvine was to arrest the chief at the first sign of any violation of even the most minor law. To be certain that Piapot broke a law, Reed promised to have an individual from Pasquah's reserve object to the council being held on that reserve in order that the accusation of trespass could be used to break up the meeting, which all the bands from Treaty 4 were attending.[53]

With a force of fifty-six men and a seven-pounder gun, Irvine caught up with Piapot shortly before the chief reached Pasquah's reserve. Irvine and the police entered the Indian camp at 2 AM, hoping to arrest Piapot and remove him from the camp before his band was aware of what happened. However, when they entered the camp, the police found themselves surrounded by armed warriors. Realizing that any attempt to arrest the chief would result in a battle, Irvine decided to hold his own council with Piapot and Reed. This impromptu council agreed that Piapot should receive a new reserve next to Pasquah, in return for which Piapot would return to Indian Head temporarily.[54]

The agreement reached between Piapot and Irvine and Reed was a victory for Piapot. By getting a reserve at Qu'Appelle again, Piapot had approximately 2000 Cree concentrated on the Qu'Appelle River and he was able to hold his council and thirst dance, for after going to Indian Head he immediately turned around and went to Pasquah's. Reed and Irvine were aware of Piapot's ruse, but did nothing to prevent his holding the council, for they were aware that the Cree at Qu'Appelle were prepared to protect Piapot from what the Indians regarded as an attack on their leader. Realizing the effect that an Indian war would have on possible settlement, and that the police were inadequate for such a clash, the Canadian officials wished to avoid giving cause for violent reaction by the Cree.[55] Piapot acted as he did because he realized that if any blood were shed the Cree would experience a fate similar to that of the Nez Percés, Blackfoot, and Dakota Sioux in those peoples' conflicts with the United States.

Dewdney and the police were to have a similar experience when they attempted to prevent Big Bear from holding a thirst dance and council at Poundmaker's reserve in June 1884. Dewdney feared that Big Bear's council, to which the old chief had invited the Blackfoot and all the Indians from Treaty 6, would result in a larger concentration of Cree than Little Pine had already effected at Battleford. Dewdney also believed that he had to undo what Little Pine had accomplished, and refused to grant Little Pine and Lucky Man the reserve sites they had requested next to Poundmaker. Big Bear was again told that he would not be granted a reserve in the Battleford district. Dewdney believed that the Cree chiefs would ignore his order to select reserve sites at some distance from Battleford, and that this could be used as a reason for arresting them. To legitimize such actions on his part, Dewdney asked the government to pass an order-in-council to make it a criminal offence for a band to refuse to move to a reserve site the commissioner suggested.[56] In order to avoid violence when he attempted to prevent Big Bear's council and ordered the arrests of Lucky Man and Little Pine, Dewdney instructed the Indian agents at Battleford and Fort Pitt to purchase all the horses, guns, and cartridges the Cree possessed. He increased the size of the police garrison at Battleford and ordered the police to prevent Big Bear from reaching Battleford.[57]

All Dewdney's efforts had little effect, for Big Bear and his band eluded the police, reached Battleford, and held their thirst dance. The Cree refused to sell their arms, and even the effort to break up the gathering by refusing to provide rations had no result other than to provoke another assault on a farm instructor on 17 June 1884. When the police sought to arrest the farm instructor's assailant, they were intimidated into leaving without a prisoner. When a larger police detachment went to the reserve on 18 June, the police were still unable to make an arrest for fear of provoking armed hostilities. Only on 20 June, when the thirst dance had concluded, were the police able to arrest the accused and only then by forcibly removing him from the Cree camp. This was done with the greatest difficulty, for the police were jostled and provoked in an effort to get them to fire on the Cree. That no violence occurred, Superintendent Crozier, in charge of the police detachment, attributed to the discipline of his men and to the actions of Little Pine and Big Bear, who did all that was humanly possible to discourage any attack of the police.[58]

The events at Battleford frightened all parties involved in the confrontation. Big Bear was very much disturbed by them, for he did not want war, as he had made abundantly clear to Dewdney in March 1884, and again to the Indian agent at Battleford, J.A. Rae, in June. However, he did want the treaties revised and establishment of an Indian territory.[59] Agent Rae was thoroughly frightened and wanted Dewdney and Ottawa to adopt a more coercive policy designed to subjugate the Cree. Superintendent Crozier argued for a less coercive policy, for unless some accommodation were reached with the Cree, Crozier believed that out of desperation they would resort to violence.[60]

On hearing of the events of May and June 1884, Ottawa decided that Dewdney, who was now Lieutenant-Governor in addition to being Indian commissioner, was to have complete control over Indian affairs in the North-West Territories. As well, the prime minister informed Dewdney that more police were being recruited for duty in the west and that the Indian Act was being amended to permit Dewdney to arrest any Indian who was on another band's reserve without the permission of the local Indian Department official.[61] Dewdney was thus being given the instruments to make his policy of compulsion effective.

Dewdney did not, however, immediately make use of his new powers. He still intended to prevent concentration of the Cree, and rejected the requests Big Bear, Poundmaker, Lucky Man, and others made for a reserve at Buffalo Lake, and later rejected Big Bear's, Little Pine's, and Lucky Man's renewed requests for reserves next to Poundmaker's.[62] However, rather than following a purely coercive policy, Dewdney adopted a policy of rewards and punishments. He provided more rations, farming equipment, oxen, ammunition, and twine, and arranged for selected Cree chiefs to visit Winnipeg and other large centres of Canadian settlement. If the Cree were not satisfied with his new approach, he would use force against them. To implement this new policy, Dewdney increased the number of Indian Department employees working on the Cree reserves, for he wanted to monitor closely the behaviour of the Indians, and, if necessary, to arrest troublesome leaders.[63]

While Dewdney was implementing his new policy, the Cree leaders continued their efforts to concentrate the Cree in an exclusively Indian territory. Little Pine went south to seek Blackfoot support for the movement.[64] Big Bear, Lucky Man, and Poundmaker went to Duck Lake for a council with the Cree leaders of the Lower Saskatchewan district. The Duck Lake council, attended by twelve bands, was initiated by Beardy and the chiefs of the Carlton District. Beardy, who acted as spokesman for the Carlton chiefs, had been relatively inactive in the Cree movements in the 1881–3 period. He, however, had been the most vehement critic of the government's failure to deliver the farm materials promised by the treaty commissioners. In the 1877–81 period, Beardy was a man of little influence in the Carlton area, but when Mistawasis and Ahtahkakoop, the principal Cree chiefs of the Carlton District came to share his views, Beardy's standing among the Carlton Cree rose dramatically.[65]

The Duck Lake Council, called by Cree leaders who Dewdney thought were loyal and docile, and of which the commissioner had no foreknowledge, was a cause of much concern. Especially vexing was the detailed list of violations of the treaty for which the Cree demanded redress from the government. The Cree charged that the treaty commissioners lied to them when they said that the Cree would be able to make a living from agriculture with the equipment provided for in the treaties. However, rather than provide all the farming goods, what the government did, according to the Cree, was to withhold many of the cattle and oxen; send inferior quality wagons, farm tools, and equipment; and provide insufficient rations and clothes, and no medicine chest. The petition closed with the statement expressing the Cree sentiment that they had been deceived by 'sweet promises' designed to cheat them of their heritage, and that unless their grievances were remedied by the summer of 1885, they would take whatever measures necessary, short of war, to get redress.[66]

Dewdney originally assumed, as did some newspapers across the west, that the Duck Lake Council was part of a plot by Louis Riel to foment an Indian and Métis rebellion. Dewdney's assumption was based on the fact that the Duck Lake Council was held a short time after Riel had returned to Canada. It was also known that Riel had attended it, and that he had advocated such an alliance and a resort to violence when he had met with the Cree in Montana in 1880.[67] Further investigation, however, made quite clear that Riel had little influence on the Cree. To allay the growing concern about the possibility of an Indian war, Dewdney had Hayter Reed issue a statement that nothing untoward was happening and that there was less danger of an Indian war in 1884 than there had been in 1881. Privately Dewdney admitted to Ottawa and his subordinates in the west that the situation was very serious.[68] After both he and Dewdney had met with Cree leaders throughout the west and after carefully assessing the situation, Hayter Reed stated that the government had nothing to fear from the Cree until the summer of 1885. What Reed and Dewdney expected at that time was a united Cree demand to renegotiate treaties.[69]

What Reed and Dewdney had learned on their tours of the Battleford, Edmonton, Carlton, and Qu'Appelle districts in the fall of 1884 was that Big Bear, Piapot, and Little Pine were on the verge of uniting the Cree to call for new treaties in which an Indian territory and greater autonomy for the Cree would be major provisions. In fact, throughout the summer and fall of 1884 Little Pine attempted, with limited success, to interest the leaders of the Blackfoot in joining the Cree movement for treaty revision. Little Pine had invited the Blackfoot to a joint council with the Cree leaders on Little Pine's reserve scheduled for the spring of 1885.[70] If the Blackfoot joined the Cree,

Ottawa's ability to govern the Indians and control the west would be seriously jeopardized.

At the moment that the Cree movement seemed on the verge of success, Big Bear was losing control of his band. As he told the assembled chiefs at Duck Lake in the summer of 1884, his young men were listening to the warrior chief, Little Poplar, who was advocating killing government officials and Indian agents as a means of restoring Cree independence. Big Bear feared that if Little Poplar's course of action were adopted the Cree would fight an Indian war that they were certain to lose.[71]

Dewdney was aware of Little Poplar's growing influence on the young men of Big Bear's and the Battleford Assiniboine bands; however, he wished to wait until after January 1885 before taking any action, because after that date the new amendments to the Indian Act would be in effect. These amendments could be used to arrest and imprison Little Pine, Little Poplar, Big Bear, and Piapot, and thereby, Dewdney hoped, destroy the movements these chiefs led.[72] In anticipation of confrontations in 1885, Dewdney ordered that the guns and ammunition normally allotted to the Cree so they could hunt for food be withheld. In addition, Indian councils were prohibited, including the one scheduled for Duck Lake in the summer of 1885, to which all the Cree in Treaty 6 had been invited. Arrangements were made to place the Mounted Police at Battleford under Dewdney's command, and serious consideration was given to placing an artillery unit there also.[73]

To get improved intelligence, Dewdney hired more men to work as Indian agents with the Cree. These men were given broad discretionary powers and were to keep the commissioner informed on Cree activities. As well, English-speaking mixed-bloods, many of whom had worked for the Hudson's Bay Company and had the confidence of the Cree, were hired as farm instructors. There would now be a farm instructor on each Cree reserve, with explicit instructions to keep the Indian agent informed of what was happening on his reserve. Staff who had personality conflicts with any of the Cree leaders were either transferred or fired. Only Thomas Quinn, Indian agent at Fort Pitt, and his farming instructor, John Delaney, were not removed before March 1885, although both were slated for transfer.[74]

Dewdney found that his most important staffing move was the employment of Peter Ballendine, a former Hudson's Bay Company trader much trusted by the principal Cree leaders. Ballendine's job was to ingratiate himself with Big Bear and report on that chief's comings and goings. Ballendine won the confidence of Big Bear and reported upon how wrong Dewdney's earlier efforts to break up Big Bear's band had been. Because so many of Big Bear's original followers either joined Lucky Man, Thunderchild, or Little Pine's bands, Big Bear by 1884 was left with only the most recalcitrant opponents of the treaty.

These individuals were only lukewarm in support of their chief's non-violent efforts to get the treaty revised. They favoured instead the course of action advocated by Little Poplar. Ballendine believed that the government could expect trouble from the Big Bear and Little Poplar bands. However, Ballendine emphasized that there was little danger of a Cree-Métis alliance, for the Cree were refusing to meet with the Métis, and were rejecting all entreaties from the Métis suggesting the two should make common cause. Instead the Cree, under the leadership of Big Bear, Beardy, and Little Pine, were planning their own council for the summer of 1885.[75]

Ballendine also developed a new source of information in Poundmaker, who was also acting as a police informer. It was from Poundmaker that Dewdney and the policy learned that Little Pine was attempting to involve the Blackfoot in the summer of 1884, and wanted to do so in January 1885, but was prevented from doing so because of temporary blindness–a possible sign of malnutrition from the hunger that most Cree experienced in the extremely harsh winter of 1884–5. Little Pine had sought to get Poundmaker to encourage Crowfoot to join the Cree movement but Poundmaker refused to aid Little Pine, and when Little Pine recovered from his blindness, he went south to meet with Crowfoot.[76]

While Little Pine met with Crowfoot, Big Bear was being challenged for the leadership of his band by his son Imases, also called Curly, and by one of his headmen, Wandering Spirit. These two men were spokesmen for the younger men of Big Bear's Band, and wanted to work with Little Poplar. In the winter of 1885, Little Poplar was journeying constantly between Pitt and Battleford enlisting support for his plan of action. Although Ballendine could not get precise information on Little Poplar's plans, he did report that by March 1885 Big Bear had asserted himself and that the influence of Imases and Wandering Spirit had seemed to wane.[77]

On the basis of these and similar reports, Dewdney and the policy were convinced that, although a number of councils were expected in 1885, no violence was to be anticipated from the Cree. Nevertheless, Dewdney wished to prevent the Cree from holding their councils. His strategy was to make the Cree satisfied with the treaties. He therefore admitted in February 1885 that the government had violated the treaties and ordered delivery to the Cree of all goods the treaties had stipulated. In addition, he ordered a dramatic increase in their rations. If this failed to placate them he planned to arrest their leaders, use the police to keep the Cree on their reserves, and to depose any chief who attempted to attend an Indian council.[78]

Dewdney had the full support of Ottawa for his policy of arresting Cree leaders. The only reservations the prime minister expressed were that Dewdney have sufficient forces to make the arrests and that he provide enough evidence to justify the charges of incitement to an insurrection. Macdonald also volunteered to communicate with the stipendiary magistrates to assure their cooperation in imposing long prison terms for any Cree leader convicted of incitement.[79] Macdonald was willing to provide this assistance because Dewdney had earlier complained that he could not use preventive detention of Indian leaders because the magistrates 'only look at the evidence and the crime committed when giving out sentences,' rather than taking into consideration the nature of the man and the harm that he might do if he were released at an inopportune time.[80] All these preparations were complete when word reached Dewdney of the Métis clash with the Mounted Police at Duck Lake in March 1885.

The Riel Rebellion of 1885 provided Dewdney with a new instrument to make his coercive policy effective. The troops sent into the North-West to suppress the rebellion could be used to destroy the Cree movement for an Indian territory. The Cree themselves would provide the excuse Dewdney needed virtually to declare war on the bands and leaders who had led the Cree movement for treaty revision. During March 1885, the Cree did engage in some acts of violence that Dewdney chose to label acts of rebellion.

These acts were unrelated to the Cree movement for treaty revision. In fact, these acts that led to the subjugation of the Cree were committed by persons not involved with the Cree movement for autonomy. It is one of the ironic quirks of history that the leaders of the Cree movement had little or nothing to do with the events which would destroy that movement to which they had devoted ten years of their lives. Nevertheless, they would be held responsible for the actions of their desperate and hungry people. To heighten the irony, it was the Métis movement, from which the Cree had held aloof, which would give Dewdney the excuse to use military force to subjugate the Cree.

The Duck Lake clash coincided with a Cree Council on Sweetgrass Reserve. The council of the Battleford area Cree had been called to consider how they could press for increased rations. When word reached the Cree at Sweetgrass of the clash at Duck Lake, they felt that circumstances would make Indian Agent Rae willing to grant them more rations. Thus the Cree, taking their women and children with them to demonstrate their peaceful intent, set out for Battleford. Fear and panic prevailed at Battleford, for on learning of the Crees' approach, the town's citizens assumed that the Cree had thrown in their lot with the Métis. The town was evacuated; most townspeople took refuge in the Mounted Police post.[81]

When the Cree arrived at Battleford they found the town abandoned. They sent word to the police post that they wished to speak to the Indian agent, who refused to leave the safety of the post. The Cree women, seeing the abandoned stores and houses filled with food, began to help themselves. Then, fearing arrest by the police, the Cree left town. On the way back to their reserves, as well as on their way to town, the Cree assisted a number of Indian Department employees and settlers to cross the Battle River to get to the police post, thus demonstrating the pacific nature of their intentions.[82]

Rather than returning to their individual reserves, the Cree went to Poundmaker's, for as the leader in the Battleford district to whom the government had shown much favour in the past, Poundmaker was seen as the man best able to explain to the government what had happened at Battleford. A second significant reason was the deaths of two prominent Cree leaders: Red Pheasant, the night before the Cree left for Battleford, and Little Pine, the night they returned. As it was the practice of the Cree to leave the place where their leaders had expired, both bands left their reserves and went to Poundmaker's, who, given the fears the whites had concerning a Cree and Métis alliance, might possibly defuse any crisis. Thus, in March 1885, Poundmaker became the spokesman of the Battleford Cree.[83]

No sooner were the Cree at Poundmaker's then they were joined by the local Assiniboine, who insisted that a soldier's (war) tent be erected, for events at the Assiniboine reserves convinced them that an attack on the Indian camp was imminent. The Assiniboine explained that when word had reached them of the Duck Lake fight, a few of their young men sought revenge on farming instructor James Payne, who was blamed for the death of a girl. The girl's male relatives killed Payne and murdered farmer Barney Tremont. The Assiniboine now assumed that the Canadian authorities would behave in a similar manner to the Americans and blame all Indians for the actions of a few individuals.[84]

Erection of the soldier's tent meant that the warriors were in control of the camp and that Poundmaker and the civil authorities had to defer to them. It was at this time that the Métis appeal for aid was received. The Cree refused to assist the Métis, although they expected an attack on their camp. Watches were set on the roads, and protection was offered to the Métis at Bresaylor, for the settlers there had earned the enmity of the Batoche Métis. As long as no military or police forces came towards the Cree camp, the Cree remained on their reserves and did not interfere with anyone going to or leaving Battleford. The Mounted Police detachment from Fort Pitt and Colonel Otter's military unit arrived in Battleford without encountering any Indians. Nevertheless, reports from the police and local officials maintained that the town was under siege.[85]

While the Battleford Cree were preparing their defences, Big Bear's band was making trouble for itself. Big Bear was absent from his camp when the members of his band heard about the fight at Duck Lake. Wandering Spirit and Imases sought to use the opportunity presented by the Métis uprising to seek revenge for the insults and abuses perpetrated against the Cree by Indian Agent Thomas Quinn and Farming Instructor Delaney. Quinn had physically abused some of the Indian men, while Delaney had cuckolded others before he brought a white bride to Frog Lake in late 1884. Big Bear's headmen demanded that the two officials open the storehouse to the Cree, and when they refused to do so, they were murdered. This set off further acts of violence that resulted in the murder of all the white men in the camp save one.[86]

On his return to camp Big Bear ended further acts of violence. Although unable to prevent a minor skirmish between his young men and a small police patrol, he convinced his warriors to allow the police detachment at Fort Pitt to withdraw from the post without being attacked and to guarantee safety to the civilian residents of the Frog Lake and Fort Pitt regions. Big Bear then led his people north, where he hoped they would be out of harm's way and not engage in further acts of violence.[87]

Beardy also lost control of his band. He and the neighbouring One Arrow band had reserves next to Batoche. Before the clash with the police, the Métis had come to the One Arrow Reserve, captured Farming Instructor Peter Thompkins, and threatened the Cree band with destruction unless the Cree aided the Métis. Some of the younger men of One Arrow's band agreed to do so.[88] The Métis made the same threat against Beardy and his band, and although a few of his young men joined the Métis, Beardy and most of his people remained neutral.[89] It is doubtful that the Cree would have aided the Métis without the threat of violence. Earlier, the Cree of the Duck Lake region had threatened hostilities against the Métis, for the Métis had settled on One Arrow's Reserve and demanded that the government turn over to them some of One Arrow's Reserve. Ottawa, fearing the Métis more than the Cree in 1880, acquiesced. Over the next four years, one task of the local Indian agent and the police was to reconcile the Cree with the Métis of the Batoche region.[90]

The Cree acts of violence in March 1885 were the excuse Dewdney needed to justify the use of troops against them. He maintained that the Battleford, Fort Pitt, and Duck Lake Cree were part of the Riel Rebellion. Privately, Dewdney reported to Ottawa that he saw the events at Battleford and Frog Lake as the acts of a desperate, starving people and unrelated to what the Métis were doing.[91] In fact, Dewdney had sought in late March to open negotiations with the Battleford Cree, but Rae refused to meet the Cree leaders. Subsequent efforts to open negotiations ended in failure because there was no way to get a message to Poundmaker, and after Colonel Otter's attack on the Cree camp any thought of negotiations was dropped.[92]

Publicly Dewdney proclaimed that the Cree were part of the Métis uprising. He issued a proclamation that any Indian who left his reserve was to be regarded as a rebel.[93] As well, to intimidate Piapot and the Treaty 4 Cree,

Dewdney stationed troops on their reserves. To prevent an alliance of Blackfoot and Cree, Dewdney announced that he was stationing troops at Swift Current and Medicine Hat. Dewdney took these steps, as he confided to Macdonald, because he feared that the Cree might still attempt to take action on their own cause, and he was concerned because in the previous year the Cree had attempted to enlist the Blackfoot in the movement to revise the treaties.[94]

The military commander in the North-West, General F.D. Middleton, was not as concerned about the problems with the Cree. He wanted to concentrate his attention on the Métis. Although he did send troops under Colonel William Otter to Swift Current, he refused to order them to Battleford to lift the alleged siege until he received word of the Frog Lake massacre. Otter was then ordered to lift the 'siege' and protect Battleford from Indian attack, but he was not to take the offensive. At the same time General Thomas Strange was ordered to bring Big Bear under control.

Otter reached Battleford without seeing an Indian. He was upset that he and his troops would not see action. He therefore proposed that he attack the Indian camp at Poundmaker's Reserve. Middleton vetoed the plan, but Dewdney welcomed it as a means to bring the Cree under government control. Taking the Lieutenant-Governor's approval to be paramount to Middleton's veto, Otter launched his attack. The engagement, known as the Battle of Cut Knife Hill, almost ended in total disaster for Otter's force. Only the Cree fear that they would suffer the same fate as Sitting Bull after the Battle of the Little Big Horn saved Otter's troops from total annihilation.[95]

The tale of the subsequent military campaigns against the Cree by Strange and Middleton and the voluntary surrenders of Poundmaker and Big Bear is found in detail in Stanley's *Birth of Western Canada* and Desmond Morton's *The Last War Drum*. With Big Bear and Poundmaker in custody, Dewdney prepared to use the courts in the manner he had planned before the Riel Rebellion. Both Cree leaders were charged with treason-felony, despite Dewdney's knowledge that neither man had engaged in an act of rebellion. Eyewitnesses to the events at Fort Pitt, Frog Lake, and Battleford all made clear that neither chief was involved in the murders and looting that had occurred. In fact, many of these people served as defence witnesses.[96] As Dewdney informed the prime minister, the diaries and letters of the murdered officials at Frog Lake showed that until the day of the 'massacre' there was 'no reason to believe that our Indians were even dissatisfied much less contemplated violence.'[97] Ballendine's reports indicated that there were no plans for violence, that the Cree were not involved with the Métis, and that they planned no rebellion. Dewdney believed that the Cree had not 'even thought, intended or wished that the uprising would reach the proportion it has ... Things just got out of control.'[98] As Dewdney related to the prime minister, had the people living in the region not been new settlers from the east, and had they not fled in panic, much of the 'raiding' and looting would not have occurred. In regions where people had not abandoned their homes no raiding occurred.[99] Therefore, the charges against Big Bear and Poundmaker were designed to remove the leadership of the Cree movement for revision of the treaties. They were charged to elicit prison sentences that would have the effect of coercing the Cree to accept government control. The trails were conducted to have the desired result, and both Big Bear and Poundmaker were convicted and sentenced to three years in Stoney Mountain Penitentiary.[100] Neither man served his full term, and both died a short time after their release from prison.

By the end of 1885, Dewdney had succeeded in subjugating the Cree. Big Bear was in prison, Little Pine was dead, and Piapot was intimidated by having troops stationed on his reserve. Dewdney had deprived the Cree of their principal leaders and of their autonomy. He used the military to disarm and impoverish the Cree by confiscating their horses and carts; he increased the size of the Mounted Police force, and used the police to arrest Cree leaders who protested against his policies; he broke up Cree bands, deposed Cree leaders, and forbade any Indian to be off his reserve without permission from the Indian Agent.[101] By 1890, through vigorous implementation of the Indian Act, Dewdney and his successor, Hayter Reed, had begun the process of making the Cree an administered people.

The record of the Canadian government in dealing with the Cree is thus not one of honourable fair-mindedness and justice as the traditional interpretation portrays. As Dewdney admitted in 1885, the treaties' promises and provisions were not being fulfilled, and Dewdney himself had taken steps to assure Canadian control over the Cree, which were themselves violations of the treaties. Thus, he had refused to grant the Cree the reserve sites they selected; he had refused to distribute the ammunition and twine the treaties required. His plans for dealing with the Cree leaders were based on a political use of the legal and judicial system, and ultimately he made use of the military, the police, and the courts in a political manner to achieve his goals of subjugating the Cree. Only by ignoring these facts can one continue to perpetuate the myth of Canada's just and honourable Indian policy from 1870 to 1885.

NOTES

This article is from *Canadian Historical Review* 64 (4) (1983). Reprinted with permission.

1 Doug Owram, *Promise of Eden: The Canadian Expansionist Movement and the Idea of the West, 1856–1900* (Toronto 1980), 131–4
2 G.F.G. Stanley, *The Birth of Western Canada: A History of the Riel Rebellions* (Toronto 1960)
3 Ibid., 206–15
4 Ibid., vii–viii, 196, 216–36. It should be noted that the traditional interpretation of a Cree rebellion in association with the Métis has been challenged by R. Allen, 'Big Bear,' *Saskatchewan History* 25 (1972); W.B. Fraser, 'Big Bear, Indian Patriot,' *Alberta Historical Review* 14 (1966): 1–13; Rudy Wiebe in his fictional biography, *The Temptations of Big Bear* (Toronto 1973) and in his biography of Big Bear in the *Dictionary of Canadian Biography* [DCB], XI, 1881–90 (Toronto 1982), 597–601; and Norma Sluman, *Poundmaker* (Toronto 1967). However, none of these authors deals with Canada's Indian policy, and none examines what the Cree were doing in the period 1876–85.
5 Alexander Morris, *The Treaties of Canada with the Indians of Manitoba and the North-West Territories* (Toronto 1880), 37; Public Archives of Manitoba, Adams G. Archibald Papers (hereafter cited as PAM Archibald Papers, letters)
6 National Archives of Canada, Record Group 10 Indian Affairs Files, vol. 3571, file 124–2, also vol. 3603, file 2036 (hereafter cited as NA, RG 10, vol., file). See also Morris, *Treaties of Canada*, 25–43, and 126–7, for a printed account of the negotiations and the texts of the original and renegotiated treaties, 313–20, 338–42. Two articles by John Taylor, 'Canada's Northwest Indian Policy in the 1870's: Traditional Premises and Necessary Innovations' and 'Two Views on the Meaning of Treaties Six and Seven' in *The Spirit of Alberta Indian Treaties* (Montreal 1980), 3–7 and 9–45 respectively, provide a good account of the Indian contribution and attitude towards the treaties.
7 Morris, *Treaties of Canada*, 44–76; on 120–3 Morris demonstrates how he had to make Treaty 3 the model for the Qu'Appelle Treaty to get the Saulteaux and Cree of the Qu'Appelle River region to accept what he originally offered them. Compare Treaties 1–6 to see what the government was forced to concede. Also see Taylor's 'Traditional Premises' for Indian contributions to the negotiation process.
8 NA, RG 10, vol. 3586, file 1137, Lieutenant-Governor Morris to Secretary of State for provinces, 13 Sept. 1872; NA, RG 10, vol. 3576, file 378 entire file; vol. 3609, file 3229; vol. 3604, file 2543; vol. 3636, file 6694–1
9 NA, RG 10, vol. 3612, file 4012, entire file: PAM Archibald Papers, W.J. Christie to George W. Hill, 26 April 1871; Archibald to Secretary of State for the Provinces, 5 Jan 1872; also letters in note 15; William Francis Butler, *The Great Lone Land* (Rutland, VT 1970), 360–2, 368; NA, Manuscript Group 26A, John A. Macdonald Papers, vol. 104, entire volume (hereafter cited as NA, MG 26A, letters); PAM, Archibald Papers, Joseph Howe to Archibald, 30 June 1872; PAM, Alexander Morris Papers, Lt Governor's Collection, Morris to Minister of the Interior, 7 July 1873 (hereafter cited as PAM, Morris Papers, letter); NA, RG 10, vol. 3625, file 5366, Morris to Minister of the Interior, David Laird, 22 July and 4 Aug. 1875; RG 10, vol. 3624, file 5152, Colonel French, Commissioner of the NWMP to the Minister of Justice, 6 and 19 Aug. 1875; Morris, 170–1; RG 10, vol. 3612, file 4012, entire file; Adams G. Archibald Papers, Petition of James Seenum to Archibald, 9 Jan. 1871, and attached letters of Kehewin, Little

Hunter, and Kiskion; Archibald to Secretary of State for the provinces, 5 Jan. 1872

10 Two excellent studies of the Cree in the pre-1870 era are those by Arthur J. Ray, *Indians in the Fur Trade: Their Role as Hunters, Trappers, and Middlemen in the Lands Southwest of Hudson Bay 1660–1870* (Toronto 1974), and David G. Mandelbaum, *The Plains Cree*, XXXVII, Part II of Anthropological Papers of the American Museum of Natural History (New York 1940).

11 Ibid. An excellent study of the Cree expansion is the unpublished MA thesis by John S. Milloy, 'The Plains Cree: A Preliminary Trade and Military Chronology, 1670–1870' (Carleton University 1972); also Henry John Moberly and William B. Cameron, *When Fur Was King* (Toronto 1929), 208–12, describes part of the last phase of this movement. The shrinking range of buffalo and how the Cree reacted are also discussed in Frank Gilbert Roe, *The North American Buffalo: A Critical Study of the Species in Its Wild State* (Toronto 1951), 282–333.

12 Henry Youle Hind, *Narrative of the Canadian Red River Exploring Expedition of 1857 and of the Assiniboine and Saskatchewan Exploring Expedition of 1858* (Edmonton 1971), vol. I, 334; Irene Spry, *The Palliser Expedition: An Account of John Palliser's British North American Expedition, 1857–1860* (London 1964), 59–60; Viscount Milton and W.B. Cheadle, *The Northwest Passage by Land, Being the Narrative of an Expedition from the Atlantic to the Pacific* (Toronto 1970), 66–7; Edwin Thompson Perry, *Five Indian Tribes of the Upper Missouri: Sioux, Arickaras, Assiniboine, Crees, Crow* (Norman, OK 1969), 99–137; J. Hines, *The Red Indians of the Plains: Thirty Years' Missionary Experience in Saskatchewan* (Toronto 1916), 78–80, 88–91

13 Morris, *Treaties of Canada*, 77–123 and 168–239, discusses the negotiations of Treaties 4 and 6 with the Cree and how he was forced to modify his offer. Also described is the Cree concern about their land. The reaction of the Mackenzie government is detailed in NA, RG 10, vol. 3636, file 6694–2, and in particular, Minister of the Interior Report to Privy Council, 31 Jan. 1877, and order-in-council, 10 Feb. 1877.

14 Milloy, 'The Plains Cree,' 250–62; Alexander Johnson, *The Battle at Belly River: Stories of the Last Great Indian Battle* (Lethbridge 1966)

15 Hind, *Narrative*, vol. I, 334, 360–1, carried reports of Mistickoos or Short Stick's comments on a council of Cree leaders that resolved to limit white and Métis hunting privileges. Milton and Cheadle, *Northwest Passage*, 66, 67, contains comments on the Cree determination to limit non-Indian involvement in the hunt. PAM, E. Adams Archibald Papers, letter #200, Macdonald to Archibald, 14 Feb. 1871; letter #170, English halfbreeds to Archibald, 10 Jan. 1871, all stress that Cree were taking action to limit non-Indian involvement in the buffalo hunt.

16 Morris, *Treaties of Canada*, 241

17 Interview with Walter Gordon, director of the Indian Rights and Treaties Program, Federation of Saskatchewan Indians, March 1974. Poundmaker made a similar statement in an interview quoted in 'Indian Affairs,' *Saskatchewan Herald*, 2 Aug. 1880. The importance of Big Bear, Piapot, and Little Pine cannot be underestimated, for of those Cree chiefs who took treaty only Sweetgrass had the standing of these men, and Sweetgrass died within a few months of taking treaty.

18 Morris, *Treaties of Canada*, 85–7. More detailed information on the adhesions of Piapot and Cheekuk is to be found in NA, RG 10, vol. 3625, file 5489, W.J. Christie to Laird, 7 Oct. 1875.

19 Morris, *Treaties of Canada*, 240, for the quotation. See 355 for the clauses in Treaty 6 respecting acceptance of Canadian laws.

20 Ibid., 174

21 Fraser, 'Big Bear, Indian Patriot,' 76–7, agrees that Big Bear was not referring specifically to hanging but to the effect the treaty would have on the Cree.

22 NA, RG 10, vol. 3656, file 9093, Agent Dickieson to Lt-Gov. Laird, 14 Sept. 1877

23 NA, RG 10, vol. 3648, file 8380; vol. 3655, file 9000, Laird to Minister of the Interior, 9 May 1878

24 NA, RG 10, vol. 3655, file 9000, Laird to Minister of the Interior, 9 May 1878; vol. 3636, file 9092, Laird to Superintendent-General, 19 Nov. 1877; RG 10, vol. 3670, file 10,771, Laird to Minister of the Interior, 12 Nov. 1878; RG 10, vol. 3672, file 10,853, Dickieson to Meredith, 2 April 1878; vol. 3656, file 9092, Inspector James Walker to Laird, 5 Sept. 1877; Department of Indian Affairs and Northern Development, Ottawa, file 1/1–11–3, Laird to Minister of the Interior, 30 Dec. 1878; Dickieson to Laird, 9 Oct. 1878; Walker to Laird, 4 and 26 Feb. 1879 (hereafter cited as DIAND, file, letter)

25 NA, RG 10, vol. 3655, file 1002, Laird to Minister of the Interior, 9 May 1878; vol. 3672, file 19,853, Dickieson to Vankoughnet, 26 July 1878; NA, MG 26A, E.D. Clark to Fred White, 16 July 1879

26 'News from the Plains,' *Saskatchewan Herald*, 18 Nov. 1878; 'From the Plains,' *Saskatchewan Herald*, 5 May 1879. 'Contradictory News from the West,' *Fort Benton Record*, 31 Jan. 1879

27 NA, RG 10, vol. 3672, file 10,853, M.G. Dickieson to Vankoughnet, 26 July 1878; *Opening Up the West: Being the Official Reports to Parliament of the North-West Mounted Police from 1874–1881* (Toronto 1973), Report for 1878, 21

28 NA, RG 10, vol. 3704, file 17,858, entire file; vol. 3648, file 162–2, entire file. Ibid., vol. 3699, file 16,580, order-in-council, 9 Oct. 1879; vol. 3766, file 22,541; E.T. Galt to Superintendent-General of Indian Affairs, 27 July 1880; vol. 3730, file 26,279, entire file; vol. 3757, file 21,397, entire file

29 House of Commons, Ottawa, *Sessional Papers*, XVII (1885), Report No. 3, 157 (hereafter cited as CSP, vol., year, report); Edward Ahenakew, *Voices of the Plains Cree*, ed. Ruth Buck (Toronto 1973), 26. Dewdney in adopting this tactic simply copied what the fur-trading companies had done in the past. The Cree tolerated such practices because they improved the opportunities to have better access to European goods. See Arthur J. Ray and Donald Freeman, *'Give Us Good Measure': An Economic Analysis of Relations between the Indians and the Hudson's Bay Company before 1763* (Toronto 1978), passim. Ray, *Indians in the Fur Trade*, passim., deals with the same practice in the post-1763 period. Mandelbaum, *The Plains Cree*, 105–10, discusses the nature of Cree political organization and leadership that explains their acceptance of such practices.

30 Morris, *Treaties of Canada*, 366–7. DIAND, Treaty Annuity Pay Sheets for 1879. More than 1000 Plains Cree took treaty for the first time in 1879 under Little Pine, Thunderchild, and Lucky Man. Others from Little Pine's and Big Bear's bands had already taken treaty a year earlier as part of Thunder Companion's band, while others joined Poundmaker, and the three Cree bands settled in the Peace Hills. A portion of the Assiniboine also took treaty under Mosquito in

1878, while many of the northern Saulteaux who had followed Yellow Sky took treaty in 1878 under the leadership of Moosomin.

31 NA, RG 10, vol. 3745, file 29506–4, vol. 2, Ray to Reed, 23 April 1883; vol. 3668, file 9644, Reed to Commissioner, 23 Dec. 1883. Although these materials refer to events in the Battleford district, as will be demonstrated, the tactics in 1883–4 were similar to, if not exactly the same as, those used in the Cypress Hills between 1879 and 1882. That they were not better recorded for the earlier period is due to the fact that the government had fewer men working with the Indians, and did not have as effective supervision in 1879–82 period as it did at Battleford. Also much of the police and Indian Affairs material relating to this region in the 1879–82 period have been lost or destroyed.

32 NA, RG 10, vol. 3730, file 36,279, entire file; vol. 3668, file 10,440, Agent Allen to L. Vankoughnet, 11 Nov. 1878. CSP, vol. XVI (1883), Paper No. 5, 197. *Settlers and Rebels: Being the Reports tc Parliament of the Activities of the Royal North-West Mounted Police Force from 1882–1885* (Toronto 1973), Report for 1882, 4–6 (hereafter cited as *Settlers and Rebels*)

33 NA, RG 10, vol. 3730, file 26,219, Report of surveyor Patrick to Superintendent-General, 16 Dec. 1880; vol. 3716, file 22,546, Assistant Commissioner E.T. Galt to Superintendent-General, 27 July 1880; vol. 3757, files 31,393 and 31,333; vol. 3757, file 20,034. NA, MG 26A, vol. 210, Dewdney to Macdonald, 3 Oct. 1880

34 NA, RG 10, vol. 3652, file 8589, parts 1 and 2, entire file; vol. 3691, file 13,893, entire file. The *Benton Weekly Record* throughout the spring and summer of 1880 carried reports of Cree and Assiniboine horse-stealing raids, and reports of what the Cree were doing in Montana. On 7 May 1880 the paper carried an article entiled 'Starving Indians,' which was a strong denunciation of Canada's Indian policy and the effect it had on the Cree.

35 NA, MG 26A, vol. 210, Dewdney to Macdonald, 29 Oct. 1880; *Saskatchewan Herald*, 14 Feb. 1881

36 NA, MG 26A, vol. 210, Dewdney to Macdonald, 26 Oct. 1880, and 23 April 1880; *Saskatchewan Herald*, 14, 28 Feb. 1881

37 NA, MG 26A, vol. 210, Dewdney to MacPherson, 4 July 1881; vol. 247, Galt to MacPherson , 14 July 1881; 'Edmonton,' *Saskatchewan Herald*, 12 Nov. 1881

38 Ibid., also NA, MG 26A, vol. 210, Dewdney to Macdonald, 19 June 1881; vol. 247, Galt to Vankoughnet, 16 July 1881. NA, RG 10, vol. 3739, file 28,748–1, Dewdney to Macdonald, 3 April 1882; Fred White to Minister of the Interior, 9 June 1882; Freylinghausen to Sackville-West, 9 June 1882. *Saskatchewan Herald*, 1 Aug. 1881 'Starving Indians,' *Benton Weekly Record*, 14 July, 25 Aug., 1 Sept., and 13 Oct. 1881

39 NA, RG 10. vol. 3739, file 28,478–1, C.G. Denny to Commissioner, 24 Oct. 1881; vol. 3768, file 33,642; vol. 3603, file 20,141, McIlree to Dewdney, 21 June 1882. Glenbow Institute, Calgary, Edgar Dewdney Papers, V, file 57, Irvine to Dewdney, 24 June 1882 (hereafter cited as Dewdney Papers, vol., file, letter). *Saskatchewan Herald*, 24 June 1882; *Edmonton Bulletin*, 17 June 1882

40 NA, RG 10, vol. 3768, file 33,642, entire file

41 NA, MG 26A, vol. 210, Dewdney to Macdonald, 19 June 1881; vol. 247, Galt to Vankoughnet, 16 July 1881. *Saskatchewan Herald*, 1 Aug. 1881. 'Starving Indians,' *Benton Weekly Record*, 14 July 1881. See also *Benton Weekly Record*, 25 Aug., 1 Sept., and 13 Oct. 1881.

42 Morris, *Treaties of Canada*, 205, 218, 352–3

43 NA, RG 10, vol. 3604, file 2589, entire file. See also *Settlers and Rebels*, 1882 Report. See also Dewdney Papers, V, file 57, White to Irvine, 29 Aug. 1882. NA, RG 10, vol. 3604, file 2589. 'The Repatriated Indians,' *Saskatchewan Herald*, 5 Aug. 1882. 'From the South,' *Saskatchewan Herald*, 21 May 1882; 'Back on the Grub Pile,' *Saskatchewan Herald*, 24 June 1882

44 Dewdney Papers, V, file 57, Irvine to Dewdney, 24 June 1882 and 25 Sept. 1882. *Settlers and Rebels*, 1882 Report, 4, 5. CSP, XVI (1883), Paper No. 5, 197. NA, RG 10, vol. 3604, file 2589. 'Repatriated Indians,' *Saskatchewan Herald*, 5 Aug. 1882

45 Ibid.; Dewdney Papers, IV, file 45, White to Dewdney, 12 Oct. 1882. *Saskatchewan Herald*, 14 Oct. 1882. 'Big Bear and Others,' and the 'I.D.,' *Edmonton Bulletin*, 21 Oct. 1882

46 Dewdney Papers, IV, file 45, White to Dewdney, 17 Oct. 1882. NA, MG 26A, vol. 289, Vankoughnet to Macdonald, 2 Nov. 1882

47 NA, MG 26A, Dewdney to J.A. Macdonald, 2 Sept. 1883. NA, RG 10, vol. 3682, file 12,667, Dewdney to Superintendent-General, 28 April 1884

48 NA, RG 10, vol. 3668, file 10,644, Reed to Commissioner, 23 Dec. 1883. Robert Jefferson, *Fifty Years on the Saskatchewan* (Battleford 1929), 103

49 NA, RG 10, vol. 3668, file 10,644, Reed to Commissioner, 23 Dec. 1883. *Edmonton Bulletin*, 9 Feb. 1884; *Saskatchewan Herald*, 24 Nov. 1883

50 NA, MG 26A, vol. 289, Vankoughnet to Macdonald, 4, 10 Dec. 1883; vol. 104, Deputy Superintendent-General to T. Quinn, 21 Sept. 1883; Dewdney to Superintendent-General, 27 Sept. 1883; Deputy Superintendent-General to Reed, 10 April 1884; vol. 212, Dewdney to Macdonald, 2 Jan. 1883 [sic! Given the contents of the letter, it is obvious Dewdney forgot that a new year had begun the previous day]; vol. 91, Dewdney to Macdonald, 24 July 1884, another letter but without a date, which was probably written in the first week of Aug. 1884; vol. 107, entire file. NA, RG 10, vol. 3664, file 9843, entire file

51 NA, RG 10, vol. 3616, file 10,181. Burton Deane, *Mounted Police Life in Canada: A Record of Thirty-One Years in Service, 1883–1914* (Toronto 1973), 140–53. Isabell Andrews, 'Indian Protest against Starvation: The Yellow Calf Incident of 1884,' *Saskatchewan History*, 28 (1975): 4–52. *Edmonton Bulletin*, 7 Jan., 3 Feb., 7, 28 July, and 4 Aug. 1883

52 Dewdney Papers, V, file 58, Dewdney to Superintendent-General, 29 Feb. 1884; NA, MG 26A, vol. 211, Dewdney to Macdonald, 6 Oct. 1883; vol. 212, Reed to Dewdney, 15 Feb. 1884; Dewdney to Macdonald, 16 Feb. and 9 April 1884

53 NA, RG 10, vol. 3682, file 12,667, Dewdney to Superintendent-General, 28 April 1884; vol. 3686, file 13,168, entire file; vol. 3745, file 29,506-4(2), Reed to Colonel Irvine, 18 May 1884

54 Ibid., vol. 3745, file 29,506–4(2), Reed to Irvine, 18 May 1884; Irvine to Comptroller Fred White, 27 May 1884; White to Vankoughnet, 19 May 1884

55 Ibid., Agent Macdonald to Commissioner, 29 May 1884; vol. 3655, file 9026, Dewdney to Superintendent-General, 13 June 1884

56 NA, RG 10, vol. 3745, file 29,506-4(2), Reed to Superintendent-General, 19 April 1884. Similar report in vol. 3576, file 309B. NA, MG 26A, file 37, Dewdney to Macdonald, 3 May 1884. Dewdney's request and actions were contrary to what the Cree had been told about how reserve sites could be chosen, as were the government's actions in denying the Cree reserves in the Cypress Hills and

forcing them to move north. See Morris, *Treaties in Canada*, passim. NA, RG 10, vol. 3576, file 309B, Vankoughnet to Dewdney, 10 May 1884; MG 26A, vol. 104, Dewdney to Superintendent-General, 14 June 1884. Campbell Innes, *The Cree Rebellion of 1884: Sidelights of Indian Conditions Subsequent to 1876* (Battleford 1926), 'Fineday Interview,' 13–15. *Saskatchewan Herald*, 19 April and 17 May 1884

57 NA, RG 10, vol. 3576, file 309B, Reed to Superintendent-General, 19 April 1884. Reed to Vankoughnet, 19 April 1884; Ray to Commissioner, 23 April 1884; Reed to Superintendent-General, 20 May 1884. Dewdney Papers, III, file 36, Dewdney to Macdonald, 12 June 1884

58 NA, RG 10, vol. 3576, file 309B, Ray to Commissioner, 19, 21 June 1884; Crozier to Dewdney, 22 June 1884. Jefferson, *Fifty Years*, 108–9. Innes, *The Cree Rebellion of 1884*, 13–17, 28

59 NA, RG 10, vol. 3576, file 309B, Ray to Commissioner, 28 June 1884; see also Rae to Dewdney, 9 June 1884. Innes, 'McKay Interview,' 44. NA, RG 10, vol. 3576, file 309A, Dewdney to Ray, 5 July 1884

60 NA, RG 10, vol. 3576, file 309B, Ray to Dewdney, 23 June 1884; Crozier to Dewdney, 23 June 1884

61 Dewdney Papers, III, file 37, Macdonald to Dewdney, 18 July 1884, 11 Aug. 1884, and 2 Sept. 1884; IV, file 45, Macdonald to White, 15 Sept. 1884. NA, RG 10, vol. 3576, file 309A, Vankoughnet to Dewdney, 27 July 1884

62 NA, RG 10, vol. 3576, file 309B, Ray to Commissioner, 30 June 1884; file 309A, Ray to Commissioner, 24, 29 July 1884. NA, MG 26A, vol. 212, Dewdney to Macdonald, 14 July 1884; J.A. MacRae to Commissioner, 7 Aug. 1884; vol. 107, Ray to Commissioner, 29 July 1884

63 NA, RG 10, vol. 3745, file 29,506–4(2), Dewdney to Superintendent-General, 7 Aug. 1884; vol. 3576, file 309A, Ray to Dewdney, 19 July 1884. NA, MG 26A, vol. 104, Dewdney to Department, 19 July 1884

64 NA, RG 10, vol. 3576, file 309B, Ray to Commissioner, 30 June 1884; file 309A, Ray to Commissioner, 24, 29 July 1884. NA, MG 26A, vol. 212, Dewdney to Macdonald, 14 July 1884; J.A. MacRae to Commissioner, 7 Aug. 1884; vol. 107, Ray to Commissioner, 29 July 1884

65 NA, MG 26A, vol. 107, Ray to Commissioner, 29 July and 2 Aug. 1884; J.A. MacRae to Commissioner, 29 July 1884

66 NA, RG 10, vol. 3697, file 15,423, J.A. MacRae to Dewdney, 25 Aug. 1884

67 Ibid., Reed to Superintendent-General, 23 Jan. 1885; Reed to Dewdney, 22, 25 Aug. 1884. NA, MG 26A, vol. 107, J.A. MacRae to Commissioner, 29 July 1884; J.M. Ray to Commissioner, 2 Aug. 1884; MacRae to Commissioner, 5 Aug. 1884; vol. 212, MacRae to Commissioner, 7 Aug. 1884. NA, RG 10, vol. 3756, file 309A, J.M. Ray to Commissioner, 24, 25 July 1884. 'Big Bear Rises to Speak,' *Saskatchewan Herald*, 5 Aug. 1882. *Saskatchewan Herald*, 25 July and 9 Aug. 1884

68 Ibid., NA, RG 10, vol. 3576, file 309A, Commissioner to Ray, 7 Aug. 1884. Ray to Commissioner, 29 July 1884; see also in NA, MG 26A, vol. 107. Dewdney Papers, VI, file 69, Crozier to Comptroller, NWMP, 27 July 1884. NA, MG 26A, vol. 212, Dewdney to Macdonald, 8 Aug. 1884

69 NA, MG 26A, vol. 107, Reed to Dewdney, 23, 24, 25 Aug., 4 Sept. 1884; Dewdney, to Macdonald, 5 Sept. 1884

70 NA, RG 10, vol. 3576, file 309A, Begg to Commissioner, 20 Feb. 1885; 'Indian Affairs,' *Saskatchewan Herald*, 31 Oct. 1884
71 Dewdney Papers, VI, file 66, Reed to Dewdney, 4 Sept. 1884
72 Statutes of Canada, 43 Vict. I, 27, 'An Act to Amend the Indian Act, 1880,' 12 April 1884. NA, MG 26A, vol. 107, Dewdney to Macdonald, 24 Aug. 1884
73 NA, MG 26A, vol. 212, Reed to Dewdney, 7 Sept. 1884; vol. 107, Dewdney to Macdonald, 24 Aug. 1884
74 NA, RG 10, vol. 3576, file 309A, Reed to Dewdney, 12 Sept. 1884; vol. 3745, file 29,506–4(2), Reed to Dewdney, 14 Sept. 1884; vol. 3704, file 17,799, entire file; vol. 3664, file 9834 and 9843; vol. 3761, file 30,836, entire file; Dewdney Papers IV, file 45, Reed to Dewdney, 12 Sept. 1884; vol. IV, file 47, Crozier to Comptroller, NWMP, 4 Nov. 1884; V, file 57, Crozier to Dewdney, 30 Jan. 1885
75 NA, RG 10, vol. 3582, file 749, Ballendine to Reed, 8 Nov. and 26 Dec. 1884
76 NA, RG 10, vol. 3582, file 949, P. Ballendine to Reed, 20 Nov., 26 Dec., 2 Jan., 1885; J.M. Ray to Commissioner, 27 Dec. 1884; Crozier to Commissioner, NWMP, 14 Jan. 1885; vol. 3576, file 309A, Magnus Begg to Dewdney, 20 Feb. 1885. NA, MG 26A, extract of Ray to Dewdney, 24 Jan. 1885. Ray, Ballendine, and Crozier when they reported on Little Pine mentioned that their principal source of information was Poundmaker, although Ballendine did get some of his information directly from Little Pine himself.
77 NA, RG 10, vol. 3582, file 949, Ballendine to Reed, 10 Oct. and 26 Dec. 1884, and 2 Jan. and 16 March 1885; Ballendine to Dewdney, 19 March 1885. NA, MG 26A, vol. 107, extract of Ray to Dewdney, 24 Jan. 1885. NA, Manuscript Group 27IC4, Edgar Dewdney Papers, II, Francis Dickens to Officer Commanding, Battleford, 27 Oct. 1884 (hereafter cited as NA, MG 27IC4, vol., letter)
78 NA, MG 26A, vol. 117, Dewdney to Macdonald, 9 Feb. 1885. NA, RG 10, vol. 3676, file 309A, Dewdney to Vankoughnet, 12 Feb. 1885
79 NA, RG 10, vol. 3705, file 17,193, Vankoughnet to Dewdney, 5 Feb. 1885; Vankoughnet to Macdonald, 31 Jan. 1885; vol. 3582, file 949, Vankoughnet to Reed, 28 Jan. 1885. Dewdney Papers, III, file 38, Macdonald to Dewdney, 23 Feb. 1885
80 NA, RG 10, vol. 3576, file 309A, Dewdney to Vankoughnet, 12 Feb. 1885
81 Jefferson, *Fifty Years*, 125
82 Ibid., 126–8. NA, MG 26A, deposition, William Lightfoot to J.A. MacKay, 31 May 1885
83 Jefferson, *Fifty Years*, 127, 130, 138
84 Innes, 'Fine Day Interview,' 185. Sluman, *Poundmaker*, 199–200, 184–5. Jefferson, *Fifty Years*, 130–8
85 Desmond Morton, *The Last War Drum* (Toronto 1972), 98–102. Jefferson, *Fifty Years*, 125–40
86 NA, RG 10, vol. 3755, file 30,973, Reed to Commissioner, 18 June 1881; see also material cited in note 72 above. William B. Cameron, *Blood Red the Sun* (Edmonton 1977), 33–61, vividly describes the slaughter at Frog Lake.
87 Cameron, *Blood Red the Sun*, passim
88 Charles Mulvaney, *The History of the North-West Rebellion of 1885* (Toronto 1885), 212–16. *Settlers and Rebels*, 1882 Report, 22, 26–7. NA, RG 10, vol. 3584, file 1130, 1, Superintendent Herchmer to Dewdney, 5 April 1885
89 Ibid.

90 NA, RG 10, vol. 3697, file 15,446 entire file; vol. 3598, file 1411, entire file; vol. 7768, file 2109–2; vol. 3794, file 46,584
91 NA, MG 27IC4, vol. 7, letters, Dewdney to White, March–Apr. 1885. This correspondence reveals that in early April Dewdney believed that he had to deal with an Indian uprising. However, he did admit that this impression was based on scanty and often faulty or false information. By mid-April, Dewdney makes clear to White, the NWMP comptroller, that he did not believe that he was dealing with either an Indian uprising or a rebellion.
92 NA, MG 27IC4, vol. 1, Dewdney to Begg, 3 May 1885; vol. 4, Dewdney to Middleton, 30 March 1885. NA, RG 10, vol. 3584, file 1130, Dewdney to Ray, 7 May 1885. Jefferson, *Fifty Years*, 128–33
93 NA, RG 10, vol. 3584, file 1120. Proclamation of 6 May 1885
94 NA, MG 26A, vol. 107, Dewdney to Macdonald, 6 April 1885
95 Morton, *The Last War Drum*, 96–110
96 Cameron, *Blood Red the Sun*, 195–204. Sandra Estlin Bingman, 'The Trials of Poundmaker and Big Bear,' *Saskatchewan History* 28 (1975): 81–95, gives an account of the conduct of the trials and raises questions about their conduct, particularly the trial of Big Bear. However, Bingman apparently was unaware of Dewdney and Macdonald's efforts to use the courts and whatever other means possible to remove Cree leaders.
97 NA, MG 26A, vol. 107, Dewdney to Macdonald, 3 June 1885
98 Ibid.
99 Ibid.
100 Bingman, 'The Trials of Poundmaker and Big Bear,' 81–95
101 A very good account of Dewdney's actions to bring the Cree under government control after 1885 is to be found in Jean Lamour, 'Edgar Dewdney and the Aftermath of the Rebellion,' *Saskatchewan History* 23 (1970): 105–16. For a discussion of the use of the Indian Act as a means of destroying Indian cultural autonomy see John L. Tobias, 'Protection, Civilization, Assimilation: An Outline History of Canada's Indian Policy,' *Western Canadian Journal of Anthropology* 6 (1976). For a discussion of specific use of this policy against the Cree, and how the Cree reacted, see John L. Tobias, 'Indian Reserves in Western Canada: Indian Homelands or Devices for Assimilation,' in *Approaches to Native History in Canada: Papers of a Conference held at the National Museum of Man, October, 1975*, ed., D.A. Muise (Ottawa 1977), 89–103.

NORTHWEST REBELLION

J.R. MILLER

The Northwest Rebellion of 1885

The rebellion that broke out in the spring of 1885 has been the subject of a great deal of misunderstanding and myth-making. Among the many distorted views of that event, none is more ingrained than the notion that rebellion was the consequence of the meeting of two distinct ways of life.[1] According to this view, both the Red River Resistance of 1869 and the trouble in the Saskatchewan country in 1885 are best understood as the lamentable consequences of the meeting of a sophisticated society and more primitive peoples. Both represented futile attempts by technologically backward peoples to resist the march of more advanced societies. In Saskatchewan in 1885 the Métis and Indians used force to defend a fading way of life against the expansion of commerce and agriculture. Led by Louis Riel, the Métis precipitated a rebellion in which some of the Indian nations joined, both groups being motivated by a desire to repel the advance of agriculture. Such an interpretation, while seductive in its simplicity, fails to appreciate the complexity of the events and the variety of the motives of the actors in the Northwest Rebellion.

A proper understanding of these events requires careful consideration of at least three distinct elements. These are the Indians, the Métis communities of the Saskatchewan, and Louis Riel. The behaviour of each was quite distinguishable from that of the others, particularly in the preliminary stages of the armed struggle. And, in the case of the Indians, there were important differences among the various nations: the use of force was confined to the more northerly bands. It is impossible to understand why some Cree killed people, while others remained quiet without analysing the situation in which the western Indians found themselves between the signing of Treaty 7 in 1877 and the outbreak of violence in 1885. And it is impossible to appreciate why a peaceful Métis struggle for redress of grievances culminated in rebellion without careful examination of both the people who had grievances and the individual whose leadership they sought. Such an analysis will demonstrate that there was no Indian rebellion in the Northwest in 1885; there were only sporadic and isolated reprisals by small groups from some bands. It will also illustrate that Louis Riel was the spark that caused the mixture of Métis and government to explode.

If any people in the North-West Territories had reason to rebel in the 1880s it was the Indians. They saw the basis of their economy shattered in the 1870s, and then watched in the 1880s as the new relationship with the Dominion of Canada that they had negotiated in the 1870s failed to provide them with the relief and assistance on which they had counted. Moreover, they watched as Ottawa deliberately and systematically violated its treaty promises in order to coerce the Indians into adopting the government's plans for settlement rather than following their own. Finally, they endured great hardship as Ottawa implemented policies of retrenchment that bore savagely on them. The underlying cause of the Indians' problems was the disappearance of the bison. It had come under greater pressure after the 1820s, as the Métis increasingly shifted into the provisioning trade for the Hudson's Bay Company and attempted to satisfy the expanding market for buffalo robes. Other factors that accounted for the depletion of the herds included the arrival of modern weapons, such as the repeating rifle, and the completion of the transcontinental railway in the United States that brought to the plains the 'sports' hunter whose only interest was the acquisition of a trophy. Buffalo hides were also in demand in eastern factories for use in the belts that drove machinery.

One final factor was American policy towards the Indians south of the forty-ninth parallel. In the 1860s and 1870s the United States was still engaged in military campaigns against various Indian nations. Among the most spectacular of these was the ill-fated foray of General G.A. Custer and the Seventh Calvary that resulted in their annihilation at the hands of Sitting Bull, Crazy Horse, and their warriors on the Little Big Horn River in 1877. The aftermath of this was the flight of Sitting Bull and hundreds of his followers across the 'medicine line,' as the international boundary was called by Indians who recognized its importance in demarcating a land of refuge from a territory in which they could be hunted. Sitting Bull's presence in what is today southwestern Saskatchewan added to the strain on the food resources of the region and encouraged the American military to undertake operations designed to compel him to stay in Canada or starve him into submission in the United States.[2] At times in the late 1870s American forces burned the prairies in an effort to prevent the southern bison herd from trekking into Canada where it might help to sustain the fugitive Sioux.

The result of this combination of factors was the near-extinction of the bison by the 1880s. Of the herds that had impeded travellers on the prairies and parkland for days at a time in the 1840s, mere hundreds were known to exist by the end of the 1870s. In 1879 a Hudson's Bay Company man wrote in shock of 'the total disappearance of buffalo from British territory this season.' By 1884 only 300 bison hides were sold at St Paul, and by 1888 an American game report said that 'only six animals were then known to be in existence!'[3] The horror of starvation, never totally absent from Indian societies, now became all too familiar in the lodges of both plains and woodlands bands.

The devastating hardships that the Indians faced as a result of the disappearance of the bison were compounded by the government's response. As the Indians, especially the Cree, moved southward into the Cypress Hills in search of game and a base from which to pursue the buffalo herds, the Canadian authorities became increasingly alarmed. When the Cree, led by Piapot, Little Pine, and Big Bear in particular, began to press for contiguous reserves in the region of the hills, Ottawa's man on the spot became determined to prevent such a concentration. The fact that all three of these Cree leaders had refused to adhere to Treaty 6 when it was signed in 1876, and that Big Bear had expressly rejected the concept of submission to Canadian law that was part of the treaty, made their actions a source of concern to uneasy officials.[4] The disappearance of the buffalo and the consequent hardships provided North-West Territories lieutenant-governor Edgar Dewdney with his opportunity.

Dewdney, who was also commissioner of Indian affairs for the territories after 1879, could use the Indians' plight to defeat their diplomatic campaign for the creation of an Indian territory and to disperse them into other parts of the territories where they might be more easily controlled.[5] In deliberate violation of treaty provisions that covered at least Piapot and Little Pine, Indian Affairs officials refused them the reserves they requested in the south. At the same time the government used denial of food aid to the starving bands as a weapon to drive them out of the Cypress Hills. In 1882 they were informed they would get no more rations in the Cypress Hills, and in 1883 the Mounted Police post, Fort Walsh, was closed. The bands were forced to make their way north to lands in the Saskatchewan country. One by one the recalcitrants accepted reserves; even Big Bear entered treaty in 1882 and in 1884 accepted a reserve well away from Little Pine and Poundmaker in the Battleford district in order to secure assistance for his starving people. But his retreat was merely a strategic withdrawal, not a surrender.

Over the next few years the Cree chieftains tried to unite the Plains Indians so as to force a revision of the treaties. Piapot in the south and Big Bear and Little Pine in the Saskatchewan district attempted to persuade various bands of Indians – even such traditional enemies as the Blackfoot and Cree – to combine in a united front in their dealings with the federal government.

Gradually, through personal appeals and the use of thirst dances that were designed to united different groups through communal ritual observances, headway was made on this diplomatic offensive. In the summer of 1884 an Indian council was held at Duck Lake by leaders of twelve bands to protest the snail-like pace with which the government was honouring its treaty promises on agricultural assistance. This was evidence of the success that Big Bear and some others were achieving in their drive to secure reserves in the same areas and in other revisions of the treaties. These consummate diplomats were confident that the next spring, 1885, would see the triumph of their strategy when the Blackfoot joined them in a council on Little Pine's reserve. Progress could not come too soon. During the winter of 1884–5, the worst on record, younger Indians were becoming very restive.

Indian Affairs officials such as Edgar Dewdney had not been sitting idly by while the Cree attempted again what they had tried but failed to do in the Cypress Hills in the late 1870s. Dewdney used a policy of 'no work no rations' to try to force the Indians into adopting agriculture speedily and to assert the government's control. At the same time, his officials and the Mounted Police did whatever they could to interfere with the movements of the Indian diplomats. Where possible they prevented chiefs from travelling to councils or disrupted council meetings. They also instructed their agents and farm instructors to use rations to force a speedy transition to agriculture. In the south some chiefs were taken by the new railway to visit Regina and Winnipeg so they would become acquainted with the numbers and power of the white population.

This tendency towards coercion was made all the more painful for the Indians by Ottawa's decision after 1883 to implement a policy of retrenchment that would necessitate a reduction in assistance to Indians. A combination of renewed recession and mounting demands on the government treasury for the completion of the Canadian Pacific Railway created a strain on the federal budget that led to cuts in many government departments, including Indian Affairs. Officials on the spot warned the department that such measures were false economy, but Macdonald's deputy minister was convinced by a quick tour of the region he made in 1883 that such reductions were possible. And the prime minister was too busy with other matters and too little informed about western affairs to overrule his senior bureaucrat. Such parsimony was as unwise as it was inhumane, given the situation that prevailed among the Indians of the western interior in 1883 and 1884.

Ironically, these economies were ordered at the same time that the Indian Affairs department began to divert an increasing share of its budget to education. Prior to the 1880s nothing that could be called an Indian educational policy existed. In eastern Canada there were schools that were run by representatives of missionary organizations, and in Ontario there were even a few boarding schools for Indians. On the prairies and in British Columbia that same chaotic approach to Indian education had been allowed to develop. Missionary societies on their own initiative had set up schools associated with their mission stations. Many of these rudimentary efforts were day schools presided over by ill-trained, and worse paid, missionaries who had far too many other duties to worry unduly about the abysmal attendance and poor academic showing of their students. A few missionaries had also begun to experiment with boarding schools in the west. By the 1880s a hodgepodge of schools had developed in the region west of Ontario: there were day schools to which the government sometimes made small grants that paid much of the teachers' stipends; and less frequently there were also boarding schools to which the government rarely contributed anything. Between 1878 and 1883 the government embarked on an extension of the day schools and the creation of a wholly new system of industrial schools. In 1883–4 costly residential schools that were designed to teach Indians trades and agriculture were opened in Battleford, Qu'Appelle, and High River in the North-West Territories. The financial impact of these schools, which were expensively built and maintained, was significant in an Indian department that was already under financial pressure as a result of the policy of retrenchment.

Indian Affairs commissioner Dewdney had one final weapon he proposed to use to cow and control the Indians of the plains and Pacific in the mid-1880s. Convinced that the policy of harassing Indian diplomats and applying pressure by restricting the flow of rations was only partially successful, he urged Macdonald to adopt a policy of 'sheer compulsion' in dealing with the leaders of those Indian bands who refused to behave as the department desired.[6] His efforts to prevent Indian leaders from meeting in 1884 had been thwarted by the small number of officials and police and by the absence of legislation enabling them to control Indians' movements. More police would be recruited by 1885, and the Indian Act would be amended to authorize officials to arrest Indians who were on reserves other than their own without department permission and to outlaw the Potlatch of the Pacific Indians. Dewdney was confident that, when these amendments came into effect in 1885, he would be equal to the challenge posed by the likes of Big Bear, Piapot, and Little Pine.

While Big Bear had been manoeuvring and Dewdney had been countering, increasing dissatisfaction had arisen within some of the Cree bands, discontent that threatened to overthrow the traditional leadership and rise up against government authority. While such experienced leaders as Big Bear and Piapot understood the need for a unified front and the futility of armed action, some of their younger followers did not. The less experienced men found it hard to bear the suffering caused by want and the indignities resulting from the actions of overbearing bureaucrats. By 1883 their anger was approaching the boiling point, and in the summer of 1884 there were confrontations on reserves, such as that of Yellow Calf in the Qu'Appelle area, between hungry Indians and outnumbered policemen. In such disputes it was all that cooler, more mature heads could do to prevent the slaughter of the constable or agent. Big Bear complained at the 1884 council in Duck Lake that he was losing control of his band to more militant young men such as Little Poplar, who advocated an all-out war as an alternative to diplomacy.

Though it did not have to be that way, it was in fact the grievances of the Métis, in combination with the influence of Louis Riel, that brought armed rebellion to the Saskatchewan country in 1885. The mixed-blood population of the region were largely Manitoba Métis who had migrated westward in search of a new home in which they could pursue their customary lifestyle of hunting, fishing, casual employment, and some agriculture. In the 1870s, while white settlers were establishing the nearby town of Prince Albert, some 1500 Métis founded villages such as St Laurent and Batoche in the South Saskatchewan Valley.

Both the Métis and the Euro-Canadians of the Saskatchewan had grievances with the federal government in the 1880s. The white farmers objected to the slowness of the land registry system, the failure of the transcontinental railway to make its expected way through their region, and the hardships resulting from several bad seasons. They responded by participating in the 1884 formation of the Manitoba and North-West Farmers' Union and by joining with the Métis in a campaign to pressure the federal government to deal with their problems. The Métis not only shared in the whites' disgruntlement with government and economic adversity, but had additional concerns of their own as well. As usual, land was at the heart of most of their grievances. As in Manitoba earlier, the Saskatchewan Métis feared that the arrival of a land registration system from Ottawa might jeopardize their customary title to river-lot farms. They could not get assurances from an ominously silent federal government that their title would be respected. Some of them also believed they had a claim for compensation for loss of aboriginal title in the territories. They argued that the dominion had by treaty extinguished the Indians' title to the lands, but not theirs. Before extensive development occurred, Canada should recognize in Saskatchewan, as it had in Manitoba, that the Métis shared in aboriginal title and should compensate them for their loss of this interest in the land. And, finally, some of the Saskatchewan Métis argued that they or their children had unresolved claims against the dominion for land grants as a result of the promises made to future generations of Métis in the Manitoba Act of 1870.

The problems the Métis experienced in advancing their case in the early 1880s were similar to those that white farmers encountered: Ottawa never seemed to deal with their complaints. In part the problem was that federal politicians were preoccupied with other, to them more important matters. In part the difficulty was simply that the ministers responsible for western matters, David Macpherson and later Sir John Macdonald, knew little about western problems. In Macdonald's case the problem was still further compounded by his age. Old Tomorrow was getting on. He was sixty-three when he returned to power in the general election of 1878; he was running out of energy. And he had little sympathy for the Métis. Macdonald mistakenly believed that much of the talk of land compensation from the Métis was nonsense that had been inspired by white land speculators who were stirring up the people of Batoche or St Laurent. So far as a repetition of the Manitoba Act's promise of land to mixed bloods by virtue of their partial Indian ancestry was concerned, Macdonald was having no part of such schemes. The promise of the Manitoba Act had been a disaster to fulfil, not least because the slowness, dishonesty, and incompetence of federal officials delayed the distribution of land so long that many Métis gave up and sold their land scrip for a pittance to speculators. Macdonald was, if possible, even more unsympathetic than he was uninterested in the complaints from the Saskatchewan country.

The response of both Métis and whites to their failure to get the federal government to deal with their grievances was a decision to ask Louis Riel to return to Canada to lead their movement. Both parties were clear that what they wanted was Riel's experience and skill in dealing peacefully with an unresponsive government. To obtain his help with their movement for redress of grievances, they sent a party south to Montana at the beginning of June 1884 to ask him to come to their assistance. Had they thought about his response to their request for any length of time, they might have been troubled about what they were doing. 'God wants you to understand that you have taken the right way,' said Riel when he met the delegates, 'for there are four of you, and you have arrived on the fourth of June.'[7]

What Riel's cryptic response to the invitation imperfectly disguised was the fact that the Louis Riel who accepted the invitation in June 1884 was a very different man from the Riel who had led the resistance fifteen years earlier. Riel had felt himself ill-used by the Canadian government in 1870. Forced to flee, denied the amnesty he had been promised, elected to Parliament but unable to take his seat for fear for his life, Riel was finally banished from the country for five years in 1875. The distressing events of the 1870s had unhinged him mentally. Riel was now convinced he had a divine mission. Like the poet-king of Israel, David, whose name he adopted, he had been chosen by God. His mission was to prepare the world for the second coming of Christ and the end of the world by transferring the papacy from Italy to the new world, replacing the bishop of Rome with the Ultramontane bishop of Montreal, and ultimately locating the Holy See at St Vital, his home parish in Manitoba. The northwest was to become a new homeland in which the oppressed peoples of Europe could join the Métis and Indians to live in peace during a millennium that would precede the final end of the world.[8]

Like most prophets, Riel found himself without honour in his own land once he began to act on the revelation of his divine mission. He spent two periods of incarceration in asylums for the mentally ill in Quebec in the 1870s, and, when he was released, he was told that his cure would last only if he avoided involvement in matters that excited him. He moved to the United States, married, became an American citizen and participated in American politics, and settled down to the life of a mission school teacher in the west. However, he had not forgotten his mission; he continued to look for a sign that it was time for its fulfilment. When, on 4 June 1884, four delegates from the Métis of Saskatchewan invited him to return with them, he knew it was the signal he sought.

In the initial months after his return with his wife and children to Canada, Riel played the role he had been asked to rather than the role he knew God ultimately intended for him. He served as an adviser and organizer of legal protests, attending meetings and helping with the preparation of yet more petitions to Ottawa. He was even at Duck Lake at the time of the Indian council in 1884, but there is no record that he sought to incite either the Indians or his own followers to acts of rebellion. It was only gradually during the winter of 1884–5 that his purpose became known to the Oblate priests with whom he was in frequent contact. One of them claimed Riel said he had personal claims – no doubt based on the terms of the Manitoba Act – that the federal government should redress. The priest informed Ottawa, but the prime minister declined to play the game of bribery, if that was the game that Riel intended.[9] The clerics became convinced that Riel was heretical if not completely deranged, as they became aware of his peculiar religious ideas. They would be the first in the community to turn against him; they would be followed during that winter by the white settlers who set their face against the conversion of the movement from peaceful protest to armed struggle.

It was clearly Riel – not the community at large, not even the Métis as a group – who pushed events in the direction of rebellion in the early weeks of 1885. For many months he had simply advanced the existing agitation; a petition of December 1884 did not include his own exalted claim for a land grant to the Métis by virtue of their sharing in the aboriginal title to the country. By March Riel was poised to attempt a recreation of the strategy that had worked so well in 1869. His pretext was the lack of response from

Ottawa. In fact, in January the federal government decided to appoint a commission to inquire into the grievances of the Métis, and, while they made that decision known to Riel through an intermediary, they did not follow up their actions until two months later when the members of the commission were appointed. By that time Riel had raised the stakes, proclaiming a provisional government, of which he would be the prophet and Gabriel Dumont the adjutant general. The insurgents demanded the surrender of Fort Carlton and its police detachment.

But, if Riel thought he was re-enacting the events at Red River in 1869, he miscalculated. The two situations were starkly different. In 1869 he had enjoyed clerical support and the backing of a reasonably united community. In 1885 the priests turned against him and the white settlers' support evaporated. It might have been possible in Rupert's Land in 1869, especially after McDougall's abortive proclamation of Canadian authority, to argue that there was a vacuum of legal authority that justified a provisional government. In 1885 there was little doubt that Canada was the effective government in the North-West Territories. Red River had been distant and vulnerable, partly because Ottawa feared that the Americans had designs upon the region. Batoche in 1885 was geographically more remote, but in actuality more accessible, thanks to the nearly complete Canadian Pacific Railway. If the dominion chose in 1885 to crush Riel rather than negotiate, his rising was doomed. That, of course, was precisely what Canada decided to do.

It was largely a matter of coincidence – certainly not a matter of design – that a series of Indian actions occurred about the same time that Riel and the Métis confronted the police. In the camp of Big Bear effective power had shifted by March 1885 to the young men in the warrior society. This transition, by no means unusual in the fluid and subtle political systems of Indian communities, meant that the authority of the elderly diplomat, Big Bear, was greatly lessened, while the ability of men such as his son Imasees and the war chiefs Little Poplar and Wandering Spirit to carry the band on their own more warlike policy was increased. Irritation had been building up against some of the white men at Frog Lake, where Big Bear's band was established, and, when news arrived of a Métis victory over the police at Duck Lake, some of the young warriors attacked the Hudson's Bay Company storekeeper and the Indian agent. Big Bear attempted to restrain them when he became aware of what was going on, but before he could make peace prevail nine whites lay dead.

The incident, essentially a bloody act of vengeance against unpopular officials, became unjustifiably known as the Frog Lake Massacre. That it was nothing of the sort was illustrated by the fact that not all the Euro-Canadians were killed; one company man and two white women were spared, thanks in part to Big Bear. Moreover, though these people were prisoners in Big Bear's camp for weeks, they were not harmed at all. If the death of nine people and the humane treatment of three others constitute a massacre, then, and only then, was Frog Lake a massacre.

But the impression that prevailed at the time was that the Indians were rising in response to the Métis initiative. The rout of the police at Duck Lake had been followed by the 'massacre' at Frog Lake. Panic set in, nowhere more obviously than in the Battleford district, where white settlers fled for refuge to the fort. Groups from Poundmaker's band who were travelling to the post in search of badly needed food looted some abandoned homesteads near the fort. In the minds of the settlers and the government these relatively innocent events became a 'siege' of the fort by Poundmaker and the Cree. Again, it was nothing of the sort, as Poundmaker's retreat to his own reserve clearly illustrated. Nonetheless, the Canadian government was convinced, and set about convincing others, that the entire northwest was threatened by a combined Métis-Indian rising.

Canada's military response was devastating and indiscriminate. In all, some 8000 troops, militia, and police were dispatched into the region along three routes: from Qu'Appelle north against the mixed-blood community in the valley of the South Saskatchewan; from Swift Current north to 'relieve' Battleford; and from Calgary north to Edmonton. The only fighting of any consequence occurred at Fish Creek, Batoche, and Cut Knife Hill. At Fish Creek Dumont persuaded Riel to let him attack the military column from hiding, but then nullified the advantage of surprise by prematurely revealing his position. The final stand came at Batoche, where the Métis dug rifle pits and established fortifications from which they rained a withering fire on their attackers. Unfortunately for the Métis the defenders quickly exhausted their ammunition and were reduced to using makeshift projectiles. The attacking Canadian forces, troops and militia, greatly outnumbered the few hundred armed Métis. Moreover, they were equipped with ample arms and ammunition, not even counting the Gatling gun that the American military had thoughtfully provided for field testing or the steamer that the commander attempted to use as a diversionary naval force. Finally, the ill-disciplined militiamen, tired of three days of feinting and long-range firing, and fed up with their general's cautious probes of Batoche, ignored their orders and overran the rifle pits.

Louis Riel, who had behaved throughout the encounters at Duck Lake and Batoche as though he was conducting a religious service rather than leading a revolt, surrendered. The truth was that, at least in his own mind, his was a religious cause. He could not fail because he was carrying out God's mission. If the deity had arranged for a defeat, it could only be because Riel was to make his case at a trial after the surrender. Dumont, practical fighter that he was, lit out for the United States.

The other military actions of the northwest campaign involved Poundmaker and Big Bear. When Colonel Otter's column 'relieved' Battleford, its leader decided to set off in search of Poundmaker, whom all held responsible for the 'siege' that had never happened. Otter caught up to Poundmaker's people at Cut Knife Hill and attacked. He and his men soon found themselves in trouble as the Cree fired from protected positions at the soldiers who were silhouetted on a hillside. The troops were astounded when they were able to retreat in an orderly fashion without suffering further losses. What they did not know was that Poundmaker had persuaded his men not to pursue and inflict any more damage on Otter's battered soldiers.

Big Bear and his followers spent much of May evading yet another Canadian force led by T.B. Strange in the bush country north of Frog Lake. The aftermath of the 'massacre' had been the restoration of the old leader's authority, and he used his control to follow his traditionally pacific paths. He allowed a frightened contingent of police to vacate Fort Pitt safely, and then he tried to take his people away from all trouble, including advancing troops. Strange caught up to Big Bear once, to his sorrow, near Frenchman's Butte, in the Fort Pitt area. Strange had to withdraw to Fort Pitt. Eventually, after Big Bear had led the soldiers a merry chase in the northern bush, his forces began to melt away. Finally, Big Bear returned to the Fort Carlton area and surrendered on 2 July. With Riel and Poundmaker already in custody, Big Bear's surrender marked the end of the rebellion.

What was at least as significant as who participated in the rising was who did not. Piapot in the Qu'Appelle area did not take up arms, perhaps because the government quickly stationed troops on his reserve to discourage his men from violence. At Round Lake, near Broadview, Assiniboia, the Presbyterian missionary noted that the Indians became excited and prepared to leave only when they heard that 'the soldiers are comming [sic] & will take us prisoner & we would rather fight & die on the battle field than to go away as a prisoner.' However, when he assured them that if the troops came and took the braves they would have to imprison the missionary as well, 'I was not a little astonished to see them take my advice & remain at home.'[10] In other words, Indians in Assiniboia either chose or were persuaded by the presence of troops not to join in the rising.

Nor did the Blackfoot confederacy in the southwest take up arms. Part of the explanation lies in how weakened the southern tribes were by hardship, hunger, and disease by 1885. Here, again, the pacific influence of older chiefs such as Crowfoot was part of the explanation. But so, too, was the southern Indians' familiarity with whites and their power. The Blackfoot, four of whose chiefs had earlier travelled by train to Regina and Winnipeg at Dewdney's invitation, appreciated the general significance of the large numbers of Euro-Canadians and the military potential of the railway.[11] The non-participation of the southern Indians, arguably the people who had suffered most since the making of the treaties and the disappearance of the bison, was further evidence that the events of 1885, whatever Edgar Dewdney said they were, were not an Indian rising.

Nonetheless, Dewdney and the government chose to portray the events as an Indian rebellion and to use that excuse to complete the 'subjugation' of the Plains Cree that they had begun in the late 1870s.[12] Although there was no reliable evidence that Poundmaker was responsible for the 'siege of Battleford' or that Big Bear was the architect of the 'Frog Lake Massacre,' both leaders were prosecuted and convicted of treason-felony. Their incarceration in a penitentiary in Manitoba, of course, made certain that the movement for revision of the treaties would not resume. Both were released before serving all of their three-year sentences; each died within a year of release. In addition to Big Bear and Poundmaker, forty-two other Indians were convicted of various offences for actions that occurred during the insurrection. Students of the trials of the Indian defendants have concluded that they were much less carefully handled than those of the Métis and white defendants.[13] The explanation of the unfairness of the Indian trials lies in a combination of Dewdney's desire to use the courts to complete the cowing of the Indian leaders and the prejudice of Euro-Canadian juries.

It is an interesting comment on the preoccupations of historians that it has been the trial of the Métis leader that has captured most attention. It is often claimed that Riel's trial was a travesty of justice. Critics objected that he should not have been charged with high treason because he was an American citizen, that he should not have been tried before a magistrate because he faced a capital charge, and that he should have been granted a change of venue to Manitoba where he would have been entitled to some French-speaking jurors rather than the six English-speaking Protestants who decided his fate during the tense days of July 1885. Finally, most observers have argued that Riel was insane and should, consequently, not have been found guilty, or, if convicted, should have had the sentence of death commuted. These criticisms are unfounded.

The charge of treason was valid, as was the venue and the composition of the court. Anyone residing, even temporarily, within a jurisdiction owes a sort of allegiance and obedience to the legitimate authority of that territory. Riel owed obedience to the laws and Queen of Canada when he came into the country in 1884.[14] Riel was not entitled under territorial law to a change of venue to another province; Regina was a legal, if not entirely appropriate, site for his trial. Where else in the territories should the trial have occurred? Battleford? Prince Albert? And there was no doubt that Magistrate Richardson was entitled to hear the case, even if it must be admitted that he did not sparkle on the bench. There was a precedent for conducting a capital trial before a territorial magistrate and jury of six.[15]

The most tangled issue surrounding Riel's trial and conviction was his mental health. That he was mentally ill, perhaps even insane, seems indisputable. However, his lawyers' opportunity to argue for a not guilty verdict on this basis was largely wiped out by Riel's public protestations to the court that he was not insane and by his cogent closing address to the jury. Riel opposed the insanity plea because he believed he was the instrument of a great cause that deserved its day in court. To have agreed to a plea of insanity would have been to deny the validity and importance of both his and the Métis cause. Riel was mentally ill, but his lawyers were unable to plead effectively that he should be acquitted on grounds of insanity. Accordingly, once the jury found him guilty, the presiding judge had no choice but to impose the ultimate sentence. The only possibility of avoiding execution, given the charge and the verdict, lay in the jury's recommendation of clemency.

Only the federal government could recommend commutation of Riel's sentence to life imprisonment. And within Quebec a demand began to develop for clemency once Ontario extremists began to demand the carrying out of the sentence in terms that were offensive to the French-speaking Catholics of Quebec. It was not that Quebec sympathized with Riel or supported his actions; it was rather that Ontarians had converted him into a symbol of Quebec itself by demanding his blood not as a Métis traitor, but as a French and Catholic rebel.[16] But if Ottawa was to accede to Quebec, on what grounds could it do so?

Many people, then and since, were prepared to come forward with arguments they thought justified commutation. Some argued that the rebellion had been justified by the federal government's neglect. Obviously, no government – certainly not Sir John Macdonald's – was going to accept such an argument. It is a painful but real fact of life that the only thing that justifies rebellion is success. The successful revolutionary is a statesman, the unsuccessful a criminal. A suggestion that Riel should receive clemency because his offence was a *political* crime received a similarly chilly reception from Ottawa. Such a category of offence did not exist, and no conventional government was interested in creating one. One person's political crime was another's act of treason. That left only the insanity argument.

The insanity issue came in two phases: the trial and the prelude to execution. If Riel had been found legally insane at the trial, he would have been acquitted by reason of insanity. But the nineteenth-century criteria of legal insanity were extremely narrow and rigid. The test boiled down to the question, 'Did the accused know right from wrong when he committed the act?' Doctors who examined Riel found that, though he held strange ideas on political and religious issues, he did know right from wrong. He was not *legally* insane. However, there was an additional point. If Riel had become insane since his conviction, it would not be humane to execute him. The federal government explored this possibility with a medical commission that, though not unanimous, concluded that the condemned prisoner in the Regina jail was not insane. The federal government misrepresented the views of one of the doctors to strengthen its case, thereby earning the opprobrium of later commentators.[17]

Advocates were running out of arguments, and Riel out of time. Since there were no medical grounds for commutation, since there were no effective arguments in favour of clemency, and since Ontario was demanding the carrying out of the sentence even more vehemently than Quebec was insisting on commutation, Macdonald and the federal cabinet concluded that the stern course of justice should be followed. The prime minister did not doubt Riel's guilt and the justness of the sentence. Macdonald believed that no matter what his government did, it would be damned by some group. If they were damned if they did and damned if they didn't, then he was damned well going to do what he personally believed was right. The federal government announced it would not interfere. And on 16 November 1885 Louis Riel was hanged.

In a sense Riel never died. Though they took down his body and transported it to St Boniface where a grieving Métis community interred it in the cathedral cemetery, he lived on. Riel became a symbol of many causes in the century after his execution. To the French-speaking people of Quebec he immediately became a token of their own vulnerability in a confederation dominated by English-speaking Protestants. They reacted by electing a so-called *parti national* government in 1886. In the twentieth century Riel has served as a representative figure for western politicians such as Saskatchewan's Ross Thatcher, who have exploited his tragic life to make their case against an unresponsive federal government. 'Whether we realize it or not, we of 1968 face a situation which is similar in some respects. If Riel could walk the soil of Canada today, I am sure his sense of justice would be outraged as it was in 1885,' intoned the Liberal premier of Saskatchewan.[18] Pierre Trudeau also exploited the Métis martyr by holding him up as a symbol of where intolerance towards ethnic and racial minorities led. At the unveiling of a monument to Riel in Regina in 1969 Trudeau warned, 'We must never forget that, in the long run, a democracy is judged by the way the majority treats the minority. Louis Riel's battle is not yet won.'[19] And in the 1960s Riel was adopted and patronized by white, middle-class student radicals who found him an acceptable substitute for the Cuban Revolution's Che Guevara. He has been the subject of innumerable stories, plays, and one important opera. Canadians find Riel or, more accurately, their own concerns that they project on Riel endlessly fascinating.

The native communities have had a more difficult time deciding how to handle the historical memory of Riel. For a time the Métis embraced him as the principal symbol of their problems at the hands of an unsympathetic government and community. In the early 1970s the Association of Metis and Non-Status Indians of Saskatchewan even petitioned Ottawa for a pardon for Riel, but later they withdrew their request, arguing that it was not Riel but the federal government that needed a pardon. The equivocal nature of the Métis attitude towards Riel is illustrated by their tendency to exalt his adjutant general, Gabriel Dumont, as a symbol. Most still admire Louis Riel greatly.

No corresponding fascination has developed with those who lost the most by the Northwest Rebellion, the Indians. One can point to a National Film Board account, *Ballad of Crowfoot,* or a major novel on *The Temptations of Big Bear,* but not to any pattern of utilizing leaders such as Poundmaker or Big Bear as symbols of various causes.[20] It is almost as though a great amnesia descended on Canadians as a result of the crushing of Indian leadership after the rising of 1885. There was no Indian rebellion in the Saskatchewan country in 1885; there were scattered and isolated acts of violence by angry young men who could no longer be restrained by cooler heads. The Indians did not rebel, yet they have suffered the most.

NOTES

This article is from *Skyscrapers Hide the Heavens: A History of Indian-White Relations in Canada.* Toronto: University of Toronto Press 1989. Reprinted with permission.

1 The earliest, and still the best, treatment of the rebellion as the clash of two ways of life is G.F.G. Stanley, *The Birth of Western Canada: A History of the Riel Rebellions,* 2nd ed. (Toronto: University of Toronto 1960; first published 1936).
2 G. Pennanen, 'Sitting Bull: Indian without a Country,' *Canadian Historical Review* (CHR) 51 (2) (June 1970): 123–41
3 Stanley, *Birth of Western Canada,* 220, 221; G. Friesen, *The Canadian Prairies: A History* (Toronto: University of Toronto Press 1984), 250
4 J.L. Tobias, 'Canada's Subjugation of the Plains Cree, 1879–1885,' CHR 64 (4) (Dec. 1983): 524, 527–8
5 This account is based on ibid., 526ff.
6 Quoted ibid., 534
7 Quoted in Friesen, *Canadian Prairies,* 227

8 The best account of Riel's millenarian thought is T. Flanagan, *Louis "David" Riel: Prophet of the New World* (Toronto: University of Toronto Press 1979).
9 T. Flanagan, *Riel and the Rebellion: 1885 Reconsidered* (Saskatoon: Western Producer Prairie Books 1983), chap. 5. How accurate the priest's report was is impossible to determine.
10 United Church of Canada Archives, Presbyterian Church Papers, Home Missions Committee, box 1A, file 18, H. McKay to 'Dear Sir,' 13 April 1885
11 H.A. Dempsey, 'The Fearsome Fire Wagons,' in H.A. Dempsey, ed., *The CPR West: The Iron Road and The Making of a Nation* (Vancouver / Toronto: Douglas & McIntyre 1984), 65
12 Tobias, 'Subjugation,' 545–7
13 S. Bingaman, 'The Trials of Poundmaker and Big Bear, 1885,' *Saskatchewan History* 28 (3) (autumn 1975): 81–94; and 'The Trials of the "White Rebels," 1885,' ibid. 25 (2) (spring 1972): 41–54; Flanagan, *1885 Reconsidered*, 118
14 D.H. Brown, 'The Meaning of Treason in 1885,' *Saskatchewan History* 28 (2) (spring 1975): 65–73
15 Flanagan, *1885 Reconsidered*, 122–4, 126–9
16 A.I. Silver, *The French-Canadian Idea of Confederation 1864–1900* (Toronto: University of Toronto Press 1982), 153–79
17 See especially Flanagan, *1885 Reconsidered*, chap. 7.
18 Quoted in Association of Metis and Non-Status Indians of Saskatchewan, 'Louis Riel: Justice Must Be Done,' mimeograph, 1978, vi
19 *Colombo's Canadian Quotations* (Edmonton: Hurtig 1974), 597
20 R. Wiebe, *The Temptations of Big Bear* (Toronto: McClelland and Stewart 1973); National Film Board, *The Ballad of Crowfoot* (1968)

A. BLAIR STONECHILD

The Indian View of the 1885 Uprising

THE INDIAN VERSION OF THE REBELLION: AN UNTOLD STORY

Although there is no shortage of written material on the North-West Rebellion of 1885, Indian elders have said that the full story of the Indian involvement has yet to be told.

As one elder put it, 'This story was told only at night and at bedtime. And not the whole story. No way. They did not want to tell on anyone who were [sic] involved. It is like when something is covered with a blanket and held down on the ground on all four sides. They talked about it in parts only. And they got nervous telling it. They were afraid of another uprising and more trouble. And they were also afraid of getting the young people into trouble.'[1]

Some elders did not like to tell the stories simply because it made them sad. Other elders did not tell their stories to any white person, even priests, since they were afraid that these stories would be used for the profit of others.

Most historians have used only written documents and official interpretations in their research. After the rebellion the Indian people did not have the freedom or luxury of doing their own research and putting forward their own views. As a result, contemporary interpretations of the Indian role have remained very biased.

HOW THE REBELLION STARTED

The first Indian involvement in the rebellion is said to have been at the Duck Lake fight on 26 March 1885. A few Indians were among Gabriel Dumont's group of about thirty men; but then, considering that the fight itself occurred on Beardy's Reserve, it should not be so surprising that Indians were present at all. One of the least understood aspects of the Duck Lake fight is why one of Chief Beardy's headmen (Assiyiwin) was shot during the purported parley preceding the fight. How did an old, half-blind, unarmed headman of the band become involved in the fracas?

What does Indian oral history have to say about this? The following story is told by Harry Michael of Beardy's Reserve. Harry Michael's grandfather was the nephew of Assiyiwin:

> Assiyiwin had gone to town, to Duck Lake to visit a friend, a half-breed by the name of Wolfe. Over there he heard that there was going to be some trouble. Something very bad was going to happen. He had gone to town on horseback and he bought some goods from the store in Duck Lake which he tied on his saddle. He then started walking home. The town of Duck Lake was not too far from the camp.
>
> The old man had very poor eyesight – he was almost blind. And as he was approaching the reserve and the camp he noticed something. He heard a lot of voices, a lot of talking. But he could not see anything until he came near the people.
>
> It was then a half-breed spoke to him – called in Cree and said, 'Stop! Don't you know what is going to happen?'
>
> Assiyiwin said, 'I am blind. Exactly what is it?'
>
> The half-breed answered, 'There is going to be a battle. Didn't you hear about it?'
>
> Assiyiwin answered, 'Yes, I heard about it.'
>
> The half-breed replied, 'You have walked right into it. Turn back where you came from.'
>
> Assiyiwin answered, 'Ha! I cannot turn back. I'm going home. This is my reserve land. If you are going to have a battle, if you are going to spill blood, you cannot do it on our reserve land.' And he remained standing there with his horse.
>
> The half-breed said, 'Go back where you came from.'
>
> Assiyiwin replied, 'No, I am going home.'
>
> This half-breed threw his coat to Assiyiwin. His name was Joe McKay. He said, 'Step over my coat ... I'll shoot you.'
>
> That was the time when Assiyiwin heard someone saying while he was standing there, 'Don't shoot each other. Don't shoot.' It was said in Cree. It was a half-breed. He must have been very brave, coming into the centre of the two sides of the people on horseback, half-breeds and Indians on one side and the Northwest [sic] Mounted Police on the other side. He was trying to tell the people not to shoot each other. He came running from the half-breed side. He did not know the name of this man. He was waving his hands shouting, 'Don't shoot each other!

> People are trying to find a way on how they can get along better. Don't try and kill each other.' He got as far as their location.
>
> It was then Assiyiwin stepped over and passed the coat of McKay and said, 'I am going home.'
>
> Assiyiwin witnessed the days of intertribal [sic] battles with the Blackfeet. Assiyiwin performed some brave acts when he had the strength and power in his legs. He had some scalps in a wooden box. He had fought and killed in battles and scalped. This was a brave man. That is why he did not back out from Joe McKay's orders. He refused Joe McKay and stepped over past the coat and said he was going to go on home. He was not about to get frightened. His bravery must have returned to him in spite [of the fact] that he was an old man.
>
> The gun went off and fired. McKay shot the old man Assiyiwin down, hitting him in the stomach. Then there were blasts of gunfire coming from all directions.
>
> They came later after the old man. He didn't die right away that night. He died at sunrise the following morning. He was the first Cree Indian killed. That's how my grandfather told this story.[2]

The official interpretation of the event at Duck Lake was that Beardy's band had joined the rebellion. The story of Assiyiwin, however, presents an entirely different view. An older man, with poor eyesight, Assiyiwin was hardly likely to be associating with young fighters. Moreover, as one of Beardy's headmen, he probably shared Beardy's disassociation from Riel's activities and Beardy's dislike of intruders on their Indian reserve land.

It appears that Assiyiwin's mistake was being in the wrong place at the wrong time, and being too bold in asserting his indignation at what was occurring. Gabriel Dumont did not see his brother Isidore or Assiyiwin approach Crozier and McKay. What was probably not so much a parley as an effort to defuse a tense situation turned into a senseless slaughter when Joe McKay pulled his trigger.

It later became clear that Chief Beardy had not ordered his men to support the rebellion, yet through the incident at Duck Lake the Indian people were fully implicated.

INDIAN TREATIES WERE A COMMITMENT TO PEACE

In order to understand the Indian attitude at the time of the rebellion more clearly, one has to look back to the period prior to the signing of the treaties. Indian nations waged tremendous battles against each other as a result of intertribal conflicts created by the expansion of the fur trade. In some battles between the Cree and the Blackfoot, such as that on the Oldman River in 1870, several hundred warriors were killed. An even greater killer – the epidemics – wiped out over half of the tribes in some outbreaks. The result of all of this was the drastic depopulation of the Indian nations, and an increasing awareness among Indian leaders that their nations had to come to grips with a very fundamental and real issue – that of survival.

Because of these experiences, a strong peace movement began to develop among the Indian nations. One famous peacemaker was the Cree Chief Maskipitoon, who strove to mend relations between the Cree and the Blackfoot during the 1860s. He eventually fell victim to a misguided warrior's bullet. The adoption of the Cree Poundmaker by the Blackfoot Chief Crowfoot was another important development in the cementing of peaceful relations between the two nations.

It was because of this sentiment for peace that Indian leaders were receptive to the signing of treaties in the 1870s. Not only had Indians never been at war with whites in the North-West, but they also sought to prevent such a thing from ever happening. Treaty Six stated, 'they will maintain peace and good order between each other, and also between themselves and others of Her Majesty's subjects.'[3] To Indian nations, that was one of the most important principles of the treaty.

For Indians, the signing of treaties was far more than a political act – it was also a sacred act. By the ceremony of smoking the Sacred Pipe, the Indian people pledged before the Creator that they would uphold the treaties. As Senator John Tootoosis puts it, 'We signed an agreement with the Crown, with the Queen not to fight any more. We were to live in peace. We had to live up to this Treaty. We promised in the name of the Creator to keep the Treaty. The Indian people feared offending the Creator.'[4] If the treaty was ever broken, it would not be the Indian people who broke it first.

Around the time of the rebellion, white people did not fully appreciate the commitment of the Indian people. They had the perception that Indian people were no more than hunters and warriors. When the Marquis of Lorne, Queen Victoria's son-in-law, met Poundmaker in 1881, he expected to hear many war stories, and was surprised that instead he heard mainly about the spiritual and political ideas of the Indian people.

THE SOLUTIONS TO TREATY PROBLEMS WOULD BE POLITICAL

The Indian leadership was aware that there were serious shortcomings in the implementation of the treaties. In the councils of the political leaders the focus of attention was on the dissatisfaction being experienced by those Indians settling on reserves. During those days of 'The Time of the Great Hunger,' Indians were seeing few of the benefits promised them under the treaty. The meager rations provided to them did little to stop the loss of life. Between 1880 and 1885 the Indian population dropped from 32,549 to 20,170 – a death rate of nearly 10 per cent per year.[5]

At the Duck Lake council, held in early August of 1884, Indian leaders presented a list of eighteen specific treaty grievances including complaints about untamed horses and cows, inadequate rations, poor implements, lack of schools and medical assistance, and general dissatisfaction with government measures. The report on their presentation stated 'that requests for redress of their grievances have been again and again made without effect. They are glad that the young men have not resorted to violent measures to gain it. That it is almost too hard for them to bear the treatment received at the hands of the government after its 'sweet promises' made in order to get their country from them. They now fear that they are going to be cheated. They will wait until next summer to see if this council has the desired effect, failing which they will take measures to get what they desire. (The proposed 'measures' could not be elicited, but a suggestion of the idea of war was repudiated.)'[6]

One measure being proposed by the chiefs was a meeting of the Grand Council to be held on Little Pine's reserve in 1885. The Blackfoot would be invited to attend. Once a united position was agreed upon, a delegation of chiefs would travel to Ottawa where it was believed someone with sufficient authority could make some changes.

Thus, the Indian people were charting their own course of action to deal with Indian problems. It was a plan which called for concerted political action, and under it any outbreak of violence would be viewed as an undesirable course of events.

THE SPREAD OF THE REBELLION TESTS INDIAN LOYALTIES

Following the outbreak of hostilities at Duck Lake, Riel, attempting to spark a territory-wide insurrection, sent messengers to many reserves urging the Indians to join him. The response of most Indian leaders was to send messages to government authorities reaffirming their loyalty.

On 28 March 1885 a delegation of Touchwood chiefs sent a message expressing 'to his Excellency the Lieutenant-Governor and through him to the Governor-General, their loyalty to their Great Mother the Queen, and further wish to express their disapproval of the course of action pursued by those at the head of the present struggle.'[7]

At a meeting called by Riel's messengers at the Crooked Lakes reserves, the Indians decided to remain loyal. Chief Kahkewistahaw made the following statement: 'Agent, you remember the time I promised I would go to my reserve. I also said that I and my young men's fighting days were over. I stick to those words no matter what may be done up north, we will remain on our reserves and attend to our work.'[8]

Chief Piapot, the main Cree leader in the south, wrote: 'It is eleven years since I gave up fighting. When I took the government Treaty I touched the pen not to interfere with the whiteman and the whiteman not to interfere with me.'[9]

Also on 28 March, Indian Agent Rae visited old Chief Mosquito on his reserve a few miles south of Battleford and received the chief's assurances that the band would remain loyal. At about the same time, Riel's messengers were visiting both Mosquito's and Red Pheasant's reserves.

On Mosquito's reserve a band member named Itka had been grieving over the death of his daughter, which he blamed on Farm Instructor Payne. A few days before her death, Payne had physically thrown the frail girl out of his house. Itka decided the time was opportune for revenge, went to the farm instructor's home, and shot him dead. Relatives of Itka, convinced that Canadian authorities would conduct an American-style retaliation against them, decided that their best alternative would be to seek refuge. They went to the house of Barney Tremont, a local farmer, demanding horses. When Tremont refused, he was shot and killed.

While these events were occurring on the Mosquito Reserve, Chiefs Poundmaker and Little Pine, concerned about the outbreak at Duck Lake, decided to travel to Battleford to express their loyalty to the Queen. Poundmaker also decided that at the same time he would take the opportunity to attempt to gain government concessions for food and other treaty provisions. Hearing this, most of the band members decided to accompany their chiefs in the hope that they would be present for the distributions.

The two chiefs and their followers met with Chief Young Sweetgrass on 28 March at the Sweetgrass Reserve, about ten miles west of Battleford. Farm instructors Jefferson and Craig debated whether or not they should accompany the Indians to Battleford, but decided against it for fear of disapproval by their superiors, who wanted Indians to remain on their reserves.

Also present was Peter Ballantyne, who was operating as a spy for Edgar Dewdney. He checked on the Indians' plans and came to the conclusion that their intentions were peaceful.

Meanwhile in Battleford, rumours were rampant that Poundmaker was approaching to attack the town.

BATTLEFORD – THE SIEGE THAT NEVER OCCURRED

When Poundmaker and his followers reached Battleford on the morning of 30 March, they were surprised to find the town deserted. The residents had taken refuge in the North-West Mounted Police barracks on the other side of the river.

Poundmaker sent a message to the fort stating his peaceful intentions and requesting a meeting with Indian Agent Rae. Rae refused to leave the fort, but Peter Ballantyne and Hudson's Bay Company Factor McKay came out to meet Poundmaker. McKay agreed to release food to the Indians from the Hudson's Bay Company store.

Governor Dewdney was sent a telegram stating, 'Indians willing to go back to reserves tomorrow if their demands for clothing are met. Strongly urge you to deal with them as we are not in a position at present to begin an Indian war.'[10] Dewdney later replied, although too late, that he would meet with Poundmaker.

There were other groups who had arrived at Battleford – some of the Stoneys from Mosquito's reserve and Riel's agitators from Duck Lake. As Ballantyne and McKay were returning to the fort after failing to arrange talks with Rae, some of the Métis took shots at them. Later that day, some of the Stoneys began to break into stores and loot. Poundmaker and Little Pine tried to restrain their followers from looting, but with only limited success.

By the next morning, Poundmaker and most of his followers were on their way home. The strain of the troubles was too great for Little Pine, who had been suffering from temporary blindness and other symptoms of starvation. He died on 31 March 1885, a few miles before reaching his reserve. Little Pine's death, and that of old Chief Red Pheasant a few days earlier, meant that Poundmaker had become the main Indian leader in the Battleford area.

Accounts of the siege were blown well out of proportion. The telegraph line had not been tampered with, allowing the Battleford residents to send out daily messages of alarm. During the twenty-five days before relief troops arrived, the five hundred settlers barricaded in the fort were even able to obtain water safely from their only source a mile outside of the barracks. According to one observer, 'one solitary individual – the cook – had the temerity to continue in residence at the old government house. He had many visitors that day, gave them to eat, when they departed without harming him.'[11]

Interestingly enough, another observer reported, 'they [the Indians] had been too hurried to take much; the principal looting was the work of white men. As soon as the coast was clear in the morning they came over in detachments and finished what the Indians had begun. They made a clean sweep.'[12]

Not the least of these raiders was Farm Instructor Craig, who 'devoted his time and attention to looting the stores and houses that had been broken into by the Indians, but his enterprise was frustrated by persistent robbing of his tent whenever he left it.'[13]

Several observers were of the opinion that looting would never have taken place had the townspeople not deserted their houses and stores. By and large, the 'siege' was a fabricated event.

BIG BEAR'S MISFORTUNE PEAKS AT FROG LAKE

Big Bear had become the principal leader of the northern Plains Cree in 1877, following the death of Chief Sweetgrass. Unfortunately, he had a poor relationship with the government. One of the tactics used by the government during treaty negotiations had been to fail to send notification of the meetings to Indian leaders who were considered difficult to deal with. Such was the reason for Big Bear's arrival at Fort Pitt a day after Treaty Six had been signed.

During a speech objecting to the lack of consultation with the several bands he was representing, Big Bear said: 'I have come off to speak for the different bands that are out on the Plains. It is no small matter we were to consult about. I expected the Chiefs here would have waited until I arrived ... I heard the Governor was to come and I said I shall see him; when I see him I will request that he will save me from that which I most dread, that is: the rope to be about my neck, it was not given to us by the Great Spirit that the red man or the white man should shed each other's blood.'[14]

The official treaty interpreter had already left and Reverend McKay, whose mastery of Cree was far from perfect, misinterpreted Big Bear's words to mean a fear of hanging (ayhahkotit). Big Bear was actually saying that he did not wish to lose his freedom, like an animal with a rope around its neck (aysakapaykinit).[15] Nevertheless, the impression created of Big Bear was that he was evil and cowardly, an image which would haunt him up to his final days.

Steadfast in his belief that he could get a revision of Treaty Six, similar to those of Treaties One and Two, Big Bear held out from signing Treaty Six longer than any other chief. He was forced to sign six years later, when it became clear that his band members would starve unless they obtained government rations.

In 1884, after years of urging, Big Bear agreed to choose a reserve next to Poundmaker's. Deputy Superintendent-General of Indian Affairs Lawrence Vankoughnet, a man who disliked Big Bear, vetoed the plan, suggesting it would not be a good idea to have too many 'idle Indians' in one area. Instead, Vankoughnet warned Big Bear to take a reserve already set aside near Fort Pitt – a location which Big Bear had already rejected – or face a cut-off of rations during the winter of 1884–5. Big Bear refused to comply.

An unhealthy blend of ingredients was being mixed. Many members of Big Bear's band, including his son Imases and the War Chief Wandering Spirit, were becoming frustrated with the state of affairs. Compounding the problem was the presence of Indian Agent Quinn, a man known to have been abusive to Indians, and Farm Instructor Delaney, who had been accused of violating Indian women. The government was aware of the unpopularity of these men with the Indians, and had been planning to relocate them.

News of the Duck Lake fight did not reach Agent Quinn until late on 31 March 1885. The next day, 1 April or 'Big Lie Day,' as the Indians called it, Quinn summoned Big Bear's band members to inform them of the incident. Imases, speaking on behalf of Big Bear, who was out hunting for food for the band, replied: 'They have already risen; we knew about it before you. They have beaten the soldiers in the first fight, killing many. We do not wish to join the half-breeds, but we are afraid. We wish to stay here and prove ourselves the friends of the white man.'[16] Imases then asked Quinn to provide rations to the band. Quinn refused, saying he would have to speak to Big Bear first.

Later that day Big Bear returned empty-handed from hunting and led a delegation to request rations from Quinn. Big Bear was upset at his refusal. Imases, hoping to win a compromise, suggested that Quinn give the Indians food for a feast as a gift to the band, and he would not then have to call it rations. Quinn, however, had decided to give them nothing.

That night, unknown to Big Bear, Wandering Spirit and several members of the Rattler's Warrior Society held a dance in secret. As dawn broke some twenty armed warriors came to the Frog Lake community, waking up the residents and herding them to Quinn's house.

That morning, when asked for food and other supplies, Quinn was willing to comply, and various Indians were allowed to have goods from the stores.

That day was Holy Thursday, and two priests who had come for the occasion asked permission to hold church services. The hostages were all allowed to attend church. By this time Big Bear had learned of the trouble and had joined the whites in the church to ensure that nothing worse occurred.

As the church services progressed the noise outside increased. The warriors had broken into the stores and had found wine, spirits, and painkillers. As these were consumed the shouting and yelling of the warriors grew louder, and they eventually began to enter the church and disrupt the service.[17]

Big Bear decided to leave the church and begin warning the other residents of the community, who were in their houses, to leave in case trouble broke out. He was at Mrs Simpson's house when he heard shots. The church service had been cut short.

Wandering Spirit, the war chief, ordered the whites to go to the Indian camp, a short distance away. Quinn refused to move, and after repeated warnings Wandering Spirit shot him dead.

Big Bear ran outside, yelling at the warriors to stop it, but it was too late. Urged on by the prompting of Wandering Spirit, the warriors soon killed eight white men.

Perhaps the violence would have been averted had Quinn simply given food to the starving band the day before. It did not appear that the band was thinking seriously of any sort of insurrection at that time. Even on the following day, had Quinn been liberal with Indian requests for food and simply complied with the warriors' orders, it is possible that bloodshed could have been averted entirely. The presence of alcohol and painkillers can be the only explanation for the gruesomeness of the murders. In Indian thinking, it was considered dishonourable and cowardly to kill an unarmed man for no reason at all.

Big Bear's hopes of peaceful dealings with government had all but vanished, yet he distinguished himself by protecting the lives of the remaining white captives and by preventing greater bloodshed at Fort Pitt.

The warriors moved to seize the provisions at Fort Pitt on 14 April. Big Bear, no longer in control of the band, argued for an attempt to arrange a peaceful surrender of the fort. He held the warriors back for one night, and the next day persuaded forty-four civilians to surrender to the band. With this achieved, the North-West Mounted Police detachment had little reason to stay and was allowed to escape down the river by boat. Big Bear's vigilance was an important factor in preventing any deaths among them.

THE UNPROVOKED ATTACK ON CUTKNIFE HILL

Although Poundmaker had been forced to relinquish power to the warrior society, he was influential in maintaining calm among the Indians camped at Cutknife Hill following the so-called siege of Battleford.

Lieutenant-Colonel Otter arrived at Battleford on 24 April 1885 with close to 550 troops. Also, part of his arsenal was a Gatling gun sent for demonstration by the United States army.

Otter's troops were sorely disappointed at not seeing action on arrival at Battleford. Otter had been ordered by Middleton to stay at Battleford and guard the townspeople. Sensing the unrest of his troops, and seeing the opportunity to gain personal glory, Otter wired Dewdney, 'I propose taking part of my force at once to punish Poundmaker leaving 100 men to garrison Battleford. Great depredations committed. Immediate decisive action necessary. Do you approve?'[18]

Dewdney, probably after consulting the prime minister, wired Otter with approval.

Otter planned to surprise Poundmaker and force him to surrender. On the evening of 28 April, he left Battleford for Cutknife Hill. Otter's timing was good and he arrived at the foot of Cutknife Hill at 5:15 the following morning. Fortunately for Poundmaker's camp, an old man, Jacob With the Long Hair, was awake and heard the sounds of the approaching soldiers. He ran through the camp shouting warnings.

At that point, Otter ordered his guns to open fire on the sleeping camp. The barrage knocked over some tipis, but all of the occupants managed to scramble to safety.

Some of the Indian warriors ran out to confront the troops while others began shooting from nearby coulees. According to Robert Jefferson, an eyewitness, 'Not more than 50 [Indians] altogether, had taken part in the battle. This was excusable since few were armed.'[19] As the battle continued throughout the morning, Otter realized that his troops were in a vulnerable position and were slowly being surrounded. Just before noon, he ordered his men to retreat.

The warriors wanted to pursue Otter. Knowing the land like the backs of their hands and gaining the advantage of nightfall, the warriors could have inflicted heavy casualties on the tiring soldiers. Poundmaker refused to agree, maintaining that while the Indians were right in defending themselves on their land, it would be wrong to go on the offensive.

There had been a split among the people at Cutknife Hill. On the one side was the pro-Riel faction consisting of the Métis agitators and the Stoney warriors. On the other side were those led by Poundmaker who wanted to have as little as possible to do with the rebellion. Poundmaker had tried to lead his followers west towards the hilly country around Devil's Lake, with plans to take refuge eventually near Crowfoot, but the warriors and Métis prevented them from leaving.

Poundmaker was essentially being used as a spokesman by the belligerent faction. An example of this was a letter to Riel dictated by Riel's sympathizers but bearing the 'signatures' of Poundmaker and several other Indians. Poundmaker's lack of verbal or written knowledge of either French or English put him at a great disadvantage. The fact was that Poundmaker was not in control, and the insinuation of support for Riel contained in the letter was out of character with his actions. That letter later became the main piece of evidence used in convicting Poundmaker.

Following the Battle of Cutknife Hill, it was decided it was no longer safe to remain on the reserve. When the pro-Riel faction decided to join Riel at Batoche, Poundmaker attempted to lead his followers west, away from trouble.

The dispute nearly led to bloodshed, but Poundmaker's poorly armed followers relented. Poundmaker's lack of cooperation and additional efforts to break away from the camp slowed the Indians' progress to Batoche by several days.

Poundmaker's stalling tactics saved many Indian lives, for as they neared Batoche on 14 May they received news that Middleton's army had just defeated the Métis. After some discussion, Poundmaker sought terms of surrender from Middleton; when refused, he surrendered unconditionally at Battleford on 26 May 1885.

Poundmaker's plan to abandon his reserve and seek refuge by moving to an isolated area was not unique. A significant number of band members, from reserves such as Mosquito's, Red Pheasant's, One Arrow's, and Thunderchild's, went north to avoid any involvement in the troubles.

During this period, Sir John A. Macdonald was attempting to exploit tribal differences by inquiring about sending Indian patrols against Poundmaker and Big Bear. He wrote Dewdney on 29 March 1885 'I understand that the Crees dread the Blackfeet like the devil. Now a corps of scouts under Crowfoot might be formed.'[20] Because of the relationship between Crowfoot and Poundmaker this plan never succeeded, despite repeated requests from the prime minister.

AT BATOCHE AGAINST THEIR WILL

Part of the strategy of Riel's Provisional Government was based on the belief that they held influence over the Indians. In a note to the English half-breeds on 22 March 1885, they wrote, 'We are sure that if the English and French half-breeds unite well in this time of crisis, not only can we control the Indians, but we will also have their weight on our side.'[21] With Indians outnumbering both Métis and whites in the North-West, their support in a conflict could be critical, but the presumption of Indian involvement was made without consultation with any of the Indian leaders.

On 18 March 1885, one day before Riel's proclamation of his Provisional Government, that process of 'controlling' Indians began. About forty Riel supporters arrived at One Arrow's Reserve, approximately two miles east of Batoche, taking the Indian agent and farm instructor prisoner. The next day, One Arrow and fifteen of his men came to Batoche. As One Arrow testified at his trial, 'I am an old man now ... I was taken to the place, Batoche's, to join Riel by Gabriel. I did not take myself to the place. They took me there. I could not say how many there were of them that took me there, but there was quite a number of them ... so when I went there and got there I was taken prisoner.'[22] Witnesses testified that One Arrow was seen in the area during both the Duck Lake fight and the Battle of Batoche. In his defence,

One Arrow testified that 'all that was said against me was thrown upon me falsely. I did not take up my gun with the intention to shoot at any man. I was on the brink of the hill the whole day, and I had my gun there, but, of course, not with the intention to use the gun against any man, and when I saw the whitemen coming down, I ran down the hill too, and ran off.'[23]

On 10 April 1885 around twenty Riel supporters arrived at Whitecap's Reserve, a few miles south of Saskatoon. Whitecap, the chief of a band of refugee American Dakota, had resisted Riel's overtures two weeks previously. Before the Métis began forcing Whitecap and twenty of his men towards Batoche, Whitecap managed to send a message to a white friend in Saskatoon, Gerald Willoughby, asking him for assistance. When the group reached Saskatoon, a group of nine citizens tried to persuade the Métis to allow Whitecap to return to his reserve. Outnumbered, their attempt was unsuccessful.

When Whitecap arrived at Batoche, he was appointed the only Indian member of Riel's council on internal matters, but because he understood neither French nor Cree he attended only one meeting.

Whitecap's men were seen at the battles of Fish Creek and Batoche. Testimony provided by the main prosecution witnesses showed that Whitecap could not be positively identified as having been among the several old Indian men at Batoche, but it was mainly because of the evidence showing that Whitecap had been coerced to fight that all charges against him were dropped.[24]

THE INDIAN TRIALS: UNWARRANTED PUNISHMENT

Poundmaker, despite evidence of his efforts to maintain peace, was convicted of treason-felony on the basis of the letter to Riel bearing his name. Speaking after hearing the guilty verdict, Poundmaker categorically denied any wrongdoing, saying, 'Everything that is bad has been laid against me this summer, there is nothing of it true.'[25] On hearing that he was sentenced to three years at Stony Mountain, Poundmaker declared, 'I would prefer to be hung at once than to be in that place.'[26] Poundmaker was released in the spring of 1886, largely because of public sympathy, but he died in June after making a trek on foot to visit his adoptive father Crowfoot.

Although the evidence was strongly in favour of Big Bear, it appeared that the outcome of his trial was predetermined and he was sentenced to the same three-year term as Poundmaker. There was less public sympathy for Big Bear, and he was not released until 3 February 1887, after a medical report confirmed his badly deteriorating health. He had no band to return to, since it had been dispersed by the government. Most of his family he would never see, since they were fugitives in the United States. With his heart broken and no cause to live for, he died on 18 January 1888.

When Chief One Arrow heard the charges of treason-felony translated to him, it came out in Cree as 'knocking off the Queen's bonnet and stabbing her in the behind with a sword.'[27] This moved One Arrow to ask the interpreter if he was drunk. The conviction of One Arrow was based on his presence at the battle sites, and his account of how he came to be there was ignored.

One Arrow was not so fortunate as to make it back to his own reserve. He was released from Stony Mountain Prison on 21 April 1886 and died four days later at Archbishop Taché's residence in St Boniface. He was baptised just before his death and lies in St Boniface cemetery in an unmarked grave.

In order to save money, a decision was made not to hold all of the rebellion trials at Regina. Several of them were held in Battleford instead. The atmosphere in Battleford was not hospitable towards Indians, as an editorial written in the *Saskatchewan Herald* on 23 April 1885, shows:

> The petted Indians are the bad ones. The Stonies have been treated as being of a superior race, and are the first to shed the blood of their benefactors. Poundmaker has been petted and feted, and stands in the front rank as a raider. Little Pine, bribed to come north and kept in comfort, hastens to the carnage. Big Bear, who has for years enjoyed the privilege of eating of the bread of idleness, shows his gratitude by killing his priests and his best friends in cold blood. Little Poplar, a non-treaty Indian has been liberally supplied with provisions and other necessaries and thus enabled to spend all his time in travelling up and down the land plotting mischief and preparing for this season's carnival of ruin. The petted Indians have proved the bad ones, and this gives weight to the old adage that the only good Indians are the dead ones.[28]

Judge Rouleau, who would pass the judgments, had narrowly missed being murdered along with Farm Instructor Payne, and was also bitter about the burning of his mansion at Battleford. He was known before the trials to advocate harsh punishment as a deterrent to future rebellious acts by Indians.

The eight Indians eventually hanged were at a disadvantage. They knew nothing of the legal system and had no legal counsel or other advice. No effective defence of any sort was mounted which might have created sympathy for the defendants – for example, the reality of their starvation under Indian Affairs administration, or the excesses brought on by alcohol and drugs at the Frog Lake massacre.

Several Indian elders are certain that at least one of the Indians, Man-Without-Blood, was wrongly hanged for the shooting of Farm Instructor

Payne. They claim it was done by the other Stoney, Man-With-A-Black-Blanket. According to one story:

> The two of the Stoney young men were arrested also. They were accused of killing the farm instructor and they were both arrested. And at that time people were very respectable. There was a lot of respect for the older people. Now the one who did not kill the Indian Agent, he was the one who was accused by his partner. So the one who was accused of killing the farm instructor, when he went to trial, the officer asked him, 'Is it true what you did? Or is it not true?' He replied, 'Maybe it is true, and maybe it is not.' And he really had nothing to do with it, he didn't shoot the Indian Agent. So when he said, 'Maybe they are telling the truth,' that was accepted as his plea, as telling the truth. So he got the blame for the death of the farm instructor. So he was one of them that got hanged. They weren't going to sympathize with him or feel sorry for him.[29]

According to another story, 'It's him who killed the ration feeder. And the one who followed him shot the dog. He was the one who got hung instead, said my father, the one who shot the dog. He did not want to report his partner.'[30]

No clear evidence of committing murder was shown against Iron Body and Little Bear, two of the six Indians tried for their role in the Frog Lake massacre. They were hanged on the basis that, by aiding and abetting the others, they were equally guilty.

Four Sky Thunder received a sentence of fourteen years for burning down the Frog Lake church. Another Indian, whose only wrongdoing was having been seen with Big Bear, was sentenced to six years in prison.[31]

Several Indians were never brought to justice. Among them was Man-Who-Speaks-Our-Language, who nearly caused the outbreak of fighting with the North-West Mounted Police on Poundmaker's reserve in 1884 and was responsible for some of the killings at Frog Lake.

The hangings at Battleford took place on 27 November 1885. Indians from several reserves were there to witness the event.

A new section was built at Stony Mountain Penitentiary to accommodate the twenty-five Indians and eighteen Métis sentenced to prison. Several of the Indians never returned to their reserves and are buried in the St Boniface cemetery.

THE AFTERMATH: SUPPRESSION OF INDIANS

The government saw the rebellion as an opportunity to achieve a goal which had eluded it since 1870 – that of gaining total control over Indians. In July

1885 Assistant Commissioner Hayter Reed drew up a list of fifteen recommendations on actions to be taken following the rebellion. Among these were the following:

> The leaders of the Teton Sioux who fought against the troops should be hanged and the rest be sent out of the country;
>
> Big Bear's band should either be broken up and scattered among other bands or be given a reserve adjacent to that at Onion Lake;
>
> One Arrow's band should be joined with that of Beardy and Okemasis and their reserve surrendered;
>
> No annuity money should be now paid any bands that rebelled, or to any individuals that joined the insurgents;
>
> The tribal system should be abolished in so far as is compatible with the Treaty;
>
> All half-breeds, members of rebel bands, although not shown to have taken any active part in the rebellion, should have their names erased from the paysheets;
>
> No rebel Indians should be allowed off the Reserves without a pass signed by an Indian Department official; and
>
> All Indians who have not during the late troubles been disloyal or troublesome should be treated as heretofore.[32]

Reed had also prepared a list of every Indian band in the North-West and had identified twenty-eight disloyal bands. In his enthusiasm he erroneously included several reserves, such as Sweetgrass and Thunderchild, which had been very loyal. Most of the others had actually been loyal, with only the odd individual implicated in the rebellion. Of all the bands identified as disloyal in the rebellion, it is clear that none of the chiefs, whether Big Bear, Poundmaker, Mosquito, Red Pheasant, Little Pine, Beardy, One Arrow, or Whitecap, politically supported the rebellion. All were drawn into the conflict by circumstances beyond their personal control. In all, less than 5 per cent of the Indian population of the North-West was involved.

The original proposal to disallow rebel Indians from leaving their reserves without a pass soon became a measure to be applied to all Indians. In approving this plan, Sir John A. Macdonald was aware that he was contravening the treaties. He noted: 'Mr. Dewdney thinks that the pass system can be generally introduced in July. If so, it is in the highest degree desirable. As to the disloyal

Bands, this should be carried out as the consequence of their disloyalty. The system should be introduced in the loyal Bands as well and the advantage of the change pressed upon them. But no punishment for breaking bounds could be inflicted and in the case of resistance on the grounds of Treaty rights should not be insisted on.'[33]

The measures taken against Indians, in particular those restricting them to reserves, were measures which would have a profound effect on subsequent Indian developments. What little influence Indian people had over their own lives was removed, and Indian people became vulnerable to government whim, manipulation, and mismanagement.

It was regrettable that Sir John A. Macdonald, who was superintendent general of Indian affairs and prime minister, never once bothered to visit the people over whom he had charge during the eight critical years he held office, from 1879 to 1887.

Had the Indian people been able to retain their freedom of movement, things might have turned out much differently. Big Bear and other Indian leaders might have met Sir John A. Macdonald in 1885. Nationally, efforts to form the League of Indians of Canada in the 1920s and the North American Indian Brotherhood in the 1940s would have been more successful and probably would have received the bulk of their strength from the prairies. Indian political development in Canada was probably put back by two generations.

The rebellion has left a legacy of a century of suspicions about Indian political abilities and loyalties, and misconceptions about the validity of Indian treaties.

In concluding, I would say that a clear understanding of the Indian view of the 1885 uprising is the least that can be done to right the blunders of the past.

NOTES

This article is from *1885 and After: Native Society in Transition*, ed. F. Laurie Barron and James B. Waldram. Regina: Canadian Plains Research Center 1986. Reprinted with permission.

1 Florence Paul, interview by Wilfred Tootoosis, One Arrow Indian Reserve, 15 March 1985
2 Harry Michael, interview by Wilfred Tootoosis, Beardy's Indian Reserve, 14 March 1985
3 Canada, *Treaty Number Six Between Her Majesty the Queen and the Plain and Wood Cree Indians and Other Tribes of Indians* (Ottawa: Queen's Printer 1964), 5
4 John B. Tootoosis, interview by Wilfred Tootoosis, Poundmaker Indian Reserve, 30 Nov. 1984

5 Canada, *Sessional Papers*, 1886, no. 36, 2
6 National Archives of Canada (NA), RG 10, vol. 3697, file 15,423, MacRae to Dewdney, 25 Aug. 1884
7 NA, RG 10, vol. 3584, file 1130, pt 3A, McBeath to Macdonald, 28 March 1885
8 Ibid., Macdonald to Indian Commissioner, 8 April 1885
9 Ibid., Piapot to Macdonald, 30 April 1885
10 Dewdney Papers, vol. 5, 1879–80, Rae to Dewdney, 30 March 1885
11 Robert Jefferson, *Fifty Years on the Saskatchewan* (Battleford: Canadian Northwest Historical Society 1929), 127
12 Ibid., 128
13 Ibid., 126
14 Alexander Morris, *Treaties of Canada with the Indians of Manitoba and the North-West Territories* (Toronto: Coles Publishing Limited 1971), 239
15 Hugh Dempsey, *Big Bear – The End of Freedom* (Vancouver: Douglas and McIntyre 1984), 74
16 W.B. Cameron, *Blood Red The Sun* (Edmonton: Hurtig Publishers 1977), 33
17 Dempsey, *Big Bear*, 155
18 Dewdney Papers, vol. 5, 1806, Otter to Dewdney, 26 April 1885
19 Jefferson, *Fifty Years*, 146
20 NA, MG 26A, vol. 526, 1404, Macdonald to Dewdney, 29 March 1885
21 Bob Beal and Rod Macleod, *Prairie Fire: The 1885 North-West Rebellion* (Edmonton: Hurtig Publishers 1984), 148
22 Canada, *Sessional Papers*, 1886, no. 52, 33
23 Ibid., 32
24 Ibid., 13
25 Ibid., 336
26 Ibid., 337
27 Beal and Macleod, *Prairie Fire*, 309
28 *Saskatchewan Herald* (Battleford), 23 April 1885
29 Lawrence Lonesinger, interview by Wilfred Tootoosis, Sweetgrass Indian Reserve, 13 March 1985
30 Alex Sapp, interview by Wilfred Tootoosis, Little Pine Indian Reserve, date not available
31 S.E. Bingaman, 'The North-West Rebellion Trials, 1885' (MA thesis, University of Regina, 1971), 133
32 NA, RG 10, vol. 3710, file 19, 550-3, Reed to Dewdney, 20 July 1885
33 Ibid., Vankoughnet to Superintendent General, 17 Aug. 1885

RELATIONS

ON THE PACIFIC

ROBIN FISHER

Indian Control of the Maritime Fur Trade and the Northwest Coast

Historians have usually characterized the maritime fur trade on the northwest coast as a trade in which gullible Indians were exploited by avaricious and unprincipled European traders. Stanley Ryerson has asserted that the maritime fur trade 'depended on ruthless exploitation of Indian labour ... backed whenever necessary by force or open threats of force.'[1] Others, with less obvious ideological commitments, have made similar comments. H.H. Bancroft wrote of Captain James Cook buying furs from the 'guileless savage,'[2] while F.W. Howay, the most meticulous student of the maritime fur trade, described it as a predatory affair, 'merely a looting of the coast.'[3] Like much historical writing on Indian-European relations, these conclusions are an attempt to pass judgment on European behaviour rather than to analyse Indian responses to the culture contact situation.

The first contact with the Indians of the area that was to become British Columbia was in July 1774 when the Spanish navigator, Juan Pérez, met a group of Haida off the northwest point of Langara Island. But this first fleeting contact between the two cultures was not renewed for four years[4] and a decade was to pass before the first fur-trading expedition came to the coast. In 1778 James Cook, leading his third voyage to the Pacific, spent nearly a month refitting at Nootka Sound. While he was there his crews obtained a number of sea otter skins from the Indians and the story has often been retold of how these pelts fetched fabulous prices in China. However, rumours of the profits to be made by selling sea otter furs in China were not confirmed until the publication of the official account of Cook's third voyage in 1784 and Captain James King's revelation that some of the best skins had sold for $120.[5] In the following year the first fur-trading vessel, appropriately named *Sea Otter*, under James Hanna, arrived at Nootka.

In the next few years, as explorers began to probe the sounds and circle the islands, the continental foreshore was opened to the maritime fur trade. For the first three seasons all the trading vessels were British, but in 1788 the first American ships arrived on the coast. In 1792 the maritime fur trade really began to burgeon. In that season there were twenty-one vessels engaged in the trade, nearly double the number of the previous year, and more than half of them were British. But in the following year the American outnumbered the English, and this trend was to continue until, by 1801, the trade was dominated by American vessels, most of them out of Boston. The peak years of the maritime fur trade were from 1792 to about 1812. By 1825 the Hudson's Bay Company was becoming active on the northwest coast and the maritime fur trade had virtually ceased to exist as a separate entity.

During the very early years of the trade it was true that pelts were relatively easily acquired and some European traders made considerable profits. On 2 July 1787 Captain George Dixon was tacking into a bay that was later to become famous as Cloak Bay when some Haida approached in their canoes. As Pérez had found, curiosity was the initial reaction of the Indians. The Haida could not, at first, be tempted to trade; 'their attention seemed entirely taken up with viewing the vessel, which they apparently did with marks of wonder and surprise.'[6] Only after the Indians had satisfied their curiosity about the vessel could they be induced to trade. Later in the day Dixon ran his snow, the *Queen Charlotte*, further up the bay and a scene is described 'which absolutely beggars all description.' The crew was 'so overjoyed, that we could scarcely believe the evidence of our senses,' because the Indians were falling over each other to trade their cloaks and furs: 'they fairly quarrelled with each other about which should sell his cloak first; and some actually threw their furs on board if nobody was at hand to receive them.' In half an hour Dixon obtained three hundred furs.[7] A month later, when he left the islands he had named the Queen Charlottes, his vessel had 1821 furs in its hold.[8] In 1789, two years after Dixon's visit, the crew of the American ship *Columbia* emulated his example. John Kendrick, the master of the *Columbia*, made one of the best deals ever when, in a few minutes, he traded 200 pelts at the rate of one chisel each at the Indian village of Kiusta on the northern end of Graham Island.[9] In the first years of the trade these furs, so cheaply purchased, brought high prices in China. It was claimed that the 560 sea otter pelts that Hanna collected on his first trip realized $20,600,[10] and that the Dixon and Portlock expedition sold 2552 furs for 54,875 Spanish dollars.[11] Prices such as these moved Dixon's associate, Nathaniel Portlock, to remark that this branch of commerce was perhaps 'the most profitable and lucrative employ that the enterprising merchant can possibly engage in.'[12]

Yet, even in these early years, the Indians were not passive objects of exploitation. Rather they vigorously asserted their demands. Northwest coast Indians were, for example, never very interested in baubles and beads as trade items. Cook noted in his journal that European beads could not supplant the Nootkans' own ornaments.[13] So the old stereotype of the avaricious trader stealing Indian furs for a few trinkets never applied to the maritime fur trade.

Furthermore, the comparatively easy trading and high profits of the first frantic years of the trade were not to continue. As vessels visited the coast with increased frequency, the maritime fur trade settled into a more consistent pattern – and it was a pattern of trade over which the Indians exercised a great deal of control. It was, after all, Indian demands that had to be satisfied before sea otter pelts changed hands.

For one thing the Indians rapidly lost their curiosity about the Europeans and their vessels. A ship under full sail was an impressive sight, but to the trading Indians it became commonplace. In contrast to the curiosity with which the *Queen Charlotte* was received in 1787, the Indians of Cloak Bay wandered all over Jacinto Caamano's ship, *Aranzazu*, in 1792 'without showing wonder at anything, nor was there any object of which they did not appear to know the use.'[14] As in most contact situations, the initial phase, when the white men were inexplicable and were perhaps even regarded as supernatural beings, soon passed. It quickly became apparent to the Indians that their visitors were quite human, and though some of their behaviour might be curious, many of their demands and desires were familiar.

As the Indians grew accustomed to the presence of the Europeans they also became shrewder in their trading with them. Even after his brief encounter with a group of Haida in 1774, Pérez declared that the Indians were expert and skilful traders.[15] The members of Cook's expedition reached similar conclusions. As one of them put it, 'they are very keen traders getting as much as they could for everything they had; always asking for more give them what you would.'[16] The consequence of their astuteness was that the Indians of Nootka 'got a greater middly and variety of things' from *Resolution* and *Discovery* than any other people that the vessels had visited.[17] When John Meares left on a trading expedition to the coast in 1787, he was warned that 'it appears that the natives are such intelligent traders, that should you be in the least degree lavish, or inattentive in forming bargains, they will so enhance the value of their furs, as not only to exhaust your present stock, but also to injure, if not to ruin, any future adventure.'[18]

The Indian demand for metals, particularly iron, was recognized by most early traders. Cook's ships left Nootka with hardly any brass left on board, and his crews had also traded a considerable amount of iron.[19] Like the explorers, the early fur traders found that the coast Indians were most partial to iron. Members of the Spanish expedition led by Pérez had noted that the Indians particularly wanted large pieces with a cutting edge, and Dixon's staple medium of exchange was 'toes,' or iron chisels.[20] Early in 1789 the crew of the *Columbia*, trading in the Straits of Juan De Fuca, were mortified to see seventy prime pelts escape them 'for want of Chizels to purchase them.'[21]

Another indication of Indian control of the maritime fur trade was the rapid increase in the price of furs in the early 1790s. Traders in those years who hoped to follow the example of those who were first in the field and purchase large numbers of furs cheaply were often disappointed. John Boit returned to the coast in 1795 and found that the price of pelts at Dadens on Langara Island had increased 100 per cent since 1792 when he had been there on the *Columbia*.[22] Archibald Menzies observed a similar rate of increase in Johnstone Strait when he returned there with Vancouver in 1792,[23] while another member of Vancouver's expedition claimed that prices generally had quadrupled since the earliest voyages.[24] At Nootka, where Meares had traded ten skins for one piece of copper in 1786, the asking rate six years later was one pelt for one piece of copper.[25] Price increases such as these led the Spaniard, Alejandro Malaspina, to conclude that the great profits of Cook's and Portlock's voyages should be forgotten as unattainable.[26] There were, of course, other factors that affected prices, including the growing scarcity of furs. However, the depletion of the sea otter was not as significant in the early 1790s as it was to be after the turn of the century. The Indians had learned to demand higher prices while furs were still relatively plentiful.

Not only did the Indians quickly learn to demand a greater quantity of goods for their furs, but they also became very discriminating about the nature of the goods they acquired. It is a commonly held view that the Indian taste in trade goods was 'strangely whimsical and constantly variable.'[27] By citing examples from widely differing points in time and place it is possible to create the impression that Indian demands were merely fickle,[28] and to obscure those patterns that their requests conformed to. Initially the Indians wanted articles that had meaning and use within pre-contact society. They possessed both iron and copper at the time of contact,[29] but these metals were not plentiful. For this reason iron and other metals were highly valued and in great demand in the early years of the maritime fur trade. The iron chisels brought by the traders were sufficiently similar to indigenous tools to be readily understood, hence the heavy initial demand for them. As the market became saturated with these items their value dropped, other needs began to operate, and new demands were made. The trade meant that the furs were not used as much for clothing as they had been prior to the arrival of the European. The need for an alternative arose, so the Indians turned their attention to trading cloth, clothing, and blankets. The demand for blankets particularly remained fairly constant, and they became a staple in the trade. As a garment they served an important function for the Indians. But the blanket was also an article that could be easily counted and compared. It was, therefore, a useful medium of exchange both in the fur trade and for Indian potlatches. During the later years of the trade the Indians acquired some more exotic tastes. A liking for rum, smoking tobacco, and molasses gradually developed, and muskets also became an important trade item.[30]

Naturally, there were exceptions to this pattern, as the Indian market was as much subject to fads as any other. Yet most of these were also related to Indian usages. The popularity of the iron collars forged aboard the brigatine *Hope* has been seen as the height of Haida fadishness,[31] but this demand was consistent with the Haida taste in personal ornamentation. Copper bracelets, for example, were frequently worn and Joseph Ingraham made his collars from the pattern of one he had seen a Haida woman wearing.[32] The same point can be made about the ermine skins that William Sturgis sold with considerable profit at Kaigani.[33] Ermine pelts were an important wealth item among the coast Indians. But demand for this kind of article was temporary and the market quickly became glutted.

There were other factors that created the impression the Indians would take a great variety of goods. At times they would receive as presents items, such as beads and trinkets, they would not accept as trade.[34] Often when Indians accepted these baubles they were as an additional gift to facilitate trade and not as a part of the actual trading transaction. These presents added to the diversity of goods that changed hands but not to the number of articles that would buy furs.

Trading Indians not only paid great attention to the type of goods they acquired but also were discriminating about the quality, and trade articles were examined closely and carefully before bargains were struck.[35] Iron that contained flaws or was too brittle was of little value to the Indians because they worked it while it was cold.[36] Indians showed great 'judgment and sagacity' when selecting firearms; [37] woollen goods of insufficient quality were turned down,[38] and porcelain imitations of dentalia shells were treated with contempt.[39] Usually the Indians knew what they wanted when they were trading and they were determined to get it.

Nor were Indian traders easily diverted from their purpose. One captain hoped that a few hours of conviviality in the house of a chief would bring him more furs, 'but no sooner was traffic mentioned, than from being the engaging master of the house, he became a Jew chapman and dealer.'[40] There are numerous comments in the journals of trading expeditions to the northwest coast about the enterprise of Indian traders whose trading acumen meant that many captains 'had the sorrow to see valuable furs escape us, the acquisition of which was the principal object of the expedition, for want of suitable objects to exchange.'[41]

As vessels came in search of furs with increasing frequency, the Indians became very tough-minded manipulators of competition. They forced prices upwards, particularly at places often visited by traders. As a consequence, in the early years furs were found to cost more at Nootka than at other places.[42] Later, harbours such as Newitty, Massett, and Kaigani became centres of trade and of high prices. At Kaigani John D'Wolf found in 1805 that the Indians were 'so extravagant in their demands ... that it was quite impossible to trade.'[43] When more than one vessel was at anchor the Indians would move from one to another comparing prices and bargaining to force them upward; and, as one trader observed, it was easy to increase one's price but always impossible to reduce it.[44] The American Richard Cleveland, while on the northern coast in 1799, was told by another captain that he could expect ten other vessels from Boston to be trading in the area that year. He was, therefore, anxious to dispose of his 'articles of traffic' before competition reduced their value, because, he said, 'the Indians are sufficiently cunning to derive all possible advantage from competition, and will go from one vessel to another, and back again, with assertions of offers made to them, which have no foundation in truth, and showing themselves to be as well versed in the tricks of the trade as the greatest adepts.'[45] Even the captains of solitary vessels who felt Indian prices were exorbitant were informed that other traders would soon follow who would be willing to pay what was asked.[46] Such exploitation of competition by the trading Indians was one of the reasons why, far from making a killing, many fur-trading voyages were ruinous to their promoters.[47] As the Indians raised their prices, captains were apt to overestimate the value of their cargo and, therefore, their margin of profit.

Indian traders were not above adding a few tricks to the trade. When Cook was at Nootka he found that the Indians were not quite as 'guileless' as Bancroft would have us believe. The explorer discovered that the Indians were deceiving his men by selling containers of oil that were partly filled with water. In fact, 'once or twice they had the address to impose upon us whole bladders of water without a drop of oil in them.'[48] Another captain found a Nootkan trying to pass off a land otter pelt as a sea otter in the dusk of evening.[49] Meares went as far as to claim that in their commercial transactions the Indians would play a thousand tricks. He was probably exaggerating when he added that Europeans were 'more or less, the dupes of their cunning,'[50] but it is undeniable that Indians behaved with confidence when they were trading.

The Indians were able to assert their demands with such vigour that European captains had to modify their trading methods to accommodate them. In the early years of trade, Dixon had largely coasted along the shore line and relied on the Indians to paddle out to him to trade. He was convinced 'that this plan was attended with better and speedier success than our laying at anchor could possibly be.'[51] Only four years later, in 1791, Ingraham collected 1400 sea otter skins off the Queen Charlotte Islands, and he attributed his success to the opposite tactic of remaining at one village until no further furs could be secured. The Indians preferred this approach to paddling out four or five miles to a moving vessel.[52] The tendency was for captains to have to spend more time in one place instead of moving about. It also became apparent that one season was insufficient time to gather a profitable cargo. Crews began to winter on the coast and, by 1806–8, to trade all year round.[53] Initially most trading was conducted over the side of vessels with the Indians remaining in their canoes, but increasingly they had to be allowed to come on deck to display their wares.

Changes such as these resulted from the fact that the Indians preferred to trade at their leisure. They had plenty of time at their disposal and liked to use it to bargain over prices. Even though captains were invariably in a hurry to fill their holds, Indian concepts of time operated increasingly. Many 'would wait alongside several hours – nay all day – to obtain their price.[54] D'Wolf complained that the Kaigani Indians would lie about the deck for days on end endeavouring to extort unreasonable prices for their furs, while affecting the utmost indifference as to whether they sold them or not.[55]

Other Indian usages had to be observed by captains hoping to acquire furs. The journals show that a considerable amount of Indian ceremonial accompanied trading contacts. One observer noted it was a constant custom to begin and terminate commercial transactions with strangers with singing.[56] Although traders often found such ceremonies irritating and time consuming, they had to be patiently accepted before the exchange of goods began. However fixed European notions of the nature of trade might be, traders also had to accede to the custom of gift exchange with Indian leaders.[57] This ritual was observed in spite of the feeling on the part of some captains that furs exchanged as presents were sure to prove the dearest they obtained.[58]

European traders were also adapting to the patterns of northwest coast Indian society by conducting most of their trading with Indian leaders rather than the general population. Some of the trading was done with individual families, but the people did not possess such an abundance of furs as their leaders.[59] Those chiefs who had the good fortune to be in the right place at the right time were able to exercise great control over the trade, and their wealth and, consequently, their prestige were greatly increased. Perhaps the most famous, if not the most powerful, was Maquinna, the leader of the Indians whose summer village was at Yuquot in Nootka Sound. Probably newly succeeded to chieftainship when the maritime fur trade began, Maquinna was able to tap the wealth of his own people as well as that of neighbouring groups. During the Nootka Sound controversy he was feted by both the Spanish and the English, and European traders recognized him as the leading trading chief in the area. By manipulating the fur trade, Maquinna became incredibly wealthy by Indian standards. In 1803, for example, it is reported that he gave a potlatch at which he dispensed 200 muskets, 200 yards of cloth, 100 chemises, 100 looking glasses, and 7 barrels of gunpowder.[60]

There were other Indian leaders whose power was comparable to that of Maquinna. It is possible that Wickaninish, the leader at Clayoquot Sound, was even more powerful.[61] On the northern Queen Charlottes, Cunneah, who resided at Kuista, was the first mentioned and best known chief. Also very important was Kow, who initially lived at Dadens, but during the 1790s moved across Dixon Entrance and established himself permanently at his summer village at Kaigani.[62] Like Maquinna, these leaders acquired great wealth. In 1799, when the author of the *Eliza* journal visited the house of Kow, the chief proudly displayed his wealth. The house was lined with boxes of goods acquired in the trade, but Kow drew particular attention to his hoard of ermine skins which were valued as gold or silver. By virtue of his collection of 120 of these pelts Kow claimed that, next to Cunneah, he was the wealthiest chief in the area.[63]

So great was the power and influence of some of these leaders that European traders found it very much in their interest to cultivate their friendship and they had to be treated with much of the deference they expected from their own people. Richard Cleveland was one trader who generally could not abide the presence of Indians on the deck of his ship. When he was at Kaigani, however, Kow had to be indulged with hospitality on board. It would, said Cleveland, 'have been folly to have prevented him.'[64] Indian leaders who were unwittingly insulted had to be mollified, while supposed insults from Indians were tolerated in the hope of driving a bargain.[65]

European traders were further subject to Indian trading patterns to the extent that those Indians who sold them furs were often middlemen who had their own mark-up. The first Europeans to arrive on the coast noticed how Indian traders made efforts to prevent other Indians from trading with them. While he was at Nootka, Cook, who by 1778 was an experienced observer of the behaviour of indigenous peoples, noted that the Indians he first contacted attempted to monopolize the trade with the *Resolution* and the *Discovery*. Whenever strangers were allowed to trade with the ships, the transactions were managed by the people of Yuquot, [66] and in such a way as to increase their own prices while lowering the value of the English commodities.[67] On other occasions the local Indians used force to prevent outsiders from trading with the ships.[68] It was evident that these explorers had not arrived in a commercial desert, but that definite trading patterns already existed. Much is often made by European historians of the trading abilities of the Yankee captains out of Boston, but it is less frequently remembered that the Indians had a long tradition of trading among themselves.

Many, perhaps most, of the furs that changed hands during the period of the maritime fur trade were not captured by the Indians who traded them.

When captains were exhorted, as they often were, to wait a day or two so that Indian traders could gather more furs, it did not mean that those Indians intended to hunt for them. Indian leaders on the outer coast collected furs from those who lived deeper inland, either as plunder or by trade. Some chiefs quite frankly told white traders that if they would wait they would go and fight for furs which they would then bring to sell.[69] No doubt this method of gathering pelts was not uncommon. It was well known that Maquinna controlled a trading network with the Indians who lived near the mouth of the Nimpkish River on the east coast of Vancouver Island. When European explorers established the insularity of Vancouver Island, they also found that the Indians who had villages along Johnstone and Queen Charlotte Straits were quite familiar with their merchandise. These Indians, in contrast to the Coast Salish to the south, had passed through the stage of high demand for iron and were also much sharper traders.[70] Maquinna nevertheless made considerable profit in his trade with these people.[71] Wickaninish, the chief of Clayoquot Sound, exercised a similar control over the trade of that area.[72] The Haida likewise traded with mainland groups. By 1799 it was considered that not half of the furs traded at the Queen Charlottes were collected there.[73] Indians on the outer coast exchanged European goods with inland Indians at 200 and 300 per cent profit margins,[74] and in this way furs were collected at the central locations of the trade with European vessels. Thus, one seaman observed, 'we see the untutored Indian influenced by true Mercantile principles.'[75] Certainly, if there was exploitation in the maritime fur trade, it was not confined to Europeans.

It has been argued that because trading captains seldom expected to return to a specific locality, they were frequently able to defraud Indian traders and regularly took violent action against them.[76] In fact there was more continuity in the trade than might be expected. There are records of some 300 fur-trading vessels coming to the northwest coast during the forty years between 1785 and 1825. Of this total, 40 per cent spent more than one season trading on the coast, and about 23 per cent made three or more visits.[77] Not only did many vessels and captains return to the coast more than once but also a large percentage of the trade was done with a few Indian leaders at a limited number of entrepôts. So a European trader who made more than one voyage was very likely to return to the same place to trade, particularly if relations with the Indians had been amicable during the first visit. The possibility of a return trip militated against the indiscriminate use of fraud and violence.

During this early period of culture contact there was a certain amount of inter-racial violence but its extent should not be exaggerated. Such were the demands made by the Indians on European traders that it was considered that 'a man ought to be endowed with an uncommon share of patience to trade with any of these people.'[78] Of course, many trading captains lacked their fair share of patience and, caught in the squeeze between increasing costs on the northwest coast and declining prices in China, they were apt to become annoyed with Indians who made what they considered to be unreasonable demands. When the early method of coasting became unfruitful, vessels had to stay longer in one place to negotiate trading terms and the extended contact added to the possibility of friction. Given these circumstances, what is surprising is not that there were some outbreaks of violence, but that hostilities were not more frequent.

It is clear that the degree of mutual hostility between the two races during the maritime fur trading period has been exaggerated in European records. Captains came to the coast expecting the Indians to be hostile and often perceived hostility where it did not exist. Some captains tried to deter others from trading with the Indians by telling tales of their 'Monstrous savage disposition.'[79] Sometimes Indian leaders also tried to prevent traders from calling on neighbouring groups by emphasizing their uncooperative and warlike nature. In an effort to protect their trading interests, both races exaggerated the hostility of the other. The anticipation of violence occasionally brought its expected result, yet the number of violent incidents was still relatively few. A delicate balance of gains and losses had to be weighed up by those who contemplated an attack. The immediate advantage of plunder had to be assessed against the long-term disadvantage of losing trade. Both races realized that trading possibilities were not enhanced by attacks on potential customers.

The Indians of the northwest coast, rather than feeling exploited by the European traders, became annoyed when opportunities to trade escaped them. If Europeans rejected offers to trade, particularly when furs were offered by the Indians in the form of reciprocal presents, the refusal could be, and sometimes was, taken as an insult.[80] Indian groups also became dissatisfied when the maritime fur trade passed them by. Sea otter were rare at Nootka Sound by the turn of the century, and vessels were neglecting the area in favour of visiting the more lucrative inner harbours. The Nootka resented this development and their resentment was part of the motivation behind their famous attack on the trading vessel, *Boston*, in 1803.

During the maritime fur-trading period the Indians of the northwest coast were not, like some pre-Marxist proletariat, the passive objects of exploitation. Rather, they were part of a mutually beneficial trading relationship over which they exercised a good deal of control. Because the amount of overt coercion used against the Indians was limited they were involved in a process of non-directed culture change.[81] Within the trading relationship they selected those goods they wanted and rejected those they did not. The maritime fur trade was not 'an unequal trade with a primitive people.'[82] The overwhelming impression that emerges from the journals is that the Indians were intelligent and energetic traders, quite capable of driving a hard bargain. John Meares, after several months of trading with the northwest coast Indians, expressed the view of many European traders when he noted that 'we learned to our cost, that these people, ... possessed all the cunning necessary to the gains of mercantile life.'[83]

NOTES

This article is from *Approaches to Native History in Canada: Papers of a Conference Held at the National Museum of Man, October 1975*, ed. D.A. Muise. National Museum of Man Mercury Series, History Division Paper No. 25. Ottawa: National Museums of Canada 1977. Reprinted with permission.

1 B. Ryerson Stanley, *The Founding of Canada: Beginnings to 1815* (Toronto 1963), 262
2 Hubert Howe Bancroft, *History of British Columbia* (San Francisco 1890), 4
3 F.W. Howay, 'An Outline Sketch of the Maritime Fur Trade,' Canadian Historical Association, *Report*, 1932, 14
4 In 1775 Juan Francisco de la Bodega y Quadra passed up the coast in the schooner *Sonora*. Although he discovered and named Bucareli Bay on the west coast of Prince of Wales Island, he did not make a landfall between latitudes 49° and 54°40′ N.
5 James Cook and James King, *A Voyage to the Pacific Ocean ... Performed under the Direction of Captains Cook, Clerke, and Gore, in His Majesty's Ships the Resolution and the Discovery. In the Years, 1776, 1777, 1778, 1779, and 1780* (London 1784), III, 437
6 George Dixon, *A Voyage Round the World; but more Particularly to the North-West Coast of America: Performed in 1785, 1786, 1787 and 1788, in the King George and Queen Charlotte, Captains Portlock and Dixon* (London 1789), 199–200. Although Dixon's name appears on the title page of this work, it was actually written by William Beresford, who was supercargo on the *Queen Charlotte*.
7 Ibid., 201
8 Ibid., 228
9 Robert Haswell, Log, [June 1789], in Frederick W. Howay, ed., *Voyages of the 'Columbia' to the Northwest Coast 1787–1790 and 1790–1793* (Boston 1941), 96
10 Dixon, *Voyage*, 315–16
11 George Dixon, *Remarks on the Voyages of John Meares, Esq. in a Letter to the Gentleman* (London 1890), in F.W. Howay, ed., *The Dixon-Meares Controversy ...* (Toronto [1929]), 30
12 Nathaniel Portlock, *A Voyage Round the World; but more Particularly to the Northwest Coast of America: Performed in 1785, 1786, 1787 and 1788 ...* (London 1789), 382
13 Juan Crespi, Diary, 21 July 1774, in Geo. Butler Griffen, ed., *Documents from the Sutro Collection, Publications of the Historical Society of Southern California* (Los Angeles 1891), II, part 1, 192. Cook, Journal, 30 March and 26 April 1778, in J.C.

Beaglehole, ed., *The Journals of Captain James Cook on his Voyages of Discovery; the Voyage of the 'Resolution' and 'Discovery,' 1776–1780* (Cambridge 1967), part 1, 297, 302, and 314

14 Caamano, Journal, 19 July 1792, Jacinto Caamano, 'The Journal of Jacinto Caamano,' *British Columbia Historical Quarterly* 2 (July 1938): 215. Cook had made similar remarks about most of the Nootka Indians as early as 1778. See Cook, Journal, 12 April 1778, in Beaglehole, ed., *Journals*, 301.

15 Pérez, Diary, 20 July 1774, in Margaret Olive Johnson, 'Spanish Exploration of the Pacific Coast by Juan Pérez in 1774' (Master of Letters thesis, University of California, Berkeley, 1911), 59

16 Beaglehole, ed., *Journals*, part 1, 302, fn 2

17 Cook, Journal, 18 April 1778, ibid., 302–3

18 The Merchant Proprietors to Meares, 24 Dec. 1787, in John Meares, *Voyages Made in the Years 1788 and 1789 from China to the North West Coast of America ...* (London 1790), app. 1, unpaginated

19 Cook, Journal, 18 April and 29 March 1778, in Beaglehole, ed., *Journals*, part 1, 302 and 296

20 Pena, Diary, 21 July 1774, in Griffen, ed., *Documents*, 123; Dixon, *Voyage*, 200–1

21 Haswell, Log, 19 April 1789, in Howay, ed., *Voyages of the 'Columbia,'* 81

22 Boit, Journal, 9 June 1795, in John Boit, Journal of a Voyage Round the Globe, 1795 and 1796 [in the *Union*] MS, Special Collections, University of British Columbia Library (hereafter cited as SC)

23 George Vancouver, *A Voyage of Discovery to the North Pacific Ocean, and Round the World ... Performed in the Years 1790, 1791, 1792, 1793, 1794 and 1795 in the Discovery Sloop of War and Armed Tender Chatham under the Command of Captain George Vancouver* (London 1798), I, 348

24 Edmund S. Meany, ed., *A New Vancouver Journal on the Discovery of Puget Sound by a Member of the Chatham's Crew* (Seattle 1915), 40

25 Cecil Jane, trans., *A Spanish Voyage to Vancouver and the North-West Coast of America: Being the Narrative of the Voyage made in the Year 1792 by the Schooners 'Sutil' and 'Mexicana' to Explore the Strait of Fuca* (London 1930), 90. See also Vancouver, *Voyage*, I, 349.

26 Alessandro (sic) Malaspina, 'Politico-Scientific Voyages around the World ... from 1789-1794,' typescript, SC, II, 244

27 F.W. Howay, 'The Voyage of the Hope: 1790–1792,' *Washington Historical Quarterly*, 11 (Jan. 1920): 28; Howay 'Outline Sketch,' 8; Paul Chrisler Phillips, *The Fur Trade* (Norman 1961), II, 54

28 See Hubert Howe Bancroft, *History of the Northwest Coast* (San Francisco 1884), I, 370–1.

29 Pena, Diary, 20 July and 8 Aug. 1774, in Griffen, ed., *Documents*, 121 and 132. Cook noted that the Nootka had a word for iron and other metals. Cook, Journal, [April 1778], in Beaglehole, ed., *Journals*, part 1, 328

30 This kind of pattern has been delineated for other areas of the Pacific. See Dorothy Shineberg, *They Came for Sandalwood: A Study of the Sandalwood Trade in the South-West Pacific* (Melbourne 1967), 145 and 150.

31 Howay, 'Voyage of the Hope,' 10

32 Ingraham, Journal, 12 July 1791, in Mark D. Kaplanoff, ed., *Joseph Ingraham's Journal of the Brigantine 'Hope' on a Voyage to the Northwest Coast of North America* (Barre, Mass. 1971), 105

33 F.W. Howay, ed., 'William Sturgis: The Northwest Fur Trade,' *British Columbia Historical Quarterly 8* (Jan. 1971): 22
34 Vancouver, *Voyage*, I, 349
35 C.P. Claret Fleurieu, *A Voyage Round the World, Performed during the Years 1790, 1791 and 1792, by Etienne Marchand* ... (London 1801), I, 449
36 Meares, *Voyages*, 368; Burney, Journal, 24 April 1778, 'Journal of the Proceedings of His Majesty's Sloop Discovery – Chas. Clerke, Commander, 1776–1779,' photocopy, British Columbia Archives and Record Service (BCARS)
37 John D'Wolf, *Voyage to the North Pacific and a Journey through Siberia more than Half a Century Ago* (Cambridge 1861), 19
38 M. Camille De Roquefeuil, *A Voyage round the World, between the Years 1816–1819* (London 1823), 87
39 G.H. Von Langsdorff, *Voyages and Travels in Various Parts of the World, during the Years 1803, 1804, 1805, 1806 and 1807* (Carlisle 1817), 413
40 Fleurieu, *Voyage*, I, 422
41 Roquefeuil, *Voyage*, 92
42 John Hoskins, Memorandum [Aug. 1792], in Howay, ed., *Voyages of the 'Columbia,'* 486; Puget, Log, 27 April 1793, Peter Puget, 'Log of the Proceedings of His Majesty's Armed Tender Chatham Lieutenant Peter Puget Acting Commander 12 Day of January 1793,' microfilm, University of British Columbia Library, 40
43 D'Wolf, *Voyage*, 18; for Newitty see 17.
44 Samuel Dorr to Ebenezer Door, 16 Aug. 1801, Ebenezer Dorr, Dorr Marine Collection, 1795–1820, MSS, BCARS
45 Richard J. Cleveland, *Voyages and Commercial Enterprises of the Sons of New England* (New York 1865), 94
46 Haswell, Log, 25 April 1792, in Howay, ed., *Voyages of the 'Columbia,'* 323
47 Howay, ed., 'William Sturgis,' 20
48 Cook, Journal, 18 April 1778, in Beaglehole, ed., *Journals*, part 1, 302; and cf Bancroft, *History of British Columbia*, 4
49 Roquefeuil, *Voyage*, 97
50 Meares, *Voyages*, 148
51 Dixon, *Voyage*, 204
52 Ingraham, Journal, 2 Sept. 1791, in Kaplanoff, ed., *Ingraham's Journal*, 146
53 Howay, 'Outline Sketch,' 10
54 Ingraham, Journal, 2 Sept. 1791, in Kaplanoff, ed., *Ingraham's Journal*, 147
55 D'Wolf, *Voyage*, 18
56 Fleurieu, *Voyage*, 283
57 See for example Meares, *Voyages*, 120; and Ingraham, Journal, 5 Aug. 1791, in Kaplanoff, ed., *Ingraham's Journal*, 126
58 Ingraham, Journal, 11 Aug. 1791, in Kaplanoff, ed., *Ingraham's Journal*, 130; Hoskins, Narrative, Jan. 1792, in Howay, ed., *Voyages of the 'Columbia,'* 265
59 Suría, Journal, 13 Aug. 1791, in Henry R. Wagner, ed., *Journal of Thomas de Suría of his Voyage with Malaspina to the Northwest Coast of America in 1791* (Glendale 1936), 274
60 Jewitt, Journal, 24 Nov. 1803, in John Jewitt, *A Journal Kept at Nootka Sound* ... (Boston 1807), 13
61 Puget, Log, 16 April 1793, in Puget, 'Log of the Chatham,' 39–40

62 Cf Ingraham, Journal, 10 July 1791, in Kaplanoff, ed., *Ingraham's Journal*, 102, and *Eliza*, Journal, 27 March 1799, [*Eliza*], 'Journal of the *Eliza*, Feb.–May 1799,' photocopy, SC, 13

63 *Eliza*, Journal, 27 March 1799, 29. Kow owned these ermine skins before Sturgis glutted the Kaigani market with them in 1806. See Howay, ed., 'William Sturgis,' 22.

64 Cleveland Log, 27 June 1799, R.J. Cleveland, 'Log Kept by Capt. Richard Cleveland, 10 January 1799 to 4 May 1804,' MS, SC

65 Cleveland, Log, 17 June 1799. Meares, *Voyages*, 128; D'Wolf, *Voyage*, 18; and Hoskins, Narrative, July 1791, in Howay, ed., *Voyages of the 'Columbia,'* 198

66 Cook did not anchor at Yuquot (called Friendly Cove by Europeans) but at Ship Cove (now called Resolute Cove) on the southwest tip of Bligh Island. But it seems likely that the people who had a summer village at Yuquot were the ones controlling the trade with the expedition.

67 Cook, Journal, 18 April 1778, in Beaglehole, ed., *Journals*, part 1, 302

68 Ibid., 1 April 1778, 299. See also Charles Clerke, Journal, [April 1778], ibid., part 2, 1326.

69 Ingraham, Journal, 2 Aug. 1791, in Kaplanoff, ed., *Ingraham's Journal*, 121

70 Vancouver, *Voyage*, I, 331–2, 346, and 349; Jane, trans., *Spanish Voyage*, 74–5; Menzies, Journal, 20 July 1792, in C.F. Newcombe, ed., *Menzies Journal of Vancouver's Voyage April to October 1792, Archives of British Columbia Memoir No. V* (Victoria 1923), 88

71 Hoskins, Narrative, Jan. 1792, in Howay, ed., *Voyages of the 'Columbia,'* 265

72 Meares, *Voyages*, 142; Magee, Log, 31 May 1793, [Bernard Magee], Log of the Jefferson, photocopy, SC

73 *Eliza*, Journal, 5 May 1799

74 Ibid., 4 March 1799, 13

75 Puget, 'Log of the Chatham,' 52

76 See Howay, 'Outline Sketch,' 9; and Criston I. Archer, 'The Transient Presence: A Re-Appraisal of Spanish Attitudes toward the Northwest Coast in the Eighteenth Century,' *BC Studies*, no. 18, 1973, 29

77 The figures are based on a series of articles by F.W. Howay, 'A List of Trading Vessels in the Maritime Fur Trade, 1785–1794,' *Transactions of the Royal Society of Canada* (TRSC), third series, 24, section 2 (1930): 111–34; 'A List of Trading Vessels in the Maritime Fur Trade, 1795–1804,' TRSC, third series, 25, section 2 (1931): 117–49; 'A List of Trading Vessels in the Maritime Fur Trade, 1805–1814,' TRSC, third series, 26, section 2 (1932): 43–86; 'A List of Trading Vessels in the Maritime Fur Trade, 1815–1819,' TRSC, third series, 27, section 2 (1933): 119–47; 'A List of Trading Vessels in the Maritime Fur Trade, 1820–1825,' TRSC, third series, 28, section 2 (1934): 11–49. The percentages of vessels making more than one visit are probably a little conservative since the records for some of the single-season voyages are of dubious authenticity. For the same reason the total figure is only approximate.

78 Ingraham, Journal, 12 Aug. 1791, in Kaplanoff, ed., *Ingraham's Journal*, 132.

79 Haswell, Log, 16 Sept. 1788, in Howay, ed., *Voyages of the 'Columbia,'* 49

80 Puget, Log, 27 July 1793, in Puget, 'Log of the Chatham,' 71; Edward Belcher, *Narrative of a Voyage Round the World Performed in Her Majesty's Ship Sulpher, during the Years 1836–1842 ...* (London 1843), I, 111

81 The distinction between 'directed' and 'non-directed' culture change is made by Ralph Linton, ed., *Acculturation in Seven American Indian Tribes* (Gloucester Mass. 1963), 502

82 F.W. Howay, W.N. Sage, and H.F. Angus, *British Columbia and the United States, the North Pacific Slope from Fur Trade to Aviation* (Toronto 1942), 12

83 Meares, *Voyages*, 141–2

JEAN USHER

Duncan of Metlakatla: The Victorian Origins of a Model Indian Community

There is a happy spot of busy life
Where order reigns where hushed the din of strife,
Harmonious brethren neath paternal rule,
Ply their glad tasks in Metlakatla's school,
There Duncan holds supreme his peaceful throne,
His power unquestioned, and their rights his own.
Anvil and hammer, saw and wheel resound,
And useful arts of industry abound
While faith and knowledge find an altar there.[1]

The inspiration for such a eulogy was Metlakatla, a Christian Indian village established in 1862 not far from the mouth of the Skeena River in British Columbia. By 1876 under the direction of William Duncan, an Anglican lay missionary, this settlement of some nine hundred Tsimshian Indians had begun to attract marked attention both in Britain and Canada as an outstanding example of missionary endeavour, and of the industrial potential of the American Indian.

The Earl of Dufferin after a vice-regal visit to Metlakatla in 1876 spoke of the 'neat Indian Maidens in Mr. Duncan's School at Metlakatla, as modest and as well dressed as any clergyman's daughter in an English parish' and advised British Columbians that 'what you want are not resources but human beings to develop them and consume them. Raise your 30,000 Indians to the level Mr. Duncan has taught us they can be brought, and consider what an enormous amount of vital power you will have added to your present strength.'[2]

With its parallel rows of neat white houses, gardens, and picket fences, its school, store, street lamps, gaol, and dominated by a church reputed to be the largest west of Chicago and north of San Francisco, the village presented an imposing picture of civilized life in the wilderness. The society developed within this environment was hardly less impressive, particularly when seen in contrast to the life of the heathen Indians of the area. Rank and class had apparently been abolished, as had liquor, potlatching, and other heathen customs. Church attendance and family prayers had become the rule, whilst day schools, evening schools, and Sunday schools were well attended by adults and children. Government was by a council of elders and enforcement of law and order was carried out by a corps of native constables. Besides encouraging the traditional pursuits of hunting and fishing, Duncan claimed to have introduced such trades as coopering, weaving, rope making, printing, and had built a variety of workshops and a saw mill for the Indians' use. European clothing and cleanliness marked the appearance of the Metlakatla Indians, who spent their leisure time in hymn singing, playing football, or participating in the activities of the village fire brigade and the Metlakatla brass band. The introduction of Christianity to the Tsimshian Indians of British Columbia had meant not only were they offered new spiritual ideas and beliefs, but an entirely different kind of life was opened for them at the Christian village of Metlakatla.

Before Duncan's arrival at Fort Simpson in 1857, the Tsimshian had had a varied and lengthy contact with European culture. From 1775 to 1825 the maritime fur trade introduced many goods and techniques to the coastal Indians with few disruptive effects.[3] Similarly the North West Company, and after 1821 the Hudson's Bay Company posts established among the Tsimshian served mainly to give impetus to a new growth of arts, technology, and social and ceremonial life.[4] The Hudson's Bay Company had had extensive experience in dealing with Indians and aimed generally, by a strict but just policy, to keep the peace that was necessary for successful trade relations. The trader, in most cases, had no desire to change native society. The Indians were asked only to accept that part of white culture they desired, and on this basis reasonably harmonious relations could be maintained. But, whereas the process of cultural diffusion in the trader-native contact situation is one of imitation, the missionary attempts to inculcate his values into the native society and asks that the native accept all the values and beliefs that he offers.[5] The missionary is of necessity a reformer and likely to make a far greater impact on native societies than other Europeans. The kind of influence he exerts and the demands he makes of prospective converts will be largely characterized by his own cultural background, mores, and social position.[6]

William Duncan began his mission to the Tsimshian Indians in 1857 under the auspices of the Church Missionary Society, the evangelical missionary society of the Church of England. Born in Beverley, Yorkshire, in 1832, the year of the great Reform Bill, he grew up in an era of great ferment in English society, in an age of reform where Evangelical and Utilitarian alike were challenging old institutions and attempting to ameliorate or change the social conditions that industrialization had produced. 'Reform – political, religious social, artistic – was more deeply a part of the early Victorian temperament than was the complacency of which it has been consistently and smugly accused.'[7] In later years the church was to claim that Duncan had been no more than a far-sighted social worker. Yet in fact he was primarily a Christian protestant missionary, but one espousing a nineteenth-century Christianity, formed in the religious, humanitarian, and middle-class framework of mid-Victorian England.

Duncan's own cultural background is found in the larger sphere of Victorian attitudes and reform movements and in the more particular policies and ideals of the Church Missionary Society and of Henry Venn. Duncan himself received little formal education and, like most children of working-class parents, was sent out to work at the age of thirteen. For nine years he was employed by the leather firm of Cussons in Beverley, spending seven years as an apprentice clerk and two years as a clerk and commercial traveller. A serious and earnest young man, Duncan appears to have shunned frivolous activities and to have spent most of his time working, reading, singing in the church choir, and teaching a Sunday school class at Beverley Minster. In his late adolescence he developed close relations with his employer, Mr G. Cussons, and with his minister, the Reverend E. Carr. Carr conducted a weekly Bible study and prayer meeting for young men, at which Duncan was a devout and regular attendant. He received particular and fond attention from Carr and it was under his influence that Duncan decided to devote part of his life to missionary work.

Duncan seems to have had no close family ties, and although from a working-class background himself, derived most of his attitudes from these middle-class men with whom he was most familiar. As an ambitious young clerk, too, it was understandable that he should try to pattern himself after his employer.

The Victorian middle classes, the small manufacturers, retailers, independent businessmen, saw their society as a dynamic one where a man was judged on his abilities and where progress and advancement depended upon the exertions and skills of the individual. The Gospel of Work was eminently suited to their own social and economic position.

Samuel Smiles's doctrine of Self-Help embodied this middle-class view of the road to individual success and progress, but was itself directed at the working classes. Smiles, like many of the middle class, feared the growth of proletarian radicalism and sought to make it unnecessary by exhorting the worker to educate himself, to find a joy in work, to persevere, to be thrifty, dutiful, and of strong character; to change himself rather than society. Smiles emphasised in his lectures to working men in Leeds the value of discipline and drill: 'Wonderful is the magic of drill! Drill means discipline, training, education.'[8] Although faith in education was characteristic of much of Victorian thinking, Smiles was less interested in the formal education of the schoolroom than in the industrial training of the workshop and the moral training of a Christian home.[9] In essence, Smiles recognized the condition of the working classes and aimed not to change society but to elevate the mass of the proletariat to the level of the middle class. Yet only by the elevation of the individual could the mass be raised. He fully accepted the Victorian ideal of a free and independent labourer, and felt that the improvement of the individual should be initiated by a personal, moral desire rather than by government pressure. 'Whatever is done *for* men and classes to a certain extent takes away the stimulus and the necessity of doing for themselves.'[10] The dominance of middle-class values and mores over a large part of Victorian society meant that Self-Help ideas were prevalent in the attitudes of many of the Victorian reformers.

The values of Victorian society were derived from the humanitarian tradition of evangelical protestantism and from the economic needs of the middle class. A dominant feature of the era was the close relationship amongst religious, economic, and social ideas. Samuel Smiles's emphasis on thrift was based on the fact that individual savings were the foundation of the national accumulation of wealth, essential to that continued economic growth and progress which so enthralled the Victorians. A thrifty worker received moral accolades too, since his savings guaranteed his independence and reinforced the Victorian faith in the idea of the free labourer. The gospel of work, like the protestant gospel, saw idleness as a sin, 'an abrogation of God's will and a dangerous opportunity to move downwards to hell.'[11] Poverty too was seen as a moral failing, since by individual action the worker could improve his position and hence improve society. Failure in this social duty was a moral offence.

The religious revival of Wesley had made Victorian religion acutely aware of the constant inner struggle with temptation and the strong necessity for leading a disciplined Christian life. This emphasis on discipline and authority is evident in many aspects of Victorian society, and the continuous efforts of Christians to discipline themselves in the struggle with evil led to a concern for self-improvement in secular life which gave added impetus to the ready acceptance of the doctrine of Self-Help.

The Victorian reform movements 'arose from the intense feelings of a few individuals acting on the sensibilities of a governing class increasingly accustomed to change, increasingly persuaded of the possibility of progress and increasingly alarmed by industrial and urban misery ... [it] found its most energetic expression in the Evangelicals and Utilitarians.'[12] The early Victorian reformers, Evangelicals like Ashley or Utilitarians like Edwin Chadwick and Kay-Shuttleworth, saw poverty as dependent upon the indolent disposition of the individual. Like Samuel Smiles they felt that the interests of the individual would best be served by freeing him from the corrupting relief and making him a free and independent agent. Such was the general philosophy behind the New Poor Law which rationalized and centralized the administration of relief.

Although they recognized the need to alleviate the overcrowding and poor sanitation they found in English cities, the reformers maintained that social conditions only reflected the moral destitution of the people. 'The absence of any sound moral training, said numerous inspectors in countless reports, caused the intemperance, pauperism and crime which threatened English society.'[13] Such ideas were eminently suited to the backgrounds of the reformers. Many Evangelicals felt that prosperity was the earthly reward for living a moral life and that poverty must thus be a reflection of immorality. Social evils were seen as due primarily to ignorance of religious and moral principles.

The emphasis of the reformers on the ignorance of the population as a general cause of social problems meant that a corresponding stress was laid on the necessity for more universal education. Education was seen by E.C. Tufnell, a government inspector, as 'the universal remedy,' the panacea for all ills. Like many Victorians, the inspectors saw education as the agent of progress and held optimistic, rational views of its power to mould human nature. Men such as Dr James Kay-Shuttleworth also believed the school had a responsibility to develop a child's skill and encouraged schools to introduce their pupils to a wide variety of subjects such as science and music. Under the influence of Swiss educators such as de Fellenberg, the school inspectors encouraged industrial training and farming as a means of reforming pauper children. Just as Samuel Smiles encouraged thrift to produce moral, independent workers, the school inspectors advocated gardening to teach the future workers the forethought and economy that would ensure their independence.

The commissioners themselves who so influenced the social life of England in these years were endowed, as so many Victorians were, with an unending zeal and energy. Their reports reflected the enthusiasm they felt for their work. 'Across the length and breadth of England, assistant commissioners reported miraculous regeneration. Their communications read like letters from missionaries describing the conversion and rebirth of the heathen.'[14] Throughout the 1840s and 1850s the steady work of the reformers resulted in sanitary and prison reform, new approaches to the treatment of lunacy, and regulation of merchant shipping, mines, smoke, and burial grounds. The initiation of reforms owes much to the humanitarianism, paternalism, and conscience of the Evangelicals. But the extensive investigation of conditions, the exhaustive research, writing, inspecting, and interviewing that characterized the work of the inspectors was a product of the rational, utilitarian ideas of Chadwick and Kay-Shuttleworth.

The number of small utopian movements in the mid-nineteenth century is evidence of the growing realization that human life and human societies were malleable and that their form and structure could be changed as desired. Historians have tended to treat these social experiments as forms of retreat from the realities of the world. In fact, they should be considered in the context of the general movement for reform in the early and mid-nineteenth century. The utopian reformers sought to exert an influence on society as a whole, to produce reform and change.[15] They established separate communities and hoped to prove the efficiency and practicality of their ideas in this microcosm of society.

In England the Moravian Brethren had several community settlements which lasted into the nineteenth century. The unity of the group in secular as in religious life was emphasized, and before admittance to the community the individual signed a 'brotherly agreement' declaring willingness to abide by the rules and discipline of the community. A council of elders was the ruling body and had general control of economic life, education, and social welfare. The rules were read aloud once a year and those guilty of disobedience were expelled from the settlement.[16] Impressed by the Moravian groups, John Minter Morgan in the 1840s proposed a similar scheme for self-supporting villages under the auspices of the established church. The Church of England Self-Supporting Village Society was formed and aimed at 'those benefits resulting in the Moravian settlements from a more intimate connection between secular and religious affairs.'[17] The economic basis of the communities was to be mainly agricultural (like the school inspectors, Morgan encouraged gardening), with some industrial and handicraft work. A committee of management was to direct the community affairs, and Morgan introduced a 'strongly authoritarian note,' in his emphasis on 'codes of conduct!'[18] The community as a whole was intended to be a practical demonstration of Christian brotherhood and unity, 'wherein each labouring for all, the exertions of each will receive their due and proper reward – wherein the weak shall be aided and supported by the strong.'[19] Although there was little implementation of these proposals on an extensive scale, the Church of England Self-Supporting Village Society did in fact receive wide attention in the press, and Morgan and his adherent, James Silk Buckingham, spoke at many meetings throughout England. The *Illustrated London News* in 1850 commented on Morgan's proposals for a model town: 'It reminds us of Bridewell or some contrivance for central inspection ... The idea is obviously borrowed from the unsuccessful efforts of the State to correct the people of Bridewell's workhouses and prisons – substituting a gentler kind of control for diet, ships, dungeons and fetters ... Mr. Morgan does not conceal his desire to organise the "destitute people" and the whole society in Reductions (formal villages) similar to those by which the Jesuits drilled the Indians in Paraguay.'[20]

'The 1840's was an age of models; model villages, model apartments, model lodging houses and even model beds.'[21] Perhaps the most spectacular model was the industrial town of Saltaire, fifty miles from Duncan's home in Beverley. Titus Salt, a former mayor of Bradford, a woollen manufacturer and himself a hero of Self-Help, alarmed by a serious cholera outbreak in Bradford, began in 1851 to build a model manufacturing town for his workers. Residential and industrial areas were separate, and schools, shops, and a literary institute were established. The mill itself, a huge structure with unusually large windows for light and ventilation, was a model of industrial architecture. Though moved by humanitarian ideals, concern for the health and welfare of his workers, Salt, a Congregationalist, felt like many Victorians that the evils of society were not all environmental. The sign across the entrance to the town read, 'All Beer Abandon ye that Enter Here.' As in many model communities, the element of discipline and authority was evident in Saltaire too.[22]

Early Victorian social work was endowed with a strong missionary zeal. Apart from the building trusts, the alleviation of hunger, and care of orphans, its main efforts were directed at the moral failings of the individual. Drunkenness and lust were seen as the basic problems of the working class and temperance societies and prostitution reform movements were active and well supported. The church sisterhoods were active in the 1850s in establishing homes for penitent and wayward ladies. The sisters had strong faith in education and example and hoped to change the character of the girls by love, prayer, and the example of a religious and pious life. By work and training in laundry and domestic work they tried to prepare the women to make an honest living for themselves.[23]

Thus although Duncan's role as a missionary to the heathen would lead him inevitably into attempts at social reform, his own cultural background was also one where reformers and their ideas had captured the imagination of many people. The nature of Victorian reform and the values which determined it were to play an important part in establishing the Christian Indian Society of Metlakatla.

There was, however, a more particular influence evident in the formation of Duncan's attitudes towards the Indians and to his conception of his task as a missionary. As an agent of the evangelical Church Missionary Society, he was directly influenced by their ideas and practices, through personal contacts, correspondence with the secretaries of the society, and through accounts of other missionary work in the various journals of the Church Missionary Society.

That body was dominated in these mid-Victorian decades by the energetic and vigorous ideas of Henry Venn, whose 'Native Church' policy established the guidelines for CMS missionaries until the late 1870s. Venn's 'Minute on the Native Pastorate and Organisation,' first published in 1851, recognised that European and American missionaries could not, even in the distant future, hope to reach all the heathen of the world. He advocated that the European missionary act purely as an evangelist, and hoped to maintain a clear distinction between the missionary who preached to the heathen and the pastor who ministered to the congregation of native Christians.[24] The role of the missionary was to establish a self-supporting and self-governing congregation of native Christians, and when this had been effected, the mission would have 'attained its euthanasia and the Missionary and all the Mission agency can be transferred to the regions beyond.'[25] From the beginning the missionary was to train a native pastor and helpers who would be capable of taking eventual control of the congregation. 'The main underlying principle which appears to have guided Mr. Venn ... is that foreign missions to the heathen must always be treated as a transition state.'[26]

The man who did not train up a native clergy was building on an insecure foundation and Venn warned particularly that the skills and technology possessed by the European would tend to make him indispensable to his converts and this might unnecessarily prolong his work among them. 'It may be said to have been only lately discovered in the science of missions, that when the missionary is of another and superior race than his converts he must not attempt to be their pastor; though they will be bound to him by personal attachment, and by a sense of benefits received from him, they will not form a vigorous, native Church, but as a general rule they will remain in a dependent condition, and make but little progress in spiritual attainments. The same congregation under competent native pastors, would become more self-reliant, and their religion would be of a more manly, home character.'[27]

Like Samuel Smiles, Venn appeared to see an intrinsic value in encouraging Self-Help and independence among the native Christians. Converts should not become dependent on a foreign mission but should become members of a native church as soon as possible. Nor should they be allowed to fall into the habit of thinking that everything should be done for them. From the beginning of the mission they should be encouraged to contribute to a native church fund and, at each stage of development of the mission, the missionary should inculcate the values of self-support, self-government, and self-extension.

Although influenced by the problems of personnel, the climatic difficulties for Europeans in tropical climates, and the vast field of work to be covered, Venn was also idealistically concerned that the result of missionary endeavour should be the establishment of national native churches. As the church in each nation assumed a national character, he hoped it would ultimately supersede the denominational distinctions introduced by foreign missionary societies, which divided the church of Christ in Europe and America.

It was important to Venn, too, that this national church be an expression to some extent of the native people themselves. Unlike Roman Catholic missions, the CMS under Venn was to make Christianity indigenous and not exotic, with many centres instead of one.[28] The missionaries when forming a national church were enjoined to avail themselves of national habits, of Christian headmen, and of a church council. 'Let every member feel himself doubly bound to his country by this social as well as religious society.'[29] It is interesting to note that many of Venn's ideas were directly influenced by Rufus Anderson, the secretary of the American Board of Commissioners for Foreign Missions. Both Venn and Anderson emphasized the importance of the work of the Apostle Paul, whose task had been the gathering and forming of local churches, and putting the power of self-government and organization in the hands of each Christian community.[30]

Detailed plans were laid out by the CMS to guide the formation of native churches. Each district brought under missionary action would have its converts formed into companies where they could receive daily instruction in Christianity and make regular contributions towards a church fund, a system comparable in many ways to that of the Methodists in England. These companies aimed at providing mutual support and encouragement for new converts. Each company was to have an elder or Christian headman, approved of or selected by the missionary. Weekly company meetings were to be held under him and to a large extent the converts were to be dependent on these headmen for their Christian instruction. The missionary was to hold monthly meetings of the headmen at which reports would be presented on the moral and religious conditions of companies. Subscriptions would be handed over and the headmen would receive spiritual counsel and encouragement from the missionary.[31]

The first step in the organization of a native church would be the formation of one or more companies into a congregation, having a schoolmaster or native teacher amongst them and supported by their own funds. Secondly, a native congregation would be formed under an ordained native pastorate paid by a native church fund. The final phase would be when the district conferences would come together to organize the future of the national church.

Venn was interested, however, not only in the expansion of Christianity but in the kind of native Christian that was to be created. He instructed his lay agent embarking for Abeokuta in 1853 to study the resources of the country in marketable products and to direct the attention of the converts towards them, so that 'these parties may rise in social position and influence while they are receiving Christian instruction and thus form themselves into a self-supporting Christian Church and give practical proof that godliness hath promise of the life that now is, as well as that which is to come.'[32]

Sir Thomas Fowell Buxton, writing in 1841,[33] recommended not only that British naval force be used to blockade the slave trade, but that Christian England should invest in Africa and attempt to stimulate agriculture and commerce and produce an industrial class of African. 'These Africans, protected by Britain, guided by the missionaries, and working with capital from European merchants would ... move inland and man factories at every strategic spot living together in little colonies, little cells of civilisation from which the light would radiate to the regions around.'[34] Venn, like Buxton, his colleague and friend, wanted to find a substitute for the profits from slave trading, and also needed to make the Christian converts self-supporting. It was thus under the influence of Venn that the Moravian ideal of a mission station catering for education, trades, agriculture, industry, and medicine besides the teaching of Christianity became the pattern upon which many Anglican missions were founded.[35]

Although in the early years of the evangelical revival there had been little concern for secular problems, the idea of taking the gospel and civilization to the heathen was no novelty in the history of the CMS. The Reverend Samuel Marsden, a missionary in Australia and New Zealand in the early decades of the century, continually pressed the CMS to find employment for the Maoris. Lacking the arts of civilization, the Maoris were not 'so favourably circumstanced for reception of the Gospel as civilized nations are ... since nothing can pave the way for the Gospel but civilization.'[36] He was able to persuade the CMS to send not ordained men but mechanics; a carpenter, a blacksmith, a twinespinner, and a man able to teach the cultivation of sugar cane, cotton, coffee, and other marketable products. An essentially practical man, Marsden himself was active in New South Wales in cattle-rearing, growing grain, and improving the breed of Australian sheep. This was the kind of man that Venn needed for his Christian settlements in West Africa. At least as important as the ordained missionary in the life of the Christian villages were the lay schoolmasters, carpenters, the men who taught the mechanics of civilization which not only enabled the village to become self-supporting but elevated the Christian African above his heathen counterpart.

Venn aimed to create an African middle class, though not necessarily in the image of its Victorian counterpart. His great insistence on the learning and transcribing of native languages, and on the toleration of native customs and systems of law were strongly felt throughout the CMS. Venn realized how difficult it was for Englishmen to show respect for national peculiarities different from their own, yet advised the missionary to 'study the national character of the people among whom you labour and show the utmost respect for national peculiarities ... from your first arrival in the country [it is best] ... to study and respect the national habits and conventionalities, till it becomes a habit with you and second nature.'[37] Yet he advocated no immediate or drastic changes in the form of native societies and recommended that although the wielding of authority in native society might seem absurd or unjust to a European, that 'nevertheless they are the framework of society and till they are replaced by a more enlightened system they must be respected.'[38] Missionaries, indeed, were to utilize the present structure of the society to further their own ends. In attempting to evangelize a nation they were exhorted to follow the example of St Paul and to concern themselves particularly with men of influence and the leaders of national thought.

As a true Evangelical, Venn did not concern himself only with the children of a nation. In fact, the conversion of the adult was of utmost importance for the future of a mission, for here was evidence to his neighbours that Christianity came not merely by habit or force of education. The adult was aware, too, of the idolatry and native customs he must renounce and not only was he often also imbued with a missionary zeal himself but 'he has some idea of the obloquy and danger to which he is exposed.'[39]

Education was to be the means to full conversion. Sunday school and religious instruction were of course of primary importance but the arts of civilization must also be taught. Venn advised that the missionary was not to develop a highly educated élite, but was to attempt to build self-supporting educational institutions by combining book learning and industrial labour. 'The separation of scholastic life and manual labour is a refinement of advanced civilisation. It may be doubted whether even in this case it is desirable, but certainly it is not desirable in a mission school or according to the example of the Apostle of the Gentiles.'[40] Venn's ideal native Christian, a man of strong but simple faith, able to read and understand the Bible and economically self-supporting, bore a strong resemblance to the Victorian ideal of Samuel Smiles's independent Christian working man.

Smiles would have found much to admire in William Duncan. Although *Self-Help* was not published until 1859, Smiles had already popularized his ideas in lectures to working men and many books for young men concentrated on similar ideals. Duncan himself was impressed by such books[41] and from a

Young Man's Own Book copied out such homilies as 'Nothing is so valuable as a good stock of information ... Success depends on having fixed principles ... be accustomed to studying your own self, for all other knowledge, without a knowledge of yourself is but splendid ignorance ... to have a good memory you must be temperate in both eating and drinking and sleeping.'[42] Energetic and ambitious, Duncan's 'lists of things to learn' ranged from 'Grammar, Histories of Great Men, Navigation, Law, Astronomy, and Farming to Manners and Politeness.'[43] Recognizing that 'one of the great lessons I have yet to learn is to be diligent and spend well the present moment,' Duncan disciplined his life strictly, allocating twenty-seven hours a week to religion, twenty-seven hours to education, fifty-four to business activities, ten hours for exercise and healthful pursuits, and allowing fifty-four hours a week for sleep. Years later Cussons commented that 'besides discharging his duties to myself most faithfully and effectually, he planned out his spare time for self-improvement and laboured most industriously to make up for his want of earlier education.'[44]

Duncan had no doubt been a model employee, and in fact in 1854 turned down Cusson's offer of double salary to go to London to train as a schoolmaster in the Highbury College of the Church Missionary Society. Besides expanding his own basic education in arithmetic, grammar, history, and geography, Duncan continued formal studies in liturgy and church history. This was combined with the practical application of pedagogical techniques and school management. Several weeks each term were spent in teaching at the model school attached to the college and students were marked on their lesson plans, their use of illustrations, their ability to keep a class attentive, and whether examination of the children had been animated, judicious, and patient.

It was at Highbury too that Duncan came into contact with the mission field, through his teachers, the missionary magazines and meetings, and through his fellow students. In 1856 he commented that his close friend at the college 'Mr. Kirkham, a missionary student, leaves this month for Abeokuta, I have learnt a good deal by being here with him.'[45] Kirkham's impressions of Abeokuta, a model CMS mission, must have been instructive for Duncan. 'The natives are naturally industrious but our converts much more so: in one corner of the yard you will see a carpenter's shop, in another a cotton cleaning establishment and in another a printing press busy at work. In the school are about sixty children receiving a sound elementary education. I have school hours from nine to two and then from three to five; they, the pupils, work at agriculture, carpentry and bookbinding.'[46]

The CMS at this time was mainly active in West Africa. It was conditions in Africa which had influenced the ideas of Henry Venn, and several Highbury students, including Duncan, anticipated a missionary career there. Captain

James Prevost's offer of a free passage to a missionary to the North Pacific coast meant that not only was Duncan unable to finish his final third year at Highbury, but that instead of following his friend Kirkham to a Christian village in West Africa, Duncan was expected to be the first bearer of the gospel to the Indians of British Columbia. In such a context, perhaps, it is less surprising that within four years Duncan had established a Christian self-supporting industrial village among the Coast Indians.

Impressed by the life and the work of Samuel Marsden, after whom he named his first convert, and like many Victorian missionaries, Duncan was convinced that civilization and Christianity were inseparable. The savage condition of the aborigines was seen as due to the free operation of the power of original sin, and it was felt civilization could only be reached by means of Christian moral teachings and the development of industrious and sober men.[47]

The Tsimshian Indians had had a lengthy and in some cases a close contact with white civilization. The maritime fur trade and the Hudson's Bay Company had so stimulated their desire for European artifacts that when the Hudson's Bay Company established a post at Fort Simpson in the 1830s, the neighbouring tribes moved from their ancient home of Metlakatla to take up residence outside the gates of the fort. Thus for twenty years the Tsimshians had been able to observe and learn the daily operations of civilized life, from people whom they held in great respect, yet such an example had apparently made no mark on their own lives. The contrast between life in the fort and in the Indian camp struck the young missionary forcibly. 'Here in the Fort steady industry marks the hours from morn till night while forethought ever directs the shortest way to the desired goal: And what is more, hundreds of Indians, in the course of the year, being employed about the Fort come within these regulation; yet in the Camp the people are content with their sloth and all its train of evils.'[48]

Indeed, Duncan saw no reason for the Indians to imitate the life of the Hudson's Bay Company, for here was civilization without the gospel. White civilization shaped the exterior of the fort but ungodliness was the rule within. Here was the answer for those who felt that if civilization were disseminated among the heathen, they would cast away their heathenism and adopt the virtues of white men. 'I think this instance alone to the contrary is sufficient to explode such an absurdity. No civilization apart from Christianity has no vitality – how then can it impart life? It is the fuel without the fire, how then can it radiate heat? Civilization appears to the eye and to the hand but not to the heart. It may prove the muscles but it cannot reach the hidden springs of life.'[49] In Duncan's eyes, the godliness of the company not only rendered it unable to civilize the Indians, but by exhibiting such a poor example of

Christian civilization was in fact likely to retard his own civilizing and religious mission. The desire to lessen the influence of the Hudson's Bay Company played no small part in Duncan's decision to move from Fort Simpson and establish a Christian Indian Village at Metlakatla.

The influx of miners into the region, almost immediately after Duncan's establishment at Fort Simpson, made the worst aspects of civilization available to the Indians. Liquor, disease, and prostitution had a devastating effect on the native population and strongly influenced Duncan's determination to establish a settlement where not only a greater control could be maintained over converts, but alternative forms of wealth and diversion could be offered to them. A self-supporting industrial village, ruled by Duncan and other Christian missionaries, would provide the society necessary for the Christian life. 'One effect the mission must have upon the Indian will be to make them desire social improvement. How necessary therefore it is that the Mission be established where social improvement is possible. But at Fort Simpson it is *not* possible.'[50]

Duncan soon recognized the difficulties facing his few converts at Fort Simpson. Open to all the temptations offered by their old way of life, they needed also to withstand the taunts and challenges of their fellows, and scattered through the various tribes they could develop no sense of group cohesion which might have helped them to bear their burden. As early as 1859, in reply to an old chief and his sons who had complained about drunkenness in the camp, Duncan mentioned 'the probability of some day dividing them. The Good going away to some good land and establishing a village for themselves where they could be free from the drunkenness and the bad ways.'[51]

Thus there were pragmatic and immediate reasons for wanting to isolate the native Christians in their own village. But as we have seen, the idea of a Christian self-supporting settlement was by no means novel and was in fact the mode of operation for CMS missionaries in other parts of the world, particularly in West Africa. The Church of England Self-Supporting Village Society had also promulgated similar ideas in England, whilst the idea of Metlakatla bore striking similarities to the cells of civilization advocated by Fowell Buxton for Africa.

Contemporaries also saw Metlakatla as a small utopian movement. 'Many, both whites and Indians were ready to ridicule our scheme. They felt sure it was Utopian and could only end in failure.'[52] To the extent that it was a gathering of converts into a communitarian society, espousing specific principles of behaviour and attitudes and attempting to find a way to reform the Indian society as a whole, Metlakatla certainly should be considered in the context of utopian movements of the mid-Victorian era.

Lord Dufferin, like other visitors to the settlement, had been most impressed by the secular industrial work undertaken at Metlakatla. Besides developing a large-scale program of public works and a thriving trading business, Duncan was constantly searching for new industries to establish in the village. Initially the purpose of the industries was to offer an alternative form of employment and means of gaining wealth to Indians who had previously gone to Victoria and had there been exposed to the evils of liquor and disease. It was in effect a means of physically preserving the Indians and was a necessary concomitant of the policy of isolation.

Duncan, like Venn, was interested in increasing the wealth of the converts so that their capital position might be elevated over that of their heathen counterpart. He realized that the adoption of civilization might tend to impoverish the Indians by 'calling for an increased outlay of their expenses without augmenting their income.'[53] A Christian Indian needed to clothe, wash, and house himself in a civilized manner and this demanded capital which was not generally available to the individual Indian.

In the early days of Christianity, evangelism had been the main means of spreading the gospel, but Duncan pointed out that 'the early days can hardly be said to apply to this Mission. The people amongst whom the early Christian Churches were first established were civilized and very differently situated socially and civilly from the poor Indians. Christianity and civilization must go on together. I think and [I mean] ... to get both fairly established at Metlakatla.'[54] He strongly advocated that the missionary should become everything to his converts. The North American Indians in particular 'are a race of people found without means or appliances necessary for advancement to civilized life, and whose labours are hunting and who are but barely able to supply their daily needs ... how can such a people as this if they become Christian be expected ever to maintain their own Church and Schools unless fresh industries are introduced amongst them and markets opened to them for what they can produce.'[55] Here again is evident the strong influence of the policies of Henry Venn. The development of native churches necessitated that the body of Christians be self-supporting and financially independent of European help. The CMS reminded those engaged in new missions that 'self-support and self-government are far more easily introduced when the first groups of Converts are formed than when the Native Christians have become accustomed to the faulty system of helpless dependence and blind subordination.'[56] The sooner a congregation became self-supporting in fact, the sooner the euthanasia of the mission could be effected and the missionary be transferred to other fields.

The industrial establishment at Metlakatla was also useful to Duncan in inculcating the social and moral attitudes desirable in a native Christian.

Sabbath observance was strictly enforced and, like Samuel Smiles, Duncan stressed the moral value of honest toil. The influence of the miners was felt to be particularly pernicious for the Indians were 'being jostled by rolling stones and reckless gamblers; hence unless we can catch up and utilise their energies and bend their backs to the yoke of steady and profitable industry, they will become at best mere hangers-on among the whites.'[57] Duncan was, in fact, creating an environment in which Victorian values of industriousness, thrift, and self-help would have relevance and could be systematically taught.

Victorians concerned with the problems of native peoples were generally convinced that cultural change necessitated economic development.[58] The alliance between the Bible and the plough has been seen as the main feature of Canadian policy from the seventeenth century,[59] and there were many Victorian theorists such as Fowell Buxton who advocated this policy. But others, like Venn, saw the possibilities of developing commercial societies, and it was under such influence, and putting to use his own mercantile talents, that Duncan chose commerce as an agent of acculturation for the Indians of the North Pacific.

Having left Fort Simpson, there were urgent practical reasons for finding a convenient method of supplying the new settlement with trade goods. By taking control of trade into his own hands, Duncan was able not only to satisfy this need, but to make it an integral part of his civilizing mission. He saw that many of the drawbacks to civilization among the Indians were traceable to the way they were treated by traders and set himself 'the task of removing away some of those drawbacks ... I saw and felt persuaded that intoxicating drink is the bane of the Indian population and the root of nearly all the crime amongst them. Hence I longed to set up a trade in this new settlement in which liquor should find no countenance.'[60] Not only would he be able to control the supply of liquor, but he could also determine the type of goods available to the new converts, 'ensuring a supply of such things (many which the traders never bring) as their new habits and tastes demanded.'[61] Within the store Duncan demanded quietness and courtesy and hoped to teach the Indians the just and honest business principles of Victorian England.

Beside having such an important educational function, the village store with its cheap, good-quality articles attracted groups of Indians from surrounding tribes, who thus came into contact with Christianity and religious teachings. By purchasing a schooner for the trade and selling shares in this to the Metlakatla Indians, Duncan aimed to encourage self-help and eventually to enable them to move into independence. Practically speaking, the most important effect of the trade was its financial success, which enabled Duncan to spend considerable sums of money on 'objects conducive to the public benefit, in the erection of public buildings and in subsidies to the people in aid of improving their wharves and canoes.'[62]

The fur trade had been long established among the coastal Indians and it was this which became the basis of Duncan's trade at Metlakatla. Following Venn's advice on adaptation to native customs, Duncan also turned to the traditional pursuits of fishing and crafts to find marketable exports. Attempts were made to export kippered, salted, and smoked fish, and barrels of oolachan oil were sent to the Victoria market. The Tsimshian were reputed to be particularly skilled in the working of metals and wood and, besides exporting numbers of curios, Duncan reintroduced old crafts such as hat-making which might find a market locally or as curios in Victoria. Several Indians were taught coopering so that casks could be made for the export of salt, oolachan, and salmon; soap-making was introduced, the product being mainly for local use to stimulate habits of cleanliness among the Metlakatlans and neighbouring tribes; and the women were encouraged to sew their own clothes and in some cases taught to spin yarn and weave blankets. Such activity aimed to encourage not only industrious habits, but taught thrift, and was to keep the Indians honestly occupied for large parts of the day. Like the school inspectors of England, Duncan also encouraged gardening to develop the forethought and economy that could maintain the independence of the individual that was so highly prized by the Victorians.

On a communal basis, Duncan introduced a saw mill and in later years a salmon cannery. Both were significant in introducing a wage labour system and regular work hours into the settlement, whilst the saw mill was particularly important in providing the means to initiate an ambitious building program.

Metlakatla was to be a model town which would provide the environment necessary for Christianity and would stimulate others to follow the Metlakatla system. Religious reform in Victorian eyes was inextricably entwined with social and moral regeneration. A man's social condition was seen as a reflection of his moral state, which was itself dependent upon the strength of his religion. Not only would the improvement in dwellings and physical conditions greatly facilitate the moral and religious improvements of the Indians, but the physical appearance of the civilized settlement would provide a significant contrast to that of the Indian camps, and would prove a constant testimony to the effect of Christian religious and moral teachings.

In building the new village Duncan's main concerns, like those of Titus Salt, were order, uniformity, health, and morality. At Abeokuta, Kirkham had commented that 'the houses are built without any regard to order, nay confusion seems to be studied for you will scarcely find two houses in the same continuous line.'[63] He noted too that much of the sickness in the settlement was caused by ill-ventilated houses and unsanitary conditions and advised Duncan that 'your determined habits of cleanliness would be very useful here.'[64] At Metlakatla, order and regularity were most apparent. Formal streets were constructed, and neat rows of identical Indian houses were built according to a rational plan, determined jointly by Duncan and the new converts.

In designing the basic plan for the model houses, Duncan was undoubtedly influenced by the many model dwellings proposed in the 1840s. Perhaps he had seen the Prince Consort's own model apartments for the working classes at the Crystal Palace Exhibition; or perhaps he had been familiar with some of the philanthropic building trusts in London. His aim at Metlakatla was to 'combine the accommodation necessary for the Indian as a Christian without offering impediment to his love of hospitality and conflicting with his habits of life.'[65] Just as he had incorporated the traditional economic activities of the Indian into the life of the new settlement, so were the house plans adapted to the traditional needs of the Indians. The old communal house, with the extended family living in one room, had provided an important form of social control, and Duncan was faced with the problem of reconciling this with his need to provide the privacy demanded by Victorian morality. The Reverend Edward Cridge noted that though 'the houses are after the European model and the habits of the people proportionately improved ... they have not forsaken the habit of living more than one family in a house, for the sake of fuel and company, they are beginning to build their houses with small apartments at each end and a common room in the centre and thus to reconcile the difficulties of their situation with a due regard to the decencies of life.'[66] In an almost romantic manner Duncan also wanted to see the Indians surrounded by all the trappings of the Victorian home. 'I wanted to see each house possessed of a stove and have chairs and tables and a clock in it and also see the walls papered and floors well matted, etc.'[67]

Education in its broadest sense was the major function of the Metlakatla settlement. As an Evangelical, Duncan was concerned with the teaching of religion through the knowledge and understanding of the word of God. The CMS desired to make Christianity indigenous, and Venn was particularly insistent on the necessity for missionaries learning and transcribing native languages. Working with the British and Foreign Bible Society, the CMS had encouraged the translation and publication of the Scriptures in many languages and dialects. Duncan's first task at Fort Simpson had been to master the Tsimshian language and to translate portions of the prayers and the gospels. Besides being trained and sent out as a schoolmaster, the Evangelical's need to teach a convert to read and understand his Bible would have perforce made formal education a major undertaking for this first missionary to the Tsimshian people.

For many years a Sunday school teacher at Beverley Minster, and trained in pedagogical techniques in the model school attached to Highbury College, Duncan was an enthusiastic and conscientious teacher.

His children's day school at Metlakatla, assembled by the ringing of a school bell and composed at times of over a hundred children, was redolent of the many schools organized on the Lancaster system both in England and abroad. As in the Lancaster schools children were divided into classes and taught by monitors who were themselves instructed by the master. Duncan noted, 'I took the first class almost exclusively in the afternoon – because I employ them as teachers in the morning.'[68] The monitorial system was well adapted to the problems of instructing large numbers, with no other help, but it also conformed to the CMS aims of encouraging the development of native teachers and evangelists. As in their English counterparts, competition was encouraged among pupils, prizes were given for advancement, and the use of slates and tickets for each child was in accordance with Lancaster's practices.[69]

As a Sunday school teacher Duncan had aimed, in teaching others, to 'Instruct, Delight, Overcome or bend the will,' and this became essentially his approach to the education of the Tsimshian. Discipline was strict and often involved corporal punishment which Duncan defended as being a very ancient mode of correction used frequently by officers of Her Majesty's Navy and one not entirely obsolete in England. Reading, writing, and Scriptural knowledge formed the basis of the curriculum, but a conscious effort was made, particularly in the adult evening school, to widen the experience of the Indian, to stimulate his curiosity about a larger world, and to attempt to get rid of what Duncan felt to be his superstitious beliefs. Systematic lectures were given on history, geography, and the physical basis of the universe, and arithmetic and composition were also taught.

The Metlakatla School, however, was also to inculcate the attitudes and values desirable in native Christians. Duncan commented proudly on the achievements of his first pupils. 'They can sing hymns and are learning God Save the Queen ... they know the consequences to us of both courses of conduct, bad and good. They have learnt what are the proper expressions in prayer. They can count alone to 100 ... They have learnt how to speak in terms of civility to their fellow men and have had several of their ways corrected.'[70]

One of the purposes in establishing Metlakatla had been to gather a community whose moral and religious training might render it safe and proper to impart secular instruction. The moral lesson of their secular learning was most important in Duncan's instruction. 'After reading and writing lessons were over I gave them a lecture on perseverance illustrating by ... George Stephenson the great Engineer.'[71]

Like Venn, Duncan believed it was undesirable to separate labour and learning. Industrial training in its most practical form was an integral part of a Metlakatla education. Unless the Christian Indian were taught a useful and profitable trade he would not rise in status above the heathen, nor could he in future contribute to the support of a native church. If the Christian Indian were 'obliged to go back to the Indian mode of getting a living ... [he would be] little better off than the Indian who have had no such education.'[72] So earnest was Duncan to encourage the Victorian habits desirable in Christian converts that he decided in 1872 that only the girls and small boys were to attend the day school. 'Let the big boys earn their bread in daylight and come to school at night, will be my rule.'[73] Perseverance, industriousness, thrift, and self-help were to be as important to the Metlakatla Indian as they were to William Duncan.

As in Victorian England, the atmosphere of a Christian family home was seen as vital to the education of the Indian child. This was partly why the CMS was insistent upon reaching all generations of natives. Not only were there individual souls to be saved, but men like Venn recognized the value of the influence of Christian parents and saw how difficult it was to isolate one generation within a community. In the training of native pastors, Venn recommended that training be given to the men and their wives not only in Scripture but in Christian habits, 'for this purpose an establishment is required rather partaking of the character of a Christian settlement than of a collegiate institution.'[74] Such was the settlement at Metlakatla.

To further his aim of producing moral Christian homes, Duncan, like Samuel Crowther at Lagos and many other missionaries of the mid-nineteenth century, established a boarding home for young girls at the Mission House. Hoping not only to eliminate some of the promiscuity in the village but to train the girls in domestic pursuits and Christian habits, Duncan tried to create a strict but kindly family atmosphere within the house. The Reverend A.J. Hall noted that 'there is a marked contrast between the women who were trained in the Mission house and others. The former are quite domesticated, many of them have clean houses and they exercise a good influence throughout the village. The girls enter the Mission House when about sixteen years of age and remain, if their conduct is good, until they are married. The training of these girls keeps a check upon the young men who are all anxious to obtain a wife from the house and are aware that good conduct is necessary to obtain such a prize.'[75] Redolent of the female homes of the Anglican sisterhoods in England, this was one of the most forceful and successful forms of acculturation and one which considerably extended the personal influence and control of the missionary.

The Metlakatla system was all-embracing. Duncan's belief that the missionary should become everything to his people meant that he was concerned with all aspects of their life, including their leisure hours. The seasonal nature of the Tsimshian economy meant that traditionally the winter season had been devoted to medicine practices and ceremonial dances. Having eliminated these from Metlakatla, the missionary had to attempt to replace such activities with those considered more conducive to the life of a Christian Indian. Thus, the education of a Metlakatlan included the informal learning of English games such as football. Duncan reported the Indians were delighted. 'They had never seen the game before. The village is in two wings east and west. So it was easy to get sides.'[76] A playground was built for the children who were also introduced to sack races and 'hunt the hare.' The year was punctuated with Christmas and Boxing Day feasts, whilst the Queen's Birthday was always celebrated with canoe races and magic-lantern shows. Duncan himself was particularly interested in music, having as a boy been a noted chorister in Beverley Minster. Regular choir practices were held at Metlakatla, and the hymn singing in church was noted by visitors to be most pleasant and hearty. In the 1870s after Duncan's return from a visit to England, a brass band was begun at Metlakatla. It is interesting to note that the 'brass band' is a peculiarly British institution and one which had its origin and found its most enthusiastic reception in that northeastern part of England from which Duncan came.[77] As in the north of England, where works bands and village bands flourished, the Metlakatla brass band was an object of pride for the whole group, and served also to utilize constructively the time and energies of the young men.

Community life at Metlakatla as in other utopian ventures had a clearly defined framework, and the formal laws were strictly enforced. Liquor, medicine work, gambling, face painting, and potlatching must be renounced by all prospective residents. Once established, the new settler must send his children to school, attend all Divine services, settle all quarrels by civil process, pay the village tax, build himself a neat house, cultivate a garden, and endeavour to be cleanly, industrious, orderly, peaceful, and honest.[78]

All ranks and class had been abolished and each Metlakatlan became equal in the eyes of the law and in the sight of God. In such a context it was almost inevitable that Duncan's authority would become supreme. He was, however, supported by the establishment of a corps of twenty uniformed native constables. With remarkable insight and perhaps influenced by Venn's ideas on the development and civilizing of native societies, Duncan felt that the proper persons for constables in Indian villages were the natives themselves. 'The results may not be satisfactory at first but such an office is good training for the natives – tends to enlist their sympathies on the side of the law – is less expensive to the Government and ultimately will afford a better guarantee of the preservation of the peace than if held by white men in their midst.'[79]

By becoming a magistrate himself, Duncan was also able effectively to control the lawlessness and liquor trade in the area, which might have threatened the success of Metlakatla. Although the CMS itself did not generally approve of its missionaries taking such posts, there were many and indeed distinguished precedents in English history for the combination of the offices of vicar and justice of the peace. Lacking any legal training, Duncan administered the law in a common-sense manner and with a firm sense of justice.

One of the aims of Metlakatla had been to set up the supremacy of the law, teach loyalty to the Queen, and conserve the peace of the country, and it was in this aspect that Duncan felt the most striking progress of the Metlakatlans was evident. 'From a great number of lawless and hostile hordes, we have gathered out and established one of the most law-abiding and peace loving communities in the province.'[80] So vital did he feel this aspect of his work to be that, when advising an American acquaintance on the treatment of the Alaskan natives, Duncan recommended that the missionary be immediately given magisterial powers. 'Let him choose a few Indian constables and be occasionally visited and supported by a ship of war and all will go well both for the Indian and the Country too.'[81]

Visitors found the internal organization of Metlakatla particularly fascinating. The men of the village were divided into ten companies, each having two constables, a Sunday school teacher and an elected elder, the latter forming a native council. Although unique in the Canadian mission scene at the time, these companies were in fact similar to the classes advocated by Henry Venn in his plans for native church organization. Sunday school work, the explaining and teaching of Scriptural texts, was carried out in the mature years of the settlement, almost entirely by native Christian teachers within each company. The constables were specifically enjoined to be responsible for the conduct of their company members, to promote their industry and improvement, and to report annually to the missionary on their progress. This was very similar to the system in practice in Sierra Leone, where to develop native leadership a portion of the church members were entrusted to the care of a Christian visitor who was 'required to assist the Minister in seeking out every case of sin, want and need and report to him.'[82]

Similarly, the native council at Metlakatla, which under Duncan's guidance administered the laws of the settlement, may be compared to the native council in Lagos. The Reverend J.A. Lamb noted that the system was most useful for 'if any member needs reproof for carelessness or improper behaviour or has been guilty of conduct which requires suspension, the case comes before the meeting for united decision. Thus personal responsibility is thrown off me, and our people are taught to respect their own people when put in a position of authority in the Church.'[83] And in such a manner did the council function at Metlakatla.

Historiographically, Duncan has been seen as a man with exceptional talent and insight into the problems of handling native peoples. There can be no doubt of his ability to understand Indian needs and society, or to lead and control the people. But he was hardly the daring innovator and social theorist he has been portrayed. Following the advice of Henry Venn to study and adapt to the native society, to utilize as much of it as was valuable, to develop leadership, independence, and industriousness among his converts, Duncan was moving along a well-trodden path. The problems facing the Tsimshian Indians in coping with the impact of white civilization were not unique. Similarly, the solutions proposed by their Victorian missionary had their origin in the ideas of men with the same ideals, who had faced similar problems in other parts of the world. For Will Duncan the cultural reference was always London, not Victoria or Ottawa. Metlakatla was not in essence a response to the wilderness or the Canadian frontier but a systematic attempt to establish a community where Victorian values and ideals could shape the future of the Indians of the North Pacific.

NOTES

This article is from *The Shield of Achilles: Aspects of Canada in the Victorian Age*, ed. W.L. Morton. Toronto: McClelland and Stewart 1968. Reprinted with permission.

The major primary sources for the study of William Duncan are to be found in the William Duncan Papers referred to here as WD/C and the Church Missionary Society Papers, referred to here as CMS/A.

1 WD/C 2156, Reverend G. Mason, *Lo! The Poor Indian:* Read before the Mechanics' Literary Institute, Victoria, 28 Oct 1875
2 WD/C 2156, Earl of Dufferin, *Speech in Victoria B.C.*, 20 Sept. 1876
3 J.A. Wike, 'The Effect of the Maritime Fur Trade on Northwest Coast Indian Society' (PhD thesis, Columbia University, 1951), 3
4 W. Duff, *The Indian History of British Columbia*, vol. I: *The Impact of the White Man* (Victoria: Provincial Museum of Natural History and Anthropology, Memoir No. 5, 1964), 53
5 V.D. Annakin, 'The Missionary, An Agent of Cultural Diffusion' (PhD thesis, Ohio State University, 1940), 50
6 R. Gordon Brown, 'Missions and Cultural Diffusion,' *American Journal of Sociology* 50 (Nov. 1944): 214

7 J.W. Dodds, *The Age of Paradox* (New York: Rinehart 1952), 348
8 Asa Briggs, *Victorian People* (London: Odhams Press 1954), 137
9 Ibid., 139
10 Ibid.
11 W.E. Houghton, *The Victorian Frame of Mind* (New Haven: Yale University Press 1957), 254
12 David Roberts, *The Victorian Origins of the British Welfare State* (New Haven: Yale University Press 1960), 88
13 Ibid., 214
14 Ibid., 221
15 A.E. Bestor Jr, *Backwoods Utopias: The Sectarian and Owenite Phases of Communitarian Socialism in America: 1663–1829* (Philadelphia: University of Pennsylvania Press 1950), vii–viii
16 W.H.G. Armytage, *Heavens Below: Utopian Experiments in England, 1560–1960* (London: Routledge and Kegan Paul 1961), 55
17 Ibid., 57
18 Asa Briggs, *Victorian Cities* (London: Odhams Press 1963), 71
19 Armytage, *Heavens Below*, 211
20 Ibid., 221
21 Briggs, *Cities*, 70
22 Many of the Utopian movements of the nineteenth century were derived to some extent from the practices and writings of Robert Owen. The fame of New Lanark was widespread but Owen's atheism did not endear his humanitarian ideas to the Victorian middle class. The ideas of Charles Fourier had less influence in England than in the United States. A major aim of the organization of his phalanxes was to make work enjoyable and attractive. Such ideas were unlikely to find a sympathetic audience in a Victorian England which saw a moral worth in toiling at unenviable tasks.
23 A.F. Young and E.T. Ashton, *British Social Work in the Nineteenth Century* (London: Routledge and Kegan Paul 1956), 218
24 W. Knight, *The Missionary Secretariat of Henry Venn B.D.* (London: Longmans, Green 1880), 305
25 E. Stock, *A History of the Church Missionary Society*, vol. II (London: Longmans, Green 1899), 83
26 Knight, *Venn*, 210
27 Henry Venn to the Bishop of Kingston, London, Jan. 1867. Cited in Knight, *Venn*, 216
28 Knight, *Venn*, 210
29 Henry Venn, *On National Churches*. Cited in Knight, *Venn*, 285
30 Rufus Anderson, *Foreign Missions: Their Relations and Claims* (New York: Charles Scribner 1869), 47ff
31 Henry Venn, *On National Churches*, second paper, 1861. Cited in Knight, *Venn*, 312
32 CMS CA/2L1, Final Instructions to Dr. E. Irving, London 23 Dec. 1853. Cited in J.F.A. Ajayi, *Christian Missions in Nigeria. 1841–1891: The Making of a New Elite* (London: Longmans, Green 1965), 81
33 T.F. Buxton, *The African Slave Trade and its Remedy* (London 1841)
34 Cited in Ajayi, *Christian Missions*, 7

35 Peter Hinchcliff, *The Anglican Church in South Africa* (London: Darton, Longman and Todd 1963), 45
36 S.M. Johnstone, *Samuel Marsden: A Pioneer of Civilization in the South Seas* (Sydney: Angus and Robertson 1932), 71
37 Henry Venn, *On Nationality*. Cited in Knight, *Venn*, 282
38 Henry Venn, *Memoir on the Character of the Reverend Edward Bickersteth*. Cited in Knight, *Venn*, 166
39 Henry Venn, *Memoir of the Character of the Reverend Edward Bickersteth*. Cited in Knight, *Venn*, 166
40 CMS CA/L2, Instructions of the Parent Committee to Mr W. Kirkham, schoolmaster, 29 Jan. 1856. Cited in Ajayi, *Christian Missions*, 144
41 The public library at New Metlakatla, Alaska (Duncan's second settlement) possessed multiple copies of all the works of Samuel Smiles.
42 WD/C2157, Notebook, April 1852
43 WD/C2157, Notebook, nd
44 CMS/A124, G. Cussons to the CMS, Beverley, 2 Jan. 1866
45 WD/C2154, Journal, 16 Jan. 1856
46 WD/C2143, W. Kirkham to Highbury Friends, Lagos, 19 July 1856
47 P. Curtin, *The Image of Africa: British Ideas and Action, 1780–1850* (Madison: University of Wisconsin Press 1964), 420
48 WD/C2154, First Report from Fort Simpson, Journal, Feb. 1858
49 Ibid.
50 CMS/A80, William Duncan to the CMS, Metlakatla, 25 Oct. 1860
51 WD/C 2154, Journal, 2 June 1859
52 CMS/A81, William Duncan to the Hon. D. Laird, minister of the interior, np, May 1875
53 Ibid.
54 WD/C2154, William Duncan to Mrs W.J. Macdonald, Metlakatla, 6 Sept. 1869
55 WD/C2154, Journal, Statement in Reference to Metlakatla, np, nd
56 WD/C2145, CMS to William Duncan, London, 8 Sept. 1876
57 WD/C2148, William Duncan to the CMS, Metlakatla, 5 Dec. 1871
58 Curtin, *Image of Africa*, 431
59 G.F.G. Stanley, 'The Indian Background of Canadian History,' Canadian Historical Association, *Annual Report*, 1952, 14–21
60 WD/C2144, William Duncan to W.F. Tolmie, Metlakatla, 9 May 1866
61 WD/C2155, Journal, 5 Aug. 1863
62 CMS/A105, Rev. E. Cridge to the CMS, Metlakatla, 27 Sept. 1867
63 WD/C2143, W. Kirkham to Highbury Friends, Lagos, 19 July 1856
64 WD/C2143, W. Kirkham to William Duncan, Lagos, 20 March 1856
65 CMS/A81, William Duncan to the CMS, Metlakatla, 29 Jan. 1874
66 CMS/A105, Rev. E. Cridge to the CMS, Metlakatla, 27 Sept. 1867
67 WD/C2155, Journal, 17 Nov. 1863
68 WD/C2155, Journal, 11 Nov. 1867
69 Joseph Lancaster, *The British System of Education* (Georgetown: Joseph Mulligan 1812), 58ff
70 WD/C2154, Journal, 18 Feb. 1859
71 WD/C2155, Journal, 22 Dec. 1864
72 CMS/A80, William Duncan to the CMS, Fort Simpson, 14 May 1861

73 WD/C2155, Journal, 2 Oct. 1872
74 Henry Venn to the Bishop of Kingston, London, Jan. 1867. Cited in Knight, *Venn*, 218
75 CMS/A106, Rev. A.J. Hall to the CMS, Metlakatla, 6 March 1878
76 WD/C2155, Journal, 26 Dec. 1864
77 John F. Russell and J.H. Elliot, *The Brass Band Movement* (London: J.M. Dent and Sons 1936). The first brass band contests were held in the 1840s at Burton Constable, twelve miles from Duncan's home.
78 WD/C2158, Notebook, Laws of Metlakatla, 15 Oct. 1862
79 WD/C2149, William Duncan to the Provincial Secretary, Metlakatla, 27 Jan. 1875
80 CMS/A81, William Duncan to Hon. David Laird, minister of the interior, May 1875
81 WD/C2154, William Duncan to Mr N. Colyer, New York, 28 Feb. 1870
82 WD/C2156, Rev. J. Johnson to the CMS, Sierra Leone, 15 April 1869
83 WD/C2156, Rev. J.A. Lamb to the CMS, Lagos, 17 April 1869

THE POLICY OF
THE BIBLE AND
THE PLOUGH

J.R. MILLER

Owen Glendower, Hotspur, and Canadian Indian Policy

Owen Glendower I can call spirits from the vasty deep.
Hotspur Why, so can I, or so can any man; But will they come when you do call for them?

Shakespeare, *Henry* IV, *Part* I

Scholarly writing on Canada's Indian policy of the late Victorian period has lagged behind analysis of other aspects of native-newcomer relations. Like American academics, Canadians have made an impressive start on revising the understanding of economic, military, and social relations in the seventeenth and eighteenth centuries. However, discussions of nineteenth-century assimilative policies have persisted in an older tendency to treat the Indians as objects rather than agents, victims rather than creators of their history. The existing literature usually examines missionaries' requests for the suppression of cultural practices such as the Potlatch and notes how their desires coincided with the government's anxiety to prevent Indians from squandering their capital or wasting their time. The standard interpretation then makes a logical leap from such policies as forbidding the Sun Dance or establishing residential schools to an implicit conclusion that such measures assimilated Indians.

In short, in this traditional version of government policy towards Canada's native peoples there is a tendency to treat the aims and results of legislation banning traditional cultural practices or inhibiting native movement as synonymous. Such treatments remind one of nothing so much as Shakespeare's dialogue between Hotspur and Owen Glendower. When the boastful Glendower claims, 'I can call spirits from the vasty deep,' Hotspur responds, 'Why, so can I, or so can any man.' Calling them is not the point. What matters is the response. 'But will they come when you do call for them?'[1] Canada legislated to control and assimilate Indians late in the nineteenth century. But did the measures work? Were the Indians simply victims of these policies?[2]

This view of late nineteenth-century policy as efficacious resembles older, outmoded views of economic, military, and social relations between Canada's indigenous peoples and European newcomers. For a long time the literature on the fur trade, for instance, treated the Indians and Inuit as victims of rapacious European traders.[3] Following Francis Parkman, military historians talked about the 'use' of Indians by various European powers in the wars of the eighteenth century in North America.[4] Similarly, accounts of Christian missions in early New France emphasized the heroism of the Jesuits while paying little attention to the activities of those whom they proselytized.

Unlike the conventional treatment of late Victorian Indian policy, however, the traditional picture of the Indian as victim of European merchants, generals, and missionaries has of late been revised. People such as A.J. Ray and Robin Fisher have demonstrated that Indians both in the Hudson's Bay Company lands and on the Pacific were in control of the commerce in furs: natives successfully insisted that the fur trade be carried on according to their formulas, and for purposes largely determined by them.[5] This work has been amplified and enriched by social historians who, while probing the role of native women in fur-trade country, discovered that the social side of the commerce in peltries was controlled by native societies, too.[6] And scholars such as Axtell, Eccles, Jaenen, and Trigger have reassessed the social and intellectual relations between Indians and Europeans in New France. They have demonstrated that missions were planted in the interior of North America primarily because the native peoples regarded them as a manifestation of the exchange of personnel with which they had for centuries cemented commercial liaisons. Jesuits were allowed into Huronia to maintain the commercial and military alliance between the Huron and the French.[7] 'Heroic' missionaries were hostages to the exchange of furs; Jesuits were 'martyrs' to commercial ambitions.

The military relationship of the colonial period has also been reinterpreted to portray the Indian peoples as agents rather than objects. This development in Canadian historiography has paralleled American writing on military relations.[8] To Canadian audiences L.F.S. Upton explained that the Micmac did not fight as the tools of the French, but rather that they embraced Catholicism and the French alliance as their best defence against the Anglo-Americans whom they feared. And students of the American War of Independence have demonstrated conclusively that Indians operated, not as 'pawns' or 'tools,' but according to carefully worked out calculations of where their self-interest lay.[9] Woodlands Indians perceived that their interests lay with the more northerly, commercially inclined European power rather than with the agriculturalists to the south.[10] Pontiac sought to repel the Anglo-American farmers who were poised to sweep across the Alleghenies after the Peace of Paris in 1763. The Brant family led the Mohawk to support the British in the Revolutionary War for personal and familial reasons and because of calculations that the British posed a lesser threat to their lands than the Americans. Tecumseh and The Prophet were operating during the War of 1812 on the same strategy that was designed to deter the advance of the agricultural frontier.[11]

What these specialists in economic, social, and military history have done is to restore indigenous peoples to their active role in Canadian history. They have demonstrated that the native peoples, at least in the early phases of contact, controlled the fur trade, that they pursued their own interests in military matters, and that they shaped the social and intellectual relationship. Similarly, some works on education and civil policy making in the early decades after the War of 1812 have recognized an active Indian role. Mississauga and other Indians north of the lower Great Lakes encouraged and supported efforts to educate their young until they recognized that the missionaries and government sought to assimilate native youths as well as make them literate. And legislative initiatives in the 1850s to assert political control over Indians in the central colony of British North America encountered stiff resistance.[12] Unfortunately, studies of Indian-white relations after Confederation have thus far proved largely resistant to reinterpretation.[13] It is now time for another look at Canada's version of the 'policy of the Bible and the plough.'

This policy, though foreshadowed in pre-Confederation programs in central Canada, became fully developed only after 1867. Legislation of 1869 and 1876, which was re-enacted in the Indian Act of 1880, presumed to define who was an Indian and to interfere with Indian self-government. At the same time, inducements were held out to Indians to encourage their 'advancement' towards full citizenship by offering those in eastern Canada the federal franchise in 1885 and by making 'allotments' of reserve land available to Indians who wished to take possession of individual plots. However, as had been the case with similar experiments earlier, Indians proved uninterested in acquiring electoral rights or freehold tenure and remarkably resistant to so-called enfranchisement, or adoption of normal citizenship status.[14] Bureaucrats responded to parallel failures in the 1870s and 1880s by resorting to what Indian commissioner Edgar Dewdney described as 'sheer compulsion.'[15]

Officialdom's inclination towards coercion culminated in a series of measures that were designed to control Indians politically and alter them culturally. Amendments to the Indian Act in 1884 prohibited the Potlatch, or 'the Indian dance known as the "Tamanawas" ' of the Pacific Indians, while in 1885 department regulations instituted a 'pass system' designed to control movement. In western Canada, Indians who wished to travel off their reserve were expected to obtain a pass signed by the agent. The pass system was designed to inhibit the movements of Indian diplomats, to discourage parental visits to residential schools, and to provide the North-West Mounted Police (NWMP) and Indian agents with the authority to stop Plains Indians from participating in ceremonies such as the Sun Dance or the Thirst Dance on distant reserves. These coercive measures were aimed at assimilating Indians by attacking their religious rituals, removing their children from home influences, and preventing their travelling when there was work to be done in the fields. They were viewed as a necessary part of a broad campaign to inculcate agriculture in the prairie west that embraced subdivision of reserves into individual lots and enforced avoidance of mechanized horticulture.[16] These policies were stiffened in 1894–5 by regulations requiring Indian children's attendance at school and by further legislation that attacked the cultural practices of both Pacific and Plains Indians by banning 'giveaway' dances or ceremonies that involved self-mutilation. Finally, in 1898 a new government withdrew the 1885 offer of the right to vote from eastern Canadian Indians.[17]

These Canadian policies were based on both British and American practices. In the British North American colonies in the middle decades of the nineteenth century, Christian missionaries and civil government had combined to promote both sedentary agriculture and education.[18] After the formation of the Dominion of Canada and the acquisition of the western plains by the new state in the 1860s, there was an increasing tendency among Canadian policy makers to look to the United States as well as to British colonial policy for suggestions as to what should be done. The destructive American Indian wars of this period were quickly rejected as a model for Canada's integration of its new lands. Recognizing that they had 'to make up their mind to one of three policies – viz: to help the Indians to farm and raise stock, to feed them or to fight them,' Canadian officials chose the first option for reasons of both economy and humanitarianism.[19] However, if the American military was not an appropriate model for Canadian policy makers, other aspects of American Indian policy were. Programs such as allotting reserve lands in individual plots in an effort to break up the reserves and atomize members of bands were largely copied from the Dawes scheme.[20] And planning in the late 1870s for a new educational policy led the federal government to send a commissioner south to investigate what its neighbours were doing by way of residential schooling.[21] Finally, the thorough cooperation of state and Christian church for the prosecution of these policies was both reminiscent of contemporary American approaches and consistent with British and British North American practice.

More important than the sources of these policies of assimilation was their effect. On the whole, scholars have treated policy intent and effect as similar, if not identical, largely because they concentrated on government fiat and documents. That assimilation and coercion were the objectives of the group of policies there is no doubt. But what were the effects? Did the measures work?

Consider, for example, the notorious pass system that was set up in 1885. First, it is important to note that little about the operation, as opposed to the purpose, of the system is known. We do not know for certain how long even a pretence of enforcing it was maintained.[22] And while it was official policy in the prairie provinces, its effects appear to have been very mixed. For one thing, it does not seem to have been implemented uniformly in the 1880s. Hayter Reed, commissioner after Dewdney's elevation to cabinet, referred in 1891 correspondence with his deputy minister to 'regulations already issued, but so far disregarded' when talking about natives' mobility.[23] Agents and farm instructors, who lacked the power and the time to make Indians obey the pass regulations, attempted to hand the duty off to the NWMP.[24] But the leaders of the NWMP had serious doubts about the system and their role in enforcing it. They believed that the requirement that Indians get a pass before leaving their reserve would not stand up in court. They also feared that if Indians tested it through litigation, their victory would discredit the whole system of law enforcement. In the aftermath of the Northwest Rebellion of 1885, the horsemen were most concerned not to undermine the law and themselves by attempting to enforce invalid regulations. They dragged their feet in response to agents' requests for help and, at times, refused outright to enforce the restrictions of the pass system.[25]

Indian Affairs bureaucrats themselves recognized the weakness of their position and were reluctant to provoke a confrontation over passes. The department's instruction to its agents was 'to issue Passes to Indians who they know will leave in any case, and so preserve an appearance at least of control, and a knowledge of their movements.'[26] It is also clear that many agents were less than thorough in their administration of the pass system. One disgruntled Mountie complained to Commissioner Reed that one of the latter's agents had given a pass to 'the biggest whore master in the band,' a man who 'had six squaws with him.'[27] In sum, what little is known about the actual operation of the pass system suggests not so much that it was effective in controlling the Indians as that it was often a nullity.

There is similar reason to doubt the efficacy of the 1884 and 1895 measures against the Potlatch and 'giveaway dances.' An 1884 amendment to the Indian Act threatened anyone 'who engages or assists in celebrating the Indian festival known as the "Potlach" or in the Indian dance known as the "Tamanawas" ' with a jail term.[28] The federal government soon found that enforcement was a problem. The provincial government of British Columbia, which quarrelled constantly with Ottawa over Indian Affairs matters, was uncooperative about enforcement of the bans on Potlatch and Tamanawas. And the federal government had few officials on the Northwest Coast through whom to compel compliance with the law.[29] Agents were helpless in most parts of the coast. At the first announcement by a group of Indians that they intended to defy the ban, the local agent avoided a confrontation by acquiescing, giving as his justification the explanation that the scheduled Potlatch was not really a Potlatch at all.[30] The young anthropologist Franz Boas noted several years after the prohibition was legislated that 'there is nobody to prevent the Indians doing whatsoever they like.' He observed that an Indian who had been appointed a constable and supplied with a uniform and flag by the agent for the purpose of preventing unlawful feasts and dances responded strangely. Since his appointment, 'he dances in his uniform with the flag.'[31] Little wonder that the Kitwanga Indians in 1890 dismissed the anti-Potlatch law, saying it 'was as weak as a baby.'[32]

When the occasional agent did try to enforce the ban, matters only got worse from the government's point of view. The agent at Alert Bay made the first arrest under the 1885 prohibition in 1889. Acting in his capacity as justice of the peace, he tried the accused and extracted a plea of guilty. Apparently in error, the agent or his superiors then committed the prisoner to trial in Victoria, the provincial capital. When friends of the accused Indian applied for a writ of habeas corpus, the justice immediately granted it on the grounds that the prisoner had already been tried and convicted. However, the jurist went on in a remarkable series of *obiter dicta* to lay waste the 1885 ban. He explained that the statute lacked a proper definition of 'Potlatch' and that the other prohibited celebration, the 'Tamanawas,' was 'unknown.' Finally, he speculated that the accused, who knew no English, probably had not understood the earlier proceedings. The judge thought, on reflection, that 'there would be some difficulty in convicting at all under the Statute.'[33] As the distraught agent who had begun the series of events lamented, the incident rendered the 1885 ban 'a dead letter.'[34]

Although a more precisely framed amendment in 1895 got around the legal difficulty, it did not lead to immediate or effective enforcement of the prohibition on potlatching. There is abundant evidence that the supposedly forbidden celebrations went on long after 1895, though no potlatcher served a prison sentence until 1920.[35] (In 1909 a Methodist missionary on Vancouver Island plaintively asked his superiors, 'Can nothing be done with the Dominion Government to compel the enforcement of the Act which prohibits Potlatching?' When the principal of a residential school wanted to find out when a particular 'great potlach' was to take place, he wrote the agent to inquire –

hardly evidence that potlatching was something kept hidden from the agent.)[36] A crackdown stopped the festivities for a few years, but by 1927 those Indians who still wanted to Potlatch were back at it. It took the Great Depression and the gradual spread of acculturation to suppress it temporarily in the 1940s.[37] Later it would revive during a general rediscovery of traditional rites, crafts, and arts in the 1960s and later.

What is too often neglected in discussions of the anti-Potlatch campaign is the role of Indian converts. The initial ban in the 1880s was a direct response to pressure from such Indians, as well as from missionaries and Indian Affairs officers.[38] Observers on the Northwest Coast noted that the minority who supported prohibition of the Potlatch were Christian converts and young people who faced many decades of paying out before they could look forward to reaping their reward from the redistributive ritual.[39] Certainly there is evidence of pressure to enforce the ban from Christian converts in British Columbia. In 1888 government commissioners appointed to establish reserve limits in the Nass River area heard complaints from Indian opponents of the Potlatch. They explained that they had protested to Indian Affairs officials about the practice. The officials had counseled them to 'go to the heathen, and advise them to stop Potlaches, but the heathen laughed at us.' They were pleased when they heard reports that the government was going to do something about the practice.[40] In 1893 the council at Kitimaat, British Columbia, ruled that 'any person in the village of Kitimaat who gives a *feast* or *Potlach* will be *punished* by a fine of One hundred and forty Dollars,' while the 'Chiefs of Kispiox' in 1914 asked for government and church help in stopping the Potlatch and 'old fashioned feasts or feasts in memory of the dead.'[41] Converts apparently absorbed some of the outlook of the non-Indian majority. When a spokesperson for a Kawkiutl band in 1919 wanted to 'give you a few reasons' why the Potlatch ban 'should not only stand but ... also be strongly enforced,' she began with a patriotic argument. Here, 'people as a whole will never own Allegiance to the Government or King as long as they are allowed to practice their Allegiance to the Potlatch system, for to them this excludes every other Government.' 'No Potlatchers,' she claimed, 'volunteered to serve overseas.'[42] As late as 1936 a public meeting at Alert Bay was the scene of a vigorous debate between Christians and traditionalists over the Potlatch and marriage customs.[43]

If not all coastal Indians opposed banning the old ways, neither did all the purveyors of new beliefs favour coercion and suppression. Some missionaries thought coercion unnecessary and undesirable. 'Leave the thing alone as far as the old people are concerned; educate along definite lines with the young people and ten years at the outside should see the end of the problem,' one argued.[44] Even the Department of Indian Affairs on occasion promoted supposedly forbidden traditions. Ironically and unintentionally it encouraged the officially illegal dances by conveying to the World Exposition of 1893 in Chicago a troupe of Kwakiutl who staged the illicit dances.[45]

Because a pattern similar to the anti-Potlatch campaign is found in the forbidden dances of Plains Indians, it is well to be sceptical about the effectiveness of nineteenth-century prohibitions of these celebrations as well. Pressure for action against festivals such as the Sun Dance of the Blackfoot Confederacy or the Thirst Dance of the Cree and Saulteaux sometimes came from Christian converts among the Indians themselves. Church of England canon H.W. Gibbon Stocken claimed to be 'writing ... at the earnest & repeated request of several of our leading Blackfoot Christians' when he asked the deputy minister for energetic action against the 'native dances, now so largely indulged in.'[46] An Indian agent among the Dakota reported that 'there were two cliques or factions on this reserve, a *pagan* faction and a *Christian* faction .... The Christians wanted to legislate the pagans into the church, first by stopping their recreations and forcing along certain lines and the pagans worked in opposition to the Christians.'[47] Indian missionaries on the plains, like converts on the Northwest Coast, often advocated suppression. The Dakota John Thunder, a Presbyterian missionary in Manitoba, argued for action against giveaway dances, which he thought retarded his people's moral growth as well as their economic advance.[48] There were, however, rare non-native missionaries who defended Indians' right to carry out these dances. The Methodist John McDougall explained to a western audience that the Sun Dance, like the Thirst Dance, was 'a religious festival.' 'And,' he added, 'I altogether fail to see why in these days of our much boasted religious liberty anyone should interfere with a few Indians in the exercise of their faith.'[49] But Plains Indians, did not have much need of the efforts of someone like McDougall. They proved quite adept at resisting, evading, and defying efforts to stamp out the Sun and Thirst Dances.

Local Indian leaders, some of them the products of residential schools, resorted to formal protests to the government, sometimes with the aid of Euro-Canadian lawyers whom they retained, against the agents' efforts to interfere with their dancing.[50] Residential school graduates like Dan Kennedy were also known to employ their influence against the missionary on the reserve, using the argument that removal of the cleric would put an end to interference with traditional dancing.[51] Indians also became adept at exploiting differing attitudes among white authority figures to defeat those who wanted to interfere with them. Numerous Plains bands cited the missionary McDougall in justification of their attempts to carry on with their dances.[52] In the 1890s the Blood Indians decided to ignore their agent, who was threatening prosecution as they set about arranging a medicine pipe dance, at least partly because they knew that other agents on the Peigan and Blackfoot reserves were permitting dancing there.[53] As the years went by, it became increasingly common for Indians to use lawyers to combat Indian Affairs and for local officials to lament their charges' greater familiarity with the law and with legal weapons.[54]

Evasion was often employed by Plains Indians intent on maintaining their religious traditions in the dance. One of the easiest ways was simply to wait until the Indian agent was not expecting a dance and then hold it, as Samson's band did in the Hobbema Agency in Alberta.[55] Another method was to seek informal approval for a modified version of the forbidden dance and then to carry out the traditional ceremony. Under the 1895 legislation against dancing, only celebrations that involved giving away property or self-mutilation were outlawed. It was a fairly simple matter for Indians to persuade the agent that they were going to hold a 'modified' dance and then to indulge in the forbidden practices.[56] In theory, agents were supposed to use the pass system to prevent Indians from traveling to other reserves to participate in dances. Near the west-central Saskatchewan town of Battleford, the Indians of the Poundmaker and Little Pine bands hit on an ingenious stratagem. Since their reserves were contiguous, they built their dance hall on the boundary line so that no official could interfere.[57] And when the Poundmaker band had to replace their community hall, they made sure they built the new one well away from the prying eyes of agent and missionary. The dancing continued largely undetected.[58] Further south, on the File Hills Colony which was designed as a Christian home for ex-pupils of the residential schools, Indian dancing also went on clandestinely.[59]

Finally, there were cases where the Indians simply defied both law and agent. An agent in northwestern Ontario who tried to dissuade a shaman from carrying on traditional feasts and dances found that the conjurer 'only laughed' at him.[60] On Red Crow's Blood reserve, after several years in which the Indians had carried on modified versions of their dances, the agent in 1900 decided to prevent dancing altogether. He withheld the beef tongues that were essential to the ritual, but Indians who were employed by the Mounted Police as scouts quietly obtained tongues from police larders. Next the agent threatened to withhold rations from any Indian who participated in the Sun Dance. When Red Crow countered by promising to slaughter every head in his considerable herd to feed his people, the agent capitulated, 'and never again was the ceremony denied to them.'[61]

Plains Indians proved so adept at resisting, evading, or defying the bans on ceremonial dancing that agents and missionaries were compelled to proceed cautiously and often to try to redirect, rather than stamp out, these activities.[62] Agents who knew they could not suppress dancing tried to create an interest in alternatives such as sports days and other summertime festivals.[63] And the Anglican missionary on the Blackfoot reserve, following in a long Christian tradition, tried to defeat 'pagan' ritual by adopting and modifying it. He 'made a bid for the transformation' of the tobacco dance by creating 'a ceremony very much like the old one of "Beating the bounds" which has almost gone out of the Church.' He formed his converts into a procession headed by a 'cross of green wood' and marched them 'round the camp stopping at the East, South, west and North. Then we formed up in the centre of the camp and planted the cross.'[64] Moreover, agents and missionaries found that efforts to discourage dancing ran up against Euro-Canadian populations that wanted the dances included in their summer fairs in order to sell tickets.[65] Efforts to stamp out dancing, like those aimed at the Potlatch, proved largely ineffective because of both Euro-Canadian and Indian obstacles.

Even residential schools, which are often described as the most coercive of church-state instruments of assimilation, were no more representative of effective policy than prohibitions on Indians' traditional cultural and religious practices. These schools – a joint enterprise of the federal government and major Christian denominations, a blend of British and American practice[66] – sought to remove the children from 'the demoralizing and degrading influences of the tepees' and surround them with an environment of bourgeois Christian values.[67] Here the children would be made over into acquisitive, individualistic Christians who would, ultimately, make the pass system and prohibitions on dancing or Potlatch unnecessary. Residential schools were intended to lead to 'not only the emancipation of the subjects thereof from the condition of ignorance and superstitious blindness in which they are, and their parents before them were sunk, but converting them into useful members of society and contributors to, instead of merely consumers of, the wealth of the country.'[68]

Residential schools are usually treated as though they were effective in capturing Indian children and in crushing their will and identity. It is sometimes said that 'it was the rule at that time that all treaty Indian children had to attend an Indian boarding school.'[69] The authority of the Department of Indian Affairs was supposedly used to ensure that children were not only sent to these schools but also kept there. At the schools native children were strictly forbidden to practise any of their people's traditional observances, and they could not speak their own languages under any circumstances. Residential schooling, in short, typified the totalitarian and assimilative spirit of Canada's Indian policy in the later Victorian era and the first half of the twentieth century.[70] It amounted, as a candid missionary put it, to an effort to 'educate & colonize a people against their will.'[71] But is this view accurate for anything more than the intentions of those who ran the residential schools? There is no doubt that the institutions were intended to convert children to Christianity and to equip them with the skills to become self-supporting in or alongside Euro-Canadian society. But what was the result?

First, the conventional view of residential schools fails to note that the system never reached more than a minority of young Indians and Inuit. There were never more than eighty residential schools supported by the government in the entire country. Atlantic Canada did not have any until Shubenacadie was established in Nova Scotia late in the 1920s, and even thereafter most Indians in the region went to day schools or to no school at all. Much the same holds true for Quebec, where vast areas were without residential schools. In southern Ontario there were only four, and in northern Ontario there were also large districts in which boarding or industrial schools did not exist. The prairie provinces, British Columbia, and the far north were the most thoroughly covered regions, not because a far-sighted federal government systematically provided full coverage, but because denominational competition among Oblates, Anglicans, Methodists, and Presbyterians fostered the rapid multiplication of missions and schools in these areas. In some cases, Indian bands petitioned unsuccessfully for the erection of a residential school for their children.[72] Many children, even in the west and the north, completely escaped the residential schools. As one Stoney put it, 'I didn't even go to one hour of school because I am an Indian.'[73] Thousands of young Indians similarly escaped the clutches of residential schools.[74]

Even where residential schools existed, they proved singularly difficult to keep filled with students. Missionaries in the early years were forever complaining that agents either failed to help them recruit students or even worked actively against their efforts to procure them.[75] Even after the department acquiesced in 1894 to the missionaries' cries for compulsory attendance legislation, the problem persisted. In 1908 a Methodist principal complained that 'there is no law to compel an Indian to educate his child,' and in 1906 the Anglican Mission Board in the Diocese of Calgary contended that Indians 'send their children to school when it suits them to do so, and they keep them at home for the same reason. The only exception to this rule is, the children are allowed to please themselves whether they go or not.'[76] Even allowing for clerical hyperbole, it is clear that attendance remained a problem. If this were not so, why was it that principals had to make numerous, expensive 'recruiting' trips in search of students, and why was it that these men of the cloth had to resort to bribing parents to get their children?[77] Once students were obtained for the schools, how could they be kept? To take only one example, Joseph Shaw was admitted to Coqualeetza Institute on 19 August 1901; he disappeared on 1 November 1903 and remained a truant until formally discharged on 3

September 1905. (He did, however, pay a visit to the school in 1906.)[78] In understaffed schools it was a lot of trouble to chase students. Agents were often uncooperative or distracted, and the police hated the chore of retrieving unhappy runaways. When the constabulary presented the bill for their services as truant officers, the evangelists became unhappy, too.[79]

It is not clear that the schools, assuming they procured and held on to the students, were very successful in eradicating traditional Indian religion and cultural practices. Certainly most schools tried to force the children to conform to Euro-Canadian standards, especially in the highly visible areas of dress and grooming. It was standard procedure to scrub the students and shear the boys of hair on arrival, a practice that caused consternation in children from nations in which cropped hair was a sign of mourning.[80] Even after the student got over the shock of thinking that one of his loved ones had died after he left home for the school, he did not necessarily get over the rough subjection to Euro-Canadian grooming. One fellow who became a Christian worker among the Indians 'never forgave the woman who cut his hair while he slept and if he followed the inclination of his own heart he would throw off all the education & go back where he would never see a white man.'[81]

One area of school life that requires reconsideration is the matter of suppressing Indian languages, usually held to have universally occurred. This seems to be an exaggeration. It would have been strange for evangelists who had laboured hard to master Indian tongues – and there were many of them among the Oblates and Church Missionary Society workers in the nineteenth century in particular – not to use their linguistic skills with the children, if only outside classrooms. In many schools, at least one church service on Sunday was conducted in the Indian language, especially in those charges where the school chapel was also the mission's church.[82] A Methodist missionary one Sunday 'held service in the schoolhouse, and had the privilege of preaching the glorious Gospel to an earnest people in the "language wherein they were born," which, after all, is the only way to reach the hearts and thoughts of any congregation.'[83] At Lejac school 'they used to pray one week in Indian and one week in ... English.'[84] At British Columbia schools the rule was, 'we must not talk Indian (except when allowed),' while at some other institutions, such as the Blood Anglican school, students were able to use their own language after seven o'clock in the evening.[85] Some schoolmasters were criticized for indifference about language.[86] But was it realistic to think all use of Indian languages could be stopped? Many schools were like Morley, Alberta, where the teachers knew that 'the children were not supposed to speak Stoney, but they really couldn't stop them.'[87]

There were even rare examples in which the schools turned out to be the place where students actually became acquainted with their culture. The daughter of parents who lived on the File Hills ex-pupils colony in Saskatchewan recalled that 'we didn't speak Cree in our house as our parents spoke two different languages.' However, when she 'went to school we learned some Cree from our schoolmates but we often found that what we learned wasn't in good taste when we repeated it to our parents.' She picked up a little Cree at school, though she never mastered the language.[88] But this daughter of supposedly converted parents also recalled that she 'learned a lot about our Indian culture and some of the language, even though we weren't allowed to speak it at school.' On occasion 'we went down to the lake to dance a pow-wow. We used a pail for a drum and Gracie Squatepew was always our main singer.'[89]

The language question could even provoke the parents to intervene in the operation of the schools, on at least one occasion in a surprising fashion. The Anglican missionary on the Blood reserve in southern Alberta was visited by a delegation of parents, whose leader told him, 'came to see you about teaching my children. They tell me that you are teaching them syllabics in the Blackfoot language.' This man said that the parents thought this 'is wrong. We want you to teach the children the English tongue, and not syllabics. They have their own language and we have ours. Teach them English and we will be satisfied.' The missionary acceded to the delegation's desire: 'I dropped teaching them syllabics right away. There the matter ended so far as the Bloods were concerned.'[90] There were other pressures generated from among Indians in favour of the use of English. When a school population contained children from two or more language groups, the use of English was promoted as a medium of communication that all could use.[91] Residential schools were not always the oppressive institutions they were thought to be in the area of the suppression of language; and Indian parents sometimes had a significant role in the running of these schools.

The traditional view that residential schools rigidly separated children from their parents, their homes, and their bands also should be qualified. Again, there can be no doubt that this was hoped for by government officials, who wanted the schools to socialize children away from the ways of their parents. But it frequently was not the result. Many of the boarding institutions were located close to, or even on, the reserves from which their inmates came. The Mohawk Institute in Ontario was close to the Six Nations Reserve. Crowstand in east-central Saskatchewan was on the reserve of the Cote band. In southern Alberta, in particular, the boarding schools run by the Catholics and Anglicans were located on the reserves of the Sarcee, Peigan, Blackfoot, and Blood. Proximity enhanced parental control of the children's movement. When 'Running Rabbit made bother about his girl remaining in the Home' on the Blackfoot reserve, it was easier for the principal to 'let her go' than to resist.[92]

Similarly, at Alberni on Vancouver Island, the Presbyterian school was only a hop, skip, and jump from the 'rancherie,' or Indian encampment.[93] It was true that the more elaborate 'industrial schools' that the Department of Indian Affairs began to establish in 1883 were deliberately located well away from reserves, but there were always far fewer of these than there were of boarding schools. For most children in residential schools it simply was not true that they were kept away from home influences for long periods. Many of them visited home at least every weekend, whatever the theory of residential schooling might have held.

For other reasons also there was a great deal more interaction between the home and the child than Indian Affairs would have liked. The children at these schools were notorious for running away whenever they became homesick or angry with the discipline or fed up with the poor food and hard work. The diary of an Anglican missionary in southern Alberta in 1917 contains at least seventeen instances, many of them multiple escapes, of children running away during the year.[94] The high incidence of runaways was part of the reason that schools such as the Anglican Blood institution provided a weekend 'monthly holiday,' as well as generous Christmas, Easter, and summer breaks.[95] On Kuper Island in British Columbia, the principal pleaded with the Department of Indian Affairs for longer summer holidays, arguing that the parents would take the children salmon fishing regardless of what he or Ottawa said.[96] The flow of personnel went the other way, too. The pass system notwithstanding, Indian parents often made their way from their reserves to the school to visit their children. The principal at Lebret school in southern Saskatchewan constructed an 'Indian porch' to house the unauthorized visitors, defending his action to annoyed Indian Affairs officials by saying that it was necessary to prevent the parents from removing their children from the school.[97] All such instances suggest that residential schools did not always keep parents and children apart, and that parents sometimes had some influence over the schools' operation.

Indeed, there were cases where it would be more accurate to say that the Indians were the guiding force behind the foundation of the residential school. Northwest Coast Indians demanded that the Presbyterians provide residence facilities at Alberni in which their children could stay while they were absent to work in the sealery or in the canneries.[98] Those at Kitimaat petitioned the Methodists in 1896 for a home and offered to help with the construction and maintenance of such a facility.[99] In the north a missionary reported that 'at Whitefish Lake some forty miles from Lesser Slave Lake ... [a] Boarding School has just been erected because the Indians would not send their children to the School at the latter place.'[100] As revealing as these examples are, they pale beside the exceptional case of the Cecilia Jeffrey school in the Lake of the Woods district, near the Ontario-Manitoba boundary.

In 1898 the Indians at Shoal Lake petitioned the Presbyterians in Winnipeg for a school, and two years later they were reported to be 'not only willing but *anxious* for a boarding school.' The local missionary warned that they 'will lose confidence in us and have no further use for us' if the church did not move to meet their wishes.[101] In January 1902 an extraordinary meeting of missionaries and Ojibwa chiefs negotiated an agreement that should be quoted at length for the benefit of people who believe that residential schools were imposed on Indians and run totally by the clergy:

> 1st. That while children are young and at school they shall not be baptized without the consent of their parents but if when they reach years of understanding they wish to be baptized, relations and friends shall be invited to the baptism.
>
> ...
>
> 4th. That a number of children shall be sent now and if they are well treated more shall be sent.
>
> ...
>
> 6th. Little children (under 8 years) shall not be given heavy work and larger children shall attend school, at least half of each school day.
>
> ...
>
> 8th. That parents shall be allowed to take their children to their religious festivals, but only one child at a time and the child shall not remain away over night.
>
> ...
>
> 11th. That in case of a child running away, police aid shall not be used, but the parents shall bring back the child.[102]

As this contract made clear, the Ojibwa not only were responsible for the establishment of the school, but largely dictated the terms on which it was to operate. Proselytization was forbidden, children could leave to observe traditional religious rites, and the police were not to be used to force runaways back.

Over the following few years, the Cecilia Jeffrey school continued as it had begun – under Indian control. When the Indians became annoyed because the staff made the children kneel for prayers and the matron meted out harsh discipline, they warned the local missionary that they wanted the original agreement obeyed. If 'we keep our promises they will send more children [,] but if they think we are trying to use the school as a trap to get them in and make Christians of them against their parents [sic] wishes, they will perhaps withdraw even the scholars we have now.' The church's capitulation on the kneeling issue quieted the parents somewhat, but the protests against the matron continued.[103] The Cecilia Jeffrey case illustrated that Indians sometimes had considerable control over their children's schools.

Parental efforts to control if and when their children entered a residential school, and how they were treated when they did, took many forms. It was quite common to keep the children out of school at the end of the summer where seasonal employment made doing so economically attractive. As the principal of the Coqualeetza Industrial Institute in the Fraser Valley noted, 'It is difficult to persuade the Indians to allow their children to come to school til after the fishing season closes.'[104] Once the children were in school, parents could sometimes influence the curriculum, as when they preferred instruction in English to syllabics. And they persisted in visiting the schools to check up on their children over the objections of Indian Affairs officers.

Parents also had ways of responding to school officials whom they found obnoxious. The mildest form of resistance to an unpopular staff member was to petition the Department of Indian Affairs to remove the person.[105] The fact that 'the Indians from the Prince Albert District have sent in a remonstrance against the conduct of the school' was a contributing factor in the dismissal of the principal at the Battleford Industrial School.[106] Indian resistance to objectionable schooling could also be violent. At the Jesuit school on Manitoulin Island in Ontario, a boy who took exception to the unfamiliar corporal punishment grabbed his teacher by the throat and roughed him up.[107] On the Blackfoot reserve, an Indian Affairs employee was killed and the missionary-principal and his family forced to flee for their lives in 1895.[108] Another spectacular altercation between a parent and a staff member took place at the File Hills school in 1949.[109] At the Kamloops school a music instructor who had mistreated students was forced to leave, and when he returned as a teaching brother the next year, an Indian leader went to the school and successfully demanded his removal.[110] Incidents of violent resistance are not numerous in the documentary evidence (usually interviews and private correspondence between missionaries and their church's headquarters staff), but it is important to remember that missionaries were not likely to advertise their unpopularity.

More often, passive resistance was just as effective as petitions and violence were. Because of the way that the schools were financed, a certain amount of parental cooperation was essential to their survival. Since funding was based on the number of students physically present, a decline in attendance hurt the missionary organization's finances. The churches involved always found revenues from per capita grants less than their needs; therefore, a drop in enrolment-related grant revenue made a tight budgetary situation critical.[111] Denominational competition compounded the financial problem and increased the need to conciliate Indian parents. When schools of different churches occupied the same district, competition for students arose. For example, parents who were unhappy with the Methodist Coqualeetza Institute in British Columbia simply transferred their children to the Roman Catholic school at Kuper Island.[112] One consequence of competition among the schools was bribery of parents to send their children to a particular school. Another was that parents, who almost always preferred to send their children to the school closest to their home, acquired bargaining power with school officials. Institutions with reputations for mistreating or overworking children or for housing them in unhealthy conditions found recruiting more difficult. In the opinion of a bishop, the death of seven students in the Anglican school at Hay River was likely 'to make recruiting impossible' in their home community the following season.[113] Parental complaints about the inadequate number of teachers and staff in their schools led the Anglicans to appeal to their members for helpers: 'We are literally fighting for our continued existence as a Missionary Church in this area due to the highly organized campaign of the roman [sic] Church against us.'[114]

The price of failing to meet such challenges by placating the parents was the demise of the schools. The Calgary Industrial School closed because it was too distant from the reserves and because the presence of other schools on the reserves allowed the parents to refuse to send their children further away.[115] As a Presbyterian missionary said of the situation in Saskatchewan, it was 'almost impossible to get some of the Indians to send their children to a school on the reserve, and, of course, it is even more difficult to secure recruits for schools at a distance.' Distance and a poor reputation for health conditions worked against the Presbyterians' Regina Industrial School. In western Manitoba, the 'Regina School is looked upon with disfavor. It is a long way off and of the seven who were sent there only one is alive to-day, all the rest dying of tuberculosis. The parents are really afraid to let their children go.'[116] In spite of herculean efforts by the Presbyterians, enrolments at Regina could not be increased sufficiently and it closed. A similar pattern developed at an Oblate school in Alberta after the First World War. Because 'Indians seem to be more and more opposed to the idea of sending their children to Dunbow,' the local bishop came 'to the conclusion that it is better to end the struggle and send back to their respective reserves, or to the Lebret School, the few pupils actually in the Dunbow school.'[117]

Some parents fought long-term campaigns to force a school to operate as they wished. Between 1922 and 1934 the Roman Catholic Indians at Fort Frances in northwestern Ontario demanded a meeting with the provincial of the Oblates, asked for an investigation of the school's administration, withheld their children, and began to urge the Department of Indian Affairs to establish a day school. Finally, they got the principal replaced.[118] Such manifestations of organized parental resistance occurred frequently in the schools of all denominations.[119]

By means ranging from evasion to resistance, passive or violent, parents often shaped their children's educational experiences so that they were tolerable to them. In unusual cases, such as the Cecilia Jeffrey school, they could set the terms on which the school was run and enforce them by withholding their children.[120] More common were the tactics of protesting, petitioning, sending the children to a competing institution, or boycotting the schools altogether. This is not to argue that the events at Cecilia Jeffrey, Lestock, Fort Frances, or Regina were typical of all residential schools. Rather, it is to suggest that the conventional picture of residential schools as totalitarian institutions run arbitrarily by all-powerful missionaries and bureaucrats is also not universally accurate.

Nor should this analysis be read as arguing that interference and coercion did not occur. For example, dances were interrupted and dancers prosecuted.[121] Moreover, even an ineffective pass system or an unenforceable prohibition on cultural practices could have a deterrent effect, dissuading natives from exercising their right to move or to celebrate religious traditions.[122] This examination of Indian policy is merely an attempt to test the conventional picture of aggressive government and missionaries controlling and reshaping Indian peoples.

Students of Canadian Indian policy need to adjust not just the conventional picture of residential schools but also the generally accepted view of the whole array of policies aimed at political control and cultural assimilation. The pass system and the prohibitions on dancing and the Potlatch were very often not applied at all or applied ineffectively. Indian peoples after the middle of the nineteenth century may have subsided into numerical inferiority to Euro-Canadian society, they may have passed into a period of economic and military irrelevance to Canadians at large, and they may have been subjected to policies intended to transform them into Christian, bourgeois citizens. However, just as their ancestors often shaped the conduct of the fur trade and served as equal partners in military alliances in the seventeenth and eighteenth centuries, Indian peoples of the late nineteenth and early twentieth centuries were actors who pursued their interests and struggled to preserve their identity. They resisted, evaded, and defied efforts to control their decision making, limit their traditional rites, and deprive them of their children. If we distinguish between the intentions of churches and government, on the one hand, and the effects of the policies, on the other, we might find that Canada's native peoples continued from the era of fur commerce and military alliance till the twentieth century to be active, if lamentably ignored, actors in the country's history.

NOTES

This article is from *Ethnohistory* 37(4) (fall 1990). Copyright 1990 by the American Society of Ethnohistory. Reprinted with permission.

I should like to express my appreciation to the Social Sciences and Humanities Research Council of Canada, whose grants financed the research for this article; to thank W.A. Waiser, a colleague who provided helpful suggestions for revisions of earlier drafts; and to acknowledge the assistance of Janice Acoose, a student who suggested several ideas and sources to me, and that of the anonymous referees of this journal.

1 William Shakespeare, *Henry IV, Part I* (Folger ed.), III, i, 57–9

2 For examples of the conventional view of the Indian as passive victim see Bruce Sealey and Verna J. Kirkness, eds., *Indians without Tipis: A Resource Book by Indians and Metis* (Agincourt, Ont.: Book Society of Canada/Canada Studies Foundation 1973), 33; James S. Frideres, *Native People in Canada: Contemporary Conflicts*, 2nd ed. (Scarborough, Ont.: Prentice-Hall 1983; first published 1974), 33; Donald Purich, *Our Land: Native Rights in Canada* (Toronto: Lorimer 1986), 121–2.

3 Stanley B. Ryerson, *The Founding of Canada: Beginning to 1815*, new ed. (Toronto: Progress Books 1960), 86–8, 262

4 Jack M. Sosin, 'The Use of Indians in the War of the American Revolution: A Re-Assessment of Responsibility,' *Canadian Historical Review* (CHR) 46(2) (June 1965). See also George F.G. Stanley, 'The Indians in the War of 1812,' CHR 31(2) (June 1950).

5 Arthur J. Ray, *Indians in the Fur Trade: Their Role as Hunters, Trappers and Middlemen in the Lands Southwest of Hudson Bay 1660–1870* (Toronto: University of Toronto Press 1974); Robin A. Fisher, *Contact and Conflict: Indian-European Relations in British Columbia, 1774–1890* (Vancouver: University of British Columbia Press 1976), chaps. 1–3. See also Kenneth Coates, 'Furs along the Yukon: Hudson's Bay Company–Native Trade in the Yukon River Basin, 1830–1893,' *BC Studies*, no. 55 (autumn 1982): 56–68.

6 Sylvia Van Kirk, *'Many Tender Ties': Women in Fur-Trade Society, 1670–1870* (Winnipeg: Watson & Dwyer nd); Jennifer S.H. Brown, *Strangers in Blood: Fur Trade Company Families in Indian Country* (Vancouver: University of British Columbia Press 1980). For examples of other fur-trade scholars who agree with Van Kirk and Brown see Daniel Francis and Toby Morantz, *Partners in Furs: A History of the Fur Trade in Eastern James Bay 1600–1870* (Kingston and Montreal: McGill-Queen's University Press 1983), 53, 90; Paul C. Thistle, *Indian-European*

Trade Relations in the Lower Saskatchewan River Region to 1840 (Winnipeg: University of Manitoba Press 1986), 9, 16; and J. Colin Yerbury, *The Subarctic Indians and the Fur Trade 1680-1860* (Vancouver: University of British Columbia Press 1986), 71–2, 91.

7 Bruce G. Trigger, *Natives and Newcomers: Canada's 'Heroic Age' Reconsidered* (Kingston and Montreal: McGill-Queen's University Press 1985), chap. 5, especially 260–71. See also James Axtell, *The Invasion Within: The Contest of Cultures in Colonial North America* (New York: Oxford University Press 1985), especially chap. 5; William J. Eccles, *The Canadian Frontier, 1534–1760* (New York: Holt, Rinehart and Winston 1969), 44–5; and Cornelius J. Jaenen, *Friend and Foe: Aspects of French-Amerindian Cultural Contact in the Sixteenth and Seventeenth Centuries* (New York: Columbia University Press 1976), 67–8.

8 Among the most important American influences have been the following: Barbara Graymont, *The Iroquois in the American Revolution* (Syracuse: Syracuse University Press 1972); Francis Jennings, *The Invasion of America: Indians, Colonialism, and the Cant of Conquest* (Chapel Hill: University of North Carolina Press 1975); Jennings, 'The Indians' Revolution,' in Alfred F. Young, ed., *The American Revolution: Explorations in the History of American Radicalism* (De Kalb: Northern Illinois University Press 1976), 319–48, especially 322; Jennings, *The Ambiguous Iroquois Empire: The Covenant Chain Confederation of Indian Tribes with English Colonies from Its Beginnings to the Lancaster Treaty of 1744* (New York: W.W. Norton 1984); Jennings, 'Iroquois Alliances in American History,' Francis Jennings, ed., *The History and Culture of Iroquois Diplomacy: An Interdisciplinary Guide to the Treaties of the Six Nations and their League* (Syracuse: Syracuse University Press 1985), 37–65; Jennings, *Empire of Fortune: Crowns, Colonies, and Tribes in the Seven Years' War* (New York: Norton 1988).

9 Leslie F.S. Upton, *Micmacs and Colonists: Indian-White Relations in the Maritimes, 1713–1867* (Vancouver: University of British Columbia Press 1979), 26; Sydney F. Wise, 'The American Revolution and Indian History,' in J.S. Moir, ed., *Character and Circumstance: Essays in Honour of Donald Grant Creighton* (Toronto: Macmillan 1970), 200

10 Jaenen, *Friend and Foe*, 192; Jennings, 'The Indians' Revolution,' 336–41

11 E. Palmer Patterson, *The Canadian Indian: A History since 1500* (Don Mills, Ont.: Collier-Macmillan 1970), 84. Again there are strong historiographical parallels in the United States: R. David Edwards, *Tecumseh and the Quest for Indian Leadership* (Boston: Little, Brown 1984), especially chaps. 7–8; R. David Edwards, *The Shawnee Prophet* (Lincoln: University of Nebraska Press 1983), chap. 6 and epilogue; Colin G. Calloway, *Crown and Calumet: British-Indian Relations, 1783–1815* (Norman and London: University of Oklahoma Press 1987), especially 22 and chap. 8.

12 Hope McLean, 'The Hidden Agenda: Methodist Attitudes to the Ojibwa and the Development of Indian Schooling in Upper Canada, 1821–1860' (MA thesis, University of Toronto, 1978); John S. Milloy, 'The Early Indian Acts: Developmental Strategy and Constitutional Change,' in Ian A.L. Getty and Anthony S. Lussier, eds., *As Long as the Sun Shines and Water Flows: A Reader in Canadian Native Studies* (Vancouver: Nakoda Institute/University of British Columbia Press 1983), 56–64; Donald B. Smith, *Sacred Feathers: The Reverend Peter Jones (Kahkewaquonaby) and the Mississauga Indians* (Toronto: University of Toronto Press 1987), especially chaps. 8–12

13 Important exceptions to this generalization include E. Brian Titley, *A Narrow Vision: Duncan Campbell Scott and the Administration of Indian Affairs in Canada* (Vancouver: University of British Columbia Press 1986); Jacqueline J. Gresko, 'Qu'Appelle Industrial School: White "Rites" for the Indians of the Old North-West' (MA thesis, Carleton University, 1970); and Hana Samek, *The Blackfoot Confederacy 1880–1920: A Comparative Study of Canadian and U.S. Indian Policy* (Albuquerque: University of New Mexico Press 1987), especially chap. 6.

14 Milloy, 'Early Indian Acts,' 59–61

15 John L. Tobias, 'Canada's Subjugation of the Plains Cree, 1879–1885,' CHR 64(4) (Dec. 1983): 534

16 Sarah A. Carter, 'The Genesis and Anatomy of Government Policy and Indian Reserve Agriculture on Four Agencies in Treaty Four, 1874–1897' (PHD dissertation, University of Manitoba, 1987), especially chap. 6. I am grateful to Dr Carter for allowing me to use her dissertation.

17 Useful summaries of these policies are Titley, *A Narrow Vision*, especially chaps. 3, 5, 6, and 8; and James R. Miller, *Skyscrapers Hide the Heavens: A History of Indian-White Relations in Canada* (Toronto: University of Toronto Press 1989), chaps. 11, 12.

18 See note 12.

19 David Laird (lieutenant-governor and Indian commissioner of the North-West Territories) to minister of the interior, 17 April 1878, National Archives of Canada (NA), Records of the Department of Indian Affairs (RG 10), Western Canada files (Black Series), vol. 3664, file 9825; Miller, *Skyscrapers*, 161–2

20 Sarah Carter, 'Two Acres and a Cow: "Peasant" Farming for the Indians of the Northwest, 1889–97,' CHR 70(1) (March 1989): 38–9

21 Nicholas F. Davin, 'Report on Industrial Schools for Indians and Half-Breeds,' confidential, 14 March 1879, in NA, Sir John Macdonald Papers, vol. 91, 35428

22 Sarah Carter, 'Controlling Indian Movement: The Pass System,' *NeWest Review*, May 1985, 8–9; Carter, 'Genesis and Anatomy of Government Policy,' 302–12. See also Purich, *Our Land*, 129–32; F. Laurie Barron, 'The Indian Pass System in the Canadian West, 1882–1935,' *Prairie Forum*, 13(1) (spring 1988): 25–42; and B. Bennett, 'Study of Passes for Indians to Leave their Reserves,' mimeo (Ottawa: Treaties and Historical Research Centre, Department of Indian Affairs and Northern Development 1974), especially 7–8. I am grateful to John Leslie of the Treaties and Historical Research office for providing me with a copy of the Bennett paper.

23 RG 10, Black Series, vol. 3675, file 11,411-4, H. Reed to L. Vankoughnet, 20 May 1891

24 See, for example, Glenbow-Alberta Institute Archives, S.B. Lucas Papers (M 699), file 9, Diary, July 1896.

25 Roderick C. Macleod, *The North-West Mounted Police and Law Enforcement 1873–1905* (Toronto: University of Toronto Press 1976), 146; Barron, 'Pass System,' 35–7; Carter, 'Genesis and Anatomy,' 307–8. For evidence that the department knew it had no legal basis for attempting to restrict Indians to their reserves see J.D. McLean, assistant deputy and secretary, to H.E. Calkin, JP, 22 Aug. 1913, RG 10, Black Series. Copy kindly supplied by John Leslie

26 NA, MG 29 E106, Hayter Reed Papers, vol. 14, H. Reed to the Hon. T. Mayne Daly, 25 March 1893. It is significant, too, that the printed 'General

Instructions to Indian Agents in Canada' that were issued in 1913 and reissued in 1933 nowhere mention passes. Glenbow Archives, Blackfoot Indian Agency Papers (M 1785), box 3, file 15

27 Reed Papers, vol. 17, Lawrence W. Herchmer to Hayter Reed, 7 Feb. 1891

28 Statutes of Canada 1884, 47 Vict., c. 27, Sec. 3. My discussion has been greatly influenced by an unpublished manuscript on the Potlatch by Douglas Cole and Ira Chaikin, which Professor Cole kindly allowed me to read.

29 Cole and Chaikin manuscript, 51–2 and 55

30 Ibid., 46–8

31 Franz Boas, 'The Indians of British Columbia,' *Popular Science Monthly* 32 (1888): 636, and 'The Houses of the Kwakiutl Indians, British Columbia,' *Proceedings of the United States National Museum* 11 (1888): 206; quoted ibid., 50–1

32 Quoted ibid., 59

33 Ibid., 52–4

34 Quoted ibid., 54

35 Royal British Columbia Museum (RBCM), Anthropological Collections Section, # 250, 834, 2777 (examples only). British Columbia Archives and Record Service (BCARS), Sound and Moving Images Division (SMID), tape 965-1, Mrs Edward Joyce interview. Cole and Chaikin manuscript, 122 and 168

36 United Church of Canada Archives (UCA), Alexander Sutherland Papers, box 5, file 97, C.M. Tate to A. Sutherland, 5 Nov. 1909. BCARS, Add. Mss 1267, Kuper Island Industrial School Papers (Add. Mss 1267), vol. 3, 266, G. Donckele to W.R. Robertson, 23 May 1903

37 Cole and Chaikin manuscript, chaps. 6–9

38 NA, Correspondence of the Secretary of State, vol. 54, no. 4355, order-in-council, 7 July 1883 (Gazetted 4 Aug. 1883)

39 Cole and Chaikin manuscript, 43

40 Glenbow Archives, Edgar Dewdney Papers (M 320), Report of meeting of reserve commissioners, Agent Todd, and Indians on board the steamer *Douglass*, 8 Sept. 1888, 1394

41 BCARS, H/D/R13/-R13.11, G.H. Raley Collection, notice of Kitimaat Council, 10 Nov. 1893; and ibid., H/D/R13.9 (III), Kispiox chiefs' statement of 13 Feb. 1914

42 Mrs S. Cook to deputy superintendent general of Indian Affairs (D.C. Scott), 1 Feb. 1919; quoted in Daisy (My-yah-nelth) Sewid Smith, *Prosecution or Persecution* (Np: Nu-yum-Balees Society 1979), 20. Supporters of non-Christian tradition could use Christians' arguments effectively, too. One wrote to the Indian Affairs office in Ottawa to inform them that he intended to hold a Potlatch. 'I don't think there are [sic] no wrong in it, if you only look up the 10 chapter of St. Mark, ver. 17–21, in the Bible, you will see that I am just going to do the right.' Dan Quatell to J.D. McLean, 14 July 1922; quoted ibid., 72

43 Archives of the Anglican Diocese of British Columbia, text 198, file 50, report of 'Special Meeting held at Alert Bay, June 1, 1936'

44 Church of England General Synod Archives (GSA), Papers of the Missionary Society in Canada (Series 75-103), Records of the Indian and Eskimo Residential School Commission (IERSC 2-15), box 23, 2433, Minutes of Commission, 14 May 1940, quoting F. Earl Anfield

45 Douglas Cole, *Captured Heritage: The Scramble for Northwest Coast Artifacts* (Vancouver/Toronto: Douglas & McIntyre 1985), 129–30
46 RG 10, Black Series, vol. 3825, file 60,511-1, H.W. Gibbon Stocken to deputy superintendent general of Indian Affairs, 6 Jan. 1900
47 Ibid., vol. 3826, file 60,511-3, J. Hollies to David Laird, 15 Feb. 1912
48 John Thunder to David Laird, 16 July 1907, RG 10, Black Series, vol. 3569, file 95-2; cited in Peter Douglas Elias, *The Dakota of the Canadian Northwest: Lessons for Survival* (Winnipeg: University of Manitoba Press 1988), 117
49 Clipping from *Winnipeg Free Press News Bulletin*, 27 Nov. 1907, RG 10, Black Series, vol. 3825, file 60,511-2. See also ibid., J. McDougall to F. Pedley, 24 May 1906. On another occasion McDougall went so far as to charge that campaigns against dancing were a violation of treaty undertakings that he, like other missionaries, had helped to convince plains Indians to accept in the 1870s. Letter to the editor, *Christian Guardian* (Methodist), 8 July 1914, 19–20
50 RG 10, Black Series, vol. 3825, file 60,511-2, Levi Thomson to F. Oliver, 19 March 1906, enclosing petition dated 9 March 1906; ibid., 60,511-1, 208133, Extract from report of the Muskowpetung's Agency (copy), Dec. 1900; ibid., file 60,511-2, E.H. Yeomans to secretary, Indian Affairs, 11 July 1907. Concerning Indian petitions re dancing see ibid., Chief Thunderchild and C. Fineday to commissioner of Indian Affairs (copy), 28 June 1907; ibid., 339198, T. Cory to secretary, Indian Affairs, 13 March 1909; ibid., file 60,511-3, Notes of representations made by delegation of Indians from the west, A. Gaddie, interpreter, Ottawa, 24 Jan. 1911.
51 UCA, Presbyterian Church in Canada, Foreign Mission Committee, Western Section, Indian Work in Manitoba and the Northwest (PC, FMC, WS, IWMNW), box 4, file 59, E. MacKenzie to R.P. McKay, 7 March 1904
52 RG 10, Black Series, vol. 3825, file 60,511-2, G.D. Mann to Indian Commissioner David Laird, 3 July 1906, and marginal note by Laird; ibid., J.P.G. Day to commissioner, 4 July 1908
53 Hugh Dempsey, *Red Crow, Warrior Chief* (Saskatoon: Western Producer Prairie Books 1980), 208, 212. Similarly, re a Saulteaux band, see RG 10, Black Series, vol. 3825, file 60,511-2, J.P.G. Day to Indian commissioner, 4 July 1908.
54 RG 10, Black Series, vol. 3825, file 60,511-2, E.H. Yeomans to secretary, Indian Affairs, 11 July 1907 (copy); ibid., file 60,511-3, R. Logan to secretary, Indian Affairs 8 Feb. 1912; ibid. G.H. Gooderham to secretary, Indian Affairs, 19 July 1912
55 Ibid., file 60,511-2, G.G. Mann to commissioner, 22 July 1907
56 Ibid., file 60,511-2, W.S. Grant to secretary, Indian Affairs, 2 July 1906; ibid., H. Nichol to secretary, Indian Affairs, 16 Feb. 1911; ibid., file 60,511-3, Father J. Hugonard to H. Nichol, 16 Jan. 1913. In another instance the Indians intended to keep their promise to conduct only a 'modified' dance, but a latecomer to the festivities carried out self-mutilation rites, to the consternation of the attending Euro-Canadian officials. See 'The Last Rain Dance' (told by Standing Through the Earth), Alexander Wolfe, *Earth Elder Stories* (Saskatoon: Fifth House 1988), 61–4.
57 Interview with Gordon Tootoosis, Poundmaker reserve, 7 May 1987. It is extraordinary to note in the official records how infrequent are the references to the actual or even contemplated use of the pass system to prevent

movement between reserves to attend festivals. See RG 10, vol. 3825-6, file 60,511, passim.

58 Stan Cuthand, 'The Native Peoples of the Prairie Provinces in the 1920's and 1930's,' in Ian A.L. Getty and Donald B. Smith, eds., *One Century Later: Western Canadian Reserve Indians since Treaty 7* (Vancouver: University of British Columbia Press 1978), 40

59 Eleanor Brass, 'The File Hills Colony,' *Saskatchewan History* 6(2) (spring 1953): 67. See also her *I Walk in Two Worlds*, (Calgary: Glenbow Museum 1987), 13, 25.

60 RG 10, Black Series, vol. 3825, file 60,511-2, R.S. McKenzie to secretary, Indian Affairs, 24 Oct. 1903

61 Dempsey, *Red Crow*, 213–24. In the Blood chronicles, 1900 was recorded as the year when 'Yellow Buffalo Stone Woman put up the Sun Dance by force.'

62 For an example of Department of Indian Affairs's pusillanimity concerning taking action against dancing see Glenbow Archives, Blood Agency Papers (M 1788), box 4, file 23, series of letters by A. de B. Owen, Joseph Howe, J.A. McGibbon, and D. Laird, 26 June to 16 July 1902.

63 RG 10, Black Series, vols. 3285–6, passim. See also Titley, *Narrow Vision*, 170; Dempsey, *Red Crow*, 210.

64 Tims Papers (M 1234), box 1, file 7, J.W. House to J.W. Tims 19 June 1939. The missionary was under no illusions about how successful this syncretic ploy was likely to be. 'At the end of the ceremony I am quite sure they went back to their old customs,' he noted. Blending Christian and Indian practices could backfire on the missionaries. One who tried to dissuade some Blackfoot from holding the dance they made 'in preparation for tobacco sowing' on a Sunday received the reply that it was all right to hold the dance on a day of prayer because 'they were going to pray.' Ibid. (M 1233), box 2, file 22, J.W. Tims Diary, 15 May 1887

65 See, for example, University of Calgary Archives, Anglican Diocese of Calgary Papers, box 8, General Files 64, F.W. Godsal to Canon Hogbin, 13 July 1910, and unidentified newspaper clipping entitled, 'The Indians and the Exhibition.' In 1895 the *Calgary Herald* (10 July) had claimed that the Cree chief Piapot held his dance every year under the nose of the Indian Affairs Department in Regina, charging twenty-five cents' admission to the white folk who drove out from the territorial capital to see the ceremonies. *Proceedings of the Church Missionary Society 1895–1896* (London: Church Missionary House 1896), 395, report from the Battleford area of Christian Indians backsliding into being 'present at the heathen Sun Dance, the interest in which revived in a painful degree in the summer of 1895, encouraged, Mr. Inkster says, by the morbid curiosity of white men and women.' Again, there are numerous more examples in RG 10, Black Series, vols. 3825–6, file 60,511, passim.

66 The parallels between U.S. and Canadian practice are many. See, for example, Margaret Connell Szasz and Carmelita Ryan, 'American Indian Education,' in Wilcomb E. Washburn, ed., *Handbook of North American Indians, vol. 4: History of Indian-White Relations* (Washington: Smithsonian Institution 1988), 288–95; and Frederick E. Hoxie, *A Final Promise: The Campaign to Assimilate the Indians, 1880–1920* (Lincoln and London: University of Nebraska Press 1984), especially chaps. 2 and 8.

67 *Calgary Herald*, 10 Feb. 1892
68 Report of the Department of Indian Affairs for 1891, Canada, *Sessional Papers (No. 14) 1892*, x
69 Brass, *Two Worlds*, 4
70 See, for example, Purich, *Our Land*, 132–4.
71 UCA, Presbyterian Church of Canada, Foreign Mission Board, Missions to the Indians of Manitoba and the North West (PC, FMB, MIMNW), box 3, file 55, H. McKay to R.P. McKay, 25 Oct. 1903
72 RG 10, School Files, vol. 6038, file 157-1-1, Petition of Massett, BC, Council to agent, 20 Jan. 1914; A. Sutherland Papers, box 5, file 95, C.M. Tate to A. Sutherland, 28 Nov. 1905
73 Nakoda Institute Archives, Oral History Program, box 1, Norman Abraham interview. Compare the comment of a chief who said he was glad they had 'a Reserve that the white man cannot encroach upon; but there are three things that I do not wish to see within the boundaries of our Reserve. I don't want Christianity, I don't want a school, and I don't want the law. I don't want Christianity, because we wish to follow the ways of our fathers. We are Indians, and we intend to remain Indians. I don't want schools, because I want the children to be happy and free from restraint. I don't want the law because we are good people. We never do anything wrong, and we have no use for the law.' *Proceedings of the Church Missionary Society 1898–1899* (London: Church Missionary House 1899), 424
74 Indeed, most Indian children for a long time escaped any kind of schooling. In 1888, when the official Indian population of Canada was 124,589, there were only 6127 enrolled in all types of schools for Indians in Canada. Report of the Department of Indian Affairs for 1888, Canada, *Sessional Papers (No. 16) 1889*, 308, 317. On the File Hills Agency in Saskatchewan in 1889, only one-third or one-quarter (depending on whether one believes the school inspector or the Indian commissioner) were in school. RG 10, Black Series, vol. 3824, file 60,470, J.A. Macrae to commissioner, 24 July 1889. For a close study of the inadequate coverage of British Columbia by residential schooling see James Redford, 'Attendance at Indian Residential Schools in British Columbia, 1890–1920,' *BC Studies*, no. 44 (winter 1979–80): 41–56.
75 Tims Papers (M 1234), box 1, file 12, J.W. Tims to bishop of Calgary, 2 July 1895. That Tims might have had some ground for complaint is borne out by the register of Old Sun's school for 1894–1908, in which twenty-two of the 128 young people did not appear. Glenbow Archives, Calgary Indian Missions Papers (M 1356), box 1, file 7, Old Sun's Boarding School – history of pupils for September 1894. For a time in the early 1890s the department itself did not try 'to enforce too rigidly attendance at schools. Everything that is likely to irritate the Indians is to be avoided as much as possible.' Hayter Reed Papers, vol. 17, H. Reed to Mr Wright, 31 Jan. 1891. Reed was concerned about Indian unrest in the United States at the time.
76 A. Sutherland Papers, box 7, file 33, Arthur Barner to A. Sutherland, 19 Sept. 1908; GSA, GS 75-103, JERSC, 2-15, box 18, file Nov./05–Oct./06, John Hines to Hon. and Dear Sir, 29 Nov. 1906
77 Brass, *Two Worlds*, 6. See also UCA, PC, FMB, MIMNW, box 1, file 21, H. McKay to R.P. McKay, 9 Jan. 1901; ibid., file 32, Quarterly Report for Round Lake ...

31 Dec. 1901. 'We have to pay $15 to $20 for any child that we get into the school,' admitted the Presbyterian missionary, although in his official quarterly report he mentioned only that his Roman Catholic opponents on the reserve 'pay $15 or $20 for a pupil & many of the Indians will give their children to those who pay most for them.' A. Sutherland Papers, box 7, file 127, John McDougall to A. Sutherland, 2 March 1906; ibid., box 6, file 118, A. Sutherland to A.R. Aldridge, 3 March 1908

78 United Church of Canada, Conference of British Columbia Archives, Coqualeetza Institute, Register of Admissions and Discharges, #157. See also ibid., #141, Simon Green: admitted Sept. 1900, did not return from holiday July 1908, discharged officially 30 June 1909. 'Visited the school at Christmas 1911.'

79 GSA, GS 75-103, IERSC 2-15, box 20, IERSC Minutes, 382, Minutes of 23 Oct. 1924. At Kuper Island, when five ran off, two priests were out in a boat looking for them till 4 AM. The man who, 'with a warrant,' returned the children and the canoes they had stolen got a '$25 fee for returning the 5 pupils.' Add. Ms 1267, vol. 31, Daily Journal for 1924, entries for 2, 4, and 5 Jan. 1924. See also Macleod, *NWMP and Law Enforcement*, 147–8.

80 Mike Mountain Horse, *My People the Bloods*, ed. H. Dempsey (Calgary: Glenbow Museum and Blood Tribal Council 1979), 15–16; Dan Kennedy [Ochankugahe], *Recollections of an Assiniboine Chief*, ed. James R. Stevens (Toronto/Montreal: McClelland and Stewart 1972), 54

81 UCA, PC, FMB, MIMNW, box 3, file 54, H. McKay to R.P. McKay, 25 Oct. 1903

82 Tims Papers (M 1234), box 2, file 21, seven pages of prayers in syllabics on the letterhead of Calgary Industrial School. Concerning preaching in the Blackfoot language see ibid., file 15, Annual Report to Church Missionary Society (draft), 31 Jan. 1901. See also the banner in an Indian language in Christ Church Anglican Church, Alert Bay, BC, Royal British Columbia Museum (RBCM), Anthropology Collections Section, #2305. Concerning Wikwemikong, see Regis College Archives, 'Synopsis of the History of Wikwemikong' (typescript), entries for 1854 and 1860; ibid., Paquin, 'Modern Jesuit Indian Missions,' and ibid., Ontario Indian Missions Papers, file: Correspondence, Spanish 1926–36, C. Belanger to Father Walsh, 19 Feb. 1936.

83 John McDougall, *Christian Guardian*, 27 Jan. 1891, 51

84 BCARS, SMID, tape 3533-3, Sister Patricia, SCJ interview. At the church on the Stoney reserve the church service was translated into Stoney. 'Prayers are offered in Stoney by some of the men and in English by the Ministers.' Telfer Collection [J. Telfer], 'The Stoney Indians,' typescript, nd

85 BCARS, H/D/R13/R13.7, Raley Collection, file of papers on Coqualeetza Industrial Institute and other schools, 'Rules,' A.E. Green, inspector of Indian Schools, 28 Oct. 1906. At the Cariboo school, 'we talk Shuswap when we're alone.' BCARS, SMID, tape 3532-2, Celestine and David Johnson interview. A student who attended Sechelt in 1915–16 said that, while they were encouraged to speak English, 'I wouldn't say [we were] punished' for speaking their own language. BCARS, SMID, tape 960-2, Clarence Joe interview. See also, re Williams Lake, ibid., tape 3533-1 (transcript), Sister Patricia, SCJ, interview. Glenbow Archives, Nurse Jane Megarry Memoirs (M 4096), third (beige) book, 191

86 Archives Deschâtelets, L 531 .M27C, Codex historicus 1907–20 for Lestock school, 15, Instructions of provincial (J.P. Magnan, omi), 27 March 1909. Ibid., L 535 .M27L 149, Brother Leach to [provincial?], [1923], reporting that the principal at Lestock 'prefered [sic] the children to speak in their own language.' Concerning the willingness of school authorities to allow an Indian language to be used when outsiders were not around, see BCARS, SMID, tape 361-1, Joe C. Clemine interview.

87 Telfer Collection, Notes of a conversation with Miss Jean Telfer, 16 May 1979

88 Brass, *Two Worlds*, 13, 64

89 Ibid., 25. This woman's interest in Cree traditions was stimulated sufficiently that she collected and published a volume of legends and stories. Eleanor Brass, *Medicine Boy and Other Cree Tales* (Calgary: Glenbow Museum 1978). The Kuper Island Conduct Book lists many instances of infractions that involved 'Indian dances,' 'talking Indian,' and 'Forbidden Games.' Add. Ms 1267, vol. 38, Conduct Book, 1891–5

90 Glenbow Archives, S.H. Middleton Papers (M 839), box 2, file 7, S.H. Middleton to R. Forsberg (copy), 7 Nov. 1960. It is also worth noting that at a day school that a Dakota band established themselves, instruction was 'in both Dakota and English.' Elias, *Dakota of the Canadian Northwest*, 73. And an Indian woman told a reporter that her father, himself highly educated, favoured her learning English early in life. Undated clipping from *Weekend Magazine*, UCA, E.E. Joblin Papers, box 2, file 7

91 BCARS, SMID, tape 3858-1, Mary Englund interview. The same informant (ibid.) said that parents took great pride in children who mastered English. John Jeffrey, a former student at the Chapleau, Ontario, school and an Anglican clergyman, also noted that the widely differing backgrounds of the students at Chapleau made the use of English appropriate. Audio tape, December 1989, in possession of author

92 Tims Papers (M 1234), box 1, file 2, Diary, 8 Sept. 1891. For a similar case in British Columbia see Add. Mss 1267, vol. 3, 733–4, G. Donckele to W.R. Robertson, 23 July 1905.

93 UCA, PC, FMB, Missions to the Indians in British Columbia (MIBC), box 1, file 10, B.I. Johnston to R.P. McKay, 20 Feb. 1896

94 Tims Papers (M 1233), box 2, file 22, Journal for 1917. In an interview a former teacher (name withheld by request) who had served briefly at the Mohawk Institute in 1934 told me that he could not recall a day when no children ran away from the school. A request from Jesuit missionaries that the department withhold annuities from parents who failed to return schoolchildren after holidays was firmly turned down. See Regis College Archives, Wikwemikong Papers, 'Various Correspondence 1909–1912,' J.D. McLean to Rev. C. Belanger, SJ, 25 July 1910.

95 Middleton Papers, box 2, file 4, School Diary for 1945, entries for 2 March, 1 April, 4 May, 23 June, 1 Sept., and 25 Dec. Significantly, before adopting the policy, the principal held a 'Meeting of Parents at the Reserve re Holidays' on 9 December. At Sechelt 'the children got home sometimes for weekends' to the nearby reserve. BCARS, SMID, tape 3533-3, Sister Patricia, SCJ, interview. There were also Saturday afternoon visits home at Kitimaat (BCARS, microfilm 1360,

Margaret Butcher Journal, 17 April 1917), and at Kuper Island, once a month 'four deserving students of the senior class' received a weekend leave. Archives of the Sisters of St Ann, RG 2, Series 39, Kuper Island school papers, file 'Chronicles 1944–1954,' entry for 29 Oct. 1948

96 Add. Ms 1267, vol. 1, 433, G. Donckele to W.H. Lomas, 3 July 1894. The same principal confessed that he was at a loss to know how to stop parents from withdrawing their children. Ibid., 583, G. Donckele to A.W. Vowell, 30 April 1895

97 Reed Papers, vol. 18, J. Hugonard to E. Dewdney, 5 May 1891. There was a cabin to house parents overnight at the Cariboo school. See BCARS, SMID, tape 3530-1, Lily Squinahan interview. See also Add. Ms 1267, vol. 31, Daily Journal for 1924, entry of 27 May. For comments concerning the 'Indian parlor' at Williams Lake see ibid., tape 3533-1 (transcript), Sister Patricia, SCJ, interview. And 'the parents of the pupils come from all parts of the Blood reserve to attend the Church service and to visit with their children after the service.' Megarry Memoirs, third (beige) book, 238. See also, Telfer Collection, 'The Stoney Indians.'

98 UCA, PC, FMB, MIBC, box 1, file 1, J.A. McDonald to H. Cassells, 12 Jan. 1892; A. Sutherland Papers, box 6, file 108, J. Edward Rendle to A. Sutherland, 8 Oct. 1909

99 H/D/R13/R13.11, Raley Collection, file on Kitimaat, letter from Chief Jessea and forty-one Indians to 'Dear Brothern [sic],' 23 March 1896. The 'Sechelt nation' built and at least partially maintained their school. BCARS, SMID, tape 960-1, Clarence Joe interview

100 GSA, GS 75-103, IERSC, 2-15, box 18, file Nov./05–Oct./06, W.D. Reeves to S.H. Blake, 15 Oct. 1906

101 UCA, PC, FMB, MIMNW, box 1, file 14, T. Hart to W. Moore, 12 Sept. 1898; ibid., file 20, A.G. McKitrick to R.P. McKay, 14 Dec. 1900

102 Ibid., box 2, file 33, J.C. Gandier to R.P. McKay, 14 Jan. 1902, and 'Agreement' of same date

103 Ibid., box 2, file 35, A.G. McKitrick to R.P. McKay, 7 March 1902; ibid., file 38, same to same, 2 June 1902; ibid., file 41, Indian petition dated 22 Sept. 1902; ibid., box 3, file 47, A.G. McKitrick to R.P. McKay, 11 March 1903; ibid., file 55, J.O. McGregor to R.P. McKay, 27 Nov. 1903

104 A. Sutherland Papers, box 5, file 89, R. Cairns to A. Sutherland, 18 Aug. 1906

105 Ibid., box 3, file 74, A.W. Vowell to Rev. Dr. Campbell, 13 May 1905, enclosing petition from Indians against a principal. See also Archives Deschâtelets, L 281 .M274 31, list of complaints against the administration of Lebret school; and GSA, GS 75-103, IERSC, 2-15, box 22, 1847, Minutes of 17 July 1934, re Lac la Ronge school.

106 Reed Papers, vol. 14, H. Reed to Archdeacon J.A. Mackay (copy), 9 Nov. 1894

107 Regis College Archives, J. Paquin, SJ, 'Modern Jesuit Indian Missions in Ontario'

108 *Alberta Tribune*, 12 Oct. 1895; Toronto *Globe*, 4 July 1895; *Canadian Churchman*, 11 July 1895; Tims Papers (M 1234), box 1, file 12, J.W. Tims to Bishop of Calgary (draft), 2 July 1895; Reed Papers, vol. 14, H. Reed to T. Mayne Daly (copy), 25 June 1895; Ian A.L. Getty, 'The Failure of the Native Church Policy of the CMS in the North-West,' in Richard Allen, ed., *Religion and Society in the*

Prairie West (Regina: Canadian Plains Research Center 1974), 30, points out that the Blackfoot had petitioned the government in 1892 to remove the missionary, whom they regarded as 'too bossy.' The crisis in 1895 led to his transfer to another reserve.

109 UCA, United Church of Canada, Woman's Missionary Society, Home Missions, Indian Work, file 9, L. McLean to J.P.B. Ostrander, 17 Feb. 1949. Concerning a girl's attack on a nun at Lebret see Archives Deschâtelets, L 286 .M27L 226, J.P. Magnan, omi, to G. Leonard, 18 June 1930.

110 Celia Haig-Brown, *Resistance and Renewal: Surviving the Indian Residential School* (Vancouver: Tillacum Library 1988), 102. At the same school a father who was angered when his daughter's head was shaved seized the priest responsible 'and shook him up.' Ibid., 103

111 At the Anglican Sarcee school, for example, the government grant in 1915 was $100 per pupil, when operating costs per child were just over $160. During the remainder of the First World War, the discrepancy grew larger. Glenbow Archives, Calgary Indian Missions Papers (M 1356), box 1, file 5, J.W. Tims' Annual Reports to the Church Missionary Society for the years end March 1915 and 31 Dec. 1919. In 1949 the Anglicans claimed that the financial shortfall in the schools' operation that was attributable to underenrolment was $51,200. GSA, GS 75-103, IERSC, 2-15, box 29, Indian School Administration circulars, Circular 14/49, 29 April 1949

112 Add. Ms 1267, vol. 2, 561, G. Donckele to A.W. Vowell, 7 July 1900

113 GSA, Bishop Lucas Papers (M 75-1), box 3, file 'Correspondence A–M 1925,' Bishop Lucas to T.B.R. Westgate, 20 June 1925. See also Add. Ms 1267, vol. 1, 602, G. Donckele to A.W. Vowell, 1 June 1895; Microfilm 1360, Margaret Butcher Journal, 17 April 1917.

114 GSA, GS 75-103, IERSC, 2-15, ISA, box 25, Reports of Superintendents with Minutes of Executive Committee 1927–52, file 1947, Circular of Alderwood to clergy, 14 Jan. 1947

115 Tims Papers (M 1233), box 1, file 6, 'Impressions regarding Missionary Effort ... Jan. 6, 1909.' For examples of opposition to sending students to far-distant schools in British Columbia and Alberta see A. Sutherland Papers, box 6, file 108, J. Edward Rendle to A. Sutherland, 8 Oct. 1909; and ibid., box 7, file 132, 'Report of the Red Deer Industrial Institute for ... 1907,' by Thompson Ferrier.

116 UCA, PC, FMB, MIMNW, box 4, file 66, F.F. Dodds to R.P. McKay, Oct. 1904; ibid., file 72, F.O. Gilbart to R.P. McKay, 28 April 1905. On the difficulties at the Regina school see also Titley, *Narrow Vision*, 80–2.

117 Archives Deschâtelets, HR 6676 .C73R 8, Mgr Grandin to Mgr J.T. McNally, bishop of Calgary, 22 Feb. 1922. For background see RG 10, School Files, vol. 6039, file 160-1, part 1, D.C. Scott to W.J. Dilworth, 9 March 1915; and ibid., Dilworth to Scott, 20 March 1915.

118 Archives Deschâtelets, L 912 .M27C 195 and 199; ibid., L 913 .M27L 63, 102, 104, and 108. Unfortunately, the next generation of parents had to take up the struggle against another unpopular priest thirty years later. See ibid., 291, group letter of Indians to Father Provincial, May 1962.

119 See, for example, ibid., L 531 .M27C 2, Codex historicus for school at Lestock, Saskatchewan, 16 Dec. 1934.

120 There are indications that some parents imposed limits on the duration of their

children's stays at Kuper Island school when it was starting up. See Add. Ms 1267, vol. 40, 43, Quarterly Return for Quarter ended 30 Sept. 1896, Remarks. See also ibid., 47, Quarterly Return for Quarter ended 31 Dec. 1896.

121 RG 10, Black Series, vol. 3825, file 60,511-1, extract from Sgt Saul Martin's report from Fort Qu'Appelle, Sask., 28 June 1902; Toronto *Globe*, 27 May 1903

122 'The Last Rain Dance,' 64

SARAH CARTER

Two Acres and a Cow: 'Peasant' Farming for the Indians of the Northwest, 1889-1897

Indian Commissioner Hayter Reed announced in 1889 that a new 'approved system of farming' was to be adopted on western Indian reserves.[1] Indian farmers were to emulate 'peasants of various countries' who kept their operations small and their implements rudimentary. In Reed's opinion a single acre of wheat, a portion of a second acre of roots and vegetables, and a cow or two could provide sufficiently for an Indian farmer and his family. He argued that it was better for Indians to cultivate a small acreage properly than to attempt to extend the area under cultivation. Moreover, this restricted acreage eliminated any need for labour-saving machinery. Peasants of other countries, Reed contended, farmed successfully with no better implements than the hoe, the rake, cradle, sickle, and flail, and he believed that Indians had to be taught to handle these simple tools. They were to broadcast seed by hand, harvest with scythes, bind by hand with straw, and thresh with flails. In some districts Indians were discouraged from growing wheat altogether in favour of root crops, and this further reduced the need for any machinery. As part of the program, Indians were required to manufacture at home, from materials readily available, many of the items they needed such as harrows, hay forks, hay racks, carts, and ox yokes.

Indian farmers were compelled to comply with the peasant farming policy until 1897, when Reed's career with the department abruptly ended. This policy, along with the permit system and the subdivision survey of portions of reserves into forty-acre plots, had a stultifying effect on Indian farming, nipping reserve agriculture development in the bud.

Agriculture was not well-established on western Indian reserves by the turn of the century. It has generally been argued that Indians, because they were hunters and warriors, were unable to adapt to farming, and that they could not be transformed into sedentary farmers.[2] The story is far more complex, however. There was an initial positive response to agriculture on the part of many reserve residents which has been overlooked in the literature to date. There were also many difficulties. Some of these problems were those experienced by all early settlers – drought, frost, hail, and prairie fire, an absence of markets, and uncertainties about what to sow, when to sow, and how to sow. There were other problems that were not unique to the Indians but were likely magnified in their case. For example, reserve land often proved to be unsuitable for agriculture. Indian farmers also had limited numbers of oxen, implements, and seed: the treaty provisions for these items were immediately found to be inadequate. Indians were greatly hampered in their work because they lacked apparel, particularly footwear. They were undernourished, resulting in poor physical stamina and vulnerability to infectious diseases.

Indian farmers were also subject to a host of government policies and regulations which hampered agricultural development. If an Indian farmer sought better railway, market, or soil advantages he was not able to pull up stakes and try his luck elsewhere, since an Indian could not take out a homestead under the 1876 Indian Act. Nor could Indians raise outside investment capital; reserve land could not be mortgaged and Indians had difficulty obtaining credit. Freedom to sell their produce and stock and to purchase goods was strictly regulated through a permit system, just as movements off the reserves were rigidly monitored through a pass system.

By the late 1880s Indian farmers of the Qu'Appelle district of Treaty Four had few tangible rewards to show for their years of effort.[3] The decade of the 1880s had been described as a 'nightmare' to the early Saskatchewan pioneers, with drought and frost causing homesteaders to desert the district in large numbers.[4] For Indian farmers, however, the 1880s were not totally disastrous. Significant strides had been taken towards alleviating many of the problems which had handicapped reserve farming in the past. For the most part, local officials of the Department of Indian Affairs, the agents and farm instructors, had played a constructive role in facilitating favourable conditions. Steps had been taken to address such problems as the scarcity of milling and threshing facilities. A cattle-on-loan policy helped to assure a larger future supply of work oxen. Farmers on the reserves experimented with such techniques as summer-fallowing and they tested varieties of seed sent from the Central Experimental Farm in Ottawa. Indians participated in the agricultural fairs held annually throughout the Territories, even taking prizes against all competitors for their wheat and cattle. During the 1880s Indian farmers had also begun to acquire some of the equipment necessary to expedite their operations. Mowers and rakes were the most common purchases, and some bands acquired self-binders. Local officials felt that mowers and rakes were essential as stock was increasing, and that self-binders both lessened the danger of the crops' being caught by frost during a protracted harvest and reduced the waste experienced in binding with short straw, thus encouraging the farmers to cultivate a larger area.[5] Almost all of this machinery was purchased from the Indian's own earnings, with purchases being made by a band or a number of farmers together and the money coming from the proceeds of crops or from pooled annuities.

Indian farmers of the 1880s, then, were learning the techniques and acquiring the machinery that their farm instructors and agents agreed were essential to dry-land farming. They were not in all cases moving towards conformity with the individualistic model of independent homesteader; bands pooled their resources for the purchase of implements and on many reserves the fields were tilled in common. Qu'Appelle white farmers remember the year 1890 as 'the turn of the tide; after that all went well.'[6] All did not go well for Indian farmers, however. Unprecedented administrative control and restriction of their farming activities in the years to 1897 helped ensure that they remained small-scale producers.

The peasant farming policy emerged during an era when the stated priorities of the Department of Indian Affairs were to dismantle what was called the 'tribal' or 'communist' system and to promote 'individualism.' After 1885 in particular these goals were undertaken with great vigour and commitment, along with an increased emphasis on the supervision, control, and restriction of the activities and movements of the Indians. Hayter Reed, a major architect of Indian policy in the Northwest in the decade following the 1885 resistance, fully endorsed these goals. Appointed commissioner in 1888 and deputy superintendent general in 1893, Reed was in a position to articulate and compel obedience to his views. He boasted that under his administration 'the policy of destroying the tribal or communist system is assailed in every possible way, and every effort made to implant a spirit of individual responsibility instead.'[7] Although Reed's ultimate goal was to see the reserves broken up, he claimed that in the meantime his department was teaching the Indians step by step to provide for themselves through their own industry, and inculcating in them a spirit of 'self-reliance and independence.'

One way to undermine the tribal system was to subdivide reserves into separate farms. Large fields worked in common fostered the tribal system; according to Reed they did not encourage pride and industry. The individual farmer did not feel it worth his while to improve land significantly when other members of the band also claimed it as their own.[8] With a certificate of ownership, it was believed, the enterprising Indian would be induced to make permanent improvements such as superior cultivation, improved housing, and better fencing, all of which would have the effect of tying the owner to the locality. Reed was also convinced that private property created law-abiding citizens. Property would render the Indians averse to disturbing the existing order of things, as 'among them as among white communities, the lawless and revolutionary element is to be found among those who have nothing to lose but may perhaps gain by upsetting law and order.[9]

Severalty was not a new idea in Canadian Indian policy, nor was Reed the first official to promote the scheme for the Indians of western Canada, but under his administration the program began in earnest. In his annual report for 1888 Reed announced that reserves in the Northwest were to be subdivided into forty-acre plots or quarter quarter sections.[10] Survey work, which began the following spring, was done on reserves where farming had met with some success – that is, where the capacity of the land for agriculture had been proven.[11] Reserves with poorer land – such as the File Hills and Touchwood Hills – were not subdivided. The forty-acre plots were located well back of the main-line Canadian Pacific Railway and the new towns along its route, well back of the fine agricultural reserve land that new settlers and townspeople were beginning to covet – the land that was eventually surrendered.

It is clear that what was in the best interests of the agricultural future of these bands was not in the minds of those who devised this policy. When the subdivision surveys were proposed, government and Indian Affairs officials had objectives in mind beyond the establishment of agriculture on an individual model. John A. Macdonald was enthusiastic about severalty, not as a method of promoting individual initiative and private ownership, but as means of defining 'surplus' land on reserves that might be sold.[12] If each Indian were allotted the land he would likely require for cultivation, the amount of surplus land available for surrender and sale could be ascertained.

Public opinion appeared to endorse heartily the department's policy of allotment in severalty, as a means of striking at the heart of the 'tribal' system. Respected spokesmen such as Father Lacombe agreed that farming Indians could be made more industrious if they were permitted to take up land in severalty.[13] The Ottawa *Journal* hailed the subdivision of the western reserves as a 'step forward' for 'as soon as the Indians are willing to throw up tribal connections and treaty money, they retain these lands as personal property, and become citizens.'[14] The Moosomin *Courier* considered severalty to be a very fine stroke of 'national policy'; 'Chief Bull Frog and his band' had already been introduced to the modern system of farming, but they now needed individual ownership since 'self-interest is a wonderful stimulant.'[15] It was proclaimed in an 1890 *Courier* that 'superior houses, better fences, larger fields, and more extensively cultivated areas' already attested to the success of the policy, although it is unlikely that reserve residents were at this date conforming to the allotment survey. These words were taken almost directly from the

Indian Affairs annual report of 1889, in which the happy results likely to attend distribution in severalty had been outlined.[16]

A letter published in a November 1890 issue of the Ottawa *Citizen* from 'Nichie' of Battleford gave a glowing appraisal of the severalty policy in terminology that bore striking similarities to department publications.[17] The author observed that Indians with allotments made worthy efforts to improve and better their condition. He felt this system annulled tribal influence, 'the bane of Indian progress,' and instead engendered a healthy spirit of rivalry between individuals and bands. Under the system of all things held in common, the industrious worker had to share whatever was harvested with the idle, discontented, and worthless. This was discouraging to progress. The author perceived that the desire to occupy separate holdings was spreading, particularly among the young men, and he predicted that the time was not far distant when the Indians would no longer be consumers of government 'grub' but producers, relieving the government larder.

The peasant farming policy, introduced at the same time as severalty, was also presented as a means of destroying the system of community ownership on reserves and enhancing individualism and self-support. The central rationale advanced in support of the policy was that it was 'the manner best calculated to render [the Indians] self-supporting when left to their own resources.'[18] Reed repeated many times in his correspondence and public pronouncements that he believed the time was not far distant when the Indians would have to depend entirely upon their own resources. 'Our policy,' he stated, 'is to make each family cultivate such quantity of land as they can manage with such implements as they alone hope to possess for long enough after being thrown upon their own resources.'[19]

The Indians were to aim, not at breaking up large quantities of land, but at cultivating a restricted amount which could be worked solely with the family's own resources. Labour-saving implements, Reed argued, were 'likely to be beyond acquisition by the majority of Indians for some time after they may have been thrown upon their own resources.'[20] Reed was not pleased that Indians tended to club together to purchase implements because this reinforced the band unit. He wanted to see the Indians become self-sufficient as individuals, not as bands. On their own, however, these individuals were not likely to be able to afford machinery. Although Reed conceded that there were individual Indians who were independent of government assistance and could not be restrained from purchasing machinery out of their own earnings, he felt such cases were rare. If Indians received any assistance at all in the way of seed grain, rations, or other goods, then they were not self-sufficient and should not be making payments on machinery. Well-to-do farmers could instead pay for the labour of other Indians.[21] Indian women, Reed hoped, could work in the fields, particularly at harvest time. Agents and inspectors were to cancel the sales of machinery to Indians, even though these were purchased by the Indians and not by the department.

According to Reed, labour-saving machinery was not required by Indians. They should cultivate root crops rather than concentrate upon extensive grain growing.[22] In Reed's view, root and not cereal crops taught Indian farmers to be diligent and attentive: 'I've always advocated growing as many root crops as possible but Indians have to be humoured a good deal in such matters; and as soon as they begin to make some little progress they become fired with an ambition to grow larger quantities of wheat and other cereals [rather than] roots which require working and weeding at the very time they like to be off hunting while the former only require to have cattle kept away by means of a good fence.'[23]

The need to go into debt to buy machinery such as self-binders seemed a further reason to halt the use of these implements. Farmers who had to obtain credit were not regarded as self-sufficient. Reed believed the system of purchase on credit of farm machinery had widely and ruinously affected white settlers, and he shared with other department officials the view that Indians were prone to run into debt and were unable or disinclined to discharge their liabilities.[24] It was wiser, he felt, to wait and see whether the climatic conditions of the country warranted the purchase of labour-saving machinery. Machinery, he argued, would not bring prosperity; it had instead been the means of ruining large numbers of settlers.[25]

Another argument Reed forwarded against Indian use of labour-saving machinery was that rudimentary implements afforded *useful* employment for all. The possession of machinery, he believed, allowed the Indians to do nothing but 'sit by and smoke their pipes while work was being done for them without exertion on their part,' a situation he believed they preferred.[26] In his view the use of such implements was justified only when manual labour was scarce, and this was not the case on Indian reserves.

The same reasons were advanced for the necessity of home manufactures. Gainful employment during spare time prevented the 'mischief which emanates from idleness,' and trained the Indians for the time when they would be totally thrown upon their own resources.[27] Indian men and women were first encouraged and then required to make an endless list of items 'in common use upon a farm.'[28] Women's manufactures included mitts, socks, willow baskets, mats, and straw hats. Men were expected to make axe and fork handles, ox collars and harnesses, wooden harrows, bob-sleighs, and Red River carts. Compliance with this policy was readily enforced when requests for the purchase of these items were simply stroked off the estimates.

Reed drew on aspects of an evolutionary argument to support his peasant farming policy. In the late nineteenth century, those who took an evolutionary view of the North American Indian and other 'primitive' people believed there were immutable laws of social evolution.[29] It was thought that man developed progressively through prescribed stages from savagery through barbarism to civilization. These stages could not be skipped, nor could a race or culture be expected to progress at an accelerated rate. The Indians were perceived to be many stages removed from nineteenth-century civilization, and while they could take the next step forward, they could not miss the steps in between.

Reed employed these notions in defending his stand on machinery. He argued that Indians should not make an 'unnatural' leap from barbarism to nineteenth-century environment, including all its appliances.[30] The Indian was 'prone to desire to imitate the white man's nineteenth century civilization too hastily and too early.'[31] Reed noted this at length in the first of his annual reports outlining the peasant policy: 'The fact is often overlooked, that these Indians who, a few years ago, were roaming savages, have been suddenly brought into contact with a civilization which has been the growth of centuries. An ambition has thus been created to emulate in a day what white men have become fitted for through the slow progress of generations.'[32]

The ban of labour-saving machinery was something of an about-face for Hayter Reed and the department. Until the peasant program was introduced, the purchase of mowers, horse rakes, threshing machines and other implements was heralded in the annual reports as evidence of a new spirit of individualism, prosperity, and overall progress. Such purchases were also used as evidence that the Indians were not 'squandering' their earnings as many believed they were prone to do.

At the outset of his career as commissioner, Reed was convinced that a means of fostering an independent, proprietary spirit among the Indians was to allow the 'industrious' to purchase some property in the way of wagons and implements out of the proceeds of the produce they were allowed to market. If individual Indians were to be allowed to acquire some personal property, their rations should not be suddenly and completely withdrawn once they met with some success, for they would be left wondering whether their exertions were worth the effort.[33] If the industrious were compelled to devote all their earnings to the purchase of food, while those who produced half the crop received the balance from the government, there would be no incentive to work. The industrious had to be allowed to invest a fair share of their earnings. Reed's policy with regard to the individual enterprising Indian was to continue to assist him for a time so that he could purchase wagons, harnesses, and implements. In that way 'he develops into the stage of being a property holder, and soon begins to look down upon those whose laziness compels them to seek assistance from the government. Meanwhile what he had purchased secures him the means of assured independence while he has been acquiring the spirit to make it safe to discontinue helping him and his position awakens a spirit of emulation in his less industrious brother.'[34] Reed believed that as the farming Indians gained a sense of pride in their prosperity, they would be less inclined to share their produce with 'impecunious neighbours,' as in the days when 'communist' ideas prevailed.[35] This would, he hoped, compel the more reluctant Indians to put themselves into the hands of the government for similar training.

What accounts for the sudden introduction and enforcement of a ban on machinery? Immigrant settlers resented Indian competition for the limited markets of the Northwest. The 1880s saw increasingly strained relations between Indian and white farmers, a situation that was aggravated by the lean times. Local department officials generally came to the defence of the Indians' interests, while more distant officials appeared willing to please the more politically powerful settlers, at the Indians' expense. The recent arrivals believed that everything should be done to encourage their enterprise. They considered themselves the 'actual' settlers, the true discoverers and developers of the country's resources. They believed that the government had bought the land from the Indians, and it was now the government's 'right and duty to look after the interests of the settlers, both present and future, for whom the land was bought, and out of whose earnings it is expected ultimately to be paid for.'[36]

By the late 1880s, farmers in some areas of the Northwest were complaining loudly about 'unfair' competition from Indians in obtaining a share of the markets for farm produce, and a share of contracts for the supply of hay, wood, and other products. They believed that government assistance gave the Indians an unfair advantage, allowing them to undersell the white farmer. Complaints from the Battleford district were particularly strident since the markets there were strictly limited and local, and competition was intense. In 1888 the residents of that town petitioned their member of parliament, stating that 'the Indians are raising so much grain and farm produce that they are taking away the market from the white settlers.'[37]

A visit to Battleford that year appears to have had an important impact on Hayter Reed. There he was 'assailed' by complaints about the effects of Indian competition.[38] As a Department of the Interior 'chief land guide' in Manitoba in 1880–1, Reed had urged settlers to consider points as far west as Battleford.[39] He had given his assurance that despite the absence of a railway, farmers could be guaranteed a market for their produce since the government's demands alone for the Indians, the Mounted Police, surveyors, and other crews would absorb all of a farmer's surplus.[40] If the Indians were able to provide for themselves as well as sell a surplus, the already limited markets were further restricted.

Following his 1888 visit to Battleford, Reed decided that until a railway extended the settlers' opportunities, his department must do what it could to prevent jealous competition.[41] Competition for markets, he claimed, was disastrous to the Indians in any case, since they were so anxious to find purchasers that they would part with their products for a 'trifling consideration.'[42] Reed arranged with the Battleford citizens to divide up the limited markets in the district. Much of the trade in cordwood was left to the Métis, since this was their mainstay over the winter. The Indians were allowed to supply wood to the agency and, for one more year, to the industrial school. The sale of grain in the district was left exclusively to the white settlers.

The peasant farming policy, introduced a year after Reed's visit to Battleford, helped eliminate the Indians from effective competition. The permit system was another means of regulating the Indians' participation in the market economy. Under the Indian Act the department could regulate the sale, barter, exchange, or gift of any grain, roots, or other produce grown on reserves.[43] The official rationale for the permit system was that Indians had to be taught to husband their resources. John A. Macdonald stated that 'if the Indians had the power of unrestricted sale, they would dispose of their products to the first trader or whiskey dealer who came along, and the consequence would be that the Indians would be pensioners on the Government during the next winter.'[44] The permit system, however, further precluded the Indians from participation in the market economy since they could not buy, sell, or transact business.

While the peasant policy excluded Indians from effective competition with white farmers, Hayter Reed may have hoped that it might, nonetheless, provide a secure means of subsistence for the Indians. In nineteenth-century liberal economic thought the peasant proprietor gained a new respectability.[45] Among others, John Stuart Mill opposed the concentration of landed property in the hands of a few great estate owners and favoured the creation of a class of peasant proprietors. This it was believed would raise agricultural productivity, lower prices, and reduce urban unemployment. Peasant proprietorship would have social as well as economic consequences since the owner would take a permanent interest in the soil. He would be 'thrifty, sober, honest and independent.'[46] With a stake in the country, former day labourers would be less inclined to 'wanton aggressions' or 'mischief,' and instead would be interested in preserving tranquility and order. These were exactly the qualities Reed attributed to his peasant proprietors.

In the 1880s these ideas had wide public support in England and America. 'Three acres and a cow' was promoted by individuals and charitable organizations as a means of reforming and controlling the behaviour of the working classes, veterans, immigrants, and criminals.[47] In 1890 the Salvation Army's founder, William Booth, published *In Darkest England and the Way Out,* in which he advocated the settlement of the poor on three- to five-acre allotments with a cottage and a cow.[48] Reed's plan bears some resemblances to Joseph Chamberlain's 1885 election cry, 'Three Acres and a Cow.'[49] Chamberlain's loosely sketched agrarian reform policy involved the compulsory purchase of land by local authorities in order to repopulate the country with independent English yeoman. A visit to Canada in 1887 may have generated interest in Chamberlain's ideas on land reform.[50]

The peasant farming policy and subdivision of reserves into forty-acre plots were probably also inspired by the general allotment policy in the United States, codified in the Dawes Act of 1887. The rhetoric was precisely the same – that individual lots and ownership would create stable, sedentary farmers. In the United States those who supported allotment in severalty argued that the policy of concentration and isolation upon reservations had failed to resolve the Indian 'problem.'[51] Private property was the key to transforming the Indians into 'civilized' agriculturalists. Pride of ownership generated individual initiative and taught the Indians self-support. Private property destroyed the tribal relationship, breaking the yoke of authoritarian chiefs and allowing 'progressive' Indians to accumulate wealth and property. Supporters of the Dawes Act felt that an end to the isolation of the reservation would enhance Indian farming since Indians would reap the benefit of close association with enlightened white farmers. Tardy progress had resulted from this isolation as the Indians' environment was closed to all progressive influences. Assimilation, through allotment in severalty, seemed to offer a permanent solution. Isolation was condemned as an obstacle to national unity, and as a means of keeping alive racial distinctions.[52] Reservations seemed to have no place in a country which championed the concept of equal rights for all.

The Dawes Act was a major triumph for humanitarian reformers who were convinced that individual ownership was the key to the 'civilization' of the Indians, but it also appealed to those with overt self-interest in mind. It was obvious from the outset that allotment would open much reserve land for settlement. By granting land to individual Indians, 'surplus' lands could be defined and made accessible. After a stipulated acreage went to each Indian family, the remaining land would be thrown open to white settlement, and sizeable portions of reservations would be sold. Many of those who supported the measure were interested in securing Indian land at a time when farm land was becoming increasingly scarce.[53]

Reed was convinced that the independent, subsistence farm could exist on the Canadian prairie, and he was not alone in cherishing the ideal of the self-sufficient farm where the family produced its own food, manufactured at home necessary non-agricultural goods such as clothing and furniture, and did not buy or sell. The notion that this was a superior way of life was widespread and persistent, and was reflected in the suspicion of labour-saving machinery and concern about the use of debt and credit. The ideal of the self-sufficient farmer continued to appeal to the general public whereas the concept of agriculture as a market and profit-focused business met with considerable criticism.[54]

Commercial agriculture required new ideas, attitudes, and knowledge. What and how much should be produced on the farm were determined by external market conditions rather than by the family's needs and desires. Under market conditions the farmer made a business decision and had to take into consideration the nature of the soil, the characteristics of commodities, access to markets, and world prices. Commercial farming involved a 'rational' approach to technology. Potential profit rather than immediate need led the commercial farmer to purchase expensive implements on credit; payment would in part come from the increased productivity contributed by the new implement. The efficient, profitable management of the farm enterprise thus required new attitudes towards technology, credit, and debt, for immigrant settlers and Indians alike. Hayter Reed felt that Indians were incapable of understanding these concepts, and could not operate farms as business enterprises. His belief in the inability of Indians to manage their own financial affairs, and to handle debt, credit, or the new technology thus precluded commercial farming.

In the United States the ideal of the self-sufficient farm was never more than 'a nice dream of a golden age'; nor was Canadian pioneer agriculture ever self-sufficient.[55] Pioneer farmers, economist Vernon Fowke has argued, were 'from the beginning tied in with the price system and the urban economy on a national and international basis.'[56] The farmer had to purchase his transportation and to outfit himself with the necessary provisions and implements. Although the farmer may not have produced a marketable staple for some years, he had products such as hay and wood to sell locally. Exchanges might be made through barter rather than cash, but these nonetheless constituted commercial transactions. Homesteaders were in need of cash and could rarely acquire enough to finance their operations. They could not borrow against their land until title was acquired, which involved a minimum three-year wait. The farmer required credit to secure his provisions, implements, and other supplies. The standard practice was to have credit advanced at the beginning of the crop season for seed, tools, and consumable goods, with payment made at harvest time.

Subsistence farming was not characteristic of the pioneer farms of the prairie west. From the beginning these farms were connected to the local, national, and international economy. Nor did the difficulties of the 1880s imply a need for self-sufficient farms. Large-scale, single-crop farming and the introduction of the techniques and technology of dry farming would be more likely to encourage agricultural prosperity on the plains. Like other western farmers, Indian farmers tended more towards commercial than subsistence farming, focusing on wheat culture, acquiring machinery to accommodate large acreages, and adopting techniques such as summer-fallowing. In their need to acquire cash, make purchases, and sell products, Indian farmers were just as linked to the larger economy as white settlers. Yet the peasant farming policy required Indian farmers to function in isolation from the rest of western Canadian society.

This attitude was unrealistic. Subsistence farming remained at best a questionable model for the arid Canadian plains, and it may even have been impossible.'[57] Western farmers were independent neither of the markets, nor of each other. Settlement of the prairies required mutual assistance and cooperation among neighbours and relatives. Working bees, pooled purchasing, and beef rings were characteristic of the pioneer years. Indians were denounced, however, when they undertook such cooperative action. Indian farmers were expected to conform to the nostalgic ideal of the independent, self-sufficient yeoman.

It soon became clear that peasant farming was a dubious model for reserve agriculture. Farm instructors, Indian agents, inspectors, and Indian farmers all protested the system. Despite this advice, Reed rigidly enforced the policy. As commissioner, he kept a vigilant eye on every kettle and lamp ordered, and he maintained close surveillance as deputy superintendent general. Agents were not allowed to spend a 'single copper' without the authority of the commissioner.[58] Reed's replacement as commissioner, Amédée Forget, had very limited powers of expenditure; even the most minute expense had to be sanctioned by Reed. Forget could under no circumstances authorize the purchase, hire, or use of machinery. When Forget requested greater powers of expenditure in 1894 in order to be able to respond to requests requiring immediate action during critical seasons, Reed replied: 'I would say that I am only too desirous that you take upon your shoulders this part of the work, and thus relieve me of it. The fear I have had – to be candid – is that my policy might not be strictly carried out, and I forsee that if it is slackened in the slightest, it will lead us not only to a largely increased expenditure but upset what I have in view, and this is, causing our Indians to work upwards by learning how to cut and sow their grain in the most crude manner possible, and not beginning at the large-end of the norm, with self-binders and reapers.'[59]

During haying and harvest time the full weight of the policy was felt. Agents and instructors were to see that the Indian farmers accomplished these tasks without the aid of any machinery. Even when bands had reapers and self-binders purchased before the policy was adopted, the farmers were to use hand implements. Larger farmers were expected to purchase the labour of others rather than revert to the use of machinery, or were to restrict their acreages to what they could handle with hand implements. 'The general principle,' Reed explained in 1893, 'is not to allow them machinery to save them work which they should with hands available on Reserves, do by help of such implements as are alone likely for long enough, to be within their reach.'[60]

Department officials in the field protested the peasant farming policy from its inception. They were dismayed by a policy which appeared to rob the Indians of any potential source of revenue. Their main objection was that the use of hand implements involved much loss in yield at harvest time. Harvesting coincided with haying, and both had to be secured with haste. As the Edmonton agent wrote in 1896: 'Personally, I do not see how any band of Indians in this district can ever raise sufficient grain or cattle to become self-supporting as long as they have to work with sickles and scythes only, as the seasons are so very short, haying and harvesting coming together. Perhaps in the south where the seasons are longer the system would work successfully, but up here no whiteman attempts to do so.'[61]

Agents throughout the Northwest – even those much further south than Edmonton – agreed that the seasons were too short for the use of hand implements. Once ready to cut, it was vital that grain remain standing for as brief a time as possible. The Carlton agent advised that because the climate brooked no delay with regard to securing grain, conditions in the Northwest could not be equated with the early days of farming in the eastern provinces when hand implements were used.[62] If not harvested as quickly as possible, grain could be lost to frost, hail, dry hot winds, or an excess of moisture. Agent Grant, of the Assiniboine reserve, protested that 'the seasons in this country are too short to harvest any quantity of grain, without much waste, with only old-fashioned, and hand-implements to do the work with.'[63] In his view it was not possible to harvest the 240 acres of grain on his reserve with hand implements without a great loss in yield. The grain had to be cut as soon as it was ready to avoid loss, since the harvest weather was generally hot, windy, and very dry. Grant estimated that the amount of grain lost in his agency would be of sufficient quantity in two years to pay for a binder. Loss occurred, not only through the grain being too ripe, but in the gathering and binding by hand as well. Grant informed Reed that the prairie straw was dry and brittle, and would not tie the grain without breaking, which caused considerable loss. While the farmers on his reserve used the long slough grass to bind grain, collecting it took up much time, leaving the grain in danger of over-ripening.

Agents also complained that the cradles broke constantly during harvest, which caused delays for repairs. The policy of employing labour to help take off a crop seldom proved feasible. Workers had their own fields to harvest.

One agent reported that farmers who hired others spent more for labour than their crop was worth.[64] He tried to get neighbours to exchange work in each others' fields, but those available to help were usually those without crops who required pay for their labour.

Inspector Alex McGibbon was also critical of the peasant farming policy. He informed Reed in 1891 that it was contrary to common sense to ban universally the use of machinery.[65] Exceptions had to be made and flexibility shown. McGibbon gave the example of the Onion Lake band which had 500 acres under crop, much of which would be lost if the department insisted it be cut with cradles. Then there was a farmer with about fifteen acres 'of as pretty wheat as could be seen anywhere.'[66] The man was in frail health, however, and could not secure the help of others who had their own fields to look after. McGibbon observed the man cradling and his wife binding but was certain that 'the waste on that field alone would be nearly half the crop.'[67]

Agents and instructors reported difficulty enforcing the peasant policy. It was almost impossible to get the Indians to cut with cradles or sickles, especially those who had implements already.[68] Agents provided Reed with numerous examples of farmers who attempted the work and gave up, refusing to return, and of others who would not even attempt it.[69] It was reported that the Indians became discouraged and lost all interest in their crops.[70] These were not 'lazy' Indians. Agent Campbell of the Moose Mountain agency, for example, cited the case of an Indian farmer whom he considered to be the most 'progressive' in the agency.[71] He began to cradle his grain but quit, declaring he would let his grain stand and never plough another acre. By no means averse to hard work, the man chose to work on the straw pile of a threshing machine, a job 'not usually considered pleasant.' Agent Grant described the reaction of 'Black Mane,' who had fifteen acres of very good wheat and, 'when told that he would have to cut and bind it by hand, gave up his oxen, and left both his wheat and *reserve*. I gave his wheat to his brother. I have been told that he is now at Wolf Point, in the States. This will show how hard it is to compel an Indian to harvest his grain by hand.'[72] It was also the case that some Indian farmers were not strong enough, either because of age or sickness, to harvest their grain by hand. In August 1890 the Pelly agent reported that 'the Indians here, from scrofulitic [sic] effects have not enough strength to mow [hay] with a scythe and put up any quantity.'[73] If they had only two or three head they could manage to put up enough hay but any more was beyond their ability with scythes and rakes.

The Indians often became discouraged when they saw white farmers using machinery. Agent Grant reported that the Indians on his reserve worked for white settlers, used binders when they stooked for them, and not surprisingly were discouraged when asked to cut and bind their own crops by hand.[74]

Indian farmers were also keenly aware of what methods were used on reserves throughout the Northwest. McGibbon reported in 1891 that 'the Indians know all that is going on at the various agencies.'[75] The Carlton agency Indians knew precisely how many binders the Crooked Lakes Indians had and how many seeders were in another agency. Chief Mistawasis demanded to know in 1891 why the Battleford Indians, and John Smith's band, had reapers when his farmers were not allowed them.[76] McGibbon informed the chief that these were purchased before the policy was adopted, that such sales were now being cancelled, and that he and his men should be out in the fields cutting and stacking grain rather than wasting valuable time talking.

Restrictions on the use of machinery were not the only aspects of the peasant policy that agents disliked. The home manufacturers program, which called for the use of Indian-made implements, also proved unrealistic. Indian-made wooden forks, for example, could not be used for loading hay, grain, or manure.[77] Iron forks were required and even these frequently broke or wore out and had to be replaced. In some districts, moreover, appropriate materials such as hides and lumber were not available to manufacture ox-plough harness, wagon tongues, or neck yokes. Poorly made or faulty neck yokes could break going down a hill, and cattle could be injured if not killed. Other items struck from agents' estimates included lanterns and tea kettles. Agents protested that Indians could not look after their cattle at night without lanterns and that not having proper kettles resulted in the waste of much time.[78]

Hayter Reed was not the slightest bit sympathetic to nor moved by the objections and complaints of his agents, inspectors, and commissioner. His response was to dismiss their claims. Reed was aware of a 'lack of sympathy' among agents and employees, but he was convinced that they were inclined to be too lenient with the Indians.[79] 'Naturally,' he wrote to McGibbon, 'Indians and their overseers prefer to take the method easiest for themselves, and it is only after a hard and long continued fight, that I am beginning to get the policy carried into effect.'[80] Officials in the field, Reed believed, desired to make things as easy as possible for the Indians and consequently for themselves.[81] Indians 'naturally' preferred to have machinery do their work for them.

Reed refused to give in to the 'whims of Farmers and Indians,' and advised that growing less grain or losing some of the crop was preferable to the use of machinery.[82] He did not believe, however, that any grain need be lost by harvesting with hand implements, but that the loss in yield was due entirely to the 'half-heartedness' of instructors and agents.[83] With greater firmness they could manage to save their crop. If grain was being lost, the solution was for the farmers to confine their acreage to what they could handle. Reed informed one official that 'any loss suffered in the course of enforcing the policy will prove in the long run true economy.'[84] Supplementary hay, Reed naïvely assumed, could be acquired after harvesting, and he saw no conflict between the two operations.

Farm instructors were told not to meddle in the issue of machinery but simply to obey orders. Agents explained to all employees working in the fields with the Indians 'that it was their duty to set aside completely any opinions they might hold regarding the feasibility, etc., of carrying out this policy, and to act and speak always as if they had full confidence in the wisdom of getting the Indians to cut their grain by hand, and in the possibility of succeeding in doing so.'[85] Inspectors were instructed neither to convene nor be present at meetings with Indian farmers, since this would give an 'exaggerated importance' to their requests for machinery.[86] Instead, they were to defend vigorously the department's policy and severely discourage labour-saving machinery. Political opposition to the peasant policy was also dismissed by Reed: 'It may distress one in opposition to the Government to see what he does not understand the reasons of, but I fancy if we were to pamper up Indians in idleness while we supply machinery to do their work, the opposition would soon give tongue to the distress occasioned by such a course.'[87]

Department employees risked dismissal if they refused to comply with the peasant farming policy. Agent Finlayson of the Touchwood Hills agency was fired because he would not 'make his Indians provide hay and harvest their crop without the use of labour saving implements as the department is opposed to for Indians use.'[88] Despite this powerful lever to enforce policy, Reed's peasant program showed signs of crumbling by the season of 1896. That year many disgruntled and angry agents defied orders and used machinery. At his Regina office, Forget was harangued by officials requesting permission to use machinery.[89] That season was subject to severe hailstorms. Seventy thousand acres of crop were destroyed in western Manitoba in one storm, and many settlers were hailed out near Regina.[90] It was of vital importance that the crop be cut as soon as it was ready. Forget granted permission to several agents to borrow or hire binders from settlers. He informed Reed that authority was granted only on the understanding that the agent 'make a bona fide effort to secure the whole crop, or as much of it as possible, by hand appliances and it is understood that only upon all such efforts failing to secure the crop with sufficient rapidity either on account of the state of the weather or the inadequacy of the workers, is the authority to employ machinery to be made use of.'[91]

During the harvest of 1896 some agents openly defied the peasant policy or complied only half-heartedly. Agent McDonald of Crooked Lakes stated that he and his staff made no efforts that season to force the Indians to harvest their grain without the aid of labour-saving machinery.[92] He noted that earlier attempts to do so had failed, and that the Indians became discouraged and would not work. The agent claimed to have done his honest best to carry out the department's policy, but the Indians were 'so far advanced' with such large acres of grain that he could make no headway. He had tried to get those with smaller crops to harvest by hand, but even they had someone with a binder cut their crop for them. Had he expressed 'violent opposition to the Indians, I should only have achieved the result of making the smaller farmers so sullen, that they would have put in no crop at all, had they the prospect to cut it with a sickle, and the large farmers would have met me with contempt, and gone their own way, with a wide breach between us.'[93] McDonald noted that the harvest of 1896, amounting to over 9000 bushels of wheat and 3500 bushels of oats, 'would have been impossible without implements.'[94]

J.P. Wright, the Touchwood Hills agent, also admitted that the harvest in his agency was accomplished with the aid of labour-saving machinery.[95] Gordon and Poor Man's bands each owned a self-binder, and it was useless, the agent claimed, to ask them to cut their grain with sickles and cradles because they would not do it. Wright reminded Reed, as all the agents did, that the Indians were busy with their haying at harvest time and the grain had to be cut with as little delay as possible. Other agents in the Northwest in 1896 claimed to have accomplished one-half or less of the harvest by hand methods before they were obliged to save the balance of the crop with machinery.[96] Reed remained adamant, demanding that the peasant policy be rigorously pursued.[97] Although he admitted that machinery might be necessary where Indians had large crops, he nonetheless expected that a strong effort be made to carry out the policy for all others.

The agents' reports reveal some glimpses of how Indian farmers reacted to the peasant farming policy. Many became angry and discouraged, while some refused to work and gave up farming altogether. The outlets for Indian protest during the 1890s were few. Grievances related to instructors and agents generally went no further. Inspectors were not allowed to hold audiences with the Indians. The published reports of agents and inspectors were to divulge only that 'which it was desired the public should believe.'[98] Visiting officials, journalists, or other observers were taken to a few select agencies. When the governor general planned a visit to the west in 1895, Reed arranged to have him visit only the most 'advanced' reserves, such as the Crooked Lakes.[99] The August visit was to be hastily diverted elsewhere, however, if the crops failed on the reserves.

An 1893 petition from the head men of the Pasquah and Muscowpetung bands, addressed to the House of Commons, succeeded in gaining the attention of officials in Ottawa.[100] The Indians resented the restrictions on their freedom and the interference of the agent in all of their affairs. Among other things they protested the permit system: 'Whenever we have a chance to sell anything and make some money the Agent or Instructor steps in between us and the party who wants to buy, and says we have no power to sell: if this is to continue how will we be able to make a living and support ourselves? We are not even allowed to sell cattle that we raise ourselves.'[101] The petitioners wished to purchase a binder, noting that taking off grain with a cradle was too slow, but 'the Commissioner objected to us buying a Binder as he said it would make the young men lazy.'[102] The Indians claimed that 'when we ask the Agent for farm implements he sends us to the Commissioner, and he in turn sends us back to the Agent. This has completely discouraged us, as our old implements are worn out,' and 'many of the fields we used to farm are now all grown over with grass.'[103]

This petition received no action; the allegations were dismissed and the document filed away and forgotten. Hayter Reed denied the legitimacy of and refuted the charges and grievances. In a memo dealing with the petition, Reed vigorously defended his department. The permit system, he argued, was a necessity. Without it, 'Indians would be defrauded, and would part with hay while their cattle was left to starve – grain and roots which they require for sustenance, etc. etc., squander the proceeds, and then come on the Government for support. Our object is to make them acquire the limit of stock to afford them an annual surplus to dispose of, meanwhile when they have a steer or other animal which can not be profitably kept longer they are allowed to sell. If left to their own discretion there would not be a head of stock left.'[104]

The 1893 petition from Pasquah and Muscowpetung Indians was dismissed, but in the 1890s this kind of protest was not unusual. Discontent over the peasant policy, permit system, and other restrictions was widespread. In 1893 the Dakota of the Oak River reserve in southwestern Manitoba protested the same issues, but even though they succeeded in receiving considerable attention through their petitions, letters, a visit to Ottawa, and their defiance of regulations, their actions did not occasion a reconsideration or revamping of policy.[105] By this time a formula response to all Indian grievances was well entrenched. Indians were dismissed as chronic complainers and lazy idlers willing to go to any lengths to avoid work. At the same time, nefarious 'outside agitators' – usually unnamed – were blamed for any discontent.

Official pronouncements of the Department of Indian Affairs emphasized that Indian interests were paramount and that such measures as the peasant policy and the permit system were undertaken out of concern for their welfare and development. In this period and well into the twentieth century, however, Indian interests were consistently sacrificed to those of the new settlers, and there was little concern to develop independent Indian production. Organized

FIGURE 1
Saskatchewan Indian Agencies
(acres under cultivation)

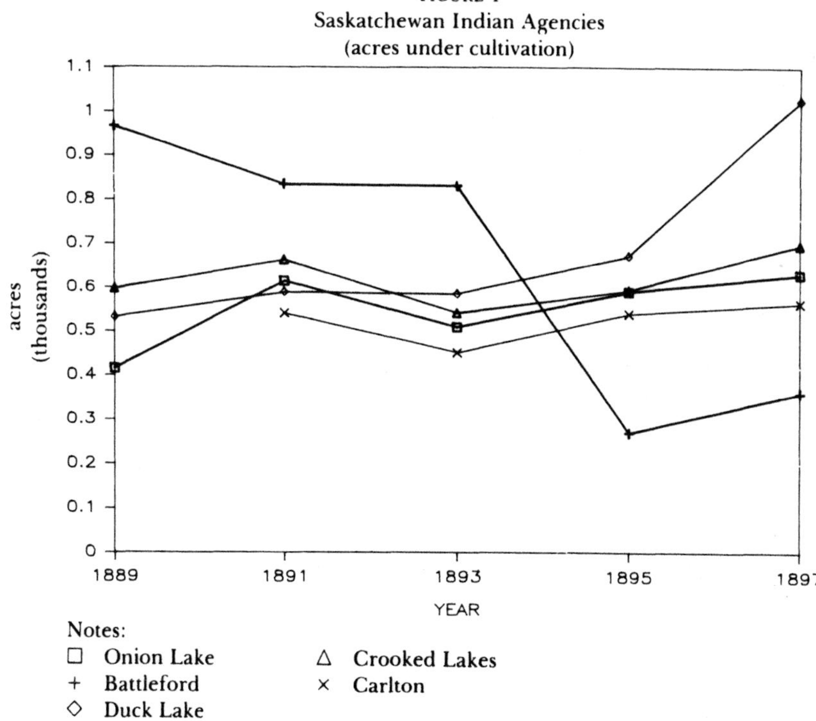

Notes:
□ Onion Lake
\+ Battleford
◇ Duck Lake
△ Crooked Lakes
× Carlton

interests were able to influence the course of Indian policy by petitioning and lobbying their members of parliament. Agents on the spot and visiting officials were pressured from neighbouring whites. The Indians' interests were easily sacrificed as they had no vote and no economic power. This pattern continued into the twentieth century when effective pressure was mounted to have the Indians surrender reserve land that was suitable for agriculture. White settlers proved loath to see the Indians establish any enterprise that might compete with or draw business away from them. Government policy reflected the economic interests of the new settlers, not the Indians.

This pattern was all too common in the British colonial world of the late nineteenth century. In Kenya, for example, the colonial administration assumed that the most effective way to exploit the country's vast resources was to establish a viable community of immigrant white farmers.[106] The economic interests of the indigenous population were thus not advanced, and African agriculture was systematically suppressed. Roads and railways by-passed African reserves, denying access to markets. Heavy taxation prevented the

FIGURE 2
Saskatchewan Indian Agencies
(acres under cultivation)

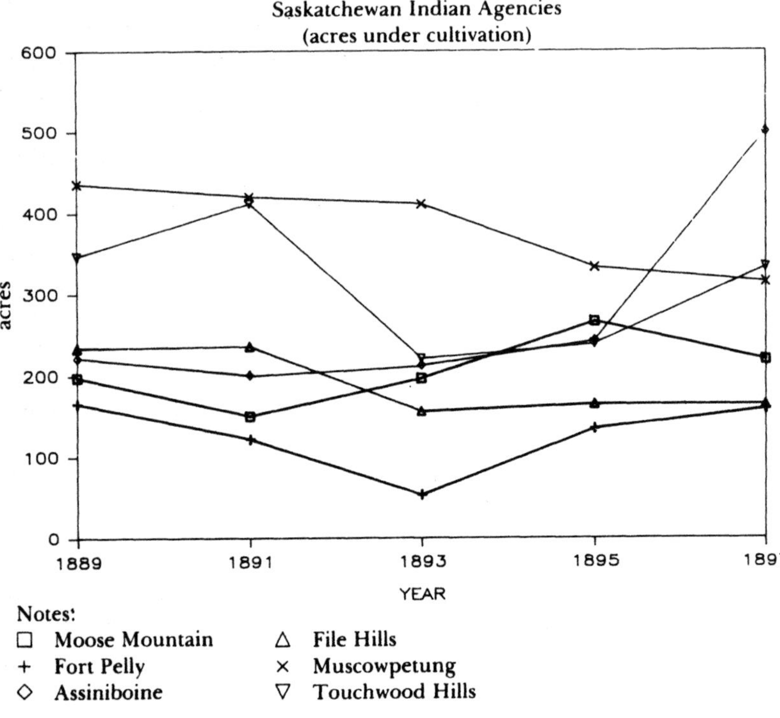

Notes:
□ Moose Mountain
\+ Fort Pelly
◇ Assiniboine
△ File Hills
× Muscowpetung
▽ Touchwood Hills

accumulation of capital necessary for efficient agriculture, ensuring instead a steady flow of cheap labour. Africans in Kenya were forbidden to grow coffee, the most lucrative cash crop.

In South Africa an African 'peasantry' emerged, responded positively to the new colonial market economy in the nineteenth century, and began to account for a large share of the agricultural exports.[107] But this stage was shortlived. The price for competing too successfully with white farmers was a barrage of legislative measures designed to inhibit African farming while white agriculture was aided by a massive program of grants and subsidies. By the 1880s peasant production began to decline, and once fertile agricultural communities became pockets of rural poverty.

Similarly, in western Canada, measures like the permit system, severalty, and peasant farming combined to undermine and atrophy agricultural development on reserves. The administration acted not to promote the agriculture of the indigenous population but to provide an optimum environment for the immigrant settler. Comparisons between the situation in colonial Africa and western Canada, however, remain dubious as the Africans were always in the majority. Yet in the 1880s and 1890s the west was sparsely settled by non-Indians, and there was a similar anxiety to see an immigrant farming class established. After 1885 immigration to the west was at a virtual standstill and the drought years of the 1880s did little to attract settlers. Consideration was not given to the possibility of enhancing Indian production as a means of creating an export sector, although it was grumbled in an 1892 item in the Regina *Leader* that it would be preferable to make farmers of Indians and have them settle on empty lands than to bring in 'Russians and Jews.'[108] Instead, new settlers were to be attracted, and policies were determined by the need to maintain the viability of this community.

Large-scale settler agriculture in Africa required access to cheap labour. Policies that were aimed at suppressing African production were also intended to force Africans into the labour market. This situation did not prevail in western Canada, where the single-family homestead became the principal economic unit. It is worth noting, however, that in the 1890s Reed promoted the Indians of the Northwest, particularly the graduates of industrial schools, as a cheap labour supply for farm or domestic work.[109] This was a clear message broadcast at national and international fairs, exhibitions, and displays aimed at prospective settlers.

In the United States, government policy of the 1880s led to a marked decline in Indian farming.[110] Before general allotment was enacted in 1887 there was a steady growth of reservation agriculture, but this was followed by stagnation and regression. American Indian policy, though distinct from Canadian in many ways, was similarly shaped by non-Indian economic interests.

Not surprisingly, there had been very little progress made in reserve farming during the 1890s. There was a modest increase in acreage on some reserves, while on others acreage stayed at about the same level or even decreased (see figures 1 and 2). The likelihood of agriculture forming the basis of a stable reserve economy faded even further after 1896, as the new administrators of Indian Affairs promoted land surrender and so further limited the agricultural capacity of reserves. Because much Indian land appeared to be 'idle,' 'unused,' or 'surplus,' the hand of those who clamoured for land surrender was strengthened. Indians were living in some cases in the midst of fine farm land that was not cultivated at all, or was worked with obsolete methods and technology. Indians appeared to cling stubbornly to the past and remain impervious to 'progressive' influences. People concluded that Indians lacked industry and were not natural farmers. These observations, reflected in the histories that have been written until very recently, obscure or overlook the Indians' positive response to agriculture in earlier years. Equally obscured and forgotten has been the role of Canadian government policy in restricting and undermining reserve agriculture in a critical period of agricultural development.

NOTES

This article is from *Canadian Historical Review* 70 (1) (1989). Reprinted with permission.

An earlier draft of this paper was read at the Western Canadian Studies Conference held at the University of Saskatchewan in October 1987. The author gratefully acknowledges the valuable comments of Barbara Angel, Jean Friesen, Don Kerr, and Jim Miller on aspects of this paper.

1 Canada, *Sessional Papers*, 1889, no. 10, 162. Hayter Reed was born in 1849 in L'Original, Prescott County, Ontario. His early training and career interests were military. In 1871 he served with the Provincial Battalion of Rifles when they were dispatched to Fort Garry as reinforcements during the Fenian scare. Reed was called to the bar of Manitoba in 1872. He retired from military service with the rank of major in 1881. In 1880 he worked out of Winnipeg as 'chief land guide' with the Department of the Interior. He was appointed to the position of Indian agent in Battleford in 1881. He had little direct experience with or knowledge of Indians before his first posting. Yet he quickly rose through the ranks of assistant commissioner in 1884, commissioner in 1888, and in 1893 he assumed the position of deputy superintendent general of Indian Affairs. In 1897 he was dismissed by Clifford Sifton, minister of the interior. Reed found employment in 1905 as manager-in-chief of the Canadian Pacific Railway's hotel department.

2 G.F.G. Stanley, *The Birth of Western Canada: A History of the Riel Rebellions* (1936; Toronto 1975), 218

3 This study focuses on the Touchwood Hills, File Hills, Muscowpetung, and Crooked Lakes agencies. These are Plains Cree and Plains Saulteaux bands.

4 G. Friesen, *The Canadian Prairies: A History* (Toronto 1984), 222

5 National Archives of Canada (NA), records relating to Indian Affairs, RG 10, vol. 3686, file 13,168, A. McDonald to Edgar Dewdney, 25 June 1884; vol. 3687, file 13,642, John Nicol to Dewdney, 30 May 1884; vol. 3812, file 55,895,W.E. Jones to Hayter Reed, 18 Sept. 1890; vol. 3795, file 46,759, H.L. Reynolds to Indian commission, 6 June 1888

6 *Qu'Appelle: Footprints to Progress: A History of Qu'Appelle and District* (Qu'Appelle Historical Society 1980), 101

7 *Sessional Papers*, 1889, no. 12, 165

8 Ibid., 166

9 McCord Museum, McGill University, Hayter Reed Papers, address on the aims of the government in its dealings with the Indians, nd, 29

10 *Sessional Papers*, 1888, no. 16, 28

11 On Pasquah's reserve, for example, 164 forty-acre plots were surveyed. Sixteen of these were divided by deep ravines, leaving 148 lots. The population of the reserve was 124, so there was little room for future expansion. This 6560 acres was only a fraction of the 38,496 acres of the reserve. See NA, National Map Collection, 0011553, Pasquah no. 179, 1889.

12 Kenneth J. Tyler, 'A Tax-eating Proposition: The History of the Passpasschase Indian Reserve' (MA thesis, University of Alberta, 1979), 114
13 NA, RG 10, deputy superintendent letterbooks, Vankoughnet to Dewdney, Nov. 1889
14 Ottawa *Journal*, 20 June 1889
15 Moosomin *Courier*, 13 March 1890
16 *Sessional Papers*, 1889, no. 12, lx
17 Ottawa *Citizen*, Nov. 1890
18 *Sessional Papers*, 1889, no. 10, 162
19 McCord Museum, Reed Papers, 'Address,' 28
20 *Sessional Papers*, 1892, no. 14, 48
21 NA, RG 10, vol. 3964, file 148,285, Reed to Amédée Forget, 24 Aug. 1896
22 Ibid., vol. 3793, file 46,062, Reed to Dewdney, 11 April 1888
23 Ibid., vol. 3746, file 29,690–3, Reed to superintendent general, 30 Sept. 1886
24 Ibid., vol. 3908, file 107,243, Reed to agent Markle, March 1895, and *Sessional Papers*, 1891, no. 14, xvii
25 NS, RG 10, vol. 3964, file 148,285, Reed to Forget, 24 Aug. 1896
26 *Sessional Papers*, 1889, no. 12, 162
27 Ibid., 1891, no. 14, 196
28 Ibid.
29 Brian Dippie, *The Vanishing Indian: White Attitudes to U.S. Indian Policy* (Middletown 1982), 164–71. See also Robert E. Bieder, *Science Encounters the Indian, 1820–1880: The Early Years of American Ethnology* (Norman 1986).
30 NA, RG 10, vol. 3964, file 148,285, Reed to Forget, 24 Aug. 1896
31 McCord Museum, Reed Papers, 'Address,' 28
32 *Sessional Papers*, 1889, no. 12, 162
33 Ibid., 1888, no. 16, 125
34 McCord Museum, Reed Papers, 'Address,' 27
35 *Sessional Papers*, 1889, no. 12, 161
36 Edmonton *Bulletin*, 17 Jan. 1881
37 House of Commons, *Debates*, 19 May 1880, 1610. See also Walter Hildebrandt, 'From Dominion to Hegemony: A Cultural History of Fort Battleford,' unpublished manuscript, 1988, Department of Environment, Parks, Prairie Region.
38 *Sessional Papers*, 1888, no. 16, 127
39 NA, RG 15, records of the Department of the Interior, vol. 245, file 23,563, part 1
40 Ibid., Hayter Reed, 'Canadian and United States Immigration,' May 1880
41 NA, RG 10, vol. 3806, file 52,332, Reed to Vankoughnet, 27 Oct. 1888
42 Ibid.
43 *The Historical Development of the Indian Act* (Ottawa 1978), 93
44 Canada, House of Commons, *Debates*, 24 March 1884, 1063
45 Clive J. Dewey, 'The Rehabilitation of the Peasant Proprietor in Nineteenth-Century Economic Thought,' *History of Political Economy* 6 (1) (1974): 17–47
46 Ibid., 32–47
47 See Clark C. Spence, *The Salvation Army Farm Colonies* (Tucson 1985), 2–7, and Frederic Impey, *Three Acres and a Cow* (London 1885).
48 William Booth, *In Darkest England and the Way Out* (London 1890)
49 Richard Jay, *Joseph Chamberlain: A Political Study* (Oxford 1981), 99

50 Willoughby Maycock, *With Mr. Chamberlain in the United States and Canada, 1877–88* (London 1914)
51 Dippie, *Vanishing Indians*, 160
52 Loring B. Priest, *Uncle Sam's Stepchildren: The Reformation of United States Indian Policy, 1865–1887* (New York 1969), 126
53 Ibid., 232
54 Rodney C. Loehr, 'Self-sufficiency on the Farm,' *Agricultural History* 26, (2) (1952): 37, and Clarence Danhof, *Change in Agriculture: The Northern United States, 1820–1870* (Cambridge 1969), 15
55 Loehr, 'Self-sufficiency,' 41
56 Vernon Fowke, *The National Policy and the Wheat Economy* (Toronto 1957), 12
57 Irene M. Spry, 'The Tragedy of the Loss of the Commons in Western Canada,' in Ian A.L. Getty and Antoine S. Lussier, eds., *As Long as the Sun Shines and Water Flows: A Reader in Canadian Native Studies* (Vancouver 1983), 221
58 NA, RG 10, deputy superintendent general letterbooks, vol. 1115, p.220. Reed to Forget, 12 June 1894
59 Ibid.
60 NA, Hayter Reed Papers, vol. 14, Reed to T.M. Daly, 10 March 1893
61 NA, RG 10, vol. 3964, file 148,285, Chas. De Cases to Reed, 19 Nov. 1896
62 Ibid.
63 Ibid., W.S. Grant to Reed, 1 Oct. 1896
64 Ibid., W.E. Jones to Reed, 1 Nov. 1896
65 NA, Reed Papers, vol. 13, no. 869, McGibbon to Reed, 16 March 1891
66 Ibid.
67 Ibid.
68 Ibid., vol. 14, no. 989, R.S. McKenzie to Reed, 16 Dec. 1890
69 NA, RG 10, vol. 3964, file 148,285
70 Ibid., Grant to Reed, 1 Oct. 1896
71 Ibid., J.J. Campbell to Reed, 8 Oct. 1896
72 Ibid., Grant to Reed, 1 Oct. 1896
73 Ibid., vol. 3812, file 55,895, W.E. Jones to Reed
74 Ibid., vol. 3964, file 148,285, Grant to Reed, 1 Oct. 1896
75 NA, Reed Papers, vol. 13, no. 869, McGibbon to Reed, 16 March 1891
76 Ibid.
77 Ibid., vol. 14, no. 989, McKenzie to Reed, 16 Dec. 1890
78 Ibid.
79 Ibid., vol. 14, no. 1206, Reed to McGibbon, 7 Nov. 1891
80 Ibid.
81 NA, RG 10, vol. 3964, file 14,285, Reed to Forget, 24 Aug. 1896
82 Ibid., deputy superintendent general letterbooks, vol. 1115, 220, Reed to Forget, 12 June 1894
83 NA, Reed Papers, vol. 14, Reed to Daly, 10 March 1893
84 Ibid.
85 NA, RG 10, vol. 3964, file 14,285, Campbell to Reed, 8 Oct. 1896
86 NA, Reed Papers, vol. 14, no. 1206, Reed to McGibbon, 7 Nov. 1891
87 Ibid., vol. 14, Reed to Daly, 10 March 1893
88 NA, RG 10, deputy superintendent general letterbooks, vol. 115, 382, memorandum relative to Mr Agent Finlayson

89 Ibid., vol. 3964, file 148,285, Forget to Reed, 20 Aug. 1896
90 Ibid.
91 Ibid.
92 Ibid., McDonald to Reed, 16 Feb. 1897
93 Ibid.
94 Ibid.
95 Ibid., J.P. Wright to Reed, 16 Feb. 1897
96 Ibid., Grant to Reed, 1 Oct. 1896; Jones to Reed, 1 Nov. 1896; de Cases to Reed, 19 Nov. 1896
97 Ibid., Reed to Forget, 25 Feb. 1897
98 Ibid., deputy superintendent general letterbooks, vol. 1115, Reed to J. Wilson, 3 Aug. 1894
99 Ibid., vol. 1117, p. 319, Reed to Forget, 20 July 1895
100 NA, Reed Papers, vol. 13, no. 960, McGirr to Reed, 8 March 1893
101 Ibid.
102 Ibid.
103 Ibid.
104 Ibid.
105 See Sarah Carter, 'Agriculture and Agitation on the Oak River Reserve, 1875–1895,' *Manitoba History* 6 (1983): 2–9.
106 See Richard D. Wolff, *The Economics of Colonialism: Britain and Kenya, 1870–1930* (New Haven 1974), and E.A. Brett, *Colonialism and Underdevelopment in East Africa: The Politics of Economic Change, 1919–1939* (London 1973).
107 Colin Bundy, *The Rise and Fall of the South African Peasantry* (Berkeley 1979)
108 Regina *Leader*, 10 Oct. 1892
109 Jacqueline Judith Kennedy, 'Qu'Appelle Industrial School: White "Rites" for the Indians of the Old North-West' (MA thesis, Carleton University, 1970), 116–23
110 Leonard A. Carlson, *Indians, Bureaucrats and Land: The Dawes Act and the Decline of Indian Farming* (Westport 1981)

EMERGENCE OF NATIVE POLITICAL ORGANIZATION

STAN CUTHAND

The Native Peoples of the Prairie Provinces in the 1920s and 1930s

Following the First World War, new social and political trends began to appear in Canadian society. The Indian people of Western Canada shared in the new political protest movements of the 1920s. The Indians' insight into what was happening and the leaders of their movement for self-determination came from native volunteers who had been in the armed forces. They came home to reactivate Pan-Indianism and to bring about a united effort for better education, ownership of property and land, and improvement in health programs. The movement towards an organized Pan-Indian movement quickly developed a broader base in Western Canada as other aims concerning treaty and hunting rights, the Indian Act, and economic development became major concerns of all the various bands and tribes.

The first national Indian leader was Lieutenant F.O. Loft,[1] a Mohawk Indian chief from Toronto who went to London, England, to ask the British Privy Council for a hearing on behalf of the Indians. He was told to organize the Indians before becoming a representative. Working out of his home in Toronto, Loft became president and secretary-treasurer of the League of Indians of Canada which held its first congress at Sault Ste Marie from 2–4 September 1919.

After the conference Loft drafted a letter to tribal leaders in Quebec, Ontario, and the Prairie provinces, calling for unity to form a body that would be a 'power to be heard and their demands recognized by governments.' The circular proclaimed:

> In politics, in the past they [Canada's Indians] have been in the background ...
>
> As peaceable and law-abiding citizens in the past, and even in the late war, we have performed dutiful service to our King, Country and Empire,

> and we have the right to claim and demand more justice and fair play as a recompense, for we, too, have fought for the sacred rights of justice, freedom and liberty so dear to mankind, no matter what their colour or creed.
>
> The first aim of the League then is to claim and protect the rights of all Indians in Canada by legitimate and just means; second, absolute control in retaining possession or disposition of our lands; that all questions and matters relative to individual and national wellbeing of Indians shall rest with the people and their dealing with the Government shall be by and through their respective band Councils.[2]

One of his first attacks against the Indian Affairs Branch concerned its intention to enfranchise returned soldiers. Loft led a public campaign to have the proposed amendments to the Indian Act dropped because they would result in the 'disintegration' of Indian bands.[3]

Although the first organizational meetings were held in Ontario, Chief Loft corresponded from the beginning with leaders in the Prairie reservations. Very few written replies were received and Chief Loft was forced to write to local Indian agents for names of leaders with the ability to read and write English.[4] The first meeting in Western Canada was held at Elphinstone, Manitoba, in June 1920. Another meeting was held the following year at Thunderchild Reserve in Saskatchewan. The purpose of these meetings was to seek strength by a united effort to change the suppressive policies of the Indian Affairs Branch and to promote religious freedom and the right to travel without passes.[5]

On 29 June 1922 a conference of Canadian Indians met at the Samson Reserve at Hobbema, Alberta.[6] Over 1500 Blackfoot, Stoney, Cree, and Assiniboine delegates attended, chiefly from Western Canada. Lieutenant Loft, as president, was known as *Natowew-Kimaw*, 'One who speaks for other.' The vice-president was Reverend S.A. Bingham from the Walpole Islands, Ontario; the provincial president of Saskatchewan was Reverend Edward Ahenakew; and provincial treasurer was James Wuttunee from Red Pheasant Reserve, Saskatchewan.[7] One of the influential leaders from Alberta was another veteran, Chief Mike Mountain House of the Blood tribe.

Thereafter, the League of Indians met annually in Saskatchewan under the leadership of Edward Ahenakew,[8] the Treaty Six area having the most active membership. Reverend Ahenakew was ideally suited to his position. He had graduated in 1912 from Emmanuel college, the Church of England theological college in Saskatoon, and he had served on numerous Saskatchewan Indian reserves. Sickness forced him to give up his dream of studying medicine at the university in Edmonton, but while he was recuperating from his illness he spent long evenings listening to the Cree elders gathered at Chief Thunderchild's home. Here he learned the old Cree traditions, the stories of Treaty Six and of the 1885 Rebellion, and the difficulties of learning to accept the white man's ways.

In *Voices of the Plains Cree* Edward Ahenakew states: 'The principal aim of the League, I would say, is equality for the Indian as citizen – equality, that is, in the two-fold meaning of privileges and responsibility; and to achieve this objective, our first emphasis must be upon improved educational and health programs ... More particularly, the Indians of Canada should have a voice in the character of legislation that is passed in Parliament when it concerns ourselves, for that is the privilege of all under our flag – personal freedom.'[9] Edward Ahenakew worked hard with the League of Indians, in which he served as president for Western Canada. He was also active in the synods of the Anglican church. Not aggressive in his approach to rectify the wrongs of his people, he was caught between two worlds, and was often more loyal to the church.

The Indian people liked what Chief Loft had to offer and the movement towards unity was revitalized in 1929 by Chief Joe Taylor at Green Lake, Saskatchewan, when the League of Indians in Western Canada was officially formed. The Saddle Lake Reserve near St Paul, Alberta, sponsored later conferences in 1931 and 1932. Resolutions were passed in 1931 that on-reserve schools be established to augment industrial and boarding schools, that the old people receive extra rations, that no further land surrenders be made, that Indian hunting, trapping, and fishing rights be preserved, and that a variety of economic assistance programs be provided by the department to individuals and to bands. There were 1344 delegates in attendance at the first Saddle Lake convention, including twenty-four chiefs and councillors from thirty Alberta reserves, and twenty-two chiefs and councillors from thirteen Saskatchewan reserves.[10] Augustine Steinhauer was elected president of the Alberta branch of the League of Indians of Canada, and it was his responsibility to help organize the yearly convention and maintain communications with the chiefs and councillors.

The resolutions passed at the 1932 convention at Saddle Lake contained more specific demands. The only one of these to which the department acceded was a request that only fully qualified teachers be employed in residential and boarding schools. To a resolution that all farm instructors and interpreters be removed form the Alberta and Saskatchewan reserves and that the money saved as a result be used to pay an old-age pension to those aged seventy years and older, the department replied, 'It is not likely the Department will assent to getting rid of Farming Instructors ... Increasing relief issues to aged Indians should depend on local conditions.' A demand that section 45 of the

Indian Act concerning permits be abolished was rejected with the comment that it was 'a move for greater freedom of action. The time has not yet come.' A general request that the government 'abolish the amendments of the Indian Act and ... follow closely the treaties of 1876 as made by Her Majesty Queen Victoria' received the ill-tempered reply: 'Too vague. What amendments are to be abolished? They have all been carefully thought out.' Further resolutions concerning individual bands, most of which dealt with land issues and requests for economic assistance, were also ignored.[11]

In 1933 various bands met at Poundmaker's Reserve, Saskatchewan, from 10 to 12 July, and a further meeting was held at Paul's Band near Duffield, Alberta, on 18 and 19 October, Chief Joe Samson from Hobbema was elected president of the Alberta league, and David Peter from Duffield secretary treasure.

Many of the issues discussed were carried forward from previous years but often with slightly different points or arguments to make. The 1934 convention was held at Enoch Reserve near Edmonton, and the 1935 convention moved back to Duffield. Some of the more unusual resolutions put forth in these years were:

> That those children who are most advanced in their studies should be sent to a school home where they can mix with the white children ...
>
> Resolved that as Canada has freedom of religious worship we Indians would earnestly petition you to grant our request to worship in our own way and according to our past customs the Most High God that created the world and all the beasts thereof and everything that pertaineth thereof, especially as we do not see anything according to our past customs, and especially that we should not be prohibited from holding our ancient Sun Dance, which should be called the Thirsty Dance and the Hungry Dance; a religious ceremony which has been dear to us for centuries and is still dear to us.[12]
>
> That when it is necessary to retain the services of a Doctor other than the doctor retained by the Indian Department, the expense of same shall be met by the Department and not from the Band funds. (This is in accordance with our Treaty) ...
>
> That where the Reservation boundary linefence extends through or into a lake we shall be given water rights within our line ...
>
> That the Department grant a Reservation on Kootenay Plain to the Nordegg Treaty people of Morley Agency.[13]
>
> That as it is now impossible to make a living from hunting and trapping and that we have a large number of Indians on our Reservations who are without the means to farm, we do hereby petition the Dominion

> Government through the Department of Indian Affairs, to assist us by providing us with horses, machinery and seed grain ...
>
> That we be given the privilege of choosing our own horses when the Department is purchasing horses for us ...
>
> That as we think it would be in the interest of the Indians to have a committee of their Chiefs and Headmen seated in the House of Parliament during the discussion of Indian matters, we humbly petition you to grant that privilege.[14]
>
> That the Dept. give us the privilege to rent out new lands to break and cultivate to any white man for five years. The only expense for [the] Indian [is] to furnish posts and get one-third of crop clear annually.[15]

These resolutions are one indication of the problems and difficulties facing Canada's treaty Indians in gaining basic educational and economic assistance and in merely running their day-to-day affairs.

During the 1930s the league was chiefly concerned with the retention of Indian reserve lands and with the question of ownership of personal property, particularly cattle. They resented the double standard – one for treaty Indians and another for non-Indians – which prevented Indians from selling their cattle. The permit system which restricted travel off one's home reserve still was being enforced by the Department of Indian Affairs. There were only minimal improvements in housing, health services, economic progress, and education. The fiftieth anniversary of the signing of Treaty Six passed during the 1920s with little real improvement for Indian people, but now, with the formation of the league, native leaders from across Canada had a national organization to lobby for changes to the Indian Act.

EDUCATION

The educational policy in the 1920s was generally directed towards improving educational facilities, but leaving curriculum content alone. Indian education was administered under the auspices of the Roman Catholic church and the three Protestant denominations – Presbyterian, Anglican, and Methodist. All the various types of schools were subject to the supervision of the Department of Indian Affairs, because the government provided financial subsidies based on attendance records. The League of Indians was concerned and wanted some improvements because many of the Indian agents were politically appointed, poorly educated white soldiers recently returned from overseas service.

In 1923 government funding was increased to include all the capital expenses at Indian residential schools, releasing the finances of the missionary societies and religious orders for better instruction, food, and clothing. Grants were offered to graduates of Indian schools showing academic promise who wished to attend high schools, universities, business colleges, and trade schools. The eligibility requirement stipulated that a student must have passed grade eight by the age of fourteen; but, in fact, many Indian children did not attend school until the age of eight or ten and some started at the age of twelve. Inevitably the program failed to place many graduates in institutions past the level of grade eight.

During the 1930s increasing emphasis was placed on manual training and vocational instruction in all types of Indian schools. Most of the Indian residential schools included self-sufficient farms of two hundred acres or more with cattle and horses. The school on the Long Plain Reserve near Portage La Prairie had large stables and well-bred stock and sold tons of potatoes every year. It had the first potato planter in the district and had drills for corn, turnips, and grain. In addition, students milked cows and made their own butter. One of the more unusual projects was a mink farm started in 1938 at the Morley Residential School in Alberta. One ill-conceived government plan involved moving the residential schools on the Blood Reserve closer to the town of Cardston, in preparation for having the north part of the reserve surrendered and sold. The Bloods refused to sell, and the controversy created a lot of suspicion among the band members.

There were two schools of thought among white administrators in connection with the education of Indians: boarding the children and teaching them away from their parents; or teaching them on the reserve in day schools in order to influence the reserve by working with the parents. Or to put it another way, some missionary societies said to 'Christianize' the Indian first and them 'civilize' them; other missionary societies said to 'civilize' the Indian first before converting them. There was a rumour among the Indian parents that the only reason the government wanted to teach their children to read and write was to make it easier to train them as soldiers if there was another war. All these attitudes were detrimental to the educational system.

The major problem with day schools was the attendance. From 1909 to 1920, for example, Little Pine Day School near Battleford, Saskatchewan, lists seventeen children, but the attendance ranged anywhere all the way down to zero. The reason for the erratic attendance was the traditional Indian culture. In the fall and spring, families moved to the bush to trap for furs, and during the winter and summer they would move back to the reserve or work on a nearby farm clearing brush. Nevertheless, the residential and day schools contributed greatly to the economy of the reserves by hiring Indians as domestic workers and by purchasing cordwood from local Indian cutters. Attendance was compulsory under the Indian Act, but enforcement varied with each reserve. Some parents wanted their children to attend school in order to understand the white man's ways, but most parents were not willing to force their children to attend school in such an alien environment. Many parents who had been at school felt short-changed by the residential schools under church control. Those who supported the churches reacted negatively to such a thought. It was a period of division and confusion on many Indian reserves. All the great Indian leaders, like Ahenakew and Steinhauer, were classically educated men and had read the government documents. At a conference held at North Battleford around 1935 they petitioned the government for improvements in education, health, and economic development.

The federal government expenditure for Indian education in 1921 was $1,112,409, but rose to $2,156,882 in 1945, $6,221,792 in 1950, and $31,291,822 in 1964. The cost of Indian education in 1921 was relatively low, because many Indian pupils were enrolled in church-operated schools and less than half of the children of school age were enrolled in any school.

During the years preceding the Second World War, a Special Joint Committee of the Senate and House of Commons made an extensive study of opinion on Indian education. Their report recommended integrated schools wherever possible, with accommodation provided for all Indian children, and decreased enrolment in residential schools. Also, to provide opportunities for vocational and university education, Indian people should assume more responsibility for the education of their own children and become actively involved in school committees.

Progress in Indian education since the 1920s and 1930s has followed many of the proposals put forth during those two decades. In September 1963 R.F. Davey, chief superintendent of Indian education, presented a statement on behalf of the Indian Affairs Branch to the Standing Committee of the Ministers of Education at the Canadian Education Association Convention. His personal observations were that eventually:

1. Indian education should be brought under the jurisdiction of the provinces.
2. Legislation to permit the organization of school units or districts on Indian reserves under provincial authority is required to extend the responsibility of the Indian in the operation of the local school.
3. Legislation [is required] to provide for Indian representation on school boards operating joint schools.
4. Increased provincial control over the integration programme is essential to simplify administration. Federal financial support to the provinces should replace tuition fees payable to local school authorities by the federal government.

5. The Indians must be recognized by the provinces as residents with equal rights and privileges with respect to Indian education.[16]

Edward Ahenakew had made many of the same points as early as 1923.[17] Many of the proposed innovations in Indian education during the 1970s closely resemble these prophetic predictions.

ECONOMIC DEVELOPMENT

Most reserve Indians had horses to sell to the new settlers coming into their area. Many sold dry wood to the farmers and town folk in the winter and hay in the summer. They cut brush most of the summers and were busy with harvesting in the fall. They trapped in the late fall and early spring for muskrats, and during the winter months some trapped weasels, fox, coyotes, and rabbits. Several families gained reputations as good farmers and ranchers.

There were a lot of old-timers past middle age who had never been to school a day of their lives, but who remembered the buffalo hunts way back in 1860, the intertribal wars, the warriors' societies, the songs and rituals. Some of them were medicine men. They witnessed the signing of Treaties Four, Six, and Seven and the Rebellion of 1885. They passed on their stories and legends at wakes and meetings, and they spoke at dances. They maintained stability in the community. They were proud and independent, preferring to reject or adapt the ideas of the Indian agents and missionaries. These men knew who they were; they reaffirmed their beliefs at sun dances, round dances, horse dances, chicken dances, hand games, the big smoke, and the singing practices. They relived the past in the sacred lodge of the Horn Society. They learned the songs and renewed their bundles.

The old people received their monthly rations from the Indian Affairs – one scoop or two pounds of tea, four pounds of rolled oats, four pounds of salt, one bar of soap, four pounds of rice, one slab of bacon or meat, four pounds of beans, two boxes of matches, twenty pounds of flour, one can of baking powder, and two pounds of lard or tallow. This diet was supplemented by rabbits, ducks, and prairie chickens. They were not too badly off, although at times the old people ran out of tobacco. Under the Veterans' Land Act an amount of up to $2320 could be granted to an Indian veteran who settled on Indian reserve lands, and the money could be used for specific purposes such as the purchase of livestock, machinery, and building materials.

In the 1930s the older generations came into conflict with the new generation who had been to school. Family-arranged marriages were opposed by the youths, and they often ran away to be married elsewhere. The younger generation refused to accept the traditional role of submitting to the wishes of their fathers and tended to question such traditional customs as giving away horses to visitors. The more educated Indians scoffed at Indian rituals and refused to participate. They danced square dances and quadrilles. They would speak English rather than their native tongue. The more traditional families ignored this and continued to show their Indianness. No matter how far removed they may have been from their hunting, fishing, and food-gathering ancestors, and in spite of opposition from the Indian Affairs policies, the elders continued to renew themselves at the sweat lodges and feasts. They restored relationships and kinship ties at sun dances. When sun dances were completely suppressed by the government, Indians met at exhibitions and fairs to meet each other and renew friendships and strengthen kinship. Kinship was strong amongst the Blackfoot and Crees. Their philosophy was, 'Know your relatives and you will know who you are.'

HEALTH SERVICES

Working with farm instructors and schoolteachers were the travelling nurses. Their job was to inspect schools and to go among the homes on the reserves giving assistance and advice. Their efforts met with some resistance. The medicine men and midwives were against the intrusion of white nurses. Often the nurses were driven away from homes. They were often suspected of causing sickness in order to further depopulate the reserves.

Government officials showed a similar misunderstanding of Indian practices. A circular written on 15 December 1921 by Duncan Campbell Scott, deputy superintendent-general of Indian Affairs, gave these instructions to the Indian agents:

> It is observed with alarm that the holding of dances by the Indians on their reserves is on the increase, and that these practices tend to disorganize the efforts which the Department is putting forth to make them self-supporting.
>
> I have, therefore, to direct you to use your utmost endeavours to dissuade the Indians from excessive indulgence in the practice of dancing. You should suppress any dances which cause waste of time, interfere with the occupations of the Indians, unsettle them for serious work, injure their health, or encourage them in sloth and idleness. You should also dissuade, and, if possible, prevent them from leaving their reserves for the purposes of attending fairs, exhibitions, etc., when their absence would result in their own farming and other interests being neglected. It is realized that reasonable amusement and recreation should be enjoyed by Indians, but they should not be allowed to dissipate their energies

> and abandon themselves to demoralizing amusements. By the use of tact and firmness you can obtain control and keep it, and this obstacle to continued progress will then disappear.
>
> The rooms, halls, or other places in which Indians congregate should be under constant inspection. They should be scrubbed, fumigated, cleansed or disinfected to prevent the dissemination of disease. The Indians should be instructed in regard to the matter of proper ventilation and the avoidance of over-crowding rooms where public assemblies are being held, and proper arrangement should be made for the shelter of their horses and ponies. The Agent will avail himself of the services of the medical attendant of his agency in this connection.

The Blood Indians of southern Alberta had a circular log building with no floor at the old Agency, the northern part of the reserve, where they held their dances. They took horses right into the building to give away at honour dances. This building was condemned by the travelling nurses and demolished. On the Little Pine Reserve there was also a circular dance hall where every week during the winter months the people danced. This also was condemned by a travelling nurse, who threatened to set it on fire. The men tore it down. For some years after this the Little Pine Band had no place to dance until Poundmaker's Reserve built their hall. The hall was across the creek and out of sight of government health officials. Periodically, big feasts and dances were held there by the community.

Despite living in what government officials considered to be unhealthy conditions, the overall health of Canadian Indians improved throughout this period. The Canadian native population in 1922 was 100,000 – the lowest in history – but in 1923 the superintendent-general, Charles Stewart, reported good progress in matters of health supervision through improved sanitation, and that notwithstanding the ravages of the 'flu,' the Indian population had been increased to 105,000 for the whole dominion.

CONCLUSION

The decades between the wars were a period of growth in awareness for native people. In the 1920s the post-treaty generations transferred their identity from that of horsemen of buffalo days to that of cowboys. They wore big hats and neckerchiefs. The ambition of every father was to see his son ride a prancing horse at the sun dance, to ride at horse races, and to ride at a rodeo, like the renowned world rodeo champion Tom Three Persons from the Blood Reserve.

Joe Samson from Hobbema writing in Cree syllabics during the late 1930s speaks of that period, lamenting the fact that the terms of the treaties signed with the Queen's representatives were not kept. The only visible evidence were the school buildings and the farmer instructors' residences. 'As far as farming is concerned, I see no sign of real help coming from the Indian Affairs,' he wrote. He also lamented that the birds and animals found on the Prairies were becoming less in numbers; some were extinct.

Conditions on Indian reserves in practically every area – social services, health, education, and living facilities – had deteriorated in the years since the signing of the treaties. There was a feeling of frustration, soon to be replaced by hopelessness and despair. But contact with other societies around the world brought a new insight and renewed hope to veterans returning from Europe. The various prairie tribes formed the League of Indians of Canada under the inspiration of Chief Loft during these two crucial decades. It laid the foundations for the creation of the Indian Association of Alberta in 1939 and of the Federation of Saskatchewan Indians in 1944. As such, it was the first expression of political unity by the Indian people of Western Canada, who began the fight for better services and for a better future.

NOTES

This article is from *One Century Later: Western Canadian Reserve Indians since Treaty 7*, ed. Ian A.L. Getty and Donald B. Smith. Vancouver: University of British Columbia Press 1978. Reprinted with permission.

1 Frederick O. Loft was a lieutenant in the Canadian militia and served overseas from June 1917 to February 1918. He was born at Grand River (Six Nations), Ontario, on 3 February 1872 and was trained as an accountant. He had two brothers, William and Harry. A major source of information on the activities of Chief Loft is found in the National Archives of Canada (NA), Record Group 10 (Red Series), volume 3211, file 527787, vol. 1 'Congress of Indians of Canada. General Correspondence, 1919-1935. 'Also on microfilm C-11, 340

2 Circular letter by chief F.O. Loft, president and secretary-treasury, League of Indians of Canada, Toronto, 26 Nov. 1919, NA, RG 10

3 The Toronto *Sunday World*, 6 June 1920; clipping enclosed in NA, RG 10. The adverse publicity raised by Loft's activities prompted the deputy superintendent-general of Indian affairs, Duncan Campbell Scott, to comment: 'He has organized a society called "The League of Indians of Canada," and he is attempting, I am credibly informed, to work against the administration of the Department, even going so far as to state that he has the ear of the Government and can supersede and circumvent the Department. He is a man of good personal appearance but has no weight, and is endeavouring to work up a reputation for himself. I am particularly anxious that he should not, in any way,

be encouraged by the Minister or the Government. At the same time, if he makes any suggestions worthy of consideration, I do not propose to turn them down on account of their source.' Memorandum to Mr. Featherston, 28 March 1922; NA, RG 10

4 Letter addressed to 'Dear Brother,' dated 25 Nov. 1919; NA, RG 10. Some of the correspondents included Teddy Yellow Fly, Blackfoot Reserve; Joe Mountain Horse, Blood Reserve; Dan Wildman, Morley Reserve; and John Barwick, Saddle Lake Reserve.

5 Ibid.

6 *Regina Leader* [June/July] 1922; clipping enclosed in NA, RG 10. The RCMP were asked by the Indian Affairs Branch to monitor the proceedings, as well as to prevent any bootlegging of liquor and killing of cattle for meat. The Mounties counted 121 tipis and reported no difficulties during the entire three-day conference. RCMP, 'Report Re – Indian League of Nations. Convention at Hobbema. July 3, 1922', NA, RG 10

7 The Reverend Canon Edward Ahenakew (1885–1961) was born at Sandy Lake, Saskatchewan, in June 1885. He compiled a series of stories from Chief Thunderchild and recorded some of his own experiences through 'Old Keyam.' These were edited by Ruth M. Buck in *Voices of the Plains Cree* (Toronto: McClelland and Stewart 1973). I worked with the editor in providing the Cree translations.

8 Ibid., 186

9 Ibid., 123–4

10 Memorandum of Resolutions passed by the Chiefs, Councillors and Voters of the various Bands of Indians assembled in council at the Convention of the League of Indians of Canada held at the Saddle Lake Indian Reserve, Alberta, on the 15th, 16th and 17th days of July 1931,' NA, RG 10. There are forty-two bands in Alberta and thirty-seven bands in Saskatchewan. *Linguistics and Cultural Affiliations of Canadian Indian Bands* (Ottawa: Department of Indian Affairs and Northern Development, Indian Affairs Branch 1970)

11 'Record and minutes of convention of League of Indians of Canada, Western Branch, held at Saddle Lake Indian Reserve, Alberta, November 3rd and 5th, 1932'; and 'Notes on Resolutions of Alberta Branch, League of Indians' [no date, initialled 'SC']; both in NA, RG 10

12 'MEMORANDUM of Resolution passed by the Chiefs, Councillors and members of the various Bands of Indians assembled in council at our convention of the League of Indians of Canada, held at Poundmaker's Reserve in the Province of Saskatchewan near Cut Knife, on July 10th, 11th and 12th, in the year 1933'; NA, RG 10

13 For an in-depth study of the importance of this resolution see the book by the chief of this Stoney Band, John Snow, *These Mountains Are Our Sacred Places* (Toronto: Samuel Stevens 1977).

14 'Record and Minutes of Convention of the League of Indians of Canada, Western Branch, held at Enoch Reserve July 2nd, 3rd, and 4th, 1934,' NA, RG 10

15 'Records and Minutes of Convention of the League of Indians of Canada, Western Branch, held at Duffield, Alberta Indian Reserve, July 26th and 27th, 1935,' NA, RG 10

16 Ahenakew, *Voices of the Plains Cree*, 186–7

17 Ibid., 128–9

HAROLD CARDINAL

Hat in Hand: The Long Fight to Organize

The time is nine o'clock any morning in the past. The setting is the outer office of the Indian agent at any reserve headquarters. An elderly Indian enters. The clerk looks up from his desk where he is reading last night's paper. He knows the man, and he knows what he wants. The clerk spent an hour yesterday talking to the agent about the old man and the agent had been explicit about how he was to be handled. The Indian waits at the chest-high counter. He is dressed in worn moccasins, blue jeans long-since faded, pale and dirt streaked, an old plaid wool shirt and a black suitcoat. Carefully he takes off his high-crowned, broad-brimmed black hat and lays it on the counter, then picks it up and holds its uncertainly in one hand.

His family is hungry. There is little food in the old man's house. His welfare cheques don't cover all that is needed. He has talked to some of the young men on the reserve about an Indian organization which would help people like him, but the agent tells him that only the government can help him. Now the time for trapping has come again, and he would be working and off relief for a few months if his traps were favoured and the fur prices were good. But he needs a loan, some money for traps. All the Indians know that the agent is empowered to disburse funds for traps, but all the Indians also know that this is a discretionary power.

The clerk motions the Indian to one of the straightback chairs against the wall and returns to his paper. The old man waits to see the agent until a few minutes before five o'clock, when he is ushered into the agent's office by the clerk. The agent has his hat and coat on, ready to go home. He looks at his petitioner in distaste, as though it is the old man's fault he isn't already on his way home. The agent says, 'I hope you understand now that the government is your only friend.' The Indian says nothing, and the agent nods to the clerk. 'You don't have to hang around here all day,' he tells the Indian. 'You'll get your trap voucher.' The clerk motions to the Indian to come with him. In the clerk's office the necessary arrangements are made in a few minutes. The old man leaves the office at five-fifteen. He knows that he could have completed his business and left at nine-fifteen that morning. He knows that the agent kept him waiting just to show him who was boss, but he also knows there was no other way he could get the traps he needed to go to work again. The agent holds dictatorial powers over him and they both know it. That night when the young men come to talk to the old man about an Indian organization, he listens.

One of the most painful lessons that Indian peoples are learning is the need for organization through which they can articulate their needs and their alternatives to the Canadian society and its government. If the situation of the Canadian Indian is to be altered, even alleviated, the central issue is the degree of sophistication that we can develop in creating organizations which are Indian controlled and representative at the reserve level.

The work of creating stable and representative organizations has been one of the most difficult challenges faced by our people. It is a task that has always drawn the attention of Indian leaders in the past, and it is primarily because of their courage in attempting to meet this responsibility that things have changed for the better as much as they have.

The average Canadian is unaware of the work that has been done and is now being undertaken by Indian leaders, largely because the government has had access to the news media and the Indian people haven't. The government carefully has doled out truthful information about the actual conditions faced by our people, but it has buttressed this with mountains of propaganda celebrating their own noble efforts and programs aimed at curing such conditions. The ordinary Canadian gets the impression that the fault for the situation rests with the Indian, because he is either unable or unwilling to take the opportunities provided by the benevolent Canadian government.

During the past forty or fifty years there have been innumerable attempts to develop organizations through which the Indian people could express their desires and through which they could suggest plans for the future to the Canadian society and its government.

In the 1920s serious attempts were made by Indian leaders to organize their people so that action could be taken to alleviate their plight. These courageous leaders sought to act positively to solve their problems in spite of overwhelming difficulties. Many factors beyond their control worked against their success. The transportation system of their day made it almost impossible for them to gather people together from across the country. No matter where a meeting was held in this vast land, days of travel by horse and wagon were required of some of the delegates. Poor communications made it extremely difficult even to get word to all areas about a proposed meeting. There was no money to pay delegates' expenses. But perhaps the most difficult task was simply that of convincing the ordinary Indian that such an organization was worth the bother. Such social structures were alien to the Indian way. The older Indians, often those with influence in their communities, saw such organizations as a waste of time. The majority were illiterate and could not be convinced with printed material.

The Indian agent, dead set against any successful Indian organization, actively worked against the leaders of the day. To the autocratic agent who enjoyed making an Indian sit uselessly all day in an office, the development of Indian organizations was a threat to his power and potentially to his job. He had many weapons and never hesitated to use them. Sometimes he openly threatened to punish people who persisted in organizational efforts. More often he used more subtle weapons such as delaying relief payments or rations to show the Indians which way the wind was blowing.

If the Indian leaders of the day were too active, they were labelled dangerous rabble rousers and were subjected to harassment by the police. By spreading gossip or falsifying facts, the government officials often were able to undermine the leaders through their own people. It was made quite obvious to people on the reserve that it was not wise to talk to certain Indians. These first leaders were genuine heroes. They had guts and they needed them. They had no money; they had no access to skilled and trained advisers; they were harassed by the white government officials and the police and they were doubted by their own people. Yet they fought on.

The work of organizing was complicated by the fact that it had to be done entirely on a voluntary basis. The Indian leaders spearheading the work had no resources but their own; they had no money for consultants and no help in the documentation of facts necessary to present their case.

Under these conditions, growth of Indian organizations was slow and difficult. The wonder is that there was any growth at all. However, although progress was slow, a basis for later organizational work was laid through the diligence and sacrifice of the leaders.

From the 1930s to the mid-1940s, development work of the early leaders began to pay off in the growth of Indian groups on a provincial basis. During these times some of the church leaders had begun to take an active interest and were encouraging their Indian parishioners to participate in organization work. Except for the odd meeting of individuals, the provincial organizations developed at this time in parallel but isolated circumstances. At this stage the first attempts were made to develop a national Indian organization. Largely because of geographical isolation and the lack of money, this effort, while moderately successful, did not take firm hold. However, the exercise was not wasted. It did awaken provincial Indian organizations to the existence of other, similar groups in other provinces, and the potential that lay in combined forces was apparent to everyone.

In fact, the provincial movements of that time were significant in that they gradually began to penetrate the isolation of the Indian communities. They assisted and encouraged local people to begin looking beyond the boundaries of their own reserves and areas. Through this opening up, they began to discover common problems. This led naturally to cooperation in seeking solutions to their problems. The leaders from far-separated reserves were able to learn from each other. In the exchange of ideas the new leaders were able to discard approaches that failed to work elsewhere and settle on those that experience had proven successful. The first efforts between reserves to help each other grew from such provincial meetings. Intertribal communication posed a major difficultly, but the use of interpreters and the commonly understood English language solved this problem.

As meetings began to develop a consistent pattern, the issues faced by the Indian people began to be defined more clearly and alternatives were presented more forcefully. The Indians began to express their concern for their rights, especially those upon which they depended for their livelihood. Nearly all were knowledgeable about such rights as hunting, trapping, and fishing. The Indian people sincerely if mistakenly believed that their treaties or their rights were secure, for the federal government itself or the queen's representatives had made sacred promises. They united in opposition to increasing attempts to infringe upon or restrict those rights.

The leaders of the developing provincial organizations grew increasingly concerned with the lack of educational opportunities for their children, for they knew that this was to be one of the crucial problems. In education lay the future of their people.

Community leaders began to express their desire for some form of economic development. They realized that it was through this channel they would make the transition to a new environment, to a world that had changed without them.

The organizations began to take on more importance to the ordinary Indian. As they gained strength they were able slowly to lift the oppressive control of autocratic government representatives. No agent could with impunity keep an old man sitting idly all day in his outer office any more.

As the leaders examined their treaties and the rights that had been pledged on a government's honour, they began to discover the wide discrepancy that had developed between the treaties as they understood them and the perverted administration that was created to implement the terms of the treaties. They discovered for the first time that the legislation called the Indian Act and the administration they knew as the Indian Affairs Branch were in no way part of those treaties and that the spirit of the treaties was in fact never envisioned or contained in the legislation and administration created by the Canadian government.

With the postwar period came strengthening of the Indian organizations and increased pressure for more freedom from control by the Indian agents, for better educational opportunities, for more emphasis on resources to develop the communities, and, most important, insistence upon the honouring and implementation of the terms of the treaties and the settlement of outstanding land claims.

As a direct result of the increased activity of Indian organizations, the Canadian government began to shift its course of action. Largely because of pressure from Indian leaders, in 1951 the Canadian government made its first attempt to change the Indian Act, an act that was created without the involvement of Indians and legislation that had not been altered significantly for fifty years. Indian pressure forced the government into action in two vital fields, education and health. For the first time the government took a serious look at its educational responsibilities. The health services, which were nearly non-existent, were upgraded. The Indian organizations gained rapid strength until the mid-1950s. Their success came entirely from the determination and initiative shown by the Indian leaders. They got no help from the government.

A number of developments in the mid-1950s resulted in a setback for the growth of Indian organizations.

In western Canada, the agitation for better educational facilities and opportunities had exposed the terrible inadequacies of the church-operated residential schools. In an effort to better the situation the government, under continuing pressure from the Indian organizations, was seeking alternatives to the moribund system. The churches, which initially had supported the Indian organization, found themselves threatened in this area of vital concern – education. They promptly reversed their stand and withdrew their support of the Indian organizations. The Roman Catholic church went a step further than the other denominations. Not only did they pull back their support, they proceeded to set up something called the Catholic Indian League. Ostensibly this new organization was supposed to be concerned with the spiritual and temporal welfare of young Catholic Indians. While the CIL supposedly devoted its energies to the encouragement of religious vocations among the younger Indians, its obvious concern was the education of the Indian children through the residential school system. The wholly predictable effect of the organization of the Catholic Indian League by the clergy of that church was to divide the Indian people. By creating yet another organization the church weakened the base of the legitimate Indian organizations, attracting from them many

Catholic members. Furthermore, the church's action increased the possibility of division among the Indians on religious lines.

This divisive move of the Catholic church may have been made innocently, without conscious intent to weaken the Indian organizations. Divisions along religious lines might not have been foreseen. The fact remains that the creation of a church-controlled organization at such a time weakened the Indian movement that had been developing strength and set the stage for denominational quarrels. No one really could have expected much else from such a move.

About the same time the Indian Affairs Branch initiated a number of steps that further weakened the organizational growth budding in Indian communities.

From the beginning the heavy expenses incurred by travelling Indian delegates to organizational meetings had been a major problem. In some cases, reserve communities were able to sponsor their representatives at least partially with proceeds from small bingos or dances. Regulations from the Indian Affairs Branch now were invoked forbidding the use of band funds or monies belonging to a reserve as contributions to Indian organizations. Even today, such contributions are limited to twenty-five cents per capita. In order to use their own money to further the work of their own organizations the Indian leaders had to go to the agent on their reserve, present their case, and ask him for money for delegates to attend conferences. Usually the answer was 'The matter will be given consideration.' And, naturally, that was the end of it.

Since the organizations functioned on a voluntary basis, without any offices or financial base, the members were expected to attend the annual meetings at their own expense and to bring to those meetings the resolutions from their respective communities. Towards the middle and latter part of the 1950s, the Indian Affairs Branch initiated a series of conferences supposedly aimed at determining the needs of the Indian people. In the province of Alberta, these meetings initially were called agricultural conferences. The reserve communities were supposed to talk about their agricultural needs and to be informed of resources available for the development of their agricultural potential. Since these were official, department-sponsored meetings, the expenses of the delegates were picked up by the branch. For the first time a per diem allowance was paid the delegates. These so-called agricultural conferences covered every conceivable topic except, possibly, agriculture and thus directly affected the strength of the Indian organizations within the provinces. Gradually the government added to the agenda of these conferences, changing their titles to meet their expanded purposes. They became economic development conferences and community development conferences and, eventually, all-chiefs' conferences. Each conference hurt the real Indian organization conferences, because most of the key members of a reserve usually chose to attend the one where all expenses were paid.

In the mid-1960s the government tried another tack. It organized provincial and national Indian advisory councils. Supposedly these councils were to advise the federal government on matters pertaining to Indians. However, the government's idea of consultation was to present to the advisory council, as a fait accompli, whatever scheme it proposed to try on the Indians next. Using its most silver-tongued speakers, the Indian Affairs Department would do its best to persuade those Indians on the council that the scheme actually had been created by them. Indians elected or appointed to the advisory councils were in a very difficult position. The department informed them that they were assembled as individuals to advise the government on the feasibility of plans drawn up by the government for the Indians, but that they must keep in mind that their advice could be accepted or rejected, at the department's discretion. The government went to considerable pains to stress to the council members that they were present only as consultants and that they should not take it upon themselves to act as representatives or spokesmen for their people. Their expenses were paid for going to meetings convened by the department, but no money was provided at all for them to travel on their own reserve or on reserves in their area. They were not to be paid one cent to circulate among their own people and find out what was wanted and needed or how the various schemes advanced by the government might be received. These advisory members were not able to report anything to their own people on the reserves because, as the government quickly pointed out, they were not representing anyone and, moreover, they had no money for the necessary travelling. At the same time, the federal government propaganda mills ground out releases telling Parliament and the Canadian public that they were consulting representatives of the Indian people on every move they made.

For the most part, when the terms of advisory councils came to an end in 1968, the Indian people themselves insisted they be dropped. All they accomplished, for all their government doubletalk, was the embarrassment of many sincere but deceived Indian workers.

Unwittingly, some private organizations also contributed to the decline of the Indian organizations during the period from the mid-1950s to the mid-1960s. For example, the Indian-Eskimo Association, a white citizens' group based in Toronto which was set up to give support to the Indian people and symbolize the concern of the non-Indian Canadian, gradually began to assume the role of spokesman for Indians rather than a supporting role. Members of that association became more of a hindrance than a help to the development of strong Indian organizations, a goal to which they were committed, because they were acquiring funds sorely needed by the Indian groups from the two sources open to our people, the private sector and the public – that is, the government.

Curiously enough, another dissipating factor at this time was the Pearson government's war-on-poverty program. This should have helped Indian people, and there was a surge of hope that it might. But the government chose a method known as community development as its vehicle to carry to Indian homes the needed aid. Under community development, workers went to Indian reserves and communities expressly to stimulate and motivate the Indians to help themselves. When the Indian Affairs Department discovered to its horror that the Indians were ready and eager to go forward on just that basis, they quickly hopped off the community development bandwagon. Carried to its proper conclusion, the program very soon would have made the jobs of the government workers unnecessary. That was not a community development department officials were anxious to promote.

At the same time and as part of the war on poverty, a peculiar group called the Company of Young Canadians was formed. While the CYC was not created to serve any particular ethnic group in Canada, a large part of its program soon was aimed at native communities. These young, instant experts on things Indian were, like community development officers, supposed to motivate the people to use their own initiative. Instead, bumbling and stumbling through community after community with little or no sensitivity to the feelings of the people they were going to help if it killed them, these dedicated amateurs discouraged and weakened Indian organizations. Some of them wanted to run the whole show, didn't want the Indians to progress except under their guiding hand. Some gave the curious impression they had invented the Indian. Nearly all were hopelessly unprepared for their tasks. The net result of their eager (and quite truly most of these young people meant well) fumbling was to weaken the base through which the Indian could express his needs and through which he had the best opportunity to press his case.

Now many of the organizational troubles and problems of the past four decades have been recognized and overcome. Strong provincial leaders are emerging and behind them, strong provincial organizations. A National Indian Brotherhood has been set up by and for Indians, with an office in Ottawa from which we can present our case for the first time on a national basis. We need more leaders and we need more leadership training, but we are not worried. The land is full of bright, eager young Indians who are better educated than their fathers, more aware of the problems and more determined to push through their own solutions.

More and more we can be confident that our future will rest in qualified but brown hands and that no gentle old man will have to sit, hat in hand, all day in any office at the whim of a petty bureaucrat.

NOTE

This article is from *The Unjust Society: The Tragedy of Canada's Indians*. Edmonton: Hurtig 1969. Reprinted with permission.

CONTEMPORARY DISPUTES

J.R. MILLER

Aboriginal Rights, Land Claims, and the Struggle to Survive

The social and economic conditions in which natives in Canada live – or, more accurately, exist – is a national disgrace. Indian children are more likely than the general population to be born outside a stable nuclear family, are far less likely to complete enough schooling to obtain a job and become self-sustaining, are much more highly represented in the figures of unemployed and incarcerated people than the rest of the population, and have shorter life expectancy than most others in the country. What is worse is the fact that these conditions have existed for close to a century and have been known by governments and churches to exist for most of that time. Ottawa and the missionaries have tried unsuccessfully to impose their programs of economic development on Indians, Métis, and Inuit.

In the last few decades natives have begun to assert themselves about how economic development should take place. They have forced governments to listen to them in large part because economic development since the end of the Second World War has focused on regions that are occupied by native groups, areas that often were not covered by the treaties of the nineteenth and early twentieth centuries. Because Euro-Canadian entrepreneurs and governments found that they wanted access to the resources in Indian and Inuit country, and because natives were insistent that they control change in their regions, development has emerged as a major point of confrontation. Disputes over economic development, as much as the political battles since 1969, have contributed to the natives' emergence from their age of 'irrelevance.'

It was natives' good fortune to find themselves occupying lands containing valuable resources as the North American economy came alive during the Second World War and expanded dramatically in the resource boom of the 1950s and 1960s. Their location was also their misfortune in that period. Being situated atop or adjacent to increasingly valuable resources was beneficial because it provided an opportunity to enrich themselves and create jobs. It was unfortunate in the early period because their rights were often ignored and their demands refused, and in later years because economic development often meant the disruption and destruction of their traditional economy and way of life.

The expansion of the economy in the 1940s was focused on energy and base minerals. To a considerable extent these resources were found in areas controlled by Indians, whether it was the Alberta Indians whose lands were in the area where Leduc #1 gushed to life in 1947, or more northerly Indians who found themselves in the path of the Alaskan Highway that the U.S. Army Corps of Engineers constructed during the Second World War. The pattern persisted after the coming of peace. The Woodland Cree discovered that their district near Lake Athabasca in Saskatchewan contained valuable deposits of uranium that Eldorado Nuclear began to develop in the early 1950s. Later Indians in neighbouring Manitoba found that projects, such as the Churchill Forests Industry complex or new hydroelectricity developments on northern rivers, provided both opportunities for employment and disruption of the habitat of the animals and fish on which they had previously depended. Much the same pattern held true in the resource-rich territories in Labrador, northern Quebec and Ontario, the northern interior of British Columbia, and the Northwest Territories. The wartime and postwar boom that was based on new sources of energy, minerals, and forest products brought rapid development to the doorstep of many Indian, Métis, and Inuit people who hitherto had resided in economically marginal lands beyond the awareness of most of the southern population.

In the early years of this boom – and in some cases for many years – the tendency of governments and developers was to ignore the interests of the native peoples. To some extent this high-handed approach to development of resources in Indian territory could be explained by the fact that the written portion of Canada's constitution, the British North America Act, gave jurisdiction over resources to the provinces. The provinces were little inclined to pay much heed to 'Indians and lands reserved for Indians,' which was an area of federal responsibility, as they set about authorizing the entrepreneurs to go after the new riches. In cases such as the Hobbema band in the Edmonton area, Indians were able to profit from the development by virtue of general rights under existing legislation, in this case provincial provisions for compensating those who held lands in which oil was found. But such materially successful bands were the minority, and even they often discovered that the problems of wealth, though different from those of poverty, were no less disturbing.

Most of Canada's native peoples who were in the path of development found that they were ignored in the process of going after the resources and left out of the division of the proceeds of their sale. Aside from some relatively low-paid jobs in unskilled categories, the Cree of north-central Saskatchewan benefited little from Eldorado's Beaver Lodge mine. Still, they were luckier than the Lubicon band of central Alberta, who were not only ignored but seriously threatened by energy developments on lands that traditionally had been theirs. Though the Lubicon had much earlier been promised a reserve, the commitment was not honoured. And when an oil company began to disrupt their territories in the 1980s, their protests were ignored by a provincial government obsessed with economic development. The plight of the Lubicon attracted the attention of Canadian and international church groups, which charged that corporate and government insensitivity during development had had 'genocidal consequences' in Alberta.[1] In British Columbia, down to and during the 1980s, similar provincial refusal to consult the Indian peoples about logging of lands that they consider theirs has led to confrontations.[2] In general, BC Indians did not prosper from the resource boom of the 1950s and 1960s as wage workers, either.[3]

Even worse were some of the government-supported programs of economic development by Indians, or adjustment to economic development by others. A depressingly large number of Indian bands found themselves moved at the whim of bureaucrats who thought that their presence impeded exploitation of a resource, as in the case of those at South Indian Lake in Manitoba who stood in the way of a hydro project, or who were deemed to require a move to another location in order to become self-sufficient. The Ojibwa of Grassy Narrows in northwestern Ontario were removed in 1964 to a new reserve where they found it very hard to make a living, and then six years later learned that the English-Wabigoon River system from which they took water and fish was polluted with mercury from industrial establishments in nearby Dryden. The closure of the waterway for fishing destroyed the band's fragile economic base, and social problems soon followed economic troubles in a depressing cascade of misery.[4] Similar horror stories from the postwar period, though fortunately not all featuring medical problems such as mercury poisoning, could be multiplied almost endlessly.[5] Whatever the type of development, the impact of socio-economic change during the thirty-year boom that followed the Great Depression was the same: the native peoples did not benefit to any great extent from expansion.

Gradually, as natives organized themselves into more effective provincial and national political bodies, they began to assert themselves to resist development or to control the way in which it occurred and the pace at which it wrought its effects. The prime examples of this new assertiveness have been the James Bay and Mackenzie Valley projects of the 1970s.

The story of the James Bay hydro project began with the election in 1970 of a Quebec Liberal government headed by Robert Bourassa. The new premier had campaigned on a platform that promised the creation of 100,000 jobs, and the key to the realization of his dream was a gargantuan project to harness the electricity potential of northern rivers. Unfortunately, Bourassa's cabinet gave no thought to the rights and interests of the approximately 10,000 Inuit and Cree who lived in the region and who hunted and fished for their livelihood. The government established a James Bay Corporation to carry out the development and then sat back to await the political benefits.

What they got instead, at least in the short run, was one of the first effective legal actions by a native group against southern developers of their homeland. Late in 1972 a coalition of Indians and Inuit from northern Quebec sought an injunction against construction of dams and generating stations until the courts could establish what rights the indigenous inhabitants had in the lands. Their case pointed out that land surrender treaties had never been signed in northern Quebec, and that whatever their rights to the territories were before the white man came were undiminished. The case lasted more than six months and heard the testimony of more than 150 witnesses. About eleven months after the native groups initiated the case, the judge issued an order to the various companies involved 'to immediately cease, desist and refrain from carrying out works, operations, and projects in the territory' and 'to cease, desist and refrain from interfering in any way with petitioners' rights, from trespassing in the said territory and from causing damage to the environment and the natural resources of the said territory.'[6] Appeals got the order to stop work lifted, but they did not remove the notion of native rights to the land that had underlain the original court order.

Eventually, government, companies, and the native peoples decided that a negotiated settlement would be preferable to more litigation. The judgment confounded developers and government, and made the Bourassa cabinet anxious to negotiate a settlement that would permit work to continue legally. For their part the native groups, unsure of the final outcome of a case based on notions of aboriginal title, also concluded that negotiations would be preferable to further litigation. The result was a massive agreement signed late in 1975 by which the Inuit and Cree surrendered their rights and claims to 400,000 square miles of northern Quebec in return for a commitment from the two senior levels of government to pay them over ten years $150 million in grants and royalties from the electricity that was to be generated, one-quarter of the royalties the province would receive for the next fifty years, control of those sites they occupied that would not be flooded, and hunting and fishing rights. Chief Billy Diamond described it as a 'big victory' when the deal was announced.[7] The general public reacted as though the native peoples of northern Quebec had received an incredible windfall. But there was much less attention paid years later when a federal study showed that the natives of James Bay were living in poverty and with inadequate educational, medical, and social services.[8] The James Bay Agreement turned out not to be an antidote to the poisonous effects of development. However, it did constitute an important precedent – a negotiated settlement to litigation that aimed at stopping development by appeal to natives' claims to the land – that would affect later events.

Three other northern incidents helped to establish the notion that native peoples who had not entered treaty had an aboriginal title that could not lightly be ignored. In 1973 the Supreme Court of Canada ruled on an argument by the Nishga of the Nass Valley, represented by lawyer Thomas Berger, that they had aboriginal title to their lands and that they could not be dispossessed of it unilaterally by legislative action. The argument fell, but in the process an important concept was established. Although the court rejected the main argument, most of the judges acknowledged that aboriginal title existed in law. A minority of them even held that the Nishga's aboriginal title had not been extinguished. A few years later another piece of litigation known as the Baker Lake case advanced the process of establishing and defining aboriginal title. The Inuit of the Hamlet of Baker Lake in the Northwest Territories (NWT) sought a prohibition on economic development on their traditional lands in order to protect their hunting economy. In considering the case the court laid down four criteria for establishing the validity of aboriginal title: first, that they (the Indians or Inuit) and their ancestors were members of an organized society; second, that this organized society occupied the specific territory over which they claimed aboriginal title; third, that the occupation was to the exclusion of other organized societies; and, finally, that the occupation was an established fact at the time sovereignty was asserted by England. The judge concluded that these criteria had been satisfied, and he agreed that the native peoples had an aboriginal title that gave them an interest in the lands for hunting and fishing, though he would not block other forms of economic development as the petitioners had asked.[9]

A political dimension was added to these legal methods by which native peoples in Canada in the 1970s began to protect their interest in their lands by two northern pipeline inquiries. In 1977 Thomas Berger, then a judge of the BC Supreme Court sitting as a federal commissioner, reported on the impact of a proposed pipeline up the Mackenzie Valley, and in the same year Ken Lysyk (then a law professor and now a judge of the BC Supreme Court) conducted an inquiry into the likely effect of an Alaskan pipeline on the southern Yukon. Both men warned against rapid development that would damage native economies and ways of life. Lysyk argued that four years would be necessary for the natives to prepare for the impact of the construction of an Alaskan pipeline, while Berger suggested that 'a period of ten years will be required in the Mackenzie Valley and Western Arctic to settle native claims, and to establish the new institutions and new programs that a settlement will entail. No pipeline should be built until these things have been achieved.'[10]

Perhaps more important than the conclusions of these investigations was the process of making the inquiries. Both commissioners spent a long time listening to the native peoples' expectations and fears about their lands and proposed development. Berger's inquiry in particular attracted a great deal of attention, and the commissioner quite deliberately extended his hearings to the south to bring northerners' views to the attention of the southern Canadians who had the political influence to affect government decisions in the sparsely populated north. Southerners were exposed to poignant statements of the natives' fear of the changes that might overwhelm them. 'Steel kills,' testified Alfred Nahanni. 'With more steel products coming in we will eventually die because we will be overpowered by something that doesn't feel the cold.'[11] Ultimately, it was a downturn in the demand for energy that accounted for the failure to proceed with northern developments. But the work of judges Lysyk and Berger, and the dozens of northerners who testified before them, helped to make rapid development of the north over the protests of its inhabitants politically unacceptable in the 1970s and early 1980s.

These new political factors, coming on top of the creative legal aspects of the Nishga and Baker Lake cases, firmly established during the 1970s that something called aboriginal title existed and had to be considered. The clearest proof that these developments had their political impact was found in the response of the federal government to the Nishga case in 1973. This was a government headed by Pierre Trudeau, a man who had claimed that political communities could not make policy on the basis of historical might-have-beens, who had argued for ignoring past wrongs in the search for a just program in the present, and who could not understand how a liberal democratic society such as he championed could have a treaty with one of its constituent elements. The Nishga case, coming fairly soon after the political firestorm over the white paper, shook the Trudeau government's confident belief in the ultimate triumph of individualism. In mid-1973 Trudeau's minister of Indian affairs and northern development, Jean Chrétien, said that the government would now deal with Indian claims to land in areas that had not been surrendered by treaties. The government was prepared to consider two types of land claims: comprehensive claims that were based on aboriginal title, and specific claims that were allegations that the government had not lived up to promises it had made, usually in treaties. Ottawa would also fund research by native bodies to support their claim cases, and the next year it set up an Office of Native Claims (ONC) with responsibility to assess the validity of native claims and to advise the Department of Indian Affairs and Northern Development (DIAND) on how to settle them.

A new procedure for handling claims was developed in the 1970s. If the Office of Native Claims thought that a claim was valid, and if DIAND decided that a negotiated settlement of the claim was in order, then officials from the ONC would participate in a government team that attempted to negotiate a settlement. Following a negotiated settlement of a native claim, the ONC would help with the implementation of, and monitor compliance with, the agreement.[12] In other words, the Trudeau government in 1973 and 1974 initiated an important new method of dealing with claims from status Indians, Inuit, Métis, and non-status Indians. This shift marked a definite retreat by Trudeau and a significant advance for aboriginal peoples.

Then ensued a protracted period of researching, presenting, and negotiating settlement of claims. The impetus that was given to this process by the events of the 1970s was strengthened by the native groups' frustrations over the constitution-making process of the period from 1977 to 1981. Failure to reach agreement in the later constitutional talks that were supposed to determine what 'existing aboriginal and treaty rights' were simply reinforced the tendency among some native groups to emphasize the claims process along with, or instead of, the drive to establish native self-government through political means. The two categories – self-government and claims – intersect because natives have long recognized that without an economic base in the ownership of extensive territories, political control of their own affairs is meaningless. In the 1980s the search for political sovereignty and drive for economic self-sufficiency marched together behind the banners of aboriginal title and land claims.

Perhaps the most difficult thing for non-natives to understand is the notion of aboriginal title that underlies both land claims and the contention that native peoples have the right to govern themselves. What is aboriginal title, and how does it relate to sovereignty? Aboriginal title is simply the right to lands that an indigenous people has by virtue of its occupation of an area 'from time immemorial.' It is a notion that Indians and other natives have always held to, though they did not always articulate it; but a notion that until recently Euro-Canadian society did not recognize or respect. European nations usually maintained that discovery or intensive use in agriculture gave them a superior right over indigenous peoples to occupancy and use of the land. (In 1988 an Australian Aborigine mocked these notions by landing at

Dover and claiming Britain for the first people of Australia.) This presumption was taken to its extreme in the Papacy's division of the western hemisphere between Spain and Portugal early in the era of Europe's expansion, without reference to the interests of either the native peoples or of other Catholic powers such as France.

But the French, while they challenged the pope's decision and the Iberian states' claim to the hemisphere, did not assert title to land and political sovereignty over the indigenous peoples of the regions with whom they came into contact. France set about the exploration and economic utilization of the eastern half of North America without much concern for pope or other European powers. But of necessity her explorers had to behave in a more circumspect manner in their relations with indigenous peoples, whatever Christian theorists may have held about the legitimacy of ignoring the rights of natives. For the most part, Frenchmen's intensive use of land was restricted to areas that the Iroquoians and Algonquians had vacated, with the result that their penetration of the continent did not threaten any aboriginal interest. French claims to title to New France were assertions made, not in the face of aboriginal title, but to forestall claims by other European powers. French pretensions to political sovereignty over the regions they explored and utilized were legal fictions based on decaying concepts of divine right kingship; they were not assented to, much less accepted by, the Indian peoples with whom the French traded and warred. The French period did not weaken aboriginal title to the land or the indigenous peoples' powers of self-government.[13]

The coming of British rule in the eighteenth century both strengthened and threatened aboriginal title and Indian sovereignty. The Royal Proclamation of 1763 established the concepts of Indian territory, Indian title, and the necessity of newcomers to arrange the extinguishment of that title by direct negotiations with the crown. Although the Royal Proclamation did not apply everywhere in present-day Canada – its application was technically only to the narrow parallelogram along the St Lawrence that constituted the Province of Quebec from 1763 to 1774 – it has had an important historical influence throughout all of Canada. By and large, as already noted, colonial and then dominion governments operated on the assumption that there was an obligation to negotiate for title to land in their dealings with Indians in Ontario, the prairies, and parts of northern Canada. While governments might have acted as though they could limit Indian self-government in various Gradual Civilizing Acts and Indian Acts, they, with the exception of colonial British Columbia, did not pretend that they could simply take territory without prior negotiations with the first occupiers.

This tradition has had the effect of continuing the influence of the Proclamation concept into post-Confederation Canada. An important step in this process was the legal decision in 1888 in the St Catharine's Milling Case. In that important ruling the Judicial Committee of the Privy Council held that there was such a thing as aboriginal title. Under the Proclamation, the decision held, Indians enjoyed a 'personal and usufructuary right, dependent upon the good will of the Sovereign.'[14] This was a minimal version of what aboriginal title meant. In the first place, a usufructuary right is merely the right to *use* something that someone else *owns*. Furthermore, the Judicial Committee's decision that even this diminished title was 'dependent upon the good will of the Sovereign' meant that the crown – and, by extension, all legislative bodies of which the crown was a part – could extinguish this title unilaterally. The Supreme Court judges who held in the Nishga case in 1973 that there was such a thing as aboriginal title but still concluded that the Nishga had no case did so largely because the BC legislature was held to have nullified the Indians' title by statute. But, as already noted, the political cost of holding to this legalistic view after granting the important point that aboriginal title existed in law was simply too great for federal governments to pay. After this decision, consonant with the Proclamation and in expansion of the St Catharine's Milling case definition of aboriginal title, the government of Canada conceded that it recognized aboriginal title. This concession was embodied, belatedly, in the 1982 Constitution Act's confirmation of 'existing aboriginal and treaty rights.'

From this important base of aboriginal title, important claims flow. In those regions of Canada where title was not extinguished, native groups argue that the land is theirs and cannot be used by anyone else without their agreement. This was the basis of the case put forward early in the 1970s by the Cree and Inuit of northern Quebec to halt the development of the James Bay project until their agreement was acquired by negotiation. It also underlay the cases of the Inuit and of the Dene Nation, as the Indian and Métis of the western Northwest Territories called themselves, in the far north who made similar arguments to the Lysyk and Berger pipeline inquiries. In the 1980s it continues to serve as the foundation of northern native claims to control their land.

Dene and Inuit maintain that southerners cannot intrude on their territories for economic development without securing the agreement of the indigenous peoples. And they also argue that they have the right to determine how their northern homeland will be governed. The Dene Declaration, a statement by the native peoples of the Territories issued in 1975, makes the point:

> We the Dene of the N.W.T. insist on the right to be regarded by ourselves and the world as a nation.
>
> ...

> What we seek then is independence and self-determination within the country of Canada. This is what we mean when we call for a just land settlement for the Dene Nation.[15]

The case for Dene control of their own political institutions is based on the argument that they were self-governing peoples before the white population arrived, that they did not sign any treaties that required recognition of Canadian sovereignty, that they were never conquered, and that, therefore, they are still sovereign and hold title to their lands.

Finally, the same arguments based on aboriginal title are at the heart of the comprehensive land claims of British Columbia's Indians. With a few exceptions, Indian groups in the Pacific province did not enter treaty with either colonial or dominion governments for title to land. Accordingly, BC Indians argue today as they have for a century that most of British Columbia is still Indian country. Here, as in most of the other cases mentioned above, solution of these claims will most likely come by negotiation rather than litigation. Neither side can afford to take the chance of losing in the courts; neither side wants to incur the costs of resolution by litigation. To date only one comprehensive land claim, that of the Inuvialuit of the western Arctic, has been settled.[16]

The Métis make a similar argument, though there are some significant differences in the foundation of their case. It is clearly a logical impossibility that the Métis argument can be one based solely on aboriginal rights if aboriginal is equated, as is usually the case, with existence and occupancy 'since time immemorial.' Even a sympathetic study of the Métis argues, obviously with tongue partly in cheek, that the mixed-blood people was not created until 'Nine months after the first White man set foot in Canada.'[17] So far as strict logic is concerned, the Métis cannot be an aboriginal people holding aboriginal title for the simple reason that they have not existed 'since time immemorial.' But history is not always logical. Since at least 1870 the mixed-blood population of Manitoba and the prairies have had a basis for claims to aboriginal status, and since 1982 the Métis and non-status Indians throughout Canada have enjoyed an even stronger one. In 1870 the Manitoba Act conferred on the mixed-blood populations of Red River a claim to land based on their share of Indian blood.[18] And the agreement on aboriginal rights in the 1982 constitution explicitly included the Métis and non-status Indians. Since then these groups have participated in first ministers' constitutional talks along with Indians and Inuit. And in the 1980s the Métis of Manitoba have asserted an extensive land claim based on the unfulfilled provisions for land grants to the offspring of mixed-blood parents under the Manitoba Act of 1870. The land claim of the Manitoba Métis is in part a comprehensive claim in that it is based on their status as an aboriginal people, and in part a specific claim based on allegations that the promises of 1870 were not carried out.

Specific claims are more limited than comprehensive land claims, and not all specific claims deal directly with land matters. Specific claims are demands for compensation or restitution based upon an allegation that a promise, usually a treaty undertaking, was not fulfilled. The cases in this category that are coming forward usually concern bands that never received any, or all, of the lands that they were promised during negotiations. In a sense, the claim of the Lubicon Indians of Alberta that was referred to earlier is such a specific claim. So far almost 300 specific claims have been preferred, but only a few have been resolved by negotiation, and they have affected small groups and limited tracts of land. Both sides are being cautious in these negotiations. The Indians recognize that any settlement must stand for a long time, and governments are aware that there are often political recriminations from white populations residing in areas where Indian reserves are expanded as a result of settling a specific land claim. Attempts in Saskatchewan to resolve some specific claims during the life of the Blakeney government (1971–82) were slowed or stopped by strong non-Indian opposition to seeing crown lands or community pastures handed over to bands. In some cases, the non-Indian neighbours were utilizing the lands that were proposed for settlement of the claims; in others they simply opposed the growth of Indian reserves. A particularly thorny instance occurred in the city of Prince Albert, where a federal-provincial proposal to grant a band a reserve within the city limits evoked ferocious opposition from the municipal council. The Prince Albert case was merely the worst example of a general disenchantment and opposition among the non-Indian population to the resolution of specific claims.

Other claims resemble specific land claims in that they are based on allegations that the government has not carried out its promises. Sometimes these are based on literal readings; other times on loose constructions of the language of the treaties. An instance of the latter was the argument of Indians in Treaty 6 that the promise of 'a medicine chest' in their treaty should be interpreted in the late twentieth century as embracing free medical care. The courts have not been persuaded to extend the meaning of Treaty 6 in this way. Claims demanding enforcement of literal promises include those that refer to the commitments in some of the numbered treaties to provide implements, ammunition, and twine. A number of Indian bands have extensive claims based on the federal government's failure to provide twine for nets and ammunition for hunting, the value of these supplies being greatly increased thanks to the magic of compound interest. Thus far claims of this nature have generally proved unsuccessful.

The final type of contemporary claim, one example of which was settled in 1985, flows not directly from aboriginal status or treaty promises, but from the special relationship in which Indians stand to the federal government by virtue of the Indian Act. The obverse of government's persistent treatment of Indians as wards, or legal minors, is the notion that Ottawa stands in a special trust relationship to Indians whose affairs it controls. From a legal standpoint, then, the role of the Department of Indian Affairs in relation to Indians is like that of a trustee administering the affairs of a minor. For more than a century Indians suffered the negative effects of this relationship: their lives were directed and their property controlled by others. But in 1985 the courts confirmed that there were certain protections inherent in this unequal relationship.

The 1985 Supreme Court of Canada decision in the Musqueam case confirmed that Ottawa had a legal obligation to discharge its trust responsibilities in a manner that advanced the interests and protected the rights of its 'wards.' The litigation stemmed from an 1958 lease that the department had negotiated on behalf of the Musqueam band with a Vancouver golf club for 160 acres of land. The lease, which was initially for fifteen years, allowed the golf club to extend it in instalments up to another seventy-five years, while limiting the increases in rent that the band could get on renewal. When band officers finally were able to see the lease some twelve years after it came into effect, they concluded that they had been misled and their interests had been abandoned by the government. The terms had not been reported accurately to them, and the rental had fallen far below the market value of the land. They took their case to court, where they were awarded ten million dollars. On appeal, the Supreme Court upheld the financial award and stated anew the notion that DIAND had a trustee relationship. Where Indian Affairs failed to discharge the duties of that role properly, it was liable for the damages those in its trust incurred.[19]

The interpretation that the Musqueam case confirmed in 1985 is a fruitful source of support for Indian claims. The concept of trust obligation on the part of the government provides those Indian bands who were deprived of their reserve lands during the western boom of the early twentieth century with an avenue for redress. If, as is often the case, they can demonstrate that the Indian Affairs officials did not properly inform their ancestors who were induced to agree to sales or leases at derisory rates, or if they can demonstrate that their band was not consulted at all, they have a good base from which to argue that the federal government is liable for the damages the band has incurred as a consequence of the unprofitable lease or fraudulent sale.

There has already been one major settlement of such a case for the White Bear reserve of southeastern Saskatchewan. In 1901 over two hundred Assiniboine were moved off their reserves by mendacious department officials and forced to move onto a Cree reserve, known as the White Bear. In 1984 Ottawa was persuaded that the dispossession of the Assiniboine had been fraudulent, and a commitment was made by the short-lived Turner government to compensate them for their losses. In 1986 land was transferred to them. Some idea of the potential for other large-scale settlements can be garnered from the fact that the Federation of Saskatchewan Indian Nations estimates that in that province alone Indians were defrauded of 416,000 acres of reserve land before the First World War.[20] There is every reason to believe that other provinces, particularly on the prairies, have similar situations.

All these claims have added up to a vast and troubled area that has absorbed Indian and federal government efforts, not to mention tens of millions of dollars of Canadian taxpayers' money, for decades. Specific claims concerning unallotted reserves, or missing twine, or annual payments continue to mount. Claims based on Ottawa's perversion of the trust relationship seem likely to increase dramatically in the wake of the Musqueam decision. But the potentially most intractable of the claims are those that fall under the heading of comprehensive claims, which are, in reality, latter-day attempts to negotiate treaties where they do not exist. The argument that various native groups have claims to extensive lands by virtue of unextinguished aboriginal title is potentially revolutionary. It is revolutionary in its scope alone, for such claims could embrace most of British Columbia, the Yukon, and the Northwest Territories. One, by the Golden Lake Algonkin band in Ontario, embraces Parliament Hill and the Petawawa armed forces base.[21] The argument on which comprehensive claims are based is also dramatic in another sense. Claims based on aboriginal rights are not only about land; they are also connected to native claims to unsurrendered political sovereignty. These contentions that Indians, Inuit, and Métis have a right to establish their own order of government within Canada are unsettling to many Canadians because they are based on assumptions about political organization that many Canadians find uncongenial and perhaps unacceptable.[22] The prospect for Indian-white relations over claims seems troubled, and the confrontation over the entwined issues of comprehensive land claims and native efforts to establish their own order of government seems likely to be protracted and painful.

For most native peoples, however, the question of what will become of comprehensive land claims and arguments over native political sovereignty must seem like idle preoccupations. For many bands the problems of maintaining or restoring an economy that will sustain them and provide a release from the stultifying welfare culture in which two-thirds of them find themselves are the most pressing concerns. Native leaders have argued that there is no such thing as a purely economic issue, that land claims and sovereignty are essential to end natives' economic problems once and for all by giving them the resources and political control to make use of them as they see fit. For a time it seemed as though those arguments had persuaded the native communities. The fact that political leaders could carry their followers with them was the result in part of the successes they won through united action and in part the side-effect of an improving economy. But the 1980s have been must less buoyant.

Interesting case studies of the economic problems Indians are facing in the harder times of the 1980s can be found in Saskatchewan. The Federation of Saskatchewan Indians, now the Federation of Saskatchewan Indian Nations (FSIN), was one of the most aggressive Indian organizations in pressing the political case and trying to advance the economic lot of Indians by their own actions. In the 1970s the FSIN established its own holding company, Sinco, to control a series of service companies based principally in the resource sector. These companies were to provide employment for Indians and to begin the process of lifting Saskatchewan's Indians out of the economic morass. After the collapse of the western resource economy in the recession of 1982, the constituent companies in Sinco began falling one by one. By 1986 only Sinco's trucking company was still in operation. Another example of attempted economic development based on the resource economy and increasing Indian political power was a technical training institute on the Thunder Child reserve in west-central Saskatchewan in the early 1980s. It was designed to train skilled Indian workers for high-paying jobs in the oil and gas industry that was booming in neighbouring Alberta. By the time the school was ready to produce its first graduates in 1986, there were no jobs to be had in the prostrate energy industry.

As these two incidents from recent western history illustrate, the economic advancement of Indian and native groups depends not just on securing a land base and political control of their own affairs. As long as most natives are located in what is sometimes called the 'Mid-Canada Corridor,' a northern region in which resource extraction and processing constitute almost the entire economy, natives also need the return of prosperity to resource industries in order to begin the long march from poverty to comfort. Just as Canada's Indians began to move out of 'irrelevance' by a combination of political assertiveness and the increase in value of the resources on which they found themselves located, a sharp economic downturn threatened to knock them back.

It was bitterly ironic that aboriginal peoples around the world found themselves in almost exactly the same position in the 1980s. The leaders of Canada's native communities began to reach out to others in similar circumstances to form a Fourth World alliance in the 1970s. Canada's Indians, Métis, and Inuit wanted to join the Saami of Scandinavia, the Maori of New Zealand, and the Melanesians and Polynesians of south Pacific states in a vast anti-imperial coalition of colonized peoples. Thanks to the recession of 1982 they also joined them in renewed poverty. Fijians saw their income from sugar collapse and Maoris participated in New Zealand's agricultural recession at the same time as lucrative jobs in the Alberta oilfields disappeared.

NOTES

This article is from *Skyscrapers Hide the Heavens: A History of Indian-White Relations in Canada*. Toronto: University of Toronto Press 1989. Reprinted with permission.

1 J. Ryan, 'Struggle for Survival: The Lubicon Cree Community Fight the Multinationals' (unpublished paper, ACSANZ '86, biennial conference of the Association for Canadian Studies in Australia and New Zealand, Griffith University, Australia, May 1986). I am indebted to Professor Ryan for providing me with a copy of her paper.
2 D. Purich, *Our Land: Native Rights in Canada* (Toronto: Lorimer 1986), 38
3 R. Knight, *Indians at Work: An Informal History of Native Indian Labour in British Columbia 1858–1930* (Vancouver: New Star Books 1978), epilogue, 201
4 A.M. Shkilnyk, *A Poison Stronger Than Love: The Destruction of an Ojibwa Community* (New Haven: Yale University Press 1985)
5 For example, P. Driben and R.S. Trudeau, *When Freedom Is Lost: The Dark Side of the Relationship between Government and the Fort Hope Band* (Toronto: University of Toronto Press 1983)
6 Quoted in B. Richardson, *Strangers Devour the Land: A Chronicle of the Assault upon the Last Coherent Hunting Culture in North America, the Cree Indians of Quebec, and Their Vast Primeval Homelands* (New York: Knopf 1975), 296
7 Quoted ibid., 319
8 Purich, *Our Land*, 56–7
9 Ibid., 188, 57
10 T.R. Berger, *Northern Frontier/Northern Homeland: The Report of the Mackenzie Valley Pipeline Inquiry*, 2 vols. (Ottawa: Minister of Supply and Services 1977), I, xxiv–xxv
11 M. O'Malley, *The Past and Future Land: An Account of the Berger Inquiry into the Mackenzie Valley Pipeline* (Toronto: Peter Martin Associates 1976), 140

12 J.R. Ponting and R. Gibbins, *Out of Irrelevance: A Socio-Political Introduction to Indian Affairs in Canada* (Toronto: Butterworths 1980), 101–2
13 C.J. Jaenen, 'French Sovereignty and Native Nationhood during the French Regime,' *Native Studies Review* 2 (1) (1986): 83–113
14 Quoted in B.W. Morse, ed., *Aboriginal Peoples and the Law: Indian, Metis and Inuit Rights in Canada* (Ottawa: Carleton University Press 1985), 97
15 The Dene Declaration (1975), reprinted in Ponting and Gibbins, *Out of Irrelevance*, 351–2. See also M. Watkins, 'Dene Nationalism,' *Canadian Review of Studies in Nationalism* 8 (1) (spring 1981): 101–13
16 Purich, *Our Land*, 60. In 1973 the Temagami Indians of northeast Ontario got a caution placed on all crown land in 110 townships (an area larger than PEI) using the argument that they had not been included in the Robinson Treaties. The case has not yet been resolved at the highest level. See B.W. Hodgins, *Aboriginal Rights in Canada: Historical Perspectives on Recent Developments and the Implications for Australia*, Macquarrie University Public Lecture (np: Macquarrie University Printery 1985), 10–11. I am indebted to Professor Hodgins for supplying me with a copy of his lecture. Finally, in 1988 the Cree of Lubicon Lake, after erecting a blockade of roads during the federal election campaign, reached agreement in principle for the settlement of their forty-eight-year-old claim to a reserve.
17 D.B. Sealey and A.S. Lussier, *The Métis: Canada's Forgotten People* (Winnipeg: Pemmican Publications 1975), 1
18 See J.R. Miller, *Skyscrapers Hide the Heavens: A History of Indian-White Relations in Canada* (Toronto: University of Toronto Press 1989), 159.
19 Purich, *Our Land*, 58–9
20 Ibid., 151–2
21 Saskatoon *Star-Phoenix*, 31 Aug. 1988
22 Miller, *Skyscrapers*, 236–7

DONALD PURICH

The Future of Native Rights

Fifteen years hence, as one drives down the road, the sign might read:

> WELCOME TO THE NATION OF OUR LAND. You are now entering the Our Land Indian Reserve governed by the Our Land Nation. You are subject to the laws and jurisdiction of the Our Land Nation. The Our Land Nation is part of the Wapati Regional Indian Government.

Driving into the reserve, one sees Ms Lonehunter working in her garden. She has just sent her children, Michael and Sarah, to Our Land Primary School, run by the Wapati Indian School Board (which operates as an independent commission of the Wapati government). Ms Lonehunter waves to Constable Squirrel, who drives by in a police car bearing the words 'Wapati Police, a division of the Wapati Regional Indian Government.' Ms Lonehunter is hoping that today's band council meeting will approve the extension of water and sewer services to her house. (Purely local matters, such as water and sewer hook-ups, are handled at the reserve level by the reserve council rather than by the regional government.)

Our Land is an Indian Reserve of 400 square kilometres; it has a population of 1200 band members. The nation's constitution states that everyone who is a descendant of the Our Land tribe and is accepted by the community is a citizen (there are rules whereby any member of the community can complain to a tribal judge about someone else's status as an Our Lander, and the judge will hear both sides and decide.)

Several years ago the Our Land nation started its own school. Because the reserve's resources are limited, the reserve found it difficult to run an education system. Eventually it joined the Wapati Indian School Board, which now has jurisdiction over the school. The board developed the curriculum, hired the teachers, and oversees the general operation of the school. Children are taught in both the native language and English. The teachers are tribal members who took teacher education at university but have now returned. Tribal elders often visit the school to talk about traditions and religious practices.

The Our Landers have also given up jurisdiction to the Wapati Regional Indian Government in other areas besides education, including policing and justice services, economic development policies, and cultural and social welfare matters. The Wapati government is made up of four neighbouring reserves. Amongst other services the Wapati government has established a medical service on the Our Land Reserve. In fact, there are clinics on each reserve, staffed on a part-time basis. The health team spends one day a week on each reserve. The cost of the health service, like all the other costs associated with the Wapati government, is shared by the four reserves. The four reserves also share a police service. Under a contractual arrangement, the police can call on the RCMP should additional help be needed. The police enforce the Criminal Code of Canada as well as traffic, liquor, and other laws made by the band council on each reserve. The laws are published and are available in each band office. They are also distributed in schools. The police spend a lot of time mediating disputes and only charge people as a last resort. A judge appointed by the Wapati government travels to each reserve once a week to hear cases. He is from one of the reserves making up the Wapati government.

Revenues to run the government are raised from selling business licences and from oil royalties. The federal government also makes an annual grant.

This fictional scenario might well be reality in Canada in another decade, as native self-government comes closer to fruition. Native self-government is the issue of the 1980s and will probably continue to be an important issue in Canadian politics well into the 1990s. The self-government debate provides a unique opportunity for the Canadian government to redefine its relationship with native people. In doing so, Canada may well reshape the nature of the federal structure. Federalism has been redefined to accommodate other pressures (such as the needs and aspirations of Quebec, and the needs of francophone citizens outside Quebec) and there is no reason why the federal structure should not be reshaped to accommodate the aspirations of Canada's native peoples.

REASONS FOR SELF-GOVERNMENT

There are two bases on which native people advance their claim for self-government. First, a natural desire on the part of people to run their own affairs. It was such a desire which fuelled the decolonization drive in much of the Third World. It is this desire that has brought blacks in South Africa into violent confrontation with the South African government.

As a signatory to the International Covenant on Civil and Political Rights, Canada has internationally recognized the desire for self-determination. The covenant states: 'All peoples have the right of self-determination. By virtue of that right they freely determine their political status and freely pursue their economic, social and cultural development.' The Helsinki Accords of 1975, to which Canada was a party, reaffirmed the right to self-determination.

Self-determination does not necessarily mean independence. It means, however, that a people (like the indigenous peoples of the world) should have a say about the terms and conditions under which they are incorporated into a nation. In other words, incorporation into a state should be a people's voluntary decision, not one forced upon them.

Canada's aboriginal people argue not only that they have the right to self-determination, but that they have had this right since time immemorial. They point out that they governed themselves before the arrival of the Europeans and have never given up their right to do so.

The second ground on which native people claim self-government is that, to date, Canadian policies regarding them have been disastrous and that the only remedy is self-government.

In negotiating self-government and changes to Indian government institutions as they are developed, Canada needs to look carefully at its past policies so that past mistakes can be avoided. It would be futile to develop native government institutions that would have to function under the shadow of past policies.

PAST NATIVE POLICIES AND SELF-GOVERNMENT

Canada's native policy so far can be characterized by a number of constants. First, there has been considerable confusion and contradiction in Indian policy. On the one hand there has been a concerted effort to assimilate the native population into the Canadian mainstream. This has been evidenced by policies such as outlawing Indian cultural beliefs, and legislative provisions whereby Indians could renounce their status (called enfranchisement). Government efforts to assimilate Indians were supported by other factions of society – such as schoolteachers who forbade the use of native languages in schools, and priests who tried to Christianize the Indians. On the other hand, policymakers saw Indians as being 'like children and unable to make their own way.' Hence the policies of segregating Indians on reserves, and the passing of special laws for Indians, including laws regarding liquor consumption and Indian will-making power. It is hard to assimilate people if you segregate them and treat them differently.

Slowly, Canada is working its way out of that conundrum thanks to the fact that Canadians are beginning to see their country as a multicultural society (multiculturalism is now constitutionally enshrined) and are rejecting the notion of assimilation.

Another constant in Canadian policy has been the failure to consult native people in a meaningful way on matters affecting them. No better example illustrates this point than the preparation of the 1969 white paper. Consultations with native leaders were being held, while at the same time senior government officials were secretly working on a policy to abolish Indian status. The constitutional conferences represent a first step in a policy change that may see more active and meaningful consultation with the Indian population.

The debate over the division of responsibility for native people between federal and provincial governments has been yet another constant in Canadian policy. Since Confederation, each level of government has tried to shift more of their responsibilities on to the other.

In the 1930s Ottawa and Quebec went to the Supreme Court of Canada to decide who was responsible for the Inuit in Quebec. Similarly, there has been an ongoing debate over who is responsible for the Métis.

In a major revision of the Indian Act in 1951 the federal government introduced a change (without consulting the Indians, of course) whereby provincial laws of general application would apply to Indian people unless they contradicted the Indian Act or any treaty made with the Indians. This change was seen by many legal scholars as Ottawa's attempt to make more provincial standards applicable to Indians and make Indian reserves into something akin to municipalities.

This was followed by the 1969 white paper, which stated: 'Propose to the governments of the provinces that they take over the same responsibility for Indians that they have for other citizens in their provinces.' Only two provinces, Ontario and Saskatchewan, supported the white paper.

Seventeen years later, in 1986, a task force reviewing federal government expenditures, under the stewardship of Deputy Prime Minister Erik Nielsen, recommended cuts in Indian programming. Such cuts, the review said, could be achieved by transferring some of the responsibility for Indians to the provinces.

In short, such constitutional squabbles, the assimilate-or-segregate contradictions, and the consistent lack of consultation with native peoples have led to policies that have hindered and set native people back rather than helping them.

WHAT IS SELF-GOVERNMENT?

No issue of native rights has provoked as much debate, concern, and fear in the non-native community as the issue of self-government. For many Canadians, self-government means independent nations – they see little countries spread across the Canadian map, each issuing its own passports, having its own embassies, and so on.

There is no one definition of self-government. It is an evolving process and ideas advocated today may no longer be advanced ten years from now. And when native government institutions are developed, time will show what works and what does not. At the present time it is impossible to define precisely the model that native governments will follow. Differing forms of government will be required for different areas of Canada. The type of governmental structures that will work for the Inuit of the north might be entirely inappropriate for the Indians of Walpole Island (in southwestern Ontario). The revenue base that will be available to native governments will also greatly influence the form of the government. In spite of the fact that it is impossible to describe a model for Indian self-government, there are certain things that can be said about it.

First, a caveat needs to be sounded. There is the danger that governments may be tempted to dictate the form native self-government should take. An equal danger is consultants defining what self-government means. If any lesson is clear from history it is that native people must be given the opportunity to define their own structures.

As a starting point, self-government means native people having a greater say about the terms under which they are incorporated into the federal system. The self-government debate should be seen as federalism growing (Canada's federal structure should not be seen as a static institution) and as a process whereby the terms of native entry into Confederation are being worked out. The Quebec-Ottawa relationship is an example of how Confederation can evolve to meet needs.

There are three basic models of native self-government. The first means a sovereign state, completely independent of Canada. With the exception of a very small minority, most native people have rejected this model. What native people are asking for is a fairer deal in Canada, not independence.

At the other end of the spectrum would be native communities having a status similar to municipalities. This model has been generally rejected by most native leaders. They see municipal government structures as being too limited to meet native aspirations. First, municipal governments are under the control of a superior government (in Canada municipalities, be they large cities or villages, are created by provincial statute and must operate within rules set by the province). Indian leaders feel that such a structure would offer them very little guarantee for the future – if they are subject to the whims of a senior government their whole government could be taken away at some future time. Moreover, native leaders want their governments to have power over things like education (including the language of instruction and the content taught), cultural affairs, and justice (the rules by which the society operates). Currently, all of those subject are beyond the jurisdiction of municipal governments in Canada (though, in fairness, large municipalities have some influence in the area of cultural policy and law enforcement). Similarly, native communities want to determine economic and industrial policy – again, an area in which municipalities have limited authority.

The third model involves something in between independent nationhood and municipal status. The model would be something close to provincehood, in which native governments would in certain areas (banking, monetary system, postal system, foreign affairs, transportation, etc.) be subject to the federal government, but would have autonomy in other areas such as education, economic policies, justice policies (including a police force, a court system, and the power to make their own laws), health care, cultural policy, and other areas. Such a native government would have authority to tax (as do provinces), and would have full control over lands within the jurisdiction of the government. Such a government might also involve some jurisdiction over criminal law and divorce. Currently, provinces have no jurisdiction in those areas. While this is a model to which many native people aspire, many Canadians, including many political leaders, are hesitant to create governments with such extensive powers.

Justice is one area that illustrates why native governments need something more than a municipal type of government. It is also an area in which considerable work has been done in developing workable models for native governments. There area several research projects under way within native organizations developing native justice systems.

Indian and Inuit leaders point out that many laws in Canada are inconsistent with native culture and traditions. They point to such areas as dispute resolution, deciding what is a wrong against the whole community (under the Canadian system wrongs against the community are called crimes and the system of law for dealing with such is known as criminal law), how wrongs against the community should be dealt with, family matters, and matters involving children. They point out, for example, that in traditional native societies the emphasis was on mediation, not punishment, and that concepts of property were that property belonged to the community, not to individuals. This does not mean that native standards are softer, rather they are different.

Native communities have often acted sternly against wrongdoers when the need arose. Under native tradition banishment from the community was not an unusual punishment. The Canadian system has not always upheld banishment as a recognized punishment. When a judge in northern Saskatchewan imposed an order banishing a thief from his home community for one year, the order was overturned by the Saskatchewan Court of Appeal. Other courts have, however, upheld banishment orders.

The conflict between the Canadian legal system and native values is most evident in the are of child welfare. In all Canadian jurisdictions, children who are abandoned or in need of protection can be apprehended and taken into state protection. There have been numerous instances of native children being seized because they were not in the care of their parents, but in the proper care of grandparents, uncles, aunts, or other relatives. In most native communities the family means not only parents but also grandparents and other immediate relatives, and it is the family, not only the parents, who are responsible for the upbringing of children. To further complicate matters, when native children were and often still are apprehended, more often than not they are placed in white foster homes rather than in a home of the extended family. (Canadian child welfare authorities have even given native children for adoption in the United States.) Such practices are gradually changing as a result of growing concern by native communities. More and more native communities are taking control over such areas as child welfare. The Spallumcheen Indian band in British Columbia was the first Indian group to take action in this area. In 1980, in a unilateral move to which federal and provincial governments later agreed, the band passed a child welfare law. Under that law the priority of placement of children in need of protection was first with the extended family on the reserve, then with extended family on another reserve, then with extended family off reserve, and only as a last resort were children to be placed in an non-Indian family.

It is because of such concerns as these that native communities speak of the need for self-government and the power to make and enforce their own laws, but there are still many problems and questions which have to be resolved before Indian government can become reality.

First and foremost is the issue of how much power these governments should have. Should native governments be able to make their own criminal laws or should their citizens be subject to the Criminal Code of Canada, as are all other Canadians? Should they have their own rules for divorce or should they be subject to the federal Divorce Act as are all other Canadians? Some native organizations have suggested that native governments should have powers to make criminal laws and deal with social questions such as divorce. They argue that such powers are necessary to ensure that native traditions and customs are reflected in those laws. The question is whether other

Canadians would be prepared to accept differing standards for the law they have to answer to and the law that citizens of native governments have to answer to.

Another area of crucial importance to native people has been wildlife. Hunting, fishing, and trapping are still an important means of livelihood for many native people. Hunting game can also be an important facet of native religion. For example, according to the beliefs of the West Coast Salish Indians it is necessary to hunt and burn fresh flesh to satisfy the hunger of one's deceased ancestors. Such practices often run afoul of provincial legislation – two Salish Indians were convicted of infringing provincial game laws and their conviction was upheld by the Supreme Court of Canada in 1985. For these reasons, native leaders argue that it is essential that native governments have the control and management of wild game. They argue that they are far more likely to effectively implement game conservation practices than any provincial government.

Another major issue is how native governments would be financed. Would they be entirely dependent on grants from federal and provincial governments or is it realistic to expect that they could finance themselves from their own tax base? Certainly the current financial position of many native communities could not provide an economic base to support government institutions.

This issue of cost is a major concern, and probably one reason why some provinces are afraid of self-government. The argument has been made that additional costs will be minimal because in large part the resources currently spent on Indians will simply be transferred to Indians. However, as is evident from the social conditions in most native communities the monies currently spent on native programming are less than adequate. The extent of the cost will not be known until the governments are in place. Costs will be dependent on the powers native governments are allowed to exercise. While land claim settlements and granting of further resource bases will help finance native governments, it is clear that, at least in the short run, transfer payments from senior governments will have to be made to ensure the financial viability of native governments. It is also the cost factor that will probably force many native communities to form regional governments in order to achieve some degree of operational efficiency.

Questions also arise as to whether the native government would have jurisdiction over non-natives who happen to be on native government territory, or over native people outside native territory. For example, an Indian child is found in Edmonton, neglected by its parents. The parents and child are originally from the Our Land Indian Reserve, located approximately 200 kilometres northeast of Edmonton. The band has a fully operational Indian government that has passed laws and put in place the administrative machinery necessary for an operational child welfare system. Should the Indian government of Our Land have any say in this case? Should Edmonton authorities turn the case over the Our Land people? Or should the Our Land system be restricted to Our Land Reserve? It should be remembered that a significant percentage, estimated to be 30 per cent and still increasing, of Canada's native population resides in urban centres. The argument against Indian governments having jurisdiction over these people is that by moving to the city these people may consciously intend to remove themselves from the jurisdiction of the Indian government. On the other hand, native governments might be in a far better position to deal with native urban issues.

A corollary problem arises: Should there be separate native governmental institutions in urban centres where there is a significant native population? Should there be, for example, separate Indian school boards? This is not a radical concept in view of the fact that separate school systems (with public funding) operate in a number of provinces. Similarly, should there be a separate native child welfare system to handle urban native child welfare?

Similar questions arise regarding the Métis. Currently they do not have a land base, which raises the question of whether you can have a government without there being some territory over which the government can rule.

The most likely scenario for southern Canada (a different situation exists in the north, which will be discussed later in the chapter) is that there will be native governments on Indian reserves and in Métis settlements, which will have jurisdiction over everyone within the geographic area covered by the government. Because of the fact that outside Alberta there are almost no lands set aside for Métis, their self-government is still in the distant future. Indian governments will probably not have the same powers as provinces, but in areas dealing with culture they are likely to have more power than provinces. There will be no jurisdiction beyond reserve boundaries. However, in some urban centres it is conceivable that there may be native school boards and child welfare systems. Similarly, arrangements are conceivable wherein natives sentenced in urban centres could serve their sentence in their home communities.

The scenario of hundreds of little provinces stretched across Canada has been painted by many critics of Indian self-government. An Ottawa writer, Ben Malkin, writing in various newspapers on the recommendations of the Special Parliamentary Committee on Indian Self-government stated: 'But it would be a provincial government based on the abhorrent apartheid principle of ethnic jurisdiction ... Besides an abhorrent principle, there is the practical problem of creating some 300 new provinces – there are approximately that many Indian bands [there are in fact 550] – each with its own bureaucracy, each with its own confrontational issue to place before a federal government already sufficiently bemused by the demands of only 10 provinces.' Another columnist, Don McGillivray, wrote; 'A serious matter such as the establishment of postage-stamp provinces here and there on a racially segregated basis should be honestly debated. Indians deserve better than apartheid.' Such critics ignore several points. Indian self-government is not apartheid. Apartheid is a policy of forced racial segregation. Indian self-government is a voluntary joining together of Indian peoples to run their own affairs. That is self-determination. No one is suggesting that Indians (or natives) will have to move back to their reserve and be subject to the rule of the reserve government. The decision to become a part of an Indian community will be voluntary. Ethnically based governments are not a novelty in Canada. The province of Quebec, for example, protects the French fact in Canada.

Nor are there likely to be hundreds of postage-stamp-size provinces. Because many Indian reserves are geographically small and have a small economic and population base, the great majority do not have, and in all likelihood never will have, the capacity to offer a full range of government services. In reality, they will have to join together in regional governments (perhaps covering all the reserves in a province or even in a region) in order to be able to offer the full range of services. Conceivably all Indian bands might unite to form one Indian government for all of Canada. In many cases Indian (or Métis) governments will decide to contract with existing agencies to provide services. Thus, it is possible that police, health, educational, and other services on reserves will be provided by existing agencies. This is not an uncommon feature on the Canadian scene. The most common example is policing – police services in a number of provinces are provided under contract by the RCMP, a federal force.

STEPS ALREADY TAKEN TOWARDS SELF-GOVERNMENT

Indian self-government has moved beyond the discussion stage. Various concrete steps have been and are being taken in that direction. It is very likely that by the year 2000 the great majority of Canada's native people will have at least some degree of self-government.

In recent years, some Indian bands have begun setting up governmental structures regardless of what the Indian Act or federal bureaucrats say about the situation. Such unilateral action has certainly acted as a stimulus for the federal government to move.

Canadian legislation has always allowed Indian bands to have some say in running their affairs (albeit a very limited one – sometimes it has been nothing more than the right to elect a chief and council, who could be thrown out of office by the Indian Affairs bureaucracy). Generally, early Canadian Indian

Act legislation provided for an elected system of chief and council (displacing traditional methods of selecting leaders) and vested limited bylaw-making power in them. Such powers could, however, be overridden by the Indian agent or other officials of the Indian bureaucracy.

There was a major rewriting of the Indian Act in 1951. Band councils were given further bylaw-making powers, including authority over such diverse subjects as regulation of traffic, control of noxious weeds, regulation of bee-keeping, control over door-to-door salespeople, some power to regulate construction work on reserves, keeping law and order on reserves, and other similar matters. However, any bylaw passed could be disallowed by the minister of Indian affairs. Also in 1951 a provision was introduced whereby, if the government felt that an Indian band had reached 'an advanced stage of development,' the band could be allowed to raise money by taxation and exercise other financial powers. Such powers could be unilaterally withdrawn from a band at any time.

The 1970s and 1980s have seen a gradual transfer of some of the powers exercised by the Indian Affairs department to band councils and regional Indian organizations. Indian Affairs runs education, health, economic development, welfare, and other programs on reserves. In 1971 some 16 per cent of the budget for services was administered by the Indian bands or organizations; by the 1982/83 fiscal year that had increased to 50 per cent. Thus while there has been a devolution of administration, this is still not self-government. Program priorities, design, and reporting are set by Indian Affairs. Self-government means setting your own priorities and designing your own programs. Such a transfer of administration does help train and create the Indian governmental structures that will be needed for functioning governments.

In 1985 federal Indian Affairs Minister Crombie announced a plan to enter into bilateral negotiations with individual Indian bands to allow them to govern their own affairs. The 650-member Sechelt Indian Band in British Columbia was the first to benefit from the plan. The federal government can, under its constitutional responsibility, proceed unilaterally in creating Indian governments. Self-government is also on the way in Ontario. In December 1985 the federal government, the Ontario government, and various Ontario Indian groups (including the Union of Ontario Indians, Association of Iroquois and Allied Indians, Nishnawbe Aski Nation, and the Grand Council of Treaty Three) signed a declaration of political intent to negotiate the establishment of Indian self-government in Ontario.

These recent events amount to a devolution of power, wherein Ottawa will give up the administration of some of its programs to Indian bands. This is not yet self-government, but it is a definite move in that direction; Indian administration of programs is replacing Ottawa-administered programs. Whether this devolution of power will lead to self-government in its true sense remains to be seen.

SELF-GOVERNMENT IN THE NORTH

It is in the Northwest Territories that the greatest progress has been made towards self-government. The Territories cover over 3.4 million square kilometres (one-third of Canada) but have a population of slightly less than 50,000. Close to 60 per cent of the population is native, including approximately 17,000 Inuit. Discussions are now under way to split the territory into a western and eastern half. The eastern half would become Nunavut, the home of the Inuit. The western half would become Denendeh, home of the Dene Indians and the Métis.

A 1982 plebiscite over the split saw 56 per cent of the voters voting in favour. Late in 1982, then Indian Affairs Minister John Munro announced that the federal cabinet had agreed in principle to dividing the Northwest Territories. Several conditions were imposed by the federal government, including the settlement of native claims, agreement on the boundary between the two territories, the choosing of new capitals, and definition of the distribution of powers between local, regional, and territorial governments.

The Nunavut Constitutional Forum was formed in the summer of 1982 for the purpose of defining a government, through consultation with the people, for Nunavut. The Dene and Métis formed a similar body in the fall of 1982 known as the Western Constitutional Forum. These two groups in combination with the Legislative Assembly of the Northwest Territories have formed the Constitutional Alliance.

The most likely dividing line between the two states will be the tree line; with everything to the north and east being Nunavut. There have, however, been some areas of contention, the most notable being the western Arctic, which is inhabited by Inuvialuit people. These people culturally are tied to the Inuit of the eastern Arctic; however, many of their economic ties are with the western portion of the territories. There are also many resources in this area and undoubtedly both governments would like to see some revenue from such resources.

The Nunavut proposal can be summed up as follows: essentially the Inuit propose a provincial form of government, with a legislative assembly having the kinds of powers that southern legislatures possess. They do, however, propose that their government have some jurisdiction in foreign affairs. Primarily they want to ensure that they will be able to maintain contact with Inuit who live in other states, such as Greenland, Alaska, and the Soviet

Union. This would be similar to the kind of arrangement that allows Quebec to participate in international forums related to francophone issues. Even today the Inuit, through the Inuit Circumpolar Conference, have active contact with the Inuit in other nations, and they have participated in United Nations conferences on whaling. Inuktitut would be one of the official languages in Nunavut.

Denendeh would also become a kind of province under proposals developed by the Western Constitutional Forum. Denendeh would probably include a greater non-native population than Nunavut (Yellowknife, which has a sizable non-native population, would probably fall within Denendeh). However, the proposals for Denendeh include various guarantees to ensure the survival of the Dene nation. Thus the Dene argue that Denendeh should have power over fisheries and navigable waters (currently areas of federal jurisdiction) to 'ensure protection of the aquatic environment of Denendeh which is basic to our traditional Dene way of life' and also control over employment and labour in order to 'preserve and develop historical Dene work styles and employment relations.' The Charter of Founding Principles for Denendeh would include entrenchment of native languages as official languages. Many of the decisions in Denendeh would involve the whole community, with community assemblies making decisions by consensus and referendums held to ensure that decisions were widely based. To ensure the cultural and political survival of the Dene, certain protections would be built into the constitution. Thus no matter what the Dene population was, they would be guaranteed a minimum of 30 per cent of the seats on community councils and in the Legislative Assembly. Secondly, there would be a Dene Senate, composed entirely of Dene, which would have the power to veto any legislation which adversely affected aboriginal rights.

Of great concern to both the Dene and the Inuit is the possibility of a migration of southerners, who would take control of government institutions. It is for that reason that the Dene are asking for the constitutional guarantees that are set out above. The lesson of Manitoba has not been lost on native people of the north. Manitoba came into being as a Métis province, with guarantees of language and land rights. As has been seen, the Métis very quickly lost their rights, and many ended up leaving Manitoba. In the past the north has attracted many migrant southerners who have come to work on resource projects. Attracted by high wages, they usually keep a home base in southern Canada. In order to ensure that such people do not gain an inordinate amount of say in government, both the Inuit and the Dene propose lengthy residence requirements for voting status. As a starting proposal, the Western Constitutional Forum recommended a ten-year residence requirement before one could vote while the Nunavut Constitutional Forum recommended a three-year requirement. Both groups feel that lengthy residence requirements will ensure that only true northerners will vote, but the fact that they would also effectively mean disenfranchisement for many has sparked considerable debate in southern Canada. Such provision may even violate the Charter of Rights and Freedoms.

To the native people in the north the division of the Territories is a challenge, and they hope to avoid the mistakes made in southern Canada. In a 1984 brief to the House of Commons Standing Committee on Indian Affairs the Western Constitutional Forum described the challenge in the following way:

> First there is the challenge and opportunity for the Dene, the Métis and the Inuit to negotiate a relationship amongst themselves. Coupled with this is the challenge and the opportunity for the aboriginal groups and the non-native population to negotiate their relationship as well. It is an uncommon event in Canadian history for these parties to attempt to reach an agreement on how they can live and work together cooperatively without using the Federal Government as a mediator. Finally there is the challenge and the opportunity for the people of the north together to negotiate their relationship with the Government of Canada.

Discussions have also been under way in the Yukon, where a sizable portion of the population is Indian. Comprehensive land-claims-settlement discussions have been under way for a number of years. In fact, two tentative settlements, one in 1976 and the other in 1983, were reached but in the end were rejected by one side or the other. The 1983 settlement fell through when the federal government pulled out, saying it had waited too long for Yukon Indians to approve the tentative settlement and that there did not appear to be sufficient support amongst Yukon's 6000 Indians for the tentative pact. The discussions included guarantees of control of internal affairs and special guaranteed participation in governmental affairs of direct interest to the Indians.

The James Bay and Northern Quebec Agreement also created Indian and Inuit governmental institutions. To a large extent, these institutions are similar to southern municipalities; however, in some areas they have extensive control.

THE AMERICAN EXPERIENCE

Lest the concept of Indian self-government seem radical it may be useful to look at the American experience. Indian self-governments have been functioning for over fifty years and have been supported by such conservative politicians as Richard Nixon and Ronald Reagan. Speaking to Congress in

1970 on Indian self-determination, Nixon said: 'Self-determination among the Indian people can and must be encouraged without the threat of eventual termination ... We must assure the Indian that he can assume control of his own life without being separated involuntarily from the tribal group. And we must make it clear that Indians can become independent of federal control without being cut off from federal concern and federal support.' Thirteen years later Ronald Reagan spoke of sovereign Indian nations and of the Indian-United States relationship as that of 'government to government.'

In American law as early as the 1830s courts recognized Indian tribes as 'dependent sovereign nations.' In 1934 Congress gave official recognition to this legal theory with the passage of the Indian Reorganization Act. The focus of the act was to allow Indian tribes a measure of self-government on their reserves.

The powers of Indian governments in the United States are fairly wide. First, Indian tribes have the power to determine their own membership. Tribes have the power to draw up their own constitution (subject to certain restriction) or they can choose to use model constitutions developed by the Bureau of Indian Affairs. They have full power to license and control businesses established on reserves and to raise revenue through taxation. They have extensive law-making powers; with the power to make laws dealing with divorce, wills, property ownership, traffic, and some criminal matters. They have the power to establish their own court systems; indeed, tribal courts are a common feature on most U.S. Indian reserves. Procedures are set out for the appointment of judges (usually someone from the community – but not necessarily a lawyer), for the establishment of a bar (association of advocates or lawyers), and for appealing judgments. Tribal courts deal with a whole range of matters including criminal, family, and civil cases.

There are, however, several limitations on the powers of Indian governments in the United States. First, there is an Indian Civil Rights Act, passed by Congress in 1968, which is a code of individual rights that Indian governments and tribal courts must respect. The act requires that all persons subject to Indian governments must be granted equal protection by the law, must have the right to a lawyer if charged, and cannot have their freedom of speech, the press, or religion curtailed. Similarly, Congress in the act has restricted the sentencing power of tribal courts to a maximum of $500 and/or six months' imprisonment. (The act is the source of much criticism in some circles; some Indian leaders see it as the imposition of white standards on Indian governments.) Congress has also defined fourteen major crimes (including murder) as being beyond the jurisdiction of Indian governments to prosecute or prescribe penalties for.

Indian governments in the United States are still dependent on the federal treasury for a significant part of their operating budgets. The Bureau of Indian Affairs still has an immense impact on Indian life. It still operates programs on some reserves and plays a supervisory role on most reserves. The social conditions that plague Canadian Indian communities – poverty, alcoholism, unemployment – are equally prevalent on many Indian reserves in the United States.

SOME QUESTIONS TO BE RESOLVED

The message to be drawn from the American experience is that native self-government will not solve all problems. There is a need to see Indian governments in realistic terms. Simply turning over management to natives will not end poverty. True self-determination requires an economic base, which in turn requires the resolution of land claims. Perhaps the aboriginal people should be looked upon as landlords who are allowing their land to be leased for development. In return for the lease they will get regular rental payments, which will in turn support native governments and native development.

Both native and Canadian governments will have to deal with the issue of the extent of development that should be allowed on Indian lands. Should there be lands left undeveloped for those native people who wish to continue to live off the land? In other words, is the industrial model of society the one that should be imposed on Indian lands?

Once it is implemented there will of course be other problems created by Indian government. In the United States there has been considerable litigation, defining where the authority of tribal governments ends. There have been disputes about jurisdiction over non-Indians doing business on the reserve, and about the extent of the powers of tribal courts. In fact, there is a whole subcategory of the legal system devoted to such questions.

There will also be those Indian people who from time to time will be unhappy with the actions of their government. These potential problems raise the question of the extent to which non-Indian institutions should be involved in such issues. For example, if an accused complains that he was sentenced to jail by a tribal court without having the right to a lawyer (in some U.S. tribal courts attorneys are discouraged or banned), should he be able to come to superior provincial court asking for an order that his conviction be overturned? Should he be able to argue that the Charter of Rights applies to the Indian court? Should a citizen of an Indian government have the right to have the election of a chief turned aside for corruption, even though the Indian court has refused to do so? Should there be recourse for the business person who has been refused a trading licence? In essence, the problem comes down to whether Canadian society will allow Indian nations full control of their affairs, or insist on minimum standards being met by the governments. These are all problems that have been grappled with in the United States. By and large, the American answer has been to impose a system of rules and standards within which Indian governments must operate. This has not always been a happy compromise, since many Indian leaders feel they are severely hampered by big government watching over them.

The American experience also shows the necessity for Indian governments to evolve over a period of time. It would be wrong to impose a model and leave no room for it to grow and change to accommodate some of the problems discussed above.

WHAT CANADA MUST DO

If there is a sad chapter in Canadian history it certainly has to be the story of relations with the native community. Canada now has an unprecedented opportunity to learn from the past and set out in new directions. Native people must be given the opportunity to manage their own affairs and they must be ensured sufficient resources to do the job adequately. In many respects, Canada has been a world leader in the last decade in dealing with aboriginal issues, but there is still much to do. By establishing effective self-government models, Canada can set a standard for other nations with indigenous populations.

Domestically, the federal government in cooperation with the provinces needs to sit down and seriously evaluate past polices with a view to correcting earlier mistakes. While Indians, Inuit, and perhaps Métis are constitutionally a federal responsibility, the reality of Canada is that the provinces need to be involved if Canada is to have a meaningful national policy on native rights. If self-government is to work, provincial cooperation is needed.

Canada also has a duty, in view of its sizable indigenous population, to speak out at international forums on the treatment of aboriginal peoples in other parts of the world. A starting-point would be to press for international standards for the treatment of indigenous peoples. International pressure is being brought to bear on South Africa to change its apartheid policies. What is happening to aboriginal peoples in many countries is as bad as or worse than what apartheid is doing to blacks in South Africa. Surely there is a need for the same type of concerted international lobbying to protect aboriginal peoples.

NOTE

This article is from *Our Land: Native Rights in Canada*. Toronto: Lorimer 1986. Reprinted with permission.

NATIVE PEOPLES AND THE ENVIRONMENT

DIAMOND JENNESS

The Indian's Interpretation of Man and Nature

It is impossible to comprehend the daily life of the eastern Indians of Canada without some knowledge of their religious beliefs, and their religious beliefs are unintelligible without an understanding of their interpretation of what they saw around them. They lived much nearer to nature than most white men, and they looked with a different eye on the trees and the rocks, the water and the sky. One is almost tempted to say that they were less materialistic, more spiritually minded, than Europeans, for they did not picture any great chasm separating mankind from the rest of creation but interpreted everything around them in much the same terms as they interpreted their own selves.

How then did they interpret themselves? Man, they believed (and in many places still believe), consists of three parts, a corporeal body that decays and disappears after death, a mind or soul that travels after death to the land of souls in the west, and an image or shadow (Latin *imago*) that roams about on earth after death, but generally remains near the grave. The body needs no further explanation, but the nature and functions of the soul and image require closer definition.

The soul or intelligent part of a man is located in the heart and is capable of travelling outside the body for brief periods, although if it remains separate too long the body will die. This is what happens in many cases of sickness; for one reason or another the soul is unable to return to the body and the patient either dies or, in a few cases, becomes insane. For the soul is the intelligent part of man's being, the agency that enables him to perceive things, to reason about them and remember them. An insane man has lost his soul and therefore has no reason. A drunken man, or a man just recovering from a bout of drunkenness, is temporarily in the same condition; his soul (or mind) moves at a distance from him, so that he consists of body and image alone and remembers nothing of what occurred during his drunkenness.

Besides being the intelligent part of man, the soul is the seat of the will. A weary Indian dragging his toboggan up a slope may feel that something is helping him along, is pulling on the toboggan with him; it is his soul – his will – that has come to his aid. So, too, it is the soul that experiences pleasure, grief, and anger. When you meet a man on the road you should never address him until you have passed him, for then your soul and his soul continue on their way and only your bodies and images stay to converse; if there should be disagreement between you it will pass away quickly, for your souls are unaffected. Even today many Indians will pass one another without speaking, then turn back to converse.

The image is slightly more indefinite than the soul and the Indians themselves often confuse them, ascribing certain attributes or phenomena now to one, now to the other. The image is located in the brain, but, like the soul, often operates apart from the body. In life it is the 'eyes' of the soul, as it were, awakening the latter to perception and knowledge. When a man is travelling his image goes before or behind him; normally it is in front, nearer to his destination. It often causes a twitching of the hunter's eyelids, informing him that it has seen game ahead. There are times when a man feels that someone is watching him, or near him, although he can see no one; it is his image that is warning him, trying to awaken his soul to perceive the danger. Throughout a man's whole lifetime it fulfils this function of enlightening the soul, or, to translate it somewhat imperfectly into the terms of our own psychologists, it is the sensation and perception that precede reasoning and knowledge. A baby's image is peculiarly sensitive and needs the most careful consideration; for example, it may easily be distressed by carelessness in swinging the hammock or cradle. As soon as a child is born its image wanders over the earth observing many things. That is why the child appears to lie dormant at this period, and to learn nothing. Actually it learns a great deal, for often you will observe it smile or laugh at something that is invisible to you yourself; its image, becoming aware of something, has enlightened the soul. So an Indian mother solicitously protects the image and soul of her baby by tying various objects to its cradle.

Generally the image is invisible, but sometimes it allows itself to be seen under the same appearance as the body. That is why you often think you see someone who is actually miles away. The phenomena of apparitions present no difficulties to the Indian.

Like the soul, again, the image must work in harmony with the other two parts of a man's being if he is to enjoy perfect health. Certain Indian methods of witchcraft, therefore, aim at breaking down this harmony by keeping the soul or the image apart from its coadjutors. Occasionally the image may divide or become double; one portion may wish to cooperate with the soul and body, the other seek to travel or go hunting. The man then becomes a centre of conflicting desires; his two images contend for the mastery, his struggling soul remains aloof from the body awaiting the issue, and the body itself falls sick. In the terminology of our psychopaths, he is the victim of neurosis. This is one of many indications that the Indians recognized the tremendous influence of psychological factors on the health of the individual.

Thus, then, the Indian interprets his own being; and exactly the same interpretation he applies to everything around him. Not only men, but animals, trees, even rocks and water are tripartite, possessing bodies, souls, and images. They all have a life like the life in human beings, even if they have all been gifted with different powers and attributes. Consider the animals, which most closely resemble man; they see and hear as we do, and clearly they reason about what they observe. The tree must have a life somewhat like out own, although it lacks the power of locomotion. When its leaves shake and murmur, surely they are talking to one another. Water runs; it too must possess life; it too must have a soul and an image. Then observe how certain minerals cause the neighbouring rocks to decompose and become loose and friable; evidently rocks too have power, and power means life, and life necessitates a soul and an image. All things then have souls and images, or, in the familiar words of Virgil:

> Spiritus intus alit, totamque infusa per artus
> Mens agitat molem et magno se corpore miscet.[1]
>
> The spirit within nourishes, and mind instilled throughout the living parts activates the whole mass and mingles with the vast frame.[2]

And all things die. But their souls are reincarnated again, and what were dead return to life. 'The tree does not die; it grows up again where it falls. When an animal is killed its soul goes into the ground with its blood; but later it comes back and is reincarnated where its blood entered the ground. Everything – trees, birds, animals, fish – return to life; while they are dead their souls are merely awaiting reincarnation.'

To the Indians, then, all objects have life, and life is synonymous with power, which may be directed for the Indian's good or ill. Just as man's power comes from his soul, or his intelligence, so does the power of the animal, tree, and stone. Therefore the Indian should treat everything he sees or touches with the respect befitting a thing that has a soul and an image not unlike his own. Let him not toss his hat idly to one side, but hang it on its peg; if his gun brings him no luck, let him not curse it, but hang it away for a time; and if he is carrying firewood, let him pile it carefully to one side, not drop it on the path. It may be that the Indian is sometimes just as careless as white people in these matters, for he realizes that the souls of hats and firewood have little power to help or harm and calmly disregards them. But he follows out his theory more strictly where greater issues are at stake. When he completes the building of a canoe he sometimes beseeches its soul to take good care of whoever may wield the paddle, and when running a rapid, or pushing out into open water, he often prays the soul of his craft to carry him safely through. Similarly when an Indian medicine man gathers roots or leaves or bark for his medicines, he propitiates the soul of each plant by placing a tiny offering of tobacco at its base, believing that without the cooperation of the soul the mere 'body' of the plant can work no cure.

Naturally, however, it is to the souls and images of animals that the Indian pays special attention, because he will secure no game if he occasions them offence. The image of the moose, the bear, etc., constantly wanders about like a man's own image, and carries back information to the animal's soul. Deer, for example, seem to know when a death has occurred, or is impending in a family, and keep away from the hunter. Some of the Indians will not cook deer-meat when they are hunting the deer, lest the animal's image be annoyed by the smell of its meat and spoil the hunter's luck. For the same reason others will not eat trout during the trout-fishing season, but cook other food instead. A man should never kill a porcupine and throw away the meat, for the image of the porcupine will be offended and harm his children. He should aim always at the head or heart of an animal in order to kill it painlessly; if he aims merely to wound, the soul of the animal will take umbrage and prevent him from securing much game. He should not think disparagingly of a bear when he is eating its flesh, or the meat will kick him in the chest (ie., cause indigestion). He should never think disparaging, indeed, of any animal or fish.

A primary rule in hunting is not to concentrate all your attention on the game that you are seeking. Look at the trees around you and consider whether they are suitable for making fish-spears or can be turned to other uses. Examine the plants at your feet and consider whether they will make beneficial medicines. For animals are subject to deception no less than human beings, and the image of the deer or moose will be thrown off its guard, will believe you are not engaged in hunting and will fail to carry back a warning. Occasionally a deer will decide, for some reason or other, that it will not allow a certain hunter to kill it. It is then hopeless for that hunter to pursue it, because its image watches his every movement; even if he succeeds in wounding the deer, he will never be able to kill it.

Not only is the animal's psychology similar to that of man, but society in the animal world is similar to human society. Animals have their families and their homes, like human beings; they meet and act in concert, like the Indians at their fishing and hunting grounds. A cricket that finds food invites all its fellows; if you kill it a messenger goes round and informs all the other crickets in the neighbourhood, who come and eat up everything. A bear, a deer, will carry information to its fellows far and wide. More than this, just as the Indians have their chiefs or leading men, so there are chiefs or 'bosses' (to use a word from the lumber camps that the Indians themselves employ) among animals, birds, and fish, even among the trees. There is no single chief ruling an entire Indian tribe, but a chief in every band; similarly there is no single boss for every species of animal or plant, but a boss in each locality. The bosses are always larger than other plants and animals of their kind, and in the case of birds, fish, and animals, always white. Now and then the Indians see and kill them, but generally they keep out of sight of human beings. They are like the government in Ottawa, one old Indian remarked. An ordinary Indian can never see the 'government.' He is sent from one office to another, is introduced to this man and to that, each of whom sometimes claims to be the 'boss'; but he never sees the real government, who keeps himself hidden.

At death a man's soul travels to the land of the west, but the souls of animals have a home in a tier or world below this earth. Sometimes many souls come up from below to be reborn, sometimes only a few; then there are correspondingly many or few animals upon this earth. The bosses of each species regulate their numbers, knowing beforehand whether an epidemic or other calamity will devastate the land. So a district may teem with hares one winter and contain hardly any the next, because their boss has ordered them to move into another district or has sent their souls back to their home below. Most of the Indians believe that the souls of dogs go to the underworld with the souls of other animals, although the dog is man's constant companion here on earth; but here and there an old man firmly believes that he will find the souls of his dogs awaiting him in the land of the west when his own soul journeys thither.

To the eastern Indians, then, all nature is one, inasmuch as everything consists of a body, soul and image; and all souls and images are alike in essence, though gifted with different forces and powers. Just as the soul of a witch can assume the form of a dog or an owl, so the souls of animals can take on human form and make themselves visible in that guise. Man does not know all the power that is imminent in the souls of animals, trees, and stones. 'You may see a log floating on the water yonder. Suddenly it disappears. Perhaps it was a water-snake, for you cannot tell what is around you.' Often a house will creak before a wind strikes it, for the 'power' of the wind has preceded its coming. You can prove that this is true because the barometer registers it.

The wind blows without man's volition, the water is stirred up into great waves, the thunder peals and the lightning flashes. The sun and the moon move daily across the sky uninfluenced by anything that man can do. They must all be sentient beings like man himself, or else the manifestations of sentient beings. Their power is infinitely greater than man's, who can only bow his head in awe and entreat their favour and assistance. They are among the greatest of the supernatural beings, but the world is full of others, most of them restricted, like man himself, to more or less definite localities, but many able to roam at will. Over them all is the Great Spirit, from whom they first received their functions and their powers.

There are innumerable myths describing the origins of various stars, of sun and moon, of wind and snow, and other phenomena about which the Indians pondered. Many Indians still believe in the historic truth of all these stories; others are frankly sceptical of some of them, regarding them as pleasant fairytales. In earlier times sceptics were probably rare, because almost anything could seem possible to people who were ignorant of the physical laws that govern natural phenomena, and who interpreted all things spiritually. We ourselves do not know what is possible, and what impossible, in the realm of mind and thought. Allowing for the Indian's ignorance of 'natural laws,' may we not say that his interpretation of nature was not only beautiful but entirely logical, provided that we can grant his initial premise that the possession of a soul (and image) is not the special heritage of man alone, but shared by him with everything else around?

NOTES

This article is from *Transactions of the Royal Society of Canada*, section II, series III, volume XXIV, May 1930. Reprinted with permission.

1 Virgil, *Aeneid* vi, 726; *The Oxford Dictionary of Quotations* (ODQ), 3rd edition (New York: Oxford University Press 1979; first published 1941), 558
2 Virgil, *Aeneid* vi, 726; ODQ, 559

WORLD COMMISSION ON ENVIRONMENT AND DEVELOPMENT (THE BRUNDTLAND REPORT)

Population and Human Resources

In 1985, some 80 million people were added to a world population of 4.8 billion. Each year the number of human beings increases, but the amount of natural resources with which to sustain this population, to improve the quality of human lives, and to eliminate mass poverty remains finite. On the other hand, expanding knowledge increases the productivity of resources.

Present rates of population growth cannot continue. They already compromise many governments' abilities to provide education, health care, and food security for people, much less their abilities to raise living standards. This gap between numbers and resources is all the more compelling because so much of the population growth is concentrated in low-income countries, ecologically disadvantaged regions, and poor households.

Yet the population issue is not solely about numbers. And poverty and resource degradation can exist on thinly populated lands, such as the drylands and the tropical forests. People are the ultimate resource. Improvements in education, health, and nutrition allow them to better use the resources they command, to stretch them further. In addition, threats to the sustainable use of resources come as much from inequalities in people's access to resources and from the ways in which they use them as from the sheer numbers of people. Thus concern over the 'population problem' also calls forth concern for human progress and human equality.

Nor are population growth rates the challenge solely of those nations with high rates of increase. An additional person in an industrial country consumes far more and places far greater pressure on natural resources than an additional person in the Third World. Consumption patterns and preferences are as important as numbers of consumers in the conservation of resources.

Thus many governments must work on several fronts – to limit population growth; to control the impact of such growth on resources and, with increasing knowledge, enlarge their range and improve their productivity; to realize human potential so that people can better husband and use resources; and to provide people with forms of social security other than large numbers of children. The means of accomplishing these goals will vary from country to country, but all should keep in mind that sustainable economic growth and equitable access to resources are two of the more certain routes towards lower fertility rates.

Giving people the means to choose the size of their families is not just a method of keep population in balance with resources; it is a way of assuring – especially for women – the basic human right of self-determination. The extent to which facilities for exercising such choices are made available is itself a measure of a nation's development. In the same way, enhancing human potential not only promotes development but helps to ensure the right of all to a full and dignified life.

THE LINKS WITH ENVIRONMENT AND DEVELOPMENT

Population growth and development are linked in complex ways. Economic development generates resources that can be used to improve education and health. These improvements, along with associated social changes, reduce both fertility and mortality rates. On the other hand, high rates of population growth that eat into surpluses available for economic and social development can hinder improvements in education and health.

In the past, the intensification of agriculture and the production of higher yields helped nations copy with the increasing population pressures on available land. Migration and international trade in food and fuels eased the pressure on local resources. They permitted and helped sustain the high population densities of some industrialized countries.

This situation is different in most of the developing world. There, improvements in medicine and public health have led to a sharp drop in mortality rates and have accelerated population growth rates to unprecedented levels. But fertility rates remain high; much human potential remains unrealized, and economic development is stalled. Agricultural intensification can go some way towards restoring a balance between food production and population, but there are limits beyond which intensification cannot go.

The very possibility of development can be compromised by high population growth rates. Moreover, most developing countries do not have the resources to wait for a few generations before population stabilizes. The option of migration to new lands is virtually closed.

A critical point of intervention is during teacher training. The attitudes of teachers will be key in increasing understanding of the environment and its links with development. To enhance the awareness and capabilities of teachers in this area, multilateral and bilateral agencies must provide support for the relevant curriculum development in teacher training institutions, for the preparation of teaching aids, and for other similar activities. Global awareness could be fostered by encouraging contacts among teachers from different countries, for instance in specialized centres set up for this purpose.

Empowering Vulnerable Groups

The processes of development generally lead to the gradual integration of local communities into a larger social and economic framework. But some communities – so-called indigenous or tribal peoples – remain isolated because of such factors as physical barriers to communication or marked differences in social and cultural practices. Such groups are found in North America, in Australia, in the Amazon Basin, in Central America, in the forests and hills of Asia, in the deserts of North Africa, and elsewhere.

The isolation of many such people has meant the preservation of a traditional way of life in close harmony with the natural environment. Their very survival has depended on their ecological awareness and adaptation. But their isolation has also meant that few of them have shared in national economic and social development; this may be reflected in their poor health, nutrition, and education.

With the gradual advance of organized development into remote regions, these groups are becoming less isolated. Many live in areas rich in valuable natural resources that planners and 'developers' want to exploit, and this exploitation disrupts the local environment so as to endanger traditional ways of life. The legal and institutional changes that accompany organized development add to such pressures.

Growing interaction with the larger world is increasing the vulnerability of these groups, since they are often left out of the processes of economic development. Social discrimination, cultural barriers, and the exclusion of these people from national political processes make these groups vulnerable and subject to exploitation. Many groups become dispossessed and marginalized, and their traditional practices disappear. They become the victims of what would be described as cultural extinction.

These communities are the repositories of vast accumulations of traditional knowledge and experience that links humanity with its ancient origins. Their disappearance is a loss for the larger society, which could learn a great deal from their traditional skills in sustainably managing very complex ecological systems. It is a terrible irony that as formal development reaches more deeply into rain forests, deserts, and other isolated environments, it tends to destroy

---

'I am here as the son of a small nation, the Krenak Indian Nation. We live in the valley of the Rio Doce, which is the frontier of Espirito Santo with the State of Minas Gerais. We are a micro-country – a micro-nation.

When the government took our land in the valley of Rio Doce, they wanted to give us another place somewhere else. But the State, the government will never understand that we do not have another place to go.

The only possible place for the Krenak people to live and to re-establish our existence, to speak to our Gods, to speak to our nature, to weave our lives is where our God created us. It is useless for the government to put us in a very beautiful place, in a very good place with a lot of hunting and a lot of fish. The Krenak people, we continue dying and we die insisting that there is only one place for us to live.

My heart does not become happy to see humanity's incapacity. I have no pleasure at all to come here and make these statements. We can no longer see the planet that we live upon as if it were a chess-board where people just move things around. We cannot consider the planet as something isolated from the cosmic.

We are not idiots to believe that there is possibility of life for us outside of where the origin of our life is. Respect our place of living, do not degrade our living condition, respect this life. We have no arms to cause pressure, the only thing we have is the right to cry for our dignity and the need to live in our land.'

Ailton Krenak
Co-ordinator of Indian Nations' Union
WCED Public Hearing, Sao Paulo, 28–29 Oct. 1985

---

the only cultures that have proved able to thrive in these environments.

The starting point for a just and humane policy for such groups is the recognition and protection of their traditional rights to land and the other resources that sustain their way of life – rights they may define in terms that do not fit into standard legal systems. These groups' own institutions to regulate rights and obligations are crucial for maintaining the harmony with nature and the environmental awareness characteristic of the traditional way of life. Hence the recognition of traditional rights must go hand in hand with measures to protect the local institutions that enforce responsibility in resource use. And this recognition must also give local communities a decisive voice in the decisions about resource use in their area.

Protection of traditional rights should be accompanied by positive measures to enhance the well-being of the community in ways appropriate to the group's life-style. For example, earnings from traditional activities can be increased through the introduction of marketing arrangements that ensure a fair price for produce, but also through steps to conserve and enhance the resource base and increase resource productivity.

Those promoting policies that have an impact on the lives of an isolated, traditional people must tread a fine line between keeping them in artificial, perhaps unwanted isolation and wantonly destroying their life-styles. Hence broader measures of human resource development are essential. Health facilities must be provided to supplement and improve traditional practices; nutritional deficiencies have to be corrected, and educational institutions established. These steps should precede new projects that open up an area to economic development. Special efforts should also be made to ensure that the local community can derive the full benefit of such projects, particularly through jobs.

In terms of sheer numbers, these isolated, vulnerable groups are small. But their marginalization is a symptom of a style of development that tends to neglect both human and environmental considerations. Hence a more careful and sensitive consideration of their interests is a touchstone of a sustainable development policy.

NOTE

This article is from *Our Common Future*, World Commission on Environment and Development [The Brundtland Report]. Oxford: Oxford University Press 1987. Reprinted with permission.

PETER JULL

Lessons from Indigenous Peoples

The Brundtland Report, *Our Common Future*, published by the World Commission on Environment and Development chaired by Norwegian prime minister Gro Harlem Brundtland, has just begun to make its impact in Australia. But since the day it was released in late April 1987 in photocopy – it is now an Oxford University Press paperback available in any bookshop – the report has created intense excitement and remarkable government attention in the northern hemisphere.

That morning I was flying with Mary Simon, the president of the world Inuit association, ICC (Inuit Circumpolar Conference), from Montreal through the Canadian Arctic to Greenland. We both read the lengthy excerpts from the report published in the morning newspapers. Mary saw at once that this was a real world breakthrough: at last a high-profile international body, strongly supported by governments around the world, was insisting on concerted political action to restore the balance between humans and the world around them, the balance which is the heart and soul of aboriginal cultures everywhere.

Whether Inuit (formerly called Eskimos), Australian Aboriginals, Torres Strait Islanders, Indians of North and South America, or others, aboriginal or indigenous peoples have developed societies based on the renewable productivity of the world we live in. In a moment of history when we have suddenly been brought up short and forced to accept that 'development' cannot be open-ended, limitless, unceasing in the changes it forces on physical nature and the human community, this should be good news.

However, as the Brundtland Report puts it in its short section on aboriginal peoples, 'Empowering Vulnerable Groups':

> These communities are the repositories of vast accumulations of traditional knowledge and experience that links humanity with its ancient

> origins. Their disappearance is a loss for the larger society which could learn a great deal from their traditional skills in sustainably managing very complex ecological systems. It is a terrible irony that as formal development reaches more deeply into rain forests, deserts, and other isolated environments, it tends to destroy the only cultures that have proved able to thrive in these environments.

One might say that the modern industrial systems which Britain was launching at the moment when Australia received its first white settlers have not lived *with* nature but lived by *overcoming* and *consuming* it. The result has been a steady loss of the world's resources, the capacities of biological systems to renew themselves, and such violence to the world's physical systems that scientists can now only speculate eerily on the shapes and sizes of catastrophes which await us.

On the plane to Greenland there was another passenger that morning. Georges Erasmus, the long-time leader of northern Indians, the Dene, in Canada's Northwest Territories was on board. Georges was for years a prophet on northern development, bringing Canadians to see that conventional development was creating more problems than it solved – politically, socially, economically, and environmentally. Now he was best known as leader of Canada's powerful national Indian movement. But he was travelling to Greenland in another capacity, as head of ISI (Indigenous Survival International), an organization of aboriginal people he and his Dene friends had founded.

ISI quickly involved Inuit, Indians, and Métis of all North America in the fight to protect the physical environment which harboured their traditional livelihoods centred on wildlife harvesting. It was no less dedicated to protecting the political climate from national and overseas lobbies provoking new laws designed to end aboriginal food hunting and gathering, fur trapping, etc. What city folk were doing was legislating aboriginal society out of existence. Legal measures by kindly intellectuals were no less brutal than bulldozers or oil slicks in traditional lands and waters.

Mary and George soon huddled to talk about the implications of Brundtland. They agreed that serious action was needed at once. From the moment they got off the plane in Greenland's capital, Nuuk (formerly Godthaab), their public statements and private conversations highlighted the importance of the new report.

They were preaching to the converted at first. Greenland, the huge arctic island which is 85 per cent ice-covered, is inhabited by 50,000 people, 80 per cent of whom are Inuit. The rest are mostly Danes, but it is an Inuit society and political life is entirely Inuit-controlled. Indeed, a major spur to the autonomy movement which resulted in Home Rule in 1979 was Inuit dissatisfaction with the white man's style of development, the imposition of white values and culture in schools and society, and the search for oil in Greenland's waters where local fishing was the mainstay of the economy. Inuit also were angry at the large European trawlers scooping up their already precarious fish stocks. When Inuit in the mid-1980s withdrew from the European community entirely, despite many blandishments from Brussels, Europe was stunned (and an 'impossible' new legal precedent was set!).

The respected British weekly, *The Economist*, had written earlier that Greenland had every good reason to stick with the wise business, financial, and resource prospects of the Europeans. But, the journal concluded in sad puzzlement, Inuit were unlikely to do so. Although *The Economist* did not explore the reasons for the Inuit rejection of the white man's industrial development, the article was one of the very few and very first acknowledgments in the northern world by the Establishment that aboriginal and European world views might be incompatible.

On that particular Greenland visit, we saw the different worlds of white and aboriginal aspiration starkly. Our purpose was to visit Qaanaaq, the northernmost municipality in the world. Here the Polar Inuit live at the top of Greenland, facing Ellesmere Island on the Canadian side of the international border. They continue their ancient lifestyles of hunting sea mammals and polar bears, and the other activities of the seasonal round. They have devised a good accommodation with modern technology. For instance, motorized skidoos are banned for environmental reasons, but the harnesses on dog teams are now nylon rather than skin, because hungry dogs won't eat nylon. Like aboriginal people elsewhere, the Polar Inuit do not oppose development *per se*. Rather, they oppose projects and activities which threaten their economic base of wildlife and wildlife habitat, and activities incompatible with their survival as a people with a distinct culture.

To reach Qaanaaq one must travel through the great American air base at Thule. Built at the height of the Cold War in the early 1950s, little thought was given to Inuit who were abruptly shifted from their age-old community site there and moved north to a seasonal campsite at present Qaanaaq. The base is utterly self-contained, and well-educated American servicemen we talked with in the Aerospace Command knew nothing whatever of local Inuit inhabitants. The base and its residents live in a cocooned world of American films and foods and pastimes and jokes. The annual golf game atop the flat-topped mountain by the bay is a favourite event, but Inuit view it bitterly as the use by intruders for play of an essential area from which they can no longer obtain their livelihood.

The purpose of our visit was to hear the concerns of the local Inuit councils and hunters. Their displacement by a military base was their major complaint, with many related grievances about specific impacts on the environment and their livelihoods. It would be hard to imagine a clearer difference of priority and outlook than those of Polar Inuit and American servicemen. Returning through the base on our way south we picked up the previous day's issue of the *New York Times*, flown in with other daily conveniences. The paper reported that Canada would soon announce the building of a fleet of nuclear submarines to use in arctic waters and was announcing this ahead of the main defence policy paper in order to let Indian and Inuit opponents get used to the idea. It would be a shame, no doubt, if mere northern residents marred a prime ministerial photo opportunity with unease about nuclear vessels prowling around their food species.

The submarine fleet has been cancelled now, to the fury of Canada's allies who fear a general retreat from defence spending. And although Inuit probably had minimal impact on that decision, they have won support from the Canadian government on other matters. In fact, northern governments in general are learning that aboriginal peoples have a lot of useful things to say, and a vast knowledge which frequently embarrasses governments and the developers they sponsor.

Gro Harlem Brundtland may have a special insight. She became prime minister when her predecessor so badly managed an environmental confrontation involving Sami (Lapp) reindeer herders on the Alta River that he, and government generally, lost all credibility. Certainly the wise words of her world report on aboriginal peoples are among the highlights of a voluminous document.

What she says is just what Torres Strait Islanders or Aboriginals or Inuit might say: that they know the lands and waters of their homelands, and they have a responsibility for them. The Brundtland report is very clear that ways must be found by governments to recognize the rights to resources of aboriginal peoples and to empower them to manage these and play a decisive role in development. Further, 'Protection of traditional rights should be accompanied by positive measures to enhance the well-being of the community in ways appropriate to the group's life-style ... In terms of sheer numbers, these isolated, vulnerable groups are small. But their marginalization is a symptom of a style of development that tends to neglect both human and environmental considerations. Hence a more careful and sensitive consideration of their interests is a touchstone of a sustainable development policy.'[2]

Whereas in Australia and Canada and the Amazon white men have tended to see progress in terms of filling in the map with towns, mines, roads, and tourist attractions, the Brundtland Report argues powerfully that relatively unspoiled nature is often a more vital resource. Aboriginal people and unspoiled environment do not appear together by accident. Rather, they allow each other to survive.

In the northern hemisphere, the Brundtland Report is taken very seriously. National and international work is racing ahead to design implementation of its ideas. Nobody suggests the work will be easy, or that governments will stop industrial projects. But governments are learning that to accommodate the self-government and resource management of aboriginal groups, so that they really run their own lives and manage their own area, is in the national interest. Such realization has not yet fully dawned in Australia, least of all in Queensland.

Many aboriginal peoples such as Australian Aboriginals have already lost much of their homeland and, in some areas, been alienated from traditional land uses by recent activities – for example, pastoralism. Where new ways are compatible with old, there may be many benefits for aboriginal people. But there are essential benefits for the whole community in securing the environmental and social well-being of aboriginal society everywhere. There are few areas left intact. Northern and central Australia, and northern Canada, are two of the largest such areas on earth. The wealthy, well-informed, and decent people who inhabit such countries must show a lead to other countries which do not have the good fortune of the First World.

The growing public awareness of and interest in aboriginal homelands in the northern hemisphere has led to many recent 'discoveries.' The newer populations who have created modern nation-states are learning that the earlier peoples who still live among them, usually on the margins of society, have different and often compelling answers to life in those lands. With the white man's world in confusion socially, crisis environmentally, and smug reaction politically, the vibrancy and richness of aboriginal culture and sense of community have become an inspiration to many. While some attempts to imitate aboriginal life may be naïve – such as Indian amusement at wealthy white youths wearing Indian headbands and jackets in the 1960s – on a deeper level there is much to be learned. After all, these societies have endured.

The Sami, among whom Gro Harlem Brundtland had her introduction to aboriginal issues, have had contact with encroaching European settlement for centuries. They have high material living standards comparable to other Scandinavians, but their homeland is under siege by developers and under laws which often make their livelihoods and needs invisible. Today Gro Harlem Brundtland and her government are introducing various political measures to strengthen Sami autonomy. And two national commission are working further on the most intractable problems of land rights, territorial administration, and self-government.

Aboriginal people worldwide are advancing their cause. The public in Australia has been a little slow to become aware of recent developments, but these will soon affect Australia through public opinion and through new international conventions. The aboriginal peoples of the world are not difficult welfare cases requiring expensive remedies, as governments tend to see them. They are the first custodians of the planet Earth, and the first survivors in a new age when our society and politics seem lost.

NOTES

This article is from *Social Alternatives* 9 (4) 1991. Reprinted with permission.

1 World Commission on Environment and Development, *Our Common Future* (New York: Oxford University Press 1987), 114–16
2 Ibid.

CONCLUSION

J.R. MILLER

Conclusion

> If there is any single issue on which Canada cannot hold its head high in the international community, any single area in which we can be accused of falling down on our obligations, it is in this area of aboriginal relations.[1]

One thing is certain about Indian-white relations in the 1990s: everyone now recognizes that a crisis exists. The country's human rights commissioner made the abysmal conditions in which aboriginal peoples live in Canada a cardinal item in his report on 1989. He called for 'a thorough-going enquiry into those problems, modelled on the Royal Commission on Bilingualism and Biculturalism of twenty-five years ago.'[2] Inquiries in three different provinces have laid bare the extent to which racial prejudice against native peoples infects the judicial system. A major English-language daily, which had anticipated the commissioner's call for a wide-ranging inquiry, applauded the suggestion, promising that such an investigation 'would be a catalyst for change in this country, bringing a critical mass of attention to such issues as native self-government.'[3] After outbreaks of violence at three reserves in Quebec in the spring and summer of 1990 took three lives and led to dangerous confrontations, the newspaper renewed its call and urged Ottawa to act.[4] However, although there is agreement that systematic inquiry and energetic action are needed, the coming years are likely to see a worsening of relations unless the non-native majority begins to realize that it has lessons to learn from the native communities.

Relations are likely to worsen before they improve in part because some native peoples in Canada have reached the end of their patience. The unusual resort to force in July 1990 by the Indians of Kanesatake to defend their blockade against efforts by the municipality of Oka to seize control of land embraced by a land claim provoked a rash of demonstrations and blockades across the country. These spontaneous actions were proof, if any more were needed, that the patience of long-suffering native peoples had worn out. Their frustration and impatience will likely make solution of the outstanding disputes more, not less, difficult. The future of relations also looks gloomy because of the persistence of issues that have been explained in some of the preceding essays. Of course, differences over such important policy issues as land claims and aboriginal self-government have not been resolved. In fact, there has been distressingly little progress in at least one of these two critically important areas.

The story of native land claims has been a troubled one, although there have been important advances in a few notable cases. As was pointed out in 'Aboriginal Rights, Land Claims, and the Struggle To Survive,' the James Bay and Northern Agreement of 1975 was the first comprehensive land claim to be settled. Although this agreement at the time was considered a breakthrough, by 1990 the Cree and Inuit of northern Quebec were arguing that it should be cancelled. 'The agreement was based on the assumption that hydroelectric development was compatible with the Cree way of life and environment, but that is obviously not true,' said Matthew Coon-Come, grand chief of the Grand Council of the Crees of Quebec.[5] At precisely the same time, Hydro Quebec, with the backing of the provincial government, initiated another huge power development project. The previous scheme of the 1970s, by flooding a vast area, had released large quantities of mercury that affected many species of fish and, indirectly, the Cree. Given that experience, noted Coon-Come, if the new project were to go ahead, 'you might as well tie rocks around our necks and dump us into a Hydro-Québec reservoir because that's what you would be doing, killing our people.'[6] Another Cree leader described what was occurring as 'environmental racism – you can do as you please to the environment in Quebec if the only direct victims are indigenous people.'[7] Given the implacability of the pro-development forces and the resentment and determination of the Quebec natives, continued disputes over land use in Quebec are certain.

In contrast, land claims in the territories north of the sixtieth parallel of latitude have made substantial headway only after long delay. The Council of Yukon Indians, for example, after many years of negotiation only reached a final agreement with the federal government in 1988. (A more definitive Umbrella Final Agreement was signed on 1 April 1990.) An Agreement in Principle covering over two million square kilometres in the Northwest Territories was signed with the Tungavik Federation of Nunavut on 30 April 1990, bringing to a conclusion the most difficult stage of resolving a claim that had been initiated in 1976. Ottawa expected it would take a further eighteen months to tidy up details and produce a final agreement.[8] One reason for the delays in settling comprehensive claims has been the scope and complexity – territory, mineral rights, self-government, monetary compensation for non-native use of the lands – that the agreements embrace. A second is the approach that the federal government has taken. Ottawa will negotiate only six claims at any one time, even in the northern territories where it controls crown lands and where it does not have to reach agreement on any settlement with a provincial government. At the present time, twenty comprehensive claims are queued up waiting for the attention of government negotiators.

Finally, as a major case in British Columbia illustrates, the attitudes of provincial governments have been serious obstacles to the settlement of comprehensive land claims. In 1973, after the Nishga case established at law the concept of aboriginal title and the federal government agreed to negotiate claims, the Gitksan Wet'suwet'en attempted to negotiate a settlement of a claim for a 55,000 square kilometre tract in the Nass valley. However, the province of British Columbia refused to participate in the negotiations, contending that its colonial predecessor had extinguished any aboriginal title prior to the province's entry into Confederation. Litigation of the question of whether there is anything to negotiate has trundled through the courts and in 1990 is still not settled. The Gitksan Wet'suwet'en case demonstrates clearly the complexity and intractability of comprehensive land claims. It also goes far to explain the deepening cynicism and bitterness of many native leaders.

The process for dealing with specific claims is not enjoying much success either. In particular, Temagami and Lubicon Lake are mired in strife. Although in the spring of 1990 the government of Ontario and the Teme-augama Anishnabai, often known as the Bear Island band, cobbled together a compromise over access to forest resources that protected a part of the old-growth forest by giving the Indians a veto over lumbering in a 40,000-hectare area in six townships, no real progress on the underlying question of a land claim against the government of Canada was achieved. Similarly, in Alberta, the agreement in principle that the Lubicon Lake Cree reached in the autumn of 1988 gave way to bickering over the amount of compensation Ottawa should pay the Lubicon for use of their lands during the five decades it took to acknowledge the band's right to a reserve. In 1989–90 Indian and Northern Affairs Canada seemed to revert to older divide-and-conquer tactics when it prepared to recognize and settle with a breakaway group of Lubicon Lake people who had become impatient with the delay in reaching a full settlement. Lubicon and Temagami, probably the most thoroughly covered claims disputes in the country, were not a favourable barometer of the climate for settling land claims in the region south of the sixtieth parallel, where in the west Ottawa's unfettered jurisdiction ended and provincial responsibility began.

Another area that required both federal and provincial cooperation – recognition and constitutional entrenchment of aboriginal self-government – has also seen disappointing developments. No progress was made after the First Ministers' Conference of 1987 ended in bitterness and recrimination. All the rationalizations for the collective failure to define and entrench self-government in the constitution boiled down to one genuine reason: native concerns were not very high on the agenda of the eleven governments. Indeed, how low the issue of aboriginal self-government was on the nation's constitutional agenda was revealed with brutal clarity in the episode of the Meech Lake Accord.

In 1987, meeting in haste behind closed doors to attempt to end Quebec's moral isolation from the constitutional discourse of the country, the ten provinces and the federal government fabricated an accommodation known as the Meech Lake Accord. This deal gave all the provinces something in return for their acceptance of Quebec's minimum demands for adhesion to the 1982 constitution, all the while ignoring the indigenous peoples. Not only was no attempt made during this frenetic phase of constitution-making to incorporate in the constitution the first peoples' demands for recognition of their right to self-government, but those areas of the country that were dominated by native voters suffered a major setback. The Meech Lake Accord provided that any proposal that Yukon or the Northwest Territories become a province had to gain the unanimous consent of all eleven governments. This was a hurdle no other province had been required to clear. As an indication of awareness of or sympathy for aboriginal peoples' request for greater control of their lives, the sorry affair was all too revealing. When the big-time constitutional players sat down to deal, natives were still unsatisfied onlookers, their nose pressed against the glass of the non-native constitutional structure. The 'sweet promises' native leaders had with great difficulty extracted from Ottawa and the provinces during the anxious winter of 1981–2 had not been honoured.

As the deadline by which all provinces had to ratify the Meech Lake Accord approached in the early summer of 1990, Indian leaders saw their chance to force the country's politicians to recognize the importance of dealing with native issues. In Manitoba, which was one of two provinces whose ratification was still required, the sole native member of the Legislative Assembly, Elijah Harper, repeatedly refused his consent to expedite procedures that were needed if the province's legislature was to deal with the accord in time. Harper's and the Manitoba Indians' success in killing the Meech Lake Accord was followed within a month by the violent confrontation at Oka, Quebec. The combination of events seemed to deliver a shock to at least some of the governments that had been major obstacles to resolving outstanding disputes. In Saskatchewan the government of Grant Devine announced that it was willing, in a reversal of its posture since 1982, to make provincial crown land available to resolve specific land claims.[9] And the premier of British Columbia, the province which since its entry into Confederation in 1871 had consistently refused to recognize the concept of aboriginal title or participate in negotiations in which Indian peoples were advancing claims based on it, suddenly said that henceforth it would participate in negotiations.[10] Possibly Meech Lake and Oka have accomplished what decades of protest and pressure have failed to do: to persuade Canada's political leaders to move native concerns to a prominent place on the national agenda.

Beyond the political and constitutional arenas, however, there are other forces at work that could, if recognized and handled sensitively, lead to a reconciliation between natives and non-natives in Canada. The reason for hopefulness is a point that was noted in the introduction: the motives for interaction between different peoples determine the nature of their contact relationship. There is now some modest reason to hope that both natives and non-natives can find a powerful reason to cooperate. The 1990s – dubbed hopefully 'the turnaround decade' – seem likely to see the dominance of environmental issues in citizens' minds and, belatedly as usual, on politicians' agenda. Such problems, actual or anticipated, as holes in the ozone layer, global warming, air and water degradation, and the awkward business of toxic waste disposal have come together in a concatenation of ecological concern. When the beluga whales that die in the Gulf of St Lawrence are so poisonous that the scientists who examine their remains have to wear gloves to handle them; when citizens' groups and native organizations fight against large-scale lumbering in British Columbia; when red maples in Ontario and Quebec die out; when the International Joint Commission in the autumn of 1987 receives United States and Canadian reports about high levels of toxic chemicals in Lake Ontario; when high levels of toxins are found astonishingly in the Arctic – when these things happen simultaneously, Canadians begin to wake up to the environmental horror that western science and economics have fashioned over the last several centuries.

But what does a dawning of citizen concern about environmental issues have to do with the future of Indian-white relations in Canada? The welfare of aboriginal peoples and newcomers is linked, of course, because they inhabit the same territory. Even in a country as large as Canada it is ludicrous for the non-native community to adopt the attitude, 'Oh, the leak is in their end of the boat.' As the president of the Council of the Haida, Miles Richardson, put it: 'We're all in trouble as a human species. There is no longer any question of that. As humans, we've developed the ability to radically affect the balance of nature and as surely as the indigenous nations are facing extinction, so is the human species.'[11] Beyond the need to keep a shared territory habitable, indigenous and immigrant Canadians are being drawn together in a cooperative relationship by danger to the environment. Non-natives must recognize and accept two facts if that cooperation is to be fruitful. At the root of the environmental problem is Western society's worldview; and the solution could lie in adoption of the aboriginal peoples' distinctly different outlook on the cosmos and humans' place therein.

As was noted in the introduction to this work, the two solitudes of natives and newcomers come from different traditions. The non-natives are the heirs of the Book of Genesis, the scientific method, and capitalist organization of economic activity; they believe the world is God's gift to them to exploit. From a different tradition native Canadians have acquired a contrasting outlook. They see humans as merely one of the creatures with whom they are interconnected. If they are created in the Great Spirit's image, then so too are the beaver, streams, and forests. That is what Miles Richardson means when he says, 'As human beings we have no divine right of survival.'[12] Indigenous peoples and European newcomers hold to profoundly different views of the world and the place of humans in it: the former are cooperative and compatible with the environment, the latter competitive and destructive.

Though it is rarely noticed, these two contrasting ways of seeing humankind and their world constitute the two positions on the environmental debate that seems likely to dominate the 1990s. The debate is over *how*, not if, we should halt the degradation and begin the rehabilitation of the environment. But if everyone is 'green' on ecological issues in the 1990s, they are different shades of green. One party to the environmental debate looks to the use of human instruments for solutions; the other prefers methods that bear but lightly on the natural world. For the sake of convenience, these two opposing viewpoints might be termed the Hard Green and the Soft Green options.

The Hard Green position is the logical result of centuries of Western social and intellectual development. Its devotees, most frequently found among engineers and other technologically inclined people, are the intellectual heirs of the Judeo-Christian tradition that treats humans as a privileged part of the created world. Theirs is the tradition that has given the world the phenomenal increase in the application of technology to the natural world. Rather than embracing nature, they seek to subdue it. Their symbol is the vertical human dominating a horizontal world. The Hard Green position on the environment is that all problems are solvable by the application of yet more technology, the utilization of more hardware. Are the foam plastic containers at fast-food restaurants a problem because they contain dangerous chemicals? Then a new hamburger box can be developed that will break down safely and relatively quickly. Acid rain emissions can be reduced and the development of the Greenhouse Effect slowed by further utilization of nuclear energy rather than the heat and power produced by burning fossil fuels. The Hard Greens are as sincere and committed to their vision of environmental protection as anyone else. They are also, like most of us, the prisoners of their own intellectual traditions.

The alternative Soft Green position in the debate over the environment that is now getting under way is different. It holds that humankind must lighten the burden on the natural world by reducing the application of technology. Where the engineers call for more hard technology, as in further development of nuclear power, Soft Greens advocate greater conservation and energetic efforts to develop alternative energy sources. They argue, correctly, that if as much money had been invested in the refinement of wind, solar, and tidal power as has been spent on developing and merchandising nuclear power, the world might have softer energy options that are both affordable and sustainable. The Soft Greens' symbol is the circle that links all creation. The Soft Greens are also rooted in a distinct intellectual tradition, one that is in many ways different from their technologically inclined adversaries. The ideas that underlie the Soft position are based on the religious and social beliefs of Asia and of indigenous peoples, particularly in North America, but also in parts of Europe and South America. The animistic religion of Indians and Inuit teaches that all existence, human and nonhuman, is a continuum. All creation is linked; all things on this planet are interdependent. The indigenous peoples are, thanks to their intellectual upbringing, natural environmentalists. As the premier of Greenland said some years ago, the Inuit are the 'soldiers and police' of the fragile arctic environment.[13]

Recently there has been growing recognition, both among indigenous peoples themselves and throughout other parts of society, that the worldview of native peoples might hold the answers to environmental and other problems. The Brundtland Report in 1987 drew the world's attention to the fact that the aboriginal 'communities are the repositories of vast accumulations of traditional knowledge and experience that links humanity with its ancient origins. Their disappearance is a loss for the larger society, which could learn a great deal from their traditional skills in sustainably managing very complex ecological systems.' The Inuit Circumpolar Conference, an organization made up of Inuit from North America and Europe, in the summer of 1989 proposed an ambitious program of species management and sustainable growth that attracted widespread attention. And both the Dene-Métis and Temagami settlements in April 1990 have provided the first peoples in the areas affected with a strong voice in the management of natural resources in the regions. Are these signs that the non-native majority is beginning to recognize that the aboriginal peoples are likely to be responsible stewards of their lands?

Western society is once again being presented with an opportunity to learn from the indigenous peoples whom it has so long and so often ignored. If it takes advantage of this chance, it might find there are other benefits that go beyond a broader consensus and quicker action on environmental issues. Learning from the native peoples might engender greater respect for the native minority on the part of the majority population, a respect that could usher in a new era of cooperation between native and newcomer. And with such new-found cooperation, Canada might begin to settle some of the unresolved issues in native affairs that are a blight on the political life of the country.

That, if only Canadians have the wit to realize it, is the 'sweet promise' of their own day.

NOTES

1 Canadian Human Rights Commission, *Annual Report 1989* ([Ottawa]: Minister of Supply and Services Canada 1990), 15

2 Ibid.

3 Toronto *Globe and Mail*, 3 April 1990

4 For example, ibid., 15 August 1990

5 Ibid., 13 April 1990

6 Ibid., 14 April 1990

7 Ibid., 18 April 1990

8 Indian and Northern Affairs Canada, press release 1-9014, 30 April 1990. In November 1990, however, this agreement collapsed when Dene and Métis sought to renegotiate terms that would extinguish aboriginal rights.

9 Saskatchewan Indian and Native Affairs press release 90-515, 23 July 1990

10 *Globe and Mail*, 10 August 1990

11 Miles Richardson, *The Graham Spry Lecture, 1989* (Montreal: CBC Transcripts 1989), 2

12 Ibid.

13 Quoted in Peter Jull, 'Aboriginal Peoples and Political Change in the North Atlantic Area,' *Journal of Canadian Studies* 16 (2) (summer 1981): 51